Inhabitants of Kent County, Maryland

1637-1787

Henry C. Peden, Jr.

HERITAGE BOOKS
2007

HERITAGE BOOKS
AN IMPRINT OF HERITAGE BOOKS, INC.

Books, CDs, and more—Worldwide

For our listing of thousands of titles see our website
at
www.HeritageBooks.com

Published 2007 by
HERITAGE BOOKS, INC.
Publishing Division
65 East Main Street
Westminster, Maryland 21157-5026

Copyright © 1994 Henry C. Peden, Jr.

All rights reserved. No part of this book may be reproduced or transmitted in any form or by any means, electronic or mechanical, including photocopying, recording or by any information storage and retrieval system without written permission from the author, except for the inclusion of brief quotations in a review.

International Standard Book Number: 978-1-58549-286-8

CONTENTS

Introduction v
Landowners and Tracts in Kent County Debt Books, 1733-1769 ... 1
Tract Index to Kent County and Patents, 1640-1787 42
Tract and Landowners in the Kent County Tax List of 1783 71
Indentured Orphans of Kent County, Maryland, 1778-1787 93
Abstracts of Kent County Court Proceedings, 1647-1676 100
Gleanings from St. Paul's P. E. Church, 1693-1724 150
Gleanings from Chester P. E. Church 153
Gleanings from Shrewsbury P. E. Church 156
Index to Convicted Servants in Kent County, Maryland, 1718-1770
.... 168
Revolutionary War (From *Archives of Maryland*, Vol. 18) 171
Kent County Committee of Correspondence Membership, June 2, 1774
.... 174
Kent County Delegates to Maryland Convention, April 24-May 3, 1775 174
Kent County Judges of Elections, August 15, 1776 174
Kent County Pensioner in 1840 174
Kent County Representatives to the Proprietary Assembly 175
Commanders of Isle of Kent and As Such Its Presiding Justice 178
Militia 178
Revolutionary War Patriots:
        From *Archives of Maryland*, Volume XVI ... 189
        From *Archives of Maryland*, Volume XXI ... 190
        From *Archives of Maryland*, Volume XLIII . 191
Index 193

INTRODUCTION

The first settlement by the English in what was later Maryland was made between 1629 and 1631 by William Claiborne of Virginia, who established an Indian trading post on Kent Island. This settlement existed when Maryland was granted to George Calvert in 1632. The struggle between the Calverts and Claibornes made a battleground of Kent Island and in 1638 an end was put to the struggle when the rule of the Calverts on the island was established (only to be interrupted again in 1645-1646 when Richard Ingle staged his rebellion). The county records of Kent, which have been in part preserved, begin in 1648, and while there are several breaks, there is a continuity in the county government of what was at first called the Isle of Kent County and the present day Kent County, which does not include the island. Kent Island is now part of Queen Anne's County and what has been known as Kent County since 1642 has not since 1695 included the island from which it derived its name.

There were several waves of immigration into Kent Island. In addition to the first settlers from Virginia under Claiborne, after Lord Baltimore gained firm control over the island in 1638, there was a constant addition to its population from St. Mary's. When the Puritan migration from lower Virginia to Maryland took place in 1649-1650, many of these non-conformists found their way to Kent Island, either directly or after a short stay in Anne Arundel County, and then subsequently to the neighboring mainland.

Until 1658 the only established settlements on the Eastern Shore of Maryland were those on Kent Island, although there may have been a few adventurers on the mainland. No patents to land on the mainland in the areas now occupied by Cecil, Kent, Talbot, Queen Anne's, and Dorchester Counties were issued before 1658, although some warrants for lands near Kent Island were issued as early as 1651. With the opening of the mainland in 1658 for settlement, many prominent Kent Islanders took out land patents while others received land for transporting themselves and others into the area (see Gust Skordas' Early Settlers of Maryland).

The order for a new county to be carved out of this widespread territory, until then under the jurisdiction of the Kent Court, cannot be found, but early in 1662 Talbot County had come into existence. Kent County then comprised the island and extended on the north in a general way to an indefinite line running east and west between the Chester and Sassafras Rivers. Until the creation of Cecil County in 1674, the bounds of Kent County northward were undefined. Baltimore County, as originally laid out circa 1660, extended around the head of the Chesapeake Bay and included not only what is now Cecil County, but also part of the present day Kent County. The line separating Kent and Cecil Counties was not finally defined until 1707 as being at the Sassafras River. For this reason about 30 tracts of land recorded in the early Baltimore County records appear later in the Kent County rent rolls. In 1695, however, Kent Island was taken from Kent County and included in

Talbot, and in 1706-1707 the island was made part of a new county, Queen Anne's, when the latter was carved out of Talbot.

Of the Court established in 1637, Capt. George Evelyn was given the title of Commander of the Isle of Kent and as such was its presiding Justice. He and six associates were empowered to sit in a Court with powers similar to an English Court of Sessions. The title of Commander was used to designate the chief civil, judicial, and military officer of the county until 1658. For additional information on the early presiding Justices and other distinguished Kent Countians, one should consult the *Archives of Maryland*, Volume 54, and *A Biographical Dictionary of the Maryland Legislature, 1635-1789*, by Edward A. Papenfuse, et al (Maryland State Archives).

This book on the early inhabitants of Kent County between 1637 and 1787 contains thousands of names with information gleaned from the following historical and genealogical material: Debt Books, 1733-1769; Land Patents, 1637-1787; Tax List of 1783; Indentured Orphans, 1778-1787; Lists of Batchelors, 1758-1763; Convicted Servants, 1719-1770; County Court Proceedings, 1647-1677; Parish Vestry Records of Shrewsbury, St. Paul, and Chester Protestant Episcopal Churches, 1693-1787; Colonial Militia List in 1748, and Officers, 1648-1769; Revolutionary War Soldiers, 1775-1783; Members of the Maryland Legislature, 1637-1787; and, gleanings from the *Archives of Maryland*, Volumes 11, 16, 18, 21, 43, and 54.

One should also consult the following source books for more information that has recently been published pertaining to early Kent Countians: *Citizens of the Eastern Shore of Maryland, 1659-1750*, by F. Edward Wright (1986); *Maryland Deponents, 1634-1799*, by Henry C. Peden, Jr. (1991); *More Maryland Deponents, 1716-1799*, by Henry C. Peden, Jr. (1992); *Maryland Eastern Shore Vital Records, 1648-1800*, by F. Edward Wright (4 volumes, 1982-1985); *Abstracts of the Prerogative Court of Maryland, 1648-1777*, by Vernon F. Skinner, Jr. (23 volumes, 1988-1993); *Maryland Calendar of Wills, 1635-1772* (14 volumes, begun by Jane Baldwin Cotton and continued by F. Edward Wright); "Index to Convict Servants in Kent County, 1719-1769," by Robert Andrew Oszakiewski, in *Maryland Genealogical Society Bulletin*, Vol. 34, No. 1, Winter, 1993; "Some Manumissions of Kent and Baltimore Counties," by Laura Elizabeth Sharp-Cooper, in *Maryland Genealogial Society Bulletin*, Vol. 34, No. 3, Summer, 1993; "Excerpts from Kent County Court Records, 1731-1735," by F. Edward Wright, in *Maryland Genealogical Society Bulletin*, Vol. 34, No. 4, Fall, 1993; *The Maryland Militia in the Revolutionary War*, by S. Eugene Clements and F. Edward Wright (1987); and, *Eastern Shore Families*, by Raymond B. Clark, Jr. (1987), as well as the classic *Old Kent: The Eastern Shore of Maryland*, by George A. Hanson (1876).

Henry C. Peden, Jr.
Bel Air, Maryland
February 1, 1994

LANDOWNERS AND TRACTS IN KENT COUNTY DEBT BOOKS, 1733-1769
(Ref: Maryland State Archives, Card File 58)

Abbott, William - Chance - 1733-1736
Absolam, William - Covent Garden - 1733-1735
Ackland, John - Stepney Fields - 1752-1769
Ackland, William - Stepney, Stepney Fields, Acklands Lot - 1733-1747
Adair, Alexander (heirs) - Comegys Fancy - 1738-1769
Aires, Thomas - Denbeigh - 1733-1735
Allford, Aaron - Last, Kennards Discovery alias Chance, Drayton, Little Drayton - 1736-1769
Alford, Moses - Last, Chance, Little Drayton - 1733-1735
Allibone, Edward - St. Martins, Millers Adventure, Allibones Addition - 1732-1735
Aldridge, Thomas - Aldridges Lott - 1733-1735
Allaby, Peter - Hens Roost - 1733-1735
Ambrose, Abraham - Whitfield, Ambrosia - 1733-1753
Ambrose, John - Whitefield, Ambrosia, Knave Stand Off - 1752-1769
Andrews, Miss, daughter of Samuel Anderson (Andrews) - Pentridge - 1743-1747
Anderson, James - 3 lots in Chester Town, Stepney, Arundel Grove - 1747-1769
Anderson, Capt. William - 2 lots in Chester Town - 1741-1769
Andrews, Stephen - Boonly - 1736-1743
Anger, John - Cammels Worthmore, Suffolk - 1760, 1769
Angle, John - Marshes - 1738-1744
Angles, Richard - Angles Lot - 1733-1737
Apsley, William - Covent Garden, Hermitage, Novels Adventure, Town Relict - 1733-1769
Arnold, John - 1 lot in Chester Town - 1736-1769
Ashley, Isaac - Ashleys Lott, Ashley Green, Worton Meadow - 1733-1769
Ashley, John - Ashleys Green, Ashleys Lott - 1736-1769
Ashley, Thomas - Ashleys Green - 1736-1769
Ashley, William - Ashleys Lott - 1736-1769
Ashworth, John - Canaday - 1769
Atkinson, John - Stannaway, Killinsworthmore - 1733-1735
Austin, John - Austins Beginning, Broad Neck - 1733-1737
Austin, Rosamond - Austins Beginning - 1738, 1739
Austin, Samuel - Austins Beginning - 1752-1769
Austin, William - Jones Venture - 1769
Ayres, Abraham - Denbigh - 1744-1769
Ayres, Robert - Hinchingham - 1769
Ayres, Thomas - Hinchingham, Denby, Ayres Wilderness Resurveyed - 1736-1760
Baird, Alexander - Morton, Adventure, Ellis Farm - 1752-1769
Baker, Amey - Chigwell - 1737
Baker, Charles - Chegwell - 1733-1736, 1752-1769
Baker, Thomas - Morton - 1752
Baldwin, John - Coxstall - 1740
Ball, John - East Huntington, Tilghmans Farm, Norris's Forrest,

Warners Addition, Warners Adventure, Arcadia, Addition to
  Tilghmans Farm - 1733-1747
Ball, Peter - 1 lot in Chester Town No. 19, Broad Oak, Green
  Forrest - 1752-1769
Barber, Francis - 1 lot in Chester Town - 1736
Barber, James - Great Oak Mannor - 1733-1735
Barker, James - Church Warden Neck - 1733, 1735
Barker, John - Church Warden Neck - 1736
Barkley, Thomas - Suffolk, Neglect - 1752
Barnes, William - Goose Haven, Partnership, Hemberry, London
  Bridge - 1742-1760
Barney, Francis - Barneys Forest, Richards Adventure, Essex,
  Barneys Forrest, White Marsh - 1733-1769
Barber, George - Providence - 1737-1747
Barton, Martha - 2 lots in Chester Town - 1753-1769
Barton, Samuel - Grove, Little Grove, Arcadia, Lot in Chester
  Town - 1736-1747
Bateman, Christopher - Harris's Forrest - 1733-1760
Bateman, Michael - Kent Lott - 1739-1756
Bathurst, Edward - Cornwallis Choice, Batchelors Resolution -
  1733-1739
Battle (Batsle?), Thomas - Grange - 1737-1744
Battershell, Henry - Arcadia - 1733-1735
Battershell, John - Arcadia - 1736-1769
Battershell, Rachel - Widows Rest - 1733-1735
Bayley, William - Cornwalleys Choice - 1736
Beck, Alexander - Neeps Choice - 1769
Beck, Aquilla - Beckworth - 1736-1769
Beck, Caleb - Boons Meadow, Calebs Discovery - 1733-1769
Beck, Edward - Neifs Choice, Beckworth, Long Compton, Becks
  Addition - 1733-1741, 1760,1769
Beck, Eliza - Fair Dealing - 1752-1769
Beck, Evan - Ruabon - 1733-1735
Beck, John - Probus, Becks Addition, Neifs Choice, Cornwallis's
  Choice, Chance alias Sally's Chance, Pacoes Poor Lot, Bounty
  Resurveyed - 1733-1769
Beck, Joshua - Barton - 1736-1757
Beck, Martha - Barton - 1760
Beck, Mary - Calebs Discovery - 1760
Beck, Samuel - Fair Dealing - 1736-1749, 1760
Beck, Vivian - Exchange - 1733
Beck, William Jr. - Probus - 1753-1769
Beck, William Sr. - Killingsworth More Enlarged - 1752-1760
Beckles, Thomas - Beckleys Recovery, Providence - 1733-1737
Beddoe, Griffin - Piney Point, Slades Chance, Neglect - 1736-1742
Bellas, Francis - Ridgely, Stanlys Hope, Hills and No Dales -
  1733-1738, 1752
Bellas, Hannah - Stratshold, Ridgly - 1769
Bellican, Ann - Friendship, Maidens Lott - 1733-1735
Bellican, Chris. - Haifield, Maiden Lott, Church Warden Neck,
  Addition, Three Friends, Lot in Chester Town - 1736-1760
Benham, Mathew - Buck Hill - 1733-1735
Bennett, John - 1 lot in George Town - 1/2 lot in Chester Town -
  1738-1769

Bennett, Richard - Bennetts Bridge, 4 lots in Chester Town - 1733-1769
Benny, Benjamin - Brothership, Stepney - 1769
Berry, Samuel - Providence - 1733-1735
Best, Henry - Eliners Delight - 1736
Best, Humphrey - Eliners Delight - 1737-1760
Best, William - Eliners Delight - 1736-1760
Bevens, Elizabeth - Margarets Delight, Saint Margaretts - 1733-1737
Billingsly, Thomas - Viaven, Chance, Dining Room - 1733-1735
Bishop, Risdon - Thornton, Gleaves Lot, Chance Resurveyed, 1 Lot in Chester Town, Batemans Farm, Outrange - 1769
Black, James - Kent Mannor - 1769
Blackiston, Benjamin - Deer Park, Reserve - 1733-1769
Blackiston, Capt. Ebenezer - Hinchingham, Division, Antonia, Saint Antoni, Blackistones Addition, Poplar Farm, Galloways Farm - 1733-1769
Blackiston, George - Spalding, Deer Park, Blackiston Lott - 1769
Blackiston (Blackston), Hannah - Boxly - 1736, 1737
Blackiston, John - Outrange, Rent Lott, Addition to Rent Lott, Ellis's Industry, Deer Park, Boxly, Chance, Broad Neck - 1733-1735, 1753-1769
Blackiston, Margaret - Partnership - 1753-1760
Blackiston, Michael - Boxly, 1/2 lot in Chester Town, Providence - 1738-1769
Blackiston, Prideaux - Boxly - 1741-1769
Blackiston (Blackistone), Thomas - Partnership - 1733-1752
Blackiston (Blackston), Vincent - Boxley, Adventure, Middle Branch, Hazard - 1736-1769
Blackiston (Blackstone), William - Deer Park, Reserve, Saint Antonia - 1733-1769
Blake, James - Strafford Manor - 1747-1769
Blakelidge, Benjamin - Orchards Neck, Galloways Farm - 1733
Blay, Edward - Little Grove, Staples Warren, Grove, Tilghmans Choice - 1733-1735
Blay, Isabell - Blays Range, Blays Addition, Blays Park, Dulltown, Mill Fork, Partnership, Ponds, Howels Outland - 1733-1736
Blay, William - Coxs Stale, Warners Marsh, Lincolne, Phillips Neglect - 1733-1735
Blay, Edward, and Pearce, William, and Blackiston, Ebenezer - Hopefull Unity - 1733-1735
Bodeen, Francis L. - Good Hope, Stewards Hope, Addition to Good Hope, Wolfs Huck - 1733-1735, 1752
Bodeen, Hannah - Shads Hole - 1733-1735
Bodeen, Henry - Addition to Good Hope, Wolfs Huck, Good Hope, Stewarts Hope, Little Brittain, Drayton, Raisins Double Purchase - 1747-1769
Bolton, John - Lot in Chester Town, Stepney - 1760, 1769
Bolton, William - Boultons Delight - 1733 - 1735
Bond, Benjamin - Neglect - 1734 - 1735
Bond, Eliza - Mothers Gift - 1736-1760
Bond, William - Neglect - 1733
Bonner, Francis - Partners Addition, Fork, Pearces Ramble, Hangmans End - 1753-1769

Boon, Joseph - Calebs Discovery - 1769
Boots, Thomas - Shads Hole - 1733-1735
Bootes, William - Ellis's Chance, Addition, Samfield Moore - 1736-1769
Bordley, Ann - East Huntington - 1756-1757
Bordley, Beal - Grumble, Partnership, Bordleys Beginning, Adventure Resurveyed, Providence, Fancy - 1769
Bordley, John - Adventure, Bordleys Gift, Adventure Resurveyed, Lots No. 8, 9, and 15 in Chester Town, Fancy, Partnership, Grumble, Bordleys Beginning - 1743-1769
Bordley, Stephen - 1/2 lot in Chester Town, Kindness, Bordleys Resurvey on Hilly Longford, Stepney, Arundel Grove - 1733-1735, 1760, 1769
Bordley, Thomas - Grumble, Arundel Grove, Fancy, Adventure, Partnership, Dale[?] - 1733-1769
Bordley, William - Stepney, Kindness - 1769
Bostock, Eliza - Pryors Neglect - 1752-1769
Bostock, James - Pryors Neglect - 1739, 1740
Bostick, Jane - Pryors Neglect - 1736-1747
Bostick, Samuel - Pryors Neglect - 1733-1735
Bostick (Bostock), Sanders - Pryors Neglect, Bosticks Addition, Dublin, Lot in George Town - 1752-1769
Bostick, Thomas - Northumberland - 1733, 1735
Bouchel, Dr. Slater - Ellis's Industry - 1752-1760
Bowdy, Elizabeth - Draycoat - 1733-1735
Bowdy, Richard - Bowdys Folly, Forrest of Dean - 1733-1735
Bower (Boyer), Augustine - Rich Level, Heaths Range, Heaths Forest, Boyers Adventure - 1733-1747
Bowers, Jane - Deans Adventure - 1752-1760
Bowers, Thomas - Essex, Arcadia, Blunt, Skidmore - 1736-1769
Bowers, William - Deans Adventure - 1736-1744
Bowles, Isaac - Comegies Fancy - 1733-1735
Bowles, James - Boulston, Cheseldine - 1733-1769
Bowles, John - Bowlston, Tullys Fancy - 1733-1747
Boyer, Augustine - Rich Levell, Forrest, Boyers Adventure, Adventure, Ponds, Philips Neglect, Heath Range - 1752-1769
Boyer, James - Milford, Adventure, Moreton - 1736-1760
Boyer, Mary - Heading - 1737-1747
Boyer, Nathaniel - Adventure, Rich Levell, Heaths Range - 1769
Boyer (Boyar), Penelope - Philips Neglect Resurveyed, Rich Level, Heaths Range, Mill Fork - 1760
Boyer, Richard - Heading - 1747-1760
Boyer, Thomas - Heading, Moreton - 1733-1743, 1769
Boyer, William - Philips Neglect, Philips Neglect Resurveyed, Rich Levell, Mackey - 1733-1769
Bradley, James - Chance - 1769
Bradshawe, William - Edwins Addition, Williams Adventure, Cuckolds Point, Hicks Hazard, New Town Resurveyed, Bradshaws Farm - 1733-1769
Brady, James - Chance - 1747-1757
Brett, John - 1 lot in George Town, 1 lot in Chestertown - 1744-1769
Breward, James - Prickle Pear, Brewards Marsh, Brewards Industry - 1736-1747

DEBT BOOKS, 1733-1769 5

Breward, Solomon - Brewards Marsh - 1736-1747
Brewer, James - Prickle Pear, Brewards Marsh, Brewards Industry - 1733-1735, 1752-1769
Brewer, William - Smiths Range, Addition, Edwins Rest, Floyds Chance - 1733-1737
Brice, Richard - Wedges Recovery - 1752-1769
Briscoe, Alexander - Providence Resurveyed, Chance - 1733-1769
Briscoe, Isaac - Providence, Whitfield, Providence Resurveyed - 1769
Briscoe, John - Howards Lot Resurveyed, Chance, Providence - 1733-1760
Briscoe, Joseph - Providence Resurveyed, Suffolk - 1769
Brooks, Edward - Agreement, Forrest - 1733-1735
Brooks, John - Popes Chance, Howels Range - 1733-1769
Brooks (Brook), Phil - Thornton, Gleaves Lott, Addition to Gleaves Lott, 1 lot in Chester Town, Chance, Ambrosia and Forrest, Out Range - 1752-1760
Brooks, Phillm. - Chance, Thornton, Addition - 1736-1747, 1756, 1769
Brooks, Ruth - Howells Range, Maiden Lot, Three Friends - 1736
Brown, Caleb - Browns Purchase - 1737
Brown, Edward - Ruerden, Prices Lott, Providence, Revoidan, [Rearden?], McConnoacan - 1756-1769
Brown, James - Browns Right, Browns Angle - 1733-1735
Brown, Jane - Trumpington, Smiths Meadows, Browns Purchase - 1736, 1752-1769
Brown, John (Major) - Bairs Grine, Grange, Phillips Neglect, Forrest - 1733-1769
Brown (Browne), Morgan - Rudren, Prices Lott, Providence, Clarks Convenience - 1733-1757
Brown (Browne), Capt. Peregrine - Child Harbour alias Hampshire, Blays Range, Blays Park, Rachels Farm, Browns Discovery, Phillips Chance, Bridges Point, Broad Oak, Broad Neck, Pasterne Hole, Levell, Providence - 1733-1769
Brown (Browne), Rachell - Rachells Farm, Blays Park, Dale Town, Howells Outland - 1733-1735
Brown, Rebecca - Rearden, Prices Lott, Providence - 1760
Brown (Browne), William - Ellis's Farm, Browns Choice, Browns Purchase, Mulberry Plains, High Park - 1733-1757
Browning, George - Indian Range, Ryleys Land Resurveyed, Denbye, Cove Tract, Cove, Pullens Refuge, Gore - 1733-1735, 1769
Browning, John - Adams Chance, Ashleys Lott - 1733-1769
Browning, Thomas - Brownings Addition, Mitchels Choice, Priers Neglect, Mitchels Range, Brownings Adventure, Cornwallis Choice - 1733-1747, 1760, 1769
Browning, Writson - Adams Choice - 1760
Bryan, Daniel - 4 lots in George Town, Pearces Rambles - 1733-1769
Bryan, Mathew - Land in East Neck Island - 1769
Buchannan, Robert - Kennards Point, Addition to Kennards Point - 1769
Buck, John - 1/2 lot in Chester Town, Indian Range - 1736-1769
Buckingham, Howell - Wrights Rest alias Heaths Chance, Middle Neck - 1749-1760
Budd, Samuel - Cornwalls Choice, Carola, Buds Discovery, Calebs

Discovery, Savorys Farm - 1752-1769
Burchinall, Jeremy - Mount Harman - 1741-1769
Burgan, John - Duncans Folly, Forrest, Ivingo - 1736-1757
Burgan, Marta - Ivingo - 1756-1769
Burgan (Burgen), Philip - Ivingo - 1733-1735
Burgan, Sutton - Ivingo, Standaway - 1738-1769
Burk (Burke), John - Providence - 1733-1735, 1760, 1769
Burk, Thomas - Burkes Lott - 1757 - 1760 - 1769
Burk, William - Providence, Burks Beginning - 1736-1769
Burne, Michael - Neglect, Folly - 1733-1735
Burn, Patrick - Lot in Chester Town - 1740
Burroughs, John - Ellis Chance - 1733-1736
Burroughs, Thomas - North Andover - 1739-1747
Burroughs, William - Conjuntion, Burroughs Purchase, Ellis Chance - 1736-1760
Butcher, Edmund - Partnership - 1741-1744
Butcher, Edward - Partnership Point - 1736-1740
Butcher, William - Partnership Point Resurveyed - 1747-1769
Byrne, Patrick - 1/2 lot in Chester Town - 1741-1757, 1769
Calder, James - Dallington, Swerstun, Howards Gift, Calders Meadows, Lot in Chester Town - 1736-1769
Campbell, Hugh - 1 lot in Chester Town - 1744-1769
Campbell, James - Cammells Farm - 1752
Campbell, Richard - Cammells Farm, Fish Hall - 1733-1735, 1752
Canaday, Edward - Long Acre - 1736-1747
Canaday, John - Hermitage - 1736-1741
Canby, Thomas - Rich Levell - 1769
Cann, James - Richards Adventure - 1739-1769
Cann, John - Richards Adventure - 1733-1738
Carman, Micager - Mitchells Chance, Cockstall - 1752-1769
Carman, Michael - Mitchells Chance - 1752-1769
Carmichael, William - Rousbys Recovery - 1769
Carroll, Charles - Exchange - 1733-1760
Carter, Edmund - Everitts Double Purchase, Everitts Addition, Rich Meadows - 1760
Carter, George - Grange - 1753-1769
Carter, James - Holt - 1733-1735
Carter, William - Grange - 1736
Carvill, John - Coney Warren, Salters Load Resurveyed, 1 lot in Chester Town, Carvilles Adventure, Heaths Long Lands, Fairlee, Packerton, Carvells Prevention, Martins Nest, Millers Satisfaction, Howell, Howells Addition - 1733-1769
Carwardin, Abrm - Poplar Farm - 1739-1747
Carwardin, Edward - Doe Neck, Cornwalleys Choyce - 1736-1744
Carwardin, Thomas - Queen Charlton - 1736-1747
Cammell, James - Cammells Farm, Howells Adventure - 1733-1735
Carman, Joseph - Mitchells Range, Mitchells Chance, Pryers Neglect, Cox Hall (Coxstall?) - 1736-1752
Camron (Carmon?), Anthony - Remainder - 1733-1735
Cann, James - Richards Adventure - 1733-1737
Carman, John - Mitchells Chance, Mitchells Range, Pryors Neglect, Fox Hole - 1733-1735
Carroll, Domk [Dominick?] - Coxstall - 1736
Carroll, Mary - Cox Hall (Coxstall?) - 1737-1739

Caslick, John - Angles Rest - 1736 - 1737
Cassaday, John - Angles Rest or Lot - 1737, 1738
Catling, Thomas - Reserve - 1736-1757
Caulk, Jacob - Stand Off, Dublin Resurveyed - 1736-1769
Caulk, John - New Forrest, Fair Harbour, Arcadia, Addition - 1769
Caulk, Oliver - Stand Off - 1769
Causdon, Jesse - Chance - 1753-1769
Caustiloe, Edward - 1/2 lot in Chester Town - 1760
Challon, James - Mitchels Chance - 1769
Chalmers, James - Harris Forrest, Popes Forrest, Forrest of Dean, Hermitage, Town Relict, 2 lots in Chester Town - 1769
Chancellor, Eliza - Town Relief - 1752-1757
Chancellor, William - Town Relief - 1736-1752
Chandler, Abel - Addition to Killingsworthmore - 1769
Chandler, Michael - Drayton, Chandlers - 1769
Chandler, Nicholas (Nath?) - Grange - 1769
Chandler, Thomas - Grange, Hamlins Lott, Intermix, Draycoat, Stoneton - 1733-1769
Chapple, John - Tilghmans and Foxleys Grove, Little Grove, Shields, Stepney - 1/2 lot in Chester Town - 1769
Cheseldine, Kenelm - Grantham - 1733
Cheston, James - Fair Lee, Swamp Resurveyed - 1769
Chevins, James - Ellis's Chance, Conjunct, Burroughs Addition - 1733-1769
Chrisfield, Rosamond - Austins Beginning - 1741-1747
Christian, Thomas - Moreton, Larkins Addition, Christians Addition - 1733-1747
Church, Samuel - Churchs Lot, 2 lots in George Town - 1760 - 1769
Church, Thomas - Cornwallis Choice, Doe Neck - 1733-1735
Clare, John - Dining Room - 1735-1742, 1752
Clarke, Dennis - Sewall alias Ulrick, Clarks Conveniency, Clarks Addition, Prices Lot, Ruardon, Vienna, Kemps Beginning - 1733-1735
Clark, George - Lot in Chester Town - 1737-1769
Clark, Henry - Partnership, Angels Rest, Mackdowgalls Chance - 1752-1769
Clarke, John - Sewall alias Ulrick, Relief, London Bridge, Partnership - 1733-1769
Clark, Martha - Vienna - 1733
Clark, Mary - Sewall alias Ulrick, Relief - 1736-1752
Clark, Robert - Duncans Folly - 1733-1740
Clark, Sarah - Vienna - 1733
Clarke, William - Clarks Addition, Ellis's Chance, Vienna - 1733-1769
Clay, Thomas - Lot in Chester Town - 1742-1752
Claypole, James - Lots in Chester Town, Heaths Long Lands, Syms's Prime Choice, Tryangle - 1752-1769
Clayton, John - Mill Fork - 1733-1769
Cleaves [Gleaves?], Nathaniel - Mangy Porky - 1733, 1735
Cleaver, John - Lords Gift - 1733-1769
Cleaver, John Jr. - Chance - 1740-1769
Cleaver (Clever), William - Piney Point Resurveyed - 1756-1760
Cloak, George - Fortune - 1769
Cloak, John - Partnership - 1753-1769
Cloake, Morris - Partnership - 1744-1752

8 INHABITANTS OF KENT COUNTY, MARYLAND, 1637-1787

Clothier, Lewis - Cock of the Game, Dublin, Lincoln, Cock Hall, Margarets Delight - 1736-1769
Clothier, Robert Napp - Cock of the Game - 1769
Clouds, Nicholas - Bradnox Creek, Clouds Range, Clouds Hermitage - 1733, 1735, 1752
Clobe, John and Co. - Sewall alias Ulrick, Orchards Neck, Galloways Fancy - 1733-1769
Coalter, Michael - Sewall alias Ulrick - 1739, 1740
Coarding, Edward - Cornwallis Choice - 1733-1735
Cockey, John - Wickliffe, Market Place - 1769
Cockey, Richard - Wickliff, Market Place - 1736-1760
Cockrell, Abraham - Ellis's Chance - 1736-1752
Codd, St. Leger - Sole, Francis Enlargement, Black Oak - 1733-1735
Cole, Benjamin - [name of tract missing from index] - 1769
Cole, George - Adventure, Fairfield - 1756-1769
Cole, John - Harefield - 1733-1735
Cole, Peter - Fork, Forrest - 1733-1769
Cole, Richard - Reroguard, Sewell alias Ulrick - 1733-1735
Collins, Bartholomew - Buckingham - 1736, 1737
Collins, Francis - Shadshole - 1733-1735
Collins, Thomas - Partnership - 1733-1737
Collins, William - St. Martins, Allebone Addition, Hales Purchase - 1736-1760
Comegys, Alphonso - Forrest, Chance - 1769
Comegys, Barton - Chance, Chester Grove, Deer Park - 1769
Comegies, Cornelius - Chester Grove, Hackney, Fork, Chance, Handle, Reward, Comegys Farm, Adventure, Sewall alias Ulrick, Meadows, Scrap - 1733-1760
Comegys, Edward - Sewall alias Ulrick, Stackney - 1736-1769
Comegys, Edward Jr. - Presbury, Littleworth, Landing, Chance Resurveyed - 1736-1769
Comegys, John - Buck Hill, Billys Lot Resurveyed, Reserve - 1769
Comegys, William - Presbury, Littleworth, Reserve, Chance, Handle, Meadow, Addition, James Lot, Remainder, Scrap, Chester Grove, Endeavor, Winters Field - 1733-1769
Comegies, William Jr. - Buck Hill, Billys Lot, Forrest, Chance, Reserve, Prickles Pear - 1733-1760
Connant, Moses - Littleworth - 1733-1735
Connor, John - Fanico, Lot in Chester Town - 1737-1752
Cook, Elizabeth - Millon Purchase, Lot in Chester Town - 1737-1752
Cooke, William - Lot in Chester Town - 1741-1769
Cooley, Anne - High Park - 1752
Cooley, Nathaniel - High Park, Bristow - 1737-1760
Cooley, Richard - [name of tract missing from index] - 1753-1757
Cooper, George - Lords Gift, Williams Lot - 1733-1757
Cooper, Hezekiah - Shads Hole, Ridgly, Addition to Shads Hold - 1769
Cooper, John - Coopers Folly, Folly, Middle Spring - 1736-1769
Coots, Hercules - Mount Pleasant, Jamaco, Lot in Chester Town - 1752-1760
Copper, Charles - Lords Gift, Williams Lot - 1760, 1769
Copper, George - Wedges Discovery, Lords Gift, Williams Lot,

Great Oak Manor - 1747-1769
Copper, William - Covent Garden, Ringgold Fortune, Ringgolds Lott
   - 1752-1769
Cornelius, Daniel - Comb Whitton - 1736-1752
Cornelious, William - Dullams Folly, Levell Ridge - 1753-1747
Coster, Richard - Lot in George Town - 1769
Coulter, Michael - Sewell alias Ulrick - 1741-1744
Course, Barney - Howards Chance, Wrights Rest, Middle Neck,
   Wilmers Addition, Barneys Forrest, White Marsh, Richards
   Adventure - 1769
Course (Corse), David - Stepney - 1769
Course, James - Heaths Chance, Chance, Wrights Neck, Middle Neck,
   Howards Chance, Courseys Meadow - 1733-1760
Course, John - Brotherly and Friendly Agreement, Heborns Farm,
   Griers Range, Courseys Meadow, Lambs Meadow - 1733-1769
Course, Michael - Whetherils Hope, Courses Meadows, Greers Range,
   Hepburns Farm, Brotherly and Friendly Agreement - 1733-1747,
   1769
Coursey, Col. William - Wrights Rest, Middle Chance, Whittfield -
   1733-1738, 1769
Coutts, Hercules - Mount Pleasant, Jamaica, Lots in Chester Town
   - 1741-1747
Cove, William - Johnsons Lot - 1737, 1738
Covington, Jeremy - Broad Neck, Coventry Marsh - 1736-1769
Covington, Samuel - Lot in Chester Town - 1769
Covington, Thomas - Broad Neck - 1733-1735
Cowarden, Abraham - Poplar Farm - 1752-1760
Cowarden, Thomas - Queen Carleton - 1752-1757, 1769
Cowardine, William - Forrest Resurveyed, Ambrosia - 1769
Cox, John - Canada - 1753-1760
Cox, William - Drayton - 1733
Cozens, Edward - Cozens Chance, Piney Point, Parks Rest
   1733-1744
Crabbin, Alexander - Lot in Chester Town - 1736-1747
Cracknell, John - Forrest of Dean - 1733-1760
Cracknell, Thomas - Draywal - 1736-1747
Craige, George - Lot in Chester Town - 1757-1769
Crane, David - Lot in Chester Town - 1739-1769
Crane, Thomas - Stepney, Lot in Chester Town - 1769
Crane, William - Lot in Chester Town, Adventure - 1752-1769
Crawly, Cornelius - Queen Carleton - 1733-1735
Crew, Edward - Fish Hall, Cammels Farm - 1736-1760
Crew, John - Fish Hall - 1769
Crew, Jonas - Cammels Farm - 1769
Crew, Mary - Killingsworthmore - 1733-1735
Crisfield, Phil - Austins Beginning - 1740
Crisfield, Rosamond - Jones's Venture - 1752-1760
Crosby, Thomas - German Point, Knock Folly - 1753-1757
Crouch, Richard - Langford Neck Resurveyed, Langford - 1738-1769
Crouch, Wedge - Wedges Discovery (Hodges Recovery?) - 1736-1752
Crouch, William - Crouches Addition - 1733-1735
Crowe, Edward - Cammells Farm, Fish Hall - 1733-1735
Crow, Isaac - Middle Plantation, Crows Chance - 1747-1760
Crow, Thomas - Crows Addition, Comegys Farm Addition - 1738-1769
Crowe, William - Middle Plantation, Crows Chance, Crows Addition

10 INHABITANTS OF KENT COUNTY, MARYLAND, 1637-1787

- 1733-1744
Crowley, Daniel - Chedle, Bristoll, High Park - 1733-1760
Cruickshank, Elizabeth - Jamaica, Lots in Chester Town - 1769
Cruickshank, Mary - Mount Pleasant, Jamaica, Lot in Chester Town - 1739, 1740
Cruickshank, Dr. James - Mount Pleasant, Jamaica, Lots in Chester Town, Kellys Longford - 1733-1744
Cruckshank, Mary - Jamaica, Lots in Chester Town - 1769
Cruckshank, Robert - Mount Pleasant - 1769
Crufield, Absalom - Jones's Venture - 1769
Cufey, Darby - Clifton - 1733-1735
Culley, Henry - Lots in Chester Town - 1736-1740
Cully, James - Forresters Delight, Dutches Folly, Whitefield - 1752-1760
Cunliffe, Foster - Buck Hill and Bettys Lot Resurveyed, Town Side - 1752-1760
Cunningham, Daniel - London Bridge, Hope - 1744-1752
Cunningham, Hugh - Mount Herman - 1752
Curry, Robert - Sewell - 1769
Dadman, Margarett - Colchester [Tolchester?], Lot in George Town - 1752-1769
Darden, Stephen - Hopewell - 1733-1735
Dare, William - Travelors Refreshment - 1733-1735
Darington, Thomas - Middle Branch, Hazard - 1747
Darnell, John - Darnalls Farm - 1733-1735
Darrack, Thomas - Tolchester, Lots in George Town - 1769
Daugherty, Walter - Sewell alias Ulrick - 1736-1738
Davis, Elizabeth - Lot in Chester Town, Hazard, Middle Branch - 1736-1769
Davis, Henry - Long Neglect, Harkol Fancy - 1733-1744
Davis, James - Duleans Folly - 1733-1735
Davis, John - Nancys Fancy, Hillens Adventure, Hazard, Middle Branch - 1733-1769
Davis, Mary - Stanaway, Tryangle - 1742-1752
Davis, Philip - Dallington, Hope, Dulleans Folly, Angels Lott - 1733-1769
Davis, Richard - Davis's Addition, Tryangle, Broad Neck, Nancys Fancy - 1733-1752
Davis, Samuel - Drawnear, Dullians Folly, Dallington, Triangle - 1741-1769
Davis, William - Broad Neck, Brints Pibbles - 1733-1769
Dawson, James - Winfield - 1733-1736
Dawson, John - Winfield - 1737
Day, John - Addition to Mathias and St. Johns Field, Mathias - 1753-1760
Day, Mathias - Addition to Mathias and St. Johns Fields, Mathias - 1733-1752
Deacon, Thomas - Friendship - 1741-1747
Deadman, Margaret - Lot in George Town, Tolchester - 1739-1747
Dean, William - Middle Branch, Hazard - 1736
Deavenish, John - Hinchingham - 1736-1744
Deavenish, Robert - Hinchingham - 1740 - 1747
Delahunty, Daniel - Kemps Beginning - 1736-1757
Debrula, William - Essex - 1733-1735

Dempster, John - Honest Dealing - 1736-1744
Denning, George - Ratlif [Ratcliffe?] - 1733-1760
Denning, John - Ratcliffe, Stannaway, Needful - 1733-1760
Denning, John - Mount Harman - 1747
Denning, Michael - Standaway - 1752
Derrick, John - Green Branch, Oversight - 1736-1738
Dicas, Ann - Kemps Beginning, Lot in Chester Town - 1736
Dicas, John - Kemps Beginning - 1737-1760
Dicas, William - Kemps Beginning - 1733-1736
Dickerson, Henry - Tilghmans Folly - 1742-1769
Dixon, Henry - Hurts Lot - 1769
Dixon, John - Hurts Lot - 1736-1760
Dixon, William - Cumberland - 1733-1735
Doile, John - Wexford - 1733 - 1735
Dollis, Robert - 5 lots in George Town - 1769
Donaldson, John - Forest - 1736-1769
Doran, James - Harbor, Lot in George Town - 1752-1769
Dougharty, Walter - Lot in Chester Town - 1744-1769
Douglas, George - Mill Fork, Larkins Addition - 1738-1769
Douglass, Joseph - Sewalls Manor, Hangmans Folly - 1747-1769
Dowdall, Richard - Ward Oak, Addition to Ward Oak, Dowdalls
    Fancy, Quaker Lot, Parsons Addition - 1733-1736
Downs, William - Mackeys Purchase - 1769
Drugan, Ann - Hepburns Farm - 1769
Druggan, Edward - Cove, Cove Tract, Grange, Nancys Fancy,
    Neglect, Drugans Lott, Cranberry Neck - 1752-1769
Drugan, Phillip - Cammels Farm, Hicks Addition - 1769
Dufey, Daniel - Kimbolton - 1733-1735
Dulany, Daniel - Dale Town, Fair Promise, Lords Gratious Grant,
    Partnership, Mitchels Park - 1733-1757
Dulany, Dennis - Lordships Gratious Grant - 1757-1769
Dulany, Dr. Edmond - Batchelors Resolution - 1736-1739
Dulany, Lloyd - Dale Town, Fair Promise, Partnership,
    Williamstown, Ponds, Adventure, Warners Marsh, Beals Gum,
    Warners Adventure - 1769
Dulany, Pricilla - Batchelors Resolution - 1741-1747
Duncan, George - Worths Folly - 1733-1760
Duncan, James - Worths Folly, Cammels Worthmore - 1753-1769
Dunkin, John - Killingsworthmore - 1733-1735
Duncan, Joseph - Worths Folly - 1753-1760
Dunn, Ann - Arcadia, Mackeys Desire, Bloomsbury, Waxford - 1769
Dunn, Darius - Broadnox, Fair Harbour - 1753-1769
Dunn, Hezikiah - Chance, Hynsons Chance, Addition - 1753-1769
Dunn, James - Arcadia, Mackeys Desire, Broadnox Resurveyed, High
    Park, Dmore [sic], Bristol, Browns Purchase, Mulberry Plains,
    Fork, Adventure - 1752-1769
Dunn, John - Dunns Folly - 1733-1735
Dunn, Capt. Robert - Broadnox, Fork, Adventure, Arcadia,
    Addition, Chance, Hynsons Chance - 1733-1747
Dunn, William - Fork, Arcadia, Mackeys Desire - 1757, 1760
Dunnaha, John - Easter Neck - 1733-1735
Durding, Joseph - Hopewell - 1736-1769
Dwyer, John - Howels Folly, Beaverdam, Georgetown, Medfords
    Mistake, Dwyers Desire - 1733-1737, 1769
Dyer, Edward - Lyons Hall - 1747-1756

Eades, Henry - Lords Gratious Grant, Addition - 1733-1760
Earle, Henry - Forrest - 1740
Earle, John - Mount Hope - 1733-1741
Earley, William - Prevention of Inconveniency, Earlys Beginning, Gibbs's Chance, Couzens Lott, Parks's Rest, Couzens Chance, Randon - 1733-1747
Edmondson, John - Whittington, Bluff Point - 1733-1735
Edwin Brewer (heirs) - Smiths Range, Addition, Edwins Rest, Floyds Chance - 1733-1735
Ellers, Benjamin - Sewell alias Ulrick - 1769
Elliott, Edward - Fork - 1733, 1735
Ellis, Benjamin - St. Marys, Golden Ridge, Kent Lot, Chesterton - 1733-1735
Ellis, John - Ellis Chance, St. Martins - 1733-1735
Ellis, William - St. Marys, North Andover, Williams Venture, Ellis Industry - 1736-1760
Elmes, William - Great Oak Manor - 1733-1735
Emory, Arthur - Broadnox Creek - 1769
England, Isaac - Millfork - 1733
England, Joseph - Plains, Denby - 1736-1747
Ennalls, Joseph - Ponds - 1737-1756
Ennalls, Col. William - Ponds - 1733-1743
Evans, Evan - Poplar Farm - 1736
Evans, Henry - Lot in Chester Town, Bright Helmstone - 1733-1744
Evans, Sarah - Poplar Farm - 1737 - 1738
Everett, Benjamin - Everetts Double Purchase, Everetts Addition, Rich Meadow - 1747-1757
Everett, Catherine - Popes Forrest, Lot in Chester Town, Everetts Double Purchase - 1739-1757
Everett, Elizabeth - Popes Forrest, Lot in Chester Town, Galloways Chance, Everetts Double Purchase - 1738
Everett, John - Broad Neck, Triangle - 1744-1757
Everett, Joseph - Popes Forrest, Gallaways Chance, Lot in Chester Town - 1733-1737
Everitt, St. Leger - Nancys Choice - 1769
Evett, Nathaniel - Reward, Chance, Cedar Grove (Chester Grove?) - 1733-1735
Fairhill, Daniel - Queen Carleton - 1733-1735
Falconar, Abram - Hemberry, Hope, Goose Haven, Partnership, London Bridge - 1738-1760
Falconar, Gilbert - Hembury, Goose Haven, Partnership, Daniel and Josephs Disappointment, London Bridge - 1733-1769
Falconar, Hannah - Goose Haven, Partnership, Hope, Hemberry, London Bridge - 1737-1760
Falconar, John - Falconars Lott, Beckwith, Hope - 1742-1769
Fanning, John - Providence, Kelly Langford - 1733-1769
Feddis, John - Stratford Manor - 1747-1760
Ferrell, Daniel - Queen Carleton, Ferrells Addition - 1733-1744, 1769
Ferrell, Eliza - Queen Charlton, Addition to Queen Charlton, Ferrells Addition, Lot in Chester Town - 1736
Ferrill, Robert - Vienna - 1736-1744
Ferrol, Thomas - Cock of the Game - 1769
Finchingham, Richard - Arcadia - 1733-1747

MILITIA 13

Fisher, William - Salisbury - 1733-1735
Fittzgerrald, Martha - Nancys Fancy - 1733-1735
Flaharty, James - Spring Garden - 1769
Fling, Laughlon - Sewall alias Ulrick, Ricerden - 1733-1735
Floyd, William - Chance - 1733
Forbush, John - Thornton, Addition, Suffolk - 1737-1740
Forbush, Mary - Thornton, Addition, Suffolk - 1741-1744
Ford, Richard - Forrest - 1736-1747
Ford, Robert - Sweatmans Insula, Bromfield - 1733-1769
Ford, Thomas - Hermitage - 1753-1760
Ford, William - Chance, Bromfield, Providence - 1733-1735, 1769
Foreman, Arthur - Black Halls Harmitage - 1733-1760
Foreman, Charles - Sewistern, Friendship - 1736-1769
Foreman, John - Foremans Poor Discovery, Good Hope - 1737-1756
Foreman, Robert - Sewsterne - 1733-1756
Forguson, Collin - Lot in George Town, Chance, Neighbours Neglect, Tobens Lott - 1756-1769
Forrester, Rev. George W. - Tolchester, Lots in Georgetown, Lots in Chestertown, Tobens Folly, Free Gift - 1738-1769
Foster, John - Margaretts End - 1747-1769
Foucher, John - Killingsworthmore Enlarged - 1752-1769
Foxen, George - Comb Hill - 1733-1735
Fraizar, George - Arcadia - 1760, 1769
Francis, John - Holt - 1769
Fray, William - Town Relief - 1769
Freeman, Ab. - Timber Levell, Addition to Timber Levell, By Chance, Peters Forrest, Marshy Point - 1769
Freeman, Isaac - Timber Levell, Verian, Tebbats, Freemans Addition, Marshy Point, Godfreys Point - 1733-1769
Freeman, William - Stannaway - 1733-1735
Free School, Kent County - Stepney - 1733-1747
French, Samuel - Hazard - 1753-1760
French, Zerobabel - Partnership, Beckwith's Addition, French's Lott, Hazard - 1733-1769
Frisby, Ann - Lot in Chestertown - 1738
Frisby, Elizabeth - Sewells Mannor - 1733-1735
Frisby, James - Hinchingham, Stephen Heaths Manor, Greshams College, Hudles Right, Tolchester, Rush More, Lot in Chester Town - 1747-1760
Frisby, Jane - Hinchingham, Sewells Manor, Stephen Heaths Manor, Hollyland, Gresham Colledge, Lot in Chestertown, New Key, Swan Island, Great Oak Manor - 1739-1769
Frisby, Peregrin - Tilghmans and Foxleys Grove, 3 Lots in Chestertown, Hinchingham, Broad Oak - 1739-1769
Frisby, Richard - Coneywarren, Griffith Calfpen, Eastern Neck, Packerton - 1757, 1769
Frisby, Thomas - Cox's Stale, Partnership - 1733-1735
Frisby, William - New York, Hinchingham, Dmore [sic], Swan Island, Thomas's Purchase, Great Oak Manor, Frisby's Purchase - 1733-1769
Froggett, John - Bounty - 1733-1735
Fulstone, Richard - Stephen Heaths Manor, Middle Plantation - 1733-1735
Gafford, Charles - Chester Grove - 1733-1760
Gale, John Jr. - Redmonds Supply - 1733-1769

Gale, Levin - Lots in Georgetown - 1738 - 1739
Gale, Mary - Moreton, Larkins Addition - 1736-1740
Gale, Raisin - Grange, Redmons Supply, Intermix - 1769
Gallaway, James - Lot in Chestertown - 1736-1739
Gamble, John - Great Oak Manor, Gamballs Farm, Hereford - 1736-1769
Garland, John - Queen Carleton, Ellis Chance, Fortune - 1733-1769
Garnett, Bartus - Addition to Queen Carlton, Lot in Chester Town - 1747-1769
Garnett, George - Strafford Manor, Lot in Chestertown, Sarahs Lot, Garnets Meadow - 1736-1769
Garnett, John - Standford, Kemps Beginning, Lot in Georgetown - 1769
Garnett, Jonathan - Stradford Mannor - 1733-1735
Garnett, Joseph - Standford, Kemps Beginning, Sadlers Lott, Garnett Branch, Lot in Georgetown, Lot in Chestertown - 1737-1760
Garnett, Mary - Stratford Mannor - 1736, 1737
Garnett, Thomas - Stepney, Stradford Mannor, Sarahs Lott, Garnetts Meadows - 1733-1735, 1769
Garrett, John - Antionio, Poplar Farm, Galloways Farm - 1752-1769
Gaskill, Capt. William - Agreement - 1736-1744
Geist, Christopher - Unity - 1733, 1735
George, Joseph - Stratford Manor - 1736-1769
George, Joshua - Chesterfield - 1737-1741
George, Mary - Morton Resurveyed - 1753-1757
George, Robert - Strafford Resurveyed, Hoziers Neglect, Shadford Mannor - 1733-1769
Gibbs, Edward - Fair Harbor - 1736-1769
Gibbs, Richard - Gibbs Chance, Prevention Illconvenient, Faire Harbour - 1733-1735
Gibbs, William - Lot in Chestertown - 1738-1769
Gibson, Richard - Angles Rest or Lot - 1737
Gibson, Robert - Adventure - 1738
Gibson, Woolman - Adventure, Angles Rest - 1733-1738
Gideon, Thomas - Galloways Farm - 1733-1735
Gilpin, George - Myers Chance, Addition to Fair Dealing - 1769
Gilpin, Thomas - Rich Level, London Bridge, Bordleys Gift, London Bridge Renewed, Pond Side, Johnsons Lot, Meers Inclosure, Little Forrest - 1757, 1760, 1769
Glafford (Glasford), Henry - Chance, By Chance - 1760, 1769
Glanvill, Stephen - Hinchingham, Grove - 1736-1769
Glanvill, William - Hinchingham, Grove - 1733-1735
Glassford, Henry - Chance, By Chance - 1757
Gleaves, George - Gleaves Lott - 1733-1735
Gleaves, John - Howels Range, Wardens Lott, Addition, Broad Neck, Thorton, Batchelors Resolution, Friendship, Resurvey on Tryangle - 1747-1769
Gleaves, Joseph - Howels Range, Maiden Lot, Addition, Three Friends - 1737-1760
Glenn, Jacob - Hynsons Choice - 1733-1769
Gleaves, Ruth - Addition - 1741-1743
Glenn, Alexander - Lot in Chestertown - 1753-1756
Gold, Thomas - Forrest - 1736

Gooding, Arno - Cuckolds Hope - 1734 - 1735
Goodwin, Elinor - Arcadia - 1733-1769
Gooding, Jacob - Cuckholds Hope - 1736-1744
Gooding, Samuel - Arcadia - 1736
Goodwin, Mary (for Jacob's heirs) - Cuckold Hope - 1752-1769
Gordon, Charles - Lot in Chestertown - 1769
Grae, Richard - Lot in Chestertown - 1741 - 1742
Granger, Mary - Ratcliffe's Cross, Wickliffe, Market Place, Lot in Chestertown, Grange, Kemps Beginning - 1753-1769
Granger, William - Grange, Ratcliffe Cross, Market Place, Wickliff, Lot in Chestertown - 1733-1752
Grant, Abigail - Grant Folly - 1752-1760
Grant, John - Langfords Neck Resurveyed - 1733-1769
Grant, William - Grants Folly - 1769
Graham, John - Grahams Fishery, Prickley Pear, Smally - 1769
Graham, Richard - Lot in Georgetown - 1755-1769
Graves, Alexander - Hinchingham - 1733-1735
Graves, Richard - Mothers Gift - 1769
Graves, Sarah - Dow Neck, Hill Top, Hill Down, Coney Warren, Prince William, Lot in Chestertown, Buck Neck Resurveyed - 1760
Graves, William - Buck Neck, Wye Hill Down, Hill Top, Coney Warren, Lot in Chestertown, Buck Neck Resurveyed - 1733-1769
Grey, James - Chance, Comb Whitten, Christophers Beginning - 1747
Grey, John - Lot in Georgetown - 1769
Gray, Richard - Hobsons Choice - 1733-1737
Green, Benjamin - Coney Warren - 1736-1769
Green, Bowles - Talley [Tulley] Fancy - 1736-1744
Green, Henry - Lovely Neck, Sewards Hope - 1733-1735
Green, John - Tulleys Fancy, Coney Warren - 1733-1752
Green, Peter - Comegys Fancy, Tullys Fancy - 1733-1735
Green, Robert - Lyons Hall, High Park - 1733-1744
Greenfield, Archibald - Oversight - 1738 - 1739
Greenleaf, Isaac - Duggans Delight - 1769
Greenwood, Daniel - Drayton - 1733-1736
Greenwood, James - Hills and No Dales, Addition to Hills and No Dales - 1733-1747
Greenwood, John - Boudys Folly and Greenwoods Advancement, Suffolk - 1733-1769
Greenwood, John Jr. - Bowdeys Folly, Greenwoods Adventure - 1736-1744
Greenwood, Joseph - Suffolk Resurveyed, Suffolk - 1752-1769
Greer, James - Greers Range - 1733-1735
Gresham, John - Batchelors Resolution, Providence, Greshams Colledge, Stiles Addition Corrected, Lots in Charlestown [sic], Huddles Right, Tolchester, Rushmore, Fishing Pond, Bluff Point, Unity - 1733-1769
Gresham, Richard - Batchelors Resolution, Lot in Chestertown, Hinchingham, Piney Point Resurveyed, Smiths Desart, Greshams Levells, Greshams Discovery, Langfords Neck Resurveyed, Lots in Chestertown, Memento More, Addition - 1733-1769
Griffin, Ann - Eastern Neck, Lot in Chestertown, Batchellors Choice, Spring Garden, Griffiths Calf Penn - 1737
Griffin, Benjamin - Eastern Neck, Batchellors Choice, Spring Garden, Griffins Calf Penn, Lot in Chestertown - 1733-1736

16 INHABITANTS OF KENT COUNTY, MARYLAND, 1637-1787

Griffin, Charles - Chidley - 1736-1747
Griffin, Jackson - Eastern Neck, Calf Pen, Lot in Chestertown, Spring Garden, Batchellors Choice - 1738-1769
Griffin, Jonas - Batchellors Choice - 1739, 1743
Griffin, Nathaniel - Eastern Neck, Griffiths Calf Pen - 1739-1769
Griffith, Cooter - Spring Garden - 1752-1769
Griffith, George - Providence - 1736-1769
Griffith, John - Queen Carleton - 1733-1735
Griffith, Samuel - Whitefield, Forrest Resurveyed, Adventure - 1757, 1760, 1769
Grindidge, Charles - Dulleans Folly - 1733-1769
Groome (Gromes), Charles - Hopeful Unity - 1769
Groome, Samuel - Clayton and Bowdeys Folly, Greenwoods Advancement, Cammels Worthmore, Cornwallis Chance, Falmouth - 1733-1769
Guibert, John - No Name - 1733-1735
Guy, Robert - Scotts Fancy - 1769
Gyant, John - Middle Neck - 1736-1747
Hackett, James - Hacketts Fancy, Chance Resurveyed, Broad Neck, Friendship, Long Neglect - 1741-1769
Hackett, Michael - Hacketts Fancy, Broad Neck, Friendship, Long Neglect - 1733-1757
Hackett, Samuel - Whittfield - 1733-1735
Hagarty, William - Nannys Hope (Nancys Hope), Lot in Chestertown - 1733-1737
Haimer, John - Comegies Chance, Hamers Lott, Standford, New Key - 1733-1735
Hales, Roger - Grange, Martins, Allebones Addition, Green Meadow, Hales Purchase - 1733-1769
Haley, John - St. Andrews Cross, Margarets Delight - 1736-1757
Haley, William - St. Andrews Cross, Margarets Delight, Fork, Adventure, Addition to Matthias and St. Johns Fields - 1753-1769
Hall, Ann - Tibballs, Castle Carey - 1736-1769
Hall, Chambers - Larkins Addition - 1742-1760
Hall, Christopher - Fork, Jerico, Christophers Beginning, Chance - 1/2 lot in Georgetown - 1733-1744, 1769
Hall, Francis - Green Oak - 1733-1769
Hall, George - Fork, Jericho - 1733-1769
Hall, John - Fork, Castle Cary, Tibballs, Tersons Neglect - 1733-1760
Hall, Michael - Pentridge - 1747
Hamblin, William - Hamblin Lott - 1757, 1760
Hamlin, John - Reading - 1733-1737
Hammond, Thomas - Larkins Addition - 1733-1737
Hanson, George - Tolchester, Tomb - 1733-1735
Hands, Beddinfield - 3 lots in Chestertown, Stephen Heaths Manor - 1738-1769
Hankin, John - Lincolne - 1733-1744
Hanmer, John - Standford, New Key - 1743, 1744
Hanson, Frederick - Tolchester, Tomb, Adventure - 1733-1769
Hanson, Gustave - Larkins Addition, Millfork - 1739-1760
Hanson, Hance - Tolchester - 1736-1769
Hanson, Mary - Tolchester, Green Branch - 1739-1760

Hanson, William - Tolchester - 1733-1735
Harbinston, William - Forrest - 1738-1769
Harkin, Cornelius - Stepney, Adventure, Lot in Chestertown - 1736-1769
Harris, Ariana W. - Millford, Coventry, Hillsdown, Fairlee, Swamp Resurveyed, Harris Addition, Lot in Chestertown - 1752-1760
Harris, Mrs. Augustine - Lot in Chestertown - 1747, 1752
Harris, Edward - Snow Hill, Forrest Resurveyed, Forrest, Level Ridge - 1733-1741
Harris, James - Coventry, Orchards Neck, Great Oak Mannor, Fairlee, Poplar Farme, Forrest of Dean, Millford, Poplar Hill, Addition, Skidmore and Bluntwell, Hillsdowne, Housleys Discovery, Knowlmans Desire, Swamp, Long Neglect, Lots in Chestertown - 1733-1741
Harris, John - Forrest - 1736 - 1737
Harris, Mathias - Frenchards Memorial, Long Neglect, Lots in Chestertown and Georgetown - 1738-1769
Harris, Susanna - Hansford, Sewell alias Ulrick, Hatchbury - 1736-1760
Harris, Thomas - Adventure, Snow Hill, Mill Hill, Forrest, Level Ridge - 1742-1769
Harris, William - Coventry, Hillsdown, Harris Addition, Lot in Chestertown, Swamp - 1736-1747, 1769
Harrison, William - Church Warden Neck - 1733-1735
Hart, John - Marshes - 1747-1760
Hastings (Hasting), George - Green Branch - 1733-1735
Hastings, Oliver - Green Bank (Branch) - 1737-1760
Hatcheson, Nathan - Stanaway, Hatchesons Addition - 1769
Hatcheson, Robert - Killingsworthmore - 1760, 1769
Hatcheson, Thomas - Stanaway - 1760
Havely, James - Stavelys Lot, Broad Oak, Childs Harbour, Suffolk - 1736-1741
Hays, John - Rippen, Partnership Point - 1736-1756
Hayley, John - St. Andrews Cross - 1733-1735
Haywood, William - Hillens Adventure, Boston - 1733-1737
Hazle, Benjamin - Williams Venture, Hazle Adventure, Borough Addition, Conjunction - 1747-1760
Hazleburst, John - Coney Warren - 1742-1744
Hearne, Darley - Macoakin - 1733-1735
Hearn, Hugh - Angells Lot, Spring Garden - 1743-1756
Heath, Charles - Herefield, Rebeccas Desire, Church Warden Neck - 1737-1744
Heath, James - Forrest, Larkins Addition, Heaths Range, 3 lots in Chestertown, Heathworth, Heath Forrest - 1733-1769
Hebron, James - Howells Farm, Luck, Hebrons Farm - 1733-1735
Hebron, John - Luck, Howels Farm, Broad Oak - 1736-1760
Hebron, Thomas - Broomfield, Luck, Marshes, Green Forrest - 1733-1769
Hedges, William - Forrest, Heaths Range, Larkins Addition, Lot in Chestertown - 1752-1760
Hemberston, George - Chance, Cock of the Game - 1733-1735
Hendrickson, John - Maiden Lott - 1733-1760
Hizard, Phillip - Down Date (Dale?), St. Margarets, Stricklands Rest - 1733-1760
Hickambotham, Oliver - Staples Choice - 1733-1735

18 INHABITANTS OF KENT COUNTY, MARYLAND, 1637-1787

Hiff, Edmond - Deptford - 1738-1740
Higgs, ---- [blank] - Coffin - 1733, 1735
Hill, Capt. Richard - Middle Neck, Pearch Meadows, Sweet Harbour - 1733-1742
Hix, John - Cammels Farm, Howards Lot, Hicks Addition - 1736-1760
Hix, Roger - Hix Hazard, Roger Hix Intent - 1736-1747
Hodges, John - Prevention of Inconvenience, Neifs Choice - 1733-1760
Hodges, Rebecca - Lot in Chestertown - 1769
Hodges, Robert - Prevention of Illconvenience - 1733-1752
Hodges, Samuel - Prevention of Inconvenience - 1753-1769
Hodges, Stephen - Prevention of Inconvenience - 1736-1769
Hodges, William - Prevention of Inconvenience, Hurts Direction - 1736-1769
Holeager, John - Rich Level, Philips Neglect - 1736-1747
Hollegar, Phillip - Rich Levell, Addition - 1733-1735
Holeman, Edward - Byman, Mackeys Purchase - 1733-1747
Holladay, Francis - Masseys Venture - 1738-1760
Holladay, Henry - Lot in Chestertown - 1736-1769
Holland, George - Denton - 1733
Holliday, Edward - Agreement - 1747-1757
Hollinsworth, John - St. Andrews Cross - 1733
Hollinsworth, William - Beginning - 1733 - 1735
Hollis, Charles - Chance - 1747-1769
Hollyday, Edward - Masseys Venture - 1733-1737
Hollyday, G. - Pondside - 1769
Holman, Henry - McCays Purchase - 1760, 1769
Holt, Rev. Arthur - Rushmore, Fishing Ponds, Huddles Right, Hope - 1736-1743
Hooper, Col. Henry - Lot in Georgetown - 1739-1769
Hopewell, Richard - Hereford, Hopewell - 1733-1736
Hopkins, Benjamin - Hopewell - 1736
Hopkins, Joseph - Buck Neck - 1733-1735
Hopkins, Philip - Thornton, Maiden Lott, Addition - 1733-1735
Hopkins, Sarah - Hangmans Folly, Duck Pye - 1733-1735
Hopkins, Capt. William - Lot in Chestertown - 1736-1769
Horney, Jeffery - Dixons Gift - 1733, 1735
Hoskins, Stephen - Fair Promise, Warners Adventure, Warners Addition - 1736-1744
Howard, Benjamin - Porters Resurvey, Grange - 1769
Howard, John - Howards Adventure, Norris's Desire, Blays Park, Cannaday - 1752-1769
Howard, Mathew - Howards Lot, Beaver Dam Neck, Georgetown, Howards Policy, Medfords Mistake, Howards Adventure - 1733-1760
Howell, John - Drayton, Cove, Cove Tract, Cranberry Neck - 1733-1747
Howell, Thomas - Cranberry Neck, Fairlee, Howells Outland - 1733-1735
Hozier, Hannah - New York, Hoziers Farm, Great Oak Manor - 1736-1769
Hozier, Henry - McCays Purchase, New York, Hoziers Addition, Bristowe, Tullys Fancy, Great Oak Manor, Hoziers Adventure, Hoziers Farm Resurveyed - 1733-1735, 1769

Hozier, Richard - Great Oak Mannor - 1753-1769
Hudson, John - Broad Oak, Chance - 1733-1738
Hudson, Philip - Shadshole - 1741, 1742
Huff (Hufe), John - Bounty, Addition, Chance, Hynsons Chance - 1733-1741
Hull, Daniel - Chance, Coney Warren, Verine - 1736-1752
Hull, David - Draton, Intermix, Weatherleys, Sandy Plantation - 1736-1760
Hull, Elizabeth - Childs Harbour, Suffolk, Snavelys Lott, Broad Oak - 1752-1757
Hull, Ferdinando - Snavelys Lot, Broad Oak, Childs Harbour, Suffolk, Shadshole - 1738-1747
Hull, Joseph - Suffolk - 1736-1760
Humberson, George - Chance, Cock of the Game - 1736-1769
Hunter, James - Lot in Georgetown, Tolchester - 1756-1769
Hunter, John - Wedges Discovery - 1733-1735
Hurley, Sarah - Providence - 1736-1741
Hurley, Timothy - Providence - 1733-1735
Hurlock, Robert - Hurlocks Chance - 1769
Hurt, Cornelius - Holy Land - 1742-1769
Hurt, Henry - Holy Land, Phillips Choice, Middle Plantation, Crows Chance - 1736-1769
Hurt, John - Walnut Neck, Woodland Neck, Hart Point, Hurts Lot, Remainder - 1733-1769
Hurt, Martha - Four Brothers, Bristol, Mulberry Plain, High Park, Scotts Lott - 1752-1769
Hurt, Morgan - Woodland Neck, Hart Point, Walnut Neck, Holy Land - 1736-1747
Husbands, Thomas - Husbands Lott, Ruerden - 1733-1752
Hutchinson, James - Warners Addition - 1769
Hutchenson, Thomas - Killingsworthmore - 1733-1744
Hutcheson, Mary - Hangmans End - 1769
Hutcheson, Vincent - Stanaway - 1736-1769
Hynson, Andrew - Castle Carey, Hynsons Adventure, Addition, Lot in Georgetown, Smiths Park, Scotts Folly, Sampsons Addition, Hynsons Desire - 1752-1769
Hynson, Col. Charles - Hynsons Durleon [sic], Bengey, Pig Neck, Maidens Lot, Fathers Gift, Hynsons Chance, Chance Addition, Hynsons Discovery, Harris Forrest, Skidmore - 1733-1769
Hynson, Charles Jr. - Thomas Hynsons Land Resurveyed, Omission, Bengey, Pig Neck, Maidens Lot, Fathers Gift, Hynsons Discovery, Addition - 1739-1769
Hynson, Francina - Forrest of Dean, Harmatage, Harris Forrest, Popes Forrest, Bavaria, 2 lots in Chestertown - 1752-1760
Hynson, James Jr. - Smiths Park, Fairfield, Partnership - 1760
Hynson, John - Lot in Georgetown, Hynsons Chance, Smith Park, Hynsons Division, Addition - 1733-1769
Hynson, Martha - Hinchingham, Widows Chance - 1733-1737
Hynson, Mathias - Forrest of Dean - 1757
Hynson, Col. Nathaniel - Hynsons Division, Addition, Sutton Underhill, Salkeld, Huddles Night, Fishing Ponds, Buck Neck, Underhill, Rushmore, Hinchingham, Partnership, Spring Hill - 1733-1769
Hynson, Nathaniel Jr. - Hynsons Division, Partnership, Spring Hill, Lot in Chestertown - 1736-1760

20 INHABITANTS OF KENT COUNTY, MARYLAND, 1637-1787

Hynson, Sarah - Buck Neck - 1736
Hynson, Thomas - New Forrest, Fair Harbour, Addition, New Hunting Fields - 1733-1752, 1769
Hynson, William - Hangmans Folly, Symonds Addition, Scotts Folly, Poplar Hill - 1736-1769
Inch, John - New York - 1733-1752
Ingrams, Elizabeth - Stepney - 1769
Ireland, Joseph - Rileys Beginning - 1769
Jackson, Benjamin - Buckingham - 1753-1769
Jackson, John - Barbarys Inlett - 1733
Jackson, Martha - Whitfield, Lot in Chestertown - 1741-1752
Jackson, Robert - Whitfield, Lot in Chestertown - 1737-1740
Jacobs, Henry - Bradfield - 1736-1757
James, Charles - Good Hope - 1733-1735
James, Jarvis - Heaths Long Lands - 1760
James, John - Petten, Brinton, Heaths Long Lands, Good Hope - 1733-1752
James, Seney - Good Hope, Simmons Prime Choice, Heaths Long Land - 1753-1756
Jarman, Robert - Galloways - 1733-1735
Jarvis, Joseph - Lot in Georgetown - 1744-1769
Jekyll, John - Lot in Chestertown - 1736-1740
Jekyll, Margaret - Lot on Chestertown - 1741-1756
Jennings, Edmond - Bright Helmstone, Lot in Georgetown, Lot in Chestertown - 1736-1769
Jennings, Thomas - Adventure - 1769
Jerrom, Sarah - [name of tract missing from index] - 1736
Jerrum, Thomas - Grassing Point alias Grays Inn - 1733-1760
Joce, Margaret - Bridge Point, New Forrest, Addition, Fair Harbour - 1736-1740
Joce, Pascoe - Philips Choice - 1752-1760
Joce, Thomas - Bridge Point, Philips Choice, New Forrest, Addition to New Forrest, Arcadia, Fair Harbour, Addition - 1733-1757
Johns, Richard - Lovelys Neck, Great Oak Mannor - 1736-1769
Johnson, Edward William - Darnals Farm - 1741-1760
Johnson, Holeman - Partnership - 1752-1769
Johnson, John - Forrest, Ingrams Lott, Bachmans Farm, Out Range, Thornton, Adventure, Ambrosia, Thorntons Addition, Forrest Resurveyed, Chance, Lot in Chestertown - 1733-1752
Johnson, Richard - Thornton, Batemans Farm, Ingrams Lott, Ambrosia, Thorntons Addition, Forrest Resurveyed, Lot in Chestertown, Chance - 1753-1757
Johnson, Richard, and Philip Brooks wife - Out Range - 1757
Johnson Samuel (Susanna) - Forrest, Ingrams Lot, Batemans Farm, Out Range, Thornton, Adventure, Chance, Ambrosia Resurveyed, Thornton Addition - 1736-1738
Johnson, Thomas - Darnals Farm - 1760
Johnson, William - Partnership - 1733-1752
Johnston, Thomas - Stepney - 1769
Jones, Benjamin (schoolmaster) - Chance - 1733-1743
Jones, Benjamin - Broad Oak - 1738-1747
Jones, David - Lively [Lovely?] Neck - 1736-1747
Jones, Griffin - Courses Meadows, Griers Range, Hebburns Farm,

MILITIA 21

Brotherly and Friendly Agreement, Grange - 1736-1760
Jones, Jacob - Brothers Annextion, Huckleberry Ridge, Jones Addition, Jones Adventure - 1736-1769
Jones, John - Londonderry, Providence - 1741-1769
Jones, John - Beckworth, Providence, Queen Carlton - 1733-1769
Jones, John - Chester Grove, Providence - 1747-1760
Jones, Mary - Grange - 1752
Jones, Peter - Jones Gore - 1733-1769
Jones, Rice - Little Grove - 1733-1735
Jones, Robert - Chester Grove - 1733-1735
Jones, Thomas - Batchelors Choice, Batchelors Delight, Coney Warren - 1733-1760
Jones, William - Williams Venture, Jones Addition, Georgetown, Isk, Broad Oak - 1733-1769
Jones, William - George Town, New York, Verina - 1733-1737, 1753-1760
Jordan, John - Have at All - 1733-1735
Josiah, Emanuel - 1/2 lot in Chestertown - 1769
Katen, Mary - Mount Hope - 1753-1757
Katon, William - Mount Hope - 1769
Kear, Benjamin - Lot in Chestertown, Ash Point - 1734-1769
Kear, James - Lot in Chestertown - 1736, 1737
Kears, Thomas - Ash Point - 1733-1735
Kelley, Alexander - Sewall alias Ulrick, Killingsworthmore Enlarged, Kellys Chance, Neglect, Kellys Addition - 1752-1769
Kelly, Benjamin - Kellys Chance, Howells Adventure - 1733-1737
Kelly, Daniel - Arcadia - 1733-1735
Kelly, James - Howells Adventure, Warners Adventure, Warners Addition - 1733-1769
Kelley, Mary - Howells Adventure - 1738-1752
Kendall, William - Bradfield, Necessitys Habitation - 1738-1769
Kennday, Elizabeth - Christophers Beginning, Chance, Comb Whitton - 1753-1769
Kennard, Ann - Fathers Care, Lot in Georgetown - 1769
Kennday, Edward - Long Acre - 1752-1760
Kennard, John - Doe Neck, Denby Resurveyed, Sole, Budds Meadow, Cornwallis Choice - 1736-1769
Kennard, Joseph - Lot in Chestertown - 1736-1740
Kennard, Nathaniel - Denbigh Resurveyed, Kennards Fancy - 1736-1769
Kennadt, Patrick - Oversight - 1752-1769
Kennard, Phillip - Tryangle, Drayton, Denby, Chance, Lynn, Addition to Lynn, Partnership, Kennards Discovery, Kennards Discovery Resurveyed - 1733-1769
Kennard, Richard - Denbigh Resurveyed - 1736-1769
Kennard, Sarah - Kennards Point, Addition to Kennards Point, Lot in Chestertown, Fathers Care, Lot in Georgetown, Denbye, Tryangle, Lynn, Addition to Lynn, Kennards Discovery, Kennards Fancy - 1741-1760
Kennard, Stephen - Denbigh, Wheelright Swamp - 1769
Kennedy, Jane - Deans Adventure - 1733-1735
Kennedy (Keneday), Patrick - Oversight - 1740-1747
Kennedy, Roger - Long Acre - 1733-1735
Kenslaugh, Dominick - Bloomsbury, Waxford, Arcadia, Town Hill, Baylys Forrest - 1733-1747, 1769

Kenslaugh, John - Bloomsbury, Waxford, Arcadia, Town Hill - 1752-1769
Kent County - Stepney - 1737-1769
Keys, William - Standford, New Key - 1733-1737
King, Elizabeth - [name of tract missing from index] - 1734, 1735
King, James - Scotts Folly - 1733-1735
King, John - Howards Gift, Chance - 1733-1735
Kinsey, Thomas - Burks Addition - 1769
Kinson, Stephen - Denbigh, Wheelright Swamp - 1769
Knap, Robert - Knapley - 1733-1735
Knight, Stephen - Hinchingham, Lot in Chestertown - 1736-1747
Knock, Benjamin - Andover, Knox Range, Chesterfield - 1760
Knock, Francis - Childs Harbour, Rachels Farm - 1747-1769
Knock, Henry - Chesterfield Resurveyed, Childs Harbour, Knocks Harbour, Knocks Range, Andover Resurveyed - 1733-1757
Knock, John - Castle Carey - 1753-1769
Knock, Nathaniel - Chesterfield - 1760, 1769
Knock, William - Childs Harbour, Rachels Farm - 1747-1769
Knoleman, Anthony - Niefs Choice - 1736-1769
Knowles, John - Chance - 1733-1735
Knowlman, Jane - Tolchester and Tomb - 1738, 1739
Knoleman, Richard - Tolchester and Tomb - 1736, 1737
Lamb, Edward - Lambs Range - 1736-1747
Lamb, Francis - Lambs Meadows, Hepburns Farm, Brotherly and Friendly Agreement, Friendship, Wetheralls Hope, Courses Meadow - 1736-1769
Lamb, George - Friendship - 1760, 1769
Lamb, Joshua - Lambs Range, Warners Adventure, Warners Addition - 1752-1769
Lamb, Peirce - Lambs Range, Lambs Meadow - 1733-1735
Lancaster, John - Lancaster - 1735
Lanham, James - Hunting Fields, Ringgolds Chance - 1735-1742
Larkins, Thomas - Larkins Addition, Hollands Delight - 1733-1735
Leatherbury, Jonathan - Lot in Chestertown, Stepney - 1769
Leech, Capt. Edward - Worths Folly - 1733-1737
Lenox, Richard - Hynsons Discovery, Fathers Gift, Addition, Maidens Lott - 1741-1747
Lewin, Abraham and wife - Lot in Chestertown - 1757-1769
Lewis, Evin - Neglect, Partnership Point - 1736-1769
Lewis, Fanny - Little Grove, Arcadia, Lots in Chestertown - 1752
Lewis, Francis - Grove, Lot in Chestertown - 1733-1737, 1752-1769
Lewis, Robert - [name of tract missing from index] - 1769
Lewis, Thomas - Arcadia, Hinchingham - 1733-1769
Lewis, William - Vienna - 1769
Leybourn, George - 1/2 lot in Chestertown - 1769
Lincolne, Jonathan - Lincolns Inn Fields - 1733-1736
Linegar, George - Spring Garden, Angells Lot Resurveyed, Conjunct - 1733-1769
Linegar, Jacob - Conjunct - 1769
Lisbey, James - Hunting Field - 1736
Lisbey, Robert - Hunting Field, Lovely Neck - 1737-1747
Lisle, Rebecca - Stepney, Lot in Chestertown - 1736-1769
Little, Adam - Adventure - 1769
Little, George - Harbor, Tolchester, Lot in Chestertown -

MILITIA 23

1757-1769
Little, Robert - Angels Lot Resurveyed, Spring Garden, Angels Rest - 1752-1769
Lloyd, Col. Edward - Worton Manor, Bennets Regulation, Standaway, Chevy Chace, Cornwallis Choice, Falmouth, Mitchels Park, Derby, Smiths Bay - 1733-1735. 1752-1769
Lloyd, James - Derby, Lot in Chesterfield - 1736-1738
Lloyd, Rebecca - Lots in Chestertown - 1736-1740
Lloyd, Richard - Smiths Bay, Durby, Coventry, Fairly, Addition to Fairly, Hills Down - 1739-1769
Lockerman, John - Adventure, Angles Rest - 1733-1740
Lorain, Thomas - Stepney - 1/2 lot in Chestertown - 1756-1769
Loullit, James - German Point, Knocks Folly, Morton - 1757-1769
Lowder, Charles - Chance - 1733, 1735
Lowe, Col. Henry - Green Oak, Lower Bennett, Darnall, Darnalls Farm - 1733-1735
Lowman, Samuel - Peach Meadows and Woodlands Intentions, Queen Charlton - 1736-1760
Lowmans, Richard - Peach Meadows and Woodlands Intention - 1769
Lusby, Draper - Knapley Green, Griffiths Delight, Addition to Knapley - 1752-1760
Lux, Richard - Lot in Chestertown - 1769
Lynch, Edmund - Cammels Worthmore - 1747-1769
Lynch, John - Cammels Worthmore - 1742-1744
Lynch, Nicholas - Town Relief, Ratcliffe - 1733-1769
Lynch, Robert - Dublin - 1733-1737
Lynch, Thomas - Ratcliff - 1736-1760
McCall, Benjamin - Free Gift, First Part - 1736-1760
McCann, Edward - Hollingsworthmore - 1760
McCintock, Alex. - Lot in Chestertown - 1769
McClacklan, James - Lot in Georgetown - 1756, 1757
McClane, William - Lot in Chestertown - 1737-1752
McClannahorn, Nathaniel - Buckingham - 1738-1747
McClean, James Jr. - Little Grove, Arcadia, Lot in Chestertown - 1753-1757
McClean, John Jr. - Dungannon - 1769
McCubbin, Charles - Grange - 1757-1769
McComes, Jacob M. - Angels Rest - 1756-1769
McComes, John - Angels Rest - 1756-1760
McComes, William - Angels Rest - 1756-1769
McCrakin, John - Bluntwell, Skidmore - 1737-1760
McDermott, Daniel - Edenburgh - 1769
McDowell, Rebecca - Adventure - 1769
McDowgall, John - McDowgalls Chance - 1733-1747
McGuire, Patrick - Deer Park - 1769
McHurd, Hugh - Lots in Chestertown - 1737-1769
McHerd, Joseph - Stepney - 1769
McHerd, Samuel - Lot in Chestertown - 1769
McIlvain, William - Lot on Georgetown - 1769
McKenny, William - Lot in Chestertown - 1739, 1740, 1769
McKey, John - Maries Rambles - 1737, 1738
McLacklin, James - Lot in Georgetown, Tolchester, Indian range - 1760, 1769
McLane, James - Grove, Calders Meadow, Hillens Adventure, Frenchards Memorial, Kellys Choice, Lots in Chestertown, Grove

Addition, Little Grove - 1737-1769
McManus, John - Plain Dealing - 1733-1735
McLane, Neal - Lot in Georgetown - 1741-1769
McNeil, John M. - Comb Whitten - 1756-1769
McVeny, Dennis - Redriff - 1760
Maccarty, Morris - Hatchberry, Hansford, Sewell alias Ulrick, Old Town - 1733-1735
Maccubbin, Nicholas - Yapp, Stone Tower, Pearces Desire Resurveyed - 1752-1769
Mackey, Alexander - Millfork - 1733-1735
Mackey, John - Pearces Rambles - 1733-1736
Mackey, Mary - Mackeys Desire, Arcadia - 1736-1740
Mackey, William - Mackeys Desire, Arcadia - 1733-1752
Macomes, James - Macomes Desire - 1752-1760
Magnor, Edward - Providence - 1736-1757
Magnor, John - Providence - 1733-1735
Mahon, Thomas - Queen Carlton, Addition to Queen Carlton, Shadford Mannor - 1733-1744
Manlove, Mary - Lot in Chestertown - 1769
Manlove, Mathews - Drayton, Blays Park, Standleys Hope, Gibbs Chance, Grange, Lavenham - 1739-1752
Mann, Joseph - Hurtleberry Tract, Norcutt, Hopewell, Chester Grove, Lot in Georgetown, Northcoat Plains - 1738-1747, 1769
Mann, G. Vansant - Vienna, Forrest - 1769
Mansell, Thomas - Lynns Prime Choice, Heaths Long Lands, Darnalls Farm - 1733-1740
Mansfield, Robert - Sewards Hope - 1733-1740
Mansfield, Samuel - Sewards Hope - 1741-1769
March, Dr. John - Stanlys Hope - 1733-1735
Marcy, Peter - Forrest - 1747
Marsh, Thomas - Lots in Chestertown - 1756-1769
Marshall, Charles - Marshalls Outlett - 1733 - 1735
Marshall, John - Hermitage - 1733-1735
Maslin, James - Ash Point - 1744-1760
Maslin, Thomas - Ash Point, Kears Addition, Broadfield, Bounty, Necessitys Habitation - 1733-1769
Mason, Hugh - Buck Hill - 1733-1735
Mason, Joseph - Clarks Conveniency - 1736-1747
Mason, Mary - Lot in Chestertown - 1760
Massey, Daniel - Partners Help, London Bridge Renewed, Angels Rest, Spring Garden and Angels Lot, Halls Harbour, Spring Garden - 1736-1769
Massey, Elijah - Angels Rest - 1769
Massey, Joseph - [name of tract missing from index] - 1769
Massey, Katharine - Partnership - 1752-1760
Massey, Milcah - Lot in Georgetown - 1769
Massey, Nicholas - Masseys Lott, Exchange, Masseys Venture - 1736-1769
Massey, Peter - Forrest, London Bridge - 1733-1769
Massey, Samuel - Brewards Marsh, Lots in Chestertown - 1733-1769
Massey, Sarah - Partnership - 1769
Massey, Thomas - Whaleys Adventure, Miers Luck, Partnership - 1736-1769
Massey, William - Masseys Lott - 1736-1760

MILITIA 25

Mathews, Dr. Hugh - Lot in Chestertown - 1736-1769
Mathews, John - Batchelors Choice, Spring Garden, Yapp - 1737-1747
Maxwell, Ann - Yapp - 1736
Mawell, James - Yapp - 1733-1735
Maxwell, John - Lot in Georgetown, Kent Manor - 1769
Maxwell, Robert - Bellakew, Addition to Bellakew, Second Addition, Partners Addition, Remainder, Hangmans End - 1733-1769
Maxwell, William - Partners Help - 1752-1769
Medford, Bullman - Gales Addition, Hebourns Chance, Suffolk, Simmins Park, Lot in Georgetown - 1733-1747
Medford, George - Millfork, Maggys Jointure, Heyborns Choice - 1736-1769
Medford, Marmaduke - Grange, Intermix, Hamlins Lott - 1769
Medford, McCall - Hepborns Choice, Sims Farm, Gales Addition, Marshes, Lot in Georgetown - 1769
Medford, Thomas - Hopewells Farm, Stanham, Hepbourns Choice, Maggys Jointure, Howards Chance - 1733, 1735, 1769
Medford, Unit - Marshes, Suffolk - 1757, 1769
Meekins, Francis - Forrest of Dean - 1733-1757
Meeks, James - Providence, Cuckolds Hope - 1741-1769
Meeks, Robert - Foremans Poor Discovery, Good Hope, Forrest of Dean, Ambrosia - 1733-1769
Melton, Abraham - Hatchbury, Hansford, Norris's Forrest, East Huntington, Wilmers Gift, Grange, Smiths Chance, Strafford Mannor - 1733-1769
Melton, Barbara - Stradford Manor, Hatchbury, Hansford - 1737-1747
Melton, Isaac - Stradford Manor, Grange - 1752-1760
Melton, John - Stratford Mannor - 1769
Melton, Joseph - Hansford, Hatchberry - 1752-1760
Melton, Phillip - Hilly Longford, Stratford Manor - 1747-1757
Melton, Samuel - Skinners Marsh - 1736-1747, 1769
Merrett, Lovering - Tullys Fancy, Long Slipe, Worton Mannor, Carola, Cornwallis Choice, Budds Meadows, Budds Discovery, Becks Addition, Locust Point - 1740-1769
Metzler, Daniel - Stepney - 1769
Middleton, John - Clayton (Layton) - 1736-1769
Middleton, Lutener - Bowdies Folly - 1733-1747
Miers, Luke - Bordleys Gift, Myers Inclosure, London Bridge, McDougals Chance, Miers Luck - 1756-1769
Mifflin, Daniel - Drayton, Hampshire, Tatums Meadow, Mount - 1753-1769
Mifflin, Sothey - Chegwell, Tilghmans Farm and Chance - 1760 - 1769
Millbery, Josh - Smiths Bay - 1736
Millborn, John - Lot in Chestertown, Suffolk - 1740-1752
Millborn, Samuel - Suffolk - 1736-1742
Millburne, William - Suffolk - 1733-1735
Miller, Arthur - Godlington Mannor, Lucys Recreation, East Huntington, Arcadia - 1733-1769
Miller, Michael - Hinchingham, Neglect, Addition, Covent Garden, Millers Purchase, Deans Adventure, Ambrosia, Providence - 1733-1769

26   INHABITANTS OF KENT COUNTY, MARYLAND, 1637-1787

Miller, Nathaniel - Millers Purchase, Neglect, Long Acre, Deans Adventure - 1740-1769
Miller, Richard - Millers Purchase, Hinchingham - 1769
Miller, Samuel - Millers Purchase - 1740-1760
Miller, Thomas - Millers Purchase - 1760, 1769
Milligan, George - Suffolk - 1753-1760
Millward, Charles - Kelleys Choice, Millwards Choice - 1736-1769
Millwood, Lowry - Howells Adventure - 1733-1735
Mitchell, Edward - Mitchells Adventure, Hens Roost - 1733-1769
Mode, William - Warners Adviser, Warners Addition - 1747
Moffett, George - Comb Whitten, Moffetts Lott, Flower of the Forrest, Rumford, Addition, Morfetts Lott, Browards Reserve, Addition to the Flower of the Forrest - 1733-1769
Moffet, Richard - Hurtleberry Tract, Moffets Chance, Browards Reserve, True Gift - 1753-1769
Moll, John - Darnalls Lott - 1733-1735
Monk, Henry - Lot in Chestertown - 1737-1760
Moore, Henry - Mount Hope - 1760
Moore, James - Maidens Lott, Three Friends, Lot in Chestertown - 1733-1769
Moore, John - Comegys Fancy, Arcadia, Baggaly Forrest, Miles End - 1733-1747, 1769
Moore, William - Haybornes Choice, Arcadia - 1736-1769
Morgan, Henry - Chance - 1733-1735
Morgan, John - Lot in Georgetown - 1739-1769
Morgan, William - Kent Lott - 1733-1752
Morrison, Hugh - Lot in Chestertown - 1753-1760
Morsell, Thomas - Prickel Pear, Smally, Great Oak Manor, Killingsworthmore - 1736-1760
Mullen, Patrick - Lot in Chestertown - 1737, 1738
Mullett, William - Chance - 1744-1760
Mullican, Daniel - Prickle Peare - 1733
Murphey, George - Hurtleberry Tract - 1733-1735
Murphey, James - Deans Reliefe - 1733-1735
Murphy, Mary - Lot in Chestertown - 1736-1757, 1769
Murphey, Samuel - Buckingham - 1752
Murray, Dr. William - Lot in Chestertown - 1737-1769
Myars, John - Hope, Mount Herman - 1753-1769
Manscoyne [Nanscoyne?], John - Mitchell Park - 1733
Neall, Edmond [Edward?] - Cammelsworthmore - 1736-1757
Neale, Edward - Lower Bennett - 1733-1735
Nemo, John - High Park - 1742-1756
Newcomb, Robert - Angles Rest or Lot - 1737-1740
Newcomb, Thomas - Pearces Rambles, Angles Rest - 1736-1769
Newton, Jonathan - Wedges Recovery - 1733-1735
Newton, Thomas - Pearces Rambles - 1747
Nicholson, Joseph - Pentridge, Stephen Heath Manor, Barwick, Lot in Chestertown, Scotts Lot, High Park, Rousbys Discovery, Addition, Thomas Purchase, Kings Prevention - 1736-1769
Nicholson, William - Lots in Georgetown - 1769
Nicols, James - Chance - 1753-1760
Noalman, Anthony - Bluntville, Niefs Choice - 1733-1735
Noble, Elizabeth - Hebborns Farm - 1736-1760
Noland, Matt - Larkins Addition - 1752-1769

Norcutt, Richard - Norcutt - 1733-1735
Norris, Daniel - Browards Reserve, Norris Rest, Tilghmans Farm - 1733-1735, 1753-1769
Norris, Richard - Rumford - 1752
Norris, Samuel - Scotts Folly, Brewers Reserve, Castle Cary - 1733-1760
Norris, Sarah - Browns [Brewards?] Reserve, Castle Carey, Rumford, Scotts Folly - 1737-1747
Norton, Richard - Hermitage - 1737-1752
Nowell, William - Nowells Adventure, No Name - 1733-1737
Nowland, Silvester - Adventure - 1769
Nusume, John - Middle Branch, Hazard - 1737-1744
Obryan, Laughlin - Kemps Beginning, Lot in Chestertown - 1736-1739
Oneall, Hugh - Lot in Chestertown - 1736-1741
Ovey, Anothony - Batchelors Resolution - 1733
Paca, Aquilla - Blays Park, Partridge, Childs Harbour, Rachels Farm, Blays Range, Phillips Neglect, Dales Town, Partnership, Pentridge, Stephen Heath Manor - 1736-1744, 1769
Page, John - Mount Herman, Lot in Chestertown - 1742-1760
Page, Jonathan - Lot in Chestertown, Mount Harmon - 1736-1743
Page, Ralph - Wolf Head, Hazard, Middle Branch - 1733-1769
Palmer, Benjamin - Palmers Hazard, Endeavour, Comb Whitten, Burk With Addition, Palmers Desire, Addition to Palmers Desire - 1733-1769
Palmer, Joseph - Palmers Desire, Addition to Palmers Desire, Chester Grove, Endeavour - 1769
Palmer, Nathaniel - Lot in Georgetown, Lot in Chestertown - 1738-1743
Palmer, Oliver - Grange - 1733-1735
Parish of Shrewsberry - Spring Garden, Hales - 1752-1769
Parker, William - Adventure - 1769
Parks, John - Symons Farm - 1733-1735
Parks, Patrick - Simms Farm - 1736-1743
Parr, John - Chance, Howards Gift - 1736, 1738, 1752
Parrott, Abner - Ratcliff Cross, Killingsworthmore, Mount Harmon - 1742-1760
Parsons, Benjamin - Good Hope - 1733-1743
Parsons, John - Well Meaning, Parsons Chance, Parsons Recovery, Quakers Lot - 1733-1735
Parsons, Joseph - Hope, Myers Luck - 1752-1769
Parsons, Rachel - Good Hope - 1741-1747
Parsons, Solomon - Myers Chance, Little Forrest - 1733-1740
Pascoe, John - Cornwallis, Denby, Pascos Poor Lott, Chance - 1736-1747
Pascoe, Stephen - Cornwallis Choice, Becks Addition, Pascoe Poor Lott, Chance alias Tullys Choice - 1760
Payton, Samuel - Grange - 1736
Peacock, John - Honey Hills - 1769
Peacock, Richard - Down Dale, Stand Off, Stony Hills - 1733-1760
Peacock, Robert - Down Dale, Standoff, Stoney Hills - 1769
Pearce, Andrew - Tibbalds, Godfreys Point - 1747
Pearce, Ann - Conjunct, Forrest, Tolchester, Adventure - 1753-1769
Pearce, Daniel - Verina, Slipe, Chance, New Holland - 1733-1735

Pearce, George - Lot in Georgetown - 1738-1760
Pearce, Gideon - Tolchester, York, Castle Cary, Partners Addition, Shaws Chance, Hangmans Folly, Reversion, St. Andrews Cross, Fork, Conquest, Addition - 1733-1752
Pearce, James - Tolchester, Lot in Georgetown - 1738-1769
Pearce, Mary - Venison, Slipe, Friendship - 1733-1744
Pearce, Rachell - Lot in Georgetown - 1738-1752
Pearce, Col. William - Tibballs, Godfrey Point, Addition, Pearces Addition, Pearces Angle, Chenish - 1733-1735
Peark, Robert - Stannaway - 1733-1735
Pearman, Jane - Killingsworthmore - 1737-1769
Peircivell, William - Providence - 1733-1735
Pell, Mary - [name of tract missing from index] - 1741
Pell, William - Grange - 1736-1740
Pennington, Henry - Wyatts Chance, Wyatts Addition, James Addition, Mistake alias Perkins Mistake - 1769
Pennington, John W. - Canada - 1769
Pennington, Rachel - Hangmans Folly - 1757, 1769
Pennington, Rosomd [sic] - Hangmans Folly - 1757, 1760, 1769
Perkins, Daniel - Millford, Unity - 1733-1769
Perkins, Ebenezer - Wyatts Chance, Addition, James, Wards Hope, Hopewell, Darnells Farm - 1737-1769
Perkins, G. - Lot in Charlestown [sic] - 1769
Perkins, Isaac - Brittain, Perkins Pollicy, Meadow, Barneys Forrest, Essex, Richards Adventure, Whitemarsh - 1769
Perkins, Jacob - Neglect - 1733, 1735
Perkins, Joseph - Batchelors Hall - 1769
Perkins, Susanna - Millford - 1753-1769
Perkins, Thomas - Ridgly, Johns Neglect, Perkins Adventure, Green Branch, Providence, Cammels Adventure - 1744-1769
Perry, Daniel - Sherin - 1733, 1735
Peters, Richard - 2 lots in Georgetown - 1769
Pettit, Barth - Sims Prime Choice - 1753-1769
Phillingham, Richard - Arcadia - 1752-1769
Phillips, Henry - Warners Levell, Nannys Choyce - 1740-1769
Phillips, John - Friendship - 1733-1737
Phillips, Thomas - Sweethall - 1733-1735
Pinar (Piner), Bartus - Kent Manor - 1769
Pinar, Edward - Phillips Choice - 1740-1752, 1769
Pinar, James - Piners Addition, Garretts Branch - 1736-1769
Pinar, Matthew - Tilghmans Choice, Staple Warren, Little Grove - 1733-1760
Pinar, Thomas - Piners Grove, Stepney, Piners Addition - 1733-1769
Pinar (Piner), William - Tilghmans Choice, Staples Warren, Little Grove, Piners Grove - 1769
Plastow, Edward - Tilghmans Farm - 1733-1735
Plater, George - Grantham - 1736-1756
Pollard, John - Chance - 1752
Pollard, Mary - Chance - 1736 - 1737
Pollows, John - Pearces Rambles - 1739-1744
Pooley, Mathew - Jerrome, Grays Inn, Chance - 1737-1747
Pope, Charles - Forrest - 1738-1752
Pope, Mary - Dale Town, Hermitage - 1733-1735

MILITIA 29

Pope, William - Popes Chance, Hermitage Resurveyed - 1742-1752
Porter, Giles - Grange - 1733, 1735
Porter, James - Lot in Chestertown, Plain Dealing, Partnership - 1747, 1752-1754, 1769
Porter, John - Plain Dealing, Partnership, Partnership Point Resurveyed, Porters Addition, Rippen - 1756, 1757
Porter, Richard - Lots in Chestertown - 1742-1760
Porter, Sarah - Plain Dealing, Partnership, Partnership Point, Rippen, Porter Addition - 1760
Potter, Capt. Martin - Forrest, Ingrams Lot, Outrange, Thornton, Adventure, Gleaves Lot, Chance, Ambrosia Resurvyed, Thornton Addition, Batemans Farm, Lot in Chestertown - 1738-1743
Potts, Capt. William - Tolchester, Whittfield - 1733-1735
Powell, Nehemiah - Thornton - 1733-1742
Power, Nichols - [name of tract missing from index] - 1733-1735
Pratt, Philemon - Hackney - 1769
Price, Edward - Howells Farm - 1733-1747
Price, James - Chandler Addition, Drayton, Stoneton - 1739-1769
Price, John - Chance, Partnership, Town Relief - 1733-1735, 1752
Price, Richard - Addition - 1736-1747
Price, William - Woodland Neck - 1733-1735
Pryor, John - Spring Garden - 1733-1735
Pryor, Phillip - Cock of the Game - 1733-1760
Pryor, Thomas - Hen Roost, Cock of the Game - 1733-1769
Quinney, John - Coney Warren - 1760, 1769
Quinney (Quinny), Sutton - Coney Warren, Addition to Honest Deal - 1733-1757
Ralph, Mary - Bradway - 1752
Randall, Benjamin - Benjamins Choice - 1733-1735
Randall, John - Rue Adam [Ranadam?] - 1769
Randall, Robert - Ruabon, Ranadam [Rue Adam?] - 1735-1747
Randall, Theophilus - Darnells Farm - 1736-1769
Rasin, Abraham - Stanleys Hope, Cammels Farm, Pool, Friendship Resurveyed, Fair Promise, Howards Lott, Bairs Grinn - 1753-1769
Rasin, George - Raisins Double Purchase, Hales, Drayton, Drayton Resurveyed - 1743-1769
Rasin, John - Georgetown, Drayton, Gibbs Choice, Standleys Hope, Blays Park, Partnership, Grange, George alias Scotland, Intermix - 1733-1760
Rasin, Mary - Standleys Hope, Cammels Farm, Pool, Friendship Resurveyed, Bares Grinn, Warners Marsh, Drayton, Hales Resurveyed, Forresters Delight, Fair Promise, Friendship - 1736-1760
Rasin, Phillip - Georgetown, Draycott, Gibbs Choice, Stanleys Hope, Blays Park, Partnership, Grange, Intermix - 1733-1742, 1752, 1769
Rasin, William - Forresters Delight, Blays Range, 10 lots in Chestertown, Tolchester, Grange, Mill Point, Bears Grin, Free Gift, Chance, Comb Whitten, Christophers Beginning, Forrest, Hackney, Adventure, Margarets Delight - 1743-1769
Rawlinson, James - Covent Garden - 1769
Rawlinson, John - Covent Garden - 1733-1760
Raymond, Michael - Stepney - 1752-1769
Read, Francis - Suburbs - 1737-1769

Read, George - Grange, Intermix, Denbye - 1736-1747
Read, James - 1/8 lot in Chestertown - 1738-1760
Read, John - Peach Meadows, Hopewell, Suburbs, Green Meadows - 1733-1769
Read, Joseph - Subbards [Suburbs] - 1736-1747
Read, John (carpenter) - Lot in Chestertown, Queen Carlton - 1736-1769
Read, Tilton - Grange - 1753-1769
Reardin, Timothy - Reserve - 1760, 1769
Reason, Joseph - Gibbs Choice, Stanleys Hope, Grange, Georgetown, Draycott, Blays Park - 1752-1769
Reason, Mary - Drayton, Stanleys Hope, Choyce Purchase, Grange, Clays [Blays?] Park, Swenham - 1736-1738
Reason, Thomas - Drayton, Stanleys Hope, Choyce Purchase, Grange, Clays [Blays?] Park, Swenham - 1736-1738
Redding, John - Chandlers Addition, Draycoat, Stoneton, Warners Adventure - 1736-1752
Redding, Nathaniel - Warners Adventure, Worths Folly - 1739-1769
Redding, Sarah - Draycoat, Stoneton, Warners Adventure - 1738
Reading, William - Draycott, Chandlers Addition, Stonetown - 1733-1735, 1769
Redgrave, Abraham - Margarets End - 1733-1744
Redgrave, Hannah - Margarets End - 1747-1760
Redgrave, Isaac - Abrams Lott, Childs Harbour - 1736-1769
Redgrave, John - Free Gift, Chance - 1733-1769
Redgrave, Joseph - Shads Hold, Ridgely - 1753-1760
Redgrave, William - Chance, Hampshire, Childs Harbour alias Hampshire - 1733-1735, 1756-1769
Reed, Benjamin - Kelly Langford, Stadford Mannor - 1760
Reed, John - Lot in Chestertown, Stepney Point Lott, Green Meadows - 1747-1769
Reed, Joseph - Providence, Subburbs - 1753-1769
Reed, Sarah - Lot in Chestertown - 1756-1769
Reid, Henry - Lot in Chestertown - 1756-1769
Reisen, Thomas - Drayton, Hales, Forresters Delight, Faire Promise, Cammells Farme, Bairs Grinn, Nancys Fancy, Friendship - 1733-1735
Rhea, John - Lot in Georgetown - 1769
Ricard, Benjamin - Middle Spring, Deprived Mischief, Long Acre, Providence - 1733-1769
Richardson, Douglas - Orchards Neck, Fair Lee, Lot in Chestertown - 1738-1757
Richardson, Matthew - Ryleys Land Resurveyed, Plumb Park - 1747-1769
Richardson, Capt. Samuel - Forrest - 1733-1741
Richardson, Thomas - Drayton, Warners Level - 1738-1747
Richford, Thomas - Pearces Rambles - 1733-1744
Ricketts, Charlotte - Queen Carlton - 1769
Ricketts, Joseph - Batchelors Resolution - 1747-1760
Ricketts, Nathaniel - Addition to Queen Carlton, Queen Carlton, Exchange, Batchelors Hall, Batchelors Resolution - 1736-1769
Ricketts, Phillip - Mayford, Browns Levitt [Levell?], Ambrosia - 1733-1769
Riddle, Andrew - Cammells Farme - 1733-1735

Ridgway, John - Margaretts Delight - 1733-1743
Riley, Richard - Forrest - 1747
Ringgold, Charles - Ringgolds Fortune, Ringgolds Lott, Stanaway - 1733-1769
Ringgold, Elias - Hunting Fields, Lot in Chestertown - 1733-1737
Ringgold, James - Timely Discovery, Pentridge, Plains, Hunting Fields - 1733-1769
Ringgold, John - Adventure, Plains, Hunting Field, Lot in Chestertown - 1741-1769
Ringgold, Joseph - Plains - 1736-1753
Ringgold, Josias - Plains, Viaven, Queen Carlton, Comegys Fancy - 1754-1769
Ringgold, Mary - Hunting Field, Lot in Chestertown - 1738-1740
Ringgold, Rebeccah - Hunting Fields - 1733-1769
Ringgold, Thomas - Lots in Chestertown, Hunting Field, Arcadia, Tilghmans Choice, Staples Warren, Little Grove, Queen Carlton, Poplar Farm, Addition to Dallington, Dallington, New York, Sadlers Lott, Savorys Farm, Calebs Discovery, Addition to Tilghmans Farm, Norrises Forrest, Tilghmans Farm, Hynsons Division, Wilmers Gift, Forrest of Dean, Tolchester, Drayton, Strafford Mannor, Greshams Levell, Maidens Lott, Adventure, Doe Neck, Bavaria, Plains, Rengate, Piney Grove - 1633-1769
Ringgold, William - Tilghmans Grove, Lots in Chestertown, Black Halls Hermitage, Chance, Doe Neck, Plains Park - 1733-1769
Rippon, Capt. Henry - Plain Dealing, Partnership Point, Lot in Chestertown - 1736-1741
Robas, James - Partnership - 1736-1738
Roberts, James - Deans Adventure, Long Acre, Arcadia, Cheddle, Addition - 1752-1769
Roberts, Robert - Viavan, Dining Room - 1736-1747
Roberts, William - Deans Adventure, Addition, Long Acre - 1733-1747
Robinett, Richard - Tibbets Adventure - 1757, 1760, 1769
Robinson, Heneage [Henery?] - Skidmore - 1733
Robinson, Margaret - Widows Chance - 1733-1735
Rochester, Francis - Partnership - 1739-1747
Rochester, Henry - Williams Adventure, Addition, Jones Adventure - 1752-1769
Rochester, John - Partnership - 1752-1760
Rogers, Edward - Himbleton, Harris Forrest - 1733-1760
Rogers, Elizabeth - Stepney Heath Manor - 1736-1738
Rogers, Hynson and wife - Chedle - 1769
Rogers, John - Partners Addition, Hangmans End - 1733-1744
Rolph, Glanvill - Pentridge - 1736-1747
Rolph, John - Broadway, Macoakin - 1733-1752
Rolph, William - Mocoakin, Bradway - 1753-1769
Rozier, Henry - Lower Bennet - 1752-1769
Ruddle, Andrew - Cammells Farm - 1737
Rush, Thomas - Widows Rest - 1736, 1737
Ryley, John - Plumb Park, Hangmans Folly, Ryleys Beginning, Indian Range, Gore - 1733-1744
Ryley, John - Rileys Beginning, Agreement, Forrest - 1747-1760
Ryley, Mary - Ryleys Beginning - 1752-1769
Ryley, Nicholas - Hangmans Folly, Ryleys Lands Resurveyed, Chance, Pearces Rambles, Plumb Park - 1733-1769

Ryley, Richard - Forrest, Rileys Fancy, Rylys Beginning - 1733-1769
Ryley, Sarah - Rileys Land Resurveyed - 1747
Sadler, Joseph - Broadnax Creek - 1753-1760
Salisbury, William - Adventure, Forrest, Chance, Free Gift - 1742-1769
Salter, John - Well Meaning - 1733-1735
Sampson, William - Sampsons Edition [Addition?] - 1733
Sanders, George - Pryors Neglect, Sanders Addition - 1733-1735
Sanders, Thomas - Pryors Neglect - 1736-1769
Sanders, William - Pryors Neglect, Chance - 1736-1769
Sappington, Thomas - Adventure, Mathias, Addition to Johns Fields, Addition to Matthias and St. John Fields - 1753-1769
Savage, William - Grange - 1733-1735
Savory, William Sr. - Probus, Galloways Chance, Popes Forrest, Cornwallis Choice, Carola, Locust Point - 1733-1752
Scaggs, Richard - Castle Carey, Exchange - 1733-1735, 1769
Scaggs, William - Castle Carey, Exchange - 1736-1760
Schee, Hermanus - Herefield, Rebeccas Desire, Church Wardens Neck - 1733-1736
Scott, Colonel - "See Joseph Nicholson" [sic] - 1741
Scott, Ann - Stepney Heath Manor, Lot in Chestertown - 1760
Scott, Charles - Lot in Chestertown, Stephen Heath Manor, Spring Garden - 1736-1769
Scott, David - Millford, Larkins Addition - 1769
Scott, Edward - Stephen Heath Manor, Rousbeys Discovery, Addition, Town Relief, Park, Scotts Lott, Thomas's Purchase - 1733-1735
Scott, Francis - Grange - 1733-1744
Scott, George - Lot in Georgetown - 1739, 1740
Scott, John - Pentridge, Lots in Chestertown, Thomas's Purchase, High Park, Viaven Resurveyed, Scotts Chance - 1733, 1735, 1752-1769
Scott, Mary - Lot in Georgetown - 1739-1769
Scott, Nathaniel - Partnership - 1733, 1735
Scott, Walter Jr. - Lot in Georgetown - 1741-1769
Scott, Edward, and Ringgold, Thomas - Pentridge, High Park, Tullys Fancy, Reward - 1733-1735
Sealy, Thomas - Chesterfield Resurveyed, Knocks Harbour, Trange - 1760 - 1769
Selbey, Thomas - Chigly (Chigwell) - 1738-1747
Seamans, Henry - Bright Hemstone, Seamans Folly - 1741-1769
Seamans, Jeremiah - Bright Helmstone - 1753-1769
Seamans, Sarah - Millfork - 1769
Seamans, Solomon - Bright Helmstone, Peareys Meadows (Pearces Meadows), Millfork - 1753-1769
Seamans, William - Bright Helmstone, Seamans Folly, Adventure - 1753-1769
Sewell, John - Phillips Choice, Scotts Folly, Bridge Point - 1769
Sewell, Mary - Simpsons Adventure, Addition to Simpsons Adventure - 1737-1747
Sewell, Richard - Simpsons Adventure, Addition to Simpsons Adventure - 1733-1736
Sewell, Thomas - Simpsons Adventure, Addition to Simpsons

DEBT BOOKS, 1733-1769 33

Adventure - 1756-1769
Shanhane, James - Comb Whitton - 1769
Shawe, Matthew - Elioners Delight - 1733-1735
Shawhawn, John - Shadshold - 1752
Shawhawn, Miles Mason - Chidley - 1747
Shawn, Darby - Darbys Desire, Shads Hole - 1733-1736
Shehan, Thomas - Joyners Fancy - 1769
Shehawn, Daniel - Bath, Shadshole - 1737-1741, 1769
Shehawn, John - Shadshole - 1741, 1742
Shields, John - Pentridge - 1747-1769
Shoobrook, Thomas - Stoke - 1733 - 1735
Shrewsbury Parish Vestry - Hales, Spring Garden - 1733-1747
Siglye [sic], William - Benjamins Lott - 1733-1735
Sill, Robert - Intermix - 1740-1747
Simcock, William - Larkins Addition and Millfork, Stanaway, Draw
  Near, Adventure - 1733-1769
Simmons, Richard - Norris Rest alias Norris Forrest, Strafford
  Manor, Garnet - 1733-1769
Simpson, Thomas - Lots in Georgetown - 1738-1769
Skidmore, Joseph - Bluntwell, Skidmore - 1733-1735
Skidmore, Jucley [sic] - Skidmore - 1736
Skinner, Andrew - Stockton - 1733-1737
Skinner, Thomas - Level Ridge - 1736, 1737
Skinner, William - Level Ridge - 1733-1737
Skirvin, George - Comegys Farm Addition, Middle Plantation, Crows
  Addition - 1733-1747
Skirven, Sarah - Comegys Farm Addition - 1736, 1737
Slipper, Thomas - Bounty, Longfords Neck Resurveyed - 1733-1735,
  1752-1769
Slipper, William - Bounty - 1736-1760
Sloss, Samuel - Tolchester - 1769
Smith, Charles - Whitfield - 1733-1757
Smith, Charles Jr. - Lot on Chestertown - 1736-1769
Smith, George - High Park - 1733-1735
Smith, James - Broad Neck, Worths Folly, Stepney, Lot in
  Chestertown, Providence, Holy Land, Tilghmans and Foxleys
  Grove, Broad Oak, Sutton, Grove - 1733-1769
Smith, John - Skinners Marsh, Smiths Chance, Coney Warren, Holy
  Land, Grantham, Smiths Point, Kings Prevention, Hinchingham -
  1733-1769
Smith, John Worldly - Londonderry, Hix's Hazard - 1747-1769
Smith, Jonathan - Grantham, Forrest - 1769
Smith, Joseph - Holy Land - 1753-1757, 1769
Smith, Joyce - Holy Land, Providence - 1737-1744
Smith, Mary - Trumpington, Smiths Meadows, Smiths Venture,
  Ratcliffe Cross, Addition, Plains - 1742-1747
Smith, Matthew - Vienna, Margarets End - 1747-1769
Smith, Nicholas - Vienna, Reserve, Tamfield, Forrest, Lot in
  Chestertown - 1733-1769
Smith, Capt. Richard - Free Gift, Beaver Dam - 1733-1735
Smith, Rosamond - Broad Neck - 1733-1735
Smith, Samuel - Holy Land - 1753-1757, 1769
Smith, Thomas - Stepney, Lot in Chestertown, Smiths Venture -
  1739, 1747, 1752-1757, 1760, 1769
Smith, Capt. Thomas - Trumpington, Smiths Venture, Smiths

34   INHABITANTS OF KENT COUNTY, MARYLAND, 1637-1787

   Meadows, Smiths Chance, Hunting Fields, Lots in Chestertown,
   Chance Resurveyed, Grange, Addition, Kimbolton, Millpoint,
   Plains, Smiths Desart, Ratcliff, Hinchingham - 1733-1769
Smith, William - Whitfield, Tolchester, Vienna, Chance -
   1733-1769
Smithers, John - Longfords Neck - 1733-1769
Smithers, William - Vienna, Addition, Rumford - 1733-1769
Smyth, William - Addition, Plains, Addition to Plains - 1753-1760
Snow, Prince - Lot in Georgetown - 1747-1769
Spalding, Andrew - Spalden - 1733-1744
Speare, Robert - Chance - 1738-1757
Speers, Robert - Exchange - 1769
Spearman, Abram - Ellis's Chance - 1741-1747
Spearman, Ann - Ellis Chance - 1740
Spearman, Charity - Warners Adventure, Addition - 1736-1769
Spearman, Francis - Partnership, Deerum - 1733-1760
Spearman, John - Partnership - 1769
Spearman, Philip - Ellis's Chance - 1738, 1739, 1752
Spearman, William - Partnership, Deer Park, Ellis Chance -
   1741-1747, 1769
Spencer, Eliza - Memento Mori - 1736
Spencer, Henry - Agreement, Killingsworthmore - 1733-1769
Spencer, Isaac - Agreement, Smally, Marrow Bone, Darby, Grantham,
   Buck Hill, Billeys Lott, Ellis Chance - 1769
Spencer, Jarvis - Darnalls Lot, Conclusion, Agreement, Smalley,
   Marrow Bone, Darby, Buck Hill, Billys Lott, Ellis Chance -
   1733-1760
Spencer, John - Vienna, Slipe, Friendship Resurveyed, Solbey,
   Langford Neck - 1733-1769
Spencer, Richard - Chettle - 1769
Spencer, Capt. Thomas - Memento Mori, Indian Range, Ryleys Land,
   Plumb Park - 1747-1769
Stalker, Martha - High Park - 1742-1747
Stalker, Thomas - High Park - 1741-1743
Stanton, Mary - Lot in Chestertown - 1757, 1760, 1769
Stavely, Eliza - Stavelys Lot, Broad Oak, Childs Harbour, Suffolk
   - 1742
Stavely, James - Stavelys Lott, Broad Oak, Childs Harbour,
   Suffolk - 1733-1743
Stavely, John - Broad Oak, Suffolk, Childs Harbour alias
   Hampshire, Stavelys Lott - 1733-1735, 1753-1769
Stead, James - Simpsons Adventure, Addition to Simpsons Adventure
   - 1752-1754
Stephens, William - Green Forrest - 1769
Sterling, Rev. James - Hinchingham, Birthright, Annarundel Grove
   - 1741-1769
Stevens, John - Broad Oak - 1742-1747
Stevens, William - Widows Rest, Stevenson - 1733-1769
Stevenson, John - Haysell Meadow, Lot in Chestertown - 1736-1769
Stevenson, William - Jones Neglect, Providence, Francis, Lots in
   Chestertown, Jones Venture - 1737-1743, 1760
Still, George - Ratcliff, Ratcliff Cross, Mount Harmon -
   1733-1747
Stiles, Nathaniel - Stiles Addition - 1733-1735

Stoop, Phil - Hangmans Folly - 1736-1738
Stoops, Benjamin Townsend - Brownings Adventure - 1769
Stoops, John - Philips Choice, Hangmans End - 1769
Stoops, William - Hangmans End, Mitchells Chance, Brownings
    Discovery - 1739-1769
Strahan, James - Comb Whitten - 1753-1760
Stratton, George - Skidmore - 1733-1735
Street, Jacob - Tolchester - 1769
Street, Robert - Tolchester, Popes Forrest - 1733-1769
Stringfellow, Capt. Elisha - Lots in Chestertown - 1736-1747
Strong, Micajah - Covent Garden - 1769
Strong, Thomas - Covent Garden - 1733-1769
Sullivane, Dennis - Pentridge - 1733-1735
Summers, Robert - Chance - 1769
Sutton, Benjamin - Macoakin, Ruardon - 1736-1769
Sutton, John - Batchelors Hope, Penrose, Macoakin, Adventure,
    Ruardon - 1733-1769
Sutton, Joseph - Ruerdon, Pentridge - 1733-1741
Sutton, Richard - Lot in Georgetown - 1738-1744
Sutton, Samuel - Batchelors Hope, Penrose - 1736-1760
Swift, John - Neifs Choice, Partnership Point, New Harbour -
    1733-1735, 1760
Swift, Samuel - Lot in Chestertown - 1736
Swiney, James - Chance - 1769
Sympson, William - Scots Folly - 1733-1735
Tarrington, Thomas - Middle Branch, Hazard - 1752-1769
Tasker, Benjamin, and Carroll, Charles - Bridgetown Common,
    Sewalls Manor - 1753-1769
Tatum, John - Tatums Mount - 1736-1747
Taylor, John - Mitchells Park - 1733-1752
Taylor, John - Fairlee, Weymouth - 1733-1769
Taylor, Phillip - Middle Branch, Hazard - 1747-1769
Taylor, Rebecca - Scots Folly, Simpsons Addition - 1737-1743
Taylor, Thomas - Deinbeigh - 1733-1735
Taylor, William - Lot in Georgetown - 1740, 1741, 1769
Tembrull, William - Lot in Chestertown - 1769
Tennant, James - Debtford, Lot in Chestertown - 1747-1769
Tennant, Capt. John - Debtford, Lot in Chestertown - 1733-1747
Tennant, Moses - Debtford, Buck Hill - 1736-1769
Terry, Ann - Suffolk - 1757, 1760
Terry, Benjamin - Suffolk - 1757, 1760
Terry, Hugh - Morton - 1752
Terry, John - Suffolk - 1757, 1760
Terry, William - Larkins Addition - 1752-1769
Thackiston, Mary - Drayton - 1736-1742
Thackstone, Thomas - Drayton, Hales, Webley - 1733-1735
Thomas, Ann - Drayton, Warners Level - 1736, 1737
Thomas, Ebenezer - Arundel Grove - 1769
Thomas, Francis - Cock of the Game - 1733-1743
Thomas, Henry - Thomas Purchase, New York, Mount Harman,
    Providence - 1736-1769
Thomas, James - Arundel Grove, Ferrits Addition, Addition to
    Queen Carlton, Lot in Chestertown, Ratcliffe, Thomas's
    Landing, Killingsworthmore, Mount Harmon, Providence -
    1733-1769

Thomas, Joanna - Tilghmans Farm, Ratcliff, Killingsworthmore, Mount Harmon - 1741, 1742, 1753-1757, 1769
Thomas, John - Newgate, Georgetown, New York - 1737-1744
Thomas, Margaret - Cock of the Game - 1737-1744
Thomas, Mary - Tilghmans Farm - 1741, 1742
Thomas, Col. Samuel - New York, Stratford Manor, Arundel Grove, Bounty, Chance - 1733-1747, 1769
Thomas, Samuel - Arundel Grove, Bounty, Chance - 1736-1752
Thomas, Thomas - Arundel Grove, Providence - 1737-1760
Thomas, William - Resurvey on part of Tilghmans Farm and Chance, Keggerton, New York, Addition, Stratford Manor, Cheapside, Ratcliff Cross, Tilghmans Farm, Killingsworthmore, Mount Harmon Resurveyed - 1733-1760
Thompson, Augustine - Lot in Chestertown - 1736-1739
Thompson, Dowdall - Lots in Chestertown, Lots in Georgetown - 1740-1769
Thompson, Eliza - Wards Oak, Addition to Wards Oak, Dowdals Fancy - 1741-1754
Thompson, Mary - Wards Oak, Addition to Wards Oak, Dowdals Fancy - 1740
Thompson, Samuel - Wards Oak, Addition to Wards Oak, Dowdals Farm [Fancy?] - 1756-1769
Thornton, John - Resurvey on Triangle, Davis Chance - 1740-1760
Thornton, Thomas - Tryangle, Broad Neck, Davis's Addition, Nancys Fancy - 1737-1744
Thorp [Throp?], Alice - Piney Point - 1733-1735
Thorp [Throp?], John - Neglect, Middle Spring - 1736-1769
Thrift, John - Simpsons Addition, Orchards Neck, Galloways Fancy - 1753-1769
Thrift, Mary Anne - Simpsons Addition, Orchards Neck, Galloways Fancy - 1753-1769
Tibbit, Grace - Cock of the Game, Millfork, Tibbits Venture - 1769
TIbbett, James - Mereton, Norrest Desire, Millfork - 1733-1736
Tibbett, Samuel - Millfork, Tibbetts Venture, Moreton, Norris Claim - 1742-1757
Tidmash, William - Whitfield, Lot in Chestertown - 1733-1741
Tilden and Raisin - Addition, Chance, Tolchester - 1752-1769
Tilden, Charles - High Park, Twillys Fancy, Reward, Garnetts Meadow, Kings Prevention, Addition to Scotts Lot - 1736-1769
Tilden, Elizabeth - Draycott - 1769
Tilden, John, and Brown, Peregrine - Blays Range, Blays Addition Resurveyed - 1756-1760
Tilden, Captain John - Blays Addition, Blays Park, Standaway, Lot in Chestertown, Lot in Georgetown, Adventure, Addition to Blays Park, Blays Park, Blays Range, Tildens Meadows, Beshford, Partnership, Dale Town, Howells Outland, Millfork - 1733-1769
Tilden, Marmaduke - Great Oak Manor, Hunting Field - 1733-1769
Tilden, William Blay - Blays Addition, Lot in Georgetown, Bishford Resurveyed - 1769
Tilghman, Edward - Force to It, Whittfield - 1752-1769
Tilghman, James - Cammelsworthmore, Providence - 1756-1769
Tilghman, Richard - Tilghman, Chester Point - 1733-1741

DEBT BOOKS, 1733-1769 37

Tillard, Edward - Ratcliff, Ratcliff Cross, Mount Harmon - 1752
Tillard, Forgitt - Tillards Addition - 1756-1769
Tillard, George - Ratcliff, Ratcliff Cross, Mount Harmon - 1753-1760
Tillard, John - Bounty - 1733-1769
Tilton, Humphrey - Grange - 1733-1735
Timbrell, William - Lots in Chestertown - 1737-1757
Tippett, James, and Tippett, Samuel - Millford, Tibbets Venture - 1747-1760
Toas, Daniel - Lower Fords - 1733-1735
Toas, John - Coney Warren, Addition to Honest Dealing - 1733, 1735
Tobin, Richard - Tobbins Lott, Pearces Rambles - 1738-1760
Tolson, Andrew - Middle Neck, Luck - 1733, 1735, 1752-1760
Tovey, Samuel - Hunting Field, Toveys Lot - 1736-1760
True, John - Sarahs Lot, Stratford Manor, New York - 1733-1769
True, William Jr. - Providence, Hansford, Hatchberry, Comegys Choice, Addition - 1733-1769
Trulock, Henry - Trulocks Right, Adventure, Nancys Fancy, Bares Grin, Drayton - 1736-1769
Trulock, Joseph - Nancys Fancy, Trulocks Right, Hales Adventure, Nancys Chance, Hailes, Bairs Grin, Redmonds Supply, Forresters Delight - 1733-1769
Trulock, William - Forresters Delight, Nancys Fancy - 1736-1752
Trumbles, Michael - Eagles Nest - 1733-1737
Tucker, John - Roger Hicks Intent, Chance - 1736-1769
Turbott, Major William - Whitfield - 1736, 1737
Turner, Jane - Warners Adventure, Warners Addition - 1736
Turner, John - Suffolk - 1733-1736
Turner, Jonathan - Suffolk - 1747-1769
Twigg, John - Redriff, Hermitage - 1733-1743
Twigg, Mary - Redriffe, Hermitage - 1747-1757, 1769
Umberstone, George - Chance - 1752
Unice [sic], John - Boonley - 1769
Unick, Thomas - Boonley, Middle Plantation - 1733-1769
Unitt (Underhill), Richard - Greens Forrest, Suffolk - 1733-1735
Urie, Thomas - Chance, Pascoes Poor Lot - 1753-1769
Usher, George - Partnership Point, Killingsworthmore Enlarged, Newborough alias New Harbour, Ushers Lott - 1736-1769
Usher, James - Partnership Point - 1739-1769
Usher, John - Mount Hope, Neglect - 1736-1752
Usher, Thomas - Killingsworthmore, Neglect, Ushers Lott, Partnership Point, Newborough, Fairfield - 1733-1735
Vanbebber, Adam - Lot in Chestertown - 1752-1769
Vandeke, Thomas - Lots in Chestertown - 1769
Vansant, Albertus - Lots in Georgetown - 1738-1769
Vansant, Benjamin - Lot in Georgetown, Marys Purchase (Mackeys Purchase), Angles Lott - 1747-1757, 1769
Vansant, Cornelius - Angels Rest, Fork Resurveyed, Reversion, Adams Chance - 1756-1769
Vansant, Ephraim - Lot in Georgetown, Free Gift - 1747-1769
Vansant, George - Adventure, Fork, Reversion, Adams Choice - 1733-1769
Vansant, George Jr. - Reversion, Adams Choice, Adventure - 1733-1757

Vansant, John - Endeavor, Vansants Landing, Lot in Georgetown - 1740-1747, 1752, 1769
Vansant, Joshua - Ellis Industry, Discovery, Burkwith Addition, Fair Dealing, Endeavour - 1733-1769
Vansant, Mary - Adams Choice, Reversion - 1757, 1760, 1769
Vansant, Nicholas - Tolchester, Reversion, Margarets Delight - 1733-1747
Vansant, Rosata - Lot in Georgetown - 1738-1769
Vestry of Chester Parish - Forrest Resurveyed - 1769
Vestry of St. Paul's Parish - Pentridge, Mackeys Desire - 1752-1769
Vestry of Shrewsbury Parish - Hales - 1733-1735, 1752
Visitors of Kent County Free School - Stepney - 1733-1769
Wades, ---- [blank] - Arcadia, Bloomberry - 1735
Walden, Edward - Blackwell Hermitage, Stepney - 1733-1735
Walker, Nicholas - Miers Chance, Little Forrest - 1741-1769
Walker, William - Broad Oak, Tolchester - 1736-1769
Wall, Renippa - Chance - 1752-1757
Wallace, John and Co. - Christophers Beginning, Chance, Comb Whitten - 1752-1769
Wallace, Ruth - Agreement - 1733-1735
Wallace, Samuel - Chester Grove, Partnership Resurveyed, Wolfs Huck, Good Hope, Darnells Farm, Addition to Good Hope - 1733-1769
Wallace, Hugh - Maidens Lot, Partnership, Husbands Lott, Three Friends, Addition, Lot in Chestertown, Prickley Pear, Harfield, Church Warden Neck - 1736-1769
Wallice, Hannah - Addition - 1741-1743
Wallice, John - Agreement, Partnership - 1736-1769
Wallice, William - Partnership - 1736-1769
Wallis, Francis - Agreement - 1769
Wallis, John - Partnership, Wallaces Fancy - 1769
Walls, John - Chance, Buttam (Brittian) - 1733-1747
Walls, Renippa - Chance Lott - 1769
Walls, William - Brittain - 1737-1747
Walters, Walter - Addition to Good Hope - 1757, 1760, 1769
Waltham, Edward - Skidmore - 1733, 1735
Waltham, John - Skidmore, Lot in Chestertown - 1736-1769
Waltham, William - Skidmore - 1736
Ward, John - Cox State [sic] - 1733-1735
Ward, Thomas - Arcadia - 1736-1752
Ware, John - Worths Folly - 1753-1769
Warner, George - Warners Adventure, Warners Addition, Drayton, Fair Promise, Stanleys Hope, Friendship, Pool, Warners Level - 1733-1760
Warner, Joseph - Drayton, Warners Level, Tilghmans Farm - 1742
Waterman, Nicholas - Warners Adventure - 1733-1735
Watkins, Esau - Hopeful Unity, Lots in Chestertown - 1740-1760
Watkins, John - Lots in Chestertown - 1769
Watson, John (schoolmaster) - Forrest, Chester Grove - 1753-1769
Watson, John (Scotchman) - Forrest, Edinburgh - 1753-1760
Watts, George - Denbigh - 1769
Watts, John - Denbigh, Exchange - 1733-1760
Wattson, James - High Park, Comegys Fancy - 1733-1737

Wattson, Capt. John - Lots in Georgetown - 1739-1741
Weatherell, George - Sandy Plantation - 1733-1735
Weatherell, Samuel - Wetherells Hope - 1733-1735
Webb, Amerial [sic] - Newtown Resurveyed, Chance - 1752-1760
Webb, James - Chance - 1769
Webb, John - Newtown, Chance, Chester Grove - 1733-1747
Webb, Robert - Phillips Neglect, New Town Resurveyed - 1752-1769
Welch, James - Agreement Resurveyed, Kent Manor - 1752-1769
Welch, John - Chester Grove, Forrest - 1736-1769
Wells, John - Broadfield, Broadnox Creek, Smiths Meadow, Trumpington - 1733-1738
Wells, Richard - Dicks Chance - 1733-1737
Wells, Ruth - Broadnox - 1739-1747
Welsh, Lewis - Grantham - 1769
West, Richard - Pentridge - 1733-1735
Wetherhead, Samuel - Lot in Georgetown - 1747-1769
Wethered, Richard - Chance, Lot in Georgetown, Blays Range, Blays Addition, Millfork, Partnership - 1737-1752
Wetherhead, William - Blays Addition, Blays Range, Beman, Reversion, Tolchester, Lots in Georgetown - 1760, 1769
Wethered, John - Neglect, Blays Park, Lots in Georgetown - 1769
Wetherspone, David - Hangmans End, Windmill Hill, Mitchells Chance, Lot in Georgetown - 1740-1760
Wetherspone, Thomas - Hangmans End, Windmill Hill, Mitchells Chance, Lot in Georgetown, Angels Rest, Adventure - 1738-1743, 1769
Whaland, John - Kimbolton - 1747-1769
Whaland, Owen - Kimbolton - 1741-1744
Whaley, Ann - Kimbolton - 1737-1740
Whaley, David - Whaleys Adventure - 1733-1747
Whaley, Owen - Kimbolton - 1733-1736
Whottotone, Stephen - Hinchingham - 1733-1735
Whitchcoat, Paul - Pearch Meadow, Hopewell, Woodlands Intention - 1739-1769
White, Martha - Neifs Chance - 1752-1757, 1769
White, Richard - Sweethall Neck - 1733-1735
White, Robert - Neifs Choice - 1736-1747
Whitehead, George and Co. - Addition to Freith - 1733, 1735
Whittington, I. (a minor) - Honest Dealing - 1736
Whittington, James - Honest Dealing - 1747-1769
Whittington, John - Honest Dealing, Plain Dealing - 1733-1735
Wicks, Benjamin - Bath - 1736-1747
Wicks, Joseph - Fairlee, Forrest of Dean, Buckingham Resurveyed, Wickliff, Partnership, Market Place, Surplus, Bath - 1733-1769
Wicks (Wickes), Lambert - Tilghmans and Foxleys Grove, Little Grove - 1739-1743
Wicks, Samuel - Wickliffe, Market Place, Partnership, Chester Point, Buckingham - 1733-1769
Widgin, Edward - Good Hope, Heaths Longlands, Simms Prime Choice, Lot in Chestertown - 1769
Wilkins, Bartus - Clarks Conveniency, Range, Relict, Chance, Stansford, Long Neglect, Godlington Manor - 1753-1769
Wilkins, John - Canada - 1769
Wilkins, Mary - Sewell alias Ulrick, Addition - 1769
Wilkins, Thomas - Comegys Farm Addition, Skiwins [Skirvins?]

40 INHABITANTS OF KENT COUNTY, MARYLAND, 1637-1787

Neglect, Relief - 1733-1769
Wilkinson, Richard (minor) - Addition to Honest Dealing, Fair
   Dealing - 1752-1760
Williams, Abraham - Whitfield - 1736, 1737
Williams, Charles - Acklands Lot - 1769
Williams, Christopher - Acklands Lott, Partnership - 1733-1735,
   1752-1760
Williams, Hopkins (Hopton) - Forrest - 1733-1735
Williams, John - Williams Fancy, Forresters Delight, Douchers
   Folly, Grange, Whitfield - 1733-1747, 1752, 1769
Williams, Lewis - Addition, Hangmans Folly, Pearces Rambles,
   Hangmans End, Moreton, Norris's Desire, Millfork - 1741-1747
Williams, Mary - Partners Addition, Fork, Hangmans End, Pearces
   Ramble - 1742-1752
Williams, Thomas - Lot in Chestertown, Piney Point, Addition,
   Fork, Hangmans Folly, Pearces Rambles, Slades Chance -
   1733-1743, 1769
Williamson, Rev. Alexander - Knapley Green, Griffiths Delight,
   Piney Grove, Addition - 1733-1769
Williamson, George - Chance - 1736-1769
Williamson, James - Griffins Delight, Knapley Green, Addition to
   Knapley Green, Reward, Tullys Fancy - 1741-1747
Williamson, John - Kindness, Keventon, Lot in Chestertown,
   Knapley Green, Addition to Knapley Green, Griffiths Delight -
   1740-1769
Williamson, Sarah - Lot in Chestertown - 1741, 1742
Willis, Richard - Coney Warren, Charlton - 1733-1769
Willkinson, Christopher - Fair Dealing, Addition to Fair Dealing,
   Addition to Honest Dealing - 1736-1747
Willson, George - Broad Oak, Square, Wendals Chance, Windale,
   Verina, Margaretts Delight, Wilsons Neglect, Tebbals and
   Castle Carey - 1733-1769
Willson, Isaac - Partnership - 1769
Willson, James - Vienna, Margaretts Delight, Broad Oak - 1733-1735
Willson, John Jr. - Verina, Peters Field, Margaretts End, Chance,
   Broad Oak, Margarets Delight - 1733-1769
Willson, John - Kemps Beginning, Lot in Chestertown, Vienna,
   Providence, Peters Town, Prevention Inconveniency, Margarets
   End - 1733-1735, 1752-1769
Willson, Mary - Coffin - 1752
Willson, Peter - Forrest, Peters Field - 1733-1735
Willson, Richard - Verina, Peters Field, Margarets End, Chance,
   Renippa Walls - 1736-1760
Willson, Sarah - Lot in Chestertown - 1769
Wilmer, Charles - Tilghmans and Foxleys Grove, Little Grove, Lot
   in Chestertown - 1743-1752
Wilmer, Lambert - Addition, Larkins Addition, Rich Level, Wilmers
   Arcadia, Wilmers Chance, Lot in Chestertown, Adventure -
   1733-1769
Wilmer, Mary Ann - Tilghmans and Foxleys Grove, Little Grove,
   Shields, Stepney, Lot in Chestertown - 1753-1769
Wilmer, Simon - Cox's Hall, Hens Roost, Cock of the Game,
   Lincoln, Rich Levell, Angels Lott Resurveyed, Hen Island,
   Boyers Adventure, Mitchells Chance, Pryors Neglect, McComes

Desire, Huckleberry Ridge, Neighbourhood, Davis Tryangle, Angels Lott, Adventure, Tryangle, Hill Top - 1733-1769
Wilmer, William - Lots in Chestertown, Wilmers Grove, St. Tantons, Howell Resurveyed, Tilghmans and Foxleys Grove - 1740-1769
Wilmore, Darcus - Lot in Chestertown - 1737, 1738
Wilmore, Mary - Lot in Chestertown - 1739-1742
Wilmore, William - [name of tract missing from index] - 1738, 1740
Wilshare, William - Neglect, Killingsworthmore - 1760
Wilson, George - [name of tract missing from index] - 1741-1743
Wilson, James - Verina, Broad Oak, Margaretts Delight - 1743-1769
Wilson, John - Kemps Beginning, Lot in Chestertown, Magruders Delight - 1747-1754
Wilson, Mary - Coffin, Broad Oak - 1753-1769
Wilson, Sarah - Lot in Chestertown - 1743-1769
Wiltshire, Eliz - Neglect, Killingsworthmore - 1769
Windall, Thomas - Coffin - 1733-1735
Winn, Penelope - Duncans Toy - 1741-1744
Withers, Samuel - Fair Promise - 1733-1735
Wood, Robert - House and land adjoining Chestertown, Dunns Folly - 1747-1769
Woodall, James - Smithers Plains, Lot in Georgetown - 1769
Woodall, John - Vienna - 1733, 1753-1769
Woodall, Thomas - Resurvey of Tryangle - 1769
Woodall, William - Addition, Rumford, Brewards Reserve, Vienna, Forrest, Palmers Hazard - 1760, 1769
Woodland, Abraham - Sturts Lott - 1769
Woodland, Christian - Orchards Neck, Fairlee - 1760
WOodland, James - Adventure, Woodlands Folly - 1736-1769
Woodland, Jonathan - Staples Choice - 1737
Woodland, Katharine - Lot in Chestertown - 1747, 1752
Woodland, William - Staples Choice, Hackney, Lincoln Inn Fields, Tolchester, Forrest, Lot in Chestertown, Margaretts Delight - 1733-1769
Woodland, William Jr. - Margaretts Delight, Lot in Georgetown, Chance, Woodlands Discovery, Free Gift, Woodlands Hazard - 1747-1769
Woodson, Richard - Elenors Delight - 1769
Worrell, Edward - Hillstone, Sweatmans Addition, Briston, Hanham, Sweatmans Insula - 1733-1769
Worral, Joseph - Bristol - 1769
Worrall, Mary - Hillstone, Bristol, Wilmores Farm, Sweatmans Addition - 1753-1769
Worrel, Simon - Wilmers Farm, Deer Park - 1760, 1769
Worrell, William - Wilmers Farm - 1760, 1769
Wright, James - Hinchingham, Widows Chance - 1738-1769
Wright, John - Forrest, Lot in Chestertown - 1737-1769
Wright, Joseph - Richards Adventure - 1733
Wright, Nathaniel - Chance, Wrights Chance - 1733, 1735, 1752
Wright, Solomon - Whittfield, Lot in Chestertown, Damson Point, Howard Gift, Chance - 1733-1769
Wright, Thomas - Forrest, Providence - 1737-1744
Wright, William - Lot in Chestertown - 1769
Wrightson, John - Adams Choice, Adventure - 1733-1738

Wroth, James - Town Relief, Forrest of Dean, Partnership - 1733-1735, 1760, 1769
Wroth, John - Harris Forrest, Town Relief - 1760, 1769
Wroth, Kelvin - Harris Forrest, Hermitage, Providence, Town Relief - 1736-1769
Wyatt, James Sr. - Wyatts Chance, Wards Hope, Charles Lot, Wyatts Addition, James Addition - 1733-1754
Wyatt, James Jr. - Wyatts Chance, Wyatts Addition, James Addition - 1733-1735, 1752-1760
Wyatt, Jane - Jennys Beginning - 1733, 1735
Wyatt, John - Wyatts Addition, Mistake alias Perkins Mistake, Skinners Marsh, Vienna, Buckingham - 1733-1760
Wyatt, Thomas - Wyatts Chance, Wyatts Addition, James Addition, Charles Lott - 1736-1747
Wydall, John - Chance - 1733-1735
Yearly, William - John [sic] - Prevention of Inconvenience, Earleys Beginning, Gibbs Chance, William and Marys Adventure - 1752-1769
Young, David - Howells Farm, Cammels Farm - 1733-1735
Young, John - Town Relief, Lot in Chestertown, Tolchester and Tomb - 1736-1744
Young, Joseph - New York - 1736, 1737
Young, Mary - New York, Gamets Meadow, Thomas Purchase - 1741-1743
Young, Thomas - Middle Spring - 1733-1735
Young, William - Partnership, Tolchester - 1733-1752
Younger, Humphrey - Sole - 1737-1769
Younger, James - Sole - 1752-1769
Younger, John - Sole - 1752-1769

TRACT INDEX TO KENT COUNTY LAND PATENTS, 1640-1787
(Ref: Maryland State Archives, Card File 55)

"Abrams Lott" - 120 acres - William Redgrave - 1719
"Acklands Lott" - 13 acres - William Ackland - 1734
"Adams Choice" - 300 acres - Matthew Adams - 1675
"Adams Choice" (part) - 150 acres - James Heath - 1713
"Adams End" - 9 acres - Wriston Browning - 1768
"Adams End Resurveyed" - 9 acres - Joshua Batts - 1775
"Addition" - 100 acres - Renatus Smith - 1705
"Addition" - 30 acres - John Denning - 1710
"Addition" - 25 acres - John Denning - 1720
"Addition" - 100 acres - Thomas Ricaud - 1720
"Addition" - 25 acres - John Denning - 1720
"Addition" - 360 acres - William Comegys - 1712
"Addition" - 27 acres - John Huff - 1733
"Addition" - 50 acres - Michael Miller - 1710
"Addition" - 30 acres - Thomas Hynson - 1743
"Addition" - 25 acres - Ralph Page - 1758
"Addition" (The) - 80 acres - John Floyd - 1667
"Addition" (The) - 200 acres - George Gouldhawke and Alexander Nash - 1670
"Addition" (The) - 100 acres - Phillip Holeager - 1684

"Abrams Lott" - 120 acres - William Redgrave - 1719
"Acklands Lott" - 13 acres - William Ackland - 1734
"Adams Choice" - 300 acres - Matthew Adams - 1675
"Adams Choice" (part) - 150 acres - James Heath - 1713
"Adams End" - 9 acres - Wriston Browning - 1768
"Adams End Resurveyed" - 9 acres - Joshua Batts - 1775
"Addition" - 100 acres - Renatus Smith - 1705
"Addition" - 30 acres - John Denning - 1710
"Addition" - 25 acres - John Denning - 1720
"Addition" - 100 acres - Thomas Ricaud - 1720
"Addition" - 25 acres - John Denning - 1720
"Addition" - 360 acres - William Comegys - 1712
"Addition" - 27 acres - John Huff - 1733
"Addition" - 50 acres - Michael Miller - 1710
"Addition" - 30 acres - Thomas Hynson - 1743
"Addition" - 25 acres - Ralph Page - 1758
"Addition" (The) - 80 acres - John Floyd - 1667
"Addition" (The) - 200 acres - George Gouldhawke and Alexander Nash - 1670
"Addition" (The) - 100 acres - Phillip Holeager - 1684
"Addition" (The) - 422 acres - William Peirce - 1684
"Addition" (The) - 72 acres - John True - 1684
"Addition" (The) - 150 acres - William Harris - 1689
"Addition" (The) - 150 acres - William Harris - 1705
"Addition" (The) - 100 acres - Edward Scott - 1709
"Addition" (The) - 180 acres - John Hynson - 1713
"Addition" (The) - 25 acres - Thomas Hynson - 1715
"Addition" (The) - 60 acres - Michael Miller - 1724
"Addition" (The) - 22 acres - Gideon Pearce - 1732
"Addition" (The) - 67 acres - Ruth Gleeves and Hannah Wallace -" 1740
"Addition" (The) - 15 acres - Thomas Wilkins - 1743
"Addition" (The) - 93 acres - Alexander Williamson - 1728
"Addition" (The) - 37 acres - Thomas Smith - 1762
"Additional Hope" - 80 acres - Nathaniel Pearce - 1723
"Addition" (Ye) - 70 acres - Phillip Hopkins - 1705
"Addition to Attix Adventure" - 3 1/3 acres - Aquila Attix - 1775
"Addition to Bellekell" - 22 acres - Robert Maxwell - 1738
"Addition to Blays Park" - 55 acres - John Tilden - 1756
"Addition to Chedley" - 8 1/4 acres - Richard Gresham - 1770
"Addition to Cheapside" - 50 acres - William Thomas - 1729
"Addition to Come Whitten" - 20 1/4 acres - Benjamin Palmer, Jr. - 1769
"Addition to Dollington" - 81 acres - Thomas Ringgold - 1759
"Addition to Faire Dealing" - 42 acres - John Salter - 1686
"Addition to Freith Land" - 725 acres - Benjamin Coole [sic], George Whitehead, Abraham Loyd, Richard Stafford, William Doune, John Sanders, and Charles Harford - 1716
"Addition to Good Hope" - 58 acres - Francis Bodean - 1730
"Addition to Hills and No Dales" - 55 acres - James Greenwood - 1732
"Addition to Howels Resurveyed" - 3 1/4 acres - John Carvil, Jr. - 1769
"Addition to Hutsons Hills" - 59 1/4 acres - John Hutson - 1787

"Addition to Kennards Discovery" - 33 acres - Philip Kennard - 1745
"Addition to Kennards Point" - 13 acres - Sarah - Mary and Ann Kennard - 1744
"Addition to Kent Lott" - 25 acres - John Blackiston - 1753
"Addition to Knaply Green" - 191 acres - Alexander Williamson - 1740
"Addition to Lynn" - 24 acres - Phillip Kennard - 1731
"Addition to Mathias and Johns Fields" - 250 acres - Mathias Day - 1732
"Addition to Moores Fishing Ground" - 31 1/2 acres - John Moore - 1775
"Addition to Palmers Desire" - 57 acres - Benjamin Palmer - 1732
"Addition to Penrose" - 16 acres - John Sutton - 1772
"Addition to Queen Catharine alias Charlton" - 109 acres - Daniel Ferrell and Thomas Machar - 1732
"Addition Resurveyed" - 114 acres - William Burke - 1747
"Addition to Scotts Lott" - 27 acres - John Scott - 1748
"Addition to Shads Hole" - 33 acres - Hezekiah Cooper - 1764
"Addition to Simsons Adventure" - 15 acres - Richard Sewell - 1732
"Addition to the Flower of the Forrest" - 120 acres - George Maffott - 1764
"Addition to Tilghmans Farm" - 50 acres - John Ball - 1731
"Addition to Timber Levels" - 46 acres - Isaac Freeman - 1745
"Addition to Viavan" - 25 acres - Robert Roberts - 1743
"Addition to Viavan" - 25 acres - John Scott - 1761
"Addition to Ward Oake" - 45 acres - John Salter - 1704
"Adventure" - 92 3/4 acres - Edward Sweatman - 1680
"Adventure" (The) - 510 acres - Bryan Omealy - 1684
"Adventure" (The) - 42 acres - Cornelius Comegys - 1685
"Adventure" (The) - 440 acres - Matthew Howard - 1741
"Adventure" - 825 acres - Simon Wilmer, Chambers Hall, Frederick Hanson, and Alexander Baird - 1753
"Adventure" (The) - 50 acres - John Tilden - 1754
"Adventure" (The) - 52 acres - Cornelius Comegys, Sr. - 1688
"Adventure" (The) - 300 acres - Cornelius Comegys - 1681
"Adventure" (The) - 54 acres - John Sutton - 1714
"Adventure" (The) - 160 acres - James Harris - 1722
"Adventure" (The) - 2900 acres - Richard Bennett - 1729
"Adventure Resurveyed" - 137 acres - John Bordley - 1753
"Agreement" (The) - 472 acres - William Comegys and Samuell Wallace - 1724
"Alfords Part of Drayton" - 102 acres - Aaron Alford - 1740
"Allens Deceipt" - 250 acres - John Wright - 1667
"Allens Neck" - 66 acres - Thomas Allen - 1640
"Allibones Addition" - 52 acres - Edward Allibone - 1709
"Ambrose" - 53 acres - Abraham Ambrose - 1723
"Ambrosia" - 100 acres - Ambrose Harriott - 1675
"Ambrosia" - 154 acres - Christian Geist and Michael Miller - 1726
"Andover Resurveyed" - 145 acres - Henry Knock - 1752
"Angels Lott Resurveyed" - 1045 acres - George Wilson and Simon Wilmer - 1740

TRACT INDEX TO LAND PATENTS, 1640-1787　　　　45

Apsleys Lott - 6 acres - William Apsley - no date given.
Apsleys Part of Towne Relief Resurveyed - 208 1/5 [sic] acres - William Apsley - 1785
Arcadia - 1500 acres - Michael Miller - 1682
Arundell Grove - 550 acres - Henry Staples - 1681
Ashby Green - 200 acres - William Elme - 1696
Ashleys Lott - 300 acres - Isaac Williams and John Ashley - 1744
Ash Point - 42 acres - Thomas Keare - 1688
Attixs Adventure - 6 1/4 acres - Aquila Attix - 1774
Austins Beginning - 33 acres - John Austin - 1728
Baggalyes Forrest - 100 acres - William Baggaly - 1675
Bagleys Forrest - 1250 acres - Dominick Kenslaugh - 1728
Bagleys Forrest Resurveyed - 1136 acres - Dominick Kinslaugh - 1725
Barneys Forrest - 150 acres - Francis Barney, Jr. - 1728
Barton - 100 acres - Edward Beck - 1707
Barwick - 25 acres - Joseph Nicholson - 1748
Basha - 100 acres - Andrew Basha and James Cloughton - 1640
Batchelors Choice - 80 acres - Suttlan Queeny - 1688
Batchellers Delight - 100 acres - Thomas Jones - 1724
Batchelors Hall - 50 acres - Nathaniel Rickets - 1747
Batchelors Hope - 290 acres - John Davis - 1668
Batchelors Lott - 20 acres - Phillip Rasin - 1767
Batchellors Resolution - 1000 acres - Henry Herman and Mathew Mason - 1666
Batemans Farm - 300 acres - William Bateman - 1707
Bath - 300 acres - Joseph Wickes - 1678
Battersay - 250 acres - Benjamin Randall - 1694
Batusgy - 250 acres - Benjamin Randall - 1682
Bavaria - 31 acres - Charles Hynson - 1732
Bavraia Resurveyed - 47 1/2 acres - Thomas Ringgold, Jr. - 1770
Bayres Grime - 100 acres - John James - 1666
Beards Part of Morton - 208 acres - Alexander Beard and wife Elizabeth Beard - no date given.
Beaver Dames (The) - 1000 acres - John Parsons - 1688
Beaver Neck - 200 acres - Isaac Hine and Zachary Wade - 1650
Beaver Neck - 200 acres - John Salter - 1658
Beavin Ridge (The) - 100 acres - John Hinson - 1667
Beckes Addition - 100 acres - John Beck - 1688
Beckles Recovery - 200 acres - Thomas Beckles - 1686
Becks Addition - 100 acres - Edward Beck - 1684
Becks Part of Bounty Resurveyed - 75 acres - John Beck - 1756
Belcher - 300 acres - Thomas Belcher - 1652
Bellakile Resurveyed - 97 acres - William Maxwell - 1768
Bellas Resurvey of Shadshold - 731 acres - Francis Bellas - 1734
Bellekelle - 80 acres - Robert Maxwell - 1736
Bengate - 50 acres - James Ringgold - 1685
Benjamins Choice - 200 acres - Benjamin Randall - 1681
Benjamins Lott - 23 acres - Gideon Pearce - 1730
Benjamins Lott - 350 acres - William Pearce - 1683
Benjamins Purchase - 200 acres - Benjamin Griffith - 1724
Bennetts Hope - 200 acres - Richard Bennett - 1665

"Bennetts Lowe" (or "Lowes Bennett") - 1400 acres - Henry Lowe
    and wife Sussannah Maria Lowe - 1715
"Bennetts Regulation" - 1733 acres - Richard Bennett - 1743
"Betsys Park" - 860 acres - Thomas Larkin - 1722
"Bettys Park" - 800 acres - Thomas Larkin - 1744
"Billys Lott" - 112 acres - William Comegys - 1730
"Biman" - 200 acres - Robert Michay - 1683
"Birth Right" (The) - 107 acres - James Sterling - 1760
"Bishford" - 200 acres - Elias King and Charles Tilden - 1686
"Bishford Resurveyed" - 294 acres - John Tilden - 1747
"Blackhalls Hermitage" - 300 acres - Ralph Blackhall - 1670
"Blackistons Case" - 115 3/4 acres - Ebenezer Blackiston - 1783
"Blackistons Lott" - 87 acres - Benjamin Blackiston - 1754
"Blackistons Lot Resurveyed" - 175 acres - George Blackiston - 1772
"Blackistons Neglect" - 89 acres - Michael Byrne - 1720
"Black Oak" - 250 acres - St. Leger Codd - 1724
"Blays Addition" - 450 acres - Edward Blay - 1767
"Blays Addition" - 450 acres - Edward Blay - 1679
"Blays Park" - 880 acres - William Blay - 1715
"Blays Range" - 200 acres - Edward Blay - 1675
"Bloomsburg" - 30 acres - John Wade - 1689
"Blountville" - 175 acres - Richard Blunt - 1659
"Bluff Point" - 700 acres - Thomas Mountford - 1670
"Boardleys Beginning" - 420 acres - Thomas Bordley - 1709
"Bobs Desire" - 36 acres - James Graham and George Tiller - 1770
"Boddys Neck" - 200 acres - William Boddy - 1650
"Boltons Retreat" - 100 acres and 32 perches - John Bolton - 1774
"Bondyes Folly" - 100 acres - Richard Bondy - 1687
"Bongay" - 200 acres - Henry Parker and John Reynolds - 1667
"Boonley" - 150 acres - Thomas Boone - 1673
"Boons Meadow" - 22 acres - Joseph Boon - 1767
"Bordleys Gift" - 525 acres - John Bordley - 1751
"Bordleys Resurvey on Killy Langford" - 229 acres - Stephen
    Bordley - 1767
"Bosticks Addition" - 120 acres - Sanders Bostick - 1754
"Boston" - 40 acres - William Haywood - 1700
"Bounty" - 200 acres - John Hynson - 1696
"Bowlston" - 500 acres - John Bowles - 1673
"Bownes Discovery" - 60 acres - Thomas Bowne - 1718
"Bowns Venture" - 37 acres - Thomas Brown [Bown?] - 1718
"Boxley" - 300 acres - John Scott - 1668
"Boyers Addition" - 58 3/4 acres - Augustine Boyer - 1768
"Boyers Adventure" - 94 acres - Simon Wilmer and Augustin Boyer - 1744
"Bradfield" - 300 acres - Thomas Bradnox - 1658
"Bradnox" - 500 acres - Thomas Bradnox - 1659
"Bradshaws Farm" - 162 acres - William Bradshaw - 1758
"Brewards Marsh" - 76 acres - James Breward - 1703
"Brewards Reserve Resurvey" - 170 acres - Samuel Norris - 1732
"Bridge Point" - 20 acres - Nicholas Hodgson - 1686
"Bridge Town Common" - 89 acres - Thomas Gilpin - 1762
"Bright Helmstone" - 1000 acres - James Fendall - 1683
"Brints Piddles" - 200 acres - William Davis - 1678

"Bristol" - 22 acres - Daniell Cooley - 1716
"Bristol" - 200 acres - Edward Sweatman - 1678
"Bristoll" - 150 acres - Henry Hosier - 1683
"Brittaine" - 200 acres - John Jones - 1685
"Broad Neck" - 700 acres - John Edmondson - 1666
"Bradnox Creek" - 700 acres - Thomas Bradnox - 1658
"Broadnox Resurveyed" - 737 acres - James Dunn - 1755
"Broad Oak" - 200 acres - Philip Holleger - 1671
"Broad Oake" - 500 acres - Philip Holleger - 1675
"Brodoway" - 100 acres - Nicholas Brodoway - 1658
"Bromfield" - 200 acres - John Bromfield and Richard Allome - 1667
"Brotherly and Friendly Agreement" (The) - 87 acres - John Course - 1731
"Browards Industry" - 122 acres - James Broward - 1733
"Browards Marsh" - 76 acres - James Broward - 1703
"Browards Reserve" - 200 acres - James Broward - 1707
"Brownings Addition" - 2 1/4 acres - Thomas Browning - 1759
"Brownings Adventure" - 22 1/2 acres - Thomas Browning - 1767
"Brownings Adventure" - 105 acres - Thomas Browning - 1768
"Brownings Discovery" - 107 acres - Thomas Browning - 1763
"Brownings Part of Adams Choice Resurveyed" - 255 1/4 acres - John Wrightson Browning - 1785
"Brownings Part of Byors Neglect Resurveyed" - 85 acres - Thomas Browning - 1767
"Browne Angle" - 280 acres - James Brown - 1669
"Browns Adventure" - 18 acres - John Brown - 1742
"Browns Choice" - 200 acres - William Brown - 1714
"Browns Discovery" - 7 1/2 acres - Peregrine Brown - 1757
"Browns Level" - 40 acres - John Brown - 1743
"Browns Lott" - 13 acres - John Brown - 1742
"Browns Purchase" - 60 acres - William Browne - 1717
"Browns Right" - 470 acres - James Brown - 1669
"Bryans Addition" - 11 acres - Daniel Bryan - 1753
"Brynton" - 200 acres - Charles James - 1663
"Buckhill" - 150 acres - Matthew Bennam and Hugh Masson - [no date given]
"Buck Hill and Bilbys Lott Resurveyed" - 333 acres - William Comegys - [no date given]
"Buckingham" - 1000 acres - Richard Turney - 1659
"Buckingham" - 1000 acres - Richard Bennitt - 1664
"Buckingham" - 1300 acres - Henrietta Maria Bennett and Susanna Maria Bennett - 1671
"Buckingham" - 500 acres - Symon Willmer - 1686
"Buck Neck" - 550 acres - Joseph Hopkins - 1667
"Buck Neck" - 493 acres - Sarah Graves - 1738
"Budds Discovery" - 295 acres - Samuel Budd - 1756
"Budds Meadow" - 150 acres - Samuel Budd - 1752
"Burcks Beginning" or "Burcks" - 50 acres - William Burck - 1719
"Burks Addition" - 20 acres - William Burk - 1722
"Burks Chance" - 221 acres - Thomas Burk - 1757
"Burks Lott" - 1 acre - Thomas Burk - 1755
"Burk With Its Addition Resurveyed" - 114 acres - William Burk - 1747

"Burrows Addition" - 100 acres - William Burrows - 1731
"Butlers Neck" - 200 acres - John Butler - 1640
"By Chance" - 60 acres - John Redgrave - 1739
"Cackaway Point" - 7 3/4 acres - Thomas Maslin - 1769
"Calders Meadow" - 45 acres - James Calder - 1735
"Calebs Discovery" - 50 acres - Caleb Beck - 1732
"Camells Fame" - 350 acres - John Camell - 1673
"Camells Worth More" - 1150 acres - Thomas Collins and William Marr - 1683
"Cannells Fancy" - 4 acres - Isaac Cannell - 1786
"Cannells Triangle" - 2 1/3 acres - Abraham Cannell - 1771
"Carrola" - 150 acres - Charles James - 1694
"Carrolls Addition" - 39 acres - Phill Carroll - 1719-20
"Carvills Adventure" - 177 acres - John Carvill - 1752
"Carvils Inheritance" - 698 acres - John Carvil - 1735
"Carviles Prevention" - 26 acres - John Carvile - 1694
"Castle Carey" - 250 acres - Thomas Erbery and Peter West - 1675
"Castledines Lot" - 13 acres - William Castledine - 1753
"Castles Point" - 150 acres - Ralph Castle - 1673
"Catons Choice Part of Kent Manor No. 12" - 101 1/4 acres - William Caton - 1782
"Cedar Branch" - 400 acres - John Coursey - 1658
"Chance" - 300 acres - John Collett and George Gouldsmith - 1663
"Chance" - 100 acres - John Mitchell - 1666
"Chance" - 500 acres - James Sedgewick - 1688
"Chance" - 250 acres - Richard Thornton - 1678
"Chance" - 200 acres - Darby Haley - 1696
"Chance" - 250 acres - Tolley and Hodges - 1705
"Chance" - 48 acres - Edward Drugan - 1757
"Chance" - 2 1/2 acres - Thomas Browning - 1767
"Chance" - 100 acres - Gideon Pearce - 1722
"Chance" - 400 acres - Michael Earle - 1752
"Chance" - 400 acres - Robert Smith - 1705
"Chance" - 30 acres - John Wyddall - 1713
"Chance" - 250 acres - Thomas Tolley - 1719
"Chance" - 75 acres - William Comegys - 1732
"Chance" - 730 acres - Gideon Pearce - 1734
"Chance" - 100 acres - William Woodland - 1734
"Chance" - 34 acres - Thomas Hynson - 1743
"Chance" - 72 acres - Thomas Wilkins - 1747
"Chance" - 200 acres - John Briscoe, Jr. - 1757
"Chance" - 400 acres - Philip Brooks and John Tucker - 1757
"Chance" - 400 acres - Philip Brooks, Michael Earle, and John Tucker - 1757
"Chance" (The) - 200 acres - Nicholas Painter and James Boullay - 1683
"Chance Addition" - 38 acres - Charles Hynson - 1709
"Chance Resurveyed" - 325 acres - Edward Harris - 1761
"Chance Resurveyed" - 127 acres - Edward Comegys - 1745
"Chance Resurveyed" - 300 acres - John Pollard - 1746
"Chandlers Addition" - 150 acres - Thomas Chandler - 1747
"Charles His Lott" - 300 acres - John Parsons - 1686
"Charleton alias Queen Catherine" - 109 acres - Daniel Ferrell and Thomas Macher - 1732

TRACT INDEX TO LAND PATENTS, 1640-1787   49

Cheapside - 500 acres - John Baker - 1685
Chedle - 50 acres - Michael Miller - 1681
Chenish - 200 acres - William Pearce - 1666
Chesterfield Resurveyed - 570 acres - Henry Knock - 1742
Chester Grove - 540 acres - William Comegys - 1730
Chester Grove Resurveyed and Vansants Part of Endeavour - 283 acres - Joshua Vansant - 1767
Chester Point - 200 acres - Matthew Ward - 1673
Chizwell - 200 acres - Simon Wilmer - 1695
Christins Addition - 515 acres - Lawrence Christin - 1686
Christophers Beginning - 43 acres - Christopher Hall - 1732
Churchs Chance - 221 acres - Samuel Church - 1755
Church Hill - 85 acres - Abrm. Haynes - 1776
Churches Lott - 1 1/8 acres - Samuel Church - 1757
Churchs Lotts Nos. 18 and 19 - 1/2 acre each - Samuel Church - 1757
Churchs Lotts Nos. 106 and 107 - 1/2 acre each - Samuel Church - 1757
Churchwarden Neck - 400 acres - Henry Woolchurch - 1668
Clarks Addition - 25 acres - Dennis Clark - 1717
Clarks Convenience - 196 acres - Dennis Clarke - 1707
Clarks Conveniency Resurveyed - 154 acres - William Clark - 1732
Clarks Conveniency Resurveyed - 380 acres - William Clark - 1745
Clarks Neglect - 36 1/2 acres - Bartus Wilkins - 1771
Clayton - 200 acres - Lukener Midleton - 1707
Clifton - 50 acres - William Bateman - 1677
Cloaks Addition - 31 acres - John Cloak - 1755
Clover Patch - 20 acres - Joseph Shawhorn - 1785
Cock of the Game - 300 acres - Thomas Pryor - 1675
Coffin - 170 acres - Edward Jones - 1737
Cokestalle - 250 acres - Thomas Prior - 1672
Colchester [Tolchester?] - 955 acres - Gideon Pearce - 1734
Colechester [Tolchester?] - 1000 acres - William Smith - 1666
Colchester [Tolchester?] Resurveyed - 1051 acres - Gideon Pearce - 1742
Colleton - 200 acres - John Collett - 1662
Comb Hill - 75 acres - Anthony Griffin - 1670
Comegys Choice - 350 acres - Cornelius Comegys - 1668
Comegys Delight - 400 acres - Corenlius Comegys - 1683
Comegys Farme - 300 acres - Cornelius Comegys - 1682
Comegys Farm Addition - 370 acres - Cornelius Comegys - 1688
Comegys Farm Addition Resurveyed - 516 acres - George Skirven and wife, and Thomas Wilkens and wife - 1738
Comegys Neglect - 22 acres - Dennis Clarke - 1716
Comegys Resurvey - 276 1/2 acres - Edward Comegys - 1769
Conclusion - 60 acres - Edward Mitchell - 1724
Conclusion (The) - 74 acres - Samuell Wallace - 1714
Conjunct - 400 acres - Gideon Pearce - 1732
Conny [Coney] Warren - 1000 acres - Vincent Elliott and John Willis - 1675
Contest (The) - 1 acre - Joseph Massey - 1763
Coopers Hill - 100 acres - William Joyner, Jr. - 1710

"Cornelius Comegys Land" - 52 acres - Cornelius Comegys - 1688
"Cornelius Fork" (or Forth) - 25 acres - Cornelius Comegys - 1732
"Cornewalleys Choice" - 1000 acres - Thomas Cornewalleys - 1658
"Corses Neglect" - 10 acres - Patrick Drugan - 1763
"Cosens Lott" - 100 acres - Edward Cosens - 1714
"Courseys Meadows" - 200 acres - James Coursey - 1705
"Courseys Neck" - 140 acres - William COursey - 1658
"Cove" (The) - 70 acres - Thomas Howell - 1672
"Covent Garden" - 500 acres - Michael Miller - 1685
"Coventry" - 100 acres - Jonathan Coventry - 1659
"Coventry Marsh" - 51 acres - Jeremiah Coventon - 1719-20
"Cove Tract" (The) - 100 acres - Nathaniel Stiles - 1664
"Cowarden Farm" - 62 acres - Abraham Cowarden - 1753
"Cowleys Calf Pasture" - 2 1/2 acres - Risdon Bishop - 1773
"Cozens Chance" - 68 acres - Edward Cozens - 1734
"Craney Neck" - 400 acres - Robert Hewett - 1657
"Crouchs Addition" - 70 acres - John Crouch - 1694
"Crowes Addition" - 107 acres - William Crow - 1729
"Crows Chance" - 100 acres - William Crow - 1722
"Cuckholds Point" - 55 acres - Edward Cozens - 1734
"Cuckolds Hope" - 100 acres - Roger Howard - 1688
"Cumberland" - 600 acres - William Dixon - 1680
"Cum Witton" - 360 acres - William Dixon - 1685
"Dale Town" - 300 acres - Nathaniel Utie - 1658
"Dale Town" - 700 acres - Thomas Howell - 1670
"Dallams Folly Resurveyed" - 317 acres - Samuel Davis - 1762
"Dallington" - 500 acres - John Swain - 1680
"Damsons Point" - 378 acres - Solomon Wright - 1754
"Daniels Disappointment" - 50 acres - John Jones - 1739
"Daniels Disappointment Resurveyed" - 150 acres - John Jones - 1746
"Daniel and Joseph Disappointment" - 2 acres - Gilbert Falconer - 1761
"Darby" - 384 acres - Jarvis Spencer - 1732
"Darbys Desire" - 50 acres - Darby Sheighane - 1716
"Darnalls Farme" - 600 acres - John Darnall - 1684
"Darnalls Lott" - 400 acres - John Darnall - 1683
"Davis's Addition" - 22 acres - Richard Davis - 1734
"Davis's Chance" - 38 acres - Richard Davis - 1731
"Davis's Desire" - 223 acres - Richard Davis - 1734
"Davis's Part of Hellens Adventure" - 261 acres - John Davis - 1734
"Davis's Part of Hillens Adventure" - 222 acres - John Davis - 1740
"Davis's Part of Hillens Adventure Resurveyed" - 261 acres - John Davis - 1734
"Davis's Triangle" - 140 acres - Phillip Davis - 1723
"Dawsons Chance" - 15 1/2 acres - William Dawson - 1769
"Deanes Adventure" - 213 acres - William Deane - 1695
"Deanes Reliefe" - 50 acres - William Deane - 1681
"Dearby" - 90 acres - Jarvis Spencer - 1722
"Deerby" - 400 acres - John Deer - 1659
"Deer Park" (The) - 2255 acres - Benjamin Blackiston - 1748
"Deerum" - 188 acres - Francis Speerman - 1700

TRACT INDEX TO LAND PATENTS, 1640-1787   51

"Delay" - 88 acres - Michael Miller - 1729
"Delay" - 2 acres - Joseph Massey and Ebenezer Massey - 1765
"Delay Resurveyed" - 43 acres - Richard Gresham - 1746
"Denby" - 220 acres - Morgan Jones - 1667
"Deptford" - 300 acres - William Comegys and John Tennant - 1728
"Deprived Mischief" - 100 acres - Benjamin Ricaud - 1695
"Dicks Chance" - 100 acres - Richard Wells - 1668
"Diligence" - 48 acres - Joseph Massey and Ebenezer Massey - 1764
"Dining Room" (The) - 500 acres - Nicholas Painter and James Boullay - 1682
"Disappointment" (The) - 2 1/4 acres - Ebenezer Massey and Joseph Massey - 1764
"Discovery" - 70 acres - Joshua Vansant - 1759
"Dispute" - 140 acres - Robert Smith - 1705
"Doctor Smyth's Lot" - 51 1/2 acres - William Smyth - 1784
"Doe Neck" - 200 acres - Caesar Prince and John Powell - 1673
"Donbey" - 275 acres - John Smith - 1730
"Double Purchase" - 46 acres - Morgan Brown - 1730
"Douches Folly" - 150 acres - Hugh Douch - 1683
"Dowdalls Fancy" - 50 acres - John Dowdall - 1713
"Draw Near" - 86 acres - William Simcock - 1743
"Drayton" - 2100 acres - Charles James - 1663
"Drayton" - 1200 acres - Charles James - 1667
"Drayton" (Alfords Part of) - 102 acres - Aaron Alford - 1740
"Drayton" (Reasons Part of) - 513 acres - George and Mary Reason - 1741
"Drecute" - 275 acres - Henry Jones - 1665
"Drugans Delight" - 221 acres - Edward Drugan - 1761
"Drugans Lott" - 13 acres - Edward Drugan - 1759
"Drugans Lotts Nos. 18 and 19" - 1/2 acre each - Edward Drugan - 1759
"Drugans Lot Number 37" - 1/2 acre - Edward Drugan - 1761
"Drugans Mistake" - 19 acres - John Corse - 1763
"Drugans Ramble" - 162 acres - Edward Drugan - 1757
"Dublin" - 18 acres - Edward Mitchell - 1728
"Dublin" - 100 acres - Robert Lynch - 1708
"Dublin Resurveyed" - 107 acres - Jacob Caulk - 1747
"Duck Pye" - 100 acres - William Pierce - 1678-79
"Dulleans Folly" - 300 acres - Phillip Davis - 1683
"Dultans Folly" - 317 acres - Samuel Davis - 1754
"Duncans Part of Worth's Folly" - 366 acres - George Duncan - 1743
"Dundale" - 150 acres - Thomas Dale - 1675
"Dundee" - 100 acres - Alexander Waters - 1680
"Dungannon" - 200 acres - George Garnet - 1760
"Dunns Discovery" - 16 1/2 acres - Hezekiah Dunn - 1769
"Dunns Folly" - 120 acres - Peter Debruler - 1720
"Dunstable" - 100 acres - John West - 1675
"Dwyers Desire" - 100 acres - John Dwyer - 1715
"Eagles Nest" (The) - 300 acres - William Toulson - 1663
"Eastern Island" (The) - 100 acres - John Meconokin - 1668
"Eastern Neck" (The) - 200 acres - Caesar Prince and John Powell - 1673
"East Huntington" - 800 acres - Andrew Skinner - 1665

"Edinburgh" - 15 acres - John Watson - 1748
"Edwins Affront" - 100 acres - Ralph Page - 1734
"Edwins Addition" - 240 acres - William Edwin - 1695
"Elias and James Ringgolds Part of Huntingfield Resurveyed" - 408 acres - James Ringgold and Elias Ringgold - 1734
"Elinors Delight" - 100 acres - Matthew Shaw - 1714
"Elliotts Choice" - 120 acres - William Elliott - 1667
"Ellis's Delight" - 500 acres - Benjamin Ellis and William Ellis - 1721
"Ellis's Industry Resurveyed" - 670 acres - William Ellis - 1744
"Ellis's Farm" - 182 acres - William Brown - 1753
"Ellis His Chance" - 1000 acres - John Ellis - 1695
"Ellis's Industry" - 150 acres - Benjamin Ellis - 1723
"Ellis's Ramble" - 162 acres - William Ellis - 1747
"Endeavour" (The) - 260 acres - William Comegys - 1707
"Essex" - 250 acres - Abraham Delap - 1697
"Everetts Discovery" - 9 1/2 acres - Hailes Everett - 1782
"Everitts Addition" - 20 acres - Benjamin Everitt - 1753
"Eversetts Double Purchase" - 222 acres - Benjamin Eversett - John Eversett - and Augustine Eversett - 1737
"Exchange" - 100 acres - John Fielder - 1752
"Exchange" (The) - 100 acres - John Falconer - 1704
"Exchange" (The) - 100 acres - Walter Meek - 1708
"Exchange" (The) - 100 acres - Nicholas Massey - 1720
"Faire Dealing" - 300 acres - John Salter - 1689
"Fairely" (or "Faire Lee") - 1900 acres - Bartholomew Browne - 1683
"Fairfield" - 60 acres - Peter Cole - 1730
"Fair Promise" - 500 acres - Samuel Withers - 1658
"Fair Promise" - 600 acres - George Warner and Elizabeth his wife - 1680
"Falconers Adventure" - 995 acres - John Falconer - 1753
"Falconers Lott" - 35 acres - John Falconer - 1754
"Fancico" - 28 acres - John Conner - 1743
"Fannys Slipe" - 47 1/2 acres - Samuel Davis - 1774
"Fare All" - 200 acres - John George - 1672
"Fare Harbour" - 200 acres - Nathaniel Evetts - 1667
"Fare Promise" - 600 acres - Godfrey Bayly - 1667
"Farley" - 650 acres - Thomas Howell - 1659
"Fathers Care" - 253 acres - Joseph Kennard - 1739
"Fathers Care Resurveyed" - 230 acres - Mary Kennard and Ann Kennard - 1754
"Fathers Gift" - 150 acres - William Harris - 1687
"Fawmouth" - 200 acres - William Salisbury - 1672
"Ferrils Addition" - 50 acres - Daniel Ferril - 1732
"First Part of Free Gift" (The) - 2000 acres - Richard Smith - 1694
"Fishall" - 225 acres - William Fisher - 1663
"Fishing Pond" (The) - 250 acres - Nathaniel Hynson - 1718
"Flannikins Hope" - 50 acres - Martin Flannikin - 1730
"Flower of the Forrest" - 100 acres - George Moffett - 1707
"Floyds Chance" - 50 acres - John Floyd - 1668
"Folly" (The) - 82 acres - John Cooper - 1728
"Folly Resurveyed" - 161 acres - John Cooper - 1746

"Folly Resurveyed" (The) - 178 acres - John Cooper - 1738
"Force To It" - 45 acres - Edward Tilghman - 1750
"Fords Part of Broomfield Resurveyed" - 86 acres - Robert Ford - 1747
"Foremans Poor Discovery" - 102 acres - John Foreman - 1733
"Fork" - 253 acres - Elizabeth Redgrave - 1756
"Fork" (The) - 300 acres - Henry Hawkins - 1667
"Forke" (The) - 500 acres - Perrigrine Browne - 1686
"Forrest" - 50 acres - Edward Harris - 1732
"Forrest" (The) - 250 acres - Walter Meeke - 1675
"Forrest" (The) - 500 acres - Phillip Holleager - 1695
"Forrest" (The) - 200 acres - Phillip Holleager - 1695
"Forrest" (The) - 440 acres - Solomon Wright - 1708
"Forrest" (The) - 900 acres - Gideon Wright - 1734
"Forrests Lodge" - 100 acres - Patrick Forrest - 1658
"Forrest of Dean" (The) - 586 acres - Francina Hynson and Matthias Harris - 1755
"Forest Resurveyed" - 360 acres - Richard Johnson - 1734
"Fortune" - 3 1/2 acres - Martha Barnes - 1783
"Four Brothers" (The) - 38 acres - Martha Hurt - 1750
"Francis Enlargement" - 200 acres - Thomas Francis - 1684
"Freeland" - 21 acres - William Freeman - 1720
"Freemans Addition" - 24 acres - Isaac Freeman - 1752
"Frenches Lott" - 22 acres - Zorobabel French - 1747
"Friendship" - 412 acres - Edward Jones and George Holland - 1683
"Friendship" - 401 acres - Thomas Macnemarra - 1709
"Friendship" - 75 acres - Michael Hackett - 1741
"Friendship" - 210 acres - Pearce Lamb - 1773
"Friendship" (The) - 200 acres - Thomas Waddy - 1666
"Friendship Resurveyed" - 555 acres - John Phillips - 1734
"Friendship Resurveyed" - 300 acres - Mary Raisin - 1746
"Gales Addition" - 20 acres - Bulmer Medford - 1740
"Gallaways Chance" - 200 acres - William Gallaway - 1737
"Galloways Fancy" - 150 acres - William Galloway - 1679
"Gamballs Farm" - 378 acres - John Gamball - 1755
"Gamballs Resurvey of Hereford" - 565 acres - John Gamball - 1737
"Garnetts Branch" - 23 acres - Joseph Garnett - 1747
"Garnetts Meadow" - 41 acres - George Garnett - 1733
"George Codd" - 100 acres - John Meconokin - 1668
"Georges Part of Morton" - 428 acres - Mary George - 1750
"Georgeton" (afterwards "Larenham") - 300 acres - George Gouldsmith - 1659
"Gibbs Choice" - 200 acres - John Gibbs - 1678
"Gilberts Lot" - 100 acres - John Gilbert - 1705
"Gilpins Town on London Bridge" - 333 1/3 acres - Thomas Gilpin - 1773
"Gleaves Addition" - 40 acres - John Gleaves - 1756
"Gleaves Adventure" - 580 acres - John Gleaves - 1756
"Gleaves Lott" - 150 acres - George Gleaves - 1713
"Glenns Neglect" - 7 1/4 acres - William Merritt - 1773
"Godfreys Point" - 350 acres - Godfrey Herman - 1662
"Godfreys Point" - 150 acres - William Peirce - 1678
"Godfreys Point Resurveyed" - 320 acres - Andrew Pearce - 1734
"Godlington Manor" - 1000 acres - Thomas Godlington - 1659

54 INHABITANTS OF KENT COUNTY, MARYLAND, 1637-1787

"Godlington Mannor" - 1000 acres - Thomas Clegatt - 1686
"Golden Ridge" - 100 acres - Benjamin Ellis - 1716
"Goldhawks Enlarged" - 70 acres - George Goldhawk - 1669
"Good Hope" - 300 acres - Henry Augustus Bodien - 1734
"Good Hope" (The) - 300 acres - John James - 1683
"Goose Haven" - 500 acres - William Hemsley - 1685
"Gore" (The) - 150 acres - Gideon Pearce - 1734
"Gouldhawkes Inlargement" - 70 acres - George Gouldhawke - 1670
"Grahams Addition" - 11 3/4 acres - James Graham - 1769
"Grahams Fishery" - 3/4 acre - John Graham - 1767
"Grahams Purchase" - 34 1/4 acres - James Graham - 1770
"Grainge" (The) - 150 acres - William Grainger - 1658
"Graising Point" - 150 acres - Hance Hanson - 1683
"Grange" (The) - 900 acres - John James - 1673
"Grangers Part of Wickliff and Market Place Resurveyed" - 414 acres - William Granger - 1771
"Grantham" - 500 acres - Kenelm Cheseldyn - 1674
"Grants Folly" - 69 acres - John Grant - 1735
"Graves Eastern Part of Cunney Warren" - 294 acres - William Graves - 1744
"Gray Inn" - 150 acres - Robert Hodges - 1723
"Grays Lot" - 1 acre and 8 perches - John Gary - 1759
"Great Folly" - 70 acres - John Grant - 1727-28
"Great Neck" - 330 acres - Richard Blunt - 1650
"Great Oake" - 1550 acres - John Vanheck - 1675
"Great Oak Mannor" - 2000 acres - Josias Fendall - 1658
"Green Bank" - 200 acres - Isaac Bowles - 1705
"Green Branch" - 200 acres - James Ringgold - 1671
"Green Branch Resurveyed" - 167 acres - Thomas Perkins and wife - 1753
"Green Forrest" - 200 acres - Richard Leake - 1679
"Greens Forrest Resurveyed" - 102 acres - Richard Bennett - 1742
"Green Meadow" - 150 acres - William Harris - 1707
"Greenwoods Chance" - 20 acres - John Greenwood - 1772
"Green Oak" - 492 acres - Henry Lowe and wife Sussannah - 1714
"Greenwoods Farm" - 115 3/8 acres - George Greenwood - 1776
"Greenwoods Part of Suffolk" - 120 acres - Joseph Greenwood - 1755
"Greers Range" - 100 acres - James Greer - 1688
"Greers Range" - 100 acres - James Corse - 1717
"Greshams Colledge" (Resurvey) - 733 acres - John Gresham - 1739
"Greshams Discovery" - 250 acres - Richard Gresham - 1750
"Greshams Levels" - 306 acres - Richard Gresham - 1743
"Griffins Hamilton" - 150 acres - Anthony Griffin and William Hamilton - 1658
"Griffiths Calfe Penn" - 30 acres - Benjamin Griffith - 1732
"Griffiths Delight" - 197 acres - Griffith Jones - 1717
"Grove" (The) - 400 acres - Cornelius Comegys - 1681
"Grove Addition" - 160 acres - James Smith - 1720
"Grove Addition" (The) - 160 acres - James Smith - 1722
"Grumble" - 250 acres - Thomas Boardley [Bordley] - 1720
"Habornes Farme" - 200 acres - James Haborne - 1683
"Hacketts Fancy" - 200 acres - Michaell Hackett - 1715
"Hackney" - 27 acres - Charles Garfutt - 1730

TRACT INDEX TO LAND PATENTS, 1640-1787   55

"Haddon" - 500 acres - William Hatton - 1658
"Hales" - 300 acres - Charles James - 1684
"Hales Adventure" - 104 acres - Roger Hale - 1723
"Hamblins Lott" - 9 acres - William Hamblin - 1754
"Hampshire" - 9 acres - Daniel Perkins - 1738
"Hanceford" - 100 acres - Hance Hanson - 1673
"Handle" (The) - 70 acres - Cornelius Comegys - 1744
"Hangmans End" - 300 acres - John Rogers - 1729
"Hangmans Folly" - 300 acres - William Pearce - 1684
"Hankam" - 70 acres - Edward Sweetman - 1683
"Hansons Choice" - 100 acres - Hans Hanson - 1682
"Hansons Choice Resurveyed" - 185 acres - Jacob Glenn - 1758
"Harbour" (The) - 34 acres - William McLean - 1747
"Harefield" - 200 acres - Thomas Birch - 1665
"Harris's Addition" - 166 acres - Margaritta Arina Harris - 1748
"Harris's Forrest" - 900 acres - James Harris - 1723
"Hatchbury" - 50 acres - Philip Everett and Joseph Everett - 1683
"Hayzells Adventure" - 28 acres - Benjamin Hayzell - 1748
"Hazard" - 280 acres - Ralph Page - 1725
"Hazard" - 50 acres - Samuel French - 1752. Certificate in the name of Zerobabel French.
"Hazzard" - 190 acres - Ralph Page - 1714
"Hazel Meadow" - 113 acres - John Stevenson - 1741. Certificate in the name of John Redgrave.
"Heading" - 150 acres - John Heading - 1707
"Heaths Gift" - 53 acres - Thomas Ruth - 1705
"Heaths Long Lands" - 150 acres - James Heath - 1700
"Heaths Range, The Second Part" - 1350 acres - James Heath - 1708
"Heaths Range, The Second Part Resurveyed" - 1986 acres - James Heath - 1761
"Hemberry" - 600 acres - Humphrey Davenport - 1683
"Hemsleys Discovery" - 200 acres - William Hemsley - 1760
"Henn Island" - 4 acres - Simon Wilmer - 1743
"Hens Roost" - 200 acres - Thomas Pryor - 1667
"Herberts Chance" - 14 acres - Charles Herbert - 1771-72
"Hereford" - 200 acres - Richard Hopewell and Joseph Hopewell - 1683
"Hereford" - 300 acres - Richard Hopewell and Joseph Hopewell - 1684
"Hermitage" - 200 acres - Samuel Massey - 1746
"Hermitage" - 300 acres - Matthew Pope and Sutthin Queeny - 1686
"Hermitage" - 230 acres - William Pope - 1741
"Hesbornes" ["Hepbornes"?] - 350 acres - George Macall - 1673
"Hicks Addition" - 10 acres - John Hicks - 1738
"High Park" - 600 acres - Daniel Cooley and wife Elizabeth - 1727
"High Park" (Part of) - 110 acres - William Brown - 1732
"High Parke" - 600 acres - Deliverance Lovely - 1665
"Hills" (The) - 400 acres - Richard Leake - 1674
"Hills Cabbin" - 100 acres - Peter Johnson - 1665
"Hillsdon" - 200 acres - William Hills - 1659
"Hills and No Dales" - 115 acres - Ambrose Ariss - 1694
"Hillston" - 300 acres - Thomas Hill - 1659
"Hill Top" (The) - 100 acres - George Higginbotham - 1683
"Hinsons Chance" - 100 acres - Charles Hinson, Thomas Hinson, and

John Hinson - 1668. Certificate in the name of their father, Thomas Hinson.
"Hinsons Division" - 876 acres - John Hinson - 1702
"Hinsons New Haven" - 100 acres - John Hinson - 1668
"Hintchingham" - 2200 acres - Thomas Hinson - 1659
"His Part of Forrestors Delight" - 300 acres - William Rasin - 1772
"Hixes Hazard" - 100 acres - Roger Hix - 1725
"Hobsons Choice" - 100 acres - Richard Gray - 1685
"Holy Land" - 425 acres - William Harris - 1704
"Holy Land" (The) - 425 acres - William Harris - 1695
"Honest Dealing" - 400 acres - Daniel Carnell [Carrell?] and John Salter" - 1688
"Hoosiers Adventure" - 160 acres - Henry Hoosier - 1707
"Hope" (The) - 210 acres - Gilbert Falconer - 1725
"Hopewell" - 300 acres - Richard Hopewell and Joseph Hopewell - 1686
"Hopewell" - 600 acres - Henry Woolchurch - 1672
"Hopewell" - 370 acres - Alexander Sims - 1683
"Hopewell" - 40 acres - William Smithers - 1737
"Hopewell" - 259 acres - Ebenezer Perkins - 1741
"Hopewell Resurveyed" - 259 acres - John Read - 1744
"Hopewell Unity" (The) - 150 acres - John Howell, Charles James, James Frisby, George Wardner, Joseph Hopkins, William Pearce, William Pullen, Ebenezer Blackstein [Blackiston], Benjamin Guury [Grury?], Edward Blay, Robert Saunders, and John James - 1683
"Hosiers Addition" - 100 acres - Henry Hosier - 1672
"Hosiers Farm" - 1052 acres - Henry Hosier - 1731
"Hosiers Neglect" - 58 3/4 acres - Robert George, Jr. - 1763
"Howards Adventure" - 240 acres - Mathew Howard - 1725
"Howards Adventure" - 570 acres - Mathew Howard - 1750
"Howards Chance" - 19 acres - Matthew Howard - 1744
"Howards Gift" - 300 acres - William Scott - 1683
"Howards Lott" - 96 acres - Matthew Howard - 1733
"Howards Lott Resurveyed" - 128 acres - Mathew Howard - 1745
"Howards Policy" - 97 acres - Matthew Howard - 1730
"Howards Purchase" - 77 acres - Matthew Howard - 1737
"Howells" - 300 acres - Thomas Howell - 1683
"Howells" - 500 acres - Thomas Howell - 1670
"Howells Addition" - 300 acres - Thomas Howell - 1670
"Howells Oateland" - 600 acres - Thomas Howell - 1683
"Howells Resurveyed" - 802 acres - John Carvill - 1740
"Huckleberry Ridge" - 372 acres - Jacob Jones - 1752
"Huckleberry Ridge" - 104 1/2 acres - Simon Wilmer - 1760
"Hulls Desire" - 45 acres - David Hull - 1745
"Hulls Part of Suffolk" - 150 acres - Joseph Hull - 1755
"Huntingfield" - 1200 acres - Thomas Ringgould - 1659
"Huntingfield" - Part of - and Ringgould's Chance - 624 acres - Thomas Ringgould - 1736
"Hunting Field and Ringgold's Chance" - 1196 1/4 acres - Thomas Ringgold, Elias Ringgold, and James Ringgold - 1735
"Hunting Field Resurveyed" - 408 acres - James Ringgold and Elias Ringgold - 1734

TRACT INDEX TO LAND PATENTS, 1640-1787   57

"Hurlocks Chance" - 20 acres - Jacob Hurlock - 1760
"Hurlocks Chance Resurveyed" - 62 1/2 acres - Jacob Hurlock - 1774
"Hurtleberry Tract" - 77 acres - George Murphey - 1731
"Hurts Direction" - 43 acres - Morgan Hurt - 1734
"Hurts Lott" - 200 acres - John Hurt - 1728
"Husbands Lott" - 100 acres - Thomas Huzband [Husband] - 1729
"Hutchisons Addition" - 45 acres - Vincent Hutchison - 1743
"Hutsons Hills" - 46 3/4 acres - John Hutson - 1787
"Hyllings Grove" - 44 acres - Nathaniel Hylling - 1694
"Hynsons Adventure" - 38 acres - Thomas Hynson, Jr. - 1730
"Hynsons Choice" - 100 acres - John Hynson and Charles Hynson - 1709
"Hynsons Chance Resurveyed" - 898 acres - Charles Hynson, Jr. - 1744
"Hynsons Desire" - 222 acres - Thomas Hynson - 1747
"Hynsons Discovery" - 75 acres - Charles Hynson - 1712
"Hynsons Division - 876 acres - John Hynson - 1702
"Indian Range" (The) - 250 acres - Jarvis Morgan - 1671
"Indian Range Resurveyed" - 240 acres - Thomas Spencer - 1749
"Indian Spring" - 100 acres - Henry Morgan - 1650
"Ingrams Lott" - 260 acres - Robert Ingram - 1707
"Intermixt" - 300 acres - Humphrey Tillton - 1706
"Iske" - 600 acres - Robert Jones - 1659
"Ivingo" - 210 acres - Phillip Burgen - 1703
"Jamaica" - 200 acres - Ellis Humphreys - 1679
"James's Addition" - 41 acres - Thomas Wyatt - 1739
"James's Adventure" - 84 acres - James Black - 1771
"James's Choice" - 300 acres - Edward James - 1699
"James's Discovery" - 11 1/2 acres - James Jarvis - 1767
"James's Hope" - 37 acres - John James - 1713
"Jane Brown's Part of Trumpinton Resurveyed" - 325 acres - John Brown - 1740
"Jericho" - 200 acres - John Salter - 1687
"Jerman Point" - 9 acres - Samuel Massey - 1743
"Johns Addition" - 330 3/4 acres - John Comegys - 1768
"John Carvil Hynsons Part of Hynsons Chance" - 260 acres - Charles Hynson and John Carvil Hynson - 1786
"Johns Chance" - 4 3/4 acres - John Vansant - 1769
"Johns Chance and Salem Resurveyed" - 995 1/2 acres - Thomas Ringgold, Jr. - 1772
"Jones Incognito" - 50 acres - Thomas Jones - 1722
"Johns Lott" - 1 3/4 acres - John Sanders - 1771
"Johns Neglect" - 20 acres - Daniell Perkins - 1723
"Johns Triangle Addition" - 128 acres - Joshua Vansant - 1764
"Johnsons Lott" - 50 acres - Gabrill Johnson - 1723
"Joiners Fancy" - 1 1/4 acres - Thomas Shehan - 1765
"Joings" - 210 acres - Philip Bergen - 1703
"Jones's Addition" - 100 acres - Thomas Jones - 1738
"Jones's Addition" - 90 acres - Jacob Jones - 1753
"Jones's Adventure" - 27 acres - Jacob Jones - 1753
"Jones's Gore" - 36 acres - Peter Jones - 1732
"Jones's Part of Broad Oak" - 110 acres - Isaac Freeman - 1748
"Jones's Neglect" - 100 acres - John Bordley - 1751

58   INHABITANTS OF KENT COUNTY, MARYLAND, 1637-1787

"Jones's Venture" - 100 acres - William Jones - 1723
"Kedgerston" - 1000 acres - Robert Kedger - 1659
"Kellys Addition" - 25 acres - Alexander Kelley - 1756
"Kellys Chance" - 18 acres - Alexander Kelly - 1747
"Kellys Choice" - 100 acres - James Kelly - 1705
"Kelly Longford" - 200 acres - Henry Staples - 1686
"Kemps Beginning" - 320 acres - Symon Willmer - 1688
"Kempshear" - 9 acres - Daniel Perkins - 1737
"Kennards Discovery" - 417 acres - Phillip Kennard, Jr. - 1731
"Kennards Fancy" - 85 acres - Phillip Kennard - 1734
"Kennards Farm" - 618 acres - Philip Kennard - 1755
"Kennards Point" - 510 acres - John Kennard - 1734
"Kent Lott" - 100 acres - Benjamin Ellers - 1716
"Kent Manor" - 8000 acres - Certificate 121 [no names?] - 1709
"Killinsworthmore" - 621 acres - William Thomas - 1730
"Killensworthmore" (Part of) - 97 acres - John Donk - 1733
"Killensworthmore" (Thomas's Part of) - 105 acres - William Thomas - 1732
"Killingsworthmore" (Part of) - 198 acres - Thomas Atchison - 1733
"Killins Worth More" - 500 acres - Gilbert Clarke - 1683
"Kimbolton" - 300 acres - Robert Vaughn - 1658
"Kindness" (The) - 500 acres - William Cox - 1681
"Kindness" (The) - 500 acres - Andy Lewellin - 1695
"Kings Prevention" - 34 acres - Elioys King - 1695
"Kinvin Wroth's Lot" - 32 1/2 acres - Kinvin Wroth - 1784
"Knapley" - 150 acres - Robert Knap - 1658
"Knapley Green" - 150 acres - Nathaniel Evetts - 1669
"Knave Stand Off" - 90 acres - Abraham Ambrose - 1725
"Knock Harbour" - 52 acres - Henry Knock - 1745
"Knocks Folly" - 7 acres - Thomas Crosby - 1753
"Knocks Range" - 70 acres - Henry Knock - 1747
"Lambs Meadow Resurveyed" - 149 acres - Francis Lamb - 1743
"Lambs Meadow Resurveyed" - 222 acres - John Lamb - 1773
"Landing" (The) - 16 1/4 acres - Abraham Milton - 1770
"Landing" (The) - 14 acres - Edward Comegys - 1752
"Langfords Neck" - 1500 acres - John Langford - 1658
"Langfords Neck Resurveyed" - 1040 acres - John Smithers - 1735-36
"Larenham" (formerly "Georgeston") - 300 acres - Thomas Godlington - 1664
"Larkins Addition" - 800 acres - John Larkin - 1669
"Last" (The) - 200 acres - John James - 1666
"Levell" - 1224 acres - Cornelius Comegys - 1680
"Level Fields" - 322 1/2 acres - Stephen Denning - 1782
"Linchs Chance" - 171 acres - Nicholas Linch - 1742
"Lincolne" - 100 acres - Jonathan Lincolne - 1675
"Lincolns Inn Field" - 400 acres - Jonathan Lincoln - 1696
"Little Drayton" - 100 acres - Charles James - 1667
"Little Forrest" - 100 acres - William Comegys - 1722
"Little Grove" (The) - 220 acres - Henry Staples - 1686
"Little Neck" - 55 acres - Phillip Conner - 1680
"Littleworth" - 15 acres - William Comegys - 1695
"Locust Point" - 13 acres - John March - 1714

"London Bridge Renewed" - 710 acres - Daniel Massey - 1753-54
"London Derry" - 70 acres - John Falconer - 1746-47
"Long Acre" - 20 acres - Michael Byrne - 1724
"Long Acre" - 46 acres - Benjamin Ricaud - 1733
"Longcomptor" - 90 acres - Edward Beck - 1700
"Long Gore" (The) - 34 acres - Robert Peacock - 1770
"Long Neglect" - 400 acres - James Harris - 1723
"Long Slipe" - 48 acres - Leverings Meriott - 1761
"Lords Gift" - 300 acres - John Hinson - 1695
"Lords Gift Resurveyed" - 213 3/4 acres - Charles Copper - 1772
"Lots 5 and 6 in Chestertown" - 26 square perches - William Ringgold - 1785
"Lots in Georgetown" - 1 acre and 129 perches - James Henry - 1787
"Lovelys Neck" - 100 acres - Deliverance Lovely - 1658
"Lowes Bennett" (or "Bennetts Lowe") - 1400 acres - Henry Lowe and wife Sussannah Maria Lowe - 1715
"Luck" - 100 acres - James Hebron - 1683
"Lucys Recreation" - 100 acres - Arthur Miller - 1763
"Lynn" - 150 acres - John James - 1683
"Lyons Hall" - 100 acres - Thomas Pinar - 1687
"McDowgals Chance" - 50 acres - John McDowgal - 1732
"Mackeys Chance" - 20 acres - Gideon Pearce - 1738
"Mackeys Desire" - 27 acres - William Mackey - 1716
"Macklin" - 100 acres - Robert Macklin - 1658
"Mackoakin" - 200 acres - John Mackoakin - 1658
"Macomes Desire" - 84 acres - James Macome - 1749
"Maggies Joynture" - 50 acres - George Macall - 1673
"Maggys Joynture Resurveyed" - 139 acres - George Medford - 1736
"Maidens Lott" - 50 acres - William Harris - 1685
"Maidens Lott" - 600 acres - Sarah Conner - 1666
"Margaretts End" - 300 acres - John Wilson - 1726
"Marrowbone" - 400 acres - Jarvis Spencer - 1730
"Marshy Hope" - 45 acres - William Comegys - 1730
"Marshey Point" - 335 acres - Andrew Pearce - 1746
"Martins Nest" - 80 acres - Thomas Martin - 1675
"Masseys Lott" - 72 acres - William Massey - 1728
"Masseys Part of Mers's Lock" - 28 3/4 acres - Abednego Massey - 1783
"Masseys Venture" - 200 acres - Peter Massey and Nicholas Massey - 1719
"Masseys Venture Resurveyed" - 254 1/2 acres - Joseph Massey and Ebenezer Massey - 1765
"Matthias" - 100 acres - Matthias Day - 1719
"Maxwells Purchase" - 501 acres - John Maxwell - 1770
"Meadows" (The) - 25 acres - Cornelius Comegys - 1748
"Mechays Purchase" - 150 acres - Alexander Mechay - 1683
"Medfords Mistake" - 6 acres - Matthew Howard - 1743
"Medfords Part of Suffolk" - 100 acres - Unity Medford - 1755
"Meeks Part of Forrest of Dean Resurveyed" - 200 acres - Robert Meeks - 1761
"Memento Mori" - 184 acres - Elizabeth Spencer, John Spencer and Thomas Spencer - 1734. Certificate in name of John Spencer.
"Merritts Addition" - 66 acres - Loving Merritt - 1769

"Merritts Discovery" - 104 acres - Lovering Merritt - 1771
"Merritts Dicovery Resurveyed" - 22 1/2 acres - Lovering Merritt - 1774
"Middle Branch" - 200 acres - Thomas Derrington - 1745
"Middle Neck" - 338 acres - Richard Bennett - 1715
"Middle Neck" (The) - 300 acres - George Strong - 1672
"Middle Neck" - 150 acres - Richard Hill - 1673
"Middle Plantation" (The) - 343 acres - William Crow - 1735
"Middle Plantation" (The) - 350 acres - Joseph Wickes - 1678
"Middle Spring" - 400 acres - John and James Ringgold - 1667
"Miers Chance" - 100 acres - Stephen Miers - 1723
"Miles End" - 100 acres - Charles Miles - 1721-22
"Milesford" - 70 acres - Charles Miles - 1723
"Millers Delight Enlarged" - 393 acres - Nathaniel Miller - 1782
"Millers Fancy" - 60 acres - John Gresham - 1739
"Millers Purchase Resurveyed" - 949 acres - Michael Miller - 1735
"Millers Satisfaction" - 78 acres - Michael Miller - 1694
"Millford" - 50 acres - William Harris - 1686
"Millford" - 284 acres - James Harris - 1724
"Mill Forks" - 595 acres - William Blay - 1715
"Mill Forks" - 808 acres - Phillip Holleger - 1695
"Mill Forks" - 820 acres - William Blay - 1715
"Mill Hill" - 170 acres - Thomas Harris - 1753
"Mill Point" - 20 acres - John Brown - 1758
"Millwards Choice" - 150 acres - Loverly Millward - 1705
"Mires Resurvey" - 98 1/4 acres - Luke Mires [Miers] - 1771
"Mitchells Adventure" - 300 acres - Edward Mitchell - 1751
"Mitchells Chance" - 300 acres - Edward Mitchell - 1727
"Mitchells Park" - 400 acres - Edward Mitchell - 1723
"Mitchells Park" - 1650 acres - Edward Mitchell - 1736
"Mitchells Proposal" - 16 acres - Mary Scincock - 1743
"Mitchells Ruque" ["Risque"?] - 300 acres - Edward Mitchell - 1718
"Mitchells View" - 19 acres - Edward Mitchell - 1726
"Moores Fishing Ground" - 67 3/4 acres - John Moore - 1775
"Moorton" - 600 acres - Richard Leake - 1670
"Morfetts Lott" - 80 acres - George Morfett - 1756
"Morpheys Chance" - 61 acres - George Morphey - 1732
"Morsalls Lot" - 100 acres - Thomas Morsall - 1730
"Morsells Part of Killingsworthmore" - 46 acres - Thomas Morsell - 1734
"Morton Resurveyed" - 630 acres - Joshua George - 1746
"Morton Resurveyed" - 632 acres - Hugh Jerrey - 1743
"Mothers Care Resurveyed" - 146 3/4 acres - Bartus Piner - 1770
"Mothers Gift" - 300 acres - Michael Miller - 1684
"Mount Airey" - 409 acres - Henry McLachlan - 1769
"Mount Hermon" - 890 acres - William Thomas - 1732
"Mount Hope" - 100 acres - Charles Hollinsworth - 1684
"Mount Hope Resurveyed" - 119 acres - John Earle - 1731
"Mount Pleasant" - 350 acres - John Wedge - 1709
"Mount Pleasant" - 40 acres - John Vansant, Jr. - 1769
"Mount Pleasure" - 400 acres - Matthew Ward - 1673
"Mulberry Plain" - 118 acres - William Brown - 1730
"Myers Inclosure" - 26 1/2 acres - Luke Myers - 1761

"Myers Lot" - 375 acres - Lukeas [sic] Myers - 1747
"Myers Luck" - 200 acres - Luke Myers - 1753
"Nancys Choice" - 200 acres - Nathaniel Hillen - 1682
"Nancys Hope Resurveyed" - 41 1/4 acres - George Garnett - 1769
"Nancys Hope" - 50 acres - William Haggerty - 1724
"Nathaniels Part of Danby Resurveyed" - 237 acres - Nathaniel Kennard - 1736
"Needfull" (The) - 10 acres - John Denning - 1732
"Neglect" - 50 acres - Jervis Spencer - 1719
"Neglect" (The) - 87 acres - Thomas Usher - 1705
"Neglect" - 320 acres - Michael Miller - 1695
"Neglect" - 55 acres - William Woodland - 1743
"Neglect" - 39 acres - Edward Drugan - 1764
"Negligence" - 45 acres - John Evans - 1732
"Neifs Chance" - 104 acres - John and Elizabeth Beck - 1741
"Neifes Choice" - 150 acres - Robert Neife - 1667
"Neifes Choice" - 250 acres - Robert Neife and William Pearce - 1663
"Neighbourhood" - 98 acres - John Browning and William Woodland - 1735
"Neighbours Neglect" - 15 1/2 acres - William Woodland - 1758
"New Forrest" - 250 acres - Cornelius Comegys and Nathaniel Evitts - 1674
"New Hunting Field" - 400 acres - Thomas Hinson - 1666
"New Key" - 200 acres - William Key - 1679
"Newtown" - 200 acres - Robert Roberts - 1715
"New Town Resurveyed" - 243 acres - Robert Webb - 1746
"New York" - 204 acres - Joseph Garnett - 1749
"New York" - 1000 acres - John Trew - 1731
"New York" - 800 acres - John Edmondson - 1667
"New York Resurveyed" - 890 acres - John Trew - 1732
"New York Resurveyed" - 969 acres - John Trew - 1737
"Neysborough" - 100 acres - Charles Hollinsworth - 1686
"Niniveth" - 600 acres - Toby Wells - 1666
"Norcutt" - 150 acres - Charles Garfutt - 1730
"Norris's Desire Resurveyed" - 55 acres - John Howard - 1747
"Norris His Forrest" - 100 acres - Thomas Norris - 1681
"North Andover" - 150 acres - William Ellis - 1736
"North East Thickett" - 200 acres - John Russell - 1650
"Northern Part of Stratfords Manor" (The) - 85 acres - George Garnett - 1750
"Nowells Adventure" - 90 acres - William Apsley - 1728
"Nowells Adventure" - 80 acres - William Nowell - 1687
"Omission" (The) - 143 acres - Thomas Hynson - 1723
"Orchards Neck" - 150 acres - William Orchard - 1663
"Out Range" (The) - 640 acres - Robert Smith - 1708
"Out Range" (The) - 640 acres - Robert Smith - 1765
"Out Range" (The) - 145 acres - Richard Johnson and Philip Brook - 1753
"Oversight" (The) - 140 acres - John Derrick - 1723
"Packerton" - 800 acres - Edward Packer - 1658
"Pages Discovery" - 15 1/2 acres - John Page - 1787
"Pages Farm" - 845 acres - John Page - 1787
"Pages Purchase" - 157 acres - Ralph Page - 1734

62   INHABITANTS OF KENT COUNTY, MARYLAND, 1637-1787

"Pages Purchase" - 445 acres - Ralph Page - 1752
"Pages Road" - 1 acre and 59 perches - John Page - 1774
"Palmers Desire" - 100 acres - Benjamin Palmer - 1730
"Palmers Hazard" - 30 acres - Benjamin Palmer, Jr. - 1753
"Palmers Hazard" - 14 acres - Benjamin Palmer - 1732
"Parkers Rest Resurveyed" - 44 acres - William Yearly - 1747
"Parsons Addition" - 28 acres - John Parsons - 1686
"Parsons Marsh Addition" - 10 acres - John Salter - 1713
"Parsons Part of Hope Resurveyed" - 130 1/2 acres - Joseph Parsons - 1759
"Parsons Point" - 500 acres - Robert Vaughan - 1650
"Parsons Recovery" - 22 acres - John Parsons - 1700
"Partnership" (The) - 200 acres - Thomas Collins and John Mitchell - 1670
"Partnership" - 750 acres - Thomas Bordley - 1719
"Partnership" (The) - 300 acres - Thomas Hinson and Joseph Weeks - 1666
"Partnership" - 234 acres - Isabella Blay, R. Brown, and J. Tilden and wife - 1731
"Partnership" - 75 acres - John Reason - 1739
"Partnership" - 970 acres - Samuell Wallace - 1715
"Partnership" - 100 acres - Maurice Cloke - 1743
"Partnership" - 3000 acres - Daniel Toas - 1684
"Partnership" - 102 1/8 acres - Isaac Briscoe - 1774
"Partnerships Point" - 700 acres - John Edmondson - 1667
"Partnerships Point" - 700 acres - Thomas Thurstone - 1667
"Partnerships Point Resurveyed" - 860 acres - William Butcher - 1744
"Part of a Lot in Chester Town" - 73 square perches - Thomas Smith - 1785
"Part of Danby Resurveyed" - 514 acres - Richard Kennard and Nathaniel Kennard - 1734
"Part of Hylens Adventure" - 164 acres - William Truelock - 1730
"Part of Irvings Resurveyed" - 132 acres - James Burgan - 1769
"Part of Level Fields" - 191 1/4 acres - Stephen Denny - 1782
"Part of Lott 53" - 32 perches - William Smyth - 1780
"Part of New York" - 204 acres - Thomas Ringgold - 1759
"Part of Partnership Resurveyed" - 334 1/2 acres - Samuel Wallis - 1769
"Part of the Forrest of Dean" - 100 acres - Thomas Ringgold - 1762
"Part of the Forrest of Dean Resurveyed" - 22 3/4 acres - Simon Wicks - 1784
"Part of Thomas's Purchase Resurveyed" - 94 1/2 acres - Joseph Nicholson, Jr. - 1771
"Pascoes Poor Lott" - 150 acres - John Pascoe - 1744
"Pearces Desire" - 150 acres - Richard Bennett - 1728
"Pearces Desire Resurveyed" - 93 acres - Nicholas Maccubins and wife Mary - 1759
"Pearces Meadow" - 57 1/4 acres - James Pearce - 1773
"Pearces Meadow" - 200 acres - Gideon Pearce - 1734
"Pearces Ramble" - 439 acres - Gideon Pearce - 1734
"Pearch Meadow" - 300 acres - Richard Hill - 1673
"Penrose" - 50 acres - Thomas Piner - 1688

TRACT INDEX TO LAND PATENTS, 1640-1787   63

"Pensilvania Border" - 50 acres - Benjamin Ellis - 1723
"Pentridge" - 1000 acres - William Hemsley - 1670
"Pentrogay" - 200 acres - John Deer - 1650
"Perees Angle" - 50 acres - William Peree - 1669
"Perkins Adventure" - 125 acres - Thomas Perkins - 1758
"Perkins Meadow" - 7 acres - Ebenezer Perkins - 1750
"Perkins Mistake" - 80 acres - John Wyatt - 1742
"Perkins Pollicy" - 90 acres - Daniell Perkins - 1723
"Perkins Pond Field No. 2" - 110 1/2 acres - Isaac Perkins - 1786
"Petersfield" - 100 acres - John Wilson - 1727
"Peters Forrest" - 34 acres - Peter Cole - 1740
"Petts Gift" - 100 acres - Thomas Pett - 1650
"Phillips Choice" - 400 acres - Phillip Holleadger - 1686
"Philips Neglect" - 400 acres - Alexander Mecay and Robert Norrest - 1696
"Philips Neglect" - 454 acres - William Boyer - 1753
"Pierces Addition" - 395 acres - William Pierce - 1678
"Pigg Neck" - 50 acres - Thomas Boone - 1674
"Pig Quarter Neck" - 100 acres - John Philips - 1650
"Piners Addition" - 289 acres - Thomas Piner - 1695
"Piners Grove" - 260 acres - Symon Wylmer - 1687
"Piney Grove" - 350 acres - Thomas Ringold - 1720
"Piney Grove" - 350 acres - Rebecca Ringold - 1730
"Piney Neck" - 50 acres - Alexander Waters - 1667
"Piney Point" - 100 acres - John Gibbs - 1687
"Piney Point Resurveyed" - 150 acres - Richard Gresham - 1754
"Plain Dealing" - 200 acres in Kent and Queen Anne's County - William Ellis - 1745
"Plaine Dealing" - 250 acres in Kent County - John Parsons - 1684
"Plaines" (The) - 600 acres - James Ringgold - 1677
"Plumb Park" - 350 acres - William Palmer - 1667
"Point Love" - 600 acres - Elizabeth Commins (widow) - 1650
"Pond" (The) - 200 acres - Thomas Howell - 1672
"Pond" (The) - 300 acres - Edward Mitchell - 1722
"Pond Side" - 50 acres - Henry Clark - 1765
"Poor Discovery" - 102 acres - John Foreman - 1742
"Popes Chance" - 57 acres - William Pope - 1743
"Popes Forest" - 300 acres - Matthew Pope - 1688
"Poplar Farme" - 400 acres - William Harris and Elias King - 1683
"Poplar Hill" - 200 acres - William Harris - 1681
"Poplar Hill Resurveyed" - 225 1/4 acres - William Hynson - 1763
"Porters Addition" - 48 acres - John Porter - 1754
"Postern Hole" (The) - 500 acres - Phillip Holeager - 1683-84
"Poverty Field" - 7 acres - Peregrine Cooper - 1785
"Presbury" - 150 acres - Thomas Norris - 1677
"Presburys Discovery" - 48 1/2 acres - George Presbury - 1771
"Prevention of Inconvenience" (The) - 1000 acres - James Ringold - 1667
"Prices Lott" - 58 acres - John Price - 1712
"Prickle Pear" - 200 acres - Thomas Norris - 1677
"Prince William" - 90 acres - William Graves - 1747
"Prince William Resurveyed" - 150 acres - William Graves - 1747
"Priors Neglect" - 250 acres - Phillip Holleadger - 1684
"Priors Neglect" - 350 acres - Phillip Holleadger - 1686

64   INHABITANTS OF KENT COUNTY, MARYLAND, 1637-1787

"Probus" - 150 acres - John Weeks - 1683
"Probus Resurveyed" - 274 acres - John Beck - 1742
"Providence" - 420 acres - William Trew and Morgan Brown - 1745
"Providence" - 300 acres - John Jones - 1714
"Providence" - 100 acres - Thomas Beckles - 1703
"Providence" - 100 acres - Thomas Beckles - 1704
"Providence" - 700 acres - Michael Miller - 1714
"Providence" - 117 acres - Ralph Page and Benjamin Ricaud - 1744
"Providence" - 300 acres - Charles Howell - 1678
"Providence" - 300 acres - John Jones - 1686
"Providence" - 100 acres - Thomas Beckles - 1705
"Providence Resurveyed" - 251 acres - Alexander Briscoe - 1747
"Pudding Dam" - 6 acres - Ebenezer Massey and Joseph Massey - 1764
"Quakes [Quakers?] Lott" - 98 acres - John Parsons - 1685
"Queen Charleton" - 400 acres - Samuel Tovey - 1678
"Rachells Farme" - 345 acres - Rachell Brown - 1731
"Radcliffe Cross" - 500 acres - Marke Pensax - 1659
"Raisins Double Purchase" - 45 acres - George Raisin - 1747
"Raisins Lott" - 1/2 acre - William Raisin - 1755
"Rasins Part of Hales Resurveyed" - 348 acres - George Rasin - 1743
"Raisins Part of the Grange" - 140 acres - John Raisin - 1749
"Raisons Part of Hales" - 227 acres - Mary and George Raison - 1734
"Ralphs" - 316 acres - Ralph Bassill - 1708
"Range" (The) - 50 acres - Thomas Wilkins - 1747
"Ratcliffe" - 296 acres - William Comegys and Samuell Wallace - 1707
"Ratcliffe Cross" - 116 acres - George Still and William Thomas - 1730
"Ratcliffe Cross" - 520 acres - Peregrine Brown - 1701
"Readbourne" - 1410 acres - Capt. John Ganely - 1701
"Reading" - 100 acres - William Reading - 1707
"Readings Addition" - 108 acres - William Reading - 1720
"Reasons Part of Drayton" - 541 acres - George Reason - 1759
"Rebeccas Desire" - 45 acres - Hermanus Schee - 1732
"Redgraves Part of Chance Resurveyed" - 150 acres - John Redgrave - 1748
"Redmonds Supply Resurveyed" - 300 acres - John Gale - 1742
"Redriffe" - 100 acres - John Tweeg - 1701
"Reergard" - 100 acres - Robert Smith - 1708
"Relief" (The) - 130 acres - John Clark and Thomas Wilkins - 1747
"Remainder" (The) - 200 acres - William Comegie [Comegys] - 1731
"Remains of His Lordship Gracious Grant" (The) - 6920 acres - Dennis Dulany - 1756
"Reserve" (The) - 150 acres - Benjamin Blackiston - 1729
"Reserve" (The) - 94 acres - William Comegey [Comegys] - 1724
"Reserve" - 100 acres - Edward Beck - 1707
"Resurvey of Angells Rest" - 1312 acres - Robert Newcomb et al - 1735
"Resurvey of Broodnoe" - 1236 acres - Robert Dunn - 1736
"Resurvey of Drayton" - 1771 acres - Mary Rasin - 1739
"Resurvey of Part of Trumpinton Smith's Meadow" - 370 acres -

TRACT INDEX TO LAND PATENTS, 1640-1787 65

Capt. Thomas Smith - 1759
"Resurvey of Trumpinton" - 623 acres - John Browne - 1735
"Resurvey of Jerusalem" - 1180 acres - James Tilghman - 1769
"Resurvey of Martha Hynsons Part of Hinchingham" - 260 acres - Martha Hynson - 1735
"Resurvey of Part of Tilghmans Farm and Chance" - 682 acres - William Thomas - 1753
"Resurveyed the Chance" - 692 acres - William Thomas - 1713
"Reversion" (The) - 100 acres - Gideon Pearce - 1725
"Reward" (The) - 100 acres - Cornelius Comegys and Nathaniel Evitts - 1674
"Reward" (The) - 500 acres - Cornelius Comegys and Nathaniel Evetts - 1674
"Reyners Adventure" - 514 acres - Ebenezer Reyner - 1773
"Rhue Adam" - 150 acres - Robert Randall - 1683
"Rhue Adam" - 255 acres - Robert Randall - 1734
"Richards Adventure" - 200 acres - Thomas Guinn - 1708
"Richards Part of Danby Resurveyed" - 298 acres - Richard Kennard - 1736
"Richardsons Security" - 31 acres - John Richardson - 1774
"Rich Levell" (Part of) - 308 acres - Lambert Wilmer - 1723
"Rich Levell" (Part of) - 273 acres - Augustine Boyer - 1723
"Rich Levell" (Part of) - 316 acres - Phillip Holleager - 1723
"Rich Meadow" (The) - 40 acres - Joseph Garnett - 1743
"Rich Neck" (The) - 1000 acres - Gregory Fox and Phillip Land - 1651
"Rich Neck" - 1000 acres - William Mitchell - 1651
"Rickets Farm" - 248 acres - Philip Rickets - 1761
"Ridgley" - 300 acres - Henry Ridgley - 1665
"Ridmore Supply" (The) - 350 acres - John Hodgson - 1683
"Rileys Beginning" - 300 acres - Nicholas Riley - 1734
"Ringgolds Chance" - 200 acres - Thomas Ringgold - 1696
"Ringgolds Discovery" - 125 acres - Thomas Ringgold - 1763
"Ringgolds Fortune" - 150 acres - James Ringgold - 1678
"Ringgolds Lott No. 55" - 144 square perches - Thomas Ringgold - 1759
"Ringgolds Lott" (Second Part of) - 57 acres - Charles Ringgold - 1712
"Ringgolds Part of Poplar Farm Resurveyed" - 98 acres - Thomas Ringgold - 1764
"Ringgolds Part of the Adventure Resurveyed" - 1448 3/4 acres - Thomas Ringgold - 1769
"Rippon" - 9 acres - John Hayes - 1741
"Rock Point" - 12 acres - Morgan Jones and William Hodges - 1688
"Roger Hicks Intent" - 100 acres - Roger Hicks - 1734
"Rousbys Recovery" - 550 acres - Christopher Rousby - 1668
"Ruerdon" - 300 acres - Robert Vaughan - 1658
"Rumford" - 123 acres - John Heyden - 1723
"Rusemore" [sic] - 100 acres - Robert Neaves - 1682
"Rushmore" [sic] - 100 acres - Robert Neives - 1682
"Ryleys Beginning" - 300 acres - Richard Ryley - 1707
"Ryleys Fancy" - 48 acres - Richard Ryley - 1758
"Ryleys Land Resurveyed" - 561 acres - Nicholas Ryley - 1736
"Sadlers Lott" - 40 acres - Joseph Garnett - 1743

66   INHABITANTS OF KENT COUNTY, MARYLAND, 1637-1787

"Saint Andrews Crosse" - 350 acres - William Pierce - 1684
"Saint Martine" - 200 acres - Nathaniel Hillen - 1682
"Saint Mary's" - 100 acres - Benjamin Ellis - 1716
"Saint Patricks Garden" - 8 3/4 acres - Christopher Williams - 1770
"Saint Pauls" - 150 acres - James Heath - 1713
"Saint Tantons" - 500 acres - Ebenezer Blackistone - 1685
"Saint Tauntons" - 665 acres - William Wilmer and wife Rose - 1753
"Salkeld" - 200 acres - George Saughier - 1659
"Sallvatory" - 225 acres - William Fisher - 1685
"Salters Land Resurveyed" - 992 acres - John Carvil - 1740
"Salters Load" (formerly called "Packerton") - 800 acres - Thomas Carvile - 1682
"Sandford" - 250 acres - William Key - 1678
"Sarahs Lott" - 74 acres - George Garnett - 1733
"Saunders Addition" - 100 acres - William Saunders - 1685
"Savorys Farm" - 210 acres - William Savory - 1743
"St. Clears Discovery" - 37 1/2 acres - William St. Clear - 1773
"St. Clears Resurvey" - 84 1/2 acres - William St. Clear - 1773
"St. Clears Venture" - 62 acres - William St. Clear - 1767
"Scotts Folly" - 200 acres - James King and William Simson - 1708
"Scotts Lott" - 118 acres - Edward Scott - 1725
"Scrap" - 20 acres - Cornelius Comegys - 1758
"Scuddamore" - 550 acres - Edward Skidmore - 1659
"Seawards Hope" - 300 acres - Thomas Seaward - 1686
"Seawell" - 900 acres - John Sewell - 1659
"Second Addition" - 23 acres - Robert Maxwell - 1745
"Second Chance" - 64 acres - Thomas Windall - 1720
"Selby" - 200 acres - John Hunt - 1667
"Sewstern" - 200 acres - Robert Foreman - 1707
"Shadshold" - 650 acres - William Jones - 1681
"Shaws Chance" - 100 acres - John Shaw - 1708
"Shield" (The) - 41 acres - Symon Willmer - 1703
"Sillimi" - 774 acres - Nathaniel Hynson - 1701
"Simmes Prime Choice" - 75 acres - Thomas Mansell - 1714
"Simmons Folly" - 60 acres - Henry Simmons - 1759
"Simmonson" - 480 acres - Dr. Simmond - 1720
"Simms Farm" - 89 acres - Patrick Parks - 1739
"Sims Farme" - 150 acres - Alexander Sims - 1683
"Sims Prime Choice" - 80 acres - Alexander Sims - 1683
"Skinners Marsh" - 115 acres - Samuel Milton - 1735
"Skinners Marsh" - 100 acres - Andrew Skinner - 1670
"Skirvens Neglect" - 13 acres - Thomas Wilkins - 1764
"Slayde Chance" - 186 acres - Thomas Williams - 1737
"Slipe" - 16 3/4 acres - Francis Wallace - 1782
"Slip [Slipe?] Renewed" - 11 acres - George Gilpin - 1765
"Slipe" - 6 1/2 acres - Joseph and Ebenezer Massey - 1764
"Slipe Along Side of Masseys Venture" - 25 acres - Peter Massey and Nicholas Massey - 1730
"Slipe Along Side of Masseys Venture" (The) - 25 acres - Nicholas Massey - 1740
"Smally" - 100 acres - Jarvis Spencer - 1730
"Smithers Part of Addition and Rumford Resurveyed" - 188 acres -

TRACT INDEX TO LAND PATENTS, 1640-1787   67

William Smithers - 1748
"Smithers Plains" - 130 acres - William Smithers - 1741
"Smiths Bay" - 400 acres - John Smith - 1658
"Smiths Chance" - 10 acres - John Smith - 1763
"Smiths Chance" - 48 acres - Thomas Smith - 1756
"Smiths Desart" - 260 acres - Thomas Smith - 1707
"Smiths Meadows" - 60 acres - Thomas Smith and John Wells - 1705
"Smiths Meadows Resurveyed" - 327 acres - Thomas Smith - 1756
"Smiths Park" - 250 acres - Thomas Smith - 1704
"Smiths Parke" - 350 acres - Thomas Smith - 1682
"Smiths Part of Worth Folley Resurveyed" - 283 acres - James Smith - 1758
"Smiths Part of Worths Folly" - 183 acres - James Smith - 1743
"Smiths Point" - 3 acres - Nicholas Smith - 1747
"Smiths Venture" - 300 acres - Thomas Smith - 1707
"Smiths Venture and Addition Resurveyed" - 560 acres - Thomas Smith - 1744
"Smyths Park" - 176 acres - Richard G. Smith - 1787
"Smyths Part of Standaway" - 204 3/4 acres - Thomas Smyth - 1786
"Smythston" - 300 acres - George Gouldsmith - 1659
"Snow Hill - 42 acres - Edward Harris - 1732
"Sole" (The) - 274 acres - Robert Hutchison and Humphrey Younger - 1722
"Soule" (The) - 450 acres - William Toulson - 1671
"Southward" - 150 acres - James Sudward - 1658
"Spalden" - 100 acres - Andrew Spalden - 1713
"Sparkes Point" - 50 acres - Edward Sparkes - 1668
"Spencers Part of Friendship" - 15 acres - John Spencer, Jr. - 1752
"Spicie Grove" - 250 acres - Benjamin Shurmur - 1716
"Sportsmans Hall" - 5 1/4 acres - Francis O. Brushank - 1702
"Spring Garden" - 265 acres - Gideon Pearce - 1724
"Spring Garden" - 50 acres - Benjamin Griffith - 1732
"Spring Garden" - 14 1/4 acres - George Presbury - 1770
"Spring Hill" - 150 acres - Robert Neife - 1667
"Stadts Hold" - 970 acres - Francis Bello - 1714
"Stanaway" - 400 acres - Phillip Holleager - 1696
"Standaway" - 169 acres - John Denning - 1739
"Standleys Hope" - 550 acres - William Standley - 1676
"Stand Off" - 100 acres - Alexander Clark - 1700
"Stand Off" - 100 acres - Gideon Pearce - 1734
"Staples Choice" - 300 acres - Henry Staples - 1686
"Staples Warren" - 100 acres - Edward Blay and wife Ann - 1700
"Stavelys Lott" - 305 acres - James Stavely - 1733
"Stavelys Lott Resurveyed" - 183 acres - John Stavely - 1756
"Stavelys Part of Broad Oak" - 72 acres - John Stavely - 1752
"Stavelys Part of Suffolk" - 65 acres - John Stavely - 1765
"Stephen Heath Manor" - 1000 acres - Samuel Pensax - 1659
"Stephens Inheritance" - 137 acres - Michael Byrnes - 1723
"Stepney" - 64 acres - William Comegys and Samuel Wallace - 1723
"Stepney" - 500 acres - Mary Bateman - 1666
"Stepney" - 500 acres - Peter Bovey - 1659
"Stepney Fields" - 47 acres - William Ackland - 1734
"Steventon" - 100 acres - Thomas Bordley - 1720

"Steventon" - 400 acres - William Steventon - 1685
"Stiles Addition" - 520 acres - St. Leger Codd - 1697
"Stiles Addition" - 550 acres - Nathaniell Stiles - 1667
"Stiles Addition Corrected" - 405 acres - John Gresham - 1751
"Stinton Erickson" - 200 acres - John Erickson - 1658
"Stocton" - 200 acres - Andrew Skinner - 1670
"Stoneton" - 500 acres - Richard Stone - 1658
"Stoneton" - 456 acres - Richard Bennett - 1726
"Stoney Hills" - 77 acres - Richard Peacock - 1745
"Stonnaway" - 500 acres - William Smith - 1666
"Stoopley Gibson" - 150 acres - Henry Stoops and John Gibson - 1658
"Stratford Mannor" - 1000 acres - Richard Chandler - 1659
"Stradford Manor Resurveyed" - 1203 acres - George Garnett - 1735
"Strouds White Stable" - 150 acres - Abraham Stroud - 1678
"Suffolk" - 742 acres - James Stavely - 1681
"Surprise" - 125 acres - William Woodland - 1743
"Surveyors Light" - 17 acres - James Smith - 1727
"Susquehannah" - 11 3/4 acres - John Day - 1786
"Sutton" - 400 acres - Humphrey Davenport - 1683
"Sutton Underhill" - 300 acres - John Underhill - 1659
"Swamp" (The) - 468 acres - James Harris - 1722
"Swamp Resurveyed" (The) - 554 acres - William Harris - 1746
"Swan Island" - 18 acres - William Frisby - 1687
"Sweatnams Addition" - 100 acres - Edward Sweatnam - 1695
"Sweet Hall Neck" - 380 acres - Richard White and Thomas Philips - 1684
"Sweet Harbour" - 700 acres - Richard Hill - 1673
"Sweetmans Insula" - 38 acres - Edward Sweetman - 1683
"Sympsons Addition" - 100 acres - William Simmons - 1713
"Sympsons Adventure" - 100 acres - William Sympson - 1722
"Tarr Kill" (The) - 150 acres - John Wright - 1668
"Tatums Meadow" - 2 acres - Daniel Perkins - 1739
"Tatums Mount" - 44 acres - John Tatum - 1736
"Temple Patrick" - 1/2 acre and 16 perches - Alexander Hutchinson - 1765
"Terrys Part of Suffolk" - 200 acres - John Terry - 1755
"Tersons Addition" - 50 acres - Andrew Terson - 1669
"Tersons Neck" - 300 acres - Andrew Terson - 1681
"Tersons Neck" - 50 acres - Andrew Terson - 1681
"Thomas's Addition" - 3 1/4 acres - James Thomas - 1769
"Thomas's Folly" - 24 1/8 acres - Samuel Thomas - 1773
"Thomas's Landing" - 20 acres - William Thomas - - 1736
"Thomas's Purchase" - 1080 acres - William Thomas - 1719
"Thomas's Purchase" - 1080 acres - Henry and William Thomas - 1740
"Thomas's Slipe" - 18 acres - James Thomas - 1769
"Thornton" - 1000 acres - Andrew Cooke - 1664
"Thorntons Addition" - 78 acres - John Johnson - 1734
"Three Friends" - 376 acres - James Moore, Ruth and Hannah Brooks, and Christopher Bellican - 1734
"Tibballs" - 550 acres - Philip Holleger - 1671
"Tibbets Venture" - 70 acres - James and Richard Tibbet - 1744
"Tildens and Browns Part of Blays Range and Blays Addition

Resurveyed" - 188 acres - Peregrine Brown and John Tilden - 1753
"Tildens Forest" - 145 acres - Charles Groom - 1786
"Tildens Meadows" - 79 acres - John Tilden - 1761
"Tildens Part of Blays Park Resurveyed" - 206 acres - John Tilden - 1744
"Tilghman and Foxleys Grove" - 1000 acres - Mary Tilghman - 1679
"Tilghmans Choice" - 200 acres - Richard Tilghman - 1673
"Tillards Addition" - 11 acres - Frogitt Tillard - 1754
"Timber Levell" - 140 acres - William Comegys and Margaret Hurt - 1730
"Timely Discovery" (The) - 125 acres - James Ringgold - 1755
"Tobins Folly" - 23 1/2 acres - George William Forrester - 1752
"Tobbins Lott" - 77 acres - John Nemo - 1753
"To Keep Blackiston Honest" - 66 acres - John Vansant, Jr. - 1771
"Tolchester" - 400 acres - William Tollson - 1659
"Tolchester" - 520 acres - William Toulson - 1676
"Tombe" - 100 acres - Abraham Coffin - 1659
"Toveys Lott" - 270 acres - Samuel Tovey - 1730
"Towcester" - 500 acres - William Palmer - 1672
"Tower Hill" - 37 acres - John Kinslaugh - 1759
"Towne Relief" (The) - 800 acres - James Rawth - 1681
"Townside" - 3 acres - Foster Conliffe - 1747
"Town Side Rebuilt" - 4 1/4 acres - John Commegys - 1774
"Travellers Refreshment" (The) - 320 acres - William Dare - 1684
"Triangle" - 8 acres - John Redgrave - 1751
"Triangle Resurveyed" (The) - 207 acres - John Everett and Mary Thornton - 1743
"Triangle Resurveyed" (The) - 15 acres - Abraham Cannell - 1774
"Truelocks Adventure" - 169 acres - Henry Truelock - 1754
"Truelocks Right of Hales Resurveyed" - 222 acres - Henry Truelock and Joseph Truelock - 1734
"Trumpington" - 400 acres - Thomas South - 1658
"Tryangle" - 80 acres - Richard Davis - 1713
"Tryangle" (The) - 100 acres - Phillip Kennard, Jr. - 1724
"Tullys Fancy" - 600 acres - John Tully - 1663 (afterwards granted to Henry Hosier).
"Turners Part of Suffolk" - 140 acres - Jonathan Turner - 1755
"Unity" (The) - 800 acres - Christopher Geist and Daniel Perkins - 1724
"Upper Blount Point" - 200 acres - Roger Baxter - 1650
"Upper Part of Darnalls Farm" (The) - 213 acres - Theophilus Randall - 1739
"Ushers Lott" - 58 acres - Thomas Usher - 1705
"Ushers Part of Killinsworthmore" - 168 acres - George Usher - 1735
"Utiesley" - 300 acres - Nathaniel Utie - 1658
"Utrick alias Sewall" - 1224 acres - Cornelius Comegys - 1686
"Vansants Bing" [Ring?]- 326 1/4 acres - John Vansant - 1769
"Vansants Ferry" - 10 acres - John Vansant - 1766
"Vansants Landing" - 7 1/4 acres - John Vansant - 1766
"Vansants Part of Endeavour and Chester Grove" - 278 acres - Joshua Vansant - 1756
"Vansants Part of Endeavour and Chester Grove Resurveyed" - 283

70   INHABITANTS OF KENT COUNTY, MARYLAND, 1637-1787

acres - Joshua Vansant - 1767
"Vansants Part of Fork Resurveyed" - 272 1/2 acres - Cornelius Vansant - 1763
"Verina" - 1000 acres - Thomas Cornewalleys - 1658
"Vianem" [Viaven?]- 300 acres - Nicholas Painter and James Boullay - 1682
"Vianna" - 600 acres - Cornelius Comegys - 1684
"Viaven Resurveyed" - 300 acres - Robert Roberts - 1747
"Wading Place" (The) - 1000 acres - Gregory Foy and Phillip Land - 1651
"Wading Place Neck" (The) - 300 acres - Phillip Conner - 1658
"Waiting Place Neck" - 1000 acres - William Mitchell - 1651
"Wallaces Fancy" - 19 acres - John Wallace - 1742
"Wallaces Fancy" - 19 acres - John Wallace - 1764
"Wallaces Meadow" - 77 acres - Henry Wallace - 1782
"Wallnutt Neck" - 100 acres - Andrew Skinner - 1665
"Walnut Neck Resurveyed" - 192 acres - Morgan Hunt - 1735
"Wardners Adventure" - 200 acres - George Wardner - 1683
"Ward Oak" - 400 acres - Matthew Ward - 1673
"Ward Oak Resurveyed" - 467 3/4 acres - Samuel Thompson - 1768
"Wards Hope" - 56 acres - Thomas Ward - 1702
"Warners Addition" - 112 acres - George Warner - 1695
"Warners Levels Resurveyed" - 315 acres - Henry Philips - 1754
"Warners Marsh" - 124 acres - George Warner - 1688
"Warners Part of Drayton Resurveyed" - 602 acres - Mary Warner - 1741
"Waters [Walters?] Lott" - 7 acres - Patrick Walter - 1746
"Waxford" - 44 acres - Dominick Kenslaugh - 1734
"Webley" - 400 acres - Edward Webb - 1673
"Webbs Chance" - 22 1/2 acres - Robert Webb - 1769
"Wedges Recovery Resurveyed" - 148 acres - Wedge Crouch - 1743
"Wedges Resurvey" - 100 acres - John Wedge - 1680
"Weecks Marsh" - 200 acres - Samuel Weecks - 1722
"Wehill Down" - 100 acres - John Williah [sic] - 1686
"Weyhill Down" - 100 acres - William Hynson Graves - 1757
"Welches Purchase" - 15 acres - James Welch - 1770
"Well Meaning" - 830 acres - John Parsons and John Salter - 1686
"Welshs Part of Agreement Resurveyed" - 129 acres - James Welsh - 1750
"Wetherell" - 100 acres - Thomas Wetherell - 1651
"Wetherill" - 100 acres - Samuel Wetherill - 1688
"Weymouth" - 50 acres - Thomas Weymouth - 1675
"Whaleys Adventure" - 100 acres - Daniel Whaley - 1731
"Wheelwrights Swamp" - 60 acres - Stephen Kennard - 1765
"White Marsh" (The) - 100 acres - Francis Barney, Jr. - 1729
"Whitfield" - 1000 acres - William Coursey - 1668
"Whittington" - 100 acres - John Edmondson - 1678
"Wickliff" - 800 acres - Joseph Wicks and Thomas Hinton - 1658
"Wicks Part of Buckingham Resurveyed" - 190 acres - Joseph Wicks - 1767
"Widows Chance" - 65 acres - Nathaniel Hynson - 1713
"Widdows Rest" (The) - 40 acres - Rachel Battershell - 1716
"Williams Addition" - 3 3/4 acres - William Maxwell - 1768
"William and Marys Adventure" - 207 acres - William Yearly - 1746

TRACT INDEX TO LAND PATENTS, 1640-1787

"Williams Fancy" - 19 1/4 acres - John Williams - 1763
"Williams Lott" - 100 acres - George Copper - 1708
"Williams Lott Resurveyed" - 182 acres - George Copper - 1743
"Williamston" - 500 acres - Nathaniel Styles - 1665
"Williamston" - 500 acres - William Yapp - 1659
"Williams Venture" - 500 acres - William Ellis - 1738
"Williams Venture" - 114 acres - William Bradshaw - 1725
"William Thomas's Part of Tilghmans Farm" - 82 acres - William Thomas - 1713
"Wilmers Addition" - 150 acres - Simon Wilmer - 1741
"Wilmers Adventure" - 250 acres - Simon Wilmer - 1741
"Wilmers Chance" - 21 acres - Lambert Wilmer - 1758
"Willmers Farme" - 500 acres - Simon Willmer - 1680
"Wilmers Gift" - 21 acres - Michael Miller - 1688
"Wilmers Grove" - 86 acres - William Wilmer - 1753
"Wilmers Grove Addition" - 10 1/2 acres - William Wilmer - 1769
"Willmores Arcadia" - 800 acres - Simon Willmore - 1696
"Wilsons Neglect" - 11 acres - George Wilson - 1753
"Winchester" - 250 acres - John Winchester - 1650
"Windalls Chance" - 50 acres - Thomas Windall - 1719
"Wind Mill Hill" - 6 acres - David Witherspoon - 1743
"Wintons Addition" - 50 acres - Nathaniel Evetts - 1667
"Wolfe Head" - 100 acres - Robert Neife - 1667
"Wolfs Huke" [sic] (The) - 238 acres - Francis Bodeen - 1730
"Wolf Trap Bridge" (The) - 169 1/2 acres - James Black - 1771
"Woodalls Hazard" - 2 acres - William Woodall - 1762
"Woodlands Discovery" - 17 1/2 acres - William Woodland - 1758
"Woodlands Folly" - 58 acres - James Woodland - 1742
"Woodlands Intention" - 80 acres - William Woodland - 1735
"Woodland Neck" (The) - 50 acres - Alexander Waters - 1668
"Woodland Neck" - 400 acres - Philemon Loyd - 1667
"Woodlands Risque" - 20 acres - William Woodland - 1742
"Woodyard Thicket" (The) - 200 acres - Philip Connor - 1650
"Worths Folly" - 1036 acres - John Worth - 1687
"Worton Mannor" - 3200 acres - Richard Bennett - 1708
"Worton Manor" - 2300 acres - Edward Carter - 1681
"Wrights Fortune" - 120 acres - Arthur Wright - 1667
"Wyatts Addition" - 44 acres - James Wyatt - 1701
"Wyfall" - 100 acres - Samuel Withers - 1659
"Wyotts Chance" - 50 acres - James Wyott - 1686
"Yapp" - 500 acres - Nathaniel Styles - 1664
"Yapp" - 500 acres - William Yapp - 1659
"Yearlys Beginning" - 60 acres - William Yearly - 1734

TRACTS AND LANDOWNERS IN THE KENT COUNTY TAX LIST OF 1783
(Ref: Maryland State Archives, Card File 66)

"Abrams Lott" - William Redgrave - 4th District
"Abrams Lott" - Joseph Stavely - 4th District
"Adams Choice" - John Browning, Jr. - 5th District
"Adams Choice" - John Browning, Sr. - 5th District
"Adams Hope" - George Reason - 4th District
"Addition" - John Day - 4th District

"Adventure Resurveyed" - Samuel Davis - 5th District
"Adventures" (Part of Morton) - Alexander Baird - 5th District
"Agreement" - John Greenwood - 4th District
"Agreement" - Thomas Smith - 4th District
"Agreement" - Francis Wallace - 4th District
"Ambrose" - Charlotte Griffith - 1st District
"Amelia" - Daniel Greenwood - 4th District
"Angels Lott" - William Geddes - 5th District
"Angels Lott" - William Hanson - 5th District
"Angels Rest" - Gideon Clark - 5th District
"Angels Rest" - John Gorden - 5th District
"Angels Rest" - William Hanson - 5th District
"Angels Rest" - Elijah Massy - 5th District
"Angels Rest" - Elisha Massy - 5th District
"Angels Rest" - John Massy - 5th District
"Angels Rest" - Cornelius Vansant - 5th District
"Arcadia" - Mathew Beck - 1st District
"Arcadia" - Thomas Bowers - 1st District
"Arcadia" - Hezekiah Dunn - Jr. - 1st District
"Arcadia" - Robert Dunn - 1st District
"Acradia" - William Granger - 1st District
"Arcadia" - John Hynson (of Cecil County) - 1st District
"Arcadia" - Richard Hynson - 1st District
"Arcadia" - John Moore - Jr. - 1st District
"Arcadia" - Thomas Reardon - 1st District
"Arcadia" - William Shaw - 1st District
"Arcadia" - Benjamin Strong - 1st District
"Arcadia" - Simon Wickes - 1st District
"Arundal Grove" - James Anderson, Jr. - 1st District
"Arundal Grove" - Henry Thomas - 1st District
"Arundal Grove" - J. Exel Thomas - 1st District
"Arundal Grove" - William Wilson - 1st District
"Ashley Green" - James Neale - 3rd District
"Ashleys Lott" - John Ashley - 3rd District
"Ashleys Lott" - Joel Willis - 3rd District
"Ash Point" - Mary Miflin - 2nd District
"Attix's Adventure" - William B. Tilden - 3rd District
"Bairds" (Part of Morton) - Alexander Baird - 5th District
"Bancks Choice" - Francis Sprusebanks - 4th District
"Barnes Venture" - Martha Barnes - 4th District
"Barneys Forrest" - Isaac Perkins - 3rd District
"Barton" - Edward Beck - 3rd District
"Batchelors Choice" - William Jones - 3rd District
"Batchelors Hall" - Thomas Vandyke - 3rd District
"Batchelors Hope" - John Sutton - 2nd District
"Batchelors Lott" - George Reason - 4th District
"Bath" - John Simmonds - 1st District
"Bavaria" - John Galloway for Thomas Ringgold's heirs - 3rd District
"Bears Grin" - Henry Truelock - 4th District
"Beaver Dam Neck" - John Dwire (Dwyer) - 4th District
"Beckworth" - John Culbert - 1st District
"Beckworth" - John Wilson - 3rd District
"Bennetts Bridge" - James Black - 4th District

TRACTS AND LANDOWNERS IN THE TAX LIST OF 1783   73

"Bennetts Low" - Rosier and Young - 4th District
"Bennetts Regulation" - John Cadwallader - 4th District
"Billys Lott" - Isaac Spencer - 4th District
"Birth Right" - Benjamin Benny - 3rd District
"Black Hall" - Philip Davis - 3rd District
"Black Hall Hermitage" - William Ringgold - 3rd District
"Blays Addition" - Richard Wheathered - 4th District
"Blays Addition" - Joseph Williams - 4th District
"Blays Park" - Stephen Causey - 4th District
"Blays Park" - John Rasin - 4th District
"Blays Range" - Richard Wheathered - 4th District
"Blays Range" - Joseph Williams - 4th District
"Blooms Berry" - Simon Wickes - 1st District
"Bluntwell" - Thomas Bowers - 1st District
"Bolston" - Malachi Ambrose - 4th District
"Bolston" - Isaac Redgrave - 4th District
"Boons Meadow" - Jacob Foreman - 3rd District
"Bordleys Beginning" - B. John Bordley - 1st District
"Bordleys Gift" - Jonathan Jester - 5th District
"Bordleys Gift" - Luke Miers - 5th District
"Bosticks Addition" - Samuel Davis - 5th District
"Bounty" - Alexander Beck - 1st District
"Bounty" - James Hurt - 2nd District
"Bounty" - Froggett Tillard - 1st District
"Bowdys Folly" - Joseph Greenwood, Jr. - 4th District
"Bowdys Folly" - Aquilla Meeks - 4th District
"Boxley" - Alexander Beck - 1st District
"Boxley" - James Bradshaw - 1st District
"Boxley" - John Page - 1st District
"Boyers Adventure" - John Wilmore - 5th District
"Bradshaws Farm" - John Page - 1st District
"Bradshaws Farm" - John Bradshaw - 1st District
"Browers Resurvey" - George Moffett, Sr. - 4th District
"Bright Helmstone" - Gilbert Semans - 5th District
"Bright Helmstone" - Lambert Semans - 5th District
"Bright Helmstone" - Richard Semans - 5th District
"Bright Helmstone" - Sarah Semans - 5th District
"Bright Helmstone" - Solomon Semans - 5th District
"Bright Helmstone" - William Semans - 5th District
"Bright Helmstone" - John Zelephrow - 5th District
"Bristol" - John Burk - 1st District
"Bristol" - Benjamin Worrell - 1st District
"Broad Neck" - Risdon Bishop - 3rd District
"Broad Neck" - Alexander Calder - 3rd District
"Broad Neck" - Arthur Emory - 2nd District
"Broad Neck" - John Gleaves - 3rd District
"Broad Neck" - John Smith - 3rd District
"Broad Neck" - John Wilson, Jr. - 3rd District
"Broad Oak" - Isaac Freeman - 5th District
"Broad Oak" - Rosier and Young - 4th District
"Broad Oak" - James Stavely - 4th District
"Broad Oak" - George Wilson (S.G.) - 5th District
"Broadfield" - William Kendal - 2nd District
"Broadnox" - Darius Dunn - 1st District
"Broadnox" - Hezekiah Dunn, Jr. - 1st District

74   INHABITANTS OF KENT COUNTY, MARYLAND, 1637-1787

"Broadway" - Benjamin Wickes - 2nd District
"Brooks Folly" - Henry Brooks - 4th District
"Broom Field" - Thomas Hebbern - 4th District
"Broom Field" - Edward Ford - 4th District
"Broomy Neck" - Griffin Jones - 4th District
"Brotherly and Friendly Agreement" - Michael Corse - 4th District
"Brotherly and Friendly Agreement" - Thomas Lamb - 4th District
"Brownings Addition" - Thomas Browning - 5th District
"Brownings Adventure" - John Wilmore - 5th District
"Browns Purchase" - James Hurt - 2nd District
"Bryans Delight" - Edward Tilghman - 5th District
"Buckingham" - Nathaniel Comegys - 4th District
"Buckingham" - Mary Jackson - 4th District
"Buck Neck" - Richard Graves - 3rd District
"Buck Neck" - Warner Rasin - 4th District
"Bucks Addition" - John Bolton - 3rd District
"Budds Discovery" - Sarah Merritt - 3rd District
"Budds Meadow" - John Kennard - 3rd District
"Budds Meadow" - Sarah Merritt - 3rd District
"Burks" - Zorobabel French, Sr. - 5th District
"Burks Addition" - John Jobson - 5th District
"Bushford" - William B. Tilden - 1st District
"Cackaway Point" - Thomas Maslin - 2nd District
"Calders Manor" - Lambert Seamans - 5th District
"Calders Meadows" - James McClain's heirs - 3rd District
"Calebs Discovery" - Jacob Foreman - 3rd District
"Camells Farm" - Edward Crew - 4th District
"Camells Farm" - Philip Drugan - 4th District
"Camells Farm" - James Kelly - 4th District
"Camells Worthmore" - John Anger - 4th District
"Camells Worthmore" - Hannah Bordley - 4th District
"Camells Worthmore" - James Dunkin - 4th District
"Camells Worthmore" - Charles Groomes - 4th District
"Camells Worthmore" - Edmund Linch - 4th District
"Camells Worthmore" - James Ware - 4th District
"Camels Worthmore" - John Willson - 4th District
"Canada" - William Armstrong - 5th District
"Canada" - Rebeckah Little - 5th District
"Canada" - John Ward Pennington - 5th District
"Canada" - John Taylor - 5th District
"Carroll" - Sarah Merritt - 3rd District
"Carviles Addition" - Ann Carville - 1st District
"Castle Carru" - Richard Scags - 4th District
"Castle Carru" - Thomas Shahawn - 4th District
"Castle Carru" - William Wilson - 4th District
"Castledines Lott" - Robert Peacock - 3rd District
"Caulders Manor" - James Baird - 5th District
"Caulders Manor" - Lewis Baird - 5th District
"Chance" - Jacob Comegys - 5th District
"Chance" - Nathaniel Comegys - 4th District
"Chance" - Hezekiah Dunn - 1st District
"Chance" - Colin Ferguson, Sr. - 5th District
"Chance" - Edward Ford - 4th District
"Chance" - George Fountain - 5th District

TRACTS AND LANDOWNERS IN THE TAX LIST OF 1783   75

"Chance" - Daniel Greenwood - 4th District
"Chance" - Isaac Hackett - 3rd District
"Chance" - Simon Hackett - 4th District
"Chance" - Jacob Humberson - 5th District
"Chance" - William Smith - 4th District
"Chance" - Robert Summers - 1st District
"Chance" - James Swaney - 5th District
"Chance" - Thomas Urie - 1st District
"Chance" - John Williamson - 5th District
"Chance" - John Young - 1st District
"Chandlers Addition" - William Reding - 4th District
"Chester Field" - Nathaniel Knock - 5th District
"Chester Grove" - Pearce Bowers - 4th District
"Chester Grove" - Benjamin Comegys - 5th District
"Chester Grove" - Jacob Comegys - 5th District
"Chester Grove" - Benjamin Palmer - 4th District
"Chester Grove" - Joshua Vansant - 4th District
"Chester Grove" - George Moffett, Jr. - 4th District
"Chester Point" - Joseph Wickes (Eastern Neck) - 1st District
"Chevy Chase" - Richard B. Lloyd - 3rd District
"Chiddle" - Thomas Smyth - 1st District
"Chiddle" - Richard Spencer - 1st District
"Chigwell" - Charles Baker, Sr. - 2nd District
"Chisley" - Mary Miflin - 2nd District
"Choice" - John T. Kennard - 3rd District
"Choice Resurveyed" - Cornelius Vansant - 5th District
"Christ Beginning" - James Swaney - 5th District
"Church Wardens Neck" - Christopher Bellican - 4th District
"Clifton" - John Page - 1st District
"Cock of the Game" - John Williams - 5th District
"Cock of the Game" - John Wilmore - 5th District
"Cockstall" - Thomas Ellis - 5th District
"Cockstall" - John Wilmore - 5th District
"Coffin" - George Wilson (S.G.) - 5th District
"Colechester" [Tolchester?] - James Pearce - 5th District
"Comb Whitton" - Bridget McNeal - 5th District
"Comb Whitton" - James Swaney - 5th District
"Comb Whitton" - Benjamin Palmer - 4th District
"Comegys Farm" - John Moore (farmer) - 3rd District
"Comegys Farm" - Josias Ringgold - 3rd District
"Comegys Farm" - Thomas Wilkins (a minor) - 3rd District
"Comegys Resurvey" - Richard Peacock - 4th District
"Coopers Folly" - John Galloway (executor for Thomas Ringgold) - 1st District
"Coopers Folly" - Thomas Smyth - 1st District
"Cornuwhitton" [Comb Whitton?] - Cornelius Ryley - 4th District
"Cornwallis" - John T. Kennard - 3rd District
"Cornwallis Choice" - Richard B. Lloyd - 3rd District
"Cornwallis Choice" - Sarah Merritt - 3rd District
"Corses Meadow" - Michael Corse - 4th District
"Cove" - William Greenwood - 4th District
"Cove" - William Howell - 4th District
"Coven [Covent] Garden" - James Rowlison - 1st District
"Coven [Covent] Garden" - William Strong, Jr. - 1st District
"Coventry" - B. John Bordley - 1st District

"Coventry" - Richard Lloyd - 1st District
"Cove Tract" - William Greenwood - 4th District
"Cove Tract" - William Howell - 4th District
"Cranberry Neck" - James Howard - 4th District
"Cranberry Neck" - John Howard - 4th District
"Crows Addition" - Edward Bird - 1st District
"Crows Addition" - Thomas Crow - 1st District
"Crows Addition" - Richard Spencer - 1st District
"Crows Chance" - James Hurt - 2nd District
"Cuckholds Hope" - William Brown - 1st District
"Cunney Warren" - Richard Frisby - 3rd District
"Cunney Warren" - Richard Graves - 3rd District
"Cunney Warren" - Martha Jones - 1st District
"Cunney Warren" - Samuel Smith, Jr. - 1st District
"Cunney Warren" - Richard Willis - 1st District
"Cunney Warren" - Simon Smith - 1st District
"Cunney Warren" - Thomas Vandyke - 3rd District
"Dallington" - Anthony Banning - 3rd District
"Daniels Disappointments" - George Gullett - 5th District
"Darby" - Isaac Spencer - 4th District
"Darlington" - John Galloway for Thomas Ringgold's heirs - 3rd District
"Darnells Farm" - John Eccleston - 4th District
"Darnells Farm" - Samuel Wallace - 4th District
"Davis Tred"(?) - Samuel Davis - 5th District
"Davis Triangle" - William Geddes - 5th District
"Deal Town" - Daniel Dulaney - 4th District
"Dean" - Joseph Wickes - 1st District
"Deans Adventure" - Benjamin Fillingham - 1st District
"Deans Adventure" - Samuel Wickes - 1st District
"Deatons Tract" - Samuel Bullock - 4th District
"Deer Park" - Benjamin Blackston - 5th District
"Dellins Fancy"(?) - Samuel Davis - 5th District
"Dembey" - Richard Spencer - 1st District
"Denbigh" - John Kennard - 3rd District
"Denbigh" - Nathan Kennard - 3rd District
"Denbigh" - Stephen Kennard - 3rd District
"Denbigh" - William Kennard - 3rd District
"Denbigh" - Absalom McCoy - 3rd District
"Denbigh" - Sarah McKinley - 3rd District
"Denbigh" - George Watts - 3rd District
"Demby" - Thomas Urie - 1st District
"Depford" - Sarah Huff - 4th District
"Depford" - Francis Rutter - 4th District
"Deprived Mischief" - Richard Richud - 1st District
"Doe Neck" - Richard Graves - 3rd District
"Doe Neck" - Edward Hall - 3rd District
"Doe Neck" - Absalom McCoy - 3rd District
"Douches Folly" - David Crane - 4th District
"Douches Folly" - John Williams - 4th District
"Down Dale" - Robert Peacock - 3rd District
"Down Range" - Mary Hisard - 3rd District
"Dracute" - Blackston Chandler - 4th District
"Dracute" - Thomas Medford - 4th District

"Dracute" - William Reding - 4th District
"Draw Near" - Samuel Davis - 5th District
"Draw Near" - Thomas Ellis - 5th District
"Drayton" - Isaac Canell [Carell?] - 4th District
"Drayton" - John Wethered - 4th District
"Drayton Resurveyed" - John Haley - 3rd District
"Drugans Discovery" - John Corse - 4th District
"Dublin" - John Wilmore - 5th District
"Dullams Folly" - Alexander Baird - 5th District
"Dunns Discovery" - Hezekiah Dunn - 1st District
"Durby and Smythby" - Jeremiah Nicols - 2nd District
"Eastern Neck" - Richard Frisby - 3rd District
"Eastern Neck" - Alexander Glenn - 1st District
"Eastern Neck" - Edward Scandlen - 1st District
"East Huntington" - Arthur Miller - 2nd District
"Edinburgh" - Francis Lennon - 5th District
"Ellis Industry" - John Blackston - 5th District
"Endeavor" - Pearce Bowers - 4th District
"Endeavour" - Benjamin Palmer - 4th District
"Essex" - Thomas Bowers - 4th District
"Essex" - Isaac Perkins - 3rd District
"Everetts Addition" - Hales Everett - 3rd District
"Everetts Discovery" - Hales Everett - 3rd District
"Everetts Double Purchase" - Hales Everett - 3rd District
"Exchange" - Ebenezer Massy - 5th District
"Exchange" - Richard Scags - 4th District
"Fair Dealing" - Samuel Beck - 5th District
"Fair Dealing" - Dennis Earle - 5th District
"Fairfield" - James Hynson, Jr. - 5th District
"Fair Harbour" - John Hynson (of Cecil County) - 1st District
"Fair Harbour" - Richard Hynson - 1st District
"Fair Promise" - Edward Crew - 4th District
"Fair Promise" - Daniel Dulaney - 4th District
"Falmouth" - John T. Kennard - 3rd District
"Falmouth" - Richard B. Lloyd - 3rd District
"Fancy" - B. John Bordley - 1st District
"Fannys Slipe" - Samuel Davis - 5th District
"Farlow" - James Frisby - 1st District
"Farlow" - Gustavus Hanson - 1st District
"Farlow" - James Lloyd - 1st District
"Farlow" - Richard Lloyd - 1st District
"Farlow" - Philip Taylor - 1st District
"Farlow" - Joseph Wickes - 1st District
"Fathers Care Resurveyed" - Joseph Rasin - 4th District
"Fish Hall" - Edward Crew - 4th District
"Fishing Pond" - Ann Dean - 1st District
"Flower of Forest" - George Moffett, Sr. - 4th District
"Fluhartys Lott" - Michael Fluharty - 4th District
"Foremans Poor Discovery" - St. Leger Meeks - 3rd District
"Forest" - George Black - 4th District
"Forest" - Elizabeth Cole - 4th District
"Forest" - Nathaniel Comegys - 4th District
"Forest" - Daniel Ferguson - 4th District
"Forest" - Daniel Greenwood - 4th District
"Forest" - Simon Hackett - 4th District

"Forest" - Charles Irons - 4th District
"Forest" - Josiah Massy - 4th District
"Forest" - George Moffett, Jr. - 4th District
"Forest" - George Moffett, Sr. - 4th District
"Forest" - James Steel - 4th District
"Forest" - Joshua Vansant - 4th District
"Forest" - Mary Welch - 4th District
"Forest" - James Woodall - 4th District
"Forest" - John Woodall - 4th District
"Forest" - William Woodall - 4th District
"Forrest Dean" - William Cowarding's heirs - 3rd District
"Forrest Dean" - Mary Meeks - 3rd District
"Forrest Dean" - Robert Meeks - 3rd District
"Forrest Dean" - James Worth - 3rd District
"Forresters Delight" - Benjamin Jones - 4th District
"Forresters Delight" - John Williams - 4th District
"Forrest Resurveyed" - Jonathan Comegys - 3rd District
"Fork" - Charles Broom - 5th District
"Forks" - Thomas Pearce - 5th District
"Forks" - James Vansant - 5th District
"Forks Addition" - Cornelius Vansant - 5th District
"Free Gift" - James Blackston - 5th District
"Free Gift" - Thomas Cooper - 5th District
"Free Gift" - George William Forrester - 5th District
"Free Gift" - Joseph Rasin - 5th District
"Free Gift" - Elizabeth Redgrave - 5th District
"Free Gift" - Joseph Redgrave - 5th District
"Free Gift" - Alexander Stuart - 5th District
"Free Gift" - Ephraim Vansant - 5th District
"Friendship" - Risdon Bishop - 3rd District
"Friendship" - Edward Crew - 4th District
"Friendship" - George Lamb - 4th District
"Friendship" - Pearce Lamb - 4th District
"Frisbys Choice" - Elizabeth Frisby - 4th District
"Gales Addition" - Susannah Medford - 4th District
"Garnetts Branch" - Ann Ringgold - 3rd District
"Georges" (Part of Morton) - Alexander Baird - 5th District
"Germany" - Jacob Falconer - 4th District
"Gibbs Choice" - Joseph Rasin - 4th District
"Gibsons Choice" - Francis Cann - 4th District
"Godlington" - Arthur Miller - 2nd District
"Good Hope" - St. Leger Meeks - 3rd District
"Goose Haven" - Richard Peacock - 4th District
"Gore" - George Browning - 5th District
"Gore Haven" - Gilbert Falconer - 5th District
"Grahams Purchase" - Rebeckah Graham - 4th District
"Grange" - Rasin Gale - 4th District
"Grange" - Isaac Hines - 4th District
"Grange" - Marmaduke Medford - 4th District
"Grange" - George Reason - 4th District
"Granthom" - John Turner - 4th District
"Grantom" - Isaac Spencer - 4th District
"Grantom" - Thomas Woodall - 4th District
"Grantom" - James Woodall - 4th District

TRACTS AND LANDOWNERS IN THE TAX LIST OF 1783   79

"Grants Folly" - Jonathan Grant - 1st District
"Great Oak" - Elizabeth Frisby - 1st District
"Great Oak" - Darius Gamble - 1st District
"Great Oak Mannor" - Charles Tilden, Jr. - 3rd District
"Great Oak Mannor" - Marmaduke Tilden - 3rd District
"Green Bank" - Hensin [Kinvin?] Wroth, Jr. - 3rd District
"Green Branch" - John Wilson - 1st District
"Green Forest" - Moses Brisco - 4th District
"Green Forest" - Thomas Hebbern - 4th District
"Green Meadow" - Samuel Reed - 1st District
"Green Oak" - Francis Hall - 4th District
"Greenwoods Adventure" - Joseph Greenwood, Jr. - 4th District
"Greenwoods Adventure" - Aquilla Meeks - 4th District
"Greenwoods Chance" - John Greenwood - 4th District
"Greenwoods Farm" - Joseph Greenwood, Jr. - 4th District
"Greers Range" - Michael Corse - 4th District
"Greshams College" - Ann Dean - 1st District
"Greshams College" - John Frisby - 1st District
"Greshams Discovery" - Thomas Smyth, Jr. - 1st District
"Greshams Folly" - John Galloway (executor for Thomas Ringgold) - 1st District
"Greshams Levels" - Thomas Smyth - 1st District
"Greys Inn" - Thomas Jerrum - 1st District
"Griffiths Calf Penn" - Richard Frisby - 3rd District
"Grove" - James McClain's heirs - 3rd District
"Groves Addition" - James McClain's heirs - 3rd District
"Grumble" - B. John Bordley - 1st District
"Grumble" - William Copper - 1st District
"Hacketts Fancy" - Isaac Hackett - 3rd District
"Hales" - Henry Truelock - 4th District
"Hamiltons Lott" - Marmaduke Medford - 4th District
"Hampshire" - Francis Knock - 4th District
"Hampshire" - John Miers - 4th District
"Hampshire" - William Redgrave - 4th District
"Hampshire" - James Stavely - 4th District
"Hangmans End" - Robert Moody - 5th District
"Hangmans End" - William Stoops - 5th District
"Hangmans Folly" - Daniel Cornelius - 5th District
"Hangmans Folly" - Nathaniel Knock, Jr. - 5th District
"Hangmans Folly" - John Wilson, Sr. - 5th District
"Hansford" - George Hastings - 2nd District
"Hansford" - William True - 2nd District
"Hansons Choice Resurveyed" - Jacob Glenn - 1st District
"Harberts Chance" - Abraham Woodland - 4th District
"Harbour" - John Bolton - 3rd District
"Harris Addition" - B. John Bordley - 1st District
"Harris Forrest" - George Hartshorn - 3rd District
"Hartford" - Darius Gamble - 1st District
"Harts Point" - Morgan Hurt - 1st District
"Haven" - Turbutt Wright - 5th District
"Hazard" - John Greenwood - 5th District
"Hazard" - James Tarrington - 1st District
"Hazel Thicket" - Benjamin Cleaves [Gleaves?] - 5th District
"Hazzard" - John Page - 1st District
"Hazzard" - Richard Richud - 1st District

INHABITANTS OF KENT COUNTY, MARYLAND, 1637-1787

"Heading" - Thomas Boyer - 4th District
"Heaths Choice" - John Dwire (Dwyer) - 4th District
"Heaths Low Lands" - J. Thomas James - 1st District
"Heaths Low Lands" - John Swift - 1st District
"Heaths Range" - Nathaniel Boyer - 5th District
"Hebberns Choice" - Susannah Medford - 4th District
"Hebberns Choice" - Thomas Medford - 4th District
"Hebberns Choice" - George Moore - 4th District
"Hebberns Farm" - John Corse - 4th District
"Hebberns Farm" - Thomas Lamb - 4th District
"Helens Adventure" - David Davis - 4th District
"Hembleton" - Thomas Smyth - 1st District
"Hembleton" - Thomas Whalon - 1st District
"Henberry" - Lovring Merrett - 5th District
"Henberry" - Selah Rawlings - 5th District
"Henberry" - Turbutt Wright - 5th District
"Henbury" - Gilbert Falconer - 5th District
"Henham" - Thomas Medford - 4th District
"Henroost" - John White - 5th District
"Henroost" - John Williams - 5th District
"Henroost" - John Wilmore - 5th District
"Hensland" - John Wilmore - 5th District
"Hermitage" - William Apsley - 3rd District
"Hermitage" - Philip Davis - 3rd District
"Hermitage" - Hensin Wroth - 3rd District
"Hibbers Farm" - William Armstrong - 4th District
"Hicks Town" - John Bradsha [sic] - 5th District
"High Park" - James Dunn's heirs - 2nd District
"High Park" - James Brown Dunn - 2nd District
"High Park" - B. Thomas Hands - 2nd District
"High Park" - Charles Tilden - 2nd District
"Hillings Adventure" - John Cowarden - 4th District
"Hills and No Dales" - Aquilla Meeks - 4th District
"Hills Downs" - B. John Bordley - 1st District
"Hills Downs" - Richard Lloyd - 1st District
"Hillston" - James Brown Dunn - 2nd District
"Hillston" - William Pearce - 2nd District
"Hill Top" - Thomas Vandyke - 3rd District
"Hillingsworthmore" - See "Killingsworthmore"
"Hilly Langford" - Arthur Bordley - 3rd District
"Hillys Chance" - Abraham Woodland - 4th District
"Hinchingham" - Robert Ayres - 1st District
"Hinchingham" - Stephen Blackstone - 1st District
"Hinchingham" - Ann Frisby - 1st District
"Hinchingham" - Elizabeth Frisby - 1st District
"Hinchingham" - James Frisby - 1st District
"Hinchingham" - Mary Gitting (Getting) - 1st District
"Hinchingham" - James Glanville - 1st District
"Hinchingham" - Richard Miller - 1st District
"Hinocks Lot" - Benjamin Blackston - 5th District
"Holy Land" - James Frisby - 1st District
"Holy Land" - John Hurt (son of C.) - 1st District
"Holy Land" - Jose [sic] Hurt - 1st District
"Holy Land" - Samuel Smith - 1st District

TRACTS AND LANDOWNERS IN THE TAX LIST OF 1783   81

"Honest Dealing" - John Whittington - 5th District
"Hope" - John Miers (Myars) - 5th District
"Hopefull Unity" - Charles Groomes - 4th District
"Hopewell" - John Brooks - 4th District
"Hopewell" - John Eccleston - 4th District
"Hopewell" - John Galloway (for Thomas Ringgold's heirs) - 3rd District
"Hopewell" - William Graves - 1st District
"Hopewell" - Simon Hackett - 4th District
"Hopewell" - Samuel Reed - 1st District
"Hosiers Farm" - John Stewart - 2nd District
"Howards Addition" - Ann Carville - 1st District
"Howards Gift" - Anthony Banning - 1st District
"Howards Policy" - John Dwire (Dwyer) - 4th District
"Howells Farm" - Thomas Medford - 4th District
"Howells Range" - Isaac Perkins - 3rd District
"Huckleberry" - Simon Hackett - 4th District
"Huckleberry Ridge" - William Geddes - 5th District
"Huddles Right" - Thomas Bowers - 1st District
"Hudson Adventure" - John Hudson - 4th District
"Huffs Addition" - Hezekiah Dunn - 1st District
"Hunting Field" - John Galloway (executor for Thomas Ringgold) - 1st District
"Hunting Field" - William Ringgold (Easton) - 1st District
"Hunting Field" - Thomas Smyth - 1st District
"Hurts Lott" - Henry Hurt - 4th District
"Husbands Lott" - John Wallace (M.C.) - 4th District
"Hynsons Addition" - Arthur Bryan - 1st District
"Hynsons Addition" - Robert Butler - 1st District
"Hynsons Addition" - Benjamin Hynson - 1st District
"Hynsons Chance" - Hezekiah Dunn - 1st District
"Hynsons Chance" - Charles Hynson - 1st District
"Hynsons Chance" - C. John Hynson - 1st District
"Hynsons Chance" - Richard Hynson - 1st District
"Hynsons Desire" - Isaac Freeman - 4th District
"Hynsons Desire" - James Jones - 4th District
"Hynsons Division" - Charles Chambers - 1st District
"Hynsons Division" - Benjamin Hynson, Jr. - 1st District
"Hynsons Division" - Nathaniel Hynson - 1st District
"Hynsons Division" - Mary Wickes - 1st District
"Inconvenience" - Frances Hodges - 1st District
"Inconvenience" - James Hodges - 1st District
"Inconvenience" - Stephen Hodges - 1st District
"Inconvenience" - John Yearly - 1st District
"Indian Range"- George Browning - 5th District
"Indian Range" - Thomas Browning - 5th District
"Inheritance - Maria Ann Ringgold - 1st District
"Intermix" - Marmaduke Medford - 4th District
"Intermix" - Francis Cann - 4th District
"Intermix" - Rasin Gale - 4th District
"Island" - Thomas Shahawn - 4th District
"Ivingo" - William Merrett - 4th District
"Jamaica" - Mary Cruikshank - 3rd District
"James Adventure" - George Black - 4th District
"James Discovery" - J. Thomas James - 1st District

"Jerico" - Cuthbert Hall - 4th District
"Johns Addition" - Samuel Comegys - 4th District
"Jones Neglect" - Hannah Bordley - 4th District
"Jones Neglect" - Joseph Porter - 5th District
"Kellys Choice" - Charles Millward - 4th District
"Kemps Beginning" - Joseph Garnett - 3rd District
"Kemps Beginning" - Mary Garnett - 3rd District
"Kemps Beginning" - Emory Sudler - 3rd District
"Kennards Discovery" - John Haley - 3rd District
"Kennards Fancy" - Nathaniel Kennard - 3rd District
"Kennards Farm" - Luke Griffith - 3rd District
"Kennards Point" - Robert Buchanan - 4th District
"Kent Lot" - Joseph Curlett - 5th District
"Kent Manor" - George Black - 4th District
"Kent Manor" - James Black - 4th District
"Kent Manor" - John Busly - 4th District
"Kent Manor" - Martha Dening - 4th District
"Kent Manor" - Stephen Dening - 4th District
"Kent Manor" - John Gilbert - 4th District
"Kent Manor" - Nathaniel Knock - 4th District
"Kent Manor" - William Maxwell, Jr. - 4th District
"Kent Manor" - Aquilla Page - 4th District
"Kent Manor" - Bartus Piner - 4th District
"Kent Manor" - Henry Wallace - 4th District
"Kent Manor (Abrams Lott)" - Joseph Stavely - 4th District
"Kent Manor Bought" - William Keyton - 4th District
"Kent Manor Bought" - William Merrett - 4th District
"Kent Manor" (Shad Hole) - John Shahawn - 4th District
"Killingsworthmore" - John Greenwood - 4th District
"Killingsworthmore" - Reuben Harding - 4th District
"Killingsworthmore" - Vincent Hatchison - 4th District
"Killingsworthmore" - William Thomas - 4th District
"Kindness" - Eliza Williamson - 1st District
"Knocks Range" - Ebenezer Blackstone - 5th District
"Knocks Range" - William Knock - 5th District
"Lambs Meadows" - John Corse - 4th District
"Lambs Meadows" - George Lamb - 4th District
"Lambs Meadows" - Joshua Lamb - 4th District
"Lambs Meadows" - Thomas Lamb - 4th District
"Lambs Meadows Resurveyed" - John Lamb - 4th District
"Lambs Range" - Joshua Lamb - 4th District
"Langfords Neck" - James Crouch - 1st District
"Langfords Neck" - William Glanville - 1st District
"Langfords Neck" - Rachel Grant - 1st District
"Langfords Neck" - Gustavus Hanson - 1st District
"Langfords Neck" - Thomas Smyth - 1st District
"Last" - John Haley - 3rd District
"Lauds Manor" - See "Lords Manor"
"Levingham" - Mary Jones - 4th District
"Levingsham" - James Hart - 4th District
"Levington" - Francis Cann - 4th District
"Linchhorn" - John Wilmore - 5th District
"Little Britain" - Isaac Perkins - 4th District
"Little Britain" - Hannah Warner - 4th District

TRACTS AND LANDOWNERS IN THE TAX LIST OF 1783

"Little Grove" - John Galloway for Thomas Ringgold's heirs - 3rd District
"Little Grove" - James McClain's heirs - 3rd District
"London Bridge" - Abraham Falconer - 5th District
"London Bridge" - Gilbert Falconer - 5th District
"London Bridge" - Lydia Gilpin - 5th District
"London Bridge" - Edward Haddin - 5th District
"London Bridge" - Ebenezer Massy - 5th District
"London Bridge" - William Miers - 5th District
"London Bridge" - John Rawlings - 5th District
"London Bridge" - Isaac Spencer - 5th District
"London Bridge Renewed" - Luke Miers - 5th District
"London Derry" - William Armstrong - 5th District
"London Derry" - Rebeckah Little - 5th District
"London Derry" - John Ward Pennington - 5th District
"London Derry" - George Smith - 5th District
"London Derry" - John Taylor - 5th District
"Long Acre" - Benjamin Fillingham - 1st District
"Long Acre" - Richard Richud - 1st District
"Long Compton" - Edward Beck - 3rd District
"Long Neglect" - Risdon Bishop - 3rd District
"Long Neglect" - John Galloway for Thomas Ringgold's heirs - 3rd District
"Long Slipe" - Sarah Merritt - 3rd District
"Lords Gift" - Charles Copper - 1st District
"Lords Gift" - Philip Copper - 1st District
"Lords Manor" - William Little - 5th District
"Lords Manor" - John Zelephrow - 5th District
Lott in Chestertown Suburbs - Valentine Bender - 3rd District
Lott in Chestertown Suburbs - William Boardly - 3rd District
Lot - Joseph Davenport - 5th District
Lot - Mary Dollis - 5th District
Lot - Mary Hynson - 5th District
Lot - John Massy - 5th District
Lot with house - Thomas Bevans - 5th District
Lot with house - Spence Budle - 5th District
Lot with house - Charles Irons - 5th District
Lot with house - Peter Issels - 5th District
Lot with house - John Jervis - 5th District
Lot with house - Mary Jervis - 5th District
Lot with house - Michael Jobson - 5th District
Lot with house - Elizabeth Jurey - 5th District
Lot with house - Thomas Ralph - 5th District
Lot with house - Sarah Rasin - 5th District
Lot with house - William Rogers - 5th District
Lot with house - Abraham Saunders - 5th District
Lot with house - Timothy Scott - 5th District
Lot with house - Oliver Smith - 5th District
Lot with house - William Smith - 5th District
Lot with house - Garradus Vansant - 5th District
Lot with house - George Vansant (S.B.) - 5th District
Lot with house - Jacob Vansant - 5th District
Lot with house - John Voorhees - 5th District
Lot with house - Thomas Wheatherspoon - 5th District
Lot with house - Margaret Wright - 5th District

"Lots Addition" - Benjamin Blackston - 5th District
"Love and Friendship" - John Corse - 4th District
"Lovely Neck" - Zachariah Smyth - 1st District
"Luck" - Thomas Hebbern - 1st District
"Luck" - Nathaniel Toleson - 1st District
"Lucys Recreation" - Martha Merritt - 2nd District
"Lyons Hall" - Morgan Brown - 2nd District
"McConnakin" - John Rolph - 2nd District
"McCoys (McCays) Purchase" - Robert Maxwell - 5th District
"McDugalls Chance" - Luke Miers - 5th District
"Mackeys Desire" - Thomas Reardon - 1st District
"Mackeys Desire" - Simon Wickes - 1st District
"Maidens Lott" - Christopher Bellican - 4th District
"Maidens Lott" - Darcus Moore - 4th District
"Maidens Lott" - John Wallace (M.C.) - 4th District
"Margarets Delight" - William James, Jr. [James William, Jr.?] - 5th District
"Margarets Delight" - William Gray - 5th District
"Margarets Delight" - William Wilmore - 5th District
"Margarets Delight" - George Wilson (S.G.) - 5th District
"Margarets End" - Benjamin Cole - 5th District
"Margarets End" - William Ellis - 5th District
"Margarets End" - Abraham Redgrave - 5th District
"Market Place Resurveyed" - William Granger - 1st District
"Marrow Bone" - Isaac Spencer - 4th District
"Marshes" - Thomas Hebbern - 4th District
"Marshes" - Susannah Medford - 4th District
"Marsh Point" - Isaac Freeman - 4th District
"Marshy Point" - James Woodland - 4th District
"Maslins Possession" - Thomas Crow - 2nd District
"Maslins Possession" - James Maslin - 2nd District
"Massys Adventure" - Ebenezer Massy - 5th District
"Massys Adventure" - Jonathan Newnham - 5th District
"Massys Lot Resurveyed" - John Jobson - 5th District
"Mathias" - John Day - 4th District
"Maxwells Purchase" - William Maxwell, Jr. - 4th District
"Meadows" (The) - Sarah Merrett - 3rd District
"Meadows" - James Pearce - 5th District
"Memento Mori" - Thomas Smyth - 1st District
"Merritts Discovery" - Martha Merritt - 2nd District
"Middle Branch" - John Page - 1st District
"Middle Branch" - Richard Richud - 1st District
"Middle Branch" - James Tarrington - 1st District
"Middle Neck" - James Corse - 4th District
"Middle Neck" - John Dwier (Dwyer) - 4th District
"Middle Neck" - Nathaniel Tolson - 4th District
"Middle Plantation" - Thomas Crow - 1st District
"Middle Spring" - John Page - 1st District
"Middle Spring" - Richard Richud - 1st District
"Miers Neglect" - Joseph Parsons - 5th District
"Miers Resurvey" - Luke Miers - 5th District
"Milford" - John Page - 1st District
"Mill" - Thomas Canby - 5th District
"Mill" - Oliver Caulk - 5th District

TRACTS AND LANDOWNERS IN THE TAX LIST OF 1783   85

"Millers Chance" - James Pearce - 5th District
"Millers Delight" - Nathaniel Miller - 1st District
"Millers Purchase" - Michael Miller - 1st District
"Millers Purchase" - Richard Miller - 1st District
"Millers Purchase" - Samuel Miller - 1st District
"Millers Purchase" - Walter Miller - 1st District
"Millford" - Daniel Perkins - 1st District
"Mill Fork" - James Clayton - 5th District
"Mill Fork" - William Clayton - 5th District
"Mill Fork" - George Medford - 5th District
"Mill Fork" - William Pell - 5th District
"Mill Land" - James Pearce - 4th District
"Mills" - John Wethered - 4th District
"Mills" - John Willson - 4th District
"Millwards Choice" - Charles Millward - 4th District
"Millwards Choice" - James Millward - 4th District
"Mitchells Chance" - Thomas Saunders - 5th District
"Mitchells Chance" - John Wilmore - 5th District
"Moffetts Chance" - Richard Moffett, Sr. - 4th District
"Moffetts Lott" - George Moffett, Sr. - 4th District
"Moggys Jointure" - Thomas Medford - 4th District
"Morgans C. Land" - Ann Dean - 4th District
"Mothers Care" - Bartus Piner - 4th District
"Mothers Gift" - Richard Graves - 4th District
"Mount Airy" - Edward Tilghman - 5th District
"Mount Harmon" - Hannah Brown - 4th District
"Mount Harmon" - Nathaniel Comegys - 4th District
"Mount Harmon" - Rebeckah Graham - 4th District
"Mount Harmon" - George Tiller - 4th District
"Mount Hope" - Francis Spry - 4th District
"Mount Pleasant" - Robert Cruikshank - 1st District
"Mount Pleasant" - Edward Tilghman - 5th District
"My Lords Gift" - Elias Deal - 5th District
"My Lords Gift" - Patrick Fowler - 5th District
"My Lords Gift" - Mary Little - 5th District
"My Lords Gracious Grant" - William Little - 5th District
"My Lords Gracious Grant" - Sarah McDonnald - 5th District
"My Lords Gracious Grant" - Robert Marley - 5th District
"My Lords Gracious Grant" - John Weaver - 5th District
"My Lords Gracious Grant" - John Webb - 5th District
"My Lords Gracious Grant" - David Spur - 5th District
"My Lords Gracious Grant" - William Rogers - 5th District
"My Lords Gracious Grant" - Martha Saunders - 5th District
"My Lords Gracious Grant" - Isaac Stanley - 5th District
"My Lords Gracious Grant" - John Stanley - 5th District
"My Lords Gracious Grant" - Richard Stanley - 5th District
"My Lords Gracious Grant" - William Turner - 5th District
"Nancys Choice" - David Davis - 4th District
"Nancys Choice" - St. Leger Everett - 4th District
"Nancys Choice" - Henry Truelock - 4th District
"Napley Green" - James Williamson - 1st District
"Napley Green" - John Williamson - 1st District
"Neglect" - Colin Ferguson, Sr. - 5th District
"Neglect" - Isaac Spencer - 4th District
"Neves (Neefs) Choice" - Alexander Beck - 1st District

INHABITANTS OF KENT COUNTY, MARYLAND, 1637-1787

"New Adventure" - William Hanson - 5th District
"Newels Adventure" - William Apsley - 3rd District
"New Forrest" - John Hynson (of Cecil County) - 1st District
"New Harbour" - Abraham Woodland - 4th District
"New Key" - James Frisby - 2nd District
"New M. Tavern" - Lambert Smith - 4th District
"New Scotland" - George Reason - 4th District
"New Town Resurveyed" - John Bradsha [sic] - 5th District
"New Town Resurveyed" - Joseph Curlett - 5th District
"New Town Resurveyed" - John Webb - 5th District
"New York" - Heirs of ---- Boot - 2nd District
"New York" - Heirs of ---- Frisby - 2nd District
"New York" - Samuel Thomas - 2nd District
"Nieces Chance" - Ann Carville - 1st District
"Nieces Chance" - J. Thomas James - 1st District
"Norris Forest" - Heirs of Thomas Ringgold - 2nd District
"Norris Forest" - Sarah Simmonds - 2nd District
"Out Lett" - Richard Scags - 4th District
"Packerton" - J. Thomas James - 1st District
"Pages Purchase" - John Page - 1st District
"Pages Road" - John Page - 1st District
"Palmers Desire" - George Moffet, Sr. - 4th District
"Palmers Desire" - Benjamin Palmer - 4th District
"Palmers Hazard" - William Merrett 4th District
"Palmers Hazard" - Benjamin Palmer - 4th District
"Partnership" - Malachi Ambrose - 5th District
"Partnership" - Isaac Brisco - 4th District
"Partnership" - Henry Clark - 5th District
"Partnership" - John Clark - 5th District
"Partnership" - William Clark - 5th District
"Partnership" - Daniel Dulany - 4th District
"Partnership" - John Eccleston - 4th District
"Partnership" - Gilbert Falconer - 5th District
"Partnership" - William Hull - 4th District
"Partnership" - James Hynson, Jr. - 5th District
"Partnership" - Andrew Kelly - 4th District
"Partnership" - Daniel Toas Massy - 5th District
"Partnership" - Hannah Massy - 5th District
"Partnership" - John Massy - 5th District
"Partnership" - Joseph Massy - 5th District
"Partnership" - Mary Massy - 5th District
"Partnership" - William Maxwell, Jr. - 4th District
"Partnership" - Selah Rawlings - 5th District
"Partnership" - George Reason - 4th District
"Partnership" - William Spearman - 5th District
"Partnership" - Joseph Turner - 5th District
"Partnership" - Francis Wallace - 4th District
"Partnership" - John Wallace (M.C.) - 4th District
"Partnership" - Samuel Wallace - 4th District
"Partnership Addition" - Charles Broom - 5th District
"Partnership Addition" - John Browning, Jr. - 5th District
"Partnership Addition" - Robert Maxwell - 5th District
"Partnership Point" - James Butcher - 4th District
"Partnership Point" - John Eccleston - 4th District

TRACTS AND LANDOWNERS IN THE TAX LIST OF 1783   87

"Partnership Point" - Francis Rutter - 4th District
"Partnership Point" - Abraham Woodland - 4th District
"Partnership Point" - John Woodland - 4th District
"Pearces Mill" - James Pearce - 5th District
"Pearces Desire" - Nicholas McCubbin - 4th District
"Pearces Meadow" - Solomon Semans - 5th District
"Pearces Ramble" - Charles Broom - 5th District
"Pearces Ramble" - George Newcomb - 5th District
"Pearces Ramble" - Charles Watts - 5th District
"Pentridge" - James Ringgold - 2nd District
"Pentridge" - Dr. John Scott - 2nd District
"Pentridge" - William Shields - 2nd District
"Perch Meadow" - Richard Lowman - 1st District
"Perch Meadow" - Samuel Reed - 1st District
"Perch Meadow" - Ann Maria Whichcoat - 1st District
"Perkins Adventure" - John Wilson - 1st District
"Perkins Meadows" - Isaac Perkins - 4th District
"Perkins Mistake" - William Maxwell, Jr. - 4th District
"Perkins Policy" - Isaac Perkins - 4th District
"Peters Field" - Frances Wilson - 5th District
"Peters Field" - John Wilson, Sr. - 5th District
"Philips Choice" - John Hurt - 4th District
"Philips Choice" - James McClure - 4th District
"Philips Neglect" - Solomon Semans - 5th District
"Piners Addition" - Ann Ringgold - 3rd District
"Piners Grove" - Sarah Piner - 3rd District
"Piney Point" - Richard Spencer - 1st District
"Piney Point" - James Williamson - 1st District
"Plain Dealing" - John Eccleston - 4th District
"Plains" - Anthony Banning - 1st District
"Plains" - James Brown Dunn - 2nd District
"Planes" - James Ringgold, Jr. - 1st District
"Planes" - Dr. John Ringgold - 1st District
"Planes" - Mary Ringgold - 1st District
"Poplar Farm" - Anthony Banning - 1st District
"Poplar Hill Resurveyed" - Simon Wickes - 1st District
"Porters Addition" - John Eccleston - 4th District
"Presbury" - Joseph Williams - 4th District
"Presbury Discovery" - Charles Tilden - 2nd District
"Prevention" - James Hodges - 1st District
"Prevention" - Stephen Hodges - 1st District
"Prevention" - John Yearley - 1st District
"Prices Lott" - Morgan Brown - 2nd District
"Prices Lott" - Rebeccah Brown - 2nd District
"Prickley Pear" - Risden Bishop - 4th District
"Prickley Pear" - Samuel Comegys - 4th District
"Prince William" - Richard Graves - 3rd District
"Probus" - William Beck - 3rd District
"Providence" - B. John Bordley - 1st District
"Providence" - Hannah Bordley - 4th District
"Providence" - James Bradshaw - 1st District
"Providence" - Isaac Brisco - 4th District
"Providence" - Moses Brisco - 4th District
"Providence" - Morgan Brown - 2nd District
"Providence" - Rebeccah Brown - 2nd District

"Providence" - William Brown - 1st District
"Providence" - George Copper - 1st District
"Providence" - William Dawson - 1st District
"Providence" - George Hastings - 2nd District
"Providence" - John Page - 1st District
"Providence" - Richard Richud [Ricaud?] - 1st District
"Providence" - James Smith (Farlow) - 1st District
"Providence" - William True - 2nd District
"Providence" - John Willson - 4th District
"Pryors Neglect" - William Pell - 5th District
"Pryors Neglect" - Thomas Saunders - 5th District
"Queen Charlton" - Anthony Banning - 1st District
"Queen Charlton" - Joseph Blackston - 1st District
"Queen Charlton" - Nathaniel Rickets - 1st District
"Queen Charlton" - William Wilmore - 1st District
"Queen Charlton" - Edward Worrell - 1st District
"Rachels Farm" - Francis Knock - 4th District
"Rachels Farm" - Cornelius Comegys - 4th District
"Rachels Farm" - John Miers - 4th District
"Rasins Purchase" - Thomas Rasin - 4th District
"Ratcliff" - Mary Garrett - 3rd District
"Ratcliff" - Emory Sudler - 3rd District
"Ratcliff" - George Tiller - 4th District
"Ratcliff Cross" - George Dening - 4th District
"Rearden" - Morgan Brown - 2nd District
"Rearden" - Rebeccah Brown - 2nd District
"Rebeccahs Desire" - Diana Shahawn - 4th District
"Rebeccahs Desire" - Henry Wallace - 4th District
"Redmores Supply" - Barsheba Gale - 4th District
"Redmores Supply" - John Gale - 4th District
"Redmores Supply" - Rasin Gale - 4th District
"Relief" - Bartus Wilkins - 2nd District
"Remainder" - Henry Hurt - 4th District
"Remainder" - William Maxwell, Jr. - 4th District
"Resurvey" - Oliver Smith - 4th District
"Reynors Adventure" - Ebenezer Reynor - 4th District
"Richards Adventure" - Isaac Perkins - 3rd District
"Rich Level" - Augustine Boyer - 5th District
"Rich Level" - Nathaniel Boyer - 5th District
"Rich Level" - William Grindage - 5th District
"Rich Level" - John Moffat - 5th District
"Rich Level" - John Wilmore - 5th District
"Rich Meadow" - Hales Everett - 3rd District
"Ricketts Farm" - William Dawson - 4th District
"Ricketts Farm" - St. Leger Everett - 4th District
"Ricketts Farm" - Charles Groome - 4th District
"Ridgeley" - Peregrine Cooper - 4th District
"Ridgeley" - Isaac Perkins - 4th District
"Ridgeley" - John Willson - 4th District
"Rileys Resurveyed" - John Wilson, Sr. - 5th District
"Ringgolds Fortune" - Hynson Smyth - 1st District
"Ringgolds Lott" - Hynson Smyth - 1st District
"Rippin" - John Eccleston - 4th District
"Rousby Discovery" - William Carmichael - 3rd District

TRACTS AND LANDOWNERS IN THE TAX LIST OF 1783

"Rule Adam" [Rue Adam?] - John Randal - 3rd District
"Rumford" - George Moffet, Sr. - 4th District
"Rumford Resurveyed" - William Woodall - 4th District
"Ryley" - Hannah Bordley - 4th District
"Ryleys Beginning" - Benjamin Ryley - 4th District
"Ryleys Beginning" - Jonathan Worth [Wroth?] - 4th District
"Ryleys Resurveyed" - Mathew Richardson, Sr. - 5th District
"St. Albans Addition" - Jesse Comegys - 4th District
"St. Andrews Cross" - Thomas Pearce - 5th District
"St. Ephraim" - George Vansant - 5th District
"St. Johns Fields" - John Day - 4th District
"St. Martins" (with a tanyard) - David Crane - 4th District
"St. Martins Addition" - Jesse Comegys - 4th District
"St. Tantans" - Marmaduke Medford, guardian to Blackston's heirs - 1st District
"St. Tantans" - Lambert Wilmore - 1st District
"St. Tantans" - Rosanna Wilmore - 1st District
"Salters Load" - Ann Carville - 1st District
"Salters Load" - Richard Frisby - 3rd District
"Sandy Hill" (with a mill) - John Eunick - 4th District
"Sarahs Lott" - John True - 2nd District
"Savories Farm" - John Bolton - 3rd District
"Savories Farm" - Samuel Hammond - 3rd District
"Savories Farm" - Hensin [Kinvin?] Wroth - 3rd District
"Scidmore" - Thomas Bowers - 1st District
"Scidmore" - Joseph Wickes (Bay Side) - 1st District
"Scotts Folly" - William Merrett - 4th District
"Scotts Lott" - James Brown Dunn - 2nd District
"Scrap" - Jacob Comegys - 5th District
"Semans Folly" - Gilbert Semans - 5th District
"Severnton" - Anthony Banning - 3rd District
"Severnton" - Charles Foreman - 3rd District
"Sewards Hope" - Samuel Mansfield - 4th District
"Sewards Hope" - Hannah Warner - 4th District
"Sewel" (Seawell) - Joseph Brown - 2nd District
"Sewel" (Seawell) - James Burchinal - 2nd District
"Sewel" (Seawell) - William Burchinal - 2nd District
"Sewel" (Seawell) - Edward Comegys - 2nd District
"Sewel" (Seawell) - Robert Curry - 2nd District
"Sewells Chance" - Bartus Wilkins - 2nd District
"Shads Hole" - Peregrine Cooper - 4th District
"Shads Hole" - John Hudson - 4th District
"Shads Hole" - John March, Sr. - 4th District
"Shads Hole" (Kent Manor) - John Shahawn - 4th District
"Shads Hole" - Abraham Taylor - 4th District
"Simpsons Addition" - William Wilmore - 4th District
"Sims Farm" - Susanah Medford - 4th District
"Skinners Marsh" - James Smyth - 2nd District
"Skinners Neck" - David Brown - 1st District
"Slipe" - Page and Miller - 4th District
"Smalley" - Isaac Spencer - 4th District
"Smiths Park" - James Hynsons - 5th District
"Smiths Point" - Isaac Spencer - 4th District
"Smothers" [Smethers?] - William Woodall - 4th District
"Smothers Plains" - Elizabeth Jurey - 4th District

90   INHABITANTS OF KENT COUNTY, MARYLAND, 1637-1787

"Smyths Addition" - Thomas Smyth - 1st District
"Smyths Chance" - Joseph Brown - 1st District
"Smythes Desert" - Thomas Smyth - 1st District
"Smyths Meadows" - Thomas Smyth - 1st District
"Smyths Venture" - Thomas Smyth - 1st District
"Sole" - Robert Buchanan - 3rd District
"Sole" - John Kennard - 3rd District
"Sole" - Joseph Younger - 3rd District
"Spaulding" - Hensin [Kinvin?] Wroth, Jr. - 3rd District
"Spring Garden" - Martha Griffith - 3rd District
"Spring Garden" - John Massy - 5th District
"Stanaway" - John Hatcheson - 1st District
"Stanaway" - Nathan Hatcheson - 1st District
"Stanaway" - Mary Hynson - 1st District
"Stanaway" - Thomas Smyth - 1st District
"Stanaway" - Joseph Williams - 4th District
"Standaway" - Alexander Baird - 5th District
"Standford" - Pearce Lamb - 2nd District
"Standoff" - George Gilbert - 1st District
"Standoff" - Richard Peacock - 3rd District
"Standoff" - Robert Peacock - 3rd District
"Standoff" - Hannah Saunders - 5th District
"Standoff" - John Wilmore - 5th District
"Stanford" - Joseph Garnett - 3rd District
"Stanleys Hope" - Francis Cann - 4th District
"Stanleys Hope" - Joseph Rasin - 4th District
"Staple Warren" - John Galloway for Thomas Ringgold's heirs - 3rd District
"Stavelys Lott" - John Miers - 4th District
"Stavelys Lott" - James Stavely - 4th District
"Stepney" - Arthur Bordley - 3rd District
"Stepney" - Simon Wilmore - 3rd District
"Stepney" - Sarah Piner - 3rd District
"Stepney Fields" - John Ackland - 4th District
"Stepney Fields" - John Kearton - 4th District
"Stepney Heath Manor" - Thomas B. Hands - 2nd District
"Stepney Heath Manor" - Joseph Nicholson, Sr. - 2nd District
"Stepney Heath Manor" - James Frisby - 1st District
"Stevenson" - Eliza Williamson - 1st District
"Stiles Addition" - Ann Dean - 1st District
"Stoneton" - Nicholas McCubbin - 4th District
"Stoney Hill" - Richard Peacock - 3rd District
"Stoney Hill" - Robert Peacock - 3rd District
"Stradford Manor" - Martha Melton - 2nd District
"Stradford Manor" - Heirs of Thomas Ringgold - 2nd District
"Stradford Manor" - Samuel Thomas - 2nd District
"Stradford Manor" - John True - 2nd District
"Stratford Manor" - Thomas Blake - 2nd District
"Stratford Manor" - Joseph George - 2nd District
"Stratford Manor" - Robert George - 2nd District
"Suburbs" - William Fray - 1st District
"Suburns" - Samuel Reed - 1st District
"Sudlers Lott" - John Galloway for Thomas Ringgold's heirs - 3rd District

TRACTS AND LANDOWNERS IN THE TAX LIST OF 1783

"Suffolk" - John Anger - 4th District
"Suffolk" - Joseph Greenwood, Sr. - 4th District
"Suffolk" - Joseph Stavely - 4th District
"Suffolk" - Benjamin Terry - 4th District
"Suffolk" - Jonathan Turner - 4th District
"Swamps Resurveyed" - James Frisby - 1st District
"Sweatnams Addition" - William Pearce - 2nd District
"Sweetmans Peninsula" - Robert Ford - 4th District
"Tanfield Moore" - Oliver Smith - 4th District
"Tatums Mount" - Robert Buchanan - 3rd District
"Thomas Purchase" - George Brown - 2nd District
"Thomas Purchase" - Isaac Cox - 2nd District
"Thomas Purchase" - Joseph Nicholson, Jr. - 2nd District
"Thomas Purchase" - Dr. John Scott - 2nd District
"Thornton" - John Brooks - 4th District
"Thornton" - William Ringgold - 4th District
"Three Friends" - Darcus Moore - 4th District
"Three Friends" - John Wallace (M.C.) - 4th District
"Tibbalds" - Isaac Freeman - 4th District
"Tibbalds" - William Wilson - 4th District
"Tildens Farm" - Charles Tilden - 2nd District
"Tilghmans and Foxleys Grove" - Ann Frisby - 3rd District
"Tilghmans and Foxleys Grove" - William Ringgold - 3rd District
"Tilghmans and Foxleys Grove" - Simon Wilmore - 3rd District
"Tilghmans Choice" - John Galloway for Thomas Ringgold's heirs - 3rd District
"Tilghmans Choice" - Sarah Piner - 3rd District
"TIlghmans Farm" - Nicholas Brown - 2nd District
"Tilghmans Farm" - Robert George - 2nd District
"Tilghmans Farm" - Mary Miflin - 2nd District
"Tilghmans Farm" - Heirs of Thomas Ringgold - 2nd District
"Timber Levell" - John Sutton - 4th District
"Tippets Adventure" - Robert Money - 5th District
"Tobins" - William Dodson - 5th District
"Tobins" - John Little - 5th District
"Tobins Folly" - George Newcomb - 5th District
"Tobins Lot" - Colin Ferguson, Sr. - 5th District
"Tolchester" - George Hynson - 1st District
"Toll Chester" - Ann Dean - 1st District
"Toll Chester" - William Granger - 1st District
"Toveys Lott" - William Ringgold (Easton) - 1st District
"Tower Hill" - William Mason - 1st District
"Town Relief" - William Apsley - 3rd District
"Town Relief" - John Bolton - 3rd District
"Town Relief" - Philip Fray - 3rd District
"Town Relief" - William Fray - 1st District
"Town Relief" - George Hartshorn - 3rd District
"Town Relief" - James Worth [Wroth?] - 3rd District
"Town Relief" - Hensin [Kinvin?] Wroth, Jr. - 3rd District
"Trenchards Memorial" [Frenchards Memorial?] - Heirs of James McClain - 3rd District
"Triangle" - Anthony Banning - 3rd District
"Triangle" - John Galloway for Thomas Ringgold's heirs - 3rd District
"Triangle" - Heirs of Thomas Woodall - 3rd District

"Triangle Resurveyed" - Isaac Canell [Carell?] - 4th District
"Truelocks Adventure" - Henry Truelock - 4th District
"Trumpington" - Joseph Brown - 1st District
"Trumpington" - William Crabin - 1st District
"Trumpington" - Thomas Smyth - 1st District
"Tullys Fancy" - Martha Merritt - 2nd District
"Valley" - Charlotte Griffith - 1st District
"Veavin" - Josias Ringgold - 3rd District
"Verina" - Isaac Freeman - 5th District
"Verina" - Page and Miller - 4th District
"Verina" - Frances Wilson - 5th District
"Verina" - George Wilson, Sr. - 5th District
"Verina" - James Wilson, Sr. - 5th District
"Verina" - John Wilson, Sr. - 5th District
"Verinnia" (with a mill) - Cornelius Comegys - 4th District
"Viana" - Oliver Smith - 4th District
"Viana" - William Smith - 4th District
"Viana" - Isaac Spencer - 4th District
"Viana" - John Woodall - 4th District
"Viana" - William Woodall - 4th District
"Wallace Chance" - John Wallace (S.) [sic] - 4th District
"Walnut Neck" - Thomas Smyth - 1st District
"Ward Oak" - Elizabeth Thompson - 4th District
"Warners Addition" - Daniel Lamb - 4th District
"Warners Addition" - Isaac Perkins - 3rd District
"Warners Adventure" - Nathaniel Reding - 4th District
"Warners Levels" - James Worth [Wroth?] - 3rd District
"Warners" (Part of Drayton) - Robert Buchanan - 4th District
"Waxford" - Simon Wickes - 1st District
"Wedges Recovery" - Judith Brice - 1st District
"Wedges Recovery" - Philip Copper - 1st District
"Whaley" - Abednego Massy - 5th District
"Wheatfield" - Charlotte Griffith - 1st District
"Wheatfield" - Daniel Perkins - 1st District
"Wheatfield" - William Wright - 1st District
"Wheelright Swamp" - Stephen Kennard - 3rd District
"Whetfield" [Wheatfield] - George Gilbert - 1st District
"White Clift" - John Cockey - 1st District
"White Marsh" - Isaac Perkins - 3rd District
"Wickes Land" - James Durety - 4th District
"W. Clift" [Wickliffe] - William Granger - 1st District
"W. Clift" [Wickliffe] - Ann Wickes - 1st District
"W. Clift" [Wickliffe] - Mary Wickes - 1st District
"William and Mary" - Alexander Beck - 1st District
"William and Marys Adventure" - George Copper - 1st District
"Williams Lott" - Charles Copper - 1st District
"Williams Lott" - Philip Copper - 1st District
"Williamson" - Griffin Jones - 4th District
"Williams Venture" - John Bradshaw - 1st District
"Williams Venture" - John Page - 1st District
"Wilmore Farm" - William Worrell - 3rd District
"Wilmore Farm" - Hensin [Kinvin?] Wroth, Jr. - 3rd District
"Wilmore Grove" - William Wilmore - 1st District
"Wilsons Neglect" - George Wilson (S.G.) - 5th District

TRACTS AND LANDOWNERS IN THE TAX LIST OF 1783

"Wolf Hook" - Hannah Warner - 4th District
"Wolf Hook" - Henry Wallace - 4th District
"Wolf Hook" - Dr. John Wallace - 4th District
"Woodlands Folly" - John White - 5th District
"Woodlands Folly" - Yeates and Grindage - 5th District
"Woodland Neck" - Morgan Hurt - 1st District
"Worths Folly" - James Dunkin - 4th District
"Worths Folly" - Nathaniel Reding - 4th District
"Worths Folly" - James Smith - 3rd District
"Worths Folly" - John Smith - 3rd District
"Worton Mannor" - Richard B. Lloyd - 3rd District
"Worton Mannor" - Aquila Meeks - 3rd District
"Worton Mannor" - Sarah Merritt - 3rd District
"Worton Mannor" - William Pearce - 3rd District
"Writes Rest" - James Corse - 4th District
"Wyatts Chance" - John Eccleston - 4th District
"Wyatts Chance" - Henry Penington - 4th District
"Wye Hill Downs" - Richard Graves 3rd District
"Yapp" - Nicholas McCubbin - 4th District
"Yeates Purchase" - Donaldson Yeates - 4th District

INDENTURED ORPHANS OF KENT COUNTY, MARYLAND, 1778-1787
(Ref: Maryland State Archives, MdHR 8811-3 and 8812-3)

Ann Comegys, Cornelius Comegys, and Benjamin Comegys, minors under the age of 14 and children of Bartus Comegys, chose John Comegys to be their guardian on February 11, 1778.
Mary Perkins, a minor under the age of 14, chose Ebenezer Ryner and Jonathan Turner as her guardians on February 12, 1778.
James Patton [no age given] was bound to James Kelly on June 10, 1778 until he reached age 21.
Sarah Ashley [no age given] was bound to John Moore on June 10, 1778 until she reached age 16.
Mary Ringgold, a minor under the age of 14, chose Charles Tilden to be her guardian on June 10, 1778.
John Cooper, a minor under the age of 14, chose Peregrine Cooper to be his guardian on June 11, 1778.
Joseph Reed, a minor under the age of 14, chose Aquilla Page to be his guardian on August 12, 1778.
Temperance Reed, a minor under the age of 14, chose Aquilla Page to be her guardian on August 12, 1778.
Joseph McHard, son of Samuel and a minor under the age of 14, chose Isaac McHard to be his guardian on August 12, 1778.
George Peacock, son of George and a minor under the age of 14, chose Richard Peacock to be his guardian on August 12, 1778.
Elizabeth Cosden and Jeremiah Cosden, minor children of Jesse Cosden, deceased, chose Bathsheba Cosden to be their guardian on October 13, 1778.
Hannah Cooper and Martha Cooper, minor daughters of Hezekiah Cooper, deceased, chose Mary Cooper to be their guardian on October 13, 1778.
James Moore [no age given] was bound to Thomas Blake on October 13, 1778 until he reached age 21.
John Cooper, son of Hezekiah Cooper, deceased, received his

father's plantation, as noted in Court on October 27, 1778.
Joseph Wilson [no age given] was bound to Edward Scantlan on
  August 15, 1778 until he reached age 21.
John Stavely and William Stavely, minors under the age of 14, -
  John Myers was appointed their guardian on December 8, 1778.
Anna Graham and William Graham, minors under the age of 14, -
  Mary St. Clair was appointed their guardian on December 10
  1778.
William Frisby and Sarah Frisby, minors under the age of 14, -
  Marmaduke Tilden was appointed their guardian on February 9,
  1779.
Joseph Frisby, a minor under the age of 14, - Richard Frisby was
  appointed his guardian on February 9, 1779.
John Battershell, a minor under the age of 14, - John Moore was
  appointed his guardian on February 10, 1779.
William Pennington [no age given] was bound to John Williamson on
  February 10, 1779 until he reached age 21.
William Brown [no age given] was bound to John Eunick on February
  9, 1779 until he reached age 21.
Benjamin Worrell, a minor under the age of 14, chose James
  Bradsha [sic] to be his guardian on April 13, 1779.
Haley Charlotte Haley [sic], a minor under the age of 14 - George
  Moffitt was appointed her guardian on April 13, 1779.
Robert Little and George Little, minors under the age of 14,
  chose Nathaniel Knock to be their guardian on June 8, 1779.
Amos Reed, George Reed, and Araminta Reed, minors under the age
  of 14, - George Sanders was appointed their guardian on June
  9, 1779.
Samuel Miller [no age given] was bound to Moses Moffet on August
  10, 1779 until he reached age 21.
Richard Semans and David Semans, minors under the age of 14,
  chose John Zelofrow to be their guardian on August 10, 1779.
Sarah Haley and Harriott Haley, minors under the age of 14, chose
  Joseph Baxter to be their guardian on October 12, 1779.
Ann Massey, a minor under the age of 14, chose Daniel Toas Massey
  to be her guardian on October 12, 1779.
Rebecca Graham, a minor under the age of 14, was noted on October
  12, 1779 as being an orphan of James Graham, deceased.
Ephraim Stoops, a minor under the age of 14, - Charles Rollison
  was appointed his guardian on December 14, 1779.
Josias Tillar, James Tillar, and Samuel Tiller, minors under the
  age of 14, chose their brother George Tillar to be their
  guardian on December 14, 1779.
John Massey, a minor under the age of 14, - Josiah Massey was
  appointed his guardian on December 15, 1779.
Joseph Massey, a minor under the age of 14, chose Abraham
  Falconer to be his guardian on December 15, 1779.
Rebecca Massey, a minor under the age of 14, chose Daniel Toas
  Massey to be her guardian on December 15, 1779.
Risdon Carter, a mulatto about age 10, was bound to Charles Roby
  [Raley?] on December 15, 1779.
Peregrine Reed, a minor under the age of 14, chose Henry Hurt to
  be his guardian on December 15, 1779.
Richard Wethered and John Wethered, minor sons of William

Wethered, deceased, and Mary Wethered, his daughter, all under
the age of 14,, chose Philip Davis to be their guardian on
December 15, 1779.
Mary Smith, Thomas Smith, and William Smith, minors under the age
of 14, chose Matthew Smith to be their guardian on February
12, 1780.
The Court appointed David Crane's father [no name given] to be
his [David's] guardian on February 12, 1780.
James Welch, a minor under the age of 14 - Thomas Smith (Smyth)
was appointed his guardian on February 12, 1780.
John Bivins [no age given] was bound to William Atkisson on June
14, 1780 to learn to be a weaver.
John Writson, a minor under the age of 14, chose Nathaniel Glenn
to be his guardian on June 14, 1780.
William Gray [no age given] was bound to John Tittle, [Little?],
Jr. on June 14, 1780 to learn to be a cordwainer.
Daniel Ashley, a minor under the age of 14, chose William Ashley
to be his guardian on June 14, 1780.
Daniel Dulany, a minor under the age of 14, chose Mary
Cruchington (Crudgenton) to be his guardian on August 8, 1780.
Mary Freeman, a minor under the age of 14, - Joseph Williams was
appointed his guardian on August 8, 1780.
Richard Boyer, Thomas Boyer, and Augustine Boyer, minors under
the age of 14, - Mary Boyer was appointed their guardian on
August 8, 1780.
William Stavely, a minor under the age of 14, chose John Myers to
be his guardian on October 11, 1780.
Ephraim Stoops, a minor under the age of 14, chose David Stoops
to be his guardian on April 11, 1781.
Richard Peacock was appointed guardian for Prissilla Peacock,
Mary Peacock, Robert Peacock, Acquilla Peacock, and Sarah
Peacock, minors under the age of 14, on April 11, 1781.
John Layborne, a minor under the age of 14, chose Thomas Corse to
be his guardian on April 11, 1781.
William Cannaday, a minor under the age of 14, chose Richard
Ricaud to be his guardian on June 12, 1781.
Henerietta Griffith, a minor under the age of 14, chose Amelia
Charlotta Griffith to be her guardian on June 13 1781
Samuel Wilkins and Mary Wilkins, minors under the age of 14,
chose Samuel Wallis to be their guardian on August 14, 1781.
Joseph Rasin, a minor under the age of 14 and son of Joseph
Rasin, chose Jeremiah Ford (Foard) to be his guardian on
August 15, 1781.
James Welch, a minor under the age of 14, chose Thomas Smith to
be his guardian on August 15, 1781.
Thomas Chandler, a minor under the age of 14, chose Blackiston
Chandler to be his guardian on November 6, 1781.
Robert Randolph, a minor under the age of 14, chose Henry Wallis
to be his guardian on November 6, 1781.
Robert Ford, Trulock Ford, and William Ford, minors under the age
of 14, chose Edward Ford to be their guardian on December 19,
1781.
William Frisby, Jr., a minor under the age of 14, chose Marmaduke
Tilden to be his guardian on February 12, 1782.
George William Blackiston, a minor under the age of 14, chose

Marmaduke Medford to be his guardian on February 13, 1782.
John Little, a minor under the age of 14, chose Malachi Ambrose to be his guardian on February 13, 1782.
Thomas Wilkins, a minor under the age of 14 - William Bordley was appointed his guardian on February 14, 1782.
Ann Cosden and Mary Cosden, minors under the age of 14 - John Cosden was appointed their guardian on April 10, 1782.
William Dellahunte [no age given] was bound to Thomas Smyth on April 10, 1782 to learn to be a blacksmith.
Samuel Wheeler [no age given] was bound to William Vickers to learn to be a house carpenter and joiner on April 11, 1782.
Ann Wilkins, a minor under the age of 14 - Bartus Wilkins was appointed her guardian on April 10, 1782.
Rebecca Massey, a minor under the age of 14, chose Daniel Turner to be her guardian on June 11, 1782.
James Robinson [no age given] was bound to Francis Lennan to learn to be a weaver on June 12, 1782.
James Salsbury, a minor under the age of 14 - Isabella Salsbury was appointed his guardian on June 11, 1782.
Catharine Broaderick [no age given] was bound to Thomas Weaver and wife Celia Weaver on June 13, 1782.
William Boots, a minor under the age of 14 - James Cann was appointed his guardian on August 14, 1782.
Ann Cosdon and Mary Cosdon, minors under the age of 14, - Simon Hacket was appointed their guardian on December 12, 1782.
Richard Gresham, Ann Gresham, John Gresham, and Mary Gresham, orphans of Richard Gresham, deceased - Ann Dean was appointed their guardian on December 11, 1782.
James Battershell (Bathershell) was bound to Robert Reid to learn to be a blacksmith on December 12, 1782.
William Connor [no age given] was bound to John Scott to learn to be a cordwainer on October 28, 1782.
Joseph McHard, a minor of the age of 14, chose William Dawson to be his guardian on April 8, 1783.
Lambert Keaton and John Keaton, minors under the age of 14 - Cuthbert Hall and Josiah Massey were appointed joint guardians on April 8, 1783.
Susannah Cowarden, a minor under the age of 14 - Nathaniel Kennard was appointed her guardian on April 8, 1783.
William Kindal [no age given] was bound to Daniel Lamb on April 8, 1783 to learn to be a weaver.
Jesse Conden [no age given] was bound to Daniel Lamb on April 8, 1783 to learn to be a weaver.
Margaret Phillips was bound to Daniel Hull on April 9, 1783 until she reached age 16 or married.
Mary Cosden, a minor under the age of 14 - John Cosden was appointed her guardian on April 10, 1783.
Margaret McKinley was bound to James Plimpton (Phlintham) on June 11, 1783 until she reached age 16 or married.
Hugh McKinley was bound to James Plimpton (Phlintham) on June 11, 1783 to learn to be a cordwainer.
Elizabeth Guird was bound to Benjamin Deabnam [sic] on June 11, 1783 until she reached age 16 or married.
Samuel Wheler, Thomas Wheler, and Mary Wheler, minors under the

age of 14, chose William Dunn to be their guardian on June 11, 1783.
Mary Merritt and Samuel Merritt, minors under the age of 14 - Arthur Miller was appointed their guardian on August 16, 1783.
Mary Gresham, a minor of the age of 14, chose Ann Dean to be her guardian on August 16, 1783.
Ann Droan, a minor under the age of 14 - Samuel Gott was appointed her guardian on October 15, 1783.
Elizabeth Cosden and Jeremiah Cosden, minors under the age of 14 - William Merritt and Acquilla Page were appointed their guardians on October 17, 1783.
Thomas Cox was bound to Jonathan Comegys on October 14, 1783 to learn to be a common labour until he reached age 21.
Henry Gray was bound to Nicholas Brown on December 9, 1783 to learn to be a common labour until he reached age 21.
James Fennell was bound to Nicholas Brown on December 9, 1783 to learn to be a common labour until he reached age 21.
John Newcomb and Thomas Newcomb, both minors of the age of 14, chose Isaac Spencer to be their guardian on December 7, 1783.
William Lane was bound to Isaac Cannel on April 13, 1784 to learn to be a common labour until he reached age 21.
James Gibbs was bound to Isaac Cannel on April 13, 1784 to learn to be a common labour until he reached age 21.
Thomas Norman was bound to William Cole on June 8, 1784 to learn to be a weaver until he reached age 21.
Thomas Kinnard, a minor of the age of 14, chose Absolom McCoy to be his guardian on June 9, 1784.
William Jobson, a minor under the age of 14 - Michael Jobson was appointed his guardian on June 15, 1784.
James Darach, a minor of the age of 14, chose George Black to be his guardian on June 24, 1784.
Benjamin Richardson was bound to Daniel Shehawn [Shahawn] on June 24, 1784 to learn to be a common labour until he reached age 21.
Mary Semans, a minor of the age of 14, and Sarah Semans and Asher Semans, minors under the age of 14, chose Solomon Semans to be their guardian on June 25, 1784.
James Dwyer, a minor of the age of 14, chose John Dwyer to be his guardian on August 10, 1784.
Robert Roberts, Jr., a minor under the age of 14 - His father, Robert Roberts, was appointed his guardian on October 13, 1784.
Elizabeth Roberts, a minor of the age of 14 - Robert Roberts was appointed her guardian on October 13, 1784.
John Wethered, a minor of the age of 14, chose Richard Wethered to be his guardian on October 13, 1784.
James Yardsley, a minor under the age of 14 - James Claypoole was appointed his guardian on August 13, 1780.
Charles Lius [Lins?] was bound to Charles Tilden on October 14, 1784 to learn to be a common labour until he reached age 21.
James Batton was bound to Charles Tilden on October 14, 1784 to learn to be a common labour until he reached age 21.
William Ford and Joseph Trulock Ford, minors of the age of 14, chose Edward Ford to be his guardian on October 15, 1784.
James Geddings, a minor of the age of 14, chose Levinus Clarkson

to be his guardian on October 16, 1784.
Robert Ford, Jr., a minor of the age of 14, chose Robert Ford (his uncle) to be his guardian on December 14, 1784.
Mathew Reid, a minor of the age of 14, chose Alexander Briscoe to be his guardian on February 9, 1785.
Araminta Turner and Joseph Turner, minors under the age of 14 - Martha Turner was appointed her guardian on February 9, 1785.
Sarah Bordley, a minor of the age of 14, chose Mary Bordley to be her guardian on February 9, 1785.
Mary Pearce and James Pearce, minors under the age of 14 - Henry Pearce was appointed her guardian on February 9, 1785.
Mary Merritt and Samuel Merritt, minors under the age of 14 - Arthur Miller was appointed her guardian on February 10, 1785.
Thomas Wilkins, a minor of the age of 14, chose Samuel Wilkins to be his guardian on April 12, 1785.
Charles McDermot, a minor of the age of 14, chose Francis Lennan to be his guardian on April 12, 1785.
William Kirton was bound to John Writson Browning on April 12, 1785 to learn the art of malting and brewing until he reached age 21.
Nathaniel Hynson, a minor under the age of 14 - Mary Hynson was appointed his guardian on June 15, 1785.
Daniel Dulaney, a minor under the age of 14 - Hannah Dulaney was appointed his guardian on August 10, 1785.
John Lemon was bound to Francis Maslin on February 10, 1785 to learn the trade of shoemaking until he reached age 21.
John Newcomb and Thomas Newcomb, minors of the age of 14, chose William Merritt to be his guardian on October 14, 1785.
Catharine Scanlan, a minor under the age of 14 - Ann Scanlan was appointed her guardian on December 13, 1785.
James Scandlan, a minor under the age of 14 - Ann Scandlan was appointed his guardian on December 13, 1785.
Peregrine Whichcote, a minor under the age of 14 - Phillip Fray was appointed his guardian on December 13, 1785.
Susannah Cowarden, a minor under the age of 14 - Samuel Hosier was appointed his guardian on December 13, 1785.
Anna Maria McClean, William McClean, and Margaret McClean, all minors under the age of 14 - Mary McLean was appointed their guardian on March 3, 1786.
Isaac Spencer, a minor under the age of 14 - Hannah Spencer was appointed his guardian on April 11, 1786.
Ebenezer Blackiston, a minor of the age of 14, chose George William Blackiston to be his guardian on April 12, 1786.
George Gleaves, a minor of the age of 14, chose William Gleaves to be his guardian on April 13, 1786.
William Wicks, a minor of the age of 14, chose Robert Buchanan to be his guardian on June 13, 1786.
Rebecca Whichcote, a minor of the age of 14, chose Richard Willis, Jr. to be her guardian on June 13, 1786.
Charles Rigby was bound to Capt. John Curry on June 13, 1786 to learn to be a farmer until he reached age 21. "The child is 7 years old this day."
John Tiller and Samuel Tiller, minors of the age of 14, chose James Hatchison (Hatchason) to be their guardian on June 15,

1786.
Mary Hynson, the widow of Nathaniel Hynson, of Easter Neck Island in Kent County, Maryland, was appointed guardian to her son Nathaniel Hynson (recorded on June 21, 1785).
Negro Saunter, aged about 8 years old and the son of free negro Hannah, was bound to Thomas Smith to learn to be a common labour on April 15, 1784 until he reached age 21.
George French was bound to Phillip Chaplin on August 10, 1786 to learn to be a common labour until he reached age 21.
Thomas Quail was bound to James Smith on October 12, 1786 to learn to be a farmer until he reached age 21. "The boy is 9 years of age this day."
Experience Halbert was bound to James Smith on October 12, 1786 until she reached age 16 or married.
Joseph Read, a minor above the age of 14, chose Alexander Briscoe to be his guardian on December 16, 1786.
Meshach Reed, Benjamin Reed, and John Reed, all minors above the age of 14, chose John Lamb to be their guardian on December 16, 1786.
Nicholas Riley, a minor under the age of 14 - John Bantham was appointed his guardian on August 8, 1786.
John Whittington, a minor above the age of 14, chose Abraham Whittington as his guardian on February 26, 1787.
Elizabeth Furguson (Furgison), of Kent County, was bound to Edward Needles, of Talbot County, on February 13, 1787 until she reached age 16 or married.
James Whittington and Abraham Whittington, minors above the age of 14, chose Abraham Whittington to be their guardian on February 26, 1787.
James Grey, a minor above the age of 16 [sic], chose James Speer to be his guardian on April 10, 1786 [actually 1787].
Ebenezer Cray, a minor under the age of 14 - Ebenezer Reyner was appointed his guardian on April 11, 1787.
Ann Redgrave, Polly Redgrave, Isaac Redgave, and Elizabeth Redgrave, all minors under the age of 14 - John Miers, Jr. was appointed their guardian on April 11, 1787.
Charles Gordon and Joseph Gordon, minors under the age of 14 - Hannah Gordon was appointed their guardian on April 12, 1787.
Ann Gordon, a minor above the age of 14, chose John Nicholson to be her guardian on April 12, 1787.
John Massy, a minor above the age of 14, chose Daniel Toas Massy to be his guardian on June 12, 1787.
Augustine Boyer, a minor above the age of 14, chose William Grindage to be his guardian on June 13, 1787.
Richard Boyer and Thomas Boyer, minors under the age of 14 - William Grindage was appointed their guardian on June 13, 1787.
James Salsbury, a minor above the age of 14, chose Daniel Greenwood to be his guardian on June 13, 1787.
Thomas Bourke, a minor above the age of 14, chose Joseph Wilkinson to be his guardian on August 14, 1787.
Isaac Spencer, a minor above the age of 14, chose Hannah Spencer to be his guardian on August 14, 1787.
Joseph Mann, a minor above the age of 14, chose Ann Martha Hackett to be his guardian on August 15, 1787.

100   INHABITANTS OF KENT COUNTY, MARYLAND, 1637-1787

Negro James was bound to Thomas Granger on September 13, 1787 to learn the trade and mystery of a husbandman. "James is 16 years old this day."
Negro William was bound to Thomas Granger on September 13, 1787 to learn the trade and mystery of a husbandman. "William is 16 years old this day."
Ruben Willis and Joshua Willis, minors under the age of 14 - Martha Willis was appointed their guardian on October 10, 1787.
Jno. Stavly, a minor above the age of 14, chose Luke Miers to be his guardian on December 11, 1787.
Thomas Ellis, a minor above the age of 14, chose Edward Clemans to be his guardian on December 11, 1787.
Lambert Cayton, a minor above the age of 14, chose William Turner to be his guardian on December 11, 1787.
Cornelius Willis, a minor above the age of 14, chose Martha Willis to be his guardian on December 12, 1787.

ABSTRACTS OF KENT COUNTY COURT PROCEEDINGS, 1647-1676
(Ref: *Archives of Maryland*, Volume 54)

KENT COUNTY COURT HELD AT PHILIP CONIER'S HOUSE, JANUARY 3, 1647
Present were Capt. Robert Vaughan, Commander, Mr. Thomas Bradnox, Mr. Philip Conier, Mr. Edward Commins, and Mr. Francis Brooke.
John Metham filed a complaint against Francis Lumbard.
John Winchester and wife filed a complaint against Edward Commins.
[Note: The following entries were made at this time, but referred to a later date. A number of other entries are also out of order.]
Henry Morgan was one of the Judges at the Court in January, 1650.
Francis Lumbard was Sheriff in 1650.
Walter Weeks of the County of Northumberland gave a bill of sale to George Croutch of Isle of Kent County for cattle on the island.

KENT COUNTY COURT HELD ON JANUARY 29, 1648
Present were Capt. Robert Vaughan, Mr. Philip Conner, and Mr. Nicholas Browne.
Capt. Robert Vaughan, Commander of this Island, filed a complaint against William Laut, planter.
John Winchester, of Isle of Kent, styled himself "cordwainer."
Henry Morgan was Sheriff in 1648.
Margaret Brent appointed Zachary Wade her lawful attorney on January 13, 1648.
Capt. Robert Vaughan filed a complaint against John Gresham on October 2, 1648.
Robert Dunn (Downe) of Isle of Kent conveyed land to William Body on March 22, 1648. Witnesses were Thomas Pett and Thomas Belcher.

KENT COUNTY COURT HELD IN 1651
Thomas Marsh, gentleman, recorded his hogs and cattle mark on January 22, 1651.

KENT COUNTY COURT PROCEEDINGS, 1647-1676   101

Thomas Marsh was chirurgeon in Kent County in 1651.
In a bill of sale from Margaret Brent to Zachary Wade and Edd
Claxston, in June, 1649, she styled herself "Attorney for my
brother Giles Brent."
In the gift of "Marie Brent" to George Deane, son of John Deane,
in 1651, styled herself "Attorney to my brother Giles Brent."
Hannah Heuett (Hewett), administratrix of her deceased husband
Robert Hewett, sold land to Mary Risbrooke, administratrix of her
deceased husband William Risbrooke, on July 28, 1651. Witnesses
were Abraham Hollman, George Crouch, and Walter Smith.
At a Court held on January 12, 1651, the following Commissioners
were present: Capt. Robert Vaughan, Commander; Mr. Philip Conner;
Mr. Henry Morgan; Mr. Thomas Ringgold; Mr. Nicholas Browne; Mr.
Thomas Bradnox; and, Mr. Joseph Wickes.

ISLE OF KENT, APRIL 5, 1652: "We, whose names are hereafter
subscribed, do promise and engage ourselves to be true and
faithful to the Commonwealth of England, without King or House of
Lords: Thomas Ward, Thomas South, *Thomas Wetherell, Thomas Pett,
*Thomas Taylor, *Henry Carlyen, Francis Lumbard, *John Hud,
*Robert Martin, *John Richeson, *Henry Taylor, Will Leedes, John
Sepsen, *Anthony Calliway, *John Gibson, Robert Vaughan, Phillip
Commins, Thomas Ringgold, *John Smith, *Henry Ashley, *John
Philips, John Gould, *Edward Ebes, *John Smyth, *Matthew Read,
*Will Jones, *John Ringgold, *Francis Bright, Edward Coppedge,
Edmt. Weebe, John Russell, Richard Slater, Marke Benton, *John
Maconick, *Will Band, *Francis Barnes, *Henry Clay, *Roger
Baxter, *James Horner, *Henry Weest, Isa. Ilive, *Thomas Weest,
*Thomas Bradnox, *Henry Morgan, Joseph Wickes, William Elliot,
*Robert Halters, Richard Blunt, George Croutch, Edward Burton,
Abraham Hollman, John Winchester, Nicholas Picurd, Nicholas
Browne, *David Geldersen, *Will Price, Thomas Hill, John Dean,
*Edward Coxe, Robert Dunn, John Coursey, John Errickson, Andrew
Hanson, and Andrew Anderson." [Note: Those with an asterisk (*)
made their marks.]

KENT COUNTY COURT HELD IN 1652
On February 25, 1650, Henry Morgan assigned his land patent to
Edward Coppedge. Witnesses were George Crouch and Deverox Godwin.
On May 29, 1652, it was recorded that Henry Morgan, planter, had
transported himself to the Island of Kent in 1637 to dwell, and
was acknowledged by William Stone, Lieutenant of the Province in
1650.
Robert Clarke was Surveyor General of the Province of Maryland on
June 2, 1652.
Deposition of John Gould, aged 40 or thereabouts, was taken in
which he stated his master was Mr. Carlyen, and he also mentioned
Francis Brights.
Deposition of Christian Hill, aged about 45, wife of Thomas Hill,
was taken in which she stated Goodman Burton had shot a goose on
January 9, 1652, and when Thomas Farington, servant of Mr. Philip
Conier, went on the ice towards the goose he fell in and drowned.

KENT COUNTY COURT HELD AT FRANCIS LUMBARD'S HOUSE AUGUST 16, 1652
Francis Lumbard was Sheriff of Kent County on August 16, 1652.
James Wilson, a Scot and servant of Capt. Thomas Bradnox, died on August 19, 1652, "of an intermitting fever with the dropsy or scurvy and the stripes given him by his Master not long before his death were not material." William Fuller served on the inquest with eleven others [not named].
Thomas Hynson was Clerk of the County of Kent in 1652.
Edward Coppedge was found guilty of living with Elizabeth Risby before he was able to prove the death of her husband William Risby. Edward was fined and Elizabeth was given 15 lashes.
Mark Benton petitioned the Court for his freedom from Robert Vaughan.
Capt. Robert Vaughan was fined for insolent language to the Court.
Thomas Ward was arrested upon "suspicion of felony" following the death of a maid who had been whipped for running away.
In November, 1652, the wife of Francis Hunt petitioned the Court that her husband "was lately slain by the Indians upon the Isle of Kent."
Thomas Marsh and John Russell arbitrated the case between Major Joseph Wickes and Dr. Thomas Ward.
Thomas Ringgold, aged 43 years, gave deposition that he heard William Jones at Thomas Hinson's house say that "he would question Thomas Ward about the death of his maid for he would bring him to his twelve God-fathers, which was John Hood, and Elizabeth Risby, and Richard Blunt, and he would prosecute the suit."
Deposition of Henry Carlein mentioned Jane Hood, wife of John Hood, and she insisted that Elizabeth Risby was the lawful wife of Edward Coppedge, "but only for the ceremony."
In December, 1652, Thomas Weest [sic], servant to Henry Morgan, gentleman, obtained his freedom.
Deposition of Thomas Pett, aged 40 or thereabouts, mentioned William Jones who had come from the Susquehanahs and who had seen Andrew the Sanyeard (Spaniard).
Giles Bleake (Blake) transported himself into this province and demanded his 100 acres on January 19, 1652.
Robert Clarke surveyed 2,000 acres for William Brantwell, gentleman, and Thomas Broadnax, planter, on the Isle of Kent on February 2, 1652.
On February 12, 1652, Zephania Smith bound over his plantation as security for his debt. William Chandler stood for him (and made his mark).
Hannah Lee chose George Crouch as her lawful attorney on July 28, 1651.
Thomas Broadnox conveyed land to Giles Blake in 1652. Witnesses were Hassadia Hill and Thomas Hill.
John Winchester conveyed land on Isle of Kent to Francis Barnes, of Severn. Witnesses were Oliver Sprye and William Drury.
William Jones, being sick in body, made his will on February 5, 1652, mentioning Mr. Marsh, Capt. Jacob, John Winchester, Mr. Ward, Gov. Stone, and Thomas Pett.
Clerk of the Court in 1652 signed his name "Thom's Hynson, Sen."

Certificate for 300 acres was granted to John Conitt for coming to this island with his wife and child on May 1, 1652. Thomas Marsh, merchant, obtained judgment against the estate of William Jones. Isaac Iler confirmed the testimony of Francis Lumbard.
On March 8, 1652, John Hood, being sick in body, made his will and mentioned his wife Joan Hood and son Robert Hood. Witnesses were John Russell and William Elleyott.

KENT COUNTY COURT HELD IN 1653
On June 1, 1653, William Elleott, planter, mentioned "Jone Dunn and her heirs and the estate that her Father Porter left her by will after her mother's decease." Jone Dunn stated she was a daughter of William Porter, deceased.
Inventory of Robert Short was taken on November 20, 1651, by Robert Martin and Richard Blunt, appraisers.
It was also recorded that Robert Shart [sic] arrived on Isle of Kent prior to December 9, 1640 and subsequently conveyed his patent to William Jones and Francis Lumbard, who then conveyed it to Thomas Belcher in 1651.
Francis Lumbard was removed from the office of High Sheriff "for neglect of duty" on August 3, 1653, and Thomas Bradnox was appointed in his place.
Depositions of John Salter, aged 27 or thereabouts, and John Winchester, aged 30 or thereabouts, were taken in 1653. John Brewer and Thomas Ringgold witnessed the statement of Francis Lumbard on August 15, 1653.
On January 21, 1641 [sic], Robert Heuett and Henry Bellamy, planters of Isle of Kent, conveyed land to Roger Baxter. "In this bill there is to be paid one peck of corn for rent at Kent Mill." Witness was John Bennett. Roger Baxter conveyed the land to Robert Dunne and John Richeson on September 18, 1652. Witnesses were George Crouch and Nicholas Peckard. Robert Donn [sic] conveyed his part to Thomas Marsh who conveyed it to Henry Carline, who then conveyed it to Thomas Hill in 1653.
Depositions of Thomas Hill, aged 50 or thereabouts, and John Dobb, aged 26 or thereabouts, were taken, the latter stating the conveyance occurred "in Cherrytime."
Statement was recorded on October 16, 1651, that Hannah Heuett, the late widow and relict of Robert Heuett, was now the wife of Hugh Love, and Edward Cummins was lately deceased.
On February 5, 1652, George Crouch conveyed land over to Henerie Carline and Frances Lumber. Witnesses were John Gould and Thomas Hill.

KENT COUNTY COURT HELD ON MARCH 1, 1654
Phillip Conier was appointed Chief Commander of the County of Kent, within the Province of Maryland. Also appointed as his assistants (Commissioners) were Joseph Weeckes, Thomas Ringgold, Thomas Hinson, John Russell, Henery Morgan, William Eliot, and Henery Carline. Signed by William Fuller and William Durand. Mentioned subsequently were Col. William Claiborne, Capt. Edmund Curtis (Commander of the Ginny Frigate). Capt. William Fuller, Leonard Strong, and Richard Ewen.

INHABITANTS OF KENT COUNTY, MARYLAND, 1637-1787

KENT COUNTY COURT was held at the house of Lieut. Hinson, High Sheriff of Kent County, on April 25, 1655.
John Deare filed a complaint against Nicolas Broune [Browne] for slander, claiming he was a thief and also slandering his wife [no name given].
Peeter Knight filed a complaint against Mr. Conier regarding the estate of Robert Short, deceased.
Izake Ilive filed a complaint against John Salter. Mrs. Broadnax was mentioned by attorney Henery Morgan.
Mathew Reade, John Salter, William Price, Henery Telior, Henery Clay, and Marie Croutch were charged with "misbehavior in deboist drinking, profaning the Sabbath, and discharging guns."
Deposition of Thomas South, aged 30 or thereabouts, was taken and mentioned "Franchis Broockes of Marieland" and "John Salter of Bevernecke."

KENT COUNTY COURT HELD ON SEPTEMBER 17, 1655
Rachell Carline, wife of Henery Carline, bound over all her hogs as security to Henery Morgan in repayment of her debt to him in June, 1655.
William Clapham gave authority to Henery Carline and William Eliott to apprehend James Goothward and wife Marie Goothward, John a Dutchman, and Elizabeth Ganeere, being runaway servants who had stolen from him. Witnesses were Thomas Madestard and John Harnoll.
John Masticke was cleared from all service due by Henery Carline on July 29, 1655. Witnesses were Mathew Reed (Read) and Henry Clay.
Andrew Hanson died and left his wife Annicak Hanson, four small children, and "she was big with the fifth child." Her oldest son, Hance Hanson, she bestowed to Joseph Weeckes until Hance reached age 21, he being at present 9 years of age.
Marke Benton conveyed some cattle to Thomas Hill. Witnesses were John Deare and Allexander Monro on August 7, 1655.

KENT COUNTY COURT HELD AT THOMAS HINSON'S HOUSE ON OCTOBER 29, 1655
Present were Mr. Philip Conier, Capt. Joseph Weeckes, Capt. John Russell, and Mr. William Eliot.
James Horner filed a complaint against Andrew Hanson, Valerus Leo, and Swan Swanson, stating these Swedes owed him two barrels of corn for his work. Henery Morgan filed a similar complaint.
Thomas Ward, aged 49 or thereabouts, gave his deposition, as did William Eliot, aged 34 or thereabouts, Thomas Hinson, aged 36 or thereabouts, and Thomas Ringgold, aged 44 or thereabouts.
Robert Gammer, planter, of the Isle of Kent, bound over his tobacco crop to Anthonie Calloway to satisfy a debt on July 16, 1655.

KENT COUNTY COURT HELD IN 1655
On November 29, 1655, Henery Morgan requested and received payment for taking care of Valerus Leo for 8 weeks and burying him after he died.
Anicak Hanson filed a complaint against the estate of Valerus Leo

KENT COUNTY COURT PROCEEDINGS, 1647-1676   105

as he was indebted to her [deceased] husband.
Deposition of Thomas Hinson, Sheriff, aged 35 or thereabouts, was taken, as was that of Anicak Hanson, widow, aged 36 or thereabouts.
John Elisse filed a complaint that Robert Gamer was indebted to him, and Richard Blunt did the same.
Thomas Hill filed a complaint that William Fletcher was indebted to him, as did Franchis Barnes against Thomas Ward, and Henery Carline against Thomas Ward.
Mathew Read filed a complaint against John Deare. William Leeds, planter, of Isle of Kent, conveyed land and all buildings to John Erickson, adjoining that of Thomas Ward. Witnesses were Morgan Williams and Robert Holton.

VITAL RECORDS:
Richard Blunt was born in 12th month, 3rd day, 1654.
Marie Baxster was born in 2nd month, 25th day, 1655.
Barberi Hanson, daughter of Anicake, was born in 8th month, 1655.
Henery Claye was born in 5th month, 22nd day, 1655.
Charles Vaughan, son of Capt. Vaughan, was born in 8th month, 30th day, 1655.
Christian Deare was born in 6th month, 1655.
Elizabeth Picket was born in 8th month, 19th day, 1655.
John Winchester's daughter was born in 2nd month, 23rd day, 1656.
Henery Morgan's daughter was born in 8th month, 1st day, 1656.
John Dabbs and Nan Eares were married in 8th month, 1655.
Roger Baxster and Mary Croutch were married in 11th month, 6th day, 1655.
Thomas Hill, Jr. and Margret Balie were married in 1st month, 4th day, 1655.
Andrew Elenor and Anicake Hanson were married in 3rd month, 5th day, 1656.
Capt. Joseph Weikes married Marie Hartwell in 5th month, 7th day, 1656.
Mr. Broadnox servant was buried in 5th month, 4th day, 1655.
Mr. Nicolas Broun was buried in 5th month, 21st day, 1655.
Valerus Leo was buried in 8th month, 4th day, 1655.
Joane Baxster was buried in 9th month, 14th day, 1655.
Thomas Boulton was buried in 9th month, 22nd day, 1655.
Edward Tarant was buried in 9th month, 23rd day, 1655.
George Croutch was buried in 10th month, 2nd day, 1655.
Elizabeth Baxster was buried in 10th month, 1655.
Andrew Anderson Hanson was buried in 4th month, 1655.
Mr. Brodnox servant John Pritchet was buried in 6th month, 1655.
John Smith's child John was buried in 7th month, 18th day, 1655.
John Elise's child named Jno. Elisse was buried in 5th month, 16th day, 1656.
Robert Dunne's child named William Dunne was buried in 5th month, 19th day, 1656.
Mr. Weikes child Joseph was buried in 6th month, 6th day, 1656.
Mr. Weikes servant Anne Gould was buried in 6th month, 14th day, 1656.
Thomas Hawkines of Poples was buried in 8th month, 12th day, 1656.
Edward Purlin: Scott was buried in 8th month, 19th day, 1656.

KENT COUNTY COURT HELD IN 1655

Edward Tarant, being very sick of body, made his will on November 21, 1655, mentioning Capt. Joseph Wickes who took care of him, his [Edward's] sisters Rebecka and Elizabeth, "my Nurst in Bristoll," and Charles Steward. Will proved on November 29, 1655, by testimony of Capt. Joseph Wickes and Charles Stuart.
On January 1, 1655, a caveat was filed by Thomas Hill, Sr., noting Mr. Thomas Hatton had lately deceased.
Thomas Witherell filed a complaint against the estate of Nicolas Broune.
Anthony Calloway filed a complaint against Thomas Poier and William Johnson, two men from Accomacke, who came to this island and carried away Robert Gamer.
Depositions were taken from John Winchester, aged 29 or thereabouts, and Henerie Telior, aged 26 or thereabouts.
Isake Ilive filed a complaint against Edward (Ned) Rogers, and James Horner, aged 43 or thereabouts, gave his deposition.
George Hall filed a complaint against William Leedes.
William Eliot and John Ringgold filed a complaint against John Salter, his wife Jane Salter, and William Price, for stealing hogs from him.
Deposition of Mrs. Francis Morgan, aged 30 years or thereabouts, was taken and she mentioned Mathew Read, Goodie Bright, and Goodie Winchester.
Mrs. [blank] Marsh filed complaints against the estates of Andrew Hanson, deceased, and Valerus Leo, deceased.
Joseph Weickes filed a complaint against the estate of Edward Tarent, deceased, as did Thomas Hinson, Robert Martin, George Hall, Mr. Broune, Capt. Weicks, Mr. Hinson, Mr. Conier, John Winchester, and Mr. Brodnox.
Roger Baxster, planter, expressed his "being truly affected in love to Marye [Marie] Croutch, widow and late relict of George Croutch, deceased, and fully determined God willing to take her to be my wedded wife." He also mentioned she has children of her own.
Isake Ilive acknowledged a sale of cattle to Thomas Wetherly.
Robert Vaughan acknowledged a gift of a cow to Rebecka Lumbar, daughter of Franchis Lumbar, and if she died before marriage it went to "Jane Salter, the wife of John Salter, natural and own mother to the said Rebecka Lumbar. The males of the stock (until marriage) to John Salter, father in law to the child."
Depositions of Isacke Ilive and Nicolas Pickard, aged [both blank], was taken on January 1, 1655, stating he met with George Croutch at the time of his sickness and mention his will to son George Croutch, daughter Marie Croutch, and his wife [not named].

KENT COUNTY COURT HELD AT THOMAS HINSON'S HOUSE ON FEBRUARY 1, 1655

Present were Mr. Phillip Connier, Capt. Joseph Wickes, Mr. Thomas Ringgold, Capt. John Russell, Mr. William Eliot, and Mr. Henery Carline.
Thomas Broadnax filed a complaint against Capt. Joseph Weickes.
Thomas Hinson filed a complaint against John Deare.
Capt. John Russell filed a complaint against the estate of

Nicolas Broune, deceased, as did also Capt. Robert Vaughan.
John Deare filed a complaint against Anthonie Calloway.
John Erickson filed a complaint against the estate of Edward Tarrent, deceased.
Mr. Thomas Coll filed a complaint against John Gibson.
Mr. Thomas Hinson filed a complaint against John Salter and John Deare.
Deposition of Margret Balie, aged 21 or thereabouts, was taken and she mentioned John Salter and wife Jane Salter, Widdow Bright, and Moll Croutch.
Deposition of Henery Morgan, aged 42 or thereabouts, was taken.
Mr. Thomas Ringgold filed a complaint against Thomas Hill, Sr.
Edmund Burton petitioned the court regarding his right to land.
Deposition of Mr. Thomas Hinson, aged 35 or thereabouts, was taken and mentioned Mr. Marsh and Roger Baxster.
Deposition of Capt. John Russell, aged 34 or thereabouts, was taken and mentioned Franchis Barnes, William Price and Mr. Marsh.
Deposition of Anthony Calloway, aged 26 or thereabouts, was taken and mentioned William Price and Mr. Marsh.
Robert Martin [Martine], planter, of Isle of Kent, sold some cows to William Leedes [Leeds] and Edward Tarrent. Witnesses were Joseph Wickes and Henery Ashley.
John Erickson and Edward Tarrant divided some land between them on October 22, 1655.
Thomas Broadnox conveyed land originally patented to Thomas Stent on May 17, 1641, to Henery Clay on May 7, 1653. Henerie Clay assigned his rights over to Robert Martin on October 13, 1655.
Robert Martin [Martine] sold some cows to Charles Steward on November 28, 1655.
Deposition of Anthonie Calloway, aged 26 or thereabouts, was taken on November 1, 1655 and he mentioned Mrs. Broadnox, Mr. Ringgold, Capt. Fleet, and Mr. Carline.

KENT COUNTY COURT HELD AT THOMAS HINSON'S HOUSE ON MARCH 1, 1655
Mr. Henery Morgan filed a complaint against John Deare.
Robert Martin was arrested by Mr. Thomas Hinson [case continued].
A warrant was issued for Edward Rogers to appear before the Court.
Mr. Thomas South filed a complaint against John Salter.
Sarah Marsh made her "S" mark on a list of attachments. Listed were Mr. Carlile, Mr. Morgan, Mr. Russell, Joseph Kent, and Gyles Blake.
Ritchard Blunt, planter, gave a heifer to his daughter Grace Blunt on March 1, 1655.
Robert Martin sold a heifer to John Dabbs, and also sold some land to John Dabbs and Thomas Witherell.
John [Johen] Erickson sold some land to Joseph Weickes on March 30, 1656.
George Hall recorded his cattle and hog marks on April 24, 1656.

KENT COUNTY COURT HELD AT THOMAS HINSON'S HOUSE ON MAY 1, 1656
Edward Rogers found guilty of a breach of an Act of Assembly (he shot a wild turkey on Sunday) and he claimed ignorance of the law.
John Smith was arrested by Mr. Thomas Hinson [case continued].

Deposition of Thomas Witherell, aged 47 or thereabouts, was taken and mentioned John Smith, Mr. Broadnox, and George Hall.
Deposition of George Hall, aged 34 or thereabouts, was taken.
An attachment against the estate of Gilles [Gyles] Bleake, deceased, on April 27, 1656, mentioned Thomas Cole.
Deposition of Henerie Carline, aged 48 or thereabouts, was taken and mentioned Thomas Cole.
Deposition of Henery Gott, aged 20 or thereabouts, was taken and mentioned Mr. Carline, Mr. Blake, and Mr. Cole.
Deposition of Thomas Cole, aged 50 or thereabouts, was taken and mentioned Gyles Bleake.
Deposition of William Price, aged 30 or thereabouts, was taken and mentioned Mr. Hinson, John Salter, and Mr. Broune's estate.
Deposition of John Salter, aged 32 or thereabouts, was taken and mentioned William Price and Mr. Hinson.
James Horner was bound by the Court to pay Henerie Morgan in 1656. Witnesses were Samuel Chew and John Hatton.
Roger Baxster was bound by the Court to pay Hugh Lee in 1656. Witnesses were John Jenkins and Richard Clarke.
Deposition of Thomas Reade, aged 17 or thereabouts, was taken and mentioned Goodman Martine, Goodie Martine, William Price, Henery Ashley, and a young Robine Martine.
Deposition of William Price, aged 31 or thereabouts, was taken and mentioned Goodman Martine, Thomas Reade, Henery Ashley, and a young Robbine Martine.

KENT COUNTY COURT HELD ON JULY 1, 1656
Roger Baxster filed a complaint against John Deare, as also did Capt. Robert Vaughana, attorney for Mr. Abott.
Deposition of Mr. Henery Carline. aged 40 or thereabouts, was taken.
Deposition of Thomas Hill, aged 52 or thereabouts, was taken.
Deposition of Robert Dunne, aged 26 or thereabouts, was taken and mentioned Goodman Martine and Edmund Burton.
John Deare, planter, paid his debt of tobacco to Robert Dunne.
John Deare sold eight cattle to Mr. Henery Carline for the use of Mr. Thomas Hawkines. Witnesses were Thomas Coll and Thomas Hill.

KENT COUNTY COURT HELD AT PHILIP CONNIER'S HOUSE ON JULY 5, 1656
Henery Carline was appointed Sheriff of Kent County. His securities were Thomas Hawkins, of Popeles Island, and Thomas Coll, of the County of Providence. Witnesses were Oliver Sprye and John Salter.
Henery Carline, attorney for Mr. Thomas Hawkines, assigned his right to a servant named James Gunsseill to John Deare.
Deposition of Ritchard Blunt, aged 35 or thereabouts, was taken and mentioned Mr. Ilive, Henery Clay, Mr. South, and Zacherie Wade.
Deposition of Mr. Thomas South, aged 38 or thereabouts, was taken and mentioned Ritchard Blunt, Mr. Thomas "at Siverne," and Mr. Owines.
Deposition of Anne Gould, aged 23 or thereabouts, was taken and mentioned that Mr. Owines "threw her upon a bed and hee allsoe forst her and had the usse of her bodie, which was much to her

greife."

KENT COUNTY COURT HELD ON SEPTEMBER 1, 1656
Deposition of Thomas Hill, agd 52 or thereabouts, was taken and mentioned Goodie Martin, William Price, Thomas Reade, and Henery Ashley.
Deposition of Thomas South, aged 38 or thereabouts, was taken and mentioned Tom Reed,
Deposition of Nicolas Pickard, aged 46 or thereabouts, was taken and mentioned Nicholas Broune, George Croutch and Capt. Vaughan.
Deposition of William Price, aged 30 or thereabouts, was taken and mentioned John Salter, John Ringgold, and Thomas Hinson, Jr.
Deposition of John Ringgold, aged 20 or thereabouts, was taken and mentioned John Salter, William Price, and Thomas Hinson, Jr., and Mr. Hatton's store.
Thomas Hawkines, of Nomeny in the County of Westmoreland [Virginia] sold half of Poplies Island and half of his land on Kent Island to Seath Foster on January 25, 1654. Witnesses were Edward Hull and Henry Vincent.

KENT COUNTY COURT HELD ON OCTOBER 11, 1656
Mr. Thomas Hinson filed a complaint against Mr. Thomas Ward.
Deposition of Joseph Weickes, aged 36 or thereabouts, was taken.
Deposition of Nicollas Broadaway, aged 24 or thereabouts, was taken.
Mr. Thomas Broadnox filed a complaint against Anthony Calloway.
Deposition of Thomas Hinson, aged 36 or thereabouts, was taken and mentioned John Deare and Thomas Broadnox.
Deposition of Henery Carline, aged 47 or thereabouts, was taken and mentioned John Deare, Anthonie Calloway, and Thomas Brodnox.
Deposition of Thomas Broadnox, aged 57 or thereabouts, was taken and mentioned John Salter, Roger Baxster, and Mr. Broockes of Marieland.
Deposition of Roger Baxster, aged 46 or thereabouts, was taken.
Thomas Hinson, Justice of the Peace, filed a complaint against Henerie Carlin.
Deposition of Hassadia Hill, aged 19 or thereabouts, was taken.
Deposition of Christian Hill [age blank], wife of Thomas Hill, was taken.

KENT COUNTY COURT HELD ON DECEMBER 2, 1656
Present were Mr. Phillip Conner, Commander, and Capt. Joseph Wicke, Mr. Thomas Ringgold, Mr. Henery Morgan, Capt. John Russell, and Mr. Will Elleyet, Commissioners.
Depositions of Nic Bradway and Charles Steward were taken.
Constable Jo: Elles brought Mary Hartwell, the now wife of Mr. Joseph Wickes, for bringing up a bastard upon the island and charging Mr. Wickes with the "begiting" of the said child.
Charged with fighting on the Lord's Day were Capt. Russell and John Gibson.
Charged with "corn planting violations" were Mr. Ward, William Leeds and John Deare.
Depositions of Thomas South, Isack Ilive and Henery Clay were taken.
Robert Martin, of the Isle of Kent in the Province of Maryland,

sold his plantation, livestock and tobacco crop to Mathew Reed on January 17, 1656. Robert Martin also released Elizabeth Martin, "my now lawful wife," from any right, title or claim to said property on January 25, 1656, and she acknowledged the same. Capt. John Russell, gentleman, of the Isle of Kent, sold his plantation to John Jenkins and Henery Goot on December 20, 1656. Statement recorded that John Deare, planter, of Isle of Kent, transported himself and his wife into Maryland in 1647 and settled on the east side of Cox Creek. He assigned over his right to this patent to Francis Hunt on May 31, 1652. Then, Margret Hunt, late wife of Francis Hunt, deceased, assigned over her right and title in this patent to John Dear on February 1, 1652.

KENT COUNTY COURT HELD ON FEBRUARY 2, 1656
Andrew Ellenor was arrested in a matter of an unpaid debt.
Nathanell Utie sued John Raby over a matter of an unpaid debt.
Depositions of Henery Teyler and Thomas Hinson, Jr. were taken.
Tabitha Short came to Court and chose Henery Morgan as her guardian.
Thomas Belcher sued John Ereckson over a matter of an unpaid debt.
Thomas Hill sued Thomas Warde over a matter of an unpaid debt.
Deposition of Ann Hinson, aged 43 or thereabouts, was taken.
Deposition of John Salter was taken and he stated that he heard Mr. Ringgold call Capt. Wickes a whore master and Capt. Wickes replied "it was better to be a whore master then a thief as he was."
Deposition of John Ringgold was taken and he stated he "was at Bever Necke sometime suddenly after Andrew Hanson died."
Depositions of James Rigby, Capt. Robert Vaughan, John Salter, Thomas South, Isack Ilive, and James Horner were taken.
Mr. Seath Foster petitioned the Court against the estate of John Squibb, deceased.
John Erecksen confessed in Court that he was indebted to Capt. William Fuller.
Deposition of Ann Murell, aged 35 or thereabouts, was taken and mentioned Edward Copedge and wife, and Mary Baxter and her husband and children (two boys).
Depositions of Thomas Bradnox and Robert Dunn were taken and mentioned John Deare.
Deposition of Gregory Murell, aged 36 or thereabouts, was taken.
Depositions of Ann Murell, John Salter, Henery Clay, John Ereckson, Is: Ilive, and Elizabeth Clay, aged 34 or thereabouts, were taken.
Francis Brookes, of St. Mary's County, sold "Bever Neck" on the Island of Kent to Thomas Hinson, of Kent County, on September 26, 1656. Witnesses were Well [William] Michell and John Sutton.

KENT COUNTY COURT HELD ON NOVEMBER 19, 1657
Present were Mr. Edward Loydd [sic], Mr. Samuel Withers, Mr. Phillip Conner, Mr. Thomas Ringgold, Capt. Joseph Wickes, and Mr. Henry Morgan.
Mathew Read filed a complaint against Thomas Hynson.
An agreement was signed between Robert Martine and Henery Ashley

on October 11, 1656, and witnessed by John Dabes.
Capt. Robert Vaughan sold a brown bull to John Salter on October 3, 1656. Witnesses were Marke Benson and Peter Parker.

KENT COUNTY ORPHANS COURT HELD ON NOVEMBER 1, 1656
Tabitha Short, orphaned daughter of Robert Short, deceased, was present.
Deposition of Mr. Henery Morgan, aged 40 or thereabouts, was taken.
Inventory of the estate of Mr. Nicolas Broune, deceased, was taken and the following persons were owed money as of July 24, 1655: John Deare, Franchis Lumber, William Joanes, John Cowrsy, Thomas Pett, Franchis Brookes, John Smith, William Heade, John Jacob, George Crouch, Owin Jeames, Thomas Keynes, Edward Claxston, Thomas Hill, Andrew Hanson, Valerus Leo, James Horner, Henery East, Misteris Mary Brent, William Wilkeson, and Mathew Reade. Witnesses were George Crouch and Nicholas Peckard.

KENT COUNTY COURT HELD ON DECEMBER 19, 1656
"It hath appeared unto the Court by Francis Barnes that John Day gave unto his wife and to her children after her death one hefer and her increase forever only the said Francis Barnes to have the maell cattell for his care in looking after them...[and including] a lame hefer of Robert Halton's marke."
Robert Dunn gave an account of "John Hud by will did give his sunn Robert a cow, a calve and a long gunn and a sow."
Roger Baxter gave an account "that he hath in his possetion of his sunn Francis three of femall cattell; that came of a sow pidg that his godfather Francis Brookes did give him, and 2 gunnes." He also acknowledged that Capt. Robert Vaughan "did give his sunn Robert a sow pidg."
Mary Baxter gave an account that "George Crouch her late husband deseased did by will give unto his sunn George Crouch two heffers."
Thomas Ward gave an account that "Mr. Comings and Francis Brookes som ten or eleven yeares since did give unto Elizabeth Comens, the daughter of the said Comings, one heffer" (cow now called Betty). "And there was alsoe given by Misteris Comings in the time of her weddowhood nien head of femall [cattle] to be equally devided between her two daughters Elizabeth and Sarah...the children of Edward Comings deseased."
A copy of the "inventory of the goods and estate of Misteris Francis Cox, deseased," as taken by Francis Lumburd and Robert Short on August 15, 1648, was recorded. A list of debts paid included the following: Doctor Hooper, for curing his hand; Mr. Ebdon, for phisicke diet and lodging; Misteris Margrit Brent, for sugar and spice and strong waters in the the time of Mister Cox's sickness; Richard Hull, for a coffin; Mr. Fenicke, for a winding sheet; Mr. John Winchester, for helping to tend Misteris Cox in the time of her sickness; Mary Martin, for tending Misteris Cox; Capt. Robert Vaughan, for tobacco due; John Dandy, for tobacco due; Mr. Bradnox, "for a shollups sayell and roopes;" Capt. Gilles Brent, attorney of Mr. Brookes, paid by order of the court; Person [Parson] Rosior "for coming to christen young Will Cox;" Mr. Conner, "for a hat which Mr. Cox had of him;" and,

Misteris Bradnox, "by an order from Severne."
Account of the estate that belonged to Elizabeth Cox, the daughter of Will Cox, deceased, and Francis [Frances], being now in the hands of Capt. Robert Vaughan, August 24, 1656, including: "An indenture for 5 yeares from Penellope Prince that ran away from Mistiris Cox in 1646; one bill dew from Capt. William Clayborne to Mr. Cox for 3 barell of mealle...and two sufficient men servents."

KENT COUNTY COURT HELD ON FEBRUARY 4, 1656
Deposition of Edward Hull, aged 35 or thereabouts, was taken and stated he was present when Mr. Haukins lived at Poplies Island and he was in sound mind and perfect memory when Mr. Haukins made his last will and testament dated October 2, 1656.
Deposition of Gershon Cromwell, aged 49 or thereabouts, was taken and he agreed with Edward Hull.
The will of Thomas Hawkins was recorded, naming his son Thomas Hawukins; Margret Hull, daughter of Edward Hull; Mr. Seath Faster; his wife, Elizabeth Haukins; and, appointing Capt. Robert Vaughan, Mr. Henery Carlien, and Mr. Seath Faster as his executors. The estate of Thomas Haukins, of Popplers Island, late deceased, was appraised by Thomas Hinson and William Elleoyet on March 30, 1656, and included, in part, two Bibles and some old rusty armour. Those named therein were: Mary Bally, Thomas Simons, and Henery Wharton (servants), Will Courttiour (ran away), Edward Coolle, George Knots, Jo: Bradsha [sic], Jo: Ealy, John Barnes, Gershon Crumwell, Henery Roch, John Deare, Mr. Faster, and Mr. Hollesis.

KENT COUNTY COURT HELD ON MARCH 2, 1656
John Deare was found by the jury to be not guilty of a felony.
John Deare was sued by Mr. Cooll, and also by Mr. Faster.
Isack Ilive was sued by John Deare.
A list of payments were due the following for killing the wild animals noted: Phillip Conner killed a wolf; William Price killed a wolf; Mathew Reed killed a wild cat; Mr. Elleoyett killed 2 wild cats; Robert Martin killed a wolf; John Deare killed 2 cats; John Smith killed 2 wolves and 1 cat; and Henery Clay killed 4 cats. Also, Mr. Bradnox gave a hog to the Indians, Mr. Russell was over charged by levy, and Mr. Hinson was paid for keeping the court at his house.
Isack Ilive sold his plantation called Bever Necke to Thomas South on February 3, 1656.
Thomas Ringgold, gentleman, sold a cow to his son John Ringgold on January 27, 1654.
Thomas Ringgold, gentleman, sold two heifers to his son James Ringgold on January 27, 1657.
An inventory of the estate of Mr. Thomas Hill was appraised by Thomas Hinson and Thomas South on July 6, 1657.
James Hornor paid his debt in tobacco to Henery Clay.
John Gibson recorded his cattle mark.

KENT COUNTY COURT HELD ON AUGUST 1, 1657
Henery Carlien requested to be dismissed from the office of

Sheriff and John Winchester was appointed in his place.
Depositions were taken from John Ringgold, Edward Hull, Margret Hull [wife of Edward], and Roger Baxter, all regarding John Deare.
Deposition of Thomas Hinson in 1657 mentioned that Thomas Hill was deceased and his daughter's name was Ruth.
Deposition of John Ringgold in 1657 mentioned he was at Thomas Hill's wedding at his father's house on the 4th of March 1655.
Deposition of Misteris Francis Morgon was taken.
Deposition of Anne Hinson in 1657 mentioned her husband [not by name] and her boy Bereson, and Mr. Wickes and his son [no name].
Deposition of Thomas Hinson in 1657 mentioned his wife, Mr. Ringgold and son, and Mr. Hill's wife and sons [no names given].
John Deare was charged with "frequenting the wield gange killing cattell both ould and young and marking of calfes all which he pretends to be his owne." The Court ordered that Deare "shall not at any time here after goe into those woods agayne alone, but that he shall take with him two honest naybours that may see he doth nothing any wayes that may injurious to any man."
Robert Martin and Mathew Reed discharged John Dobb and Thomas Wetherell from their debt obligation on May 1, 1657.
John Winchester sold 100 acres of land to John Gibson and Henery Stoupe on August 1, 1657.
Deposition of Morgon Williams was taken on February 2, 1656 and mentioned that he visited Mary Hartwell in Virginia last year.
Deposition of William Leeds was taken on February 2, 1656 and mentioned that Mary Hartwell was with child by Joseph Wickes and that Mary Hartwell's oath was taken before Mr. Daues [Davis] of Virginia at the house of Morgon Williams.

KENT COUNTY COURT HELD ON SEPTEMBER 1, 1657
Deposition of Thomas Bradnox, aged 58 or thereabouts, was taken and mentioned that John Salter bought a plantation from Frances Brookes sometime in July, 1654. Roger Baxter, aged 46 or thereabouts, affirmed the same.
Depositions were taken from Capt. Robert Vaughan, Henery Morgon, and Thomas Ringold.
Deposition of An: Stanly, aged 21 or thereabouts, was taken in 1657 and mentioned that his master was Thomas Snockes.
Deposition of Thomas Snockes, aged 22 or thereabouts, was taken.
Deposition of Richard Smith, aged 40 or thereabouts, was taken.
Deposition of Thomas Dickes (Dikes), aged 21 or thereabouts, was taken.

KENT COUNTY COURT HELD ON NOVEMBER 2, 1657
Thomas Bradnox filed a complaint against John Salter, as did also Capt. Robert Vaughan.
William Leedes recorded his cattle mark.
Thomas Bradnoxc sold the Craford plantation to John Ellis on September 14, 1657.
Deposition of An [sic] Stanly, aged 21 or thereabouts, was taken.
Depositionof Joseph Wickes, aged 37 or thereabouts, was taken and mentioned Thomas Bradnox and Thomas Belcher.

114 *INHABITANTS OF KENT COUNTY, MARYLAND, 1637-1787*

KENT COUNTY COURT HELD ON NOVEMBER 18, 1657
Insufficient proof from the evidences to make Joseph Wickes guilty of bastardy.
Henry Morgan filed a complaint against Thomas Ringgold who had married the administratrix of the estate of Thomas Hill, Sr.
Thomas Bradnox filed a complaint against Margreet Mannering, a servant of Thomas South, for slander.
Deposition of Elisabeth Ward, aged 40 or thereabouts, was taken in 1657 and mentioned Walter Smith and Joane Hudd.
Robert Houlton and Thomas Hill, Jr. were appointed Constables.

KENT COUNTY COURT HELD ON JANUARY 1, 1657
The estate of Luis Palpilion, deceased, was appraised and debts were recorded as being owed to William Leed, Capt. Russell, Francis Barnes, John A. Morgan, Mrs. Ward, and Andrew Elinor.
The will of Luis Palpilion was written on December 13, 1657, and named his mate William Leedes and Andrew the Spaniard. Witnesses were Thomas Dikes and Robert Holton. Proven on January 1, 1657.
John Salter filed a complaint against John Raby.
John Jenkins filed a complaint against Elisabeth Ward, wife of Thomas Ward.
Richard Blunt, assignee of Antony Calaway, filed a complaint against Robert Gaimer.
Indenture made October 30, 1657, between Capt. Robert Vaughan and Margrett Anderson with consent of her father and mother [no names given]; mentioned her father in law Andrew Elinor and "until the said Margrett Anderson shall come to age." Witnesses were Thomas Wetherill, John Salter, Andrew Anderson and Annecke Elinor.

KENT COUNTY COURT HELD ON FEBRUARY 1, 1657
Mr. Weeckes filed a complaint against Thomas Ringgold who married the relict and administratrix of the late Thomas Hill, Sr.
Mr. Ward was fined in 1652 [sic] "for unlawful correction to his servant Alse Lutt, both by himself and his wife."
Will Davis recorded his cattle mark.
Will Richards recorded his cattle mark.
Thomas Ringgold and Christina, his wife and the late wife of Thomas Hill, deceased, sold land to Thomas Hill on February 5, 1657. Witnesses were Hassadia Hill and James Ringgold.
Thomas Hynson entered a cavet on February 9, 1657, concerning 200 acres adjoining the land of Will Body.

KENT COUNTY COURT HELD ON MARCH 1, 1657
Present were Phillip Conier, Thomas Ringgold, Thomas Hynson, Henry Morgan, John Russell, and Henry Carlyne, Commissioners.
Charles Steward filed a complaint against Phillip Conier.
Mathew Read brought in a servant maide named Elisa Lockett "at the age of sixteene years without indentures."
John Erickson entered a caveat for 100 acres of land.
Morgan Williams entered his wife and Sarah his child for rights of land in 1652 "on the easterne shore or elsewhere in the province."
Joseph Wickes entered a cavet of land for 15 servants or rights due to him viz: Joseph Wickes, John Meconnikin, William Davies in

1650; John Morgan and Edd Tarrant in 1654; Ann Gold and a negro in 1655; Mrs. Wicks and her two children in 1656; John Longthorne, Ric: Huson and Eliz Eles in 1657; and, Thomas Brookes in 1656.
Thomas Hinson, of Isle of Waight [Wight] in Virginia, bound himself twice to Giles Webb, planter, of Nancemume, on January 5, 1646 [sic] for a total of 968 pounds of tobacco to be paid in Chuckatucke by October 20th next. Witnesses were George Gwillin, Clem: Thrush and John Fouckes. Received by Robert Small and Lewis William, and endorsed by John Cowrsey, Clerk.

VITAL RECORDS: (entered by John Cowrsey and Tobias Wells, Clerks)
Edward Winchester was born on March 18, 1657.
Penelope Hemsley was born on December 7, 1657.
John Jenkins was bornon February 11, 1657.
Sarah Helena was born on August 11 1658.
Sarah Gott was born on October 21, 1658.
Marie Salter was born on October 21, 1658.
William Pickard was born on December 4, 1658.
Sarah Ellis was born on November 11, 1658.
Sarah Dabb was born on January 7, 1658.
Darby Phelpe was born on February 11, 1656.
Edward Phelpe was born on January 8, 1658.
Elizabeth Foster was born on February 19. 1658.
Thomas Bridges was born on March 11, 1657.
Margret Morgan was born on March 29, 1659.
Richard Bridges was born on November 9, 1659.
John Gott was born on November 24, 1659.
Sarah Erickson was born on March 25, 1659.
Rachell Hill was born on February 15, 1659.
Mattilda Hemsley was born on March 3, 1659.
John Deere and Elizabeth Robinson married on August 22, 1658.
Deliverance Lovly and Elizabeth Ward married on August 24, 1658.
William Richards and Mary Short married on December 27, 1658.
Anthony Calloway and Martha Thomas married on September 10, 1658.
Hasidia Hill and Ann Sheares married on April 26, 1659.
William Davies and Sarah Coming married on February 19, 1659.
Christian Deare was buried on July 14, 1658.
Mary Gold was buried on August 6, 1658.
Sarah Bedle was buried on August 7, 1658.
Richard Huson was buried on October 3, 1658.
Elizabeth Eles was buried on August 12, 1658.
Lawrance Felt was buried on August 16, 1658.
Benjamin Glover was buried on August 29, 1658.
Barbary Morgan was buried on September 5, 1658.
Sarah Gott was buried on November 1, 1658.
Abraham Hooper was buried on August 20, 1658.
Sandy Fife was buried on September 25, 1658.
John Jenkins, Jr. was buried on January 12, 1658.
Maria Salter was buried on August 14, 1659.
Ann Garland was buried on July 9, 1659.
Margret Morgan was buried on September 5, 1659.
John Olliver was buried on December 24, 1659.
Francis Baxter was buried on February 13, 1659.

KENT PROVINCIAL COURT HELD AT THOMAS BRADNOX HOUSE ON JULY 20, 1658

Present were: Capt. Josias Fendall, Governor; Phillip Calvert, Esq., Secretary; Mr. William Britan, Provincial Clerk; Mr. Nathanniall Uty "which came in after judgment past in Salter's case;" Capt. Robert Vaughan and Mr. Phillip Connier, of the Quorum; and, Mr. Joseph Wickes, Mr. Thomas Bradnox and Mr. Henry Morgan, Commissioners.
John Salter's complaint against Thomas South was heard and tried.
Depositions of Elizabeth Clay, wife of Henry Clay, and Henry Clay were taken on July 19, 1658 and attested "jurat coru me" by William Bretton, Clerk. Elizabeth Clay also answered interrogatories.
Deposition of Henry Cowrsey, aged 29 or thereabouts, was taken on October 3, 1657 and attested "corum me" by Richard Preston.
Deposition of Thomas South, aged 36 or thereabouts, was taken on April 25, 1655.
Deposition of Thomas Ringgold was taken in Court on July 20, 1658.
Deposition of Thomas Bradnox, aged 58 or thereabouts, was taken on September 16, 1657, and his wife Mary Bradnox affirmed the same.
Deposition of Roger Baxter, aged 46 or thereabouts, was taken.
Deposition of Henry Morgan was taken in Court on July 20, 1658.
John Salter, planter, of Isle of Kent, appointed John Cowrsey, gentleman, to be his attorney on April 7, 1658. Witnesses were Edd Coppage and Peter Parker.
The Court ruled in favor of the plaintiff, John Salter.
Margret Brent filed a complaint against Abraham Holeman in 1658.
William Boreman filed a complaint against John Deere in 1658.
Henry Gott, Sheriff, arrested Charles Stuard in a matter involving "certain cattle in the hands of Charles Stuard which were made over by Mr. Thomas Ward, decedent, to Mr. Henry Morgan, in the behalf of the orphan Tabytha Short but now the wife of the said Stuard."
Nicolas Pickard and Mary Baxter asked the Court to have George Crouch, son of George Crouch, deceased, left in the custody of the said Nicolas Pickard, in 1658. It was so ordered.
In 1658 the following persons "agreed that the oath of fidelity should not be pressed upon the inhabitants then residing within this province" - Henry Carline, John Westley, John Ellis, Robert Martin, Edmond Burton, William Elliot, Francis Barnes, Edward Coppage, and Robert Dunn.
Pattericke Forest represented the estate of Thomas Hatton, deceased.
Depositions were taken from Thomas Bradnox, Thomas Hinson, Joseph Wickes, Capt. Robert Vaughan, and Henry Morgan in July, 1658.

KENT COUNTY COURT HELD ON SEPTEMBER 1, 1658
Present were Capt. Robert Vaughan and Mr. Phillip Conner, of the Quorum, and Capt. Thomas Bradnox, Mr. Henry Morgan, Mr. Seth Foster, and Mr. Joseph Wickes, Commissioners. John Cowrsey, Clerk.
Robert Horwood filed a complaint against Robert Gamer.

Nicholas Picmard and Henry Gott were sworn in as Constables for the Isle of Kent.
Mrs. Elizabeth Lovely sworn in court for her rights of land, viz: Thomas Ward in 1650, Deliverance Lovely in 1657, and John Silvester in 1657.
Mrs. Elizabeth Lovely acknowledged her sale of 200 acres to Henry Gott.
"Andrew Hellena makes 350 acres of land appeare upon oath, as rights due to him, viz: first himself, next Andrew Hanson, Annikeck Hanson, Hanse Hanson, Fredricke Hanson, Katteren Hanson, Margret Hanson, which rights came in the year 1653."
Henry Stoope demanded his 50 acres of land in 1658, as did also Henry Tailer, John Gold, William Richards, and John Raby.
Thomas Bradnox, gentleman, conveyed land to William Richards and George Hall in 1658 which was his by patent dated August 1, 1645.

KENT COUNTY COURT HELD AT PHILLIP CONNER'S HOUSE ON OCTOBER 1, 1658
Thomas Snookes demanded his 50 acres of land, as did also Peter Parker, Thomas Wetherell, John Morgan, John Dabb, William Williams, Nicholas Bradway, Edward Rogers, and Thomas Reade.
William Granger demanded 100 acres of land as his rights which was entered as a caveat in "An Arundale Court."
Henry Tailer assigned his tobacco crop to Henry Morgan on October 4, 1658. Witnesses were John Cowrsey and Edward Sparkes.
Edward Rogers assigned his 50 acres of land over to John Deere, as did also Thomas Reade.

KENT COUNTY COURT HELD AT THOMAS BRADNOX HOUSE ON NOVEMBER 15, 1658
Gregory Murell assigned his tobacco crop over to Henry Morgan.
John Mecanackey gave a calf to Sarah Dabb, daughter of John Dabb.
Thomas Ringgold gave a heifer to Thomas Hill. Witnesses were James Ringgold and John Ringgold.
Thomas Ringgold gave a calf to Ruth Hill, daughter of Thomas Hill, of Isle of Kent, late deceased. Witnesses were John Morgan, James Ringgold, and Ed Copedge.
Gertian Cromwell demanded his 150 acres of land for transporting himself, wife Ann Cromwell and daughter Rebecka Cromwell in 1653.
Cudbeard Phelpe demanded rights of land for transporting himself his wife Mary Phelp, and Cudbeard and Darby Phelp his children, in the year 1654 into this province, which is 200 acres.
Robert Mecarter demanded his 50 acres of land.
Mr. Henry Morgan demanded 150 acres for transporting three servants, Margret Hill, Rachell Metcalfe and Mary Gold,
John Deere filed a complaint against Henry Carline.
John Smith filed a complaint against John Deere.
John Raby filed a complaint against Henry Carline.
John Deere filed a complaint against John Smith.
Henry Morgan filed an attachment against the estate of Peter Parker, as did also Thomas Ringgold.
William Granger filed an attachment against the estate of Robert Tyler.
Depositions were taken from William Price, Gregory Murell (mentioning his house at Kent Point), and Mrs. Mary Bradnox.

Henry Gott acknowledged that he gave a calf to Mary Barnes, daughter of Francis Barnes.

KENT COUNTY COURT HELD ON DECEMBER 15, 1658
Cases heard were: John Raby vs. Henry Carline; Henry Morgan vs. Peter Parker; William Granger vs. Robert Tyler; Thomas Dickes vs. Peter Parker; Thomas Ringgold vs. Peter Parker; Richard Blunt vs. Anthony Calloway; Gregory Murell vs. Edward Hull; John Winchester vs. John Deere.
Henry Ashley and Robert Gamer were fined for not planting corn.
Mr. Edward Lloyd attached the estate of Samuel Edsell, and also in Richard Owens vs. Estate of Peter Parker.
John Temple filed a complaint against Thomas Hinson.
Thomas Hill filed a complaint against Richard Turny.
Capt. Thomas Bradnox filed a complaint against William Williams.
Phillip Conner filed a complaint against Thomas Ringgold.
William Williams filed a complaint against Capt. Thomas Bradnox.
Thomas Ringgold filed a complaint against Henry Stoope.
John Deere assigned his tobacco crop over to William Boreman in August, 1658. Witnesses were Frances Morgan and Peter Parker.
John Raby assigned his tobacco crop over to John Salter.
George Hall assigned a heifer to Sarah Dabb, daughter of John Dabb, on December 15, 1658, until she is 15 years old and her father to have the male increase until that time.
Thomas Ringgold gave a heifer to Hasidia Hill on October 31, 1658.

KENT COUNTY COURT HELD ON JANUARY 15, 1658
Cases heard were: John Jenkins vs. John Russell; Edward Rogers vs. John Deere. Warrants demanded in: Edward Rodgers vs. John Deere; Gregory Murell vs. Anthony Griffin.
Henry Gott demanded his 50 acres of land, as did Robert Gamer.

KENT COUNTY COURT HELD ON FEBRUARY 15, 1658
Cases heard were: John Russell vs. John Jenkins; Henry Morgan vs. Robert Knap; Thomas Hill vs. Thomas Ringgold; Thomas Ringgold vs. William Price; William Leeds vs. John Jenkins; William Leeds vs. Capt. Thomas Bradnox; Matthew Reade vs. Anthony Griffin; William Price vs. Thomas Ringgold; Anthony Griffin vs. Powell Lawson; Richard Blunt vs. Powell Lawson; William Hopkins vs. Henry Morgan.
William Champe took the oath of fidelity and demanded his rights to 50 acres of land for his own transportation into the province.
John Meconnikin turned over 600 pounds of tobacco to John Jenkins.
Nicholas Wadilo, of the County of North Hampton in Virginia, was bound by the court to deliver two sufficient man servants to Thomas Bradnox, of the Isle of Kent in Mariland [Maryland], by December. Witnesses on June 22, 1658, were John Russell and William Williams.
John Russell was ordered to deliver a mare fole to Nicholas Wadeloe of Acamacke in Virginia by one year from December 15, 1658.

DEPOSITION DATED AT LONDON, ENGLAND ON AUGUST 27, 1658
"Sir Richard Chiverton, Knight Lord Mayor of the City of London, and the Alderman or Senator of the same city, greetings. Personally came before us in the Chamber of the Guildhall of the said city, Henry Hide of the Parish of Bennet Pauleswharfe London waterman, aged 66 or thereabouts, and Henry Bicke of the Parish of St. Andrew in the Wardrobe London waterman, aged 54 or thereabouts, being persons well known and worthy of good credit, depose they have known Robert Browne of the Parish of Margrets in Westminster in the County of Midd. waterman for 30 years or more, and likewise know Nicholas Browne (who about 24 years since went into Virginia and is there lately deceased; and that the said Robert and Nicholas did own each other for Brethren; and further these deponents did know the mother of said Robert and Nicholas Browne who came out of Wiltshire to live in the said Parish of Bennets about 2 years before the said departure of Nicholas Browne for Virginia, and afterwards died and was buried in the Church of the said Parish, so that these deponents do undoubtedly believe the said Robert Browne to be the natural and lawful brother of the said Nicholas Browne, deceased." [Note: This document was read and recorded in the Court of Kent County, Maryland on December 15, 1658].
Property transaction between Robert Browne and Henry Tailer, both of Isle of Kent, on February 14, 1658. Witness was Charles Stuard.

KENT COUNTY COURT HELD ON MARCH 15, 1658
Warrants demanded in: William Hopkins vs. Mr. Foster; Capt. Robert Vaughan vs. George Hall; Henry Morgan vs. Henry Gott; William Wickes vs. Joseph Wickes; William Richards vs. William Williams; Richard Blunt vs. John Deere; John Russell vs. Henry Gott; and, Richard Blunt vs. Deliverance Lovly. Also for Edward Hull "for an open lyer and defamer" and for Gregory Murill "for a common swearer and disturber of the peace."
Cases heard were: Anthony Griffin vs. Edward Hull; William Williams vs. Joseph Wickes; Anthony Griffin vs. Capt. Thomas Bradnox; and, William Price vs. Thomas Ringgold.
Richard Bridges demanded his right to land for transporting himself into this province, desiring "to take up on the Easterne Shore of Chesapiack Bay."
Deposition of Francis Brooke, aged 24 or thereabouts, was taken in 1658, and mentioned William Williams and Mr. Wickes.
John Deere assigned a cow to Henry Clay on February 15, 1658. Witnesses were Anthony Griffin and William Hopkines.
Robert Browne, now of Isle of Kent, sold cattle to Henry Morgan on February 29, 1658. Witnesses were Robert Vaughan and John Cowrsey.

KENT COUNTY COURT HELD ON APRIL 15, 1659
Cases heard were: William Hopkins vs. Seth Foster, and Thomas Ringgold vs. Gregory Murill.
Joseph Wickes demanded his right to land for transporting one maid servant named Ann Garland into this province.
An attachment was issued for Mr. Edward Lloyd on March 16th last [1658] against the estate of Samuell Edsell, a non resident.

Thomas Wetherill gave a heifer to Margret Winchester, wife of John.
Thomas Wetherill sold cattle to John Dabb on February 16, 1658.
Henry Morgan demanded his right to land for transporting a woman servant named Hanna Grinley into this province in 1658.
Deposition of Henry Clay, aged 40 or thereabouts, was taken on April 15, 1659, and mentioned William Elliot and Gregory Murill fighting last winter.
Deposition of John Salter, aged 36 or thereabouts, was taken also.
Deposition of John Cowrsey was taken in Court on April 15, 1659.

KENT COUNTY COURT HELD ON MAY 16, 1658
Court was "prevented by the season" so the only Commissioners present were Capt. Robert Vaughan and Mr. Phillip Conner.
Thomas Bennet took the oath of fidelity and demanded his right to land, desiring to live on the Eastern Shore.
Mr. Robert Browne demanded his rights to land for his own transport this last year [1658] and also the rights of his brother Nicholas Browne, deceased, which was never taken up. He also demanded land for one man servant named David, a Scotchman, transported by his brother Nicholas Browne, deceased, which David deceased in his service about some 8 years since.
John Cowrsey recorded his cattle mark.
John Dabb recorded his cattle mark.
Henry Tailer recorded his cattle mark.

KENT COUNTY COURT HELD ON JULY 1, 1659
Allexsander Towrson recorded his cattle mark.
Deposition of Thomas South, aged 40 or thereabouts, was taken and mentioned Thomas Hinson, Gregory Murill, and Robert Knapp.
Deposition of Thomas Hinson, Jr., aged 20 or thereabouts, was taken.
Deposition of John Browne, aged 19 or thereabouts, was taken and apparently he was a servant to Robert Knapp.
Francis Ashe's demanded rights to land were assigned by him over to Henry Morgan.
John Jenkins demanded his rights to land for his own transport into this province in 1653.
Anthony Calloway's demanded rights to 50 acres were assigned by him over to Allexsander Towrson.
Robert Browne sold a cow to John Erickson on March 15, 1658.

KENT COUNTY COURT HELD ON OCTOBER 1, 1659
Sarah Tailer filed a complaint against her Master and Mrs., Capt. Thomas Bradnox and Mary his wife, and she was placed in custody of the Constable, Henry Gott.
John White stated he "can testify nothing in this matter affirmatively" in behalf of the servant Sarah Tailer.
John Jenkins swore in Court "he never saw Capt. Bradnox or his wife strike his servant Sarah Tailer."
Tobias Wells on oath stated "he saw Sarah Tailer stript and on her backe he saw severall blacke spots and on her arme a great blacke spot about as broad as his hand."

KENT COUNTY COURT PROCEEDINGS, 1647-1676 121

Mr. Joseph Wickes informed the court "Mrs. Bradnox broake the peace in strikinge her servant before him being a Magistrate."
Katteren Gamer gave deposition in Capt. Bradnox vs. John Deere.
Cases heard were: Capt. Thomas Bradnox vs. John Deere; Sarah Tailer vs. Capt. Thomas Bradnox; Capt. Thomas Bradnox vs. John Smith; Mr. Seth Foster vs. John Deere; and, Mr. Edward Lloyd vs. John Deere.
John Olliver demanded his right to land for his own transport into this province in 1653.
John Erickson, Jr., son of John, recorded his cattle mark.
John Cowrsey gave a calf to John Erickson, Jr. on October 1, 1659.
Andrew Helena recorded his cattle mark.
Hasadia Hill recorded his cattle mark.

KENT COUNTY COURT HELD ON NOVEMBER 1, 1659
Constable Henry Gott presented Thomas Dickes for contempt against the government.
Robert Knapp presented Constable Henry Gott for being drunk.
Constable Henry Gott presented John Deere for default of planting.
Warrants demanded in Deliverance Lovly vs. Ann Murill, and John Salter vs. Ann Murill, and Robert Browne vs. Capt. Thomas Bradnox, and Thomas Hinson vs. John Deere, and subpoenas for Henry Gott, John Silvester, Elizabeth Lovly, Capt. Thomas Bradnox, John Deere, and John Erickson, and William Hemsly.
Constable Nicholas Pickard presented John Hardiman alias Stoill, and a subpoena for Mrs. Jane Fox, who kept company with said John Stoill as his wife. Stoill stated he was married by Mr. Ladamore.
John Stuard took the oath of fidelity and demanded his right to land for his own transport into this province.
John Stoill demanded his right to land for his own transport, his daughter Ann Stoill, and Jane Fox. John Salter informed the Court that he heard David Phillips had taken up land for these 3 persons.
Depositions were taken from Deliverance Lovly and John Stoill.
Nicholas Browne and Henry Morgan, both of Isle of Kent, obligated themselves on April 25, 1655, to pay 5,000 pounds of tobacco to "Leiftent. Hinson, High Sheriff of Kent."

KENT COUNTY COURT HELD ON DECEMBER 1, 1659
Cases heard were: Henry Morgan vs. John Smith; Thomas Bradnox vs. Dilliverance Lovly; Thomas Byam vs. Francis Barnes; Robert Knapp vs. Thomas Hinson; Matthew Reade vs. John Smith; Robert Martin vs. John Smith; Capt. Thomas Bradnox vs. John Smith; Thomas Hinson vs. John Deere; Capt. Thomas Bradnox vs. John Morgan.
Warrants demanded for: Capt. Thomas Bradnox vs. John Morgan; John Stoill vs. David Phillips; Robert Knapp vs. Thomas Hinson, Sr.; Thomas Bradnox vs. Dilliverance Lovly; Thomas Byam vs. Francis Barnes; Matthew Reade vs. Ann Reade; Thomas Hinson, Sr. vs. John Deere; Matthew Reade vs. John Winchester; Matthew Reade vs. John Smith; Robert Martin vs. John Smith; Hasadia Hill vs. John Erickson; John Dabb vs. Henry Stoppe; John Dabb vs. John Gibson; Rice Mattocks vs. Edward Hull; Robert Knapp vs. Seth Foster;

Thomas Dickes vs. Henry Gott; Nathanuniall Uty vs. Richard Arie; Henry Tailer vs. John Erickson; John Ringgold vs. Henry Carline.
Thomas Hill was sworn into office as Constable of Kent County.
John Meconnikin assigned over "his patent of land and and what theiron remaineth belonginge therto, with all priviliges to the Inhabitants of Kent where the Court is now kept."
Depositions of Nicholas Bradway and Tobias Wells were taken.
Deposition of Mary Meconnikin, aged 18 or thereabouts, was taken in 1659, and mentioned Margret Smith and her husband John Smith.
Robert Knapp demanded his right to land he should have had last year.
Hasadiah Hill sold land called "Crany Necke" on September 10, 1659, to his brother Thomas Hill, which was formerly his father's, Thomas Hill, deceased. Witnesses were John Erickeson and John Gould.
John Jenkins and Charles Stuard recorded their cattle marks.
Deposition of Nicholas Bradway, aged 29 or thereabouts, was taken.
Mr. Robert Browne recorded his cattle mark, which was the same mark made by his brother Nicholas Browne, deceased, during his lifetime.

KENT COUNTY COURT HELD ON JANUARY 1, 1659
Thomas Haulkins gave a cow to Margret Hull, daughter of Edward Hull.
Edward Hull recorded his cattle mark.

KENT COUNTY COURT HELD ON FEBRUARY 1, 1659
Cases heard were: Antony Griffin vs. John Erickson, John Stuard vs. Antony Calloway, and Thomas Hinson vs. John Deere.
Warrants demanded for: John Stuard vs. Antony Calloway; Antony Griffin vs. John Erickson; John Browne vs. John Jenkins; John Brown vs. Hasadia Hill; Capt. Robert Vaughan vs. Edmund Burton; and. Nathauniall Stilds vs. Thomas Ringgold.
Anthony Griffin appointed Matthew Reade as his lawful attorney.
Deposition of Allexsander Towrson was taken, and mentioned William Hambleton and John Erickson.
William Richards recorded his cattle mark.
John Coursey is noted as the Sheriff of Kent County in 1659 and verified by John Cowrsey, Clerk of Kent County.

KENT COUNTY COURT HELD ON FEBRUARY 16, 1659
Cases heard were: Capt. Thomas Bradnox vs. John Burage; and, Seth Foster vs. Edward Coppage.
Warrants demanded for: Capt. Thomas Bradnox vs. John Burage; John Dabb vs. Capt. Robert Vaughan; Seth Foster vs. Edward Coppage; William Bagar vs. David Maine; Martin Evens vs. William Bagar.
Matthew Reade brought his man Mouse to Court for being a constant runaway from his master's service. Court ordered 25 sound lashes.
John Burage, of Ann Arundale, planter, appointed "my loving friend Mr. John Russell, of the Isle of Kent, as his lawful attorney on February 8, 1659. Witnesses were William Hemsley and Steven Benson.
Thomas Bradnox petitioned the Court for compensation for he and

his wife having kept "one of the sonnes of Mistris Parker, by name of Francis Maulden" for six years before they forcibly took him away from them.
Deposition of William Granger, aged 43 or thereabouts, was taken in 1659.

VITAL RECORDS: (recorded by John Course, Tobias Wells and Disborough Bennett, 1660-1669, and one recorded in 1673)
Elesabeth Dobb, daughter of John, was born on July 29, 1660.
Joane Dobb, daughter of John, was born on November 12, 1662.
Henry Morgan, son of Henry, was born on January 28, 1651.
Barbary Morgan, daughter of Henry, was born on July 28, 1654.
Frances Morgan, daughter of Henry, was born on October 1, 1656.
Margrett Morgan, daughter of Henry, was born on March 29, 1659.
Barbary Morgan, daughter of Henry, was born on November 5, 1660.
Robert Hood, son of John, was born on December 28, 1650.
Shusana Dunn, daughter of Robert, was born on July 21, 1656.
Joane Dunn, daughter of Robert, was born on March 5, 1660.
Ann Price, daughter of William, was born on November 17, 1662.
Edward Price, son of William, was born on January 9, 1660.
Margrett Benton, daughter of Marke, was born on December 4, 1662.
Ann Steuard, daughter of Charles, was born on February 17, 1661.
Jonathan Gotte, son of Henry, was born on March 1, 1662.
Alexander Nash, son of Alexander, was born on January 16, 1662.
Margrett Hill, daughter of Thomas, was born on April 1, 1658.
Rachell Hill, daughter of Thomas, was born on February 15, 1659.
Elezabeth Jonnes and Ruth Jonnes, twin daughters of Edward, were born on February 1, 1661.
Ann Bright, daughter of Thomas, was born on December 24, 1662.
Alexander Jonson, son of Peter, was born on December 16, 1662.
John Meconicon, son of John, was born on June 18, 1663.
Josias Blunt, son of Richard Blunt, was born on October 21, 1662.
Nathanell Hull, son of Edward, was born on April 30, 1663.
Rebecka Osborne, daughter of Thomas, was born on September 5, 1663.
Francis Benton, son of Marke, was born on November 10, 1663.
Mary Southren, daughter of Valentine, was born on June 13, 1664.
Benjamin Elles, son of John, was born on April 1, 1664.
Rebecka Dunn, daughter of Robert, was born on July 29, 1664.
Jonathan Gotte, son of Henry, was born on July 31, 1664.
Penelope Hill, daughter of Thomas, was born on March 8, 1664.
Abell Magison, son of John, was born on June 11, 1665.
Thomas Osborne, son of Thomas, was born on April 16, 1665.
Francis Finch, son of Francis, was born on May 26, 1665.
John Dobs, son of John, was born on February 15, 1664.
Sarah Nash, daughter of Alexander, was born on August 19, 1664.
Presillia Jonson, daughter of Peter, was born on December 2, 1665.
Apprell Blunt, daughter of Richard, was born on April 3, 1666.
Eastor Benton, daughter of Marke, was born on November 19, 1666.
William Osborne, son of Thomas, was born on July 12, 1667.
Barbary Hill, daughter of Thomas, was born on July 26, 1667.
Alexander Meconicon, son of John, was born on November 6, 1667.
Dorethy Sutherin, daughter of Vallentyne and Mary, was born on February 16, 1668.

INHABITANTS OF KENT COUNTY, MARYLAND, 1637-1787

Elizabeth Carter, daughter of Henry and Mary, was born on March 25, 1669.
Henry Morgan, son of John and Mary, was born on May 26, 1668.
Ellin Wallters, daughter of Alexander and Margret, was born on August 16, 1669.
Mary Morris, daughter of Richard and Ellen, was born on May 18, 1664.
Ann Morris, daughter of Richard and Jeane, was born on July 20, 1669.
Hannah Baxter, daughter of Thomas and Hannah, was born October 1, 1669.
Morgan Browne, son of Edward and Sarah, was born on October 11, 1669.
Robert Blunt, son of Richard and Ann, was born on September 16, 1668.
John Osborne, son of Thomas and Katherin, was born on March 22, 1668.
Charles Stuard, son of Charles and Tabytha, was born on March 9, 1664.
Eadey Stuard, daughter of Charles and Tabytha, was born on February 13, 1666.
George Hale and Margrett Hill married on May 10, 1660.
Alexander Nash and Ruth Hill married on January 20, 1662.
Edward Jonnes and Margrett Hale married on May 10, 1661.
Thomas Bright and Elezabeth Cripes married in May 11, 1662.
Toby Wells and Mary Richards married on August 20, 1665.
John Magisson and Janne Shears married on May 9, 1665.
Ralph Ward and Elezabeth Bogges married on November 20, 1664.
Henry Williames and Femety Albus married on November 20, 1664.
Robert Humphreys and Elezabeth Bromton married on September 2, 1664.
John Winchester and Janne Muntrose married on September 7, 1665.
John Ingram and Hannah Jenkins married on August 10, 1669.
Richard Morris and Jeane Putbery married on July 29, 1668.
Thomas Baxter and Hannah Fordah married on December 19, 1668.
Edward Browne and Sarah Williams married on October 28, 1668.
Francis Pine and Mary Vicaris married on February 24, 1669.
Elezabeth Jonnes, daughter of Edward, died on January 23, 1662.
Walter Jenkens died on July 26, 1663.
Ann Pickard died on July 27, 1663.
Heugh Prosser died on August 20, 1663.
Ed Price, son of William, died on January 14, 1661.
Francis Finch, son of Francis, died on July 22, 1665.
Ann Dobbs, wife of John, died on December 5, 1665.
Mary Meconicon, wife of John, died on December 6, 1667.
John Winchester, Sr. died on August 22, 1669.
Nicholas Pleade, son of William and Mary, died on August 6, 1669.
Mary Pleade, wife of William, died on September 12, 1669.
Dorethy Williams, wife of Mr. Morgan Williams, died on December 2, 1669.
Mary Sutherin, wife of Valentine, died on November 5, 1669.
Capt. John Vicaris died on October 24, 1669.
William Osborne, son of Thomas, was buried on October 3, 1669.
Joseph Englesby was buried on October 3, 1669.

Mr. Richard Blunte was buried on September 16, 1669.
Thomas Blunt, son of Ann, was buried on October 31, 1669.
Tabytha Stuard, wife of Charles, was buried on October 3, 1669.
Elizabeth White was buried on October 24, 1669.
Rice Griffin's wife died on June 22, 1673.

KENT COUNTY COURT HELD ON DECEMBER 1, 1660
Present were Capt. Robert Vaughan, Commander, and Mr. John Coursey, Mr. Seth Foster, Mr. William Coursey, and Mr. James Ringgould, Commissioners.
John Salter was appointed Constable for the south end of Kent County and Will Richards for the north end.
Warrants demanded for Thomas Sutherne vs. Capt. Thomas Brodnox, Mr. Lovely vs. Rogere Ladimoore, Richard Grimes vs. Arthur Write, Gregory Murrell vs. Joseph Weekes, and Gregory Murrell vs. Thomas Hinson.

KENT COUNTY COURT HELD ON DECEMBER 20, 1660
Deposition of David Fillips, aged 53 or thereabouts, was taken.
Deposition of John Silvester, aged 20 or thereabouts, was taken.
Deposition of Mr. James Ringgold, aged 23 or thereabouts, was taken.
Deposition of William Davise, aged 25 or thereabouts, was taken.
Deposition of Judeth Hemsly, aged 27 or thereabouts, was taken.
Macume Meconny, aged 23 or thereabouts, was taken.
Deposition of Nicklus Brodway, aged 30 or thereabouts, was taken.
Deposition of John White, aged 22 or thereabouts, was taken.
Deposition of William Hemsly, aged 26 or thereabouts, was taken.
Deposition of Thomas Snow, aged 20 or thereabouts, was taken.
John Smith was ordered to take into custody the estate of John Stowell, deceased.
Mathew Reade was ordered to take into custody the estate of Thomas Reade, deceased.
Mrs. Conner was given power to possess the estate of Mr. Conner, deceased, her late husband, and dispose of debts by law.
Warrants were demanded in the following complaints: Samuell Scipwith vs. Fransis Barnes; Robert Knape vs. William Mullins; Mr. Lovely vs. William Hemsly; Mr. John Hatten vs. John Winchester; John Morgan vs. Henry Gott; Mrs. Mary Conner vs. Thomas Ringgold; William Hambleton vs. Anthony Griffen; John Salter vs. Henry Clay; John Dabb vs. Mathew Reade, and subpoenas for John Spurdance and Elesabeth Lockett; Mr. Henry Morgon vs. William Champe; Nickholas Pickard vs. Will Tayler; Mrs. Mary Conner vs. Morgon Williams; John Spurdance vs. Mathew Reade, and subpoenas for Ann Reade and Elesabeth Lockett; Isabella Barns vs. John Winchester; and, a subpoena for William Collins.
Samuel Brockworth demanded subpoenas for Mr. Henry Morgon, Roger Baxter, George Halle, Nickholas Pickard, Capt. Thomas Brodnox and Mary his wife, to give tesimony concerning John Abatt.

KENT COUNTY COURT HELD ON JANUARY 21, 1660
Cases heard were: Robert Knape vs. William Mullins; Mrs. Mary Conner vs. Mr. Thomas Ringgould; John Spurdance vs. Mathew Reede; John Dabb vs. Mathew Reede; Samuel Scipwith vs. Fransis Barnes; Mrs. Mary Conner vs. Mr. Morgane Williams; John Morgon vs. Henry

Gott.
Depositions were taken from Capt. Robert Vaughan, Richard Hutchins, Roger Baxter (aged 50 or thereabouts), and Luther Ayers (aged 22 or thereabouts).
Ann Hill was admitted as adminstratrix of her late husband Hasadia.
"Left: William Evans and John Jarbo" assigned their warrant for land, dated August 28, 1649, to John Grimsditch and Isacke Ilive on November 20, 1650. Witnesses were Richard Willan, Charles Maynard, Walter Packer and Thomas Howard. They in turn assigned their rights over to Thomas March, merchant, on April 5, 1651. Witnesses were Leo: Stronge and Henry Morgan.
Capt. Thomas Brodnox sold a horse to John Coursey, gentleman, on December 1, 1660. Witnesses were Anthony Griffin and Tobye Wells.
Deliverance Lovely let his plantation to Thomas Bennett for five years, and he also gave him use of man servant John Selvester and maid Jane Brigs for five years.
Margret Hanson recorded her cattle mark.
Tobias Wells was appointed Clerk of Kent County in 1660.
William Champe signed over his land patent to Robert Martine, Sr. on March 2, 1660. Witnesses were James Ringgold and Toby Wells.
Margaret Hall, executrix of Thomas Hill [sic], deceased, signed over 100 acres of land called "Hillstone" to Amoze Hill on June 1, 1661.

KENT COUNTY COURT HELD ON MARCH 2, 1660
Mrs. Lovely petitioned the Court that her husband had let land to Thomas Bennett that by rights belonged to her child [not named].
Elexander Mancater and Daniel Glover demanded their right to land for transporting themselves into this province.
Depositions were taken from Richard Blunt, Robert Martine, Jr. and Fransis Nash.
John Bennett, mariner, did freely give his cattle on Kent to Margrett Marsh in April, 1657.
Subpoenas issued for Ann Dobb, Ann Hill, Elesabeth Deere, Catheren Gamer and Sarah Tourson to appear in next Court in 1661.
Elesabeth Stope gave a calf to William Granger, son of William, on November 20, 1661.
John Knight demanded his 50 acres of land for transporting himself into this province.
Thomas Ringgould gave half of his land called "Hunting Field" to his sons John Ringgould and James Ringgould on December 2, 1661.
Warrants issued in October, 1661, for the following complaints: Oliver Spry vs. William Hambleton, Anthony Griffin vs. Thomas Stagwell, William Hemsley vs. Capt. Robert Vaughan, William Piper vs. Deliverance Lovely, Robert Knape vs. Thomas Williams, Deliverance Lovely vs. Thomas Williams.
Mrs. Mary Bradnox recorded her cattle mark.
George Halle wrote his will on September 20, 1660, naming his daughter Cristian, daughter Margrett, daughter Rachell, and his wife Margrett who may or may not be with child. He left his wife his plantation called "The New Invention" where William Richards now lives. Witnesses were James Ringgould, Thomas Hills and Ruth Knowles, and Robert Mecartna and Tobye Wells witnesses the

codicil on February 4, 1660. George Halle died prior to March 2, 1660.
John Browne, "of Salam in New Ingland, marriner," appointed his loving friend Mr. Sammuell Wethers, "inhabitant of Providence on the south side of Severen in the County of Anorndale," to be his lawful attorney to collect any debts due him in Anorndale [Anne Arundel] or Kent. Witnesses were Daniel Walker and William Ramsse [sic] on March 19, 1660.

KENT COUNTY COURT HELD ON APRIL 1, 1661
Edward Leeke, merchant of Rode Iland [Rhode Island] in New England appointed his trusty friend Joseph Weekes as his lawful attorney.
Depositions were taken from William Piper, Ann Doob, Ann Hill, Catheren Gammer, Sarah Tourson, and Elesebeth Lockett.
Elesebeth Lockett and Thomas Bright were convicted of bastardy. She was given 20 lashes on her back, and he paid all charges plus the cost of Mrs. Conner's keeping of their child.
Thomas Williams assigned all rights to servant Thomas Bradly over to John Winchester on March 6, 1660. Witnesses were William Granger and Andrew Ellenor.
Marke Benton demanded his 100 acres for transporting himself and his wife into this province, and he assigned 50 acres of said land to John Jenkens.
Sarah Raby, destitute, prayed before the Court for some relief.
Capt. Thomas Brodnox presented his case against John White and Sarah Tayler who had stolen from him and then runaway. Members of the jury were Mathew Read, Edward Hull, John Ringgould, Charles Steward, Arthur Writte, John Smith, Richard Blunt, Morgon Williams, Thomas Stagwell, John Jenkings, John Winchester and Thomas Osborne.
John Wedg [sic] recorded his cattle mark on October 10, 1667 [sic].
Richard Deaver filed a complaint against Thomas Bennett's estate.
William Leeds filed a complaint against Hasadia Hill's estate.
Robert Vaughan filed a complaint against Robert Mecart's estate.
William Leeds filed a complaint against Robert Mecart's estate.
Thomas Brodnox, planter, reported that he transported himself and Mary his wife, plus two men servants, John Phillips and Edward Williams, into this province in 1644, and later took in two other men servants, Anthony Callaway and Thomas Snookes. He took up land bounded on the north by Elesabeth Commins, widow, and on the south by Phillipe Conner, and on the west with the "Bay of Chesepiake." On April 1, 1661, he assigned this land over to William Richards.
William Richards sold a cow and calf to Macume Meconny on June 9, 1660. Witnesses were William Hensley and Robert Holton.
John Deere wrote his will on July 21, 1659, naming his son George Deere (not of age), his daughter Christian Deere, and his wife Eleasabeth Deere. Witnesses were John Smith and Thomas Hill. John Deere died by May 1, 1661 when the Court appointed John Winchester to watch over the cattle of John's son George Deere.

KENT COUNTY COURT HELD ON MAY 1, 1661
Henry Morgon filed a complaint against John Salter's estate.

Statements were taken from George Collison and William Mouse.
Mary Conner sold two cows to Petter Jonson on April 14, 1661.
Witnesses were Thomas Phillips and Tobye Wells.
John Salter wrote his will on March 20, 1660, naming his wife Janne Salter and "daughter law" Rebecka Lumbard (whom he later referred to as "my said wife and child"). Witnesses were Moyses Stagwell and Tobye Wells. John was dead by July 27, 1661, when his widow appointed Anthony Griffin as her lawful attorney. Witnesses were John Newman and Attwell Bodwell.
William Elliott refused to take the oath of a Constable "for contiens sake" and the Sheriff was ordered to bring him to Court.
Deposition of Robert Burle, aged 51 or thereabouts, was taken.
Deposition of William Neale. aged 30 or thereabouts, was taken.
Members of the jury were Mr. Thomas Ringgould, Richard Blunt, John Dobbes, John Winchester, Mr. Henry Morgon (Foreman), William Hemsley, William Hambleton, Thomas Phillips, John Morgon, Mathew Reade, Thomas Osborne, and John Erecson.
John Winchester filed a complaint against Eseable Barnes.
Depositions were taken from John Dobes (who mentioned the death of John Winchester's wife), John Morgon, Jr. (who mentioned Goody Barnes and Sarah Raby), John Winchester, Jr., Grace Granger (who mentioned Margarett Winchester), William Granger, and William Hemsley. Margarett Winchester was the wife of John Winchester.
Janne Salter, by her attorney William Coursey, filed a complaint against the estate of Gey [sic] Knowles.

KENT COUNTY COURT HELD ON AUGUST 7, 1661
Sarah Tayler, servant of Capt. Thomas Brodnox, filed a complaint against him and his wife for beating her without just cause. The deposition of Joseph Newman was taken. Capt. Robert Vaughan, William Leeads, James Ringgould and Nickholas Pickard, Commissioners, ruled that Sarah Tayler was freed from her apprenticeship due to "the invetterat mallice of hur master and mistress toward hur."

KENT COUNTY COURT HELD ON SEPTEMBER 2, 1661
Thomas Brodnox appointed his wife Mary to be his lawful attorney to sue and implead Sarah Tayler in his behalf.
Richard Blunt filed a complaint against Thomas Snow.
Deposition of Richard Blunt was taken, and mentioned Thomas Osborne and Edmund Weeb [Webb].
Richard Deaver filed a complaint against Thomas Snow.
John Stowell's estate was sold by order of the Court on January 29, 1661, and the purchasers of various items were John Smith, Nickholas Pickard, Mathew Read, Allexander Tourson, Mary Baxter, Thomas Hills, William Price, Luther Ayers, and Thomas Phillips. Creditors paid were Capt. Brodnox, John Smith, Roger Baxter, Mathew Read, Luther Ayers, Thomas Hills, William Price, Ann Hills, Richard Blunt, Anthony Griffin, John Maconikin, and Mr. Coursey.

KENT COUNTY COURT HELD ON OCTOBER 1, 1661
William Colleman, servant of Seth Foster, judged to be 11 years old.

KENT COUNTY COURT PROCEEDINGS, 1647-1676   129

Henry Morgan appeared and declared he had not taken up the rights to land of his servants John Barnes, William Rennoulds, and Janne Seares.
Court permitted Ann Hill, relict of Hasadia Hill, deceased, to take possession of said estate and dispose of it in payment of debts.
Debts were due and payable out of the estate of Robert Macartny to Mr. Nathaniel Stoyles, Capt. Robert Vaughan, Mr. Henry Morgan, William Richards (funeral charges), Margaret Hale, Capt. Thomas Brodnox, and John Barke [sic].

KENT COUNTY COURT HELD ON NOVEMBER 1, 1661
John Dobes acknowledged he received a cow and heifer from Thomas Hills for the use of Christian Deeare, daughter of John Deeare, deceased, late of Isle of Kent.
Statement of Oliver Sprye dated October 20, 1661 was received and mentioned William Hambleton, Mrs. Katheren Coursey, John Morgan, Anthony Griffin, Mr. Penington, and Mr. Weekes.
Oliver Sprye filed a complaint against William Hambleton.
Deposition of John Morgan, aged 27 or thereabouts, was taken.
Anthony Griffin filed a complaint against Thomas Stagwell.
William Hemsley filed a complaint against Capt. Robert Vaughan.
Deposition of John Whit, aged 30 or thereabouts, was taken, and stated that "the skin of Thomas Wattson's members did drape away from him in his sickness."
The following were paid by the Court for various services rendered: Mathew Read "for 3 men to dayes," Capt. Brodnox "for boat prest to attend the Jeury men," Anthony Griffin "for charge and attendance," Mr. Morgan "for the Burgises sent in Fendalls time," Capt. Leeads "for powder and shot for 3 soldiers sent to the Susquahanakes," Mr. Weekes "for his boat to attend the Burgises in fendalls time," Thomas Osborne "for a fleck of bacon for the soldiers," John Elles "for 12 pounds of bacon," Morgan Williams "for 10 pounds of beef," William Davis "for 5 pounds of beef," Abraham Bishep "for 2 woules [wolves]," Richard Brides "for one wolf," and John Ringgould "for one wolf."
Josias Fendall ordered on August 20, 1651 that John Smith had 400 acres due him under the Conditions of Plantations and therefore granted him a parcel called "Smithsby" on the Chester River. John Smith assigned said land to James Thomson on December 16, 1661. Witnesses were Thomas Leves and Tobye Weells.

KENT COUNTY COURT HELD ON DECEMBER 16, 1661
Ann Blunt was ordered to be paid out of the estate of Thomas Read, late deceasd, "95 pounds of tobacco and two bottles of drames."

KENT COUNTY COURT HELD ON JUNE 7, 1662
John Ereckson filed a complaint that his servant Mary Stedhed was with child by Mathew Reade that "was begotten on Candlemuse Day last in the night." A jury of women was summoned to decide if Mary Stedhed's situation was true or not, viz: Mrs. Mary Broadnox, Mrs. Frances Morgon, Mrs. Alice Woolman, Mrs. Mary Conner, Elizabeth Ereckson, Mary Scott, Ann Reade, Mary Baxter, and Mary Meconicon. They could not make a determination, so the

Court ordered Mathew Reade to post a bond of 5,000 pounds of tobacco "to save the county harmless from the said woman's child if in case it be proved to be his."
Henry Stoope declared he had paid James Maxfield on November 21, 1660 as ordered. Witnesses were Mich. Billett and John Winchester.
In the matter of setting free Sarye [Sarah] Tayler, late servant of Mrs. Mary Brodnox, a Commission was appointed by Charles Calvert, Lieutenant General of this Province, namely Edward Lloyd and Henry Coursey. They determined on June 7, 1662 that Capt. Robert Vaughan, Capt. William Leeads, Mr. James Ringgould, and Mr. Nickholas Pickard, Commissioners of Kent County, had erred in this matter and ordered each of them to pay Mary Brodnox 250 pounds of good casked tobacco by October 20, 1662.
Thomas Ringgould requested that the following matter be recorded: "Capt. Edward Streator, of the County of Nantcimomb in Virginia, and Elezabeth his wife and late relict and executrix of Col. Thomas Burbage, deceased, and William Burbage, of the County of Nantcimomb aforesaid, gentleman brother of the said Col. Thomas Burbage, for the sum of 2,500 pounds of good sound merchantable casked tobacco have sold to Thomas Ringgould, gentleman, of the Isle of Kent in Maryland, a 100 acre tract of land lying between Craney Creek and Crafford Fort on the Isle of Kent, on December 6, 1655. Witnesses were W. Michell, Judeth Vial, Catherine Cooper and Isaack Bovey."

[Note: There is an obvious gap in court records between 1662 and 1667. Footnotes in the *Archives of Maryland*, Vol. 54, pp. 234-235, state, in part: "A gap of six years separates the contents from the preceding liber. The first few entries were made by clerk Tobias Wells in January, 1668. After him the entries are by John Wright. Clerks John Wright, Disborough Bennett, and Peter Sayer bore their several shares in its making. The records show a gap of nearly four years in the succession of courts. Evidently the original records had already disappeared when the liber was assembled in 1727. Peter Sayer had continued as clerk until 1672 at least and Charles Bancks became clerk in 1674 and he closes the liber records in August, 1676." Additional comments are made that many pages were damaged by deterioration of the paper].

Francis Barnes, who was about to go to England, appointed his wife Esabella Barnes and son-in-law John Stevens as his lawful attorneys on April 30, 1667. Witnesses were Simon Carpender and John Morgan.
Thomas Bright sold some cattle to Thomas Linsted on March 20, 1667 on Isle of Kent. Witnesses were John Ereckson, Elexander Nash and John Maggison.
Major Thomas Ingram recorded his cattle mark.
Bridgett Downes, wife of Henry Downes, acknowledged her consent to selling a piece of land on Elk River on January 28, 1667. Witnesses were Thomas Linsted and William Morgan.

KENT COUNTY COURT HELD ON JANUARY 28, 1667
Present were Capt. Robert Vaughan, Mr. Richard Blunt, Mr. William

KENT COUNTY COURT PROCEEDINGS, 1647-1676   131

Head, Mr. John Vickerice, Mr. John Dobbs, and Mr. Thomas Osborne, Conmissioners.
Phillip Conner, aged about 14 years, son of the late Phillip Conner, came into Court and chose John Wright as his guardian.
Capt. John Vickerice filed a complaint against Toby Wells.
Edmond Burton filed a complaint against John Browne.
George Gouldhauk filed a complaint against Mr. John Vickerice and a jury was selected as follows: Charles Steuard, John Ereckson, John Trew, Robert Kent, Peter Scale, Allexander Thourson, Francis Finch, William Granger, John Meconicon, John Maggisson, Marke Benton, and Thomas Southern. Charles Steward [sic], was Foreman.
Thomas Collens filed a complaint against Mr. John Vickerice.
Frances Sembreck, servant to John Meconicon, came into Court and demanded her freedom as she had served her time. It was granted.
Henry Downes, planter, had 300 acres due him for transporting into this province himself and his wife, plus James Dardon, Richard Whitten, Frances Sewell and Richard Chapman on September 22, 1658, so Charles Calvert, Lieutenant General of Maryland, granted to him a tract called "Hay Downe" which laid "on a river on the east side of the bay in Baltimore County called Elk River and one the south side of said river in a creek called Capt. John's Creek [and] by a branch called Gouldsmith Branch." Given at St. Mary's on September 15, 1665. Henry Downes and wife Bridgett, of Kent County, assigned this land over to Obadiah Judgkins, of Talbot County, on January 28, 1667. Witnesses were Thomas Linsted and William Morgan.
Heugh Jones was indebted to Thomas Linsted for 280 pounds of tobacco due by bill assigned from Henry Guttrick for work done by said Henry Gudrick [sic]. Court ordered the Sheriff "to pay Thomas Linsted out of the wages due to Heugh Jones for his service in Capt. Durgos his march, 380 pounds of tobacco and cask."

KENT COUNTY COURT HELD ON MARCH 31, 1668
Present were Capt. Robert Vaughan, Mr. Morgan Williams, Mr. Matthew Read, Mr. Thomas Osborne, Mr. Nickolas Pickard, Mr. William Head, Mr. Richard Blunt, and Mr. John Dabb, Commissioners.
Toby Wells filed separate complaints against Valentine Southerne and Kathorine Scale. Kathorine Scale, with the consent of her husband Peter Scale, acknowledged Mr. John Vicaris as her attorney.
John Wright filed a complaint against Thomas Ringgold.
John Floyd filed separate complaints against Anthony Callaway and John Vicaris.
Matthew Read brought to Court a servant maid named Jane Padbury who came in without indenture. Court ordered her to serve four years and no more as servant to said Read.
John Vicaris filed a complaint against Toby Wells.
John Currer filed a complaint against John Dobb (Dabb).
Henry Downes, of Upper Hundred, and John Magison, of Lower Hundred, were nominated for Constables.
John Floyd, of Talbot County, appointed Charles Steward his lawful attorney on February 26, 1667. Witnesses were John Tassell

and Toby Wells.
Robert Palmer, of Isle of Kent, appointed his well beloved friend Robert Dunn, of Isle of Kent, as his lawful attorney. Witnesses were Francis Gill and Ninian Beall.
On February 3, 1667, Mrs. Sarah Brookes "sett and lett" to John Trew and William Trew one plantation and orchard on Kent Island (formerly Henry Gott's plantation) for 7 years for the yearly rent of 1600 pounds of tobacco. Witnesses were John Cooper and Toby Wells.
Roger Baxtor, planter, of Isle of Kent, sold to John Mackconica, of said island, a 60 acre parcel of land on January 12, 1658. Witnesses were Robert Vaughan, Joseph Wickes and Nickolas Bradaway.
John Maggison recorded his cattle mark.

KENT COUNTY COURT HELD JUNE 30, 1668
John Vicaris, gentleman, was appointed and sworn in as Commissioner in Kent County and also admitted as a Quorum of said commission.
Robert Fuller filed a complaint against Toby Wells.
Edmond Burton brought to Court two servants named Humphrey Hubbert and Mary Ewens and they were ordered to serve 5 years each.
Isabella Barnes brought to Court a servant named William Whatly and he was ordered to serve 6 years.
John Wright brought to Court a servant without indenture named Thomas Henfrey and he was ordered to serve 6 years.
Marke Benton brought to Court a servant without indenture named James Dee and he was ordered to serve 7 years.
Christian Deare, daughter of John Deare, deceased, was ordered to serve Robert Dunn for 4 years or until she married.
Thomas Collins filed a complaint against John Ereckson.
John Dabb bound his daughter Sarah Dabb to Mr. Morgan Williams and his wife for 4 years "to serve them in such occasions as required."
Isaac Winchester and John Wright recorded their cattle marks.
Pasco Dunn assigned over all his "right and title of this within specified bill of sale" to Henry Downes on April 16, 1667.
Frances Shambrooke bound herself to Thomas Bright for 3 years on June 18, 1668. Witnesses were Thomas Thechiley and Robert Hawkshaw.
Alexander Thourson entered a cattle mark for his son Andrew Thourson.
Peter Scales, Mary Sacle, Robert Humphreys and William Pledge recorded their cattle marks.

KENT COUNTY COURT HELD ON AUGUST 25, 1668
Following a petition of Edward Hull, the Court ordered his servant Matthias Smith to received 20 lashes on his bare back and then be set free "in consideration of his curing of his leg and to pay him his corn and clothes."
John Woolcott brought to Court a servant named Ellenor Hutchins who was ordered to serve him for 6 years, but in case an indenture is found to serve but 4 years. [A subsequent entry in

June, 1669, was made that an indenture had been found so she serves only 4 years.]

KENT COUNTY COURT HELD ON SEPTEMBER 29, 1668
Present were Capt. Robert Vaughan, Capt. John Vicaris, Mr. Matthew Read, Mr. Morgan Williams, Mr. William Head, Mr. Thomas Osborne, and Mr. John Dabb, Commissioners.
John Wright filed a complaint against Thomas Chitcherley.
Thomas Chitcherley appointed George Gouldhawke as his attorney.
Thomas Collins filed a complaint against John Foord [sic].
Court ordered that Mary Tennant, servant to John Wright, shall serve 5 years from her first arrival into the country [no date].

KENT COUNTY COURT HELD ON OCTOVER 13, 1668
Hannah Jenkins, daughter-in-law of Mr. George Harris, was reported to have delivered a man child and murdered same. A jury of women to investigate the matter, viz: Mary Vicaris, Rebecka Denny, Christian Ringgold, Elizabeth Coppage, Dorothy Williams, Margarett Jones, Elizabeth Winchester, Hannah Dabb, Kathorine Osborne, Ann Blunt, Mary Southerne, and Kathorine Scale. The jury ordered that Hannah Jenkins "shall be cleared by proclamation."

KENT COUNTY COURT HELD ON NOVEMBER 24, 1668
Complaints were filed as follows: Capt. John Vicaris vs. Henery Downes; Rebecka Burton vs. Henery Hudson; William Grainger vs. Richard Harrington; Hannah Jenkins vs. Isabella Head; John Wright vs. Edward Hull; John Wright vs. Robert Humphreys; William Elleyeott vs. Robert Humphreys; Robert Dunn vs. Matthias Peterson; Richard Blunt vs. Thomas Currey; Henery Coursey vs. William Lippin; John Dabb vs. John Morgan; Thomas Currey vs. Thomas Chitcherley; Hannah Jenkins vs. John Stephens.
Major Thomas Ingram attached Robert Kent for 400 pounds of tobacco due by bill to Thomas Francis, which the Court ordered to be paid.
On October 31, 1668, Thomas Hill and wife Barbery Hill assisgned some land over to Richard Pether. Witnesses were John Wright and Mark Benton.

KENT COUNTY COURT HELD ON JANUARY 26, 1668
Complaints were filed as follows: Capt. John Vicaris vs. Edmond Mustian; Nathaniel Stinchcombe vs. John Tassell; Mr. John Dabb vs. Alexander Waters; Mr. John Dabb vs. Matthias Peterson; Mrs. Mary Vaughan vs. John Maggison; Mr. William Head vs. Richard Pether; Mr. William Head vs. John Lawrence; Capt. John Vicaris vs. Peter Scale; Mr. William Head vs. Peter Scale; Mr. William Head vs. John Tassell; Mr. George Harris vs. Christopher Denny; John Wright vs. George Harris; John Lawrence vs. Toby Wells; Mr. Thomas Marsh vs. Richard Pether; Mr. Thomas Marsh vs. John Winchester; Mr. Thomas Marsh vs. Thomas Ringgould; Richard Pether vs. Rebecka Burton; John Wright vs. Alexander Nash; Mr. Richard Tilghman vs. Edward Hull; Rebecka Burton vs. Henery Fedes; Rebecka Burton vs. Samuel King; Mr. Matthew Read vs. Mr. William Head; John Wright vs. George Gouldhawke; James Collyer vs. Thomas Ringgould; Mr. Matthew Read vs. Thomas Ringgould; John Cooper vs.

INHABITANTS OF KENT COUNTY, MARYLAND, 1637-1787

Mr. George Harris.
Capt. Jonathana Silbrey informed the Court that there is due him, out of the estate of Mr. Nickolas Pickard, 163 pounds of tobacco which can be verified by Samuel King who married the said Pickard's widow. Court ordered it paid on December 31, 1669.
Thomas Marsh, of Anarundell County, appointed his friend Alexander Nash, of Kent County, his lawful attorney to sue and recover debts owed by Richard Pether, Thomas Ringgould, John Winchester, William Head, John Vicarige, and Edward Hull, on November 16, 1668.
William Richards sold a cow to Thomas Southern on April 20, 1663 [sic]. Witnesses were William Pyper and Charles Steward.

KENT COUNTY COURT HELD ON MARCH 30, 1669
Complaints were filed as follows: John Wright vs. George Harris; Christopher Denny vs. Robert Humphreys; Mr. John Dabb vs. John Stevens; Henery Coursey vs. John Currer; Capt. John Vicaris vs. Edmond Mustian; John Cooper vs. George Harris; Samuel King vs. Mr. William Head.
Jury named in the case of John Cooper vs. George Harris: William Hemsley, Thomas Southern, John Erreckson, John Stevens, Thomas Bright, Robert Humphreys, Christopher Denny, Richard Pether, Thomas Heath, Thomas Linstead, Arthur Ginn, and John Winchester, Sr.
On November 14, 1668, John Currer, grocer, of London, England, appointed his loving friend Ezekiell Croscombe, Commander of the good ship King Solomon, and his [John's] loving nephew John Currer, as his lawful attorneys to recover all monies due him from John Wright, planter, of Maryland. Witnesses were Thomas Truman and William Currer.
Alexander Tourson brought to Court a servant named Hans Rosemason who came in without indenture. Court ordered him to serve 5 years.
Robert Hawkshaw recorded his cattle mark.

APPOINTMENTS ON APRIL 16, 1669:
Charles Calvert, Lieutenant General of Maryland, appointed Robert Dunn, John Vicaris, Mathew Read, Morgan Williams, Richard Blunt, Thomas Osborne, William Head, John Wright, and William Bishop, gentlemen, to serve as Justices of the Peace and Commissioners to keep the law in Kent County. He also appointed Robert Dunn and John Vicaris to be Commissioners "to enquire by the oathes of good and lawfull men of your county aforesaid of all manor of felonies, witchcraftes, inchantments, sorcery, magick arts, trespasses, forestallings, ingrosseings, and extortioners whatsoever."

KENT COUNTY COURT HELD ON JUNE 28, 1669
Mr. William Bishop petitioned the Court for tobacco due him from the estate of Capt. Robert Vaughan, deceased.
Thomas Thurston petitioned the Court for tobacco due him from the estate of Edmond Burton, deceased.
Mary Wilkins was presented to the Court for having a bastard child. She was not able to prove who the child's father was,

although she had formerly slandered Capt. John Vicaris to be the father. The Court ordered her to maintain the child herself, and also ordered her to receive 30 lashes on her bare back for slandering Capt. Vicaris.
Barbra [sic] Hill, widow, petitioned the Court for a barrel of Indian corn which Thomas Heath owed her husband at the time of his death.
James Cullums filed separate complaints against Robert Humphreys and Richard Mor [sic].
Thomas Thurston, of Baltimore County, shoemaker, appointed Henry Howard, of Ann Arundel County, to be his lawful attorney on June 4, 1669, to recover money owed him from Edmond Burton, late of Kent Island, deceased. Witnesses were George Skipwith [Skipworth] and Edward Skidmore.
Robert Kent recorded his cattle mark.
Samuel Ward was appointed Under Sheriff of Kent County by Thomas Ingram on June 28, 1669.
James Cullums, of Calvert County, appointed his well beloved friend Edward Burton, of Kent County, to be his lawful attorney on March 29, 1669, to recover monies owed from Robert Humphrey. Witnesses were William Gannocke and Allexander Beaven.

KENT COUNTY COURT HELD AT SAMUEL KING'S HOUSE ON JULY 10, 1669
Inventory of the goods and chattels of Nicholas Pickard, deceased, was presented by Samuell King as appraised in September, 1668, by Edward Joanes and George Goldhauke. Names mentioned therein were John Lewis, Mr. William Head, Mr. Thomas Ringgould, John Lawrence, Anthony Callaway, Esabella Barnes, Arthur Ginn, Thomas Sutherne, Mr. Marsh, Thomas Hill, Richard Fitts Alleyn [Fitzallen?], and John Woolcott. Also mentioned were the four minor children of Nicholas Pickard, to wit: William, John, [blank], and Sarah. Recorded by Disborough Bennett, clerk.

VITAL RECORDS:
Elizabeth Mustian, daughter of Edmond and Elizabeth Mustian, was born on October 9, 1668.
Elizabeth King, daughter of Samuell and Ellenor King, was born on December 18, 1669.
John Martin, son of John and Barbra Martin, was born on November 15, 1662.
Elizabeth Copedge, daughter of Edward and Elizabeth Copedge, was born on July 7, 1654.
Sarah Copedge, daughter of Edward and Elizabeth Copedge, was born on January 1, 1656.
John Copedge, son of Edward and Elizabeth Copedge, was born on March 31, 1660.
Phillip Copedge, son of Edward and Elizabeth Copedge, was born on November 11, 1663.
Elizabeth Harrington, daughter of Richard and Katherine Harrington, was born on August 20, 1670.
Charles [sic]
Robert Banckes was born on January 31, 1675/6.
Elizabeth King, daughter of Samuell and Ellenor King, was buried on March 24, 1669/70,
Elizabeth Copedge, wife of Edward, died on September 9, 1669.

Edward L---well [sic] died on July 18, 1669.
Elizabeth Morton died on November --, 1669.
Mary Southeran died on November 5, 1669.
Susannah Banckes died on March 12, 1675/6.
Elizabeth Dowland, daughter of William and Amy Dowland, was born on March 6, 1680.

KENT COUNTY COURT HELD ON AUGUST 24, 1669
Complaints were filed as follows: Mr. William Head vs. William Bayeley; Moses Staggall vs. John Cooper; John Cooper vs. Mr. George Harris; Isaac Burger vs. Arthur Wright.
Indenture was made on August 17, 1669 between Morgan Williams and George Harris, both gentlemen of Kent Island, whereby Williams sold to Harris a tract called "Past Hope" on Kent Island adjacent to land now in possession of Tobias Wells, formerly sold to William Richards. Witnesses were George Yate, Thomas Knighton, and John Ingram.
On August 24, 1669, John Machoakin, planter, of Kent County, sold to Capt. Jacob Brimington, of Talbot County, a parcel of land called "Machoakin" on the north side of the Chester River and on the east side of Langford's Bay, adjoining land lately laid out for Nicholas Broadway. Witnesses were Robert Dunn and John Wright.

KENT COUNTY COURT HELD IN SEPTEMBER, 1669
William Stanley filed a complaint against Mathias Peterson. The following jury was named: Tobyas Wells (Foreman), John Wallton, Edward Leake, Richard Nash, Arthur Wright, Samuell King, John Currer, John Browne, Robert Kent, Joseph Wharton, Edward Burton, and William Lawrence. The jury found for the defendant.
Mr. Edward Pomfrett entered a caveat against the estate of Thomas Linstead for 1,600 pounds of tobacco.
Court ordered that Mr. Mitchell DeContie shall have 1,000 pounds of tobacco paid by the County "for the curing of Joseph Inglesby."

KENT COUNTY COURT HELD ON OCTOBER 9, 1669
"This day according to Act of Assembly appoynted for the makeing of highwayes that the old Path coming from Kent Poynt be made goode and pasable according to the said Act to the head of Broad Creeke and allsoe a path from the Court house to meete with the said highway. And allsoe the highway to be made from the Court house to the Piqqquarter Creeke and from thence along the Gunn ridge to Isaac Winchester's and soe to the old Path that goeth by Mr. Morgan Williams and soe to Love Point. And it is allsoe ordered that a Roade be made from the head of Piggquarter Creeke unto the house of Mr. Robert Dunn and from thence by John Dabb's Plantation, and soe alonge down to the house of William Granger; it is allsoe ordered that a Roade be made from Major Thomas Ingram's house upp the said neck and soe by Marke Benton's Plantation and soe to the head of Stowell's Branch. And then by Mr. Robert Dunn's Plantation ---- [blank] Dunn's Plantation and soe to Mr. William Head's Old ---- [blank] from thence into the mayne Roade. And It is further ordered [blank] Harris be overseer

KENT COUNTY COURT PROCEEDINGS, 1647-1676   137

for the upper hundred and [blank] for the lower hundred."
On May 7, 1669, Mrs. Margrett Brent, of Virginia, appointed Edward Leake, of Kent, as her attorney to collect rents due from persons whatsoever for Kent Manor. Witnesses were John Eglon and Arthur Wright.
Thomas Taylor recorded his cattle mark.
Persons paid by the County for various services rendered in 1669: John Nuttwell, Daniell Janeffer, Edward Kanne, Richard Blunt, John True, Disboro Bennett, Richard Nash, Mrs. Blunt, Edward Joanes, Samuel King, John Davis, Matthew Reade, William Bishop, David Joanes, Francis Russell, and Joseph Englesby.

KENT COUNTY COURT HELD ON NOVEMBER 23, 1669
Complaints were filed as follows: Mrs. Ann Blunt vs. William Dowland; Mr. George Harris vs. John True; Mr. Thomas Osborne vs. John Morgan; Capt. Philemon Lloyd vs. Mr. Mathew Read and Mr. John Wright; Mr. Mitchell Conty vs. Petter Johnson; Mrs. Ann Blunt vs. Richard Pether; Mrs. Ann Blunt vs. John Winchester.
Court ordered Isaac Winchester, administrator of the estate of John Winchester, Sr., his deceased father, to deliver over to George Deare the cattle of his that were in John's possession when he died.
Claims made against the estate of Richard Blunt, deceased, by Richard Nash, Henry Feddes, William Towlson, and John Wright.
Claims made against the estate of Allexander Towrson, deceased, by Edward Burton and Tobyas Wells.
Claims made against the estate of William Elliyott, deceased, by Mosses Stagoll, Robert Kent, Tobyas Wells, and John Wright.
Claims were made against the estate of John Winchester, deceased, by Tobyas Wells, Mr. Matthew Reade, Mr. John Wright, Mr. Jeremyah Eaton, Charles Edgerton, William Joanes, and John Lawrence.
Claim was made against the estate of Henry Downes, deceased, by Tobyas Wells.
Claim was made against the estate of Thomas Linstead, deceased, by Edward Pomfrett.
Richard Pether recorded his cattle mark.
John Winchester recorded his cattle mark.

KENT COUNTY COURT HELD ON JANUARY 5, 1669
Present were Henry Coursey, Esq., Mr. Robert Dunn, Mr. Matthew Read, Mr. Thomas Osborne, Mr. William Head, Mr. William Bishopp, and Mr. John Wright, Commissioners.
Complaints were filed as follows: William Baytman vs. John True; William Baytman vs. Joseph Weekes; Mr. Robert Dunn vs. Charles Steuard; Mr. Robert Dunn vs. Mr. Mitchell Conty; George Yate vs. George Harris; Mr. Johnathan Sybrey vs. Mr. William Head; Mr. Johnathan Sibery vs. Allexander Nash; Mr. Mitchell Conty vs. Mr. John Dabb; Mr. Mitchell Conty vs. Sarah Towerson; John Currer vs. Mr. Mitchell Conty; Tobyas Wells vs. Francis Finch; Tobyas Wells vs. John Maggison; Tobyas Wells vs. Cornelious Monteag; George Harris vs. Mr. William Head; Mrs. Mary Vicaris vs. Arthur Ginn; Mr. Mitchell Conty vs. Thomas Knighton; Tobyas Wells vs. Arthur Ginn; Nathaniell Stinchcomb vs. John Browne; Thomas Cole vs. John True.

Edward Browne was appointed Constable for the Upper Hundred.
William Batteman, of Talbot County, appointed his friend Joseph Wicks as his lawful attorney to collect debts due from John True and William True on November 18, 1669. Witnesses were John Tassell and James Cowlee.
George Yate, of Ann Arrondell County, appointed Robert Willson as his lawful attorney to collect 1,000 pounds of tobacco from George Harris on November 28, 1669. Witnesses were Francis Waters and John Shearing.
Claims against the estate of Capt. John Vicaris, late of this county, deceased, were made by Henry Coursey, Disborough Bennett, Thomas Taylor, William Royden, John Currer, Mrs. Ann Blunt, and Mr. William Head.
Claims against the estate of Mr. Richard Blunt, late of this county, deceased, were made by John Currer, William Royden, and Edward Cowell.
Robert Dunn filed a claim against the estate of Henry Downes, late of this county, deceased.
Claims against the estate of John Winchester, Sr., late of this county, deceased, were filed by John Winchester, Mrs. Ann Blunt, and Mrs. Mary Vicaris.
Mr. Johnathan Sybrey filed a claim against the estate of Thomas Hill, late of this county, deceased.
John Wallton, Isaac Burgger, and Richard More recorded their cattle marks.
Philip Calvert granted a marriage license to Francis Pine and Mary Vicaris on February 2, 1669.
George Deare, son of John Deare, received cattle due him from the estate of John Winchester, Sr., deceased, on March 12, 1669/70.
Robert Kent purchased the 100 acre tract called "Ship-Poynt" from Major Thomas Ingram and then sold it to John Walton. Alienation fees were paid by both men.

KENT COUNTY COURT HELD ON MARCH 22, 1669/70
Complaints were filed as follows: John Maggison vs. Richard Pether; Mr. William Bishopp vs. George Lancester; Allexander Maxwell vs. John Dabb; Mr. George Harris vs. John True; Tobyas Wells vs. Henry Norman.
Valentine Hues was charged "for divers scandelous words spoaken against the Commissioners of Kent County."
Thomas Taylor brought a servant named James Bringgergrass to Court and he was judged to be 14 years old and was ordered to serve for 8 years "unless he can produce indentures or his age out of England."
Elizabeth Lyppins, daughter of William Lyppins, late of this county, deceased, "being a child of six yeare old the first of this instant March, [1669/70] and left the county," was ordered to serve William Granger and his wife Grace until she becomes age 18, as they now already had the child in their possession.
Henry Carter bought a 50 acre tract called "Dunns Hazard" from Mr. Robert Dunn, and paid the alienation fee.
Ezekiel Croscomb certified that Humphrey Hubberd, aged 21, was indentured to Edmond Burton for 4 years on January 2, 1669. Witnesses were Robert Dunn and William Currer.

Charles Edgerton was paid out of the estate of Capt. John Vicaris.
Petter Johnson was paid out of the estate of Capt. John Vicaris.
Charles Edgerton was paid out of the estate of Henry Downes.
Mr. William Head was paid out of the estate of Henry Downes.
Edward Burton was paid out of the estate of William Elliott.
Christopher Denney was paid out of the estate of Allexander Towerson.
Mr. John Wright was paid out of the estate of John Ellis.
Richard Pether was paid out of the estate of Thomas Hill.
John Winchester recorded his cattle mark for the future for his daughter-in-law Elizabeth Montrosse.
Mr. Francis Pyne recorded his cattle mark.

KENT COUNTY COURT HELD ON JUNE 28, 1670
Complaints were filed as follows: Tobyas Wells vs. Arthur Ginn; Tobyas Wells vs. Henry Norman; John Maggison vs. Richard Pether; John True vs. Mr. George Harris; Edward Burton vs. Samuel King; Edward Burton vs. John Maggisson; Mr. Francis Pyne vs. Mr. Robert Burle; Thomas Ringgold vs. Samuel King; John Stevens vs. Jacob Johnson.
Mr. William Head gave a heifer to Ruth Joanes, daughter of Edward.
Ann Nash, wife of Richard Nash, confirmed "a former gift of hers in her former husband's life: Mr. Richard Blunt of a heifer by her given unto Abell, son of John Maggisson."
Samuell Kinge [sic] was appointed Constable for the Lower Hundred.
Francis Pyne, of the City of Bristoll, merchant, appointed his well beloved friend Robert Burle, of Arrundell County, gentleman, to be his lawful attorney on "this eight day of 7ber, 1669." Witnesses were Thomas Marsh and Anto Mayl: [sic].
Richard Nash, boatwright, of the Island of Kent, appointed his wife Ann Nash to be his lawful attorney in his absence on April 20, 1670. Witnesses were Francis Pyne, John Cooper and Christopher Goodhande.
Mr. Robert Dunn gave a calf to Elizabeth, daughter of Henry Carter.
Henry Carter recorded his cattle mark.
Valentine Sutherin presented an account of the cattle in his possession that belong to Mary Scale, daughter of Peter Scale, late of this county, deceased.
Court ordered all know goods of William Lyppins, late of this county, deceased, to be brought to the house of Mr. Thomas Osborne and "sould att an out cry on satterday com fortnight being the 16th day of July [1670] next."
Edward Browne, Constable, presented Frances Shembrooke for having a bastard child, the father thereof not known.

KENT COUNTY COURT HELD AT RICHARD NASH'S HOUSE ON JULY 16, 1670
Frances Shembrooke complained against her masters Mr. William Bishop and Robert Palmer for abuse, and won her case. They had to pay her 100 pounds of tobacco until she was able to work.
James Phillips was declared to be the father of the bastard child of Frances Shembrooke. His masters were William Bishop and Robert

Palmer, who entered bond for him and the maintenance of the child.
Inventory and sale of the goods of William Lippins, deceased, was recorded and some of the purchasers were John Ingram (a gun), Mitchell DeConty (bedding), Thomas Osborne (looken glass), Richard Pether (bedstead), and Tobyas Wells (Irish stockens).

KENT COUNTY COURT HELD ON AUGUST 23, 1670
Complaints were filed as follows: Mr. William Head vs. Mr. James Ringgold; Edward Burton vs. Samuel and Ellenor King; John True vs. Mr. George Harris; William Crosse vs. Mr. George Harris; Mr. William Bishop vs. William Pledge; Jeremuah Eaton vs. John Morgan; Isaac Winchester vs. Thomas Heath; Jeane Griffen vs. Mr. Francis Pyne; John Quigley vs. William Joyner.
Jury selected in August, 1670: Tobyas Wells, Francis Pyne, Robert Palmer, Thomas Hinson, Johnathan Hopkins, Edward Winckles, John Browne, Arthur Wright, Petter Johnson, Thomas Heath, Isaac Winchester, and Allexander Walters.
Tobyas Wells was paid by the Court for taking care of the funeral of William Lippins.
Jere: Eaton appointed his friend Tobyas Wells to be his lawful attorney on August 13, 1670. Witness was John Rye: [sic].
John Maggison, of the Island of Kent, declared that he was indebted to Thomas Bright, of the Island of Kent, and therefore conveyed his plantation to him. Witnesses were Robert Dunn and Disboro: Bennett.

KENT COUNTY COURT HELD ON SEPTEMBER 27, 1670
Complaints were filed as follows: Mr. William Head vs. Mr. James Ringgold; Mr. William Head vs. Tobyas Wells; Tobyas Wells vs. Mr. William Head; Mr. William Head vs. John Morgan; John True vs. George Harris; Jean Griffen vs. Mr. Francis Pyne; Tobyas Wells vs. John Tassell; Mr. William Bishop vs. John Morgan; Mr. John Wright vs. Mr. Francis Pyne; Mr. Francis Pyne vs. Mr. John Wright.
Jury selected in September, 1670: James Ringgold, John Dabb, Henry Carter, John Winchester, Allexander Walters, Edward Joanes, George Goldhauke, John Cooper, Charles Stuard, Ralph Blackhall, William Yeamans, and Jeremiah Eaton.
Mr. William Head brought his servant named Thomas Guinn to Court for being absent from his service some 34 days. The Court ordered him to serve his master for 340 days and receive 10 lashes upon his bare back "for stealeing of peopls connoas from theyer landings."
John Stevenson, mariner of the Parish of Deptforde in Kent County, appointed his friend Robert Dunn to be his lawful attorney. Witnesses were Thomas Cooper and Griffen Stevens.
Caesar Sutton, chirurgion on the good ship King Solomon commanded by Ezekiel Croscombe, appointed Robert Dunn of Kent County to be his lawful attorney. Witnesses were John Ingram and Thomas Cooper.
Richard More, William Joyner, and Vallentine Sutherin recorded their cattle marks.

KENT COUNTY COURT PROCEEDINGS, 1647-1676   141

KENT COUNTY COURT HELD ON OCTOBER 10, 1670
John Dabb was appointed overseer of roads for the Upper Hundred.
Edward Burton was appointed overseer of roads for the Lower
Hundred.
Thomas Chicherley recorded his cattle mark.

KENT COUNTY COURT HELD ON NOVEMBER 22, 1670
Complaints were filed as follows: John Clemons vs. John Ingram;
Charles De la Roch vs. George Harris; Mr. Richard Tilghman vs.
George Lancester; Mr. Richard Tillman vs. Arthur Ginn; Mr.
William Head vs. Thomas Snow; Rice Cookeman vs. Christopher
Denney; Henry Norman vs. Thomas Ringgold; Mr. William Head vs.
Robert Tallent; William Granger vs. Richard Harrington; Anthony
Hillson vs. Richard Harrington; Richard More vs. Matthias Smith;
Matthias Smith vs. Katherin Wright; John Browne vs. Robert Kent;
James Thompson vs. Thomas Norris; Johnathan Hopkins vs. Mr.
William Head; Isaac Winchester vs. Edward John; Jeane Griffen vs.
Mr. Francis Pyne.
Jury was selected in 1670: Allexander Maxwell (Foreman), Edward
Browne, Daved Joanes, Richard Nash, Henry Carter, John
Winchester, Petter Johnson, William Granger, Arthur Wright,
Richard Pether, George Lancester, and Thomas Bright.
Richard Nash recorded the sale of a man servant named Richard
Kempstone to Thomas Taylor for four years and no more, from the
arrival of the ship on November 2, 1670.
Peter Johnson sold 100 acres on Isle of Kent to Mitchell De Conty
on November 22, 1670. Witnesses were Mi: [sic] Miller and Thomas
Baxter. Acknowledged by Peter Johnson and Mary Johnson who made
their marks on the conveyance.
Richard Tilghman appointed Charles De la Roch his lawful attorney
on November 2, 1670. Witnesses were John Keelee and Cornelius
Comegys.
Mr. John Wright was ordered paid out of the estate of Henry
Fedes.
Francis Pyne appointed his trust servant Christopher Goodhand to
be his lawful attorney "on 11th 9ber 1670." Witnesses were John
Norwood and Toby Appleford.
Anthony Hillson, of London, Mariner, appointed his trusty friend
William Granger, of Kent County, Planter, to be his lawful
attorney on February 12, 1669. Witnesses were Benjamin Grove and
William Currer.
John Clemons, of Talbot County, appointed his good friend John
Ingram to be his lawful attorney in 1670. Witnesses were Edward
Roe and William Crosse.
George Harris, of Kent County, appointed his wife Sarah Harris to
be his lawful attorney on November 21, 1670. Witnesses were Caleb
Baker and Heneri [sic] Cragg.

LEVY LIST IN 1670: Danie Clocker, Robert Gealiam, Thomas Spincke,
Thomas Gilpin, Richard Rider, Daniell Junifer, John Webster,
Richard Nash, John Areckson, Mitchell De Conty, Robert Dunn, John
Winchester, Disborough Bennett, Thomas Ingram, and Henry Downes.

KENT COUNTY COURT HELD ON JANUARY 24, 1670
John Winchester and Marke Benton were appointed Constables.

Complaints were filed as follows: Richard Tillman vs. Arthur Gin; William Dennes vs. John Dobbs; Thomas Heath vs. Tobias Appleford; Jeremiah Eaton vs. Michaell De County; John Currer vs. John Dobbs; Jeremiah Eaton vs. Richard Pether; William Bateman vs. Tobyas Wells; Thomas Baxter vs. Michaell De County; Hannah Sheurty vs. George Harris; Francis Pyne vs. William Davis; Mr. Matthew Reade vs. Peter Johnson; Michaell De County vs. John Currer; Tobias Wells vs. Joseph Wickes; John Cooper vs. Francis Pyne; Tobyas Wells vs. John Magisson.
Samuell King was ordered to be released from prison.
Phillomon Loyde was ordered paid out of the estate of Nicholas Pickard.
Sara Towrson appointed Michaell Miller to be her attorney.
John Magisson appointed Michaell Miller to be his attorney.
Samuell King appointed Tobias Wells to be his attorney.
Michaell De County appointed Michaell Miller to be his attorney.
William Davis appointed Tobyas Wells to be his attorney.
William Lawrence took the oath of Constable for the Lower Hundred.
John Ellison ordered to keep an orphan [not named] for 1,000 pounds of tobacco per year.
Edward Leake, of Kent County, appointed his trusty friend Michael Miller, of Talbot County, to be his lawful attorney on January 19, 1670. Witnesses were William Hemsly and Isaac Winchester.
John Cooper, of Talbot County, appointed his trusty friend Charles De la Roch, of Kent County, to be his lawful attorney on January 4, 1670/1. Witnesses were John Wright and Laurance Arnell.
Deposition taken from Roger Price, aged about 31, in 1670.
Deposition taken from Gabriell Cox, aged about 28, in 1670 and mentioned William Davis, Francis Pyne, his man Christopher, and Robert Boise.
Deposition taken from Abraham Holse, aged about 23, in 1670.

KENT COUNTY COURT HELD ON MARCH 28, 1671
Present were Mr. Mathew Reade, Mr. John Wright, Mr. Morgan Williams, Mr. William Head, and Mr. Thomas Osburne, Commissioners.
Complaints were filed as follows: William Granger vs. William Bishop; Francis Pyne vs. William Davis; Jeremiah Eaton vs. Richard Harrington; Thomas Evans vs. John Dobbs; Jeremiah Eaton vs. Alice Stevens; Richard Tillman vs. Richard Huching; Joseph Choape vs. Richard Moore; Caesar Sutton vs. George Goldhauke; Richard Moore vs. George Goldhauke; John Cooper vs. Francis Pyne; Hanna Sheurty vs/ George Harris; Francis Pyne vs. William Davis.
Jury was selected in 1671: Ralph Blakhall (Foreman), Richard More, Richard Pether, John Davis, Edward Browne, Edward Joanes, Edward Hull, Charles De la Roch, John Winchester, John Webster, John Ereckson, and John Currer.
Agreement signed by Robert Kent and Frances Ashbury on February 21, 1671. Witnesses were William Dennis and Catharin Wright, and also mentioned were Arthur Wright and John Davis.
Marke Benton brought his servant John Smith into Court and he was ordered to serve 7 years.

KENT COUNTY COURT HELD ON JUNE 27, 1671
Complaints were filed as follows: Jeremiah Eaton vs. William Head; Francis Pyne vs. William Davis; Jeremiah Eaton vs. Alice Stevens; Thomas Cole vs. John Tassell; Thomas Cole vs. Christopher Barnes; Francis Pyne vs. William Davis; Samuell Hall vs. Edward Hull; John Clemens vs. Henry Lambe; William Powell vs. John Tassell; John Stedman vs. John Ingram.
Samuell King charged with embezzling the estate of the orphans of Nicholas Pickard and the Court ordered Arthur Wright to take the orphans [not named] into his possession.
Henry Beedle requested the Court "in behalfe of Moyses Stagoll that those cattle given by William Ellson and hand [sic] his wife unto Thomas Staggoll the sonne of Thomas Stagoll" be delivered as ordered in 1665.
Mary Burton appointed Tobyas Wells to be her attorney.
Roger Baxter appointed Michael Miller to be his attorney.
John Stedman appointed Michaell Miller to be his attorney.
On June 21, 1671, Charles Calvert ordered "that for the future the north east side of the Chester as far as the bounds of Talbott County ware formerly on that side shall now bee added to Kent County and that part to belong to Kent as alsoe Poplers Island."

KENT COUNTY COURT HELD ON AUGUST 28, 1671
Complaints were filed as follows: John Clemans vs. Henry Lambe; John Dobbs vs. George Harris; Jeames Ringould vs. William Smith; Mr. Thomas Osburne vs. Michaell Miller; William Powell vs. John Tassell; Robert Chapman vs. Elizabeth Lewis; John Winchester vs. William Hodges; Mary Burton vs. Jeremiah Eaton; Jonathan Hopkings vs. Richard Cadmore; Jonathan Hopkings vs. William Head; Nicholas Wyott vs. Christopher Barnes; Francis Pyne vs. William Davis.

SESSION OF THE COMMISSIONERS was held at the house of Mr. Robert Dunn on November 18, 1671.
Charles Calvert appointed Thomas South, Joseph Wickes, Henry Hosier, and Francis Pyne, gentlemen, as Commissiones of Kent County, and Thomas South and Joseph Wickes of the Quorum, and all as Justices of the Peace, effective October 18, 1671.
Court ordered the following to be paid for services rendered: John Webster (for keeping an orphan); Arthur Wright (for use of his boat for 45 days); Mr. King (for attendance for 30 days); Richard Stevens (for a wolfes head); John Wright (for a wolfes head); Edward Rogers (for a wolfes head); John Ereckson (for keeping an orphan for 4 months); and Peter Sayer [service not listed].
Richard Nash appointed overseer of roads for the Upper Hundred.
Philip Thomas appointed overseer of roads for the Lower Hundred.
John Ringould appointed overseer of roads for Chester Hundred.

VITAL RECORDS: (recorded by Charles Bancks, clerk)
Susannah Bancks, daugter of Charles and Susannah Bancks, was born on January 16, 1673/4.
Susannah Bancks, daughter of Charles and Susannah Bancks, died on October 11, 1674.
Susannah Bancks died on March 12, 1675/6.

Mr. Tobias Wells died on February 16, 1675/6.
Samuell Richards died on April 3, 1676.
Robert Dunn died on May 12, 1676.
Alice Dunn, daughter of Robert and Joan Dunn, died on August 9, 1678 [sic].
Mr. Disboro Bennett married Mary Wells on April 21, 1676.

KENT COUNTY COURT HELD ON AUGUST 23, 1675
Present were Mr. Joseph Weicks, Mr. James Ringold, Mr. John Hinson, and Mr. Henry Hosier, Commissioners.
Complaints were filed as follows: Elizabeth Erreckson vs. Mr. Arthur Wright; Michaell Miller vs. Ralph Blackhall; Richard Moy vs. John Wells; John Mitchell vs. Jeremiah Eaton; John Gilbert vs. John Ingram; John Darby vs. Mr. Richard Tilghman and William Smith and wife Joan Smith.
Richard Moy appointed Michaell Miller to be his attorney.
John Mitchell appointed Michaell Miller to be his attorney.
John Gilbert appointed Michaell Miller to be his attorney.
Court declared they would pay reasonable expenses for any house keeper who would give food and lodging to Robert Bartrum.
Ralph Blackhall informed the Court that he was too ill to attend.

KENT COUNTY COURT HELD ON NOVEMBER 5, 1675
Court ordered the following paid for services rendered: Mr. Van Swaringen, Mr. Keene, Abraham Hall, John Summers, Mr. Dunn, Mr. Darby (for dyatt of Robert Bartrum), Mr. Darby's wife, Anthony Workeman, Mr. Dunn (prison expences), Mr. Dunn (for boat and hands to carry Mr. Bishop), Mrs. Wright (for Samuell King seven months), Mr. Darby (for one year's house room), Roger Price, Mr. Dunn (for two levy's lost), Henry Ridgley (for 1 wolfes head), Thomas Parker (for 3 wolfes heads), Thomas Baxter (for 1 wolfes head), Abraham Esseter (for 1 wolf), Cornelius Comegys (for 1 wolf), Mr. Wheeler (for 1 wolf), William Bateman (for 1 wolf), Mr. Dabbs (for Richard Redding), Mr. Tobias Wells, and Charles De la Roach.

KENT COUNTY COURT HELD ON DECEMBER 7, 1675
Complaints were filed as follows: Charles Carpenter vs. Edward James; Jonathan Hopkinson vs. William Shears; John Darby vs. Thomas Eavans; Thomas Eavans vs. William Ladds; Richard Tilghman vs. Richard Hudson; Thomas Mason vs. Richard Hudson; Thomas Mason vs. Michaell Miller; John Darby vs. John Erreckson; John Darby vs. Edward Hull; John Darby vs. Thomas Bruss; John Cooper vs. John Ingram.
Jury selected in 1675: Cornelius Comegys (Foreman), Edward James, Edward Rodgers, William Sheares, Richard Hudson, John Wright, Thomas Thexston, William Smith, William Savidge, Thomas Moore, John Cooper, and John White.
Court appointed Mr. Cornelius Comegys as overseer of roads in Langford Bay Hundred, and to clear a road from Richard Joanes' house to Swan Creek, and from Mr. Joseph Wickes' house to Swan Creek Road.
Court appointed Christopher Andrews and Robert Griffin as overseers of roads in Chester Hundred.

Court appointed John Dabb as overseer of roads for the Upper
Hundred of Kent Island.
Court appointed Issack Winchester as overseer of roads for the
Lower Hundred of Kent Island.
William Vaughan recorded his cattle mark.
Charles Bancks recorded his cattle mark.
Samuell Tovy recorded his cattle mark.
Hance Hanson recorded his cattle mark.
Richard Fillingham recorded his cattle mark.
John Bowles, Constable, brought the following persons into Court:
Mary Browne, servant to Mr. Comegys, for having a bastard child
born the last of June and died on July 6, 1675; and, Ann Tumees,
servant to Larrence Simons, "for scandiliseing William Joanes for
she said he gott her with childe the 6th or 7th day of March last
past in the yeare 1675." Signed by Nathaniell Evatts, foreman.
Richard Tilghman petitioned the Court in December, 1675, that
"aboot two monthes since did take in George Hayes to cure of the
bones of his cubit being lacerated & torne by an accident in your
county, whereby he is like to loose the use of his right cubit
for ever, and William Smith of your county did promise to pay for
one halfe of the cure, the said George Hayes not being in any
capacity to make satisfaction for the other half, [pray] order
the poore man be maintained."

KENT COUNTY COURT HELD ON JANUARY 25, 1675
Summoned to Court to take the oath of Constables were Thomas
Warren, Jr., Christopher Andrews, Henry Carter, and Thomas Brite.
Complaints were filed as follows: John Darby vs. Edward Hull;
Richard Hatton vs. James Bath; Mr. James Ringold vs. Michaell
Miller; Patrick Gordon vs. Richard Pearce; William Darvall vs.
Steven Whetston; William Darvall vs. Bennett Staires; Christopher
Pitt vs. John Larrance; Thomas Eavans vs. William Ladds;
Christopher Andrews vs. Steven Whettston; Lawrence Simons vs.
John Jackson; Michael Miller vs. Edward Browne; Thomas Marsh vs.
Thomas Chicherly; Richard Pearce vs. Patrick Gordon; John Bowles
vs. Jane Spencer; Jonathan Hopkinson vs. William Sheers; Michaell
Miller vs. John Ingram; Elizabeth Head, executrix of William Head
vs. John Ingram; Christopher Andrews vs. John Wright; Capt.
Phillamond Loyde vs. Mr. Tobyas Wells; Michaell Miller vs. Edward
Browne; Mr. Natthaniell Stile vs. Bennett Staires; John Tarkinton
vs. Steven Whettston; Charles Banckes vs. John Dabb; Mr. Joseph
Wicks vs. Charles Banckes; Mr. Matthew Warde vs. William Harriss;
John Darby vs. Zacaryah Mahew; Mr. Matthew Warde vs. John Wells;
Lewis Blangy vs. William North; Michaell Miller vs. Mr. Arthur
Wright, executor of Richard Pearce; Mr. Joseph Wicks and Mr. John
Hinson, executors of John Radway vs. William Davis, John Bowles,
John David and William Ladds; Mr. Vincent Lower vs. Mr. Arthur
Wright.
John Darby and John Dabb were ordered to be paid out of the
estate of Walter Spencer.
Elizabeth Norman, servant to Frances Finch, was judged to be 21
years old.
Owen Walter, servant to Mr. Joseph Wicks, was judged to be 13
years old, having come into this country without indentures.
Lewis Davy, servant to Morgon Williams, was judged to be 14 years

old.
Christopher Andrews became Constable for Chester Hundred.
Thomas Warren, Jr. became Constable for Langfords Bay Hundred.
Henry Carter became Constable for the Upper Hundred.
Thomas Brite became Constable for the Lower Hundred.

KENT COUNTY COURT HELD ON APRIL 20, 1676
Robert Neave, Constable, presented Mary Howten for having a bastard child.
Bennett Staires recorded a calf he gave to Martha Chicken, daughter of Edward Chicken.
Edward Chicken recorded his cattle mark.
William Bateman, planter, of Kent County, conveyed a tract called "Greene Branch" to Richard Lowder, planter, of Kent County, on March 30, 1674, located near a tract called "Middle Spring" laid out for John Ringgold. Witnesses were William Harris and Jan Hendricksen. This was acknowledged by Richard Lowder in Court on March 28, 1676.
Thomas Warren, Sr. paid his alienation fee for 125 acres of land called "Pentridge" which he had bought from John Hendrickson.
Ellis Humphrey and Thomas Warren, Sr. recorded their cattle marks.
John Hendrickson, of Kent County, conveyed a tract called "Pentridge" to Thomas Warren, Sr. and Thomas Warren, Jr. on January 20, 1675, located on Langfords Bay near Richard Hudson's land. Witnesses were John Hinson and Cornelius Comegys.
Ellis Humphrey paid his alienation fee for 125 acres of land called "Pentridge" which he bought from Lawrence Simonds and wife Seath.
Wiliam Davis, cooper,of Kent County, conveyed a tract called "Pentridge" to Morgon Jones, of Kent County, on February 15, 1675/6. Witnesses were John Jackson and Ellis Humphrey.

KENT COUNTY COURT HELD ON MARCH 28, 1676
Complaints were filed as follows: Thomas Bright vs. Michaell Miller; Edward Skidmore vs.Thomas Lewis; John Darby vs. William Harris; John Darby vs. John Jackson; John Darby vs. Robert Parkes; Mr. Vincent Lowe vs. Mr. Arthur Wright; Thomas Marsh vs. Thomas Chicherly; Mr. Joseph Wicks and Mr. John Hinson, executors of John Radway vs. John Bowles, Vincent Atchison, William Davis, and Thomas Warren; John Darby vs. Thomas Currer; Richard Brewerton vs. Robert Griffin; Christopher Andrews vs. Richard Brewerton; Thomas Thexston vs. William Davis; Edward Lowder vs. Edward James; Thomas Parker vs. Thomas Warren; Thomas Warren, Jr. vs. Thomas Parker; Samuell Hill vs. George Browne; Christopher Andrews vs. John Wright.
Mr. Henry Hosier, guardian of Richard Phillipps, ordered to be paid out of the estate of Richard Hudson, deceased, money due the orphan.
Mary Phillipps was recorded as one of the orphans of Richard Phillipps, and William Ladds was to deliver her cattle to Richard Fillingham.
Mr. Joseph Wicks brought a woman servant named Christian Gordan to Court and she declared she was 19 years old. The Court ordered

her to serve for 6 years from her first arrival [no date given].
Jury selected in 1676: Thomas Worren, Sr. (Foreman), Thomas
Parker, John White, William Smith, Morgon Joanes, Charles
Steward, Thomas Evans, John Martin, William Key, John Chanler
[sic], Charles Tilden, and William Huddell.

KENT COUNTY COURT HELD ON JUNE 27, 1676
Present were Mr. Joseph Wicks, Mr. John Hinson, Mr. Henry Hosier,
Mr. William Lawrence, Mr. Nathaniell Evatts, Mr. Samuell Tovy,
Mr. Cornelius Comegys, and Mr. Disboro Bennett, Commissioners.
Complaints were filed as follows: Mr. Henry Coursey vs. Richard
Peddar; John Tarkinton vs. Steven Whettston; Robert Griffin vs.
Richard Brewerton; Thomas Frances vs. Richard Brewerton;
Christopher Andrews vs. Richard Brewerton; Mr. John Hinson vs.
Vincent Atchison; Edward Skidmore vs. Thomas Lewis; Michaell
Miller vs. Edmond Roe.
Edward Swettnam was sworn in as Deputy Sheriff of Kent County.
Thomas Arnoll, son of Lawrence Arnoll, was ordered to live with
Michaell Miller until he is 21 years old.
Ruth and Edward Joanes, orphans of Edward Joanes, late of Kent
Island, deceased, were ordered to live with John Erreckson and
Matthew Erreckson until the Court can dispose of them elsewhere.
John and Phillip Coppidge were ordered to live with William
Rawles.
Elizabeth Hudson, administratrix of Richard Hudson, acknowledged
she owed Mr. Henry Hosier money due an orphan of Thomas Phillips.
Mr. Thomas Marsh, Patrick Gordon, George Greene, and Michaell
Miller were ordered to be paid out of the estate of Edward
Joanes.
Mary Phillipps, one of the orphans of Thomas Phillips, was
ordered to live with William Harris until age 18 or the day of
her marriage.
John Wicks was ordered to be paid out of the estate of Edward
Coppidge.
John Maconakin entered a caveat against the estate of Thomas
Baxter.
Jury selected in 1676: John Wells (Foreman), John Wedge, Patrick
Gordon, William Harris, John Bowles, Matthew Erreckson, Thomas
Cooper, Peter Harrison, William Rawles, Thomas Boone, Vincent
Atchison, and John White.
Edward Swettnam brought a servant to Court named Edward Ayres who
was judged to be 12 years old, having come in without indentures.
Robert Hood was ordered to pay Arthur Wright 400 pounds of
tobacco for making a false return of a writ against him.
Mr. William Lawrence, Mr. Disboro Bennett, the Sheriff, and Clerk
were ordered to secure the estate of Alexander Towerson, late of
this county, deceased, in behalf of his two orphans [no names].
Mr. Disboro Bennett recorded his cattle mark.
Mr. Disboro Bennett recorded that he gave a heifer to Lettis
Dabb, daughter of John and Annikin Dabb, and if she should die
before she becomes of age or marries, the calf goes to John
Mecenny, her half brother.
Mr. Disboro Bennett recorded that he gave a calf to Charles
Lowder, son of Edward and Ann Lowder.
Thomas Williams, William Harris, William Frisby, William Trews,

Thomas Warren, Jr., and Abraham Messeter recorded their cattle marks.
Johan Dunn, executrix of Robert Dunn, late of this county, deceased, delivered to Mr. John Hynson all of the weights and measures that were in her possession as ordered by the Court.
"Thomas Brite issued a capias to take the body of John Curer and the Sheriff hath returned a non est inventus."

KENT COUNTY COURT HELD ON AUGUST 22, 1676
Complaints were filed as follows: Thomas Francis vs. John Cooper; Michaell Miller vs. Peter Harrison; Michaell Miller vs. Edmond Roe; Samuell King vs. Arthur Wright; John and Mathew Erreckson vs. Thomas Warren, Jr.; Mr. Samuell Tovy vs. Samuell Hall; Thomas Bruss vs. William Carter; John Moll vs. William Harris; William Bishopp vs. Christopher Grainger; Abraham Wilde vs. Thomas Moore; George Robbins vs. James Coursy; John Darby vs. Richard Hill; Thomas Francs [Francis] vs. John Coop [Cooper]; John Mill vs. Vincent Atchison; William Bishopp vs. Richard Harrington; Thomas Williams vs. John Wells; Samuell King vs. Michaell Miller; Mr. John Moll vs. William Harris; Mr. John Moll vs. Vincent Atchison; Michaell Taylor vs. Richard Pedder; Symond Stevenson vs. Richard Mason; Christopher Andrews vs. Ellis Humphrey.
Joan Dunn, John Darby, Thomas Marsh and Michael Miller were ordered to be paid out of the estate of Richard Moore.
John Slaughter was ordered to be paid out of the estate of Robert Dunn.
John Darby was ordered to be paid out of the estate of Tobias Wells.
Elizabeth De la Roach, administratrix of Charles De la Roach, was ordered to be paid out of the estate of Richard Moore, as was also Moses Stagoll. "Copy to Mr. Winchester on April 12, 1677."
Jacob Singleton was ordered to be paid out of the estate of Mr. John Rye.
Thomas Eavans was ordered to be paid out of the estate of Edward Joanes.
Patrick Sullavant, Christopher Andrews, and Jenkins Smith were ordered to be paid out of the estate of Robert Dunn.
John Ellis came to Court and chose Michael Miller as his guardian.
Edward Rogers brought a servant to Court named Thomas James who came to this country without indentures. He was judged to be 15 years old and was ordered to serve 7 years from his first arrival.
Mr. Henry Hosier brought a servant to Court named John Shaw who came into this country without indentures. He was judged to be 17 years old and was ordered to serve 5 years from his first arrival.
William Jackman was fined 100 pounds of tobacco for swearing in open Court and for being drunk. He was a servant of Christopher Andrews, who also brought suit against him for other damages.
The Sheriff was ordered to secure John Bowles for making several diverse and scandalous remarks against Commissioner Joseph Wicks. Thomas Warren, Jr. posted a ten pound bond in behalf of said John Bowles.

Deposition was taken from William Jackman, aged 24 or thereabouts in 1676.
Deposition was taken from Ann Tumes, aged 44, a servant of Ellis Humphrey who stated Wiliam Jackman had called her master a son of a whore.
Deposition was taken from William Davis, aged 31, and mentioned Andrew Taylor.
Deposition was taken from Morgon Joanes, age 24, and mentioned William Jackman.
The Sheriff was ordered to secure William Dowland for abusing Mr. Disboro Bennett in a very unseemly manner at his home. William Joyner posted a ten pound bond in behalf of said William Dowland.
Cornelius Comegys, Jr. recorded his cattle mark.

KENT COUNTY COURT HELD ON OCTOBER 24, 1676
Present were Mr. Joseph Wicks, Mr. John Hinson, Mr. Henry Hosier, Mr. Nathaniell Evatts, and Mr. Cornelius Comegys, Commissioners.
Complaints were filed as follows: John and Matthew Erreckson vs. Thomas Warren, Jr.; and, Thomas Brite vs. John Currer.
John David was ordered to be paid out of the estate of Robert Dunn.

[End of Kent County Court Proceedings in *Archives of Md.*, Vol. 54].

INHABITANTS OF KENT COUNTY, MARYLAND, 1637-1787

GLEANINGS FROM ST. PAUL'S P. E. CHURCH VESTRY MINUTES, 1693-1724
(Ref: Maryland State Archives, Microfilm M302)

VESTRYMEN, 1693-1697: William Frisby, Thomas Smyth (Smith), Hans Hanson, Charles Tilden, Michael Miller, Simon Wilmer, and Matthew Ward, clerk.

VESTRYMEN, 1697-1702: Stephen Bordley, William Frisby, Thomas Smith, Michael Miller, John Hynson, Charles Tilden, Simon Wilmer, and George Worsley, clerk.

VESTRYMEN, 1703-1708: Col. Hans Hanson, Col. Thomas Smyth, Capt. Thomas Ringgold, Lt. Col. Elias King, Capt. John Wells, Capt. William Potts, Robert Dunn, Stephen Bordley, William Frisby, William Glanville, William Harris, Nathaniel Hynson, Thomas Covington, and George Worsley, clerk.

VESTRYMEN, 1709-1714: Alexander Williamson, Capt. Edward Scott, Col. Thomas Smyth, William Scott, William Harris, William Frisby, Jr., William Ringgold, Capt. James Harris, Charles Hynson, Major Thomas Ringgold, Capt. St. Leger Codd, Michael Miller, and Col. Nathaniel Hynson.

VESTRYMEN, 1715-1724: Col. Nathaniel Hynson, Major William Scott, Col. Edward Scott, Robert Dunn, Alexander Williamson, Capt. St. Leger Codd, Major William Potts, Edward Worrell, Thomas Piner, Marmaduke Tilden, Samuel Thomas, Thomas Ringgold, Charles Ringgold, James Smith, William Crow, Thomas Hynson, and Simon Willmer.

1716 - Church Wardens: Abram Ambrose and Hans Hanson.
1720 - Church Wardens: John Brown and Daniel Ferrell.

1699, November 11 - The following parishioners were assigned to value two acres of land adjacent to St. Paul's Church by Elias King, Sheriff of Kent County: William Smith, George Smith, James Watson, Thomas Hill, David Davis, Rice Jones, Jno. Blackston, Benjamin Ricaud, Thomas Ricaud, Richard Mason, and John Hodges.

PEWHOLDERS IN ST. PAUL'S PROTESTANT EPISCOPAL CHURCH IN 1720:
1 - Alexander Williamson, Col. Nathaniel Hynson
2 - Col. Thomas Smyth
3 - John March, Solomon Wright
4 - James Smyth, Thomas Bown [sic]
5 - James Harris, Esq.
6 - Col. Edward Scott
7 - Major William Potts, Richard Simmonds
8 - John Moll, William Bateman
9 - Samuel Thomas, Edward Davis, John Evans
10 - Simon Willmer, Thomas Piner
11 - John Fulston, Richard Fulston, William Jones, John Williams
12 - William Worrell, Samuel Tovey
13 - Rebecca Willmer, Thomas Ringold, Charles Hynson
14 - William Frisby, James Frisby

ST. PAUL'S VESTRY MINUTES, 1693-1724   151

15 - William Glanvill, William Pope
16 - Frances Crawford, Ann Frisby
17 - Oliver Higgenbottom, John Green, John Rolph
18 - Marmaduke Tilden, Thomas Hynson
19 - Arthur Miller, Edward Worrell
20 - John Moore, John Fanning
21 - St. Leger Codd, Hans Hanson
22 - Daniel Duffy, John Hynson
23 - James Murphey, Jacob Glenn [Glann?]
24 - Michael Hacket, Philip Davis
25 - Ebenezer Blackston, John Blackston
26 - John Rogers, John Tilden
27 - Michael Miller, Samuel Berry
28 - Robert Dunn, William Dunn
29 - John Taylor, William Simcocks
30 - William Ringgold, Charles Ringgold
31 - Edward Rogers, Jr., Samuel Wickes
32 - George Hanson, Frederick Hanson
33 - For the Minister, Thomas Bordley, Stephen Bordley
34 - Richard Philligem, Samuel Gooden, Edward Jarvis

GLEANINGS FROM CHESTER P. E. CHURCH VESTRY MINUTES, 1766-1780
(Ref: Maryland State Archives, Microfilm 356)

CHURCH OFFICIALS, 1766-1774 (who took their oaths of office and swore allegiance to King George of Great Britain):

Chester P. E. Church, February 18, 1766: Aron Alford, vestryman; Thomas Perkins, vestryman; Joseph Rasin, vestryman; Macall Medford, vestryman; William Cowardin, church warden; Robert Peacock, church warden; Charles Groome, register.

Chester P. E. Church, May 5, 1767: William Ringold, vestryman; Joseph Rasin, vestryman; Luke Griffith, vestryman; R. Buchanan, vestryman; R. Frisby, vestryman; Rasin Gale, church warden; John Ashley, church warden; Charles Groome, register.

September 1, 1767: James Wroth, church warden.

October 21, 1767: Matthias Harris (Reverend).

April 16, 1768: ---- Griffith, vestryman; James Wroth, vestryman; Thomas Wilkins, church warden; Hezekiah Cooper, church warden.

April 4, 1769: Macall Medford, vestryman; Edward Beck, church warden; Thn[?] Medford, church warden.

May 1, 1770: St. Leger Everitt, vestryman; William Cowardin, vestryman; Nathaniel Reading, church warden; John Dwyer, church warden.

1771: Joseph Rasin, vestryman; Jno. Dwyer, vestryman; Rasin Gale, church warden; Jno. Augier, church warden.

152   INHABITANTS OF KENT COUNTY, MARYLAND, 1637-1787

May 5, 1772: Simon Worrell, vestryman; Thomas Wilkins, vestryman; Edward Beck, church warden; Jos. Ringgold, church warden.

December 1, 1772: Moses Alford, vestryman.

May 4, 1773: Nathaniel Kennard, vestryman; A. Calder, vestryman; John Kennard, church warden; Marmaduke Medford, church warden.

September 6, 1774: Thomas Ringgold, church warden.

CHURCH OFFICIALS, 1779-1787 (who took their oaths of office but swore no allegiance or obedience to the King of Great Britain):

Chester P. E. Church, July 5, 1779: John Scott, vestryman; J. Bolton, vestryman; St. Leger Codd, vestryman; J. Kennard, vestryman; Has. Everett, vestryman; Thomas Van Dyke, vestryman; Joseph Rasin, vestryman; Michael Corse, church warden; Simon Wickes, church warden; and, Charles Groome, register.

April 5, 1780: J. Bolton, vestryman; James Wroth, vestryman; Jno. Sturgis, church warden; David Davis, church warden.

October 2, 1780: Marmaduke Tilden, vestryman.

May 7, 1781: Thomas Van Dyke, vestryman; B. Wilmer, vestryman; Simon Wilmer, church warden.

June 3, 1782: James Smith, vestryman; Marmaduke Medford, vestryman; William Dawson, church warden; Robert Constable, church warden.

June 2, 1783: J. Piper, church warden.

August 4, 1783: Joseph Forman, church warden.

November 3, 1783: Josiah Johnson, church warden.

May 3, 1784: R. Frisby, church warden; Simon Wilmer, church warden; Jno. Tilden Kennard, church warden.

June 7, 1785: Thomas Van Dyke, vestryman; St. Leger Everett, vestryman; Jere. Nicols, vestryman; Mar. Tilden, church warden; J. Kennard, church warden.

May 1, 1786: R. Buchanan, vestryman; Mar. Tilden, vestryman; William Clark, church warden.

October 19, 1786: John Scott, vestryman; John Sturgis, church warden.

May 7, 1787: John Tilden Kennard, vestryman; Simon Wilmer, vestryman; John Sturgis, church warden.

PEWHOLDERS IN CHESTER PROTESTANT EPISCOPAL CHURCH IN 1768:
1 - Kinvan Wroth, Nathaniel Kennard, John Kennard, Jr.
2 - Stephen Bordley, William Bordley, Thomas Wilkins, William Redding
3 - John Randdall, John Bonger, Henry Pennington for Jas. W. Hines
4 - Mary Davis, Thomas Wooddall, David Davis, John Ricketts
5 - William Pearce, Robert Buchanan, William Beck
6 - Philip Davis, Barna[?] Course, George Labourn
7 - Joseph Rasin, William Rasin (of George), Philip Rasin
8 - Thomas Smith, Lloyd Dulaney, Emory Sudler, Thomas Garrett
9 - William Ringgold, Joseph Wickes
10 - Robert Peacock, Richard Peacock, Moses Alford
11 - John Dwire, Macall Medford, John Gale, Jr.
12 - Charles Groome, Sarah Tilden for Charles, son of Marmaduke Tilden, Richard Hosier
13 - William Cowarden, Samuel Groome, William Fray
14 - Joseph Boon, Philip Drugan, Stephen Kennard
15 - John Ecleston for Ebenezer Perkins' heirs, John Ecleston, John Wallace, Nathaniel Redding
16 - John Gleaves, Jonas Crew (1/2 assigned to Gustavus Hanson)
17 - Edward Beck, George Ford, John Wroth
18 - Nathaniel Ricketts, Richard Gresham, Isaac Perkins, John Crew
19 - William Ford, Henry Phillips, James Phillips
20 - Thomas Jones, Richard Willis
21 - Richard Frisby, Lovering Marriott, Shadrick Reed
22 - Nathaniel Course, John Augier, John Lamb
23 - Richard Graves, Elizabeth Cruikshanks and Mary Cruikshanks, William Ringgold, James Chalmers
24 - William Apsley, James Wroth, Benjamin Howard
25 - Nathaniel Comegys for Bellican's heirs, John March, Benjamin Terry for Jo. Briscoe's heirs, Michael Chandler
26 - John Kennard, Jr., John Shawan, John Williams
27 - Robert Meeks, Jr., Frederick Perkins, Nathaniel Chandler, Robert Meeks, Sr. (1/4 assigned to Robert Meeks, Jr.)
28 - Alexander Caulder, James Hackett
29 - William Lynch (1/4 to Jno. Bolton), Edmond Lynch, Margarett Brooks for Jno. Brooks' heirs, Thomas Medford
30 - Hales Everett, and Hales Everett for William Cours' sons
31 - Minister of the Parish for the time being, James Hart (assigned to Jas. Auger), Francis Hall (to William Ringgold and from William Ringgold to Col. Edward Lloyd)
32 - Thomas Ringgold, Esq., William Rasin (of William), Robert Adair
33 - Risdon Bishop for Phil. Brooks' heirs, Charles Foarman, Henry Truelock
34 - Samuel Griffith for Phil. Ricketts' heirs, Samuel Griffith for daughter Mary Griffith, and Samuel Griffith for himself
35 - Robert Buchanan, John Weathered, Joseph Rasin
36 - [Note: There is no number 36 in the ledger.]
37 - Thomas Pinar, James Pinar, James McClain, Sarah Graves
38 - Benjamin Terry, Jonathan Turner, Thomas Perkins
39 - James Smith, Jr., Josias Ringgold, Jr., James Smith, Jr. (1/3 for Isaac Perkins)

40 - Hezekiah Cooper, William Watts, Samuel Bullock
41 - Rebecca Moore, John Chappel, Benjamin Benny, Peregrine Frisby
42 - Nicholas McCubbin, Benjamin Kelley for James Kelley's heirs, Andrew Toulson (assigned to David Crane)
43 - John Maxwell, Luke Griffith for Phil. Kennard's heirs, Marmaduke Tilden
44 - Simon Worrell, William Worrall [sic], George Blackiston (1/3 assigned to S.[or G.?] Worrell)
45 - St. Ledgar Everett, Benjamin Jackson, Chs. and James Milward, Marmaduke Medford
46 - John Augier for son, Margaret Hall (1/3 to Abrm. Cannel), Henry Rosier (1/3 to Ben. Briscoe)
47 - Griffith Jones, James Dunkan, John Ware
48 - Rasin Gale, George Moore, Roger Hales
49 - William Dullehunter, John Greenwood, Isaac Briscoe
50 - Robert Roberts, Robert Roberts for Jno. Ashley's heirs, William Ashley

PEWHOLDERS IN CHESTER PROTESTANT EPISCOPAL CHURCH IN 1772:
1 - Robert Buchanan, George Leybourn
2 - Joseph Nicholson, Sr.
3 - Emory Sudler
4 - William Ringgold
5 - Elizabeth Ingram
6 - Simon Wickes, James Porter
7 - John Williamson
8 - Dr. William Bordley
9 - James McClain
10 - Thomas Ringgold
11 - Stephen Bordley
12 - Samuel Wickes
13 - William Anderson, Richard Lloyd
14 - Peregrine Frisby, James Moore's heirs
15 - Thomas Piner's representatives
16 - Dr. William Murray's heirs
17 - James Calder's devisees
18 - Dr. James Anderson
19 - Simon Wilmer
20 - Charles Gordon
21 - William Smyth, Solomon Wright
22 - Thomas Smyth
23 - Thomas Beddingfield Hand
24 - John Chappel
25 - John Watkins, James Claypole [Claypoole]
26 - Thomas Marsh
27 - Joseph Nicholson, Sr.
28 - John Bolton
29 - John Scott, Mary Wickes
30 - Dennis Dulaney
31 - Mathias Harris
32 - Capt. Thomas Luran [?]
33 - Capt. Benjamin Benney

CHESTER P.E. CHURCH   155

34 - Robert Cruikshanks
35 - William Slubey
36 - Philip Davis, Thomas Crain
37 - Arthur Holt
38 - James Hackett, Rosannah McHard
39 - Blackiston Wilmer
40 - [Blank]
41 - Johnathan Leatherbury, William Murray
42 - [Blank]
43 - William Ringgold
44 - Samuel Wallis
45 - James Williamson
46 - Rebecca Claypole for George Claypole and William Yardsley
47 - Thomas Ringgold, Jr.
48 - Sarah Graves
49 - Isaac McHard, Joseph McHard
50 - Joseph Condon [Coudon, Cosden?]
51 - John Findley's heirs
52 - [Blank]
53 - Tobias Ashmore
54 - John Carvill [Carrell?], Jr.
55 - Robert Buchanan
56 - William Frisby, Daniel Ferrell
57 - Francina Hynson
58 - John Ringgold
59 - Edward Worrell, Simon Worrell
60 - Rebecca Claypole
61 - [Blank]
62 - Elizabeth, Ann, Sarah, and Catharine Murray
63 - John Ball, John Green
64 - [Blank]
65 - [Blank]
66 - Arthur Bordley, Arthur Miller
67 - Thomas Smyth, carpenter
68 - Joseph Garnett

PERSONS WHO DONATED MERCHANTABLE GRAIN TO THE CHESTER PARISH FOR A CLERGYMAN AND CHURCH REPAIRS ON AUGUST 7, 1780 (NAMES AND BUSHELS):
John Scott, 20; Edward Worrell, 4; Thomas Smyth, Jr., 4; Emory Sudler, 15; Benjamin Benney, 15; J. Nicholson, 10; Josiah Ringgold, 8; William Embleton, 20; Robert Constable, 3; Donald McQueen, 3; James Barnes, 3; James Piper, 3; Tobias Ashmore, 2; Thomas M. Forman, 10; Edward Wright, 3; Ann Gresham, 15; Elizabeth Williamson, 4; Charles Hackett, 2; Sarah Callister, 2; Anthony Banning, 10; Daniel Matchler, 10; Simon Wickes, 5; James Anderson, 10; William Bordley, 10; Edward Hopkins, 2; Benjamin Andrews, 3; Anna M. Ringgold, 10; Benjamin Chambers, 5; Wiliam Vickers, 2; John Sturgis, 3; Robert Reed, 3; William Ringgold, 10; Joseph Garnett, 8; William Russel, 2; Thomas Smith, carpenter, 2; A.[?] Frisby, 10; Joseph Cowder[?], 5; Mary Ringgold, 10; James Tilghman, 15; John Bolton, 5; Ann Piner, 5; Robert Buchanan, 10; John Frisby, 6; Robert Anderson, 5; Mary Garnett, 3; Sarah Piner, 6; James Anderson, Jr., 5; Miss

INHABITANTS OF KENT COUNTY, MARYLAND, 1637-1787

Cruikshanks and sister, 5; James McClane, 8; Charles Milward, 5; St. Ledgar Everitt, 10; Jonathan Turner, 6; Marmaduke Medford, 10; Henry Truelock, 5; Isaac Hackett, 3; Nathaniel Kennard, 3; John Eunick, 6; John Augier, 10; William Worrell, 5; Thomas Lamb, 2; Edward Beck, 3; B. Wilmer, 4; Jacob Forman, 1; George Rasin, 5; John Wallis (M.C.), 8; David Davis, 3; Simon Wilmer, 5; John Williams, 4; Edward Lynch, 2; Richard Graves, 20; Richard Lloyd, 20; Arther Dillen, 1; Richard Frisby, 12; Edward Sims, 1; William Marlin, 1; Daniel Groome; Owen Kennard, 3; Charles Tilden, Jr., 3; Richard Hosier, 4; Marmaduke Tilden, 10; William Pearce, 5; Thomas Van Dyke, 10; John Kennard, 10; Charles Groome, 10; James Smith (M.C.), 7; John T. Kennard, 3; George Hartshorn, 3; Benjamin Terry, 3; John Ashley, 3; Nehemiah Crouch, 1; William Jones, 2; James Neal, 3; William Beck, 4; Richard Willis, 5; John Willis, 4; William Kennard, 3; Sarah Merritt, 5; Kinvin Wroth, Sr., 5; Rasin Gale, 5; William Ashley, 1; William Ashley, Jr., 5; William Hamer, 1; Hales Everitt, 5; Peregrine Cooper, 4; Griffith Jones, 5; John Little [Tittle?], 1; James Hawkins, 2; Richard Hopkins, 1; Mary Meeks, 5; James Philips, 1; Alexander Caulder, 4; Kinvin Wroth, Jr., 5; Elizabeth Fray, 6; John Forman, 2; John Smith, 4; Thomas Woodall, 3; James Wroth, 10 (of corn); John Wilson, 5; Isaac Perkins, 7; William Apsley, 1.

VESTRYMEN OF SHREWSBURY PROTESTANT EPISCOPAL CHURCH, 1695-1730

1695 - William Pearce, William Harris, Edward Blay, William Elms, Edward Skiddimore, George Skirton (or Stourton)

1702 - Edward Blay, Phillip Hopkins, William Husband, Abraham Redgrave

1703 - Edward Blay, Phillip Hopkins, Samuel Wallis, William Comegys

1704 - Col. William Pearce, Col. Edward Blay, Phillip Hopkins, James Wilson (William Davis was Church Warden)

1705 - Col. William Pearce, Col. Edward Blay, Phillip Hopkins, James Willson, Phillip Burgan, George Browning (Thomas Windall and Francis Spearman were Church Wardens)

1706 - William Haywood, Phillip Hopkins, James Willson, Phillip Burgan, George Browning, Humphrey Tillton (Edward Holman and Richard Campbell were Church Wardens)

1708 - Col. Edward Blay, William Comegys, James Willson, Phillip Burgan, George Browning, Thomas Christian (Richard Vuett? and John Browning were Church Wardens)

1709 - Col. Edward Blay, James Willson, William Comegys, Phillip Hopkins, Richard Campbell, Samuel Wallis (Henery Knock was Church Warden and Abraham Redgrave was Clerk)

1710 - James Willson, William Comegys, Phillip Hopkins, Richard Campbell, William Blay, George Browning, George Sanders (Luttner Middleton and John Lincoln were Church Wardens)

1711 - George Browning, John Willson, Richard Campbell, Henery Knock, William Comegys, William Blay (Thomas Medford was Church Warden)

1712 - William Comegys, Richard Campbell, Henery Knock, John Willson, Samuel Wallis, Col. Edward Blay (James Campbell was Church Warden)

SHREWSBURY P.E. CHURCH

1713 - Richard Campbell, Henry Knock, John Willson, Samuel Wallis, James Willson, Lambert Willmer (John Risdon and William Millborn were Church Wardens and Abraham Redgrave was Clerk)
1714 - John Willson, Samuel Wallis, James Willson, Gidion Pearce, Lambert Wilmer, William Boyer (John Dining was Church Warden)
1715 - John Willson, Samuel Wallis, James Willson, John Hall, Lambert Willmer, William Blay (Edward Holeman and Richard Skeggs were Church Warden)
1716 - Samuel Wallis, William Comegys, Gidion Pearce (in room of William Blay, deceased), James Willson, Lambert Willmer, Henry Lowe, Thomas Heborn (Nicholas Reley, John Jones and John Cole were Church Wardens)
1718 - Lambert Willmer, Capt. Daniel Pearce, Gidion Pearce, Thomas Heborn, Samuel Wallis, Edward Holeman (Mathias Day and William Debruler were Church Wardens)
1719 - Lambert Willmer, Capt. Daniel Pearce, Samuel Wallis, Gidion Pearce, John Hall, John Willson (Thomas Chanler and John Clark were Church Wardens and Abraham Redgrave was Clerk)
1720 - Capt. Daniel Pearce, Samuel Wallis, John Willson, John Hall, John Dining (John Brooks and George Reed were Church Wardens), and The Rev. James Williamson
1721 - Samuel Wallis, John Hall, Capt. Daniel Pearce, John Brooks, Lambert Willmer (Roger Hicks and Roger Halles, or Hailes, were Church Wardens)
1722 - Capt. Daniel Pearce, Samuel Wallis, William Milborn, Roger Hicks, John Johnson (Phillip Brooks and William Smethers were Church Wardens)
1723 - Capt. Daniel Pearce, Samuel Wallis, John Brooks, William Comegys, Roger Hicks, Lambert Willmer, John Hall (Phillip Brooks, Petter Marcey, Daniel Perkins and William Smethers were Church Wardens)
1724 - John Brooks, Lambert Willmer, John Hall, William Comegys, Roger Hicks, Thomas Hepbourn in the room of Samuel Wallis, deceased (Daniel Perkins, Petter Massey, Jarvies Spencer, and Christopher Hall were Church Wardens)
1725 - John Hall, Thomas Hepbourn, John Willson, John Brooks, John Dining, Lambert Wilmer (Jarvice Spencer, Christopher Hall, George Willson and Joseph Hull were Church Wardens and Abraham Redgrave was Clerk), and The Rev. Richard Sewell
1726 - Lambert Willmer, John Brooks, John Hall, Christopher Hall, John Dining, Thomas Medford, George Wilson (John Rogers and Mathew Howard were Church Wardens)
1727 - Lambert Wilmer, John Brooks, Christopher Hall, Jarvice Spencer, George Wilson, Mathew Howard (William Woodland and Sutton Burgan were Church Wardens)
1728 - Christopher Hall, Mathew Howard, George Wilson, Jarvis Spencer, Sutton Burgin, William Woodland (Lambert Willmer and John Hall were Church Wardens and William Thornton was Clerk)
1729 - Christopher Hall, Jarvis Spencer, Mathew Howard, Sutton Burgin, William Woodland, John Hall, Henry Evins (Griffen Jones was Church Warden, as was subsequently Christopher Hall)
1730 - Sutten Burgin, William Woodland, James Stavely, Samuel Norris (John Browning and Edward Crue were Church Wardens), and The Rev. Richard Sewell.

158   INHABITANTS OF KENT COUNTY, MARYLAND, 1637-1787

PERSONS WHO GAVE MONEY FOR BUYING THE GLASS FOR SHREWSBURY P. E. CHURCH ON SEPTEMBER 18, 1727: Richard Sewell, Lambert Willmer, Mrs. Rebeckah Tilden, William Woodland, Jarvice Spencer, Dr. Thomas Williams, Gidion Pearce and his son William Pearce, John Brooks, William Comegys, Sr., John Hall, and Robert Streett.

SHREWSBURY PROTESTANT EPISCOPAL CHURCH VESTRY MINUTES, 1745-1787 (Ref: Gleanings from Maryland Historical Society Microfilm. This information is also on Maryland State Archives Microfilm M339).

VESTRYMEN, 1745: Griffith Jones, Christopher Bellikin, John Gleaves, Christopher Hall, John Jones, William Comegys, Henry Trulock (George Medford and Nicholas Massy were Church Wardens)

VESTRYMEN, 1746: Cornelius Comegys, John Gleaves, Jacob Jones, Fardinando Hull, George Medford (Thomas Chandler and John Donaldson were Church Wardens)

PERSONS CHARGED WITH UNLAWFUL COHABITATION, 1747-1754
1747 - Timothy O'Bryand and Jane Varine, Jonathan Knots and Ann Holyday, Richard Givenup and Elizabeth Banthram, Mark Dove and Mary Cater
1750 - John Spencer and Mary Clothier, William Moor and Rachel Farrel, ---- [name not given] and Elisabeth Denning "for lewdness and adultery"
1751 - Peregrine Brown and Elisabeth Eldridge
1753 - Thomas Dyer and Margaret Meeds, Thomas Price and Elizabeth Schags
1754 - John Gyant and Ann Toulson, John Thrift and Mary Sympson

VESTRYMEN, 1747: Jacob Jones (Upper Sassafras), John Gleaves (Lower Sassafras), Fardinando Hull (Lower Sassafras), George Medford (Lower Sassafras), Nicholas Massy (Upper Chester), Samuel Mansfield (Morgans Creek), and Rev. Mr. Forestor, Rector (George Wilson, Jr. and William Comegys, Jr. were Church Wardens)

VESTRYMEN, 1748: Nicholas Massy, Lambert Wilmer, John Donaldson, George Medford, Samuel Mansfield, Thomas Chandler (in the room of Fardinando Hull, deceased), John Gleaves (Peter Massy and Samuel Davis were Church Wardens)

VESTRYMEN, 1749: Samuel Mansfield, John Donaldson, Nicholas Massy, Philip Hudson, William Smith, John Hicks, Lambert Wilmer (Zorobable French and William Smith were Church Wardens)

APPOINTMENTS, JUNE 6, 1749: William Resin, Abraham Falconar and Samuel Davis were appointed by Gov. Samuel Ogle to be Inspectors of the Inspecting Houses of George Town and were sworn in before John Williamson and Hugh Wallace, Magistrates for Kent County.

VESTRYMEN, 1750: Lambert Wilmer, Phillip Hudson, William Comegys, Jr., John Hicks, Peter Massy, John Donaldson (Richard Boyer and Frederick Hanson were Church Wardens)

SHREWSBURY P.E. CHURCH

NAMES OF PERSONS WHO SUBSCRIBED TO THE NEW CHURCH BUILDING IN 1750: G. W. Forester, Jeremy Burchinal, Samuel Mansfield, Phillip Hudson, John Hicks, John Woodall, Robert Hutcheson, William Haley, Richard Boyer, John Browning, Fredrick Hanson, Edward Piner, John Smith, Collin Farguson, John Watson (merchant), Jas. Straghon, Richard Moffet, John Page, Edward Comegys, William Comegys, Jr. and son John Comegys, Edward Tillard, John Jones, William Redgrave, John Brooks, Ebenezer Reyner, Nathaniel Reading, Robert Peacock, William Woodland, William Walls, James Doran, Richard Riley, Joseph Redgrave, John Riley, W. Coursy, John Tilden, Peter Massey, William Stoops, William Kenton, Mrs. Sarah Kennard, Jr., John Johnstone (Chester River), John Burgin, Jr., Benjamin Burgin, John Thrift, Hugh Wallis, John Hamner, Jonathan Smith, Philip Brooks, P. Leonard, William Smith, Jonathan Turner, John Knock, Isaac Freeman, Richard Wilson, Peter Cole, Jr., Thomas Perkins, Jacob Jones, Edmond Linch, Joseph Riley, Nathaniel Wright, John Wright, George Medford, Thomas Chandler, Andrew Toleson, Thomas Cooper, Pasco Joce, Peregrine Brown, Philip Hudson, Jr., Richard Canster.

SUNDRY PERSONS INDEBTED TO SHREWSBURY PARISH FOR THEIR PEWS IN 1750: Rev. Mr. Forester, John Hamner for Forster Cunliff, Esq., Hugh Wallis, John Hicks, Jeremy Burchinal, Samuel Mansfield, William Woodland, Philip Hudson, Sr., Peter Massey, William Smith, Jos. Riley, William Walls, James Stranhon, Jonathan Smith, William Stoops, John Watson, Richard Moffet, Isaac Freeman, Jno. Johnston, William Redgrave, Jos. Redgrave, Robert Hatcherson, John Page, William Comegys, Jr. and son John Comegys, Richard Riley, Edward Tillar, Nathaniel Reading, John Brooks, John Smith, Edmond Lynch, Thomas Chandler, Jonathan Turner, George Medford, William Haley, Richard Canster, Benjamin Burgin, John Thrift, Ebenezer Reyner, Richard Boyer, Frederick Hanson, John Browning, Edward Piner, John Jones, Jas. Doran, Jno. Tilden, Philip Kennard, Mrs. Sarah Kennard, William Keaton, Richard Wilson, Thomas Perkins, Peter Cole, Andrew Toleson, Thomas Cooper, Pasco Joce, Peregrine Brown, Philip Hudson, Jr., Collin Farguson, Jno. Woodall, Jno. Burgin, Jr., Philip Brooks, Ed. Comegys, John Riley.

PEWHOLDERS IN SHREWSBURY PROTESTANT EPISCOPAL CHURCH IN 1755 [sic]:
1 - Ebenezer Reyner, Jonathan Turner, John Angier, Joseph Brisco
2 - Hugh Wallis, Philip Brooks (1/3 to his son), Richard Riley (1/3 John Brooks sold), John Hurt
3 - Mr. Forester, John Scott (1/3 to John Hynson), Samuel Thompson
4 - Thomas Perkins, Gustavis Hanson, John Crew
5 - Thomas Chandler, Jno. Corse (1/3 for son Thomas Hynson Corse), George Medford
6 - Given by the Vestry, and the Subscribers, for Strangers
7 - James Loutill, Samuel Grooms, John Gleaves
8 - Nicholas Smith, Simon Wilmer, Mary Keating (daughter of William Keating, Sr.), Joseph Ireland (1/3 part by John Smith, son of Nicholas Smith)
9 - John Brooks, John Johnston, Edmond Lynch

10 - John Knock, Charles McCubbins

PEWHOLDERS IN THE NEW ADDITION TO SHREWSBURY P. E. CHURCH IN 1751:
1 - William Haley, John Woodall, Pasco Joce (sold to John Stoops who sold to Chr. Fisher, Jr.), Edward Piner
2 - Rev. G. W. Forester, Mrs. Sarah Kennard, William Stoops
3 - James Dearan, Giles Cooke, John Maxfield, Theophilus Randall
4 - Peter Cole, Jr., Nathaniel Reading, John Thrift, William Walls, Sr.
5 - George Tillar, Richard Canster, Richard Boyer, Jr. and Stephen Boyer, sons of Richard Boyer, Sr.
6 - John Smith (sold to his brother Oliver Smith), Jonathan Smith, William Smith, Jr., Richard Riley
7 - Edmond Lynch, Jonathan Turner, John Jones, John Brooks
8 - John Tilden (sold his part to Mathew Hazel), Peregrine Brown, Robert Hatcherson, Peter Massey (room of Phil. Kennard)
9 - Hugh Wallis, John Comegys son of William (to A. Comegys), Samuel Mansfield, Jesse Cosden
10 - Isaac Freeman, Richard Boyer, Ebenezer Reyner, Hugh Wallis
11 - Foster Cunliff, Esq. and sons, William Comegys, Jr., John Hicks, Peter Massey
12 - John Farguson, Joseph Riley, Richard Moffet, Dennis Shaughen
13 - Philip Brooks, Thomas Perkins, Fredric Hanson, William Keaton
14 - John Burgin, Jr., Benjamin Burgin (sold to Jas. Loutill, who sold his part to Donaldson Yeates on December 1, 1780), John Page, Mrs. Susannah Hudson, widow (who married George Hill and they sold their 1/4 part of this pew to Michael Jobson and his heirs)
15 - George Medford, William Redgrave, Sr., Thomas Chandler, Andrew Toleson
16 - William Woodland, John Nemoe (sold to William Rasin), John Browning, Joseph Redgrave
17 - Jeremy Burchinal, James Straughan, John Johnson, John Riley (sold to Joseph Ireland)

PEWHOLDERS IN SHREWSBURY P.E. CHURCH WHO PAID 100 POUNDS OF TOBACCO OR 20 SHILLINGS CURRENT MONEY TO THE VESTRY ON DECEMBER 3, 1752: Rev. G. W. Forester, Hugh Wallis, John Hicks, Richard Wilson, Thomas Charles Fletcher, William Stoops, Ann Comegys, Ebenezer Reyner, Peter Massey, Sarah Kennard, Andrew Toulson, George Medford, Richard Boyer, William Haley, Jeremy Burchinal, Isaac Freeman, James Straughan, William Smith, Jonathan Smith, Collin Ferguson, John Nemoe, Joseph Riley, Samuel Mansfield, William Redgrave, Nathaniel Reding, Jno. Riley, Jno. Johnston, Jno. Browning, Richard Riley, Robert Hatcherson, Jno. Brooks, Josh. Redgrave, Edward Piner, William Woodland, William Keaton, Phillip Brooks, John Jones, John Smith, Pasco Joce, John Burgin, Jr., Benjamin Burgin, John Page, Jonathan Turner, Dennis Shaughen, Susanna Hudson, John Thrift, Thomas Perkins, Thomas Chandler, Fredric Hanson, John Tilden, Philip Kennard, Peregrine Brown, Peter Cole, Jr., William Walls, Edmond Lynch, Richard Moffet, James Dearan.

SHREWSBURY P.E. CHURCH

POOR PEOPLE WHO RECEIVED CHARITY FROM WILLIAM BOYER, APRIL 6, 1756: John Morris, Jane Howard, James Pennington, Widdow Pennington, Richard Tobin, Dennis McHanny, Rachel Caughron, Peter Kincaid, Elisabeth Francis, Mary Asthr.[?] O'Bryant, Patrick Shirkey, Margarett Jones, Mary Smythers, Joseph Parsons, William Parkinson, Thomas Barret, Elisabeth Booker, Elisabeth Biss, Rebecca Deparney, Mary Kerton, Oba[diah] Fisher, Ann Rain, and Jane Massey.

LIST OF PEWS SOLD IN THE OLD PART OF SHREWSBURY P. E. CHURCH:
1 - Abraham Freeman (1/8 part conveyed from Thomas Sewell on April 17, 1758)
2 - John Gleaves (1/4 part by Mathew Howard), and Robert Peacock (1/8 part by Abraham Spearman)
3 - Thomas Williams' heirs sold 1/4 part to Benjamin Riley on March 13, 1770, and William Simcocks, Jr. sold 1/4 part to Isaac Boyd on September 27, 1774.
4 - Michael Chandler "heir to Thomas Chandler sold to Joseph Stavely"
5 - Daniel Massey (1/4 part by John Browning), Joseph Ireland (1/4 part by John Smith, son of Nicholas Smith), and Oliver Smith (1/4 part by Joseph Ireland)
6 - John Gleaves (1/4 part by William Boyer), and Edward Price Wilmer (1/4 part by Mrs. Rebecca Wye)
7 - Samuel Wallis sold 1/4 part to George Cole
8 - John Spencer (1/4 part by Jacob Caulk), and John Spencer sold 1/8 part to William Haley and other 1/8 part to Edward Piner. Bartus Piner, heir of Edward, sold his part to William Haley on May 4, 1762.
9 - Robert Hart (1/4 part by Peter Jones) and Robert Hart sold his 1/4 part to John Auger [Anger?].
10 - [Page torn]
11 - Benjamin Palmer, Sr. sold 1/4 part to Benjamin Palmer, Jr.
12 - Jacob Falconer "and paid 7/6 for repairs from Jos. Hull and Jacob Falkconer bt. of Jos. Hull his right of a pew in the old part of the Church No. 12."
13 - [Page torn]
14 - Gideon Pearce, Sr. (1/4 part by Henry Evans), Gideon Pearce, Jr. (1/4 part by John Rogers), William Boots (1/4 part from William Thornton), and James Pearce (1/4 part from William Pearce, son of Gideon Pearce, Jr.)
15 - Daniel C. Bryan (1/4 part by Samuel Norris)
16 - Thomas Wyatt's heirs sold their 1/4 part to Isaac Wilson, and from Isaac Wilson to Abrm. Woodland on June 7, 1768.
17 - William Salsbury (1/4 part by Daniel Bryan)
18 - George Wilson (1/4 part by Benjamin Jones)
19 - Stephen Denning sold his 1/4 part to Michael Haggit on January 6, 1752)
20 - Henry Jones, grandson to Henry Spencer (1/4 part by John Ackland), and Benjamin Riley (1/4 part from Nicholas Riley)
21 - Andrew Hynson, son of Capt. Hynson (1/4 part by Jno. McKey), Isaac Freeman, Jr. (1/4 part by Joshua Vansant), Richard Moffit (1/4 part by Nicholas Smyth, son of Mathew Smyth, who claims his right from George Vansant, Sr.)
22 - Chr. Belikin (1/4 part by John Redgrave)

23 - [Blank]
24 - Samuel Greenwood, heir to James Greenwood, sold 1/4 part to William Merritt who then "gave up his right to the pew and the 1/4 part was sold by James Black and then to William Knock, May 1, 1770, Ebenezer Reyner, clerk."
25 - Daniel Perkins (1/4 part by John Browning), Daniel Cunningham (1/4 part by Thomas Pryer). "Isaac Perkins comes in heir at law for 1/4 of this pew by Daniel Perkins his grandfather. Determined by the Vestry on April 16, 1770. Joseph Burchinal and Elisabeth Burchinal, his wife, sold 1/8 of the above pew to Isaac Perkins, the said Elisabeth Burchinal was daughter of Daniel Cunningham on April 24, 1782."
26 - John Donaldson (1/4 part by Edward Windall). "William Ford and paid 7/6 for repairing from Robert Ford. John Donaldson 4th part he wills to his grandson George Little."

SUBSCRIBERS TO THE BUILDING OF THE SHREWSBURY VESTRY HOUSE IN 1746: Rev. Mr. Forester, John Gleaves, John Burgin, Mrs. Isabella Wethered, Mrs. Sarah Kennard, Jr., William Comegys, Jr., Nicholas Smith, William Smith, John Stevens, Sutton Burgin, John Donaldson, Fardinando Hull, John March, Buttmer Medford, Francis Barney, and Thomas Barkly.

LIST OF BATCHELORS IN SHREWSBURY PARISH ON JULY 11, 1758, RETURNED BY HERCULON COUTTS, SHERIFF OF KENT COUNTY (TAX AMOUNT IN POUNDS): Upper South Sassafras Hundred - Thomas Browning, 300; John Browning, 100; Dennis Dulany, 300; Thomas Gilpin, 300; George Pearce, 300; John Scott, 300; Solomon Massey, 300; Samuel Sloss, 300; John Schaw, 300; Christopher Vansant, 100; William Blaxton, 100; Joseph Rogers, 100.
Lower South Sassafras Hundred - Peregrine Brown, 300; John Tilden, 300; Abraham Rasin, 300; Charles McCubbins, 300.
Morgan's Creek Hundred - Bartis Piner, 100; Edward Piner, 100; John Egelston, 300; Thomas Williams, 300.

AT A MEETING OF THE VESTRY OF SHREWSBURY P.E. PARISH ON JULY 10, 1759, THE FOLLOWING BATCHELORS WERE "TAXED AS PER LIST OF 25 YEARS AGE": Dennis Dulany, Esq., 300; John Scott, 300; John Tilden, 300; Peregrine Brown, 300; James McLachlan, 300; Samuel Sloss, 300; Thomas Browning, 300; George Pearce, 300; Abraham Rasin, 300; John Schaw, 300; Thomas Gilpin, 300; Solomon Massey, 300; Christopher Vansant, 100; Arthur Lee, 100; Bartus Piner, 300; Charles McCubbins, 300; William Comegys, son of C. Comegys, 300; John Browning, 100; Jonas Crew, 100; Thomas Bowers, 100; Henry Dixon, 100; Joseph Rogers, 100; Edward Piner, 100; Darby Schawhan, 100; Charles Hunter, 100; Joseph Greenwood, 100; and, Samuel Walls, 100. Signed per Order of the Vestry, W. Haley, clerk.

PEWHOLDERS IN THE CHAPEL OF SHREWSBURY P. E. PARISH IN 1756:
1 - "The Incumbent for time being," and Rev. Mr. Forester
2 - Jacob Jones and Richard Gresham
3 - Richard Wethered, Jarvis Spencer, and William Comegys, Jr. in the room of Richard Wethered

SHREWSBURY P.E. CHURCH   163

4 - John Rochester and George Hall
5 - Richard Wilson and Henry Clark
6 - Cornelius Comegys, Abraham Falconer, and William Comegys in
     the room of Cornelius Comegys. "William the son of Cornelius
     Comegys conveyed by Henry Comegys the son of said Cornelius
     above mentioned William Comegys by an order to the Vestry from
     said Henry Comegys bearing date March 6, 1658."
7 - James Boyer and Benjamin Hazle
8 - Benjamin Blackston and John Nicholson
9 - Samuel Beck and John Brocksolm
10 - Gideon Pearce, John Kennard, William Wethered and John
     Wethered in the room of Mr. Kinnard's heirs, James Pearce by
     order of Robert Buchanan, and Miss Ann Kinnard
11 - John Clayton, Sr.
12 - Thomas Saunders and John Gleaves
13 - Charles Smith and Thomas Barns
14 - John Burgen and Fredrick Hanse [Hanson]
15 - Benjamin Marlow and Ebenezer Blackiston
16 - William Massey's executor
17 - Jacob Spendlove and Abraham Woodland
18 - William Hudson and Daniel Massy
19 - Nicholas Massy and Solomon Massy
20 - William Massy and George Wilson
21 - Thomas Massy and Benjamin Hazle
22 - Simon Wilmer, Nicholas Smith, and George Moffitt "half by
     John Smith, son of Nicholas Smith, said George Moffitt has
     ordered the said part of this pew to be registered to his son
     Jesse Moffitt."
23 - George Lenegar and John Webb
24 - William Stoops and Thomas Jones
25 - John Stanly and Ambross Howard
26 - William Saunders and Daniel Bryand
27 - Jacob Spendlove and Ebenezer Blaxstone [Blackstone]
28 - William Woodland
29 - James Dearan and Richard Riley
30 - Christopher Hall and John McDoughal
31 - Thomas Blackstone (2 seats), William Smythers, William Boots
32 - William Johnson (paid to Capt. Spencer), and Jno. Holeadger
33 - Augustin Boyer and Isaac Freeman
34 - William Boyer and Thomas Hynson

PEWHOLDERS IN THE NEW ADDITION TO SHREWSBURY CHAPEL IN OCTOBER,
1756:
1 - Mathew Richardson and Nicholas Riley
2 - David Scott and William Saunders
3 - Rev. Mr. Forester and William Haley
4 - William Salisbury and Thomas Burk
5 - Mrs. Elizabeth Falconer and Henry Comegys (sold)
6 - Ebenezer Blackstone and William Blackstone
7 - Thomas Richford
8 - Augustine Boyer, Jr. and William Boyer
9 - Samuel Church and Dennis Dulany
10 - Alexander Baird and John Baird
11 - John Wattson and Nehemiah Coventon
12 - Joseph Redgrave and John Browning

13 - John Falconer and Charles McDermot
14 - Daniel Massy and William Spearman
15 - Cornelius Comegys and William Comegys, son of Edward Comegys
16 - "The Rev. Mr. Forester 1/2 for loss in the Old, The Incumbent"
17 - James Perce [Pearce] and George Pearce
18 - Samuel Davis and Ebenezer Reynar
19 - John Williams and Edward Williams
20 - William Symonds
21 - Oliver Smith "bt. 1/2 of John Smith"
22 - Henry Clark and Josh. [Joseph] Rogers
23 - Simon Wilmer and William Woodland

"The above Pew No. 5 - one half of the same convaid by Henry Comegys to Zorobable Massy on April 20, 1767."

"The Pew No. 15 above mentioned a proprietor Mrs. Charity Comegys in the room of Cornelius Comegys, deceased, the said Charity was the late wife of said Cornelius Comegys conveyed by Henry Comegys the son of the aforesaid Cornelius to the said Charity Comegys all his rite and title of the above pew by order to the Vestry bearing date March 6, 1758, per Ebenezer Reyner, clerk."

LIST OF BATCHELORS IN SHREWSBURY P. E. PARISH ON JULY 8, 1760, OF THE AGE OF 25 YEARS AND UPWARDS AND TAXED (POUNDS) AS FOLLOWS:
Dennis Dulany, Esq., 300; Peregrine Brown, 300; James McLachlan, 300; Samuel Sloss, 300; Thomas Browning, 300; George Pearce, 300; Abraham Rasin, 300; John Schaw, 300; Thomas Gilpin, 300; Solomon Massy, 300; John Browning, 300; Charles McCubbins, 300; Bartus Piner, 300; William Comegys, son of C. C., 300; Joseph Ireland, 300; Robert Eavens, 300; Jonas Crew, 100; Thomas Bowers, 100; Henry Dickson, 100; Joseph Rogers, 100; Edward Piner, 100; Darby Shawhan, 100; Charles Hunter, 100; Arthur Lee, 100; Joseph Greenwood, 100; Thomas McDarmont, 100; William Boyer, 100; John Course, Jr., 100; and, Joseph Zellefroe, 100.

LIST OF BATCHELORS IN SHREWSBURY P. E. PARISH ON JULY 14, 1761, OF THE AGE OF 25 YEARS AND UPWARDS AND TAXED (POUNDS) AS FOLLOWS:
Dennis Dulany, Esq., 300; Peregrine Brown, 300; James McLachlan, 300; Samuel Sloss, 300; Thomas Browning, 300; George Pearce, 300; Abraham Rasin, 300; John Shaw, 300; Thomas Gilpin, 300; Solomon Massy, 300; John Browning, 300; Charles McCubbins, 300; Bartus Piner, 300; William Comegys, 300; Isaac Spencer, 300; Jacob Comegys, 300; Jonas Crew, 300; Joseph Greenwood, 300; Samuel Walls, 300; William Boyer, 300; John Boyer, 300; Thomas Bowers, 100; Henry Dixon, 100; Darby Shawhan, 100; Arthur Lee, 100; Thomas McDarmont, 100; John Course, Jr., 100; Joseph Zellefroe, 100; Ruloph Moor, 100; Philip Warner, 100; Thomas Kinson, 100; and, John Peacock, 100.

LIST OF BATCHELORS IN SHREWSBURY P. E. PARISH ON JULY 13, 1762, OF THE AGE OF 25 YEARS AND UPWARDS AND TAXED (POUNDS) AS FOLLOWS:
Dennis Dulany, 300; Peregrine Brown, 300; Thomas Browning, 300; George Pearce, 300; Abraham Rasin, 300; John Schaw, 300; Thomas Gilpin, 300; Solomon Massy, 300; John Browning, 300; Charles McCubbins, 300; Bartus Piner, 300; Jonas Crew, 300; Joseph

SHREWSBURY P.E. CHURCH   165

Greenwood, 300; Samuel Walls, 300; William Boyer, 300; John
Boyer, 300; Thomas McDarmont, 300; John Course, Jr., 300; George
Browning, 300; Lowl. Drumgold, 300; Isaac Spencer, 300; Lawrence
Welsh, 300; William Reding, 300; Par. Drugan, 300; William
Rogers, 300; Henry Dixson, 100; Darby Shawan, 100; Arthur Lee,
100; Joseph Zellefroe, 100; Ruloph Moore, 100; Phil. Warner, 100;
Thomas Kinson, 100; John Peacock, 100; Abraham Connell, 100; and,
William Hall, 100.

LIST OF BATCHELORS IN SHREWSBURY P. E. PARISH ON JULY 12, 1763,
OF THE AGE OF 25 YEARS AND UPWARDS AND TAXED (POUNDS) AS FOLLOWS:
Dennis Dulany, 300; James McLachlan, 300; Peregrine Brown, 300;
Thomas Browning, 300; George Pearce, 300; Solomon Massy, 300;
John Browning, 300; Jonas Crew, 300; Joseph Greenwood, 300;
Samuel Walls, 300; Thomas McDarmott, 300; John Course, 300;
George Browning, 300; Lowl. Droomgould, 300; Isaac Spencer, 300;
William Reding, 300; Par. Drugan, 300; William Rogers, 300;
Joseph Massy, 300; Henry Dixson, 100; Darby Shawhan, 100; Ruluff
Moore, 100; Thomas Kinsey, 100; John Peacock, 100; William
Taylor, 100; Andrew Boyer, 100; and, James Maslin, 100.

PEWHOLDERS IN THE NEW GALLERY IN SHREWSBURY CHAPEL IN AUGUST,
1767:
1 - Augustine Boyer (2 seats), William Downs, and William Brown
2 - Isaac Boyer, Nathaniel Knock, and Luke Myers (3 seats)
3 - G. William Forester, Jr., William Haley, Jr., and Joseph
    Redgrave, Jr. (2 seats)
4 - Bartus Comegys, Ebenezer Massy (3 seats), and Jacob Comegys
5 - Mary Weeks, James Hynson (3 seats), and William Merritt
    (sold to Thomas Little)
6 - Phil. Davis, George Moffett, Jr., and Richard Moffett, Jr.
7 - Edward Price Wilmer, John Wilson, Jr., and Jacob Reyley
8 - John Sperman [Spearman], Benjamin Blackston, and John Clark
9 - William Weithred [Wethered] and Isaac Freeman
10 - Dr. Samuel Thompson (the whole pew)
11 - Jesse Causden [Cosden], Joseph Massy, Jr., and G. Nathan
     Massy [George Nathaniel Massey]
12 - Margaret Parsons, Thomas Ellis, and John Frances

LIST OF PARISHIONERS WHO PRESENTED A NEAT VELVET CUSHION AND
CLOATH FOR THE PULPIT AND DESK ON MARCH 1, 1768, AS TESTIMONY OF
THE TRUE REGARD AND HONOUR THEY HAD FOR THE HOUSE OF GOD AND THE
LOVE AND ESTEEM FOR THE REV. GEORGE WILLIAM FORESTER WHO HAD
CARED FOR THIS PARISH UPWARDS OF 30 YEARS: James Pearce, John
Maxwell, Ebenezer Reyner, Christopher Hall, Charles Hynson,
Theophilus Randall, John Wallis, Jr., Abraham Freeman, John
Weithred [Wethered], Nicholas Smith, Samuel Sloss, John Donnalson
[Donaldson], Joseph Redgrave, John Browning, John Voorhees,
Collin Ferguson, William Haley, William St. Clear, Isaac Freeman,
William Downs, James McLachlan, Thomas Boyer, Jr., Samuel Davis,
William Blay Tilden, John Comegys, Robert Garry, Robert Maxwell,
William Freeman, Jesse Causden [Cosden], John Graham, Isaac
Spencer, Dr. Samuel Thompson, Dr. William Rogers, Thomas Pirkins
[Perkins], and Joseph Ireland.

166   INHABITANTS OF KENT COUNTY, MARYLAND, 1637-1787

SUBSCRIPTION LISTS FOR RAISING THE PARSONS SALARY FOR THE YEAR 1781 TO COMMENCE FROM JANUARY 22ND LAST FOR THE REV. JAMES J. WILMER OF SHREWSBURY P.E. PARISH (Note: w = bushels of wheat; c = bushels of corn; and, specie/money: lb. = pound, sh. = shilling, p = pence):

SUBSCRIBERS: Elijah Massy, 8w; Daniel Cornalus, 2w; Robert Moody, 2w; Stephen Massy, 1w; Daniel Toes Massy, 4w; James Brady, 4w; Henry Clerk, 4w; John Clerk, 1w; John Rogers, 1w; George Wilson, Jr., 1w; Cornalus Comegys, 6c; Hannah Massy, 6c; William Turner, 4w; Thomas Fowler, 4w; David Spear, 4w; Robert Marley, 5c; Isaac Stanly, 2w; Joseph Clayton, 5c; Jacob Clayton, 3c; Michael Bryan, 1w; John Berckiston [Blackiston?], 2w; Rebecca Little, 2w; John Ward Pennington, 3w; John Webb, 2c; Abednago Massy, 3c; Samuel Beck, 3w; Nathaniel Covington, 3c; George Sanders, 2c; William Greenwood, 3c; William Pryer, 2w; John Wright, Jr., 1w; Joseph Clayton, Jr., 2c; John Cosden, 15 sh.; Robert Maxwell, Jr., 4w; Joshua Browning, 2w; Robert Gay, 3w; Richard Moffitt, Jr., 2w; Cuthbert Hall, 1w; William Wilmer, 4w; Britain Maslin, 1w; John Runnels, Sr., 6c; John Runnels, Jr., 2w; Abraham Boyer, 3w; Absolum Chrisfield, 5c; Isaac Clayton, 3c.

VESTRY LIST: Isaac Freeman, 17w; John Hart, 10w; William Keatting, 5w; George Moffitt, 6w; George William Forester, 6w; Ebenezer Reyner, 10w; William Merritt, 6w; Michael Jobson, 4w; George Moffitt, Jr., 5w; Richard Moffitt, Sr., 5w; Moses Moffitt, 2w; Christopher Hall, 8w; John Read, 2w; James Larrance, 2w; and, Richard Scaggs, 2w.

SUBSCRIBERS: John Day, 6w; Nathaniel Comegys, 10w; Bartis Piner, 6w; Thomas Hynson, 4w; James Woodland, 4w; Christopher Fields, 5w; James Hynson, 6w and 10c; Sarah Massy, 5w; Derrick William Parker, 2w; Ephraim Vansant, Jr., 2w; John Beazly, 3w; Benjamin Terry, 5w; Benjamin Reyle, 6w; John Greenwood, 2w; William Reyle, 5w; Levering Alley, 2w; John Wilson, Jr., 1w; Benjamin Reyle, Jr., 2w; Nicholas Reyle, 2w; William Smith, of William, 2w; George Denning, 2w; Sarah Huff, 2w; Benjamin Palmer, 3w; John Gilbert, 2w; Abraham Woodland and John Woodland, 4w; William Hull, 2w: James Sappington, 2w; William Spearman, 6w; Vinsant Hatcheson, 4w; William Stewart, 3w; Thomas Boyer, 3w; William Maxwell, Jr., 5w; William Brisco, 3w; Phillip Davis, 3w; John Hickman, 2w; John Williams, 4w; David Crane, 3w; Nathaniel Toleson, 2w; James Wilmer, 2w; John Wallis, 4w; Thomas Smith, 2w; James Stavely, 2w; John Stavely, 1w; Thomas Rasin, 3w; Alexander Briscoe, 2w; Samuel Comegys, 4w; Thomas Pryer, 15 sh.; John Gears, 10 sh.; Robert Hodgson, 15 sh.; John Williams, 15 sh.; William Hanson, 1 lb.; William Pell, 7 sh. 6 p.; John Wilmer, 7 lbs, 10 sh.; John Cadwalleder, 10w; Nathaniel Knock, 10c; Robert Money, 10c; Thomas Fowler, 15c; Jacob Vansant, 5c; Charles Irons, 10c; Nathaniel Gleen, 2w; John Browning, Sr., 10c; Thomas Sanders, 2w; Aquila Page, 20c; William Stewart, farmer, 5c; William Wilson, 2w; Joseph Redgrave, 3w; William Little, 10c; John Massy, 5w; John Myars, 5c; and, Morgin James, 5c. Church Register: Ebenezer Reyner.

VESTRY MEETING OF SHREWSBURY P. E. PARISH HELD ON AUGUST 6, 1787
Vestrymen: Isaac Freeman, John Woodland, Edward Wright, Cornalus
Comegys, William Briscoe, and Vinsent Hatcheson. Church Wardens:
Josiah Massy and John Miers. On this day the Vestry and Wardens
agreed with the Rev. John Bisset for his becoming the Rector for
Shrewsbury Parish. By Order of the Vestry, Ebenezer Reyner, Reg.

168   INHABITANTS OF KENT COUNTY, MARYLAND, 1637-1787

AN INDEX TO CONVICTED SERVANTS IN KENT COUNTY, MARYLAND,
1718-1770

(Note: Since the following is only an index, one should consult the article by Robert Andrew Oszakiewski in the *Maryland Genealogical Society Bulletin*, Vol. 34, No. 1, Winter, 1993, pp. 43-84, entitled "Index to Convict Servants in Kent County, 1719-1769," for more information.)

John Abbott, 1719; John Adams, 1732; Mary Adams, 1720; John Addicott, 1733; William Addicott, 1733; Roger Affell (Affet), 1739; George Alcock, 1732; Elizabeth Alexander, 1761; Arthur Algar, 1732; Hester Anderson, 1743; Rachel Anderson, 1759; Rachel Anderson, 1761; Rachel Anderson, 1766; Elizabeth Andley, 1736; Richard Arfcot, 1743; Thomas Arland, 1732; John Arney, 1719; Mary Arnold, 1732; John Arthur, 1734; Isaac Ashmore, 1735; William Ashmore, 1743; William Athey (Atkey), 1733; Charles Bailey, 1736; William Baker, 1736; Lewis (Louis) Baker, 1719; John Ball, 1719; Katherine Banks, 1726; Elizabeth Barman, 1743; Daniel Barnard, 1732; Edward Barnstaple, 1736; Adolphus Barrett, 1736; Pasto Barriball, 1736; Nicholas Bartlet, 1744; John Bartlet, 1744; Robert Barton, 1719; George Batt, 1732; James Bendy, 1739; George Bennett, 1719; Samuel Bennett, 1719; William Bennett, 1732; Robert Beray (Berry), 1744; John Berry, 1732; Henry Blake, 1732; William Bodway (Bodye), 1736; Joseph Bonison, 1732; Jonas Boor, 1736; Roger Bouker, 1737; William Bragg, 1743; Nicholas Brayler, 1736; John Brenton, 1719; Edward Brewer, 1735; John Brockington, 1743; Philip Brockington, 1743; Alphonso Brooking, 1719; Ann Bryan, 1718, 1750; Susannah Buckwell, 1768, 1770; John Budbrook, 1744; William Bunt, 1720; Thomas Burch, 1720; Joseph Burridge, 1736; George Bussell, 1719; Anne Butler, 1749; William Caine, 1719; John Calmer, 1735; Elizabeth Cannah, 1753; Amos Carder, 1719; Elizabeth Carr, 1725; Elizabeth Carr, 1729; George Carter, 1732; Sarah Carter, 1743; Thomas Carwithy (Wythell), 1737; James Case, 1732; Samuel Chaplaine (Chaplin), 1732; Henry Chappell, 1720; Ambrose Chapple, 1732; Joseph Chapple, 1737; Nicholas Chilew, 1734; John Chubb, 1733; Horius (Honor) Chubb, 1732; Jane Churchill, 1732; William Clapp, 1720; Mary Clark, 1769; Joseph Clarke, 1732; Jane Clements, 1719; Jane Clocke, 1719; Richard Cocks, 1734; Maria (Ulalia) Cole, 1737; Richard Coles, 1732; Elizabeth Coles, 1737; John Collins, 1734; Walter Collins, 1719; John Collipriest, 1737; Thomas Combe, 1719; William Combe, 1735; Temperance Connor, 1734; Robert Cook, 1736; William Cook, 1719; Elizabeth Coram, 1749; Thomas Corham, 1733; Richard Cork, 1732; Mary Crapp, 1719; Elizabeth Crocker (Cracker), 1734; Ann Croscombies (spinster), 1739; William Crossing, 1744; Mark Curtis, 1737; George Davy, 1719; Honore Davy, 1735; John Devo, 1734; Richard Diggle (Digle), 1732; William Dingle, 1732; Henry Dinks, 1732; Ezekiel Dodd, 1732; Anne Dowes, 1743; Henry Dunnicombe, 1736; Benjamin Dyer, 1743; James Dyers, 1744; Richard Eddy, 1736; Samuel Edwards, 1732; Robert Eglan (Eglon), 1737; Mathias Eldes, 1736; Robert Ellett (Ellott), 1733; Joseph Ellis, 1732; Nathaniel Emmitt, 1735; Elizabeth England (spinster), 1746; Francis Eplatt (Eylatt), 1736; Edward Evans, 1733; William Eyres, 1737; John Fackers, 1744; Thomas Falker, 1735; William Farell,

1743; Joannah Farr, 1732; Jasper Farranton, 1743; William Farren, 1719; William Farrow, 1719; Samuel Farthing, 1735; Ann Farthing (spinster), 1739; Richard Fferet, 1737; George Ford, 1736; John Fountaine, 1732; John Francis, 1736; Thomas Francis, 1737; Walter Freestone, 1719; George French, 1733; William Frost, 1732; William Frost (weaver), 1732; James Gaffney, 1732; Mary Gaire, 1744; Richard Gale, 1719; John Galloway, 1743; Mary Garman, 1734; Vallentine Garrett, 1732; William Gauntlett, 1734; Richard Gay, 1732; Agness Geller, 1734; Thomas Geoff (Goff, Gough), 1734; John Giam, 1736; William Gibb, 1732; Benjamin Gibbs, 1732; Perry Gilbert, 1743; James Goach, 1732; John Goodyear, 1732; William Grant, 1720; John Grantlett, 1719; Mary Graves (servant to Arthur Miller), 1733; William Gray, 1736; James Green, 1719; Anthony Gregory, 1719; Edward Griffin, 1743; David Griffith, 1735; James Grigg, 1719; John Harris, 1744; John Hart, 1729; Anna Harthing, 1732; Thomas Hary, 1719; William Hath (Hatch), 1737; William Hawkings (Hawkins), 1719; Jane Hawkins, 1743; Henry Heard, 1732; John Hearst, 1736; Robert Hermann, 1735; Henry Hibbert, 1733; Elizabeth Hill, 1732; Thomas Hill, 1719; William Hingston, 1732; William Hoalden, 1733; Robert Hob, 1743; John Hobb, 1739; Thomas Hocombe, 1719; George Hosegood (Hosgood), 1732; William Houady, 1732; Thomas How, 1732; William Huxtable, 1744; Richard Ingram, 1737; Thomas Jacob, 1719; Michael Jarvis, 1743; Richard Jeffrey, 1732; William Jenkins, 1743; Robert Johns, 1734; John Jolly (Jolle), 1735; Anne Jones, 1733; Thomas Jones, 1733; Mary Jones, 1735; John Jones, 1720; Jane Jones, 1719; William Jones, 1743; David Judd, 1719; Anthony Kansbeare, 1719; Mary Kerrill, 1735; Isaac Knighton, 1737; Jane Knock, 1747; John Knowles, 1733; James Knowloes, 1743; John Lacy, 1720; William Landers (Landoss, Launders), 1732; Edward Lane, 1732; Robert Lane, 1719, 1734; Humphrey Lane, 1732; James Lang, 1735; John Lang, 1736, 1744; Abel Lashbrook, 1720; James Lashington, 1737; James Leadhorn, 1733; Joseph Leanard, 1719; Robert Leane, 1719; William Legg, 1719; Henry Legg, 1743; Grace Legg, 1732; Sarah Lellwood, 1719; Thomas Lettou, 1732; William Light, 1737; John Lippen, 1719; George Lippesley (Hippesfoy), 1732; Thomas Liscombe, 1732; John Loach, 1732; Richard Loan, 1734; Jane Loudwell, 1736; Robert Lovell, 1737; William Luke, 1734; John Lusslake, 1719; Abraham Maine, 1737; William Mallett (Mullett), 1720; Joseph Mallett, 1735; Peter Manley, 1719; Mary Manning, 1736; Nicholas Marks, 1734; Thomas Marshall, 1732; William Martyn, 1744; William Massey, 1734; Richard Mathers (Matters), 1732; William Matthews, 1732; William May, 1737; Catherine May, 1734; Mary Mayo, 1743; William Mays, 1734; Agnes McChush (Melhuish), 1719; William Meager, 1737; William Meuson, 1719; William Micon(?), 1732; Richard Mitchell, 1743; Mother Telah Moad (Mead), 1733; William Moore, 1735; John Moore, 1734; Job Morgan, 1735; William Morris, 1743; Thomas Morris, 1735; John Morro, 1719; Ruth Moses, 1768; Joseph Muggeridge, 1732; Jane Mullins, 1734; Thomas Munday (Mumday), 1734; Willmott Neuman, 1732; Thomas Newberry (Norberry), 1734; George Newport, 1732; Daniel Newtown, 1719; Peter Norman (Knolman), 1719; William O'Bryan, 1719; Margaret Olivier (spinster), 1745; Anne Osmond, 1743; William Paggesty, 1736; Robert Palmer, 1736; Anne Parkins, 1720; William Parl, 1744; Mary Parry, 1743; Love Partridge, 1733; John Pascoe, 1732;

Johnathan Passinger, 1744; David Patty, 1737; Charles Patty, 1719; John Pavior, 1735; John Pearce, 1732; John Pearce, 1732; John Pearce (Pearse), 1743; Richard Pearce, 1732; Sarah Pearce, 1736; Thomas Pearce, 1733; William Pearce (Pearse), 1732; Elizabeth Pearse, 1734; James Peddle, 1720; George Peirce, 1732; Ralph Perry, 1737; Hugh Peters, 1732; Jane Phelps, 1768; Mark Pickford, 1737; John Pingstone (Pringston), 1736; Francis Platt, 1736; Elizabeth Please, 1719; William Pockard, 1720; Richard Pointer, 1739; Alexander Pongslly [sic], 1732; John Preston, 1744; Mary Price, 1769; Bernard Purse, 1737; William Pyle, 1720; Thomas Quick, 1719; Anne Radford, 1732; Cornelius Radford, 1720; Richard Randle, 1737; Valentine Rice, 1736; John Rickman, 1737; James Roberts, 1736; Robert Rodd, Sr., 1732; William Rogers, 1733; Sarah Ronnett, 1743; John Rossiter, 1719; Philop Rutter (husband of Amy Rutter), 1736; Amy Rutter (wife of Philop Rutter), 1736; Ambrose Sampson, 1732; Thomas Saner, 1743; Sarah Saul, 1732; Andrew Sayer, 1719; Joseph Scarborough, 1719; Robert Sealy (Sowly), 1732; Daniel Searell, 1737; Thomas Seaver, 1744; Elizabeth Sevier, 1733; Henry Shute, 1719; Anthony Skinner, 1735; Thomas Slee, 1735; John Sly, 1732; Anne Smith, 1743; John Smith, 1732; John Smith, 1737; John Somers (Somerhays), 1735; John Sparke, 1732; Mary Sparles, 1735; Martha Spencer, 1720; Sarah Spencer (and mentions her son John Spencer), 1762; Burchett Spettigue, 1719; Sarah Spratt, 1737; William Stansbury, 1733; Thomas Stephens, 1733; Thomas Stephens, 1735; William Stevens, 1719; Thomas Stone, 1719; Edith Street, 1732; Lady Street, 1735; Mary Sullivan, 1767; Sarah Sumners, 1761; Alexander Symond, 1732; Edward Taimbin (Tambin, Timbin), 1737; Phillip Tauton, 1736; William Taylor, 1719; Thomas Taylor, 1734; Peter Teague (Teage, Lleage), 1732; Elizabeth Thomas, 1743; John Thomas, 1719; John Thomas, 1735; John Thomas, 1735; John Thomas, 1736; William Thorn, 1737; Richard Thorne, 1732; William Thorne, 1732; Hannah Tiley, 1737; Thomas Tippett, 1719; Martha Tippett, 1733; Elizabeth Tomson, 1735; Christopher Toole, 1734; Mary Townsend, 1737; Mary Treany, 1737; John Treise (Troife), 1732; Arthur Trevascus (Trevaseus, Trevstus), 1732; Robert Trottle, 1719; James Tuck, 1720; Peter Tucker, 1732; Richard Tuckor, 1736; John Tush, 1737; James Tyer (Wheeler), 1739; Francis Tylor, 1732; Robert Underhill, Jr., 1719; Jonas Vanstone, 1737; Hugh Vicary, 1744; Richard Vincent, 1737; William Vivian, 1719; Grace Waldrond (Walrond), 1732; Hugh Wall, 1743; John Wallmutt (Woolmutt, Woolacutt), 1735; Richard Walters, 1733; Anne (Anna) Ward (servant to Joseph Young), 1729; Job Ward, 1739; Robert Warren, 1735; Richard Webb, 1735; Thomas Webb, 1734; Timothy Webb, 1719; Humphrey Webber, 1739; Philip Welcocks, 1736; James Welles, 1736; Hugh Wells, 1735; Joseph Wells, 1733; Mary Wells, 1735; Joseph Westlake, 1719; William Wheeler, 1737; Henry White, 1732; Mary Wilkerson, 1747; Richard Wilkerson, 1737; Philis Wilkins, 1739; Samuel Wilkins, 1737; Jane Williams, 1735; John Williams, 1737; Thomas Williams, 1734; Richard Williamson, 1737; James Willis, 1736; Jane Witheridge, 1735; Thomas Wobbler, Thomas Womsley (Wonsley), 1732; John Wood, 1719; Mary Woolsy, 1736; John Wooms, 1732; Michael Wooton (Wooten), 1732; and, William York, 1734.

KENT COUNTY, MARYLAND TROOPS IN THE REVOLUTIONARY WAR, 1775-1783, (Gleaned from *Archives of Maryland*, Volume 18, "Muster Rolls of Maryland Troops, 1775-1783." The lists herein contain names of soldiers who served in the Continental Army from Kent County. For those who served in the militia, see S. Eugene Clements and F. Edward Wright's The Maryland Militia in the Revolutionary War (Westminster, Maryland: Family Line Publications, 1987), and Kent County, Maryland and Vicinity, Lists of Militia and Oaths of Allegiance, June, 1775, by Mrs. William G. Bruckey (Decorah, Iowa: The Anundsen Publishing Company, 1975, and reprinted by Family Line Publications in 1985).

January 2, 1776: Officers of the 7th Independent Maryland Company (Queen Anne's and Kent Counties) elected by the Convention: Capt. Edward Veazey, 1st Lt. William Harrison, 2nd Lt. Samuel Turbutt Wright, and 3rd Lt. Edward DeCourcy.

January 29, 1776: "A List of the Minute Company from Kent County under the Command of William Henry, who marched from said County on January 29, 1776, and now stationed in Northampton County, Virginia on February 29, 1776" -- Capt. William Henry, Lt. John Hyland, Lt. G. W. Forrester, Ensign William Clarke, Surgeon William Tillotson, Adjutant Robert Campbell, Sgt. Enos Reeves, Sgt. William Sprot, Sgt. George Vansant, Sgt. Charles Irons, Cpl. John Day, Cpl. Robert Gay, Cpl. James Henry, Cpl. Garrett Vansant, Drummer Joseph Purden, Fifer William ---- [blank]. Privates: John Bond, Stephen Boddy, Benjamin Brockson, Henry Bostick, Lambert Boyer, John Burnsides, Henry Clarke, Edward Clayton, James Campher, John Cole, John Cry, Isaac Cornelius, William Davis, Samuel Davis, Samuel Eades, Isaac Freeman, Daniel Furgusson, Abraham Freeman, Salathiel Freeland, Lambert Flowers, Benjamin Garland, James Greedy, Oliver Gallop, William Gray, William Haley, John Hurt, James Hurt, Peter Justice, William Johnson, Nathaniel Knock, David Keain, Francis Lemon, George Littles, Sr., George Littles, Jr., John Miller, John McGowan, William Miers, Enoch Massey, Nathaniel McClelland, John Massey, Samuel Money, Joseph Newsom, John Newland, Richard Nab, William Pettegrew, Charles Philipshill, Andrew Park, Benedict Pennington, Matthew Richardson, Sampson Redgrave, Thomas Read, John Richardson, Jacob Richardson, Thomas Sewell, Thomas Sappington, John Stephenson, Benjamin Stoops, John Stoops, Marlow Taylor, William Peregrine Thrift, John Vansant, Christopher Vansant, Benjamin Vansant, James Wilson, Sr., John Wilson, James Wilson, Jr., William Wilson, John Wilmer, James Woodland, Robert Young. [Note: This list was also published in The Patriotic Marylander, Vol. III, No. 4, June, 1917, pp. 230-231, in an article entitled "Kent County Militia in the Revolutionary War," by Percy G. Skirven].

At Chestertown, two companies were enlisted in July, 1776, for service in the Continental Army. The officers of these two companies and the dates of their commissions were as follows: First Company -- Capt. Thomas Smyth, Jr., July 9, 1776; 1st Lt. James Williamson, July 10, 1776; 2nd Lt. Nathaniel Kennard, July

20, 1776; Ensign Josiah Johnson, July 22, 1776. Second Company --
Capt. Isaac Perkins, July 5, 1776; 1st Lt. Abraham Falconer, July
--, 1776; 2nd Lt. Jesse Cosden, July 4, 1776; Ensign James Henry,
July 11, 1776 (Ref: The Patriotic Marylander, Vol. III, No. 1,
September, 1916, page 232).

July 17, 1776: Soldiers enlisted by Capt. Isaac Perkins and
passed by William Henry -- Benjamin Burchinall, John Williams,
William Apsley, William Mann, John Phillips, Abednegoe Jackson,
John Rollison, William Dauherty, Dennis Hurley, David Newell,
Benjamin Everitt, Conrod Whiteman, David Tulley, Nathaniel
Herring, Adam Laurence, Froggitt Tillard, Augusteen Spencer,
James Butcher, John McKinney, Daniel Knock, Joseph Greenwood,
John Lynch, Richard Kennard, John Pearce, David Crane, Daniel
Turner, Thomas Norman, Edward Stewart, William Jones, Samuel
Sinnett.

July 19, 1776: Soldiers enlisted by Lt. Abraham Falconer and
passed by William Henr -- Daniel Ahern, Benjamin Roberts, William
Hunter, Benjamin Pharow, Benjamin Garland (or Gavland), Joseph
Morris, Robert Little, Daniel Toas Massy, Jeremiah Collins, James
Ragan, Michael Thomas, Daniel Mulcahy, Nazareth Freeland, Love
Alley (or Alby), William Herring, James Wise, Ebenezer Costillo,
John Walls, Jr., William Walls, Jr.

July 13, 1776: Soldiers enlisted by Lt. Jesse Cosden and passed
by William Henry -- Lambert Boyer, William Hammon, John Cosden,
Cornelius Comegys, John Finley, John Woodall, Matthew Smyth,
Hartley Sappington, William Smith, Samuel Eades, Daniel Sevell
(or Serell?), Edward William Johnson, John Smith, William
Wiltshire, James Reyley, William Hill, James Greenwood, Johnson
Brooks, Joshua Vansant, James Copper (or Cooper?).

July 10, 1776: Enrolled by Lt. James Williamson and passed by
Edward Worrell on July 29, 1776, part of Capt. Thomas Smyth,
Jr.'s Company -- Thomas Punney, James Wilson, James Dunn, Jr.,
William Hynson, Charles Scott, John Holder, John Rolph, Charles
Scoone, Owen Whaland, Thomas Rolph, Frogget Younger, John Hughes,
Caleb Catlin, Thomas Ridiford, Anthony Dunn, Stephen Kindle,
James Saunders, Daniel McConnican, John Phillips, James
Carmichael.

July 22, 1776: Enlisted by Lt. Nathaniel Kennard, Jr. and passed
by William Henry -- William Foreman, Francis Lamb, Joseph Howard,
Charles Jones, John Punney, John Sillivin, William Giant, Stephin
Giant, Anguish McDonnold, Benjamin Jones, Richard Lane, Phillip
Reed, William Foster, William Kinnard, Francis Armstrong, John
Curtain, Benjamin Connerwey, Isaac Smith, Thomas Knimptum, John
Husselton.

July 27, 1776: Enlisted by Ensign Josiah Johnson and passed by
William Henry -- George Tolson, George Foard, William Meeks,
Robert Meeks, George Scone, Theophilius Lowmuth, John Patten,
George Connor, Thomas Jones, Morriss Marrah, John Rosse, Henry

Truelock, Jr., Daniel Donnowin, William Jones, William Dugan, Nathan Brooks.

1781: Partial list of discharged soldiers raised for the Continental Army in 1781 -- Nathaniel Basnett, Thomas Frazier, James Griffith, William Hall, James Hickenbottom [Higginbottom], Edward Kelly, John Kelly, Benjamin Kinnard, William John Lazenby, Charles Ogelsby, John Perkins, John Pearce, Hugh Pearce, Daniel Norris, Peregrine Read, Starling Thomas, Beal Thomas.

May 16, 1781: Kent County Recruits (All enlisted for 3 years) -- Henry Williams, Henry Harris, James Bryne, Reubin Elbon, John Collins, William Lynes, William Wilson, James Sheppard, George Finley, William Dunkin, Richard Dolvin, William Elbon, Thomas Wood, William Brada, Daniel B. Bayley, James Reynolds, William Grace, Richard Green, Abraham Reynolds, Smyth Bagwell, John Thomas, Ishmael Wroth, John Harris, William Guggon, James Chambers, Timothy Conner, John Gleen, Jacob Jefferies, William Taylor, James Wilson, Augustine Bryan, Thomas Farmer, Edward Chambers, Shadrick Sap, John Starkey, Absolom Scott, Richard Demby. "Agreeable to the assessment we made out thirty-nine Classes of sixteen thousand pounds each & every Class (except one) has furnished a recruit for three years according to the above list. The deficient Class was drafted on the fifth day of May and I hope that a recruit for three years will be produced for that Class. Alexander Boys passed by Class No. 35, we discovered was subject to fits, who we have since discharged, the Class agreeing to pay their proportion to the State. The said Boys having received but a small sum. Signed: W. Bordley."

Isaac Beckett was listed as a defective from the Maryland Line on June 26, 1781.

August 23, 1781: Kent County Recruits, Chester Town (All enlisted for 3 years) -- Charles Ogilsby, John Pearce, William Caulk (during the war), John Pearce, William Grant (during the war), Daniel Norris, John Kelly, Samuel Whitehouse (dead), Nicholas Smith, Peregrine Reed, Beal Thomas, Samuel Binn, Hugh Pearce, Daniel Herrin, Starling Thomas, Thomas Frasier, James McDoal, John Perkins, William Paul, Nathan Basnett, William Hall, James Kelly, Henry Thomas, Simon Beck, John Lesley, William Bogue, Edward Kelly, George Jones, George Thomas, James Higinbottam, William John Lessenby, James Griffith, Daniel Ashley.

INVALID PENSIONERS BY JOHN NICHOLSON, KENT REGISTER OF WILLS, 1789
John Davis (down county), Private, Continental Army, resident of Chester Town, pension commenced in 1781, and died in 1790.
James Carmichael, Private, 1st Maryland Regiment, pension commenced in 1781, and died in 1785.
Robert Sharpless, Corporal, Continental Army, resident of Chester Town, pension commenced in 1785, struck off rolls on November 9, 1789 because the Court thought him able to labor and a great drunkard.
John Davis (up county), Private, 6th Maryland Regiment, resident

of Chester Town at this time, pension commenced in 1785, and has been paid through October 22, 1789.
Hugh McClean, Private, 1st Maryland Regiment, pension commenced in 1785 and struck off rolls on October 22, 1789 because the Court thought him able bodied at this time.
George 2nd, Corporal, Continental Army, pension commenced in 1786, paid through August, 1789, and the Court was of the opinion he ought not be allowed in the future.
Daniel Smith, Private, Continental Army, pension commenced in 1786, and paid through January 18, 1789.
John Lynch, Corporal, Continental Army, pension commenced in 1786, and paid through August 28, 1789.

KENT COUNTY COMMITTEE OF CORRESPONDENCE MEMBERSHIP ON JUNE 2, 1774
Elected to serve at the Chestertown, Maryland, Courthouse, with future meetings to be held at the home of Edward Worrell: Chairman, Thomas Smyth; Clerk, William Hall. Committeemen -- William Ringgold (Eastern Neck), Robert Buchanan, John Maxwell, Emory Sudler, Col. Richard Lloyd, Col. Joseph Nicholson, John Cadwallader, Joseph Nicholson, Jr., Thomas Ringgold, Thomas B. Hands, Joseph Earle, Ezekiel Foreman, James Anderson, James Hynson, James Pearce, Isaac Spencer, William Carmichael, John Vorhees, Donaldson Yeates, William Ringgold (Chestertown), Eleazer McComb, Dr. John Scott, Jeremiah Nicols, Dr. William Bordley, and Capt. James Nicholson (Ref: *History of Maryland*, Vol. II, by J. Thomas Scharf, pp. 149-150 (Hatboro, Pennsylvania: Tradition Press, 1967).

KENT COUNTY DELEGATES TO MARYLAND CONVENTION, APRIL 24-MAY 3, 1775
Col. Richard Lloyd, Thomas Smyth, William Ringgold, Joseph Nicholson, Jr., Joseph Earle, Thomas Bedingfield Hands, and Thomas Ringgold (Ref: *Calendar of Maryland State Papers, Red Book No. 4*, Part 1, page 31 (Maryland Hall of Records Commission, 1950).

KENT COUNTY JUDGES OF ELECTIONS, AUGUST 15, 1776: William Rogers, William Bordley, and John Page (Ref: *Red Book, loc. cit.*, page 46).

KENT COUNTY PENSIONER IN 1840: John Humphries, 1st District, age 85, resided with L. M. Recaud [Ricaud] as of June 1, 1840 (Ref: *Census of Pensioners for Revolutionary or Military Services in 1840*, page 127 (Baltimore: Genealogical Publishing Company, 1967).

KENT COUNTY REPRESENTATIVES TO THE PROPRIETARY ASSEMBLY OF
MARYLAND (Ref: *A Biographical Dictionary of the Maryland
Legislature, 1635-1789*, by Edward C. Papenfuse, et al (Baltimore:
The Johns Hopkins Press, 1979).
1637/1638 - Robert Philpott, Thomas Bradnox, and Edward Beckler
1638/1639 - Nicholas Brown and Christopher Thomas
1640/1641 - Giles Brent, Thomas Adams, Thomas Allen, John Abbott
1641/1642 - William Lodlington [sic] and Richard Thompson
1642 - Richard Thomas and Robert Vaughan
1647 - Robert Vaughan, Thomas Bradnox, and Philip Conner
1649 - Philip Conner
1650/1652 - Robert Vaughan
1654 - Thomas Hynson and Joseph Wickes
1657 - Robert Vaughan and Joseph Wickes
1658 - Philip Conner
1659/1660 - Joseph Wickes, Thomas Hynson, Henry Morgan, John
    Russell
1661 - Thomas Stagwell and William Leeds
1662 - Robert Vaughan and Richard Blunt
1663/1664 - Henry Carline and Robert Dunn
1666 - Nicholas Pickard and Richard Blunt
1669 - Robert Dunn and Richard Blunt
1671/1675 - Arthur Wright and William Bishop
1676/1682 - Joseh Wickes, Thomas Marsh, Henry Hosier, Samuel
    Tovey, John Hynson, and Thomas Smith
1682/1684 - Joseph Wickes and Henry Hosier
1686/1688 - Henry Hosier, Michael Miller, and William Harris
1689/1692 - William Harris, Michael Miller, Hans Hanson, Thomas
    Davis

KENT COUNTY REPRESENTATIVES TO THE ROYAL ASSEMBLY OF MARYLAND
1692/1693 - William Harris, Hans Hanson, Elias King, Samuel
    Wheeler
1694/1697 - Hans Hanson, John Hynson, Thomas Smith, William
    Frisby
1796/1700 - Michael Miller, Thomas Smith, John Whittington, Simon
    Wilmer, Solomon Wright, and Charles Hynson
1701/1704 - Thomas Smith, John Whittington, John Hynson, John
    Salter
1704/1707 - Thomas Smith (Speaker of the Lower House), William
    Frisby, Elias King, and John Wells
1708 - William Frisby, Samuel Wallis, John Carvile, Thomas
    Covington, and Daniel Pearce
1708/1711 - Daniel Pearce, Thomas Covington, Edward Bathurst,
    John Carvile, Thomas Ringgold, James Harris, and Edward Scott
1712/1714 - Daniel Pearce, Edward Scott, St. Leger Codd, Edward
    Blay, and William Blay
1715 - James Harris, William Blay, St. Leger Codd, Andrew
    Hamilton

KENT COUNTY REPRESENTATIVES TO THE PROPRIETARY ASSEMBLY OF
    MARYLAND
1716/1718 - St. Ledger Codd, James Harris, Edward Scott,
    Nathaniel Hynson

176 INHABITANTS OF KENT COUNTY, MARYLAND, 1637-1787

1719/1722 - Nathaniel Hynson, James Smith, St. Ledger Codd, Lambert Wilmer
1722/1724 - Samuel Wallis, Robert Dunn, Philip Kennard, William Blackiston, Ebenezer Blackiston
1725/1727 - James Harris, Philip Kennard, Simon Wilmer, Marmaduke Tilden, Ebenezer Blackiston
1728/1731 - James Harris, Philip Kennard, George Willson, Ebenezer Blackiston
1732/1734 - Ebenezer Blackiston, George Willson, Matthew Howard, Christopher Hall
1734/1737 - James Harris (Speaker of the Lower House), Christopher Hall, George Willson, Philip Kennard
1738 - George Willson, Philip Kennard, Thomas Smith, Charles Hynson
1739/1741 - Charles Hynson, George Willson, William Harris, James Calder
1742/1744 - Richard Gresham, George Willson, James Calder, John Gresham
1745 - Richard Gresham, George Willson, John Gresham, Matthias Harris
1745/1748 - John Gresham, George Willson, Richard Gresham, Matthias Harris
1749/1751 - Matthias Harris, Richard Lloyd, Simon Wilmer, Nicholas Smith
1751/1754 - Alexander Williamson, William Rasin, John Gresham, Abraham Falconar, Richard Gresham, Hugh Wallis
1754/1757 - Alexander Williamson (Speaker of the Lower House), Richard Gresham, Hugh Wallis, William Hynson
1757/1758 - John Tilden, William Rasin, William Hynson, Alexander Williamson
1758/1761 - Alexander Williamson, Richard Gresham, John Tilden, William Hynson, Thomas Ringgold
1762/1763 - William Hynson, Richard Lloyd, Simon Wilmer, Thomas Ringgold
1765/1766 - Thomas Ringgold, Robert Buchanan, Richard Lloyd, William Hynson
1768/1770 - Robert Buchanan, Thomas Ringgold, Stephen Bordley, Richard Gresham
1771 - Thomas Ringgold, Richard Gresham, Stephen Bordley, Robert Buchanan, William Ringgold
1773/1774 - Robert Buchanan, William Ringgold, John Maxwell, Emory Sudler

KENT COUNTY REPRESENTATIVES TO THE MARYLAND PROVISIONAL GOVERNMENT
June 22, 1774 - First Convention: Thomas Smyth, William Ringgold, Joseph Nicholson, Jr., Thomas Ringgold, Joseph Earle, William Hall.
December 8, 1774 - Third Convention: Thomas Ringgold, Joseph Earle.
April 24, 1775 - Fourth Convention: Richard Lloyd, Thomas Smyth, William Ringgold, Joseph Nicholson, Jr., Joseph Earle, Thomas Bedingfield Hands, Thomas Ringgold.
July 26, 1775 - Fifth Convention: William Ringgold, Richard

REPRESENTATIVES TO THE PROPRIETARY ASSEMBLY   177

Lloyd, Thomas Smyth, Joseph Earle, Thomas Bedingfield Hands, Thomas Ringgold, Joseph Nicholson, Jr.
August 29, 1775 - First Council of Safety: Richard Lloyd, Edward Lloyd, Thomas Smyth.
June 21, 1776 - Eighth Convention: Robert Buchanan, Peregrine Letherbury, Thomas Smyth, Emory Sudler, William Sluby, Thomas Ringgold.
January 18, 1776 - Second Council of Safety: Thomas Smyth, Thomas Bedingfield Hands.
May 27, 1776 - Third Council of Safety: Thomas Smyth, Thomas Bedingfield Hands.
July 6, 1776 - Fourth Council of Safety: Thomas Bedingfield Hands, Thomas Smyth, Joseph Nicholson, Jr.
August 14, 1776 - Ninth Convention: Thomas Ringgold, William Ringgold, Joseph Earle, Thomas Smyth.
November 12, 1776 - Fifth Council of Safety: Joseph Nicholson, Jr., William Hemsley, James Lloyd Chamberlaine, Turbutt Wright.

KENT COUNTY DELEGATES TO THE MARYLAND GENERAL ASSEMBLY
1777 - First Session: Peregrine Letherbury, Isaac Perkins, John Maxwell, Donaldson Yeates
1777/1778 - Peregrine Letherbury, John Maxwell, Ezekiel Foreman, John Cadwalader, Richard Gresham, James Lloyd
1778/1779 - Peregrine Letherbury, Richard Gresham, James Lloyd, John Lambert Wilmer
1779/1780 - Richard Gresham, John Lambert Wilmer, Peregrine Letherbury, William Stevenson, John Cadwalader
1780/1781 - William Stevenson, Peregrine Letherbury, John Lambert Wilmer, John Cadwalader
1781/1782 - John Cadwalader, William Stevenson, James Lloyd, Marmaduke Tilden
1782/1783 - Thomas Smyth, Jr., John Cadwalader, James Pearce, James Lloyd
1783 - Peregrine Letherbury, William Stevenson, Robert Maxwell, James Brown Dunn
1784 - Peregrine Letherbury, John Scott, Richard Graves, John Cadwalader
1785 - Peregrine Letherbury, Robert Maxwell, Richard Graves, James Pearce
1786/1787 - Isaac Perkins, Richard Miller, Josiah Johnson, Robert Wright.

INHABITANTS OF KENT COUNTY, MARYLAND, 1637-1787

COMMANDERS OF ISLE OF KENT AND AS SUCH ITS PRESIDING JUSTICE
(Ref: *Archives of Maryland*, Volume 54)
Capt. George Evelyn, 1637
Capt. Robert Philpot, 1637-1638
Capt. William Brainthwaite, 1638-1639
Capt. Giles Brent, 1639-1644
Capt. John Wyatt, 1644
Capt. Robert Vaughan, 1645-1652
Capt. Philip Conner (Conier), 1652-1658

COLONIAL MILITIA OFFICERS GLEANED FROM CHURCH RECORDS, 1703-1724
1703-1708: Col. William Pearce, Col. Edward Blay, Col. Hans Hanson, Col. Thomas Smyth, Lt. Col. Elias King, Capt. Thomas Ringgold, Capt. John Wells, and Capt. William Potts.
1709-1714: Col. Edward Blay, Col. Nathaniel Hynson, Major Thomas Ringgold, Capt. Edward Scott, Capt. St. Leger Codd, and Capt. James Harris.
1715-1724: Col. Nathaniel Hynson, Col. Edward Scott, Major William Scott, Major William Potts, Capt. St. Leger Codd, and Capt. Daniel Pearce.
(Also: Capt. ---- Lovering in 1750, and Capt. ---- Spencer in 1756)

COLONIAL MILITIA OFFICERS GLEANED FROM COUNTY DEBT BOOKS, 1733-1769
[Note: The following officers appeared in the Kent County Debt Books as owning land between the years noted after each name. Whether or not they actually lived in Kent County is another matter, and some of the Captains could have been Ship Captains.]
Colonel William Coursey, 1733-1769
Colonel William Ennalls, 1733-1747
Colonel Henry Hooper, 1739-1769
Colonel Charles Hynson, 1733-1769
Colonel Nathaniel Hynson. 1733-1769
Colonel ---- [blank] Scott, 1741
Colonel Samuel Thomas, 1733-1769
Colonel Edward Lloyd, 1733-1769
Colonel Henry Lowe, 1733-1735
Colonel William Pearce, 1733-1735
Major John Brown, 1733-1760
Major William Turbutt, 1736-1737
Captain John Wattson, 1739-1741
Captain John Tilden, 1733-1769
Captain Edward Leech, 1733-1747
Captain Martin Potter, 1738-1743
Captain William Potts, 1733-1742
Captain Samuel Richardson, 1733-1741
Captain Henry Rippin, 1735-1741
Captain Richard Smith, 1733-1735
Captain Thomas Spencer, 1733-1769
Captain Elisha Stringfellow, 1736-1747
Captain John Tennant, 1733-1747
Captain Ebenezer Blackiston, 1733-1769

Captain Peregrine Brown, 1733-1769
Captain Robert Dunn, 1733-1747
Captain William Gaskill, 1736-1742
Captain Richard Hill, 1733-1742
Captain William Hopkins, 1736-1769

KENT COUNTY MILITIA IN CAPT. PEREGRINE BROWN'S COMPANY CIRCA 1748
(Ref: *Colonial Soldiers of the South, 1732-1774*, by Murtie June Clark, pp. 109-110). [Note: Although not identified as such, it is obvious from the surnames listed that they were Kent Countians who were called to duty for 15 days service probably in 1748 or 1749. It should also be noted that there are other lists in Clark's book for colonial soldiers on Kent Island, formerly in Kent County, but then part of Queen Anne's County, so they are not included herein.]

Capt. Peregrine Brown, Ensign Joseph Rasin, Sgt. Rasin Gale, Sgt. Henry Trulock, Sgt. Joseph Trulock, Sgt. John McGuire, Cpl. David Hull, Cpl. John Craig, Cpl. William Collins, Cpl. McCall Medford, Drummer Benjamin Foreman, and Clerk Thomas Chandler. The soldiers (Privates) were: John Boggs, James Greenwood, Thomas Hart, Nicholas Parsons, John Tuckwell, John Everett, John Brisco, Luke Middleton, Jacob Trulock, Michael Raimon, Charles Tombs, John Ricketts, Joseph King, John Castledine, Robert Ford, Jr., John Angier [Augier?], Joseph Greenwood, William Ford, Joshua George, Andrew Toalson, John Yoarkley, William Course, Samuel Warner, Mark Noble, Tilton Reed, William Reading, Joseph Ashbur, Thomas Hepburn, Thomas Chandler, Jr., Isaac Briscoe, Henry Talbott, Joseph Hull, John Mitchell, John Hickes, Charles Ford, and John Davis.

GLEANINGS FROM COLONIAL MILITIA ACCOUNTS NOW BEFORE THE COMMITTEE OF ACCOUNTS, FOR KENT COUNTIANS [UNDATED, BUT PROBABLY CIRCA 1748] (Ref: Clark, loc. cit., pp. 120-123): #5 - Jonathan Leatherbury; #6 - John Chapple; #26 - Thomas Ringgold; #27 - John Bolton; #28 - John Bordley; #29 - George Brown; #30 - John Carvill; #129 - Batrix Johnson; #149 - James Reed's executors (assigned to Col. Richard Lloyd); #166 - William Weatherhead (George Town); and, #167 - Isabella Weatherhead. Also, although not identified as Kent County accounts, these names certainly appear in that county during this time period: #136 - Thomas Perkins; #137 - James Porter; #138 - Edward Forener; #139 - Thomas Ringgold; #140 - Sarah McDermott; #141 - Abraham Wood; and, #142 - Jonathan Barrett (all of these accounts were assigned to Col. Richard Lloyd); plus, #146 - Simon Wilmer, and #147 - Thomas Spencer (who were also Kent Countians).

KENT COUNTY MILITIA, 13TH BATTALION UNDER COL. RICHARD GRAVES, 1778
(Ref: The Patriotic Marylander, Vol. III, No. 2, December, 1916) [Note: Several sources have copied these lists and indicated that they served in 1775. According to the distinguished historian and genealogist Francis B. Culver these lists were recorded in 1778. The 13th Battalion was formed in the lower part of the county.]

13TH BATTALION OFFICERS: Col. Richard Graves, Lt. Col. Benjamin Chambers, Major William Frisby, Major Isaac Perkins, and the following Captains and their respective companies:

13TH BATTALION, FIRST COMPANY UNDER CAPT. ROBERT CRUIKSHANK, 1778
Pvt. Edward Alford, Pvt. Nathan Atkins, 1st Lt. Anthony Banning, Pvt. John Burk, Pvt. Arthur Bordley, Pvt. John Burk, Jr., Pvt. Joseph Blackiston, Pvt. William Buckingham, Pvt. Henry Bashwell, Pvt. William Boddy, Pvt. Edward Cannon, Pvt. George Clark, Pvt. Nathaniel Dyer, Pvt. James Dunn, Jr., Pvt. Edward Davis, Pvt. William Dowling, Pvt. George Duncan, Pvt. Thomas Delahunty, Pvt. Mordica Delahunty, Pvt. John Dew, Pvt. John Eads, Pvt. Henry Eads, Pvt. James Eads, Pvt. Jonathan Eads, Pvt. William Fray, Jr., Pvt. John Frisby, Pvt. John Frazier, Pvt. James Frazier, Ensign George Gilbert, Pvt. Thomas Granger, Pvt. William Glenn, Pvt. John Gird, Pvt. James Griffith, Pvt. James Grant, Pvt. William Greenfield, Pvt. Joseph Hopkins, Pvt. James Hurt, Pvt. Thomas Hadley, Pvt. Thomas Ireland, Pvt. John Jones, Pvt. William Kendoll, Pvt. James Kendoll, Pvt. Richard Lennox, Pvt. John Lowman, Pvt. John Lynch, Pvt. Thomas Lord, Pvt. Richard Lane, 1st Lt. Thomas Masling, Pvt. William Matthews, Pvt. Boutain Masling, Pvt. James Masling, Pvt. William Money, Pvt. Hamon Masling, Pvt. John Magnor, Jr., Pvt. William Mason, Jr., Pvt. John Grey Parish, Pvt. James Ringgold, Pvt. James Ringgold, Jr., Pvt. John Ringgold, Jr., Pvt. Edward Smith, Pvt. William Shield, Pvt. William Strong, Pvt. Major Stewart, Pvt. Francis Skervin, Pvt. Richard Smyth, Pvt. John Simmonds, Pvt. William Shaw, Pvt. Joseph Scow, Pvt. John Wiles, Pvt. Valentine Warum.

13TH BATTALION, SECOND COMPANY UNDER CAPT. MORGAN BROWN, 1778
Pvt. Patrick Ahern, Pvt. John Ashley, Pvt. Edward Beck, Pvt. Joseph Byram, Pvt. James Byram, Pvt. William Byram, Pvt. John Byram, Pvt. Stephen Byram, Pvt. Nicholas Brown, Pvt. Charles Baker, Pvt. James Blackiston, Pvt. Abraham Boots, Pvt. John Boddy, Pvt. William Baker, Pvt. John Barratt, Pvt. William Burchinall, Pvt. James Casemark, Pvt. Elisha Clark, Pvt. Jesse Clark, Pvt. James Clark, Pvt. John Clark, Jr., Pvt. Elijah Clark, Pvt. William Clark, Pvt. Henry Curry, Pvt. Jesse Comegys, Pvt. Edward Comegys, Pvt. William Dennison, Pvt. John Grimes, Pvt. Peregrine Glenn, Pvt. Joseph George, Pvt. Robert George, Pvt. Alexander Green, Pvt. John Gleaves, Pvt. Joseph Hopkins, Pvt. William Harwood, Pvt. James Harrison, Pvt. William Ivey, Pvt. James Lovegrove, 2nd Lt. Lovrin Merritt, Pvt. William Mansfield, Pvt. Morris Megonigil, Pvt. William Mason, Pvt. Abraham Milton, Pvt. Richard Milton, Pvt. Francis Masling, Ensign Charles Neil, Pvt. Jeremiah Nicols, Pvt. William Pearce, Jr., Pvt. Charles Pearce, Pvt. Henry Price, Pvt. Thomas Punney, 1st Lt. John Rolph, Pvt. Elias Ringgold, Pvt. William Solway, Pvt. James Smith, Pvt. John Sutton, Pvt. John Stewart, Pvt. William Smith, Pvt. Thomas Sudler, Pvt. Thomas Stapleford, Pvt. Aaron Trencher, Pvt. William Trew, Pvt. Henry Troth, Pvt. Samuel Thomas, Pvt. George Wilson, Pvt. Richard Wilson.

MILITIA   181

13TH BATTALION, 3RD COMPANY UNDER CAPT. ALEXANDER ANDERSON, 1778
Pvt. John Ashby, Pvt. Robert Anderson, Pvt. Tobias Ashmore, Pvt.
John Beverlin, Pvt. James Brewer, Pvt. Moses Berry, Pvt. Benjamin
Binney [Benney], Pvt. James Blake, Pvt. Barney Corse, Pvt.
Cornelius Connway, Pvt. Thomas Chipchase, Pvt. James Covington,
Pvt. Thomas Covington, Pvt. Charles Copper, Pvt. Samuel Crouch,
Pvt. Joseph Conden, Pvt. Thomas Caton, 2nd Lt. Philip Davis, Pvt.
Robert Davis, Pvt. Matthew Dean, Pvt. Solomon Dawson, Pvt. John
Deighton, Pvt. Philip Fray, Pvt. Bartholomew Foreman, Pvt. Samuel
Foreman, 1st Lt. George Hartshorn, Pvt. Samuel Hammond, Pvt.
Thomas Humphrey, Pvt. Thomas Huff, Pvt. Daniel Holyoak, Pvt.
Simion Halbert, Pvt. William Hall, Pvt. James Hamilton, Pvt.
Isaac Hackett, Pvt. Shem Hadley, Pvt. Thomas Kent, Pvt. John
Lorian, Pvt. Simon Moore, Pvt. Jere. McHaffey. Pvt. John Moore,
Pvt. George Moore, Pvt. Thomas McCoppin, Pvt. Charles Miller,
Pvt. Henry Price, Pvt. William Pearce, Pvt. William Roberts, Pvt.
James Riedderford, Pvt. Josias Ringgold, Pvt. Thomas Ringgold,
Pvt. John T. Ricketts, Pvt. Samuel Sinnett, 2nd Lt. John Sturges,
Pvt. John Shaves, Pvt. William Senby, Pvt. James Smith, Pvt. John
Scott, Pvt. John Sullivan, Pvt. John Smith, Pvt. James Earle
Thomas, Pvt. William Trew, Pvt. Thomas Thomas, Ensign William
Worrell, Pvt. Thomas Woodal, Pvt. Samuel Wallis, Pvt. James
Wilson, Pvt. Benjamin Wroth, Pvt. Thomas Weaver, Pvt. George
Waller, Pvt. John Wethered, Pvt. Kinvin Wroth, Pvt. Thomas
Woodard, Pvt. James Wilmer, Pvt. Charles Whealer, Pvt. Simon
Worrell.

13TH BATTALION, FOURTH COMPANY UNDER CAPT. JOHN MOORE, 1778
2nd Sgt. Benjamin Andrews, Pvt. Lewis Atkinson, Pvt. Peter
Arnold, Ensign Samuel Beck, Pvt. Richard Brice, Pvt. James
Brummel, Pvt. Richard Brummel, Pvt. Samuel Buttew, Pvt. Stephen
Boddy, Pvt. John Boddy, Pvt. John Brice, Pvt. John Burk, Jr., 1st
Lt. Thomas Crow, 3rd Sgt. William Copper, 4th Cpl. James Crouch,
Pvt. John Costley, Pvt. Patrick Carr, Pvt. Andrew Childs, Pvt.
John Carradine, Pvt. John Curry, Pvt. John Clark, Pvt. William
Hynson Crabbin, Pvt. Benjamin Clever, Pvt. William Caulk, Pvt.
Thomas Crosley, Pvt. Norris Copper, Pvt. James Dovin, Pvt. John
Dickey, Pvt. Hezekiah Dunn, Pvt. William Drummond, Pvt. Darius
Dunn, Pvt. James Dunn, Pvt. Robert Dunn, Pvt. William Dunn, Pvt.
James Darrington, Pvt. James Evans, Pvt. John Elliott, Pvt.
Richard Fillingham, Pvt. Benajah Fillingham, Pvt. James Frisby,
Jr., Pvt. Benjamin Forster, Pvt. John Fitzgerald, 4th Sgt.
William Grant, Pvt. Samuel Grant, Pvt. Jonathan Grant, 2nd Cpl.
William Glanville, Pvt. Thomas Griffith, Pvt. William Griffith,
Pvt. Edward Gibbs, 3rd Cpl. Vincent Hatchison, Pvt. Samuel
Hutson, Pvt. John Carvill Hynson, Pvt. Charles Hynson, Jr., Pvt.
Morgan Hurt, Pvt. John Hartley, Pvt. Samuel Hammond, Pvt.
Benjamin Hatcheson, Pvt. Nathan Hatcheson, Pvt. John Hatcheson,
Pvt. Philip Holmes, Pvt. William Hall, Pvt. John Housroof, Pvt.
Richard Kirkwood, Pvt. Richard Kirkwood, Jr., Pvt. Richard
Munjar, Pvt. Samuel Munjar, Pvt. John Martin, Pvt. Thomas
Mansfield, Pvt. James Mansfield, Pvt. James Massey, Pvt. Kelly
McCarty, Pvt. Charles Morgan, Pvt. John McGregory, Pvt. William
Merchant, Pvt. Elisha Nabb, 1st Cpl. Henry Prosser, Pvt. John
Pearce, Pvt. Thomas Quick, 1st Sgt. John Ricketts, Pvt. James

182   INHABITANTS OF KENT COUNTY, MARYLAND, 1637-1787

Ross, Pvt. Joseph Reed, Pvt. Thomas Reardon, Pvt. Joseph Rumney, Pvt. William Robertson, Pvt. James Saunders, Pvt. William Shaw, Pvt. Ephraim Stoker, Pvt. Richard Spencer, Pvt. John Tiller, Pvt. John Taylor, Pvt. James Thrap, Pvt. George Tucker, 1st Lt. Simon Wickes, Pvt. Samuel Wickes, Pvt. Joseph Wickes, Jr., Pvt. Robert Wharton, Pvt. Thomas Wharton, Pvt. James Wilson, Pvt. William Wilson, Pvt. Elisha Winters, Pvt. Thomas Whaland, Pvt. Edward Whaland, Pvt. William Watson, Pvt. John Young.

13TH BATTALION, FIFTH COMPANY UNDER CAPT. MARMADUKE TILDEN, 1778
4th Cpl. Aquilla Attix, Jr., Pvt. Aquilla Attix, Pvt. Alexander Apsley, Pvt. Edward Apsley, Pvt. Moses Alford, 1st Sgt. Alexander Beck, 2nd Sgt. Joshua Beck, 1st Cpl. Daniel Beck, Pvt. John Beck, Pvt. Edward Beck, Jr., Pvt. James Beck, Pvt. Samuel Beck, Pvt. James Benton, Pvt. William Brassett, Pvt. Nathan Beswick, Pvt. Moses Berry, Pvt. John Blanchford, 3rd Cpl. Jonathan Comegys, Pvt. Nehemiah Crouch, Pvt. James Chalmers, Pvt. Stephen Causey, Pvt. John Cowarden, Pvt. Daniel Davis, Pvt. John Dever, Pvt. Arthur Dillen, Pvt. Hales Everitt, Pvt. William Forster, Pvt. Jacob Foreman, Pvt. John Griffith, Pvt. John Gidley, Pvt. John Hil, Pvt. William Hening, Pvt. William Hurst, Pvt. Thomas Horny, Pvt. William Hamer, Pvt. Philip Jones, Pvt. Thomas Jones, Pvt. John Jones, Pvt. John Kennard, Jr., Pvt. Stephen Kennard, Pvt. William Kennard, Jr., Pvt. Daniel Kennard, Pvt. Dennis Kennard, Pvt. John Kennard, Pvt. William Kenny, Pvt. Robert Kendal, Pvt. Christ. Knight, Pvt. John Merry, Pvt. St. Leger Meeks, Pvt. Robert Meeks, Pvt. William Meeks, Pvt. John Nusom, 2nd Lt. Andrew Pearce, 2nd Cpl. John Patton, Pvt. James Pullet, Pvt. Bartus Punney, Pvt. Richard Peacock, Pvt. Edward Pearce, Pvt. William Pearce, 1st Lt. Samuel Reed, 3rd Sgt. John Reed, Pvt. John Roberts, Pvt. Isaac Redgrave, Pvt. William Riley, Pvt. ---- [blank] Randal, Pvt. John Randal, Pvt. Daniel Spencer, Pvt. Hugh Spencer, Pvt. Richard Spencer, Pvt. Pere. Spencer, Pvt. Jonathan Spencer, Pvt. George Shakes, Pvt. James Stein, Ensign Charles Tilden, Pvt. James Thompson, Pvt. John Timms, Pvt. Samuel Tishe, Pvt. Thomas Trew, 4th Sgt. John Whaland, Pvt. Samuel Whitehouse, Pvt. George Watts, Pvt. Joshua Willis, Pvt. James Wroth, Pvt. James Wroth, Jr., Pvt. Kinvin Wroth, Jr., Pvt. Kinvin Wroth.

13TH BATTALION, SIXTH COMPANY UNDER CAPT. RICHARD GRESHAM, 1778
2nd Lt. Samuel Bullock, Pvt. Henry Blackiston, Pvt. John Blackiston, Pvt. Thomas Broadaway, Pvt. Henry Brooks, Pvt. Samuel Bennett, Pvt. Matthew Brooking, 1st Lt. David Crane, Pvt. Thomas Corse, Pvt. James Cannon, Pvt. Thomas Ceetly [Costly?], Pvt. Isaac Cammell, Pvt. John Corse, Pvt. Richard Carpenter, Pvt. Lambert Cavender, Pvt. William Daugherty, Pvt. John Daily, Pvt. James Dunkin, Pvt. William Dugan [Drugan?], Pvt. Edward Engram, Pvt. George Ferguson, Pvt. Jacob Falconer, Pvt. Michael Flaharty, 3rd Cpl. James Greenwood, Pvt. William Greenwood, Pvt. James Groom, Pvt. Alexander Glens, Pvt. Charles Groome, 4th Sgt. Abraham Haynes, Pvt. John Hudson, Pvt. John Hix, Pvt. Dennis Hurley, Pvt. Richard Hynson, Pvt. Benjamin Iston, 4th Cpl. Abednego Jackson, Pvt. Thomas Jones, Pvt. Benjamin Jones, Pvt. Daniel King, 1st Sgt. Edmond Lynch, Pvt. John Lynch, Pvt.

MILITIA 183

Nicholas Lynch, 2nd Cpl. James Lawrence, Pvt. Pearce Lamb, Pvt. Pearce Lamb, Jr., Pvt. Charles Milward, Pvt. Isaac Macany, Pvt. William Mears, Pvt. John Matthews, Pvt. Aquila Meeks, Pvt. Joseph Numbers, Pvt. John Numbers, Ensign John Rollingson, Pvt. John Russell, Pvt. Richard Redding, Pvt. George Reed, Pvt. John Strahan, Pvt. William Smith, Pvt. Noble Simmonds, Pvt. Edward Stewart, Pvt. John Sullivan, Pvt. Joseph Sill, Pvt. Andrew Scott, 2nd Sgt. Daniel Turner, Pvt. John Turner, 1st Cpl. Robert Taylor, Pvt. William Taylor, Pvt. Abraham Taylor, Jr., Pvt. William Tennant, Pvt. Thomas Trew, Pvt. Jacob Trulock, Pvt. Frogget Tillard, Pvt. John Ustleton, Pvt. Abner Vickers, 3rd Sgt. John Williams, Pvt. James Ware, Pvt. John Willis, Pvt. John Watson, Pvt. James Woodal.

13TH BATTALION, SEVENTH COMPANY UNDER CAPT. JOHN PAGE, 1778
Pvt. William Ayers, Pvt. Michael Atkinson, Pvt. David Ashley, Pvt. Alexander Beck, Pvt. Alexander Beck, Jr., Pvt. Edward Bird, Pvt. Benjamin Benton, Pvt. Francis Benton, Pvt. Nathan Brooks, Pvt. John Berry, Pvt. James Bradshaw, Pvt. Stephen Blackiston, Pvt. William Brice, Pvt. William Browny [Browning?], Pvt. Robert Butler, Pvt. Joseph Copper, Pvt. William Crabbin, Pvt. Charles Coleman, Pvt. Thomas Collins, Pvt. Samuel Crouch, Pvt. William Davis, Pvt. Benjamin Dedman, Pvt. William Elburn, Jr., Pvt. John Enloes, Pvt. George Frazier, Pvt. William Frazier, Pvt. John Frazier, Pvt. William J. Fry, Pvt. George Gibbs, Pvt. John Gordon, Pvt. William Hynson, Pvt. Nathaniel Hynson, Pvt. John Hinds, Pvt. William Hurst, Pvt. John Holden, Pvt. Sabret Huxter, Pvt. James Hague, Pvt. James Hodges, Pvt. John Hurt, Pvt. John Jones, Pvt. John Jones (Hill Point), Pvt. Richard Jones, Pvt. Benjamin Joiner, Pvt. Richard Knight, Pvt. Michael Miller, Pvt. James Miller, Pvt. Thomas Miller, Pvt. Thomas Miller (son of Thomas), Pvt. Richard Miller, Pvt. Samuel Miller, Pvt. Nathan Miller, Pvt. George Merchant, Pvt. Peregrine McFall, Pvt. Andrew Martin, Pvt. William Parker, Pvt. Isaac Redue, Pvt. John Rogers, Pvt. Nathaniel Rogers, Pvt. William Ringgold, Pvt. James Scone, Pvt. Nathan Shaw, Pvt. Thomas Smith, Pvt. William Smith, Pvt. Robert Summers, Pvt. John Stinson, Pvt. William Stivens [Stevens?], Pvt. Samuel Taylor, Pvt. James Williamson, Pvt. Joseph Wickers [Vickers?], Pvt. John Yearley.

13TH BATTALION, EIGHTH COMPANY UNDER CAPT. WILLIAM FRISBY, 1778
Pvt. William Ashley, Pvt. James Ashley, Pvt. Edward Ashley, Pvt. Edward Ashley, Jr., Pvt. John Ashley, Sr., Pvt. John Ashley, Jr., Pvt. Abram Ashley, Pvt. Anthony Bannon, Pvt. Thomas Bowers, Pvt. Thomas Bowers, Jr., Pvt. Joseph Briscoe, Pvt. George Burk, Pvt. Solomon Bennett, Pvt. David Brown, Pvt. Edward Carroll, Pvt. James Clark, Pvt. Thomas Carter, Pvt. John Culbert, Pvt. Benjamin Conaway, Pvt. James Copper, Pvt. John Claton, Pvt. John Dinson, Pvt. John Davis, Pvt. William Dial, Pvt. William Dawson, Pvt. Thomas Dunk, Pvt. Thomas Dew, Pvt. Thomas Edwards, Pvt. Joseph Frisby, Pvt. Richard Frisby, Pvt. Patrick Flinn, 4th Cpl. Thomas Gamble, Pvt. Darius Gamble, Pvt. John Griffith, Pvt. Robert Greenfield, 2nd Cpl. Joel Higinbottom, Pvt. Oliver Higinbottom, Pct. George Higinbottom, Pvt. Benjamin Higinbottom, Pvt. John Hiag, Pvt. Joseph Harris, Pvt. Gustav Hanson, 3rd Cpl. John

Jones, Pvt. John Jones, Pvt. Darius Jones, Pvt. Thomas James, Pvt. Richard Kennard, Pvt. William Kennard, 1st Lt. James Lloyd, Pvt. James Lynch, Pvt. Richard Lowman, Pvt. Thomas Mansfield, Pvt. Absolum McCoy, Pvt. James Niel, Pvt. James Plimton, 1st Sgt. James Rolinson, 2nd Sgt. Simon Smith, 1st Cpl. Richard Smith, Pvt. John Smith, Jr., Pvt. Stephen Smith, Pvt. James Smith, Pvt. Sutton Smith, Pvt. George Smith, Pvt. Hynson Smyth, Pvt. John Swift, Pvt. William Skirvin, 3rd Sgt. Philip Taylor, Pvt. John Tharp, Pvt. Hyth. Taylor, Pvt. Charles Tilden, Pvt. Sterling Thomas, Pvt. Mich. Underhill, 2nd Lt. William Wilmer, Pvt. Blackiston Wilmer, 4th Sgt. Joel Willis, Pvt. Richard Willis, Pvt. Owen Whaland, Pvt. William Yeates.

13TH BATTALION, NINTH COMPANY UNDER CAPT. PEREGRINE LETHERBURY, 1778

Pvt. Walter Anderson, Pvt. Thomas Anderson, Pvt. James Anderson, Jr., Pvt. Charles Baker, Jr., Pvt. William Bowers, Pvt. Barrett Boddy, Pvt. Philip Brooks, Pvt. John Blakeway, Pvt. David Boyd, Pvt. Jeremiah Bannon, Pvt. Samuel Chaplin, Pvt. William Collins, Pvt. Joshua Clarke, Pvt. James Corse, Pvt. Blackiston Chandler, Pvt. Alexander Danskin, Pvt. William Dunkan, Pvt. John Elbert, Pvt. Ezekiel Foreman, Pvt. Daniel Fisher, Pvt. William Forbes, Pvt. C. Joshua Guthery, Pvt. John Green, Pvt. John Hartley, Pvt. John Harragan, Pvt. James Hendley, Pvt. Cuthbert Hall, Pvt. Jacobus Hinds, Pvt. Edward Hopkins, Pvt. Charles Hackett, Pvt. Owen Kennard, Pvt. John Kenedy, Pvt. William Kenedy, Pvt. Thomas Kemp, Pvt. James Kelly, Pvt. Joseph Lusby, Pvt. Donald McQuinn, Pvt. David Matzler, Pvt. John McKim, Pvt. William McKim, Pvt. Dennis McNamara, Pvt. Hugh McKinly, Pvt. Timothy Marah, Pvt. Richard Morris, Pvt. John Offley, Ensign James Piper, Pvt. William Pattin, Pvt. John Palmer, Pvt. William Perkins, Pvt. Samuel Perkins, Pvt. William Rowell, Pvt. William Ramsey, Pvt. John Ringgold, Pvt. William Russell, Pvt. Dean Reed, Pvt. Samuel Roberts, Pvt. Robert Reed, Pvt. Robert Roberts, Pvt. William Robertson, Pvt. James Simpson, Pvt. Jacob Shaffer, Pvt. Richard Thomas, Jr., Pvt. Richard Thomas, Sr., Pvt. Lazarius Tittle, Pvt. John Tittle, Pvt. Thomas Thornton, Pvt. Philemon Tilghman, Pvt. William Vickers, Pvt. James Vickers, 1st Lt. John Watkins, Pvt. John Watkins, Pvt. Thomas Whaland, Pvt. William Wallis, Pvt. John Wright, Pvt. William Woolaston, Pvt. William Yardsley.

KENT COUNTY MILITIA, 27TH BATTALION UNDER BY COL. DONALDSON YEATES, 1778 (Ref: The Patriotic Marylander, Vol. III, No. 2, December, 1916). [Note: Several sources have copied these lists and indicated that they served in 1775. According to the distinguished historian and genealogist Francis B. Culver these listed were recorded in 1778. The 27th Battalion was formed in the upper part of the county.]

27TH BATTALION, FIRST COMPANY UNDER CAPT. WILLIAM MAXWELL, 1778
Pvt. Joseph Briscoe, Pvt. John Briscoe, Pvt. John Burgen, Pvt. Henry Breese, Pvt. John Bolton, Pvt. Alphonso Comegys, Pvt. William Comegys, Pvt. John Cahoon, Pvt. Blackston Chandler, Pvt. James Chappell, Cpl. William Dixson, Pvt. John Dixson, Pvt.

MILITIA

Joseph Duyer, Pvt. Samuel Dulee, Pvt. Moses Foard, Pvt. William Folkes, Sgt. John Greenwood, Pvt. John Greenwood, Pvt. William Gay, Pvt. John Howard, Sr., Pvt. Isaac Hynes, Pvt. John Hartt, Pvt. Richard Hartt, Pvt. Walter Harris, Pvt. James Howard, Pvt. John Joyant [Giant?], Pvt. Stephen Joyant [Giant?], Pvt. Benjamin Johnston, Pvt. Michael Jobson, Pvt. Samuel Jones, Pvt. James Jones, Pvt. Francis Knock, Jr., Pvt. William Knock, Jr., Pvt. Andrew Kelley, Pvt. George Lamb, Ensign William Merritt, Pvt. Edward Murphy, Pvt. John Mires, Pvt. James Myres, Pvt. William Maxwell, Cpl. James Norris, Cpl. David Newell, Pvt. George Newcomb, Pvt. Samuel Norris, Pvt. Aquila Page, Pvt. John Parsons, Pvt. James Pennington, Pvt. Moses Price, Pvt. William Quillen, 1st Lt. John Reason, Pvt. George Reason, Pvt. Thomas Rasin, Pvt. Robert Redgrave, Pvt. William Redgrave, Jr., Pvt. Amos Reed, Pvt. John Read, 2nd Lt. Thomas Sewell, Cpl. James Staple, Pvt. James Sullivan, Pvt. Joseph Stavely, Pvt. Richard Scaggs, Pvt. Asa Stewart, Pvt. William Stewart, Pvt. John Stewart, Pvt. Isaac Shawhorn, Pvt. Thomas Shawhorn, Jr., Pvt. Thomas Shawhorn, Sr., Pvt. Richard Sewell, Sgt. Nathaniel Toulson, Pvt. Pere. Thrift, Pvt. James Taylor, Pvt. William Turner, Pvt. James Uslington, Sgt. John Woodall, Pvt. James Woodall.

27TH BATTALION, SECOND COMPANY UNDER CAPT. JESSE COSDEN, 1778
Sgt. Thomas Armstrong, Pvt. Benjamin Arno, Pvt. Jeremiah Arno, Cpl. Joshua Browning, Pvt. John Burgus, Pvt. William Boots, Pvt. Alfonso Boots, Pvt. Thomas Boyer, Pvt. James Broxton, Pvt. John Broxton, 1st Lt. Samuel Comegys, Cpl. George Cornelius, Pvt. Ebenezer Castleton, Pvt. John Comegys, Pvt. Elisha Dayley, Pvt. David Ferguson, Pvt. William Graham, Pvt. William Graham, Sr., 2nd Lt. Cuthbert Hall, Ensign John Haley, Sgt. George Hall, Pvt. Simon Hackett, Pvt. Hynson Hall, Pvt. William Hales, Pvt. Vincent Hatchinson, Pvt. William Hunter, Sgt. Edward William Johnston, Cpl. John Kerton, Pvt. William Lawrence, Sgt. Haley Moffett, Pvt. Jacob Moffett, Pvt. Moses Moffett, Pvt. Robert Moffett, Pvt. George Moffett, Pvt. Jesse Moffett, Pvt. Richard Moffett, Pvt. Josiah Massey, Pvt. Isaac McCay, Pvt. John Palmer, Pvt. Bartley Palmer, Pvt. Richard Peacock, Pvt. Francis Rutter, Pvt. Isaac Redgrave, Pvt. James Redgrave, Pvt. Joseph Reynolds, Pvt. John Rolinson, Pvt. George Smith, Pvt. John Smith, Pvt. Lambert Smith, Pvt. Matthew Smith, Pvt. William Smith, Sr., Pvt. Nicholas Smith, Pvt. James Smith, Pvt. William Smith (son of John), Pvt. James States, Pvt. David Stoops, Pvt. Nicholas Stoops, Pvt. Francis Spry, Pvt. Francis Sherrard, Pvt. Isaac Spencer, Pvt. Jonas Tiller, Pvt. George Tiller, Pvt. John Turner, Pvt. Lambert Vansant, Pvt. George Vansant, Cpl. John Woodall, Pvt. John Woodall, Pvt. Thomas Woodall, Pvt. Edward Woodall, Pvt. William Woodall, Pvt. James Woodall, Pvt. Joseph Williams, Pvt. John Weaver, Pvt. Christopher Williams.

27TH BATTALION, THIRD COMPANY UNDER CAPT. JEREMIAH FORD, 1778
Pvt. John Anger [Auger?], Pvt. John Anger [Auger?], Sr., Sgt. Jacob Briscoe, Cpl. Alexander Briscoe, Pvt. William Briscoe, Pvt. Moses Briscoe, Pvt. James Berrywalls, Pvt. Robert Buckhannon, Pvt. James Butler, Pvt. Michael Corse, Pvt. Michael Corse, Jr., Pvt. James Corse, Pvt. Ceazer Corse, Pvt. Francis Cann, Pvt.

James Cann, Pvt. Thomas Chandler, Pvt. John Crew, Pvt. Edward Crew, Pvt. Richard Colsy, Pvt. Isac Copper, Pvt. William Collins, Pvt. David Cunningham, Pvt. Phillip Drugan, Pvt. Thomas Drugan, Pvt. William Dugan [Drugan?], Pvt. Robert Daugherty, Pvt. David Davis, Pvt. St. Leger Everitt, Pvt. James Elborne, Pvt. John Eunock, Pvt. John Effield, Jr., Pvt. Charles Ford, Sgt. Daniel Groom, Cpl. Daniel Greenwood, Pvt. George Greenwood, Pvt. John Gale, Pvt. William Gale, Pvt. Rasin Gale, Pvt. Benjamin Gilbert, Pvt. Cornelius Howard, Pvt. John Howard, Jr., Pvt. Benjamin Howard, Pvt. Thomas Howard, Pvt. Linard Howard, Pvt. Joseph Howard, Pvt. Joseph Hart, Pvt. Nathaniel Howell, Pvt. William Howell, Pvt. John Hickman, Pvt. James Hartt, Pvt. Robert Hartt, Pvt. Thomas Hebborn, Cpl. Griffith Jones, Cpl. James Jones, Pvt. Charles Jones, Pvt. Thomas Jones, Pvt. Jacob Jackson, Pvt. James Kelley, Sgt. Thomas Lamb, Pvt. Francis Lamb, Jr., Pvt. James Lamb, Pvt. Francis Lamb, Sr., Pvt. John Lamb, Pvt. John Lasaells, Lt. Marmaduke Medford, Pvt. McCall Medford, Pvt. George Moore, Pvt. Joseph Middleton, Pvt. James Miller, Sgt. John Newell, Pvt. John Pavin, Pvt. Anthony Pushpin, Sgt. Lambert Phillips, Pvt. William Redgrave, Sr., Pvt. William Reding, Pvt. Robert Rasin, Pvt. James Strong, Lt. James Smith, Pvt. John Sullivan, Pvt. John Tatom, Pvt. Richard Trusty, Pvt. Ebenezer Turner, Pvt. Robert Usilton, Pvt. William Usselton, Pvt. Francis Usselton, Pvt. John Wetherhead.

27TH BATTALION, FOURTH COMPANY UNDER CAPT. WILLIAM KNOCK, 1778
Sgt. Azariah Bostick, Pvt. James Bostick, Pvt. John Blackston, Pvt. James Bryan, Pvt. James Black, Pvt. Joseph Burch, Pvt. Benjamin Cleaves, Pvt. Nathan Cleaves, Pvt. John Colgan, Pvt. Elias Deal, Pvt. John Deal, Pvt. John Dixon, Sgt. Thomas Fowler, Pvt. Patrick Fowler, Pvt. Zorababel French, Jr., Pvt. Christopher Field, Pvt. Thomas Galalee, Sgt. William Harper, Pvt. James Hynson, Pvt. William Hogans, Pvt. John Jobson, Pvt. Benjamin Kithison, Lt. William Little, Cpl. Robert Little, Lt. Daniel Toes Massey, Ensign Stephen Massey, Sgt. Joseph Massey, Pvt. Ebenezer Massey, Pvt. Robert Marby, Pvt. Isaac Middlebrook, Pvt. Jeremiah McDonald, Pvt. Andrew McMullin, Pvt. Joel Newman, Pvt. Rubin Neal, Pvt. John W. Pennington, Pvt. William Pitt, Pvt. Robert Reynolds, Pvt. John Reynolds, Cpl. John Spearman, Pvt. Lambert Simmons, Pvt. William Simmons, Jr., Pvt. Archibald Simmons, Pvt. John Skaggs, Pvt. Isaac Stanley, Pvt. John Stanley, Pvt. Ebenezer Stanley, Pvt. John Smith, Pvt. James Speer, Sgt. Joseph Turner, Cpl. William Turner, Pvt. William Turner, Pvt. John Taylor, Pvt. James Waters, Pvt. William Ward, Pvt. John Webb, Pvt. David Wells, Pvt. John Zelefro.

27TH BATTALION, FIFTH COMPANY UNDER CAPT. GILBERT FALCONER, 1778
Pvt. John Arno, Pvt. Eben Blackiston, Pvt. John Blackiston, Pvt. John Bradshaw, Pvt. James Boyer, Pvt. James Bruer, Pvt. Joseph Burchanell, Pvt. Samuel Beck, Pvt. Pearce Bowers, Pvt. George Barcus, Pvt. Abraham Comegys, Pvt. Peter Covington, Pvt. William Dawson, Pvt. Dennis Earle, Pvt. George Fountain, Pvt. Terey Glandby, Pvt. Archibald Hannah, Pvt. James Hynson, Pvt. James Harrison, Pvt. Stephen Howard, Pvt. Jacob Humberson, Sgt.

MILITIA 187

Jonathan Jobson, Pvt. Jonathan Jester, Pvt. William Jones, Pvt.
William King, Pvt. Nathaniel Knock, Pvt. George Lyons, Lt.
William Mires, Ensign Stephen Mires, Pvt. William Mires (son of
Stephen), Pvt. Luke Mires, Pvt. Stephen Mires, Pvt. John Mires,
Sgt. Abednego Massey, Pvt. William Molt, Sgt. Andrew Parkes, Sgt.
Joseph Parsons, Pvt. Spier Piper, Pvt. Stephen Phillips, Pvt.
Richard Pratt, Pvt. Thomas Rawlins, Pvt. Joseph Rawlins, Pvt.
James Readis, Pvt. John Roulins, Pvt. Charles Rialy, Pvt. George
Sanders, Pvt. Daniel Shawhorn, Pvt. Benjamin Sill, Pvt. Lewis
Turey, Pvt. John Thomas, Pvt. John Thomas (Dr.), Cpl. Garrett
Vansant, Lt. John Whittington, Cpl. John Walls, Pvt. Joseph
Wilkinson, Pvt. John White, Pvt. Isaac Weaver, Pvt. Robert Webb,
Pvt. Abraham Whittington, Pvt. William Walls, Pvt. David Welldin.

27TH BATTALION, SIXTH COMPANY UNDER CAPT. JOHN DAY, 1778
Pvt. William Armstrong, Pvt. George Browning, Pvt. Spencer
Biddle, Pvt. Nathaniel Browne, Pvt. Smith Bagwell, Pvt. John
Bevans, Pvt. Benjamin Cole, Pvt. William Clark, Pvt. Cornelius
Comegys, Pvt. Edward Comegys, Pvt. Daniel Cornelius, Cpl. William
Dolles, Pvt. John Dolles, Pvt. Jonathan Devanport, Pvt. Joseph
Devanport, Pvt. Benjamin Everitt, Lt. Isaac Freeman, Sgt. Edward
Freeman, Pvt. William Forrester, Pvt. William Grant, Pvt. James
Grudy, Pvt. John Hurt, Pvt. John Harris, Jr., Pvt. James Henry,
Pvt. William Hirrin, Pvt. Charles Irons, Pvt. Henry Knock, Pvt.
Nathaniel Knock, Pvt. Francis Leonard, Pvt. Robert Latham, Pvt.
Joseph Lary, Pvt. James Lawrence, Cpl. Robert Maxwell, Pvt.
Robert Maxwell, Sr., Pvt. George Mason, Pvt. John Mitchell, Pvt.
James Pearce, Pvt. Joseph Pennington, Pvt. James Pennington, Pvt.
Benjamin Riley, Pvt. Joseph Redgrave, Pvt. Abraham Redgrave, Pvt.
William Richardson, Pvt. William Rogers, Pvt. Joshua Rasin, Pvt.
William Rasin, Pvt. William Smith, Pvt. Lambert Smith, Pvt.
Alexander Stewart, Pvt. Barnett Thompson, Pvt. Thomas Taylor,
Pvt. William Taylor, Pvt. Isaac Toney, Pvt. James Tenant, Pvt.
Jacob Vansant, Pvt. George Vansant, Pvt. Christopher Vansant, Lt.
James Woodland, Pvt. Abraham Woodland, Ensign William Wilson,
Sgt. James Wilson (son of James), Pvt. James Wilson, Pvt. George
Wilson, Pvt. George Wilson, Pvt. John Wilson (son of George),
Pvt. William Wise, Pvt. William Williams, Pvt. Archibald Wright,
Pvt. John Wright.

27TH BATTALION, SEVENTH COMPANY UNDER CAPT. NATHANIEL COMEGYS,
1778
Pvt. Lovering Alley, Pvt. Frederick Armington, Pvt. Malichi
Ambrose, Pvt. James Baley, Pvt. George Bell, Pvt. James Butcher,
Pvt. William Burgin, Pvt. Christopher Bellican, Pvt. Edward Beck,
Pvt. Benjamin Busby, Pvt. George Black, Pvt. Prince Buckskin,
Sgt. John Cray, Sgt. John Cosden, Pvt. Isaac Cork (Caulk), Pvt.
Thomas Corse, Pvt. George Cole, Cpl. George Dennan, Cpl. Jonas
Denning, Pvt. Stephen Denning, Pvt. Nicholas Denning, Cpl. Isaac
Dawson, Pvt. Mordecai Dillehunte, Pvt. Jams Durity, Pvt. James
Farrow, Pvt. John Gibbs, Pvt. Richard Green, Pvt. Cuff Gibbs,
Pvt. William Herrin, Pvt. Nathaniel Herrin, Pvt. William Herrin,
Pvt. James Hynson, Pvt. William Hull, Pvt. Nathaniel Hartt, Pvt.
James Hatchinson, Pvt. Richard Hurtt, Pvt. Richard Hurtt, Pvt.
John Hanvey, Pvt. William Ireland, Pvt. Simon Irons, Pvt. William

Jackson, Pvt. John Jones, Pvt. Andrew Kerr, Pvt. William Keyton, Pvt. William Kelly, Pvt. Samuel Lynch, Pvt. Simon Lovemoney, Cpl. Samuel Mansfield, Pvt. James Miney, Pvt. James Martin, Pvt. John Murphey, Pvt. Robert Mansfield, Pvt. Robert Maxwell, Jr., Pvt. William Mann, Pvt. John May, Pvt. Michael Parsons, Pvt. Nathaniel Piner, Sgt. William Parker (Dr.), Pvt. Henry Pennington, Sgt. Charles Robson, Pvt. William Riley, Pvt. Jacob Riley, Pvt. Nicholas Riley, Pvt. Peregrine Reed, Pvt. Hartley Sappington, Pvt. James Sappington, Pvt. James Steel, Pvt. Thomas Smith, Pvt. John Smith, Pvt. James Smith, Pvt. Edward Sutton, Pvt. Edward Stewart, Pvt. Edward Tiller (Tyler), Pvt. Abraham Taylor, Pvt. John Vansant, Lt. James Willmer, Lt. Francis Wallis, Ensign John Woodland, Pvt. Henry Wyatt, Pvt. Samuel Wyatt, Pvt. William Wyatt, Pvt. John Wallace, Sr., Pvt. Henry Wallis, Pvt. Hugh Wallis, Pvt. John Wallis (Dr.), Pvt. John Wallis, Jr., Pvt. Samuel Wallis, Pvt. James Willson, Pvt. William Worth [Wroth?], Pvt. George Williamson.

27TH BATTALION, EIGHTH COMPANY UNDER CAPT. JOHN LAMBERT WILMER, 1778
Pvt. William Boyer (son of John), Pvt. William Boyer, Pvt. James Boyer, Pvt. William Boyer, Sr., Pvt. Thomas Boyer, Pvt. Jonas Blackskin [Blackston?], Pvt. Richard Bautham, Pvt. Henry Bautham, Jr., Pvt. John Brown, Pvt. Charles Brown, Pvt. James Bentley, Pvt. Nathaniel Clark, Pvt. Gideon Clarke, Pvt. Peter Carr, Pvt. Absolom Christfield, Pvt. Joseph Carroll, Pvt. Joseph Deford, Pvt. Charles Deford, Pvt. William Ellith, Pvt. Thomas Elliss, Pvt. William Elliss, Pvt. Thomas Emsson, Pvt. William French, Pvt. Samuel Freeman, Pvt. Thomas Ferrell, Pvt. Nathaniel Glann [Glenn?], Pvt. James Greenwood, Pvt. William Gundage [Grindage?], Pvt. William Gibson, Pvt. Jesse Heath, Pvt. Cornelius Hartt, Pvt. William Hanson, Pvt. Robert Hacheson [Hatcheson], Pvt. Enoch Johns, 2nd Lt. Robert Moodey, Ensign George Medford, Cpl. Elisha Massey, Pvt. Elijah Massey, Pvt. William Mansfield, Pvt. Robert Money, Pvt. Elijah McKey, Pvt. Samuel McDowell, Pvt. William McDowell, Pvt. William McDowell, Pvt. James McDowell, Pvt. Isaac Newland, Pvt. John Newland, Pvt. Thomas Price, Pvt. Benjamin Price, Pvt. Richard Pennington, Sgt. Samson Redgrave, Pvt. Richard Redgrave, Pvt. James Russell, Sgt. Thomas Sanders, Pvt. Abraham Sanders, Pvt. Thomas Stevens, Pvt. Lambert Scott, Pvt. Richard Simons, Pvt. David Simons, Pvt. William Vansant, Pvt. James Vansant, 1st Lt. John Wilson, Sgt. Samuel Wilson, Pvt. Hiram Wilson, Pvt. John Wilson, Pvt. John Wilson, Jr., Cpl. John Williams, Pvt. Eli Williams, Pvt. Benjamin Webb, Pvt. Eli White, Pvt. John White, Pvt. Peter Watson, Pvt. Charles Watts, Pvt. John Williamson, Pvt. John Zelefroth [Zelefrow?].

KENT COUNTY REVOLUTIONARY WAR PATRIOTS GLEANED FROM THE *ARCHIVES OF MARYLAND*, VOL. XI, JOURNAL OF MARYLAND COUNCIL OF SAFETY, 1775-1776
Thomas Ringgold, Joseph Earle, and William Ringgold (Eastern Neck) were appointed "Collectors of all the gold and silver coin that can be procured in Kent County to comply with the Resolve of the Congress...taking for granted that Continental Money will be

ordered us in exchange." (January 27, 1776).

Capt. William Henry's Company of Kent County, Maryland Militia were stationed at Northampton County, Virginia on February 29, 1776 (see complete list herein which has been gleaned from Volumes XI and XVIII). Capt. Henry reported that the following men were sent home on March 1, 1776: John Wilmer, George Little, Sr., Salathiel Freeland, John Burnsides, Francis Lennon, William Miers, Nathaniel Knock, Charles Irons, George Little, Jr., and John Hurt.

Commissions were issued to 1st Lt. Samuel Griffith, 2nd Lt. Richard Finley, and Ensign James Robinson of Capt. William Frisby's Company of Militia in Kent County (March 15, 1776).

Treasurer of the Western Shore was ordered to pay Thomas Ringgold for the use of Elisha Winters, of Chester Town in Kent County, to enable said Winters to comply with his contract for manufacturing firearms (June 10, 1776).

Commission was issued to 3rd Lt. Richard Gresham of Capt. Thomas Smyth's Company of Militia of Light Infantry in Kent County, belonging to the 13th Battalion (June 26, 1776).

The Committee of Safety requested that the Committee of Observation for Kent County deliver to Joseph Middleton all of the public powder now lodged in Mr. Sluby's warehouse at Chester Town (June 27, 1776).

KENT COUNTY REVOLUTIONARY WAR PATRIOTS GLEANED FROM THE *ARCHIVES OF MARYLAND*, VOLUME XVI, JOURNAL OF THE COUNCIL OF MARYLAND, 1777-1778
Commissions were issued to Col. William Bordley, Lt. Col. William Ringgold, Jr., 1st Major Richard Graves, 2nd Major John Page, and Quartermaster Jeremiah Nichols, of the 13th Battalion of Kent County Militia, and to Col. Isaac Spencer, Lt. Col. William Henry, 1st Major Jonathan Worth, and 2nd Major William Maxwell, Jr., of the 27th Battalion of Kent County Militia (May 8, 1777).

Justices of the Orphans Court for Kent County were Thomas Smyth, Robert Cruckshank [Cruikshank], John Eccleston, William Ringgold, Jr., and Richard Frisby (June 4, 1777).

Treasurer of the Western Shore was ordered to pay William Bordley, Lt. of Kent County, money for the use of Robert Blake, David Boyd, John Sturgis, and Thomas Vandycke (November 22, 1777).

Ezekiel Forman was appointed Collector of Clothing for Kent County and to procure clothing for the American Army (November 27, 1777).

Treasurer of the Western Shore was ordered to pay Donaldson Yates

[Yeates] money to purchase beef and pork for the State, to John Bolton for purchasing beef and pork, and to William Merrit, Sheriff of Kent County, money to be delivered to the recruiting officer in Kent County (January 29, 1778).

William Houston was appointed the Agent for Purchasing Provisions in Kent County for the Army of the United States (March 25, 1778).

KENT COUNTY REVOLUTIONARY WAR PATRIOTS GLEANED FROM THE *ARCHIVES OF MARYLAND*, VOLUME XXI, JOURNAL OF THE COUNCIL OF MARYLAND, 1778-1779
Col. William Bordley, Esq., was Lt. of Kent County in 1778.

Commissions were issued to Lt. Col. Isaac Perkins, Major William Frisby, Capt. George Hanson, Capt. Simon Wickes, 1st Lt. Thomas Crew, 2nd Lt. Samuel Beck, Capt. Philip Davis, 1st Lt. William Warrell, 2nd Lt. Samuel Sinnett, Ensign William Sturges, Capt. James Williamson, 1st Lt. Morgan Hunt [Hurt?], in the 13th Battalion of Kent County Militia (June 4, 1778).

Judges of the Court of Appeal for Kent County were Joseph Nicholson, James McClean, Samuel Davis, Ezekiel Forman, and Richard Lloyd (June 4, 1778).

Thomas Masslin was discharged from military service, having been drafted for nine months and having procured a substitute to serve in the continental service for three years (June 11, 1778).

Petition of Silas Snow and confession of George Mann, lately an inhabitant of Kent County in this State, that said Mann was in company with a party of men who took the said Snow in the government of the three lower counties of Delaware and carried him to the enemy who afterwards imprisoned him in the New Jail in Philadelphia. The Sheriff was ordered to obtain George Mann and put him in prison for treason until the matter could be resolved (June 12, 1778).

Commissions were issued to Capt. David Crane, 1st Lt. Samuel Bullock, 2nd Lt. Henry Truelock, Ensign John Williams, of the 13th Battalion of Kent County Militia, and also to Capt. William Knock, 1st Lt. William Little, 2nd Lt. Daniel Tres [Toes] Massey, and Ensign Stephen Mires, of the 27th Battalion of Kent County Militia (September 12, 1778).

Justices of the Peace for Kent County were John Maxwell, John Scott, William Bordley, Robert Maxwell, James Claypoole, John Wilmer, William Henry, Marmaduke Tilden, Jonathan Worth, Morgan Hurt, Isaac Freeman, Joseph Rasin, and Samuel Davis (November 21, 1778).

Judges of the Orphans Court for Kent County were John Maxwell, John Scott, William Bordley, Robert Maxwell, and James Claypoole (November 21, 1778).

Commissions were issued to Capt. John Day, 1st Lt. Isaac Freeman, 2nd Lt. James Woodland, Ensign William Wilson, of the 27th Battalion of Kent County Militia, and Capt. George Hartshorn, 1st Lt. James Rollison, 2nd Lt. Simon Smyth, Ensign Joel Willis, and also 2nd Lt. Joseph Wicks and Ensign Stephen Glenvill of Capt. Simon Wicks' Company in the 13th Battalion of Kent County (March 11, 1779).

Jeremiah Baron and Andrew Miers, two of the militia from Kent County who were on guard of some British prisoners to Wilmington [Delaware], were themselves imprisoned there by a regular officer for a trifling inattention which he considered an insult. County Lieutenant William Bordley wrote to the Council of Maryland in behalf of Baron and Miers (August 16, 1779).

Commissions were issued to William Bordley, William Henry, and Marmaduke Tilden to receive subscriptions for Kent County (August 19, 1779).

Patrick Ewing, of Cecil County, was commissioned Assistant Deputy Commissary of Purchases for Cecil and Kent Counties (September 10, 1779).

Commissions were issued to Capt. Jesse Cosden, 1st Lt. Samuel Comegys, 2nd Lt. Cuthbert Hall, and Ensign John Haley, of the 27th Battalion of Kent County Militia, and to 2nd Lt. James Dunn (son of Ezekiah) of Capt. Williamson's Company, and to Ensign Robert Weeks [Wicks?] of Capt. Tilden's Company in the 13th Battalion of Kent County Militia (September 18, 1779).

KENT COUNTY REVOLUTIONARY WAR PATRIOTS GLEANED FROM THE *ARCHIVES OF MARYLAND*, VOL. XLIII, JOURNAL OF THE COUNCIL OF MARYLAND, 1779-1780
William Hall was elected and commissioned Sheriff of Kent County (November 5, 1779).

Justices of the Peace for Kent County were John Scott, William Bordley, Robert Maxwell, James Claypoole, William Henry, Jonathan Worth, Morgan Hunt, Samuel Davis, Thomas Smyth, Jr., William Granger, Jesse Cosden, Willam Maxwell, and Richard Miller (November 17, 1779).

Judges of the Orphans Court for Kent County were William Bordley, James Claypoole, William Henry, and Thomas Smyth, Jr. (November 17, 1779).

Abraham Falconer and John Moore were Recruiting Officers for Kent County (January 14, 1780).

Maryland Council correspondence to William Merrit, late of Kent: "Mary Gittings hath by her petition set forth to us that she was in September, 1777, plundered by the enemy, of household furniture, wearing apparel, etc., to a very considerable amount, and it appearing to us by her deposition with a list of her losses and the depositions of others, that the said facts are true, and we esteeming it proper that the Collection of Assessment of the said Mary Gittings for the year 1779 amounting to the sum of 269 pounds, 15 shillings, should be suspended." (February 23, 1780).

John Page, also Commissioner of Supplies for Kent County (March 11, 1780), was appointed Sheriff of Kent County in the room of William Hall, deceased (April 5, 1780).

Ensign John Sears, of the 2nd Maryland Regiment, was ordered to be paid by the Collector of the Tax for Kent County for said Sears' recruiting service (March 14, 1780).

John Page, Isaac Perkins, and Josiah Johnson were Commissioners of Supply for Kent County and were paid for obtaining provisions for the Army (April 8, 1780).

Capt. Edward Wright, of the 7th Maryland Regiment, was ordered to be paid by the Collector of the Tax for Kent County for said Wright's recruiting service (May 18, 1780).

John Voorhees was appointed Commissary for Purchases in Kent County (July 8, 1780).

John Bolton was ordered to be paid by the Collector of the Tax for Kent County to be expended in necessaries for the recruits, etc. at Chestertown (July 26, 1780).

William Rasin (or Raisin) was Contractor for Horses in Kent County (August 14, 1780).

Abraham Falconer was Contractor for Horses and Wagons in Kent County (August 23, 1780).

Nathaniel Ricketts was appointed Inspector of Tobacco for Langford's Bay in Kent County (August 30, 1780).

Ezekiel Forman, Clerk of Kent County, reported the death of Mr. Hall, Sheriff of Kent County, to the Council (March 25, 1780).

Col. Isaac Perkins reported to the Council that "my invaluable set of mills were burned to the ground on the 27th instant at night before I reached home from Annapolis, my conjectures are that the Tories in the upper part of this county [were responsible]." The deposition of John Cooper, aged 17, supported Perkins' statement and said Perkin's blacksmith Daniel Greenwood awakened him and told him the mill was on fire at one o'clock in the night (correspondence dated June 29, 1780).

Note: the same name may appear several times on the same page. Check the entire page.

-A-
AARNELL, Laurance, 142
ABATT, John, 125
ABBOTT, John, 168, 175
William, 1
ABOTT, Mr., 108
ABRAMS LOTT, 30, 42, 43, 71, 82
ABSOLAM, William, 1
ACKLAND, John, 1, 90, 161
William, 1, 42, 43, 67
ACKLANDS LOT, 1, 40
ACKLANDS LOTT, 40, 42, 43
ADAIR, Alexander, 1
Robert, 153
ADAMS, John, 168
Mary, 168
Matthew, 42, 43
Thomas, 175
ADAMS CHANCE, 5, 37
ADAMS CHOICE, 5, 37, 38, 41, 42, 43, 71
ADAMS END, 42, 43
ADAMS END RESURVEYED, 42, 43
ADAMS HOPE, 71
ADDICOTT, John, 168
William, 168
ADDITION (The), 2, 4, 5, 7, 8, 11, 12, 13, 14, 15, 17, 18, 19, 20, 22, 25, 26, 28, 29, 31, 32, 33, 34, 36, 37, 38, 40, 41, 42, 43, 71
ADDITION RESURVEYED, 44
ADDITION TO ATTIX ADVENTURE, 43
ADDITION TO BELLAKEW, 25
ADDITION TO BELLEKELL, 43
ADDITION TO BLAYS PARK, 36, 43
ADDITION TO CHEAPSIDE, 43
ADDITION TO CHEDLEY, 43
ADDITION TO COME WHITTEN, 43
ADDITION TO DALLINGTON, 31
ADDITION TO DOLLINGTON, 43
ADDITION TO FAIR DEALING, 14, 40
ADDITION TO FAIRE DEALING, 43
ADDITION TO FAIRLY, 23
ADDITION TO FEITH LAND, 43
ADDITION TO FREITH, 39
ADDITION TO GLEAVES LOTT, 5
ADDITION TO GOOD HOPE, 3, 38, 43
ADDITION TO HANGMANS FOLLY, 40
ADDITION TO HILLS AND NO DALES, 15, 43
ADDITION TO HONEST DEAL, 29
ADDITION TO HONEST DEALING, 37, 40
ADDITION TO HOWELS RESURVEYED, 43
ADDITION TO HUTSONS HILLS, 43
ADDITION TO JOHNS FIELDS, 32
ADDITION TO KENNARD DISCOVERY, 44
ADDITION TO KENNARDS POINT, 5, 21, 44
ADDITION TO KENT LOTT, 44
ADDITION TO KILLINGSWORTHMORE, 7
ADDITION TO KNAPLEY, 23
ADDITION TO KNAPLEY GREEN, 40
ADDITION TO KNAPLY GREEN, 44
ADDITION TO LYNN, 21, 44
ADDITION TO MATHIAS AND JOHN FIELDS, 44
ADDITION TO MATTHIAS AND ST JOHN FIELDS, 10, 16, 32
ADDITION TO MOORES FISHING GROUND, 44
ADDITION TO NEW FORREST, 20
ADDITION TO PALMERS DESIRE, 27, 44
ADDITION TO PENROSE, 44
ADDITION TO PLAINS, 34
ADDITION TO QUEEN CARLETON, 14
ADDITION TO QUEEN CARLTON, 24, 30, 35
ADDITION TO QUEEN CATHARINE, ALIAS CHARLTON, 44
ADDITION TO QUEEN CHARLTON, 12
ADDITION TO RENT LOTT, 3
ADDITION TO SCOTTS LOT, 36
ADDITION TO SCOTTS LOTT, 44
ADDITION TO SHADS

194   INHABITANTS OF KENT COUNTY, MARYLAND, 1637-1787

HOLD, 8
ADDITION TO SHADS
    HOLE, 44
ADDITION TO
    SIMPSONS
    ADVENTURE, 32,
    34
ADDITION TO SIMONS
    ADVENTURE, 44
ADDITION TO THE
    FLOWER OF THE
    FORREST, 26, 44
ADDITION TO
    TILGHMANS FARM,
    2, 31, 44
ADDITION TO TIMBER
    LEVELL, 13
ADDITION TO TIMBER
    LEVELS, 44
ADDITION TO VIAVAN,
    44
ADDITION TO WARD
    OAK, 11
ADDITION TO WARD
    OAKE, 44
ADDITION TO WARDS
    OAK, 36
ADDITIONAL HOPE, 43
ADVENTURE, 1, 3, 4,
    8, 9, 11, 14,
    16, 17, 20, 22,
    23, 27, 29, 31,
    32, 33, 35, 36,
    37, 39, 40, 44
ADVENTURE
    RESURVEYED, 4,
    72
ADVENTURE, THE, 44
ADVENTURES, 72
AFFELL, Roger, 168
AFFET, Roger, 168
AGREEMENT, 5, 14,
    18, 31, 34, 38,
    44, 72
AGREEMENT
    RESURVEYED, 39
AHERN, Daniel, 172
    Patrick, 180
AIRES, Thomas, 1
ALBUS, Femety, 124
ALBY, Love, 172
ALCOCK, George, 168
ALDRIDGE, Thomas, 1
ALDRIDGES LOTT, 1
ALEXANDER,
    Elizabeth, 168
ALFORD, Aaron, 44,
    51
    Aron, 151
    Edward, 180
    Moses, 1, 152,
    153, 182
ALFORDS PART OF
    DRAYTON, 44
ALGAR, Arthur, 168
ALIBONE, Edward, 1
ALLABY, Peter, 1
ALLEBONE ADDITION,
    8
ALLEBONES ADDITION,
    16
ALLEN, Sara, 193
    Sherwood, 193
    Thomas, 44, 175
ALLENS DECEIPT, 44
ALLENS NECK, 44
ALLEY, Levering,
    166
    Love, 172
    Lovering, 187
ALLEYN, Richard
    Fitts, 135
ALLFORD, Aaron, 1
ALLIBONE, Edward,
    44
ALLIBONES ADDITION,
    1, 44
AMBROSE, 44, 72
    Abraham, 1, 44,
    58
    Abram, 150
    John, 1
    Malachi, 73, 86,
    96
    Malichi, 187
AMBROSIA, 1, 5, 9,
    20, 25, 30, 44
AMBROSIA
    RESURVEYED, 20,
    29
AMELIA, 72
AMOS, Ann, 193
    Benj., 193
    Charles, 193
    Dave, 193
    James, 193
    John, 193
    Jos., 193
    Ransome, 193
    William, 193
ANDERSON,
    Alexander, 181
    Andrew, 101, 114
    Hester, 168
    James, 1, 72,
    154, 155, 174,
    184
    Margrett, 114
    Rachel, 168
    Robert, 155, 181
    Thomas, 184
    Walter, 184
    William, 1, 154
ANDLEY, Elizabeth,
    168
ANDOVER, 22
ANDOVER RESURVEYED,
    22, 44
ANDREW, The
    Spaniard, , 102
ANDREW, Elenor,
    105, 114
ANDREWS, Benjamin,
    155, 181
    Christopher, 144,
    145, 146, 147,
    148
    Miss, 1
    Samuel Anderson,
    1
    Stephen, 1
ANGELLS LOT, 17
ANGELLS LOT
    RESURVEYED,
    George, 22
ANGELLS LOTT, 37
ANGELS LOT, 24
ANGELS LOT
    RESURVEYED, 23
ANGELS LOTT, 10,
    41, 72
ANGELS LOTT
    RESURVEYED, 40,
    44
ANGELS REST, 23,
    24, 37, 39, 72
ANGER, John, 1, 74,
    91, 161, 185
ANGIER, John, 159,
    179
ANGLE, John, 1
ANGLES, Richard, 1

ANGLES LOT, 1, 7,
26
ANGLES REST, 7, 26
ANGLES REST OR LOT,
14
ANNARUNDEL GROVE,
34
ANTIONIO, 14
ANTONIA, 3
APPLEFORD, Tobias,
142
Toby, 141
APSLEY, Alexander,
182
Edward, 182
William, 1, 45,
61, 80, 86, 91,
153, 156, 172
APSLEYS LOTT, 45
APSLEYS PART OF
TOWNE RELIEF
RESURVEYED, 45
ARACADIA, 72
ARCADIA, 2, 4, 7,
11, 12, 13, 15,
20, 21, 22, 23,
24, 25, 26, 28,
31, 38, 45
ARECKSON, John, 141
ARFCOT, Richard,
168
ARIE, Richard, 122
ARISS, Ambrose, 55
ARLAND, Thomas, 168
ARMINGTON,
Frederick, 187
ARMSTRONG, Francis,
172
Thomas, 185
William, 74, 80,
83, 187
ARNEY, John, 168
ARNO, Benjamin, 185
Jeremiah, 185
John, 186
ARNOLD, John, 1
Mary, 168
Peter, 181
ARNOLL, Lawrence,
147
Thomas, 147
ARTHUR, John, 168
ARUNDAL GROVE, 72
ARUNDEL GROVE, 1,
4, 35, 36
ARUNDELL GROVE, 45
ASH POINT, 21, 24,
45, 72
ASHBUR, Joseph, 179
ASHBURY, Frances,
142
ASHBY, John, 181
ASHBY GREEN, 45
ASHE, Francis, 120
ASHLEY, Abram, 183
Daniel, 95, 173
David, 183
Edward, 183
Henery, 108, 109,
110
Henry, 101, 118
Isaac, 1
James, 183
Jno., 154
John, 1, 45, 72
151, 156, 180,
183
Sarah, 93
Thomas, 1
William, 1, 95,
154, 156, 183
ASHLEY GREEN, 1, 72
ASHLEYS GREEN, 1
ASHLEYS LOTT, 1, 5,
72
ASHMORE, Isaac, 168
Tobias, 155, 181
William, 168
ASHSLEYS LOTT, 45
ASHWORTH, John, 1
ATCHISON, Thomas,
58
Vincent, 146,
147, 148
ATHEY, William, 168
ATKEY, William, 168
ATKINS, Nathan, 180
ATKINSON, John, 1
Lewis, 181
Michael, 183
ATKISSON, William,
95
ATTIX, Aquila, 43,
45
Aquilla, 182
ATTIX'S ADVENTURE,
72
ATTIXS ADVENTURE,
45
AUGER, Jas., 153
John, 161, 185
AUGIER, Jno., 151
John, 153, 154,
156, 179
AUSTIN, John, 1, 45
Rosamond, 1
Samuel, 1
William, 1
AUSTINS BEGINNING,
1, 7, 9, 45
AYERS, Luther, 126
William, 183
AYES, Luther, 128
AYRES, Abraham, 1
Edward, 147
Luther, 128
Robert, 1, 80
Thomas, 1
AYRES WILDERNESS
RESURVEYED, 1

-B-
BACHMANS FARM, 20
BAGAR, William, 122
BAGGALY, William,
45
BAGGALY FORREST, 26
BAGGALYS FORREST,
45
BAGLEYS FORREST, 45
BAGLEYS FORRET
RESURVEYED, 45
BAGWELL, Smith, 187
Smyth, 173
BAILEY, Charles,
168
BAIRD, Alexander,
1, 44, 72, 77,
78, 90, 163
James, 74
John, 163
Lewis, 74
BAIRDS, 72
BAIRS GRIN, 37
BAIRS GRINE, 5
BAIRS GRINN, 29, 30
BAKER, Amey, 1
Caleb, 141
Charles, 1, 75,
180, 184
John, 49
Thomas, 1

196 INHABITANTS OF KENT COUNTY, MARYLAND, 1637-1787

William, 168, 180
BALDWIN, John, 1
BALEY, James, 187
BALIE, Margret,
  105, 107
BALL, John, 1, 44,
  155, 168
  Peter, 2
BALLY, Mary, 112
BANCKES, Charles,
  145
  Robert, 135
  Susannah, 136
BANCKS, Charles,
  130, 143, 145
  Susannah, 143
BANCKS CHOICE, 72
BAND, Will, 101
BANKER, Lewis, 168
  Louis, 168
BANKS, Katherine,
  168
BANNING, Anthony,
  76, 81, 87, 88,
  89, 91, 155, 180
BANNON, Anthony,
  183
  Jeremiah, 184
BANTHAM, John, 99
BANTHRAM,
  Elizabeth, 158
BARBARYS INLETT, 20
BARBER, Francis, 2
  George, 2
  James, 2
BARCUS, George, 186
BARES GRIN, 37
BARES GRINN, 29
BARKE, John, 129
BARKER, James, 2
  John, 2
BARKLEY, Thomas, 2
BARKLY, Thomas, 162
BARMAN, Elizabeth,
  168
BARNARD, Daniel,
  168
BARNES,
  Christopher, 143
  Esabella, 130,
  135
  Eseable, 128
  Franchis, 105,
  107

Francis, 101,
  102, 111, 114,
  116, 118, 121,
  130
Fransis, 125
Goody, 128
Isabella, 132
James, 155
John, 112, 129
Martha, 53, 72
Mary, 118
William, 2
BARNES VENTURE, 72
BARNEY, Francis, 2,
  45, 70, 162
BARNEYS FOREST, 2
BARNEYS FORREST, 2,
  9, 28, 45, 72
BARNS, Thomas, 163
BARNSTAPLE, Edward,
  168
BARON, Jeremiah,
  191
BARRATT, John, 180
BARRET, Thomas, 161
BARRETT, Adolphus,
  168
  Jonathan, 179
BARRIBALL, Pasto,
  168
BARTLET, John, 168
  Nicholas, 168
BARTON, 2, 45, 72
  Martha, 2
  Robert, 168
  Samuel, 2
BARTRUM, Robert,
  144
BARWICK, 26, 45
BASHA, 45
  Andrew, 45
BASHWELL, Henry,
  180
BASNETT, Nathan,
  173
  Nathaniel, 173
BASSILL, Ralph, 64
BATCHELLORS CHOICE,
  15, 16
BATCHELORS CHOICE,
  21, 25, 45, 72
BATCHELORS DELIGHT,
  21, 45
BATCHELORS HALL,

  28, 30, 45, 72
BATCHELORS HOPE,
  35, 45, 72
BATCHELORS LOTT,
  45, 72
BATCHELORS
  RESOLUTION, 2,
  11, 14, 15, 27,
  30, 45
BATEMAN,
  Christopher, 2
  Mary, 67
  Michael, 2
  William, 45, 49,
  142, 144, 146
BATEMANS FARM, 3,
  20, 29, 45
BATH, 33, 39, 45,
  72
  James, 145
BATHERSHELL, James,
  96
BATHURST, Edward,
  2, 175
BATSLE, Thomas, 2
BATT, George, 168
BATTEMAN, William,
  138
BATTERSAY, 45
BATTERSHELL, Henry,
  2
  James, 96
  John, 2, 94
  Rachel, 2, 70
BATTLE, Thomas, 2
BATTON, James, 97
BATTS, Joshua, 42
BATUSGY, 45
BAUTHAM, Henry, 188
  Richard, 188
BAVARIA, 19, 31,
  45, 72
BAVARIA RESURVEYED,
  45
BAXSTER, Elizabeth,
  105
  Joane, 105
  Marie, 105
  Roger, 105, 106,
  107, 108, 109
BAXTER, Francis,
  115
  Hannah, 124

INDEX

Joseph, 94
Mary, 110, 111, 128, 129
Roger, 69, 101, 103, 111, 113, 116, 125, 126, 128, 143
Thomas, 124, 141, 142, 144, 147
BAXTOR, Roger, 132
BAYELEY, William, 136
BAYLEY, Daniel B., 173
William, 2
BAYLY, Godfrey, 52
BAYLYS FORREST, 21
BAYRES GRINE, 45
BAYTMAN, William, 137
BEALL, Ninian, 132
BEALS GUM, 11
BEARD, Alexander, 45
Elizabeth, 45
BEARDS PART OF MORTON, 45
BEARS GRIN, 72
BEAVEN, Allexander, 135
BEAVER DAM, 33
BEAVER DAM NECK, 18, 72
BEAVER DAMS, 45
BEAVER NECK, 45
BEAVERDAM, 11
BEAVIN RIDGE, 45
BEAZLY, John, 166
BECK, Alexander, 2, 73, 85, 92, 182, 183
Aquilla, 2
Caleb, 2, 48
Daniel, 182
Edward, 2, 43, 59, 64, 72, 83, 151, 152, 153, 156, 180, 182, 187
Eliza, 2
Elizabeth, 61
Evan, 2
James, 182
John, 2, 45, 61, 64, 182
Joshua, 2, 182
Martha, 2
Mary, 2
Mathew, 72
Samuel, 2, 77, 163, 166, 181, 182, 186, 190
Simon, 173
Vivian, 2
William, 2, 87, 153
BECKES ADDITION, 45
BECKETT, Isaac, 173
BECKLER, Edward, 175
BECKLES, Thomas, 2, 45, 64
BECKLES RECOVERY, 45
BECKLEYS RECOVERY, 2
BECKS ADDITION, 2, 25, 27, 45
BECKS PART OF BOUNTY RESURVEYED, 45
BECKWITH, 12
BECKWITH'S ADDITION, 13
BECKWORTH, 2, 21, 72
BEDDOE, Griffin, 2
BEDLE, Sarah, 115
BEEDLE, Henry, 143
BEGINNING, 18
BELCHER, 45
Thomas, 45, 100, 103, 110, 113
BELIKIN, Chr., 161
BELL, George, 187
BELLAKEW, 25
BELLAKILLE RESURVEYED, 45
BELLAMY, Henry, 103
BELLAS, Francis, 2, 45
Hannah, 2
BELLAS RESURVEY OF SHADSHOLD, 45
BELLEKELLE, 45
BELLICAN, Ann, 2
Chris., 2
Christopher, 68, 75, 84, 187
BELLICAN'S heirs, 153
BELLIKIN, Christopher, 158
BELLO, Francis, 67
BEMAN, 39
BENDER, Valentine, 83
BENDY, James, 168
BENGATE, 45
BENGEY, 19
BENHAM, Mathew, 2
BENJAMINS CHOICE, 29, 45
BENJAMINS LOTT, 33, 45
BENJAMINS PURCHASE, 45
BENNAM, Matthew, 47
BENNETS REGULATION, 23
BENNETT, Disboro(ugh), 123, 130, 135, 137, 138, 140, 141, 144, 147, 149
George, 168
Henrietta Maria, 47
John, 2, 103
Richard, 3, 44, 45, 46, 47, 54, 60, 62, 68, 71
Samuel, 168, 182
Solomon, 183
Susanna Maria, 47
Thomas, 126, 127
William, 168
BENNETTS BRIDGE, 3, 72
BENNETTS HOPE, 45
BENNETTS LOW, 73
BENNETTS LOWE, 46, 59
BENNETTS REGULATION, 46, 73
BENNEY, Benjamin, 154, 155, 181
BENNY, Benjamin, 3, 73, 154
BENSON, Marke, 111
Steven, 122
BENTLEY, James, 188

198 INHABITANTS OF KENT COUNTY, MARYLAND, 1637-1787

BENTON, Benjamin,
  183
  Eastor, 123
  Francis, 123, 183
  James, 182
  Margrett, 123
  Mark, 102, 133
  Marke, 101, 104,
    123, 127, 131,
    132, 136, 141,
    142
BERAY, Robert, 168
BERCKISTON, John,
  166
BERGEN, Philip, 57
BERRY, John, 168,
  183
  Moses, 181, 182
  Robert, 168
  Samuel, 3, 151
BERRYWALLS, James,
  185
BESHFORD, 36
BEST, Henry, 3
  Humphrey, 3
  William, 3
BESWICK, Nathan,
  182
BETSYS PARK, 46
BETTYS LOT
  RESURVEYED, 10
BETTYS PARK, 46
BEVANS, John, 187
  Thomas, 83
BEVENS, Elizabeth,
  3
BEVERLIN, John, 181
BICKE, Henry, 119
BIDDLE, Spencer,
  187
BILLETT, Mich., 130
BILLEYS LOTT, 34
BILLILNGSLY,
  Thomas, 3
BILLYS LOT
  RESURVEYED, 8
BILLYS LOTT, 34,
  46, 73
BIMAN, 46
BINN, Samuel, 173
BINNEY, Benjamin,
  181
BIRCH, Thomas, 55
BIRD, Edward, 76,
  183
BIRTH RIGHT, 73
BIRTH RIGHT, THE,
  46
BIRTHRIGHT, 34
BISHFORD, 46
BISHFORD
  RESURVEYED, 36,
  46
BISHIP, Abraham,
  129
BISHOP, Risden, 87
  Risdon, 3, 50,
    73, 78, 83, 153
  William, 134,
    137, 139, 140,
    142, 175
BISHOPP, William,
  137, 138, 148
BISS, Elisabeth,
  161
BISSET, John, 167
BIVINS, John, 95
BLACK, George, 77,
  81, 82, 97, 187
  James, 3, 57, 71,
    72, 82, 162, 186
BLACK HALL, 73
BLACK HALL
  HERMITAGE, 73
BLACK HALLS
  HARMITAGE, 13
BLACK HALLS
  HERMITAGE, 31
BLACK OAK, 8, 46
BLACKHALL, Ralph,
  46, 140, 144
BLACKHALLS
  HERMITAGE, 46
BLACKISTON,
  Benjamin, 3, 46,
    50, 64
  Eben, 186
  Ebenezer, 3, 46,
    56, 98, 163,
    176, 178
  George, 3, 46,
    154
  George William,
    95, 98
  Hannah, 3
  Henry, 182
  James, 180
  John, 3, 43, 166,
    182, 186
  Joseph, 180
  Margaret, 3
  Michael, 3
  Prideaux, 3
  Stephen, 183
  Thomas, 3
  Vincent, 3
  William, 3, 176
BLACKISTON LOTT, 3
BLACKISTONE,
  Ebenezer, 66
  Thomas, 3
BLACKISTONES
  ADDITION, 3
BLACKISTONS CASE,
  46
BLACKISTONS LOT
  RESURVEYED, 46
BLACKISTONS LOTT,
  46
BLACKISTONS
  NEGLECT, 46
BLACKSKIN, Jonas,
  188
BLACKSTEIN,
  Ebenezer, 56
BLACKSTON,
  Benjamin, 76,
    80, 84, 163, 165
  Ebenezer, 151
  Hannah, 3
  James, 78
  Jno., 150
  John, 77, 151,
    186
  Jonas, 188
  Joseph, 88
  Vincent, 3
BLACKSTONE,
  Ebenezer, 82,
    163
  Stephen, 80
  Thomas, 163
  William, 163
BLACKSTON'S HEIRS,
  89
BLACKWELL
  HERMITAGE, 38
BLAKE, Ancibel, 193
  Ancibel Crampton,
    193
  Giles, 102
  Gyles, 107

Henry, 168
James, 3, 181
John, 193
Mr., 108
Robert, 189
Thomas, 90, 93
BLAKELIDGE,
 Benjamin, 3
BLAKEWAY, John, 184
BLAKHALL, Ralph,
 142
BLANCHFORD, John,
 182
BLANGY, Lewis, 145
BLAXSTONE,
 Ebenezer, 163
BLAXTON, William,
 162
BLAY, Ann, 67
 Edward, 3, 46,
 56, 67, 156,
 175, 178
 Isabell, 3
 Isabella, 62
 William, 3, 46,
 60, 157, 175
BLAYS ADDITION, 3,
 39, 46, 73
BLAYS ADDITION
 RESURVEYED, 36
BLAYS PARK, 3, 5,
 18, 24, 27, 29,
 30, 36, 39, 46,
 73
BLAYS RANGE, 3, 27,
 29, 36, 39, 46,
 73
BLEAKE, Giles, 102
 Gilles, 108
 Gyles, 108
BLOOMBERRY, 38
BLOOMS BERRY, 73
BLOOMSBURG, 46
BLOOMSBURY, 11, 21,
 22
BLOUNTVILLE, 46
BLUFF POINT, 12,
 15, 46
BLUNT, 4
 Ann, 124, 125,
 129, 133, 137,
 138
 Apprell, 123
 Grace, 107

Josias, 123
Mrs., 137
Richard, 46, 54,
 101, 102, 103,
 105, 107, 108,
 114, 118, 119,
 123, 124, 126,
 127, 128, 130,
 131, 133, 134,
 137, 138, 139,
 175
 Robert, 124
 Thomas, 125
BLUNTE, Richard,
 125
BLUNTVILLE, 26
BLUNTWELL, 23, 33,
 73
BOARDLEY, Thomas,
 54
BOARDLEYS
 BEGINNING, 46
BOARDLY, William,
 83
BOBS DESIRE, 46
BODDY, Barrett, 184
 John, 180, 181
 Stephen, 171, 181
 William, 46, 180
BODDYS NECK, 46
BODEAN, Francis, 43
BODEEN, Francis, 71
 Francis L., 3
 Hannah, 3
 Henry, 3
BODIEN, Henry
 Augustus, 54
BODWAY, William,
 168
BODWELL, Atwell,
 128
BODY, Will, 114
 William, 100
BODYE, William, 168
BOGGES, Elezabeth,
 124
BOGGS, John, 179
BOGUE, William, 173
BOISE, Robert, 142
BOLSTON, 73
BOLTON, J., 152
 Jno., 153
 John, 3, 46, 74,
 79, 89, 91, 154,

155, 179, 184,
 190, 192
 William, 3
BOLTONS RETREAT, 46
BOND, Benjamin, 3
 Eliza, 3
 John, 171
 William, 3
BONDY, Richard, 46
BONDYES FOLLY, 46
BONGAY, 46
BONGER, John, 153
BONISON, Joseph,
 168
BONNER, Francis, 3
BOOKER, Elisabeth,
 161
BOON, Joseph, 4,
 46, 153
BOONE, Thomas, 46,
 63, 147
BOONLEY, 37, 46
BOONLY, 1
BOONS MEADOW, 2,
 46, 73
BOOR, Jonas, 168
BOOT, Heirs of, 86
BOOTES, William, 4
BOOTS, Abraham, 180
 Alfonso, 185
 Thomas, 4
 William, 96, 161,
 163, 185
BORDLEY, Ann, 4
 Arthur, 80, 90,
 155, 180
 B. John, 73, 75,
 79, 80, 87
 B.John, 77
 Beal, 4
 Hannah, 74, 82,
 87, 89
 John, 4, 44, 46,
 57, 179
 Mary, 98
 Sarah, 98
 Stephen, 4, 46,
 150, 151, 153,
 154, 176
 Thomas, 4, 46,
 54, 62, 67, 151
 W., 173
 William, 4, 96,
 153, 154, 155,

174, 189, 190, 191
BORDLEYS BEGINNING, 4, 73
BORDLEYS GIFT, 4, 14, 25, 46, 73
BORDLEYS RESURVEY ON, HILLY LONGFORD, 4
BORDLEYS RESURVEY ON KILLY LANGFORD, 46
BOREMAN, William, 116, 118
BOROUGH ADDITION, 17
BOSTICK, Azariah, 186
James, 186
Jane, 4
Samuel, 4
Sanders, 4
Thomas, 4
BOSTICKS ADDITION, 4, 46, 73
BOSTOCK, Eliza, 4
James, 4
Sanders, 4
BOSTON, 17, 46
BOSTRICK, Henry, 171
BOSTWICK, Sanders, 46
BOUCHEL, Slater, Dr., 4
BOUDYS FOLLY AND, Greenwoods Advancement, 15
BOUKER, Roger, 168
BOULLAY, James, 48, 51, 70
BOULSTON, 4
BOULTON, Thomas, 105
BOULTONS DELIGHT, 3
BOUNTY, 13, 19, 24, 33, 36, 37, 46, 73
BOUNTY RESURVEYED, 2
BOURK, Thomas, 163
BOURKE, Thomas, 99
BOVEY, Isaack, 130
Peter, 67

BOWDEYS FOLLY, 15
BOWDIES FOLLY, 25
BOWDY, Elizabeth, 4
Richard, 4
BOWDYS FOLLY, 4, 73
BOWER, Augustine, 4
BOWERS, Jane, 4
Pearce, 75, 77, 186
Thomas, 4, 72, 73, 77, 81, 89, 162, 164, 183
William, 4, 184
BOWLES, Isaac, 4, 54
James, 4
John, 4, 46, 145, 146, 147, 148
BOWLSTON, 4, 46
BOWNE, Thomas, 46
BOWNES DISCOVERY, 46
BOWNS VENTURE, 46
BOXLEY, 46, 73
BOXLY, 3
BOYAR, Penelope, 4
BOYD, David, 184, 189
Isaac, 161
BOYER, Abraham, 166
Andrew, 165
Augustin, 46, 163
Augustine, 4, 46, 65, 88, 95, 99, 163, 165
Isaac, 165
James, 4, 163, 186, 188
John, 164, 165, 188
Lambert, 171, 172
Mary, 4, 95
Nathaniel, 4, 80, 88
Penelope, 4
Richard, 4, 95, 99, 158, 159, 160
Stephen, 160
Thomas, 4, 80, 95, 99, 165, 185, 188
William, 4, 63, 157, 161, 163,

164, 165, 188
BOYERS ADVENTURE, 73
BOYERS ADDITION, 46
BOYERS ADVENTURE, 4, 40, 46
BOYS, Alexander, 173
BRADA, William, 173
BRADAWAY, Nickolas, 132
BRADFIELD, 20, 21, 46
BRADLEY, James, 4
BRADLY, Thomas, 127
BRADNOX, 46
Capt., 121
Mary, 116, 117, 120, 126
Misteris, 112
Mr., 111, 112
Mrs., 121
Thomas, 46, 47, 100, 101, 102, 103, 110, 113, 114, 116, 117, 118, 119, 120, 122, 126, 175
BRADNOX CREEK, 8, 47
BRADSHA, James, 94
Jo:, 112
John, 80, 86
BRADSHAW, James, 73, 87, 183
John, 73, 92, 186
William, 46, 71
BRADSHAWE, William, 4
BRADSHAWS FARM, 4, 46, 73
BRADWAY, 29, 31
Nic, 109
Nicholas, 117, 122
BRADY, James, 4, 166
BRAGG, William, 168
BRAINTHWAITE, William, 178
BRANTWELL, William, 102
BRAODNOX, Mrs., 107
Thomas, 107

INDEX

BRASSETT, William, 182
BRAYLER, Nicholas, 168
BREESE, Henry, 184
BRENT, Giles, 101, 175, 178
  Gilles, 111
  Margaret, 101
  Margret, 116
  Margrett, 137
  Margrit, 111
  Marie, 101
  Mary, 111
BRENTON, John, 168
BRETT, John, 4
BRETTON, William, 116
BREWARD, James, 4, 46
  Solomon, 5
BREWARDS INDUSTRY, 4, 5
BREWARDS MARSH, 4, 5, 24, 46
BREWARDS RESERVE, 27, 41
BREWARDS RESERVE RESURVEY, 46
BREWER, Edward, 168
  Edwin (heirs), 12
  James, 5, 101
  John, 103
  William, 5
BREWERS RESERVE, 27
BREWERS RESURVEY, 73
BREWERTON, Richard, 146, 147
BRICE, John, 181
  Judith, 92
  Richard, 5, 181
  William, 183
BRIDES, Richard, 129
BRIDGE POINT, 20, 32, 46
BRIDGE TOWN COMMON, 46
BRIDGES, Richard, 115, 119
  Thomas, 115
BRIDGES POINT, 5
BRIDGETOWN COMMON, 35
BRIGHT, Ann, 123
  Francis, 101
  Goodie, 106
  Thomas, 123, 124, 127, 130, 134, 140, 141, 146
  Widdow, 107
BRIGHT HELMSTONE, 12, 32, 46
BRIGHT HELMSTSONE, 20, 73
BRIGHT HEMSTONE, 32
BRIGS, Jane, 126
BRIMINGTON, Jacob, 136
BRINGGERGRASS, James, 138
BRINTON, 20
BRINTS PIBBLES, 10
BRINTS PIDDLES, 46
BRISCO, Isaac, 86, 87
  Joseph, 159
  Moses, 79, 87
  William, 166
BRISCOE, Alexander, 5, 64, 98, 99, 185
  Allexander, 166
  Ben., 154
  Isaac, 5, 62, 154, 179
  Jacob, 185
  Jo., 153
  John, 5, 48, 184
  Joseph, 5, 183, 184
  Moses, 185
  William, 167, 185
BRISICO, John, 179
BRISTOL, 11, 19, 41, 47, 73
BRISTOLL, 10, 47
BRISTON, 41
BRISTOW, 8
BRISTOWE, 18
BRITAN, William, 116
BRITE, Thomas, 145, 146, 148, 149
BRITTAIN, 28, 38
BRITTAINE, 47
BRITTIAN, 38
BROAD NECK, 1, 3, 5, 9, 10, 12, 14, 16, 33, 36, 47, 73
BROAD OAK, 2, 5, 13, 17, 19, 20, 21, 33, 34, 38, 40, 41, 47, 73
BROAD OAKE, 47
BROADAWAY, Nicollas, 109
  Thomas, 182
BROADERICK, Catharine, 96
BROADFIELD, 24, 39, 73
BROADNAX, Mrs., 104
  Thomas, 102, 106
BROADNAX CREEK, 32
BROADNOX, 11, 73
  Mary, 129
  Mr., 105, 108
  Thomas, 102, 109
BROADNOX CREEK, 12, 39
BROADNOX RESURVEYED, 47
BROADWAY, 31, 74
  Nicholas, 136
BROCKINGTON, John, 168
  Philip, 168
BROCKSOLM, John, 163
BROCKSON, Benjamin, 171
BROCKWORTH, Samuel, 125
BRODNOX, Capt., 128, 129
  Mary, 125, 127, 128, 130
  Mr., 105, 106
  Thomas, 109, 125, 127, 128, 129
BROD(O)WAY, 47
  Nicholas, 47
  Nicklus, 125
BROMFIELD, 13, 47
  John, 47
BROMTON, Elezabeth, 124
BROOCKES, Franchis, 104
  Mr., 109

BROOK, Philip, 61
  Thornton, 5
BROOKE, Francis,
  100, 119
BROOKES, Frances,
  113
  Franchis, 111
  Francis, 110, 111
  Mr., 111
  Sarah, 132
  Thomas, 115
BROOKING, Alphonso,
  168
  Matthew, 182
BROOKS, Edward, 5
  Hannah, 68
  Henry, 74, 182
  Jno., 153
  John, 5, 81, 91,
    158, 159, 160
  Johnson, 172
  Margarett, 153
  Nathan, 173, 183
  Phil., 153
  Philip, 20, 48,
    159, 160, 184
  Phillip, 157
  Phillm., 5
  Ruth, 5, 68
  Thornton, 5
BROOKS FOLLY, 74
BROOM, Charles, 78,
  86, 87
BROOM FIELD, 74
BROOMFIELD, 17
BROOMY NECK, 74
BROTHERLY &
  FRIENDLY
  AGREEMENT, 9,
  21, 22
BROTHERLY AND
  FRIENDLY
  AGREEMENT, 47,
  74
BROTHERS ANNEXTION,
  21
BROTHERSHIP, 3
BROUN, Nicholas,
  105
BROUNE, Mr., 106,
  108
  Nicholas, 104,
    106, 107, 109
  Nicolas, 111

BROWARD, James, 47
BROWARDS INDUSTRY, 47
BROWARDS MARSH, 47
BROWARDS RESERVE,
  26, 27, 47
BROWN, Caleb, 5
  Charles, 188
  Christopher, 175
  David, 89, 183
  Edward, 5
  George, 91, 179
  Hannah, 85
  James, 5, 47
  Jane, 5
  John, 5, 47, 57,
    60, 122, 150,
    178, 188
  Joseph, 89, 90,
    92
  Morgan, 5, 51, 64,
    84, 87, 88, 180
  Nicholas, 97, 175,
    180
  Peregrine, 5, 47,
    64, 69, 158,
    159, 160, 162,
    164, 165, 179
  R., 62
  Rachell, 5, 64
  Rebecca, 5,
  Rebeccah 87,
    88
  Thomas, 46
  William, 5, 47,
    52, 55, 60,
    76, 88, 94,
    165
BROWNE,
  Bartholomew, 52
  Edward, 124, 138,
    139, 141, 142,
    145
  George, 146
  John, 65, 120,
    122, 127, 131,
    136, 137, 140,
    141
  Mary, 145
  Morgan, 5, 124
  Nathaniel, 187
  Nicholas, 100,
    101, 104, 119,
    120, 121

  Peregrine, 5
  Perrigrine, 53
  Rachell, 5
  Robert, 119, 120,
    121, 122
  Sarah, 124
  William, 5, 47
BROWNE ANGLE, 47
BROWNING, George,
  5, 78, 81, 156,
  165, 187
  John, 5, 61, 71,
    86, 156, 159,
    160, 161, 162,
    163, 164, 165,
    166
  John Wrightson, 47
  Joshua, 166, 185
  Thomas, 5, 47, 48,
    74, 81, 162, 164, 165
  William, 183
  Wriston, 42
  Writson, 5
BROWNINGS ADDITION,
  5, 47, 74
BROWNINGS
  ADVENTURE, 5,
  35, 47, 74
BROWNINGS
  DISCOVERY, 35,
  47
BROWNINGS PART OF
  ADAMS CHOICE
  RESURVEYED, 47
BROWNINGS PART OF
  BYORS NEGLECT
  RESURVEYED, 47
BROWNS ADVENTURE,
  47
BROWNS ANGLE, 5
BROWNS CHOICE, 5,
  47
BROWNS DISCOVERY,
  5, 47
BROWNS LEVEL, 47
BROWNS LEVELL, 30
BROWNS LEVITT, 30
BROWNS LOTT, 47
BROWNS PURCHASE, 5,
  11, 47, 74
BROWNS RESERVE, 27
BROWNS RIGHT, 5, 47
BROWNY, William,
  183

BROXTON, James, 185
John, 185
BRUCKEY, William
G., Mrs., 171
BRUER, James, 186
BRUMMEL, James, 181
Richard, 181
BRUS, Thomas, 148
BRUSBANK, Francis
O., 67
BRUSS, Thomas, 144
BRYAN, Ann, 168
Arthur, 81
Augustine. 173
Daniel, 5, 47, 161
Daniel C., 161
James, 186
Mathew, 5
Michael, 166
BRYAND, Daniel, 163
BRYANS ADDITION, 47
BRYANS DELIGHT, 74
BRYNE, James, 173
BRYNTON, 47
BUCHANAN, R., 151, 152
Robert, 82, 90, 91, 92, 98, 153, 154, 155, 163, 174, 176, 177
DUCHANNAN, Robort, 5
BUCK, John, 5
BUCK HILL, 2, 8, 10, 24, 34, 35
BUCK HILL AND BILBYS LOTT RESURVEYED, 47
BUCK NECK, 15, 18, 19, 47, 74
BUCK NECK RESURVEYED, 15
BUCKHANNON, Robert, 185
BUCKHILL, 47
BUCKINGHAM, 8, 20, 23, 26, 39, 42, 47, 74
Howell, 5
William, 180
BUCKINGHAM RESURVEYED, 39
BUCKS ADDITION, 74
BUCKSKIN, Prince, 187
BUCKWELL, Susannah, 168
BUDBROOK, John, 168
BUDD, Samuel, 5, 47
BUDDS DISCOVERY, 25, 47, 74
BUDDS MEADOW, 21, 47, 74
BUDDS MEADOWS, 25
BUDLE, Spence, 83
BUDS DISCOVERY, 5
BULLOCK, Samuel, 76, 154, 182, 190
BUNT, William, 168
BURAGE, John, 122
BURBAGE, Thomas, 130
William, 130
BURCH, Joseph, 186
Thomas, 168
BURCHANELL, Joseph, 186
BURCHINAL, Elisabeth, 162
James, 89
Jeremy, 159, 160
Joseph, 162
William, 89
BURCHINALL, Benjamin, 172
Jeremy, 6
William, 180
BURCKS BEGINNING, 47
BURGAN, James, 62
John, 6
Marta, 6
Philip, 6
Phillip, 156
Sutten, 157
Sutton, 6
BURGEN, John, 163, 184
Philip, 6
Phillip, 57
BURGER, Isaac, 136
BURGES, Capt., 131
BURGGER, Isaac, 138
BURGIN, Benjamin, 159, 160
John, 159, 160, 162

Sutton, 162
William, 187
BURGUS, John, 185
BURK, George, 183
John, 6, 73, 180, 181
Thomas, 6, 47
William, 6, 47
BURK WITH ADDITION, 27
BURK WITH ITS ADDITION RESURVEYED, 47
BURKE, John, 6
William, 44
BURKES LOTT, 6
BURKS, 74
BURKS ADDITION, 22, 47, 74
BURKS BEGINNING, 6
BURKS CHANCE, 47
BURKS LOTT, 47
BURKWITH ADDITION, 38
BURLE, Robert, 128, 139
BURN, Patrick, 6
BURNE, Michael, 6
BURNSIDES, John, 171, 189
BURRIDGE, Joseph, 168
BURROUGHS, John, 6
Thomas, 6
William, 6
BURROUGHS ADDITION, 7
BURROUGHS PURCHASE, 6
BURROWS, William, 48
BURROWS ADDITION, 48
BURTON, Edmond, 116, 131, 132, 134, 135, 138
Edmund, 108, 122
Edward, 101, 107, 135, 136, 137, 139, 140, 141
Goodman, 101
Mary, 143
Rebecka, 133
BUSBY, Benjamin,

204 INHABITANTS OF KENT COUNTY, MARYLAND, 1637-1787

187
BUSHFORD, 74
BUSLY, John, 82
BUSSELL, George, 168
BUTCHER, Edmund, 6
Edward, 6
James, 86, 172, 187
William, 6, 62
BUTLER, Anne, 168
James, 185
John, 48
Robert, 81, 183
BUTLERS NECK, 48
BUTTAM, 38
BUTTEW, Samuel, 181
BY CHANCE, 13, 14, 48
BYAM, Thomas, 121
BYMAN, 18
BYRAM, James, 180
John, 180
Joseph, 180
Stephen, 180
William, 180
BYRNE, Michael, 46, Micl
Patrick, 6
BYRNES, Michael, 67

-C-
CACKAWAY POINT, 48, 74
CADMORE, Richard, 143
CADWALADER, John, 177
CADWALLADER, John, 73, 174
CADWALLEDER, John, 166
CAHOON, John, 184
CAINE, William, 168
CALAWAY, Antony, 114
CALDER, A., 152
Alexander, 73
James, 6, 48, 154, 176
CALDERS MANOR, 74
CALDERS MEADOW, 23, 48
CALDERS MEADOWS, 6, 74
CALEBS DISCOVER, 2
CALEBS DISCOVERY, 2, 4, 5, 31, 48, 74
CALF PEN, 16
CALLAWAY, Anthony, 127, 135
CALLISTER, Sarah, 155
CALLIWAY, Anthony, 101
CALLOWAY, Anthonie, 104, 107, 109
Anthony, 106, 109, 115, 118, 120
Antony, 122
CALMER, John, 168
CALVERT, Charles, 130, 134, 143
Philip, 138
Phillip, 116
CAMELL, John, 48
CAMELLS FAME, 48
CAMELLS FARM, 74
CAMELLS WORTH MORE, 48
CAMELLS WORTHMORE, 74
CAMELS WORTHMORE, 74
CAMMELL, Isaac, 182
James, 6
CAMMELLS FARM, 6, 31
CAMMELLS FARME, 30
CAMMELS ADVENTURE, 28
CAMMELS FARM, 9, 11, 18, 29, 42
CAMMELS WORTHMORE, 1, 11, 16, 23
CAMMELSWORTHMORE, 26, 36
CAMPBELL, Hugh, 6
James, 6, 156
Richard, 6, 156, 157
Robert, 171
CAMPHER, James, 171
CAMRON, Anthony, 6
CANADA, 9, 28, 74
Thomas, 39
CANADAY, Edward, 6
John, 6
CANADY, 1
CANBY, Thomas, 6, 84
CANDLEMUSE, Day, 129
CANELL, Isaac, 77, 92
CANN, Francis, 78, 81, 82, 90, 185
James, 6, 96, 186
John, 6
CANNADAY, 18
William, 95
CANNAH, Elizabeth, 168
CANNEL, Abrm., 154
Isaac, 97
CANNELL, Abraham, 48, 69
Isaac, 48
CANNELLS TRIANGLE, 48
CANNELLS FANCY, 48
CANNON, Edward, 180
James, 182
CANSTER, Richard, 159, 160
CARDER, Amos, 168
CARELL, Isaac, 77, 92
CARLEIN, Henry, 102
CARLIEN, Henery, 112
CARLIN, Henerie, 109
CARLINE, Henerie, 103, 108
Henery, 104, 105, 106, 109
Henry, 103, 116, 117, 118, 122, 175
Mr., 107
Rachell, 104
CARLYEN, Henry, 101
Mr., 101
CARLYNE, Henry, 114
CARMAN, Joseph, 6
Micager, 6
Michael, 6
CARMICHAEL, James, 172, 173

William, 6, 88,
  174
CARMON , Anthony, 6
CARNELL, Daniel, 56
CAROLA, 5, 25, 32
CARPENDER, Simon,
  130
CARPENTER, Charles,
  144
  Richard, 182
CARR, Elizabeth,
  168
  Patrick, 181
  Peter, 188
CARRADINE, John,
  181
CARRELL, Daniel, 56
  John, 155
CARROLA, 48
CARROLL, 35, 74
  Charles, 6
  Dominick , 6
  Domk, 6
  Edward, 183
  Joseph, 188
  Mary, 6
  Phill, 48
CARROLLS ADDITION,
  48
CARSVILLES
  ADDITION, 74
CARTER, Edmond, 6
  Edward, 71
  Elizabeth, 124,
  139
  George, 6, 168
  Henry, 124, 138,
  139, 140, 141,
  145, 146
  James, 6
  Mary, 124
  Risdon, 94
  Sarah, 168
  Thomas, 183
  William, 6, 148
CARVELLS
  PREVENTION, 6
CARVIL, John, 43,
  48, 66
CARVILE, John, 48,
  175
  Thomas, 66
CARVILES
  PREVENTION, 48

CARVILL, John, 6,
  48, 56, 155, 179
CARVILLE, Ann, 74,
  81, 86, 89
CARVILLES
  ADVENTURE, 6
CARVILLS ADVENTURE,
  48
CARVILS
  INHERITANCE, 48
CARWARDIN, Abrm., 6
  Edward, 6
  Thomas, 6
CARWITHY, Thomas,
  168
CASE, James, 168
CASEMARK, James,
  180
CASLICK, John, 7
CASSADAY, John, 7
CASTLE, Ralph, 48
CASTLE CAREY, 16,
  19, 22, 27, 32,
  48
CASTLE CARRU, 74
CASTLE CARY, 27, 28
CASTLEDINE, John,
  179
  William, 48
CASTLEDINES LOT, 48
CASTLEDINES LOTT,
  74
CASTLES POINT, 48
CASTLETON,
  Ebenezer, 185
CATER, Mary, 158
CATLIN, Caleb, 172
CATLING, Thomas, 7
CATON, Thomas, 181
  William, 48
CATONS CHOICE PART
  OF KENT MANOR
  NO. 12, 48
CAUGHRON, Rachel,
  161
CAULDER, Alexander,
  153, 156
CAULDERS MANOR, 74
CAULK, Isaac, 187
  Jacob, 7, 51, 161
  John, 7
  Oliver, 7, 84
  William, 173, 181
CAUSDEN, Jesse, 165

CAUSDON, Jesse, 7
CAUSEY, Stephen,
  73, 182
CAUSTILOE, Edward,
  7
CAVENDER, Lambert,
  182
CAYTON, Lambert,
  100
CEDAR BRANCH, 48
CEDAR GROVE, 12
CEETLY, Thomas, 182
CHALLON, James, 7
CHALMERS, James, 7,
  153, 182
CHAMBERLAINE, James
  Lloyd, 177
CHAMBERS, 16
  Benjamin, 155,
  180
  Charles, 81
  Edward, 173
  James, 173
CHAMPE, William,
  118, 125, 126
CHANCE, 1, 2, 3, 4,
  5, 7, 8, 9, 11,
  12, 13, 14, 15,
  16, 17, 18, 19,
  20, 21, 22, 23,
  26, 27, 28, 29,
  30, 31, 32, 34,
  35, 36, 37, 38,
  39, 40, 41, 48,
  74, 75
  Henry, 26
CHANCE ADDITION,
  19, 48
CHANCE ALIAS TULLYS
  CHOICE, 27
CHANCE LOTT, 38
CHANCE RESURVEYED,
  3, 8, 16, 34, 48
CHANCE, THE, 48
CHANCELLOR, Eliza,
  7
  William, 7
CHANDLER, Abel, 7
  Blackiston, 95,
  184
  Blackston, 76,
  184
  Michael, 7, 153
  Nath , 7

206   INHABITANTS OF KENT COUNTY, MARYLAND, 1637-1787

Nathaniel, 153
Nicholas, 7
Richard, 68
Thomas, 7, 48,
  95, 158, 159,
  160, 179, 186
William, 102
CHANDLER ADDITION,
  29
CHANDLERS, 7
CHANDLERS ADDITION,
  30, 48, 75
CHANLER, John, 147
  Thomas, 157
CHAPLAINE, Samuel,
  168
CHAPLIN, Phillip,
  99
  Samuel, 168, 184
CHAPMAN, Robert,
  143
CHAPPEL, John, 154
CHAPPELL, Henry,
  168
  James, 184
CHAPPLE, Ambrose,
  168
  John, 7, 179
  Joseph, 168
CHARLES, 35
CHARLES HIS LOTT,
  48
CHARLES LOT, 42
CHARLETON ALIAS
  QUEEN,
  CATHERINE, 48
CHARLTON, 40, 44
CHEAPSIDE, 36, 49
CHEDDLE, 31
CHEDLE, 10, 31, 49
CHEGWELL, 1, 25
CHENISH, 28, 49
CHESELDINE, 4
  Kenelm, 7
CHESELDYN, Kenelm,
  54
CHESTER GROVE, 21
CHESTER FIELD, 75
CHESTER GROVE, 8,
  13, 24, 27, 38,
  39, 49, 75
CHESTER GROVE , 12
CHESTER POINT, 36,
  39, 49, 75
CHESTERFIELD, 14,
  22
CHESTERFIELD
  RESURVEYED, 22,
  32
CHESTERTON, 12
CHESTON, James, 7
CHESTSERFIELD, 22
CHESTSERFIELD
  RESURVEYED, 49
CHETTLE, 34
CHEVINS, James, 7
CHEVY CHACE, 23
CHEVY CHASE, 75
CHEW, Samuel, 108
CHICHERLEY, Thomas,
  141
CHICHERLY, Thomas,
  145, 146
CHICKEN, Edward,
  146
  Martha, 146
CHIDDLE, 75
CHIDLEY, 16, 33
CHIGLY, 32
CHIGWELL, 1, 32, 75
CHILD HARBOUR, 5
CHILDS, Andrew, 181
CHILDS HARBOUR, 17,
  19, 22, 27, 30,
  34
CHILEW, Nicholas,
  168
CHIPCHASE, Thomas,
  181
CHISLEY, 75
CHITCHERLEY,
  Thomas, 133
CHIVERTON, Richard,
  119
CHIZWELL, 49
CHOAPE, Joseph, 142
CHOICE, 75
CHOICE RESURVEYED,
  75
CHOYCE PURCHASE, 30
CHRISFIELD,
  Absolum, 166
  Rosamond, 7
CHRIST BEGINNING,
  75
CHRISTFIELD,
  Absolom, 188
CHRISTIAN, Thomas,
  7, 156
CHRISTIANS
  ADDITION, 7
CHRISTIN, Lawrence,
  49
CHRISTINS ADDITION,
  49
CHRISTOPHER, 142
CHRISTOPHERS
  BEGINNING, 15,
  16, 21, 29, 38,
  49
CHUBB, Honor, 168
  Horius, 168
  John, 168
CHURCH, Chester P.
  E., 152
  Samuel, 7, 49,
  163
  Thomas, 7
CHURCH HILL, 49
CHURCH WARDEN NECK,
  2, 38
CHURCH WARDENS
  NECK, 17, 32, 75
CHURCHES LOTT, 49
CHURCHILL, Jane,
  168
CHURCHS CHANCE, 49
CHURCHS LOTTS NO.
  18 AND 19, 49
CHURCHS LOTTS NOS.
  106 AND 107, 49
CHURCHWARDEN NECK,
  49
CLAIBORNE, William,
  103
CLAPHAM, William,
  104
CLAPP, William, 168
CLARE, John, 7
CLARK, Alexander,
  67
  Dennis, 49
  Elijah, 180
  Elisha, 180
  George, 7, 180
  Gideon, 72
  Henry, 7, 63, 86,
  163, 164
  James, 180, 183
  Jesse, 180
  John, 64, 86,
  157, 165, 180,

INDEX 207

181
Martha, 7
Mary, 7, 168
Murtie June, 179
Nathaniel, 188
Robert, 7
Sarah, 7
William, 49, 86, 152, 180, 187
CLARKE, Dennis, 7, 49
Gideon, 188
Gilbert, 58
Henry, 171
Joseph, 168
Joshua, 184
Richard, 108
Robert, 101, 102
William, 7, 171
CLARKS ADDITION, 7, 49
CLARKS CONVENIENCE, 5, 49
CLARKS CONVENIENCY, 7, 24
CLARKS CONVENIENCY RESURVEYED, 49
CLARKS NEGLECT, 49
CLARKSON, Levinus, 97
CLATON, John, 183
CLAXSTON, Edd, 101
Edward, 111
CLAY, Elizabeth, 110, 116
Henery, 104, 107, 109, 110
Henrery, 112
Henry, 101, 104, 116, 119, 120, 125
Thomas, 7
CLAYBORNE, William, 112
CLAYE, Henery, 105
CLAYPOLE, George, 155
James, 7
John, 154
Rebecca, 155
CLAYPOOLE, James, 97, 190, 191
John, 154
CLAYS PARK, 30

CLAYTON, 25, 49
Edward, 171
Isaac, 166
Jacob, 166
James, 85
John, 7, 163
Joseph, 166
William, 85
CLAYTON AND BOWDEYS FOLLY, 16
CLEAVER, John, 7
William, 7
CLEAVER, JOHN, JR., 7
CLEAVES, Benjamin, 79, 186
Nathan, 186
Nathaniel, 7
CLEGATT, Thomas, 54
CLEMANS, Edward, 100
John, 143
CLEMENS, John, 143
CLEMENTS, Jane, 168
S. Eugene, 171
CLEMONS, John, 141
CLERK, Henry, 166
John, 166
CLEVER, Benjamin, 181
William, 7
CLIFTON, 10, 49, 75
CLOAK, George, 7
John, 7, 49
CLOAKE, Morris, 7
CLOAKS ADDITION, 49
CLOBE, John and Co., 8
CLOCKE, Jane, 168
CLOCKER, Danie, 141
CLOKE, Maurice, 62
CLOTHIER, Lewis, 8
Mary, 158
Robert Napp, 8
CLOUDS, Nicholas, 8
CLOUDS HERMITAGE, 8
CLOUDS RANGE, 8
CLOUGHTON, James, 45
CLOVER PATCH, 49
COALTER, Michael, 8
COARDING, Edward, 8
COCK HALL, 8
COCK OF THE GAME,

8, 12, 17, 19, 29, 35, 36, 40, 49, 75
COCKEY, John, 8, 92
Richard, 8
COCKOLDS POINT, 4
COCKRELL, Abraham, 8
COCKS, Richard, 168
COCKSTALL, 6, 75
CODD, St. Ledger, 46, 176
St. Leger, 8, 68, 150, 151, 152, 175, 178
COFEY, Darby, 10
COFFIN, 18, 40, 41, 49, 75
Abraham, 69
COKESTALLE, 49
COLCHESTER, 10, 49
COLCHESTER RESURVEYED, 49
COLE, Benjamin, 8, 84, 187
Elizabeth, 77
George, 8, 161, 187
John, 8, 157, 171
Maria, 168
Peter, 8, 52, 63, 159, 160
Richard, 8
Thomas, 108, 137, 143
Ulalia, 168
William, 97
COLECHESTER, 49, 75
COLEMAN, Charles, 183
COLES, Elizabeth, 168
Richard, 168
COLGAN, John, 186
COLL, Thomas, 107, 108
COLLEMAN, William, 128
COLLENS, Thomas, 131
COLLETON, 49
COLLETT, John, 48, 49
COLLINS,

208 INHABITANTS OF KENT COUNTY, MARYLAND, 1637-1787

Bartholomew, 8
Francis, 8
Jeremiah, 172
John, 168, 173
Thomas, 8, 48,
  62, 132, 133,
  183
Walter, 168
William, 8, 125,
  179, 184, 186
COLLIPRIEST, John,
  168
COLLISON, George,
  128
COLLYER, James, 133
COLSY, Richard, 186
COMB HILL, 13, 49
COMB WHITTEN, 15,
  24, 26, 27, 29,
  35, 38
COMB WHITTON, 9,
  21, 33, 75
COMBE, Thomas, 168
  William, 168
COMEGEY, William,
  64
COMEGIE, William,
  64
COMEGIES, William,
  8
COMEGIES CHANCE, 16
COMEGIES FANCY, 4
COMEGYS, A., 160
  Abraham, 186
  Alphonso, 8, 184
  Ann, 93, 160
  Barton, 8
  Bartus, 93, 165
  Benjamin, 75, 93
  C., 162
  C. C., 164
  Charity, 164
  Cornalus, 166,
    167
  Cornelius, 8, 44,
    49, 50, 54, 55,
    58, 59, 61, 65,
    66, 69, 70, 88,
    92, 93, 141,
    144, 146, 147,
    149, 158, 163,
    164, 172, 187
  Edward, 8, 48,
    49, 58, 89, 159,
    164, 180, 187
  Edward, Jr., 8
  Henry, 163, 164
  Jacob, 74, 75,
    89, 164, 165
  Jesse, 89, 180
  John, 8, 57, 93,
    159, 160, 165,
    185
  Jonathan, 78, 97,
    182
  Mr., 145
  Nathaniel, 74,
    77, 85, 153,
    166, 187
  Samuel, 82, 87,
    166, 185, 191
  William, 8, 42,
    43, 44, 46, 47,
    48, 49, 51, 52,
    58, 59, 64, 67,
    69, 156, 157,
    158, 159, 160,
    162, 163, 164,
    184
COMEGYS CHOICE, 37,
  49
COMEGYS DELIGHT, 49
COMEGYS FANCY, 1,
  15, 26, 31
COMEGYS FARM, 8, 75
COMEGYS FARM
  ADDITION, 9, 33,
  39, 49
  RESURVEYED, 49
COMEGYS FARME, 49
COMEGYS NEGLECT, 49
COMEGYS RESURVEY,
  49, 75
COMENS, Elizabeth,
  111
COMING, Sarah, 115
COMINGS, Edward
  Mr., 111
COMINGS, Sarah, 111
COMINGS, Elizabeth,
  111
COMMEGYS, John, 69
COMMINS, Edward,
  100
  Elesabeth, 127
  Elizabeth, 63
CONAWAY, Benjamin,
  183
CONCLUSION, 34, 49
CONDEN, Jesse, 96
  Joseph, 181
CONDON, Joseph, 155
CONEY WAARREN, 33
CONEY WARREN, 6,
  15, 17, 19, 21,
  29, 37, 40
CONEYWARREN, 13
CONIER, Mr., 104,
  106
  Philip, 100, 101,
    104, 178
  Phillip, 103, 114
CONITT, John, 103
CONJUNCT, 7, 27, 49
  George, 22
CONJUNCTION, 17
CONJUNTION, 6
CONLIFFE, Foster,
  69
CONNANT, Moses, 8
CONNELL, Abraham,
  165
CONNER, John, 52
  Mary, 125, 128,
    129
  Mr., 111, 125
  Mrs., 125, 127
  Philip, 100, 101,
    175, 178
  Phillip, 58, 70,
    109, 110, 112,
    116, 117, 118,
    120, 131
  Phillipe, 127
  Sarah, 59
  Timothy, 173
CONNERWEY,
  Benjamin, 172
CONNIER, Philip,
  108
  Phillip, 106, 116
CONNOR, George, 172
  John, 8
  Philip, 71
  Temperance, 168
  William, 96
CONNWAY, Cornelius,
  181
CONNY WARRN, 49
CONQUEST, 28
CONSTABLE, Robert,
  152, 155

CONTEST, THE, 49
CONTY, Mitchell, 137
COOK, Elizabeth, 8
  Robert, 168
  William, 168
COOKE, Andrew, 68
  Giles, 160
  William, 8
COOKEMAN, Rice, 141
COOLE, Benjamin, 43
COOLEY, Anne, 8
  Daniell, 47
  Nathaniel, 8
  Richard, 8
COOLLE, Edward, 112
COOP, John, 148
COOPER, Catherine, 130
  George, 8
  Hannah, 93
  Hezekiah, 8, 44, 93, 151, 154
  James, 172
  John, 8, 52, 53, 93, 132, 133, 134, 136, 139, 140, 142, 144, 148, 192
  Martha, 93
  Mary, 93
  Peregrine, 63, 88, 89, 93, 156
  Thomas, 78, 140, 147, 159
COOPERS FOLLY, 8, 75
COOPERS HILL, 49
COOTS, Hercules, 8
COPEDGE, Ed, 117
  Edward, 110, 135
  Elizabeth, 135
  John, 135
  Phillip, 135
  Sarah, 135
COPPAGE, Edd, 116
  Edward, 116, 122
  Elizabeth, 133
COPPEDGE, Edward, 101, 102
COPPER, Charles, 8, 59, 83, 92, 181
  George, 8, 71, 88, 92

Isac, 186
James, 172, 183
Joseph, 183
Norris, 181
Philip, 83, 92
William, 9, 79, 181
COPPIDGE, Edward, 147
  John, 147
  Phillip, 147
CORAM, Elizabeth, 168
CORHAM, Thomas, 168
CORK, Isaac, 187
  Richard, 168
CORNALUS, Daniel, 166
CORNELIOUS, William, 9
CORNELIUS, Daniel, 9, 79, 187
  George, 185
  Isaac, 171
CORNELIUS COMEGYS LAND, 50
CORNELIUS FORK, 50
CORNELIUS FORTH, 50
CORNEWALLEYS, Thomas, 50, 70
CORNEWALLEYS CHOICE, 50
CORNUWHITTON, 75
CORNWALLEYS CHOICE, 2
CORNWALLEYS CHOYCE, 6
CORNWALLIS, 27, 75
CORNWALLIS CHANCE, 16
CORNWALLIS CHOICE, 2, 5, 7, 8, 21, 23, 25, 27, 32, 75
CORNWALLIS'S CHOICE, 2
CORNWALLS CHOICE, 5
CORSE, Barney, 181
  Ceazer, 185
  David, 9
  James, 54, 84, 93, 184, 185
  Jno., 159
  John, 51, 77, 80,

82, 84, 182
  Michael, 74, 75, 79, 152, 185
  Thomas, 95, 182, 187
  Thomas Hynson, 159
CORSES MEADOW, 75
CORSES NEGLECT, 50
COSDEN, Ann, 96
  Bathsheba, 93
  Elizabeth, 93, 97
  Jeremiah, 93, 97
  Jesse, 160, 165, 172, 185, 191
  John, 96, 166, 172, 187
  Joseph, 155
  Mary, 96
COSDON, Ann, 96
  Mary, 96
COSENS, Edward, 50
COSENS LOTT, 50
COSTER, Richard, 9
COSTILLO, Ebenezer, 172
COSTLEY, John, 181
COSTLY, Thomas, 182
COUDON, Joseph, 155
COULTER, Michael, 9
COURS, William, 153
COURSE, Barna..., 153
  Barney, 9
  David, 9
  James, 9
  John, 9, 47, 123, 164, 165
  Michael, 9
  Nathaniel, 153
  William, 179
COURSES MEADOW, 9, 22
COURSES MEADOWS, 20
COURSEY, Henery, 133, 134
  Henry, 130, 137, 138, 147
  James, 50
  John, 48, 101, 122, 125, 126
  Katheren, 129
  Mr., 128
  William, 9, 50,

70, 125, 128, 178
COURSEYS MEADOW, 9
COURSEYS MEADOWS, 50
COURSEYS NECK, 50
COURSY, James, 148
W., 159
COURTTIOUR, Will, 112
COUTTS, Hercules, 9
Herculon, 162
COUZENS CHANCE, 12
COUZENS LOTT, 12
COVE, 5, 11, 18, 75
William, 9
COVE TRACT, 5, 11, 18, 76
COVE TRACT, THE, 50
COVE, THE, 50
COVEN, 75
COVENT, 75
COVENT GARDEN, 1, 9, 25, 29, 35, 50
COVENTON, Jeremiah, 50
Nehemiah, 163
COVENTRY, 17, 23, 50, 75, 76
Jonathan, 50
COVENTRY MARSH, 9, 50
COVINGTON, James, 181
Jeremy, 9
Nathaniel, 166
Peter, 186
Samuel, 9
Thomas, 9, 150, 175, 181
COWARDEN, Abraham, 9, 50
John, 80, 182
Susannah, 96, 98
Thomas, 9
William, 153
COWARDEN FARM, 50
COWARDIN, William, 151
COWARDINE, William, 9
COWARDING, William (Heirs), 78

COWDER, Joseph, 155
COWELL, Edward, 138
COWLEE, James, 138
COWLEYS CALF PASTURE, 50
COWRSEY, Henry, 116
John, 115, 116, 117, 119, 120, 121, 122
COWRSY, John, 111
COX, Elizabeth, 112
Francis, 111
Gabriell, 142
Isaac, 91
John, 9
Mistiris, 112
Thomas, 97
Will, 112
William, 9, 58
COX HALL, 6
COX STATE, 38
COXE, Edward, 101
COX'S HALL, 40
COX'S STALE, 13
COXS STALE, 3
COXSTALL, 1, 6
COXSTALL , 6
COZENS, Edward, 9, 50
COZENS CHANCE, 9, 50
CRABBIN, Alexander, 9
William, 183
William Hynson, 181
CRABIN, William, 92
CRACKER, Elizabeth, 168
CRACKNELL, John, 9
Thomas, 9
CRAGG, Heneri, 141
CRAIG, John, 179
CRAIGE, George, 9
CRAIN, Thomas, 155
CRANBERRY NECK, 11, 18, 76
CRANE, David, 9, 76, 89, 95, 154, 166, 172, 182, 190
Thomas, 9
William, 9
CRANEY NECK, 50

CRANY NECKE, 122
CRAPP, Mary, 168
CRAWFORD, Frances, 151
CRAWLY, Cornelius, 9
CRAY, Ebenezer, 99
John, 187
CREW, Edward, 9, 74, 77, 78, 186
John, 9, 153, 159, 186
Jonas, 9, 153, 162, 164, 165
Mary, 9
Thomas, 190
CRIPES, Elezabeth, 124
CRISFIELD, Phil, 9
Rosamond, 9
CROCKER, Elizabeth, 168
CROMWELL, Ann, 117
Gershon, 112
Gertian, 117
Rebecka, 117
CROSBY, Thomas, 9, 58
CROSCOMB, Ezekiel, 138
CROSCOMBE, Ezekiel, 140
Ezekiell, 134
CROSCOMBIES, Ann, 168
CROSLEY, Thomas, 181
CROSSE, William, 140, 141
CROSSING, William, 168
CROUCH, George, 101, 102, 111, 116
James, 82, 181
John, 50
Nehemiah, 156, 182
Richard, 9
Samuel, 181, 183
Wedge, 9, 70
William, 9
CROUCHES ADDITION, 9

CROUCHS ADDITION,
    50
CROUTCH, George,
    100, 101, 105,
    106, 109
  Marie, 104, 106
  Mary, 105
  Marye, 106
  Moll, 107
CROW, Isaac, 9
  Thomas, 9, 76,
    84, 181
  William, 50, 60,
    150
CROWE, Edward, 9
  William, 9
CROWES ADDITION, 50
CROWLEY, Daniel, 10
CROWS ADDITION, 9,
    33, 76
CROWS CHANCE, 9,
    19, 50, 76
CROWS PLANTATION, 9
CRUCKSHANK, Mary,
    10
  Robert, 10, 189
CRUDGENTON, Mary,
    95
CRUE, Edward, 157
CRUFIELD, Absalom,
    10
CRUICKSHANK,
  Elizabeth, 10
  James, 10
  Mary, 10
CRUIKSHANK, Mary,
    81
  Robert, 85, 180,
    189
CRUIKSHANKS,
  Elizabeth, 153
  Mary, 153
  Miss, 156
  Robert, 155
CRUMWELL, Gershon,
    112
CRUNCHINGTON, Mary,
    95
CRY, John, 171
CUCKHOLDS HOPE, 76
CUCKHOLDS POINT, 50
CUCKOLD HOPE, 15
CUCKOLDS HOPE, 15,
    25, 50

CULBERT, John, 72,
    183
CULLEY, Henry, 10
CULLUMS, James, 135
CULLY, James, 10
CULVER, Francis B.,
    179, 184
CUM WITTON, 50
CUMBERLAND, 11, 50
CUMMINS, Phillip,
    101
CUNLIFF, Forster,
    159
  Foster, 160
CUNLIFFE, Foster,
    10
CUNNEY WARREN, 76
CUNNINGHAM, Daniel,
    10, 162
  David, 186
  Hugh, 10
CURER, John, 148
CURLETT, Joseph,
    82, 86
CURRER, John, 131,
    134, 136, 137,
    138, 142, 149
  Thomas, 146
  William, 134,
    138, 141
CURREY, Thomas, 133
CURRY, Henry, 180
  John, 98, 181
  Robert, 10, 89
CURTAIN, John, 172
CURTIS, Edmund, 103
  Mark, 168

-D-
DAB, John, 133
DABB, Annikin, 147
  Hannah, 133
  John, 117, 118,
    120, 122, 125,
    131, 132, 133,
    134, 136, 137,
    138, 140, 141,
    145, 147
  Lettis, 147
  Sarah, 115, 117,
    118, 132
DABBS, John, 105,
    107
  Mr., 144

DABES, John, 111
DADMAN, Margarett,
    10
DAILY, John, 182
DALE, Thomas, 51
DALE , 4
DALE TOWN, 5, 11,
    28, 36, 50
DALES TOWN, 27
DALLAMS FOLLY
  RESURVEYED, 50
DALLINGTON, 6, 10,
    31, 50, 76
DAMSON POINT, 41
DAMSONS POINT, 50
DANDY, John, 111
DANIEL & JOSEPHS
  DISAPPOINTMENT,
    12, 50
DANIELS
  DISAPPOINTMENT,
    50
DANIELS
  DISAPPOINTMENT
  RESURVD, 50
DANIELS
  DISAPPOINTMENTS,
    76
DANNING, John, 42
DANSKIN, Alexander,
    184
DARACH, James, 97
DARBY, 34, 50, 76
  John, 144, 145,
    146, 148
  Mr., 144
DARBYS DESIRE, 33,
    50
DARDEN, Stephen, 10
DARDON, James, 131
DARE, William, 10,
    69
DARINGTON, Thomas,
    10
DARLINGTON, 76
DARNALL, 23
  John, 50
DARNALLS FARM, 10,
    23, 24
DARNALLS FARME, 50
DARNALLS LOT, 34
DARNALLS LOTT, 26,
    50
DARNALS FARM, 20

DARNELL, John, 10
DARNELLS FARM, 28, 29, 38, 76
DARRACK, Thomas, 10
DARRINGTON, James, 181
DARVALL, William, 145
DAUES, Mr., 113
DAUGHERTY, Robert, 186
  Walter, 10
  William, 182
DAUHERTY, William, 172
DAVENPORT,
  Humphrey, 55, 68
  Joseph, 83
DAVID, John, 145, 149
  Samuel, 171
  William, 171
DAVID, 120
DAVIES, William, 114, 115
DAVIS, Daniel, 182
  David, 80, 85, 150, 152, 153, 156, 186
  Edward, 180
  Elizabeth, 10
  Henry, 10
  James, 10
  John, 10, 45, 50, 137, 142, 173, 179, 183
  Mary, 10, 153
  Mr., 113
  Phil., 165
  Philip, 10, 73, 80, 95, 151, 153, 155, 181, 190
  Phillip, 50, 51, 166
  Richard, 10, 50, 69
  Robert, 181
  Samuel, 10, 50, 51, 52, 72, 73, 76, 77, 158, 164, 165, 190, 191
  Thomas, 175
  Will, 114
  William, 10, 46, 129, 142, 143, 145, 146, 149, 156, 183
DAVIS CHANCE, 36
DAVIS TRED, 76
DAVIS TRIANGLE, 76
DAVIS TRYANGLE, 41
DAVISE, William, 125
DAVIS'S ADDITION, 10, 36, 50
DAVIS'S CHANCE, 50
DAVIS'S DESIRE, 50
DAVIS'S PART OF HELLENS, ADVENTURE, 50
ADVENTURE RESURVEYED, 50
DAVIS'S TRIANGLE, 50
DAVY, George, 168
  Honore, 168
  Lewis, 145
DAWSON, Isaac, 187
  James, 10
  John, 10
  Solomon, 181
  William, 50, 88, 96, 152, 183, 186
DAWSONS CHANCE, 50
DAY, John, 10, 68, 71, 84, 89, 111, 171, 187, 191
  Mathias, 10, 44, 157
  Matthias, 59
DAYLEY, Elisha, 185
DE CONTY, Mitchell, 141
DE LA ROACH,
  Charles, 144, 148
  Elizabeth, 148
DE LA ROCH,
  Charles, 141, 142
DEABNAM, Benjamin, 96
DEACON, Thomas, 10
DEADMAN, Margaret, 10
DEAL, Elias, 85, 186
  John, 186
DEAL TOWN, 76
DEAN, 76
  Ann, 77, 79, 85, 90, 91, 96, 97
  John, 101
  Matthew, 181
  William, 10
DEANE, George, 101
  John, 101
  William, 50
DEANES ADVENTURE, 50
DEANES RELIEFE, 50
DEANS ADVENTURE, 4, 21, 25, 26, 31, 76
DEANS RELIEFE, 26
DEAR, John, 110
DEARAN, James, 160, 163
DEARBY, 50
DEARE, Christian, 105, 115, 132
  George, 137, 138
  John, 104, 105, 106, 107, 108, 109, 110, 111, 112, 113, 132, 138
DEATONS TRACT, 76
DEAVENISH, John, 10
  Robert, 10
DEAVER, Richard, 127, 128
DEBRULA, William, 10
DEBRULER, Peter, 51
  William, 157
DEBTFORD, 35
DECONTIE, Mitchell, 136
DECONTY, Mitchell, 140
DECOUNTY, Michaell, 142
DECOURCY, Edward, 171
DEDMAN, Benjamin, 183
DEE, James, 132
DEEARE, Christian,

INDEX 213

129
John, 129
DEER, John, 50, 63
DEER PARK, 3, 8, 23, 34, 41, 76
DEER PARK, THE, 50
DEERBY, 50
DEERE, Christian, 127
Eleasabeth, 127
Elesabeth, 126
George, 127
John, 115, 116, 117, 118, 119, 121, 122, 127
DEERUM, 34, 50
DEFORD, Charles, 188
Joseph, 188
DEIGHTON, John, 181
DEINBEIGH, 35
DELAHUNTY, Daniel, 10
Mordica, 180
Thomas, 180
DELAP, Abraham, 52
DELAY, 51
DELAY RESURVEYED, 51
DELL, Richard, 193
DELLAHUNTE, William, 96
DELLINS FANCY, 76
DEMBEY, 76
DEMBY, 76
Richard, 173
DEMPSTER, John, 11
DENBBY RESURVEYED, 21
DENBEIGH, 1
DENBIGH, 1, 22, 38, 76
DENBIGH RESURVEYED, 21
DENBY, 1, 12, 21, 27, 51
DENBYE, 5, 21, 30
DENING, George, 88
Martha, 82
Stephen, 82
DENNAN, George, 187
DENNES, William, 142
DENNEY, Christopher, 139, 141
DENNING, Elisabeth, 158
George, 11, 166
John, 11, 43, 61, 67
Jonas, 187
Michael, 11
Nicholas, 187
Stephen, 58, 161, 187
DENNIS, William, 142
DENNISON, William, 180
DENNY, Christopher, 133, 134
Rebecka, 133
Stephen, 62
DENTON, 18
DEPARNEY, Rebecca, 161
DEPFORD, 76
DEPRIVED MISCHIEF, 30, 51, 76
DEPTFORD, 18, 51
DERBY, 23
DERRICK, John, 11, 61
DERRINGTON, Thomas, 60
DEVANPORT, Jonathan, 187
Joseph, 187
DEVER, John, 182
DEVO, John, 168
DEW, John, 180
Thomas, 183
DIAL, William, 183
DICAS, Ann, 11
William, 11
DICKERSON, Henry, 11
DICKES, Thomas, 113, 118, 121, 122
DICKEY, John, 181
DICKS CHANCE, 39, 51
DICKSON, Henry, 164
DIGGLE, Richard, 168
DIGLE, Richard, 168
DIKES, Thomas, 113, 114
DILIGENCE, 51
DILL, Richard, 193
Stephen, 193
DILLEN, Arther, 156
Arthur, 182
DINGLE, William, 168
DINING, John, 157
DINING ROOM, 3, 31
John, 7
DINING ROOM, THE, 51
DINKS, Henry, 168
DINSON, John, 183
DISAPPOINTMENT, THE, 51
DISCOVERY, 38, 51
DISPUTE, 51
DIVISION, 3
DIXON, Henry, 11, 162
John, 11, 186
William, 11, 50
DIXONS GIFT, 18
DIXSON, Henry, 165
John, 184
William, 184
DMORE, 11, 13
DOBB, Ann, 126
Elesabeth, 123
Joane, 123
John, 103, 113, 123, 131
DOBBES, John, 128
DOBBS, Ann, 124
John, 124, 131, 142, 143
DOBES, John, 128, 129
DOBS, John, 123
DOCTOR SMYTH'S LOT, 51
DODD, Ezekiel, 168
DODSON, William, 91
DOE NECK, 6, 7, 21, 31, 51, 76
DOILE, John, 11
DOLLES, John, 187
William, 187
DOLLIS, Mary, 83
Robert, 11
DOLVIN, Richard,

173
DONALDSON, John,
  11, 158, 162,
  165
DONBEY, 51
DONK, John, 58
DONN, Robert, 103
DONNALSON, John,
  165
DONNOWIN, Daniel,
  173
DOOB, Ann, 127
DOOLEY, Daniel, 55
  Elizabeth, 55
DORAN, James, 11,
  159
DOUBLE PURCHASE, 51
DOUCH, Hugh, 51
DOUCHERS FOLLY, 40
DOUCHES FOLLY, 51,
  76
DOUGHARTY, Walter,
  11
DOUGLAS, George, 11
DOUNE, William, 43
DOVE, Mark, 158
DOVIN, James, 181
DOW NECK, 15
DOWDALL, John, 51
  Richard, 11
DOWDALLS FANCY, 11,
  51
DOWDALS FANCY, 36
DOWDALS FARM, 36
DOWES, Anne, 168
DOWLAND, Amy, 136
  Elizabeth, 136
  William, 136,
  137, 149
DOWLING, William,
  180
DOWN DALE, 17, 27,
  76
DOWN DATE, 17
DOWN RANGE, 76
DOWNE, Robert, 100
DOWNES, Bridgett,
  130, 131
  Henery, 133
  Henry, 130, 131,
  137, 138, 139,
  141
DOWNS, William, 11,
  165

DOWRSEY, John, 116
DRACUTE, 76, 77
DRATON, 19
DRAW NEAR, 51, 77
DRAW NECK, 33
DRAWNEAR, 10
DRAYCOAT, 4, 7, 30
DRAYCOTT, 29, 30,
  36
DRAYTON, 3, 7, 9,
  15, 18, 21, 24,
  25, 29, 30, 31,
  35, 37, 38, 51,
  77
  Little Drayton, 1
DRAYTON RESURVEYED,
  29, 77
DRAYTON, ALFORDS
  PART OF, 51
DRAYTON, REASONS
  PART OF, 51
DRAYWAL, 9
DRECUTE, 51
DROAN, Ann, 97
DROOMGOULD, Lowl.,
  165
DRUGAN, Ann, 11
  Edward, 48, 51,
  61
  Par., 165
  Patrick, 50
  Philip, 74, 153
  Phillip, 11, 186
  Thomas, 186
  William, 182, 186
DRUGANS DELIGHT, 51
DRUGANS DISCOVER,
  77
DRUGANS LOT NUMBER
  37, 51
DRUGANS LOTT, 11,
  51
DRUGANS LOTTS NOS.
  18 AND 19, 51
DRUGANS MISTAKE, 51
DRUGANS RAMBLE, 51
DRUGGAN, Edward, 11
DRUMGOLD, Lowl.,
  165
DRUMMOND, William,
  181
DRURY, William, 102
DUBLIN, 4, 8, 23,
  51, 77

DUBLIN RESURVEYED,
  7, 51
DUCK PYE, 18, 51
DUFEY, Daniel, 11
DUFFY, Daniel, 151
DUGAN, William,
  173, 182, 186
DUGGANS DELIGHT, 15
DULANEY, Daniel,
  76, 77, 98
  Dennis, 154, 165
  Hannah, 98
  Lloyd, 153
DULANY, Daniel, 11,
  86, 95
  Dannis, 163
  Dennis, 11, 64,
  162, 164
  Edmond, 11
  Lloyd, 11
  Priscilla, 11
DULEANS FOLLY, 10
DULEE, Samuel, 185
DULLAMS FOLLY, 9,
  77
DULLEANS FOLLY, 10,
  16, 51
DULLEHUNTER,
  William, 154
DULLIANS FOLLY, 10
DULLTOWN, 3
DULTANS FOLLY, 51
DUNCAN, George, 11,
  51, 180
  Joseph, 11
DUNCANS FOLLY, 6, 7
DUNCANS PART OF
  WORTH'S FOLLY,
  51
DUNCANS TOY, 41
DUNDALE, 51
DUNDEE, 51
DUNGANNON, 23, 51
DUNK, Thomas, 183
DUNKAN, James, 154
  William, 184
DUNKIN, James, 74,
  93, 182
  John, 11
  William, 173
DUNN, Alice, 144
  Ann, 11
  Anthony, 172
  Daraius, 11

INDEX 215

Darius, 73, 181
Ezekiah, 191
Hezekiah, 51, 72,
 73, 74, 77, 81,
 181
Hezikiah, 11
James, 11, 47, 172,
 180, 181, 191
James (heirs), 80
James Brown, 80,
 87, 89, 177
Joan, 144, 148
Joane, 123
Johan, 148
John, 11
Jone, 103
Mr., 144
Pasco, 132
Rebecka, 123
Robert, 11, 64,
 72, 100, 101,
 110, 111, 116,
 123, 132, 133,
 134, 136, 137,
 138, 139, 140,
 143, 144, 148,
 149, 150, 151,
 175, 176, 179,
 181
Shusana, 123
William, 11, 97,
 151, 181
DUNNAHA, John, 11
DUNNE, Robert, 103,
 105, 108
 William, 105
DUNNICOMBE, Henry,
 168
DUNNS DISCOVERY,
 51, 77
DUNNS FOLLY, 11,
 41, 51
DUNNS HAZARD, 138
DUNSTABLE, 51
DURAND, William,
 103
DURBY, 23
DURBY AND SMYTHBY,
 77
DURDING, Joseph, 11
DURETY, James, 92
DURITY, Jams, 187
DUTCHES FOLLY, 10
DUYER, Joseph, 185

DWIER, John, 84
DWIRE, John, 72,
 80, 81, 153
DWYER, James, 97
 Jno., 151
 John, 11, 51, 72,
 80, 81, 84, 97,
 151
DWYERS DESIRE, 11,
 51
DYER, Benjamin, 168
 Edward, 11
 Nathaniel, 180
 Thomas, 158
DYERS, James, 168

-E-
EADES, Henry, 12
 Samuel, 171
EADESS, Samuel, 172
EADS, Henry, 180
 James, 180
 John, 180
 Jonathan, 180
EAGLES NEST, 37
EAGLES NEST, THE,
 51
EALY, Jo:, 112
EARES, Nan, 105
EARLE, Dennis, 77,
 186
 Henry, 12
 John, 12, 60
 Joseph, 174, 176,
 177, 188
 Michael, 48
EARLEY, William, 12
EARLEYS BEGINNING,
 42
EARLYS BEGINNING,
 12
EAST, Henery, 111
EAST HUNTINGTON, 1,
 4, 25, 51, 77
EAST NECK ISLAND,
 LAND IN, 5
EASTER NECK, John,
 11
EASTERN ISLAND,
 THE, 51
EASTERN NECK, 13,
 15, 16
EASTERN NECK, THE,
 51

EASTERNNECK, 77
EATON, Jeremiah,
 140, 142, 143,
 144
 Jeremuah, 140
 Jeremyah, 137
EAVANS, Thomas,
 144, 145, 148
EAVENS, Robert, 164
EBDON, Mr., 111
EBES, Edward, 101
ECCLEESTON, John,
 76
ECCLESTON, John,
 81, 86, 87, 88,
 93, 189
ECLESTON, John, 153
EDDY, Richard, 168
EDENBURGH, 23
EDGERTON, Charles,
 137, 139
EDINBURGH, 38, 52,
 77
EDMONDSON, John, 12,
 47, 61, 62, 70
EDSELL, Samuel, 118
 Samuell, 119
EDWARD, Thomas, 183
EDWARDS, Samuel,
 168
EDWIN, William, 52
EDWINS ADDITION, 4,
 52
EDWINS AFFRONT, 52
EDWINS REST, 5, 12
EFFIELD, John, 186
EGELSTON, John, 162
EGLAN, Robert, 168
EGLON, John, 137
 Robert, 168
ELBERT, John, 184
ELBON, Reubin, 173
 William, 173
ELBORNE, James, 186
ELBURN, William,
 183
ELDES, Mathias, 168
ELDRIDGE,
 Elisabeth, 158
ELENORS DELIGHT, 41
ELES, Eliz, 115
 Elizabeth, 115
ELIAS AND JAMES
 RINGGOLDS PART

OF HUNTINGFIELD
Resurv, 52
ELINERS DELIGHT, 3
ELINOR, Andrew, 114
  Annecke, 114
ELINORS DELIGHT, 3,
  52
ELIONERS DELIGHT,
  33
ELIOT, William,
  103, 104, 106
ELIOTT, William,
  104
ELISE, John, 105
ELISSE, Jno., 105
  John, 105
ELLENOR, Andrew,
  110, 127
ELLEOTT, William,
  103
ELLEOYET, Mr., 112
  William, 112
ELLERS, Benjamin,
  12, 58
ELLES, Benjamin,
  123
  Jo, 109
  John, 123, 129
ELLETT, Robert, 168
ELLEYEOTT, William,
  133
ELLEYET, Will, 109
ELLEYOTT, William,
  103
ELLIOT, William,
  101, 116, 120
ELLIOTT, Edward, 12
  John, 181
  Vincent, 49
  William, 52, 128,
  139
ELLIOTTS CHOICE, 52
ELLIS, Benjamin,
  12, 52, 54, 63,
  66
  John, 12, 52,
  113, 116, 139,
  148
  Joseph, 168
  Sarah, 115
  Thomas, 75, 77,
  100
  William, 12, 52,
  61, 63, 71, 84

ELLIS CHANCE, 6,
  12, 14, 34
ELLIS FARM, 1
ELLIS HIS CHANCE,
  52
ELLIS INDUSTRY, 12,
  38, 77
ELLISON, John, 142
ELLISS, Thomas, 188
  William, 188
ELLIS'S CHANCE, 4,
  7, 8, 34
ELLIS'S DELIGHT, 52
ELLIS'S FARM, 5, 52
ELLIS'S INDUSTRY,
  3, 4, 52
ELLIS'S INDUSTRY
  RESURVEYED, 52
ELLIS'S RAMBLE, 52
ELLITH, William,
  188
ELLIYOTT, William,
  137
ELLOTT, Robert, 168
ELLSON, William,
  143
ELME, William, 45
ELMES, William, 12
ELMS, William, 156
EMBLETON, William,
  155
EMMITT, Nathaniel,
  168
EMORY, Arthur, 12,
  73
EMSSON, Thomas, 188
ENDEAVOR, 8, 38, 77
ENDEAVOUR, 27, 38,
  77
ENDEAVOUR, THE, 52
ENGLAND, Elizabeth,
  168
  Isaac, 12
  Joseph, 12
ENGLESBY, Joseph,
  124, 137
ENGRAM, Edward, 182
ENLOES, John, 183
ENNALLS, Joseph, 12
  William, 12, 178
EPLATT, Francis,
  168
ERBERY, Thomas, 48
ERECKSEN, John, 110

ERECKSON,
  Elizabeth, 129
  John, 110, 129,
  130, 131, 132,
  142, 143
ERECSON, John, 128
ERICKESON, Thomas,
  122
ERICKSON, Johen,
  107
  Johkn, 120
  John, 68, 105,
  107, 114, 121,
  122
  Jokhn, 121
  Sarah, 115
ERRECKSON,
  Elizabeth, 144
  John, 134, 144,
  147, 148, 149
  Mathew, 148
  Matthew, 147, 149
ERRICKSON, John,
  101
ESSETER, Abraham,
  144
ESSEX, 2, 4, 10,
  28, 52, 77
EUNICK, John, 89,
  94, 156
EUNOCK, John, 186
EVANS, Edward, 168
  Evan, 12
  Henry, 12, 161
  James, 181
  John, 61
  Sarah, 12
  Thomas, 142, 147
  William, 126
EVATTS, Nathaniell,
  145, 147, 149
EVELYN, George, 178
EVENS, Martin, 122
EVERETT, Benjamin,
  12
  Catherine, 12
  Elizabeth, 12
  Hailes, 52
  Hales, 77, 88,
  153
  Has., 152
  John, 12, 69, 179
  Joseph, 12, 55
  Philip, 55

INDEX

St. Ledgar, 154
St. Leger, 85,
    88, 152
EVERETTS ADDITION,
    12, 77
EVERETTS DISCOVERY,
    52, 77
EVERETTS DOUBLE
    PURCHASE, 12, 77
EVERITT, Benjamin,
    52, 172, 187
    Hales, 156, 182
    St. Ledgar, 156
    St. Leger, 12,
    151, 186
EVERITTS ADDITION,
    6, 52
EVERITTS DOUBLE
    PURCHASE, 6
EVERSETT,
    Augustine, 52
    Benjamin, 52
EVERSETTS DOUBLE
    PURCHASE, 52
EVETT, Nathaniel,
    12
EVETTS, Nathaniel,
    52, 58, 65, 71
EVIN, Abraham, 22
EVINS, Henry, 157
EVITTS, Nathaniel,
    61
EWEN, Richard, 103
EWENS, Mary, 132
EWING, Patrick, 191
EXCHANGE, 2, 6, 24,
    30, 32, 34, 38,
    52, 77
EXCHANGE, THE, 52
EYLATT, Francis,
    168
EYRES, William, 168

-F-
FACKERS, John, 168
FAIR DEALING, 2,
    38, 40, 77
FAIR HARBOR, 14
FAIR HARBOUR, 7,
    11, 20, 77
FAIR LEE, 7, 30
FAIR PROMISE, 11,
    18, 29, 38, 41,
    52, 77

FAIRALEE, 35
FAIRE DEALING, 52
FAIRE HARBOUR, 14
FAIRE LEE, 52
FAIRE PROMISE, 30
FAIRELY, 52
FAIRFIELD, 8, 19,
    37, 52, 77
FAIRHILL, Daniel,
    12
FAIRLEE, 6, 17, 18,
    39, 41
FAIRLY, 23
FALCONAR, Abraham,
    158, 176
    Abram, 12
    Hannah, 12
    John, 12
FALCONARS LOTT, 12
FALCONER, Abraham,
    83, 94, 163,
    172, 191, 192
    Elizabeth, 163
    Gilbert, 50, 56,
    78, 80, 83, 86,
    186
    Jacob, 78, 161,
    182
    John, 52, 59, 164
FALCONERS
    ADVENTURE, 52
FALCONERS LOTT, 52
FALKCONER, Jacob,
    161
FALKER, Thomas, 168
FALMOUTH, 16, 23,
    77
FANCICO, 52
FANCY, 4, 77
FANNING, John, 12,
    151
FANNYS SLIPE, 52,
    77
FARAREN, William,
    169
FARE ALL, 52
FARE HARBOUR, 52
FARE PROMISE, 52
FARELL, William,
    168
FARGUSON, Collin,
    159
    John, 160
FARINGTON, Thomas,
    101
FARLEY, 52
FARLOW, 77
FARMER, Thomas, 173
FARR, Joannah, 169
FARRANTON, Jasper,
    169
FARREL, Rachel, 158
FARROW, James, 187
    William, 169
FARTHING, Ann, 169
    Samuel, 169
FASTER, Seath, 112
FATHERS CARE, 21,
    52
FATHERS CARE
    RESURVEYED, 52,
    77
FATHERS GIFT, 19,
    22, 52
FAWMOUTH, 52
FEDDES, Henry, 137
FEDDIS, John, 12
FEDES, Henery, 133
    Henry, 141
FELT, Lawrance, 115
FENDALL, James, 46
    Josias, 54, 116,
    129
FENICKE, Mr., 111
FENNELL, James, 97
FERGUSON, Colin,
    74, 85, 91
    Collin, 160, 165
    Daniel, 77
    David, 185
    George, 182
FERRELL, Daniel,
    12, 43, 48, 150,
    155
    Eliza, 12
    Thomas, 188
FERRELLS ADDITION,
    12
FERRIL, Daniel, 52
FERRILL, Robert, 12
FERRILS ADDITION,
    52
FERRITS ADDITION,
    35
FERROL, Thomas, 12
FFERET, Richard,
    169
FIELD, Christopher,

186
FIELDER, John, 52
FIELDS,
  Christopher, 166
FIFE, Sandy, 115
FILLINGHAM,
  Benajah, 181
  Benjamin, 76, 83
  Richard, 145,
  146, 181
FILLIPS, David, 125
FINCH, Frances, 145
  Francis, 123,
  124, 131, 137
FINCHINGHAM,
  Richard, 12
FINDLEY, John, 155
FINLEY, George, 173
  John, 172
  Richard, 189
FIRST PART, 23
FIRST PART OF FREE
  GIFT, THE, 52
FISH HALL, 6, 9, 77
FISHALL, 52
FISHER, Chr., 160
  Daniel, 184
  Oba[diah], 161
  William, 13, 52,
  66
FISHING POND, 15,
  18, 19, 77
FISHING PONT, THE,
  52
FITTZGERRALD,
  Martha, 13
FITZALLEN, Richard,
  135
FITZGERALD, John,
  181
FLAHARTY, James, 13
  Michael, 182
FLANNIKIN, Martin,
  52
FLANNIKINS HOPE, 52
FLEET, Capt., 107
FLETCHER, Thomas
  Charles, 160
  William, 105
FLING, Laughlon, 13
FLINN, Patrick, 183
FLOWER OF FOREST,
  77
FLOWER OF THE

FORREST, 26, 52
FLOWERS, Lambert,
  171
FLOYD, John, 42,
  52, 131
  William, 13
FLOYDS CHANCE, 5,
  12, 52
FLUHARTY, Michael,
  77
FLUHARTYSE LOTT, 77
FOARD, George, 172
  Jeremiah, 95
  Moses, 185
FOARMAN, Charles,
  153
FOLKES, William,
  185
FOLLY, 6, 8
FOLLY RESURVEYED,
  52
FOLLY, THE, 52
FOORD, John, 133
FORBES, William,
  184
FORBUSH, John, 13
  Mary, 13
FORCE TO IT, 36
FORD, Charles, 179,
  186
  Edward, 74, 95,
  97
  George, 153, 169
  Jeremiah, 95, 185
  Joseph Trulock,
  97
  Richard, 13
  Robert, 13, 53,
  91, 95, 98, 162,
  179
  Thomas, 13
  Trulock, 95
  William, 13, 95,
  97, 153, 162,
  179
FORDAH, Hannah, 124
FOREMAN, Arthur, 13
  Bartholomew, 181
  Benjamin, 179
  Charles, 13, 89
  Ezekiel, 174,
  177, 184
  Henry, 128
  Jacob, 73, 74,

182
  John, 13, 53, 63
  Robert, 13, 66
  Samuel, 181
  William, 172
FOREMANS POOR
  DISCOVERY, 13,
  25, 77
FORENER, Edward,
  179
FOREST, 11, 77, 78
  Pattericke, 116
FORESTER, G. W.,
  159, 160
  G. William, 165
  George William,
  165, 166
  Mr., 159
  Rev. Mr., 162,
  163, 164
FORGUSON, Collin,
  13
FORK, 3, 8, 11, 12,
  16, 28, 37, 40,
  78
FORK RESURVEYED, 37
FORKS, 78
FORKS ADDITION, 78
FORMAN, Ezekiel,
  189, 190, 192
  Jacob, 156
  John, 156
  Joseph, 152
  Thomas M., 155
FORREST, 4, 5, 6,
  8, 12, 13, 14,
  17, 24, 27, 28,
  29, 30, 31, 32,
  33, 38, 39, 40,
  41
  Patrick, 53
FORREST DEAN, 78
FORREST OF DEAN, 4,
  7, 9, 17, 19,
  25, 39, 42
FORREST RESURVEYED,
  9, 16, 20, 38,
  78
FORRESTER, G. W.,
  171
  George W., 13
  George William,
  69, 78
  William, 187

INDEX 219

FORRESTERS DELIGHT,
  10, 29, 30, 37,
  40, 78
FORRESTS OF DEAN,
  31
FORRESTS
  RESURVEYED, 17
FORSTER, Benjamin,
  181
  William, 182
FORTUNE, 7, 14
FOSTER, Elizabeth,
  115
  John, 13
  Mr., 119
  Seath, 109, 110
  Seth, 116, 119,
  121, 122, 125,
  128
  William, 172
FOUCHER, John, 13
FOUCHES, John, 115
FOUNTAIN, George,
  74, 186
FOUNTAINE, John,
  169
FOUR BROTHERS, 19
FOWLER, Patrick,
  85, 186
  Thomas, 166, 186
FOX, Gregory, 65
  Jane, 121
FOX HOLE, 6
FOXEN, George, 13
FOY, Gregory, 70
FRAIZAR, George, 13
FRANCES, Thomas,
  147
FRANCIS, 34
  Elisabeth, 161
  John, 13, 169
  Thomas, 53, 133,
  148, 169
FRANCIS
  ENLARGEMENT, 8
FRANCS, Thomas, 148
FRASIER, Thomas,
  173
FRAY, Elizabeth,
  156
  Philip, 91, 181
  Phillip, 98
  William, 13, 90,
  91, 153, 180

FRAZIER, George,
  183
  James, 180
  John, 180, 183
  Thomas, 173
  William, 183
FREE GIFT, 13, 23,
  30, 32, 33, 37,
  41, 78
FREE SCHOOL, 13
FREELAND, Nazareth,
  172
  Salathiel, 171,
  189
FREEMAN, Ab., 13
  Abraham, 161,
  165, 171
  Edward, 187
  Isaac, 13, 44,
  53, 57, 73, 81,
  84, 91, 92, 159,
  160, 161, 163,
  165, 166, 167,
  171, 187, 190,
  191
  Mary, 95
  Samuel, 188
  William, 13, 53,
  165
FREEMANS ADDITION,
  13
FREESTONE, Walter,
  169
FRENCH, George, 99,
  169
  Samuel, 13, 55
  William, 188
  Zerobabel, 13, 55
  Zorababel, 186
  Zorobabel, 53, 74
  Zorobable, 158
FRENCHARDS
  MEMORIAL, 17,
  23, 91
FRENCH'S LOTT, 13
FRIENDSHIP, 2, 10,
  13, 14, 16, 22,
  28, 29, 30, 38,
  78
FRIENDSHIP
  RESURVEYED, 29,
  34
FRISBY, Heirs of,
  86

A., 155
Ann, 13, 80, 91,
  151
Elizabeth, 13,
  78, 79, 80
James, 13, 56,
  77, 80, 86, 90,
  91, 150, 181
Jane, 13
John, 79, 155,
  180
Joseph, 94, 183
Peregrin, 13
Peregrine, 154
R., 151, 152
Richard, 13, 76,
  77, 79, 89, 94,
  153, 156, 183,
  189
Sarah 94
Thomas, 13
William, 13, 68,
  94, 95, 147,
  150, 155, 175,
  180, 183, 189,
  190
FRISBYS CHOICE, 78
FRISBY'S PURCHASE,
  13
FROGGETT, John, 13
FROST, William, 169
FRY, William J.,
  183
FULLER, Robert, 132
  William, 102,
  103, 110
FULSTON, John, 150
  Richard, 150
FULSTSONE, Richard,
  13
FURGISON,
  Elizabeth, 99
FURGUSON,
  Elizabeth, 99
FURGUSSON, Daniel,
  171

-G-
GAFFNEY, James, 169
GAFFORD, Charles,
  13
GAIMER, Robert, 114
GAIRE, Mary, 169
GALALEE, Thomas,

186
GALE, Barsheba, 88
  John, 13, 64, 88,
    153, 186
  Levin, 14
  Mary, 14
  Raisin, 14
  Rasin, 78, 81,
    88, 151, 154,
    156, 179, 186
  Richard, 169
GALES ADDITION, 25,
  78
GALLAWAY, James, 14
  William, 53
GALLAWAYS CHANCE,
  12
GALLOP, Oliver, 171
GALLOWAY, John, 72,
  75, 76, 79, 81,
  83, 90, 91, 169
GALLOWAYS, 20
GALLOWAYS CHANCE,
  12, 32
GALLOWAYS FANCY, 8,
  36
GALLOWAYS FARM, 3,
  14
GAMBALL, John, 53
GAMBALLS FARM, 14
GAMBLE, Darius, 79,
  183
  John, 14
  Thomas, 183
GAMER, Catheren,
  126
  Katternen, 121
  Robert, 105, 106,
    116, 118
GAMETS MEADOW, 42
GAMMER, Catheren,
  127
  Robert, 104
GANEERE, Elizabeth,
  104
GANELY, John, 64
GANNOCKE, William,
  135
GANTT, Richard
  Judge, 193
  Sara, 193
  Susanna, 193
  Thomas, 193
GARFUTT, Charles,
  54, 61
GARLAND, Ann, 115,
  119
  Benjamin, 171,
    172
  John, 14
GARMAN, Mary, 169
GARNET, 33
  George, 51
GARNET'S MEADOW, 14
GARNETT, Bartus, 14
  George, 14, 53,
    61, 66, 68
  John, 14
  Jonathan, 14
  Joseph, 14, 53,
    61, 65, 82, 90,
    155
  Mary, 14, 82, 155
  Thomas, 14
GARNETT BRANCH, 14
GARNETTS BRANCH, 78
GARNETTS MEADOW, 36
GARNETTS MEADOWS,
  14
GARRETT, John, 14
  Mary, 88
  Thomas, 153
  Vallentine, 169
GARRETTS BRANCH, 28
GARRY, Robert, 165
GARY, John, 54
GASKILL, William,
  14, 179
GAUNTLETT, William,
  169
GAVLAND, Benjamin,
  172
GAY, Richard, 169
  Robert, 166, 171
  William, 185
GEALIAM, Robert,
  141
GEARS, John, 166
GEDDES, William,
  72, 76, 81
GEDDINGS, James, 97
GEIST, Christian,
  44
  Christopher, 14,
    69
GELDERSEN, David,
  101
GELLER, Agness, 169
GEOFF, Thomas, 169
GEORGE, John, 52
  Joseph, 14, 90,
    180
  Joshua, 14, 60,
    179
  Mary, 14, 53
  Robert, 14, 56,
    90, 180
GEORGE ALIAS
  SCOTLAND, 29
GEORGE TOWN, 21
GEORGES (PART OF
  MORTON), 78
GEORGESTON, 58
GEORGETOWN, 11, 18,
  21, 29, 30, 36
GERMAN POINT, 9, 23
GERMANY, 78
GETTING, Mary, 80
GIAM, John, 169
GIANT, John, 185
  Stephen, 172, 185
  William, 172
GIBB, William, 169
GIBBS, Benjamin,
  169
  Cuff, 187
  Edward, 14, 181
  George, 183
  James, 97
  John, 53, 63, 187
  Richard, 14
  William, 14
GIBB'S CHANCE, 12
GIBBS CHANCE, 14,
  24, 42
GIBBS CHOICE, 29,
  78
GIBBS PARK, 30
GIBERT, George, 180
GIBSON, John, 68,
  101, 107, 109,
  112, 113, 121
  Richard, 14
  William, 188
  Woolman, 14
GIBSONS CHOICE, 78
GIDEON, Thomas, 14
GIDLEY, John, 182
GIFT, 29
GILBERT, Benjamin,
  186
  George, 90, 92

John, 53, 82,
    144, 166
  Perry, 169
GILL, Francis, 132
GILPIN, George, 14,
    66
  Lydia, 83
  Thomas, 14, 46,
    53, 141, 162,
    164
GIN, Arthur, 142
GINN, Arthur, 134,
    135, 137, 139,
    141
GIRD, John, 180
GITTING, Mary, 80
GITTINGS, Mary,
    191, 192
GIVENUP, Richard,
    158
GLAFFORD, Henry, 14
GLANDBY, Terey, 186
GLANN, Jacob, 151
  Nathaniel, 188
GLANVILL, Stephen,
    14
  William, 14, 151
GLANVILLE, James,
    80
  William, 82, 150,
    181
GLASFORD, Henry, 14
GLASSFORD, Henry,
    14
GLEAVES, Benjamin,
    79
  George, 14, 53,
    98
  John, 14, 53, 73,
    153, 158, 159,
    161, 162, 163,
    180
  Joseph, 14
  Ruth, 14
  William, 98
GLEAVES ,
  Nathaniel, 7
GLEAVES LOT, 3, 29
GLEAVES LOTT, 5, 14
GLEEN, John, 173
  Nathaniel, 166
GLEEVES, Ruth, 43
GLENN, Alexander,
    14, 77

INDEX

Jacob, 14, 55,
    79, 151
  Nathaniel, 95,
    188
  Peregrine, 180
  William, 180
GLENS, Alexander,
    182
GLENVILL, Stephen,
    191
GLOVER, Benjmain,
    115
  Daniel, 126
GOACH, James, 169
GODFREY POINT, 28
GODFREYS POINT, 13,
    27
GODLINGTON, 78
  Thomas, 53, 58
GODLINGTON MANNOR,
    25, 54
GODWIN, Deverox,
    101
GOFF, Thomas, 169
GOLD, Ann, 115
  John, 117
  Mary, 115, 117
  Thomas, 14
GOLDEN RIDGE, 12,
    54
GOLDHAUKE, George,
    135, 140, 142
GOLDHAWK, George,
    54
GOLDHAWKS ENLARGED,
    54
GOOD HOPE, 3, 13,
    20, 25, 27, 38,
    39, 54, 78
GOODEN, Samuel, 151
GOODHAND,
  Christopher, 141
GOODHANDLE,
  Christopher, 139
GOODING, Arno, 15
  Jacob, 15
  Samuel, 15
GOODWIN, Elinor, 15
  Mary, 15
GOODYEAR, John, 169
GOOSE HAVEN, 2, 12,
    54, 78
GOOT, Henery, 110
GOOTHWARD, James,

221

    104
  Marie, 104
GORDAN, Christian,
    146
GORDEN, John, 72
GORDON, Ann, 99
  Charles, 15, 99,
    154
  Hannah, 99
  John, 183
  Joseph, 99
  Patrick, 145, 147
GORE, 5, 31, 78
GORE HAVEN, 78
GORE, THE, 54
GOTT, Henery, 108
  Henry, 116, 117,
    118, 119, 120,
    121, 122, 125,
    126, 132
  John, 115
  Samuel, 97
  Sarah, 115
GOTTE, Henry, 123
  Jonathan, 123
GOUGH, Thomas, 169
GOULD, Anne, 105,
    108
  John, 101, 103,
    122
GOULDHAUK, George,
    131
GOULDHAWKE, George,
    42, 54, 133
GOULDHAWKES
  INLARGEMENT, 54
GOULDSMITH, George,
    48, 53, 67
GRACE, William, 173
GRAE, Richard, 15
GRAHAM, Anna 94
  James, 46, 54, 94
  John, 15, 165
  Rebecca, 94
  Rebeckah, 78, 85
  Richard, 15
  William, 94, 185
GRAHAMS ADDITION,
    54
GRAHAMS FISHERY,
    15, 54
GRAHAMS PURCHASE,
    54, 78
GRAINGE, THE, 54

GRAINGER,
  Christopher, 148
  William, 54, 133
GRAISING POINT, 54
GRANGE, 2, 5, 6, 7,
  11, 14, 15, 16,
  18, 21, 23, 24,
  25, 27, 28, 29,
  30, 32, 34, 37,
  40, 78
GRANGE, THE, 54
GRANGER, Grace,
  128, 138
  Mary, 15
  Thomas, 100, 180
  William, 15, 54,
  72, 84, 91, 92,
  117, 118, 123,
  126, 127, 131,
  136, 138, 141,
  142, 191
GRANGERS PART OF
  WICKLIFF AND
  MARKET PLACE
  Resurvey, 54
GRANT, Abigail, 15
  James, 180
  John, 15, 54
  Jonathan, 79, 181
  Rachel, 82
  Samuel, 181
  William, 15, 169,
  173, 181, 187
GRANT FOLLY, 15
GRANTHAM, 28, 33,
  34, 39, 54
GRANTHAMM, 7
GRANTHOM, 78
GRANTLETT, John,
  169
GRANTS FOLLY, 15,
  54, 79
GRASSING POINT
  ALIAS GRAYS INN,
  20
GRAVES, Alexander,
  15
  Mary, 169
  Richard, 15, 74,
  76, 85, 87, 93,
  153, 156, 177,
  180, 189
  Sarah, 15, 47,
  153, 155

Verlinda, 193
William, 15, 54,
  63, 81
William Hynson,
  70
GRAVES EASTERN PART
  OF CUNNEY
  WARREN, 54
GRAY, Henry, 97
  Richard, 15, 56
  William, 84, 95,
  169, 171
GRAY INN, 54
GRAYS INN, 20, 28
GRAYS LOT, 54
GREAT FOLLY, 54
GREAT NECK, 54
GREAT OAK, 79
GREAT OAK MANNOR,
  2, 12, 17, 18,
  19, 20, 54, 79
GREAT OAK MANOR, 9,
  13, 14, 26, 36
GREAT OAKE, 54
GREEDY, James, 171
GREEM MEADOW, 54
GREEN, Alexander,
  180
  Benjamin, 15
  Bowles, 15
  Henry, 15
  James, 169
  John, 15, 155
  Peter, 15
  Richard, 173, 187
  Robert, 15
GREEN BANK, 17, 54,
  79
GREEN BRANCH, 11,
  16, 28, 54, 79
  George, 17
GREEN BRANCH
  RESURVEYED, 54
GREEN FOREST, 79
GREEN FORREST, 2,
  17, 34, 54
GREEN MEADOW, 16,
  79
GREEN MEADOWS, 30
GREEN OAK, 16, 23,
  54, 79
GREENE, George, 147
GREENE BRANCH, 146
GREENFIELD,

Archibald, 15
Robert, 183
William, 180
GREENLEAF, Isaac,
  15
GREENS FORREST, 37
GREENS FORREST
  RESURVEYED, 54
GREENWOOD, Daniel,
  15, 75, 77, 99,
  186, 192
  George, 54, 186
  James, 15, 43,
  162, 172, 179,
  182, 188
  John, 15, 54, 72,
  79, 82, 154,
  166, 185
  Joseph, 54, 73,
  79, 91, 162,
  164, 165, 172,
  179
  Samuel, 162
  William, 75, 166,
  182
GREENWOODS
  ADVANCEMENT, 16
GREENWOODS
  ADVENTURE, 15,
  79
GREENWOODS CHANCE,
  54, 79
GREENWOODS FARM,
  54, 79
GREENWOODS PART OF
  SUFFOLK, 54
GREER, James, 15,
  54
GREERS RANGE, 9,
  15, 54, 79
GREGORY, Anthony,
  169
GREN, John, 184
GRENWOOD, Daniel,
  72
GRESHAM, Ann, 96,
  155
  John, 15, 54, 60,
  68, 96, 100, 176
  Mary, 96, 97
  Richard, 15, 43,
  51, 54, 63, 96,
  153, 162, 176,
  177, 182, 189

GRESHAMS FOLLY, 79
GRESHAMS COLLEDGE, 15
GRESHAMS COLLEDGE (RESURVEY), 54
GRESHAMS COLLEGE, 13, 79
GRESHAMS DISCOVERY, 15, 54, 79
GRESHAMS LEVELL, 31
GRESHAMS LEVELLS, 15
GRESHAMS LEVELS, 54, 79
GREY, James, 15, 99
John, 15
GREYS INN, 79
GRIERS RANGE, 9, 20
GRIFF, James, 169
GRIFFEN, Anthony, 125
Jean, 140
Jeane, 140, 141
GRIFFIN, Ann, 15
Anthony, 49, 118, 119, 122, 126, 128, 129
Antony, 122
Benjamin, 15, 54
Charles, 16
Edward, 169
Jackson, 16
Jonas, 16
Nathaniel, 16
Rice, 125
Robert, 144, 146, 147
GRIFFINS DELIGHT, 40
GRIFFINS HAMILTON, 54
GRIFFITH, ----, 151
Amelia Charlotta, 95
Benjamin, 45, 67
Charlotte, 72, 92
Cooter, 16
David, 169
George, 16
Henerietta, 95
James, 173, 180
John, 16, 182, 183
Luke, 82, 151, 154
Martha, 90
Mary, 153
Samuel, 16, 153, 189
Thomas, 181
William, 181
GRIFFITH CALFPEN, 13
GRIFFITHS CALF PEN, 16
GRIFFITHS CALF PENN, 15, 79
GRIFFITHS CALFE PENN, 54
GRIFFITHS DELIGHT, 23, 40, 54
GRIMES, John, 180
Richard, 125
GRIMSDITCH, John, 126
GRINDAGE, William, 88, 99, 188
GRINDIDGE, Charles, 16
GRINLEY, Hanna, 120
GROMES, Charles, 16
GROOM, Charles, 69
Daniel, 186
James, 182
GROOME, Charles, 16, 88, 151, 152, 153, 156, 182
Daniel, 156
Samuel, 16, 153
GROOMES, Charles, 74, 81
GROOMS, Samuel, 159
GROVE, 2, 3, 14, 22, 23, 33, 79
Benjamin, 141
GROVE ADDITION, 23, 54
GROVE, THE, 54
GROVES ADDITION, 79
GRUDY, James, 187
GRUMBLE, 4, 54, 79
GRURY, Benjamin, 56
GUDRICK, Henry, 131
GUGGON, William, 173
GUIBERT, John, 16
GUINN, Thomas, 65, 140
GUIRD, Elizabeth, 96
GULLETT, George, 76
GUNDAGE, William, 188
GUNSSEILL, James, 108
GUTHERY, C. Joshua, 184
GUTTRICK, Henry, 131
GUURY, Benjamin, 56
GUY, Robert, 16
GWILLIN, George, 115
GYANT, John, 16, 158

-H-
HABORNE, James, 54
HABORNES FARME, 54
HACHESON, Robert, 188
HACKET, Michael, 151
Simon, 81, 96
HACKETT, Ann Martha, 99
Charles, 155, 184
Isaac, 75, 79, 156, 181
James, 16, 153, 155
Michael, 16, 53
Michaell, 54
Samuel, 16
Simon, 75, 77, 81, 185
HACKETTS FANCY, 16, 54, 79
HACKNEY, 8, 29, 41, 54
HADDIN, Edward, 83
HADDON, 55
HADLEY, Shem, 181
Thomas, 180
HAGARTY, William, 16
HAGGERTY, William, 61
HAGGIT, Michael, 161
HAGUE, James, 183

HAIFIELD, 2
HAILES, 37
  Roger, 157
HAIMER, John, 16
HALBERT,
  Experience, 99
  Simion, 181
HALE, George, 124
  Margaret, 129
  Margrett, 124
  Roger, 55
HALES, 27, 29, 30,
  33, 35, 38, 55,
  79
  Roger, 16, 154
  William, 185
HALES ADVENTURE,
  37, 55
HALES PURCHASE, 8,
  16
HALES RESURVEYED,
  29
HALEY, Charlotte,
  94
  Darby, 48
  Harriott, 94
  John, 16, 77, 82,
  185, 191
  Sarah, 94
  W., 162
  William, 16, 159,
  160, 161, 163,
  165, 171
HALL, Abraham, 144
  Ann, 16
  Chambers, 16, 44
  Christopher, 16,
  49, 157, 158,
  163, 165, 166,
  176
  Cuthbert, 82, 96,
  166, 184, 185,
  191
  Edward, 76
  Francis, 16, 79,
  153
  George, 16, 106,
  107, 108, 117,
  118, 119, 163,
  185
  Hynson, 185
  John, 16, 157,
  158
  Margaret, 126,
  154
  Michael, 16
  Mr., 192
  Samuell, 143, 148
  William, 165,
  173, 174, 176,
  181, 191, 192
HALLE, Christian,
  126
  George, 125, 126,
  127
  Margrett, 126
  Rachell, 126
HALLES, Roger, 157
HALLS HARBOUR, 24
HALTERS, Robert,
  101
HALTON, Robert, 111
HAMBLETON, William,
  122, 125, 126,
  128, 129
HAMBLIN, William,
  16, 55
HAMBLIN LOTT, 16
HAMBLINS LOTT, 55
HAMER, William,
  156, 182
HAMERS LOTT, 16
HAMILTON, Andrew,
  175
  James, 181
HAMILTONS LOTT, 79
HAMLIN, John, 16
HAMLINS LOTT, 7, 25
HAMMER, John, 16
HAMMON, William,
  172
HAMMOND, Samuel,
  89, 181
  Thomas, 16
HAMNER, John, 159
HAMPSHIRE, 25, 30,
  34, 55, 79
HAMPSHIRE BLAYS
  RANGE, 5
HANCEFORD, 55
HAND, Thomas
  Beddingfield,
  154
HANDLE, 8
HANDLE, THE, 55
HANDS, B. Thomas,
  80
  Beddinfield, 16
  Thomas B., 90,
  174
  Thomas
  Bedingfield,
  174, 176, 177
HANGMANS END, 3,
  19, 25, 31, 35,
  39, 40, 55, 79
HANGMANS FOLLY, 11,
  18, 20, 28, 31,
  35, 40, 55, 79
HANHAM, 41
HANKAM, 55
HANKIN, John, 16
HANNAH, Archibald,
  186
HANSE, Fredrick,
  163
HANSFORD, 17, 24,
  25, 37, 79
HANSON, Anderson
  Hanson, 105
  Andrew, 101, 104,
  106, 110, 111,
  117
  Anicak, 104, 105
  Anicake, 105
  Annicak, 104
  Annikeck, 117
  Barberi, 105
  Frederick, 16,
  44, 151, 158
  Fredric, 160
  Fredrick, 159,
  163
  Fredricke, 117
  George, 16, 151,
  190
  Gustav, 183
  Gustave, 16
  Gustavis, 159
  Gustavus, 77, 82,
  153
  Hance, 16, 54,
  55, 104, 145
  Hans, 55, 150,
  151, 175, 178
  Hanse, 117
  Katteren, 117
  Margret, 117, 126
  Mary, 16
  William, 17, 72,
  86, 166, 188
HANSONS CHOICE, 55

HANSONS CHOICE
  RESURVEYED, 55,
  79
HARBERTS CHANCE, 79
HARBINSTON,
  William, 17
HARBOR, 22
  James, 11
HARBOUR, 79
HARBOUR, THE, 55
HARDIMAN, John, 121
HARDING, Reuben, 82
HAREFIELD, 8, 55
HARFIELD, 38
HARFORD, Charles,
  43
HARKIN, Cornelius,
  17
HARKOL FANCY, 10
HARMATAGE, 19
HARNOLL, John, 104
HARPER, William,
  186
HARRAGAN, John, 184
HARRINGTON,
  Elizabeth, 135
  Katherine, 135
  Richard, 133,
  135, 141, 142,
  148
HARRIOTT, Ambrose,
  44
HARRIS, 136
  Ariana W., 17
  Augustine, 17
  Edward, 17, 48,
  53, 67
  George, 133, 134,
  136, 137, 138,
  139, 140, 141,
  142, 143
  Henry, 173
  James, 17, 44,
  55, 59, 60, 68,
  150, 175, 176,
  178
  John, 17, 169,
  173, 187
  Joseph, 183
  Margaritta Arina,
  55
  Mathias, 17, 154
  Matthias, 53,
  151, 176

Sarah, 141
Susanna, 17
Thomas, 17, 60
Walter, 185
William, 17, 43,
  52, 54, 56, 59,
  60, 63, 68, 146,
  147, 148, 150,
  156, 175, 176
HARRIS ADDITION,
  17, 79
HARRIS FORRESST, 19
HARRIS FORREST, 7,
  19, 42, 79
HARRIS FORRESTS, 31
HARRISON, James,
  180, 186
  Peter, 147, 148
  William, 17, 171
HARRISS, William,
  145
HARRIS'S ADDITION,
  55
HARRIS'S FORREST,
  2, 55
HART, James, 82,
  153
  John, 17, 166,
  169
  Joseph, 186
  Robert, 161
  Thomas, 179
HART POINT, 19
HARTFORD, 79
HARTHING, Anna, 169
HARTLEY, John, 181,
  184
HARTS POINT, 79
HARTSHORN, George,
  79, 91, 156,
  181, 191
HARTT, Cornelius,
  188
  James, 186
  John, 185
  Nathaniel, 187
  Richard, 185
  Robert, 186
HARTWELL, Marie,
  105
  Mary, 109, 113
HARWOOD, William,
  180
HARY, Thomas, 169

HASTING, George, 17
HASTINGS, George,
  17, 79, 88
  Oliver, 17
HATCH, William, 169
HATCHASON, James,
  98
HATCHBERRY, 24, 25,
  37
HATCHBURY, 17, 25,
  55
HATCHERSON, Robert,
  159, 160
HATCHESON,
  Benjamin, 181
  John, 90, 181
  Nathan, 17, 90,
  181
  Robert, 17, 188
  Thomas, 17
  Vinsant, 166
  Vinsent, 167
HATCHINSON, James,
  187
  Vincent, 185
HATCHISON, James,
  98
  Vincent, 82, 181
HATH, William, 169
HATTEN, John, 125
HATTON, John, 108
  Mr., 109
  Richard, 145
  Thomas, 106, 116
  William, 55
HAUKINS, Elizabeth,
  112
  Mr., 112
HAULKINS, Thomas,
  122
HAVE AT ALL, 21
HAVELY, James, 17
HAVEN, 79
HAWKINES, Thomas,
  105, 108, 109
HAWKINGS, William,
  169
HAWKINS, Henry, 53
  Jane, 169
  Thomas, 108, 112
  William, 169
HAWKSHAW, Robert,
  134
HAWUKINS, Thomas,

112
HAY DOWNE, 131
HAYBORNES CHOICE, 26
HAYES, George, 145
  John, 65
HAYLET, John, 17
HAYNES, Abraham, 182
  Abrm., 49
HAYS, John, 17
HAYWOOD, William, 17, 46, 156
HAYZELL, Benjamin, 55
HAYZELLS ADVENTURE, 55
HAZARD, 3, 10, 13, 27, 35, 55, 79
HAZEL, Mathew, 160
HAZEL MEADOW, 55
HAZEL THICKET, 79
HAZLE, Benjamin, 17, 163
HAZLE ADVENTURE, 17
HAZLEBURST, John, 17
HAZZARD, 55, 79
HCHARD, Isaac, 93
  Joseph, 93
  Samuel, 93
HEAD, Elizabeth, 145
  Isabella, 133
  William, 131, 133, 134, 135, 136, 137, 138, 139, 140, 141, 143, 145
HEADE, William, 111
HEADING, 4, 55, 80
  John, 55
HEARD, Henry, 169
HEARN, Hugh, 17
HEARNE, Darley, 17
HEARST, John, 169
HEATH, Charles, 17
  James, 17, 42, 55, 66
  Jesse, 188
  Thomas, 134, 135, 140, 142
HEATH FORREST, 17
HEATH RANGE, 4

HEATHS CHANCE, 5, 9
HEATHS CHOICE, 80
HEATHS FORREST, 4
HEATHS GIFT, 55
HEATHS LONG LANDS, 6, 7, 20, 24, 55
HEATHS LONGLANDS, 39
HEATHS LOW LANDS, 80
HEATHS RANGE, 4, 17, 80
HEATHS RANGE, THE SECOND PART, 55 RESURVEYED, 55
HEATHWORTH, 17
HEBBERN, Thomas, 74, 79, 84
HEBBERNS FARM, 80
HEBBERNSCHOICE, 80
HEBBORN, Thomas, 186
HEBBORNS FARM, 26
HEBBURNS FARM, 20
HEBORN, Thomas, 157
HEBORNS FARM, 9
HEBOURNS CHANCE, 25
HEBRON, James, 17, 59
  John, 17
  Thomas, 17
HEBRONS FARM, 17
HEDGES, William, 17
HELENA, Andrew, 121
  Sarah, 115
HELENS ADVENTURE, 80
HELLENA, Andrew, 117
HEMBERRY, 2, 12, 55
HEMBERSTON, George, 17
HEMBLETON, 80
HEMSLEY, Judeth, 125
  Mattilda, 115
  Penelope, 115
  William, 54, 55, 63, 121, 122, 125, 126, 128, 129, 134, 142, 177
HEMSLEYS DISCOVERY, 55

HEN ISLAND, 40
HEN ROOST, 29
HENBERRY, 80
HENBURY, 80
HENDLEY, James, 184
HENDRICKSEN, Jan, 146
HENDRICKSON, John, 17, 146
HENFREY, Thomas, 132
HENHAM, 80
HENING, William, 182
HENN ISLAND, 55
HENROOST, 80
HENRY, James, 59, 171, 172, 187
  William, 171, 172, 189, 190, 191
HENS ROOST, 1, 26, 40, 55
HENSLAND, 80
HENSLEY, William, 127
HEPBORNES, 55
HEPBORNS CHOICE, 25
HEPBOURN, Thomas, 157
HEPBOURNS CHOICE, 25
HEPBURN, Thomas, 179
HEPBURNS FARM, 9, 11, 22
HERBERT, Charles, 55
HERBERTS CHANCE, 55
HEREFIELD, 17, 32
HEREFORD, 14, 18, 55
HERMAN, Godfrey, 53
  Henry, 45
HERMANN, Robert, 169
HERMITAGE, 1, 6, 7, 13, 24, 27, 28, 37, 42, 55, 80
HERMITAGE RESURVEYED, 29
HERRIN, Daniel, 173
  Nathaniel, 187
  William, 187

INDEX 227

HERRING, Nathaniel, 172
William, 172
HESBORNES, 55
HEUETT, Hannah, 101, 103
Robert, 103
HEWETT, Hannah, 101
Robert, 50, 101
HEYDEN, John, 65
HIAG, John, 183
HIBBERS FARM, 80
HIBBERT, Henry, 169
HICKAMBOTHAM, Oliver, 17
HICKENBOTTOM, James, 173
HICKES, John, 179
HICKMAN, John, 166, 186
HICKS, John, 55, 158, 159, 160
Roger, 65, 157
HICKS ADDITION, 11, 18, 55
HICKS HAZARD, 4
HICKS TOWN, 80
HIDE, Henry, 119
HIFF, Edmond, 18
HIGGENBOTTOM, Olivor, 151
HIGGINBOTHAM, George, 55
HIGGINBOTTOM, James, 173
HIGGS, 18
HIGH PARK, 5, 8, 10, 11, 15, 19, 26, 32, 33, 34, 36, 55, 80
HIGH PARK, PART OF, 55
HIGH PARKE, 55
HIGINBOTTOM, Benjamin, 183
George, 183
James, 173
Joel, 183
Oliver, 183
HIL, John, 182
HILL, Amoze, 126
Ann, 126, 127, 129
Barbary, 123

Barbery, 133
Barbra, 135
Christian, 101, 109
Elizabeth, 169
George, 160
Hasadia, 121, 122, 126, 127, 129
Hasadiah, 122
Hasidia, 115, 118
Hassadia, 102, 109, 114
Margret, 117
Margrett, 123, 124
Penelope, 123
Rachell, 115, 123
Richard, 18, 60, 62, 68, 148, 179
Ruth, 113, 117, 124
Samuell, 146
Thomas, 55, 101, 102, 103, 104, 105, 106, 107, 108, 109, 110, 111, 112, 113, 114, 117, 118, 122, 123, 126, 127, 133, 135, 138, 139, 150, 169
William, 172
HILL DOWN, 15
HILL TOP, 15, 41, 80
HILL TOP, THE, 55
HILLEN, Nathaniel, 61, 66
HILLENS ADVENTURE, 10, 17, 23
HILLINGS ADVENTURE, 80
HILLINGSWORTHMKORE, 80
HILLS, Ann, 128
Thomas, 126, 128, 129
William, 55
HILLS AND NO DALES, 2, 15, 55, 80
HILLS CABBIN, 55
HILLS DOWN, 80

HILLS, THE, 55
HILLSDON, 55
HILLSDOWN, 17
HILLSDOWNE, 17
HILLSON, Anthony, 141
HILLSTON, 55, 80
HILLSTONE, 41, 126
HILLY LANGFORD, 80
HILLY LONGFORD, 25
HILLYS CHANCE, 80
HIMBLETON, 31
HINCHINGHAM, 3, 10, 13, 14, 15, 19, 22, 25, 26, 33, 34, 39, 41, 80
Robert, 1
HINDS, Jacobus, 184
John, 183
HINE, Isaac, 45
HINES, Isaac, 78
Jas. W., 153
HINGSTON, William, 169
HINOCKS LOT, 80
HINSON, Ann, 110
Anne, 113
Charles, 55
John, 45, 56, 59, 144, 145, 146, 147, 149
Leiftent, 121
Lieut., 104
Mr., 106, 108, 112
Thomas, 56, 61, 62, 102, 103, 104, 105, 106, 107, 109, 110, 112, 113, 115, 116, 118, 120, 121, 125, 140
HINSONS CHANCE, 55
HINSONS DIVISION, 56
HINSONS NEW HAVEN, 56
HINTCHINGHAM, 56
HINTON, Thomas, 70
HIPPESFOY, George, 169
HIRRIN, William, 187
HIS PART OF

228 INHABITANTS OF KENT COUNTY, MARYLAND, 1637-1787

FORRESTORS
  DELIGHT, 56
HISARD, Mary, 76
HIX, John, 18, 182
  Roger, 18, 56
HIX HAZARD, 18
HIXES HAZARD, 56
HIX'S HAZARD, 33
HIZARD, Phillip, 17
HOALDEN, William,
  169
HOB, Robert, 169
HOBB, John, 169
HOBSONS CHOICE, 15,
  56
HOCOMBE, Thomas,
  169
HODGES, Frances, 81
  James, 81, 87,
  183
  John, 18, 150
  Rebecca, 18
  Robert, 18, 54
  Samuel, 18
  Stephen, 18, 81,
  87
  William, 18, 65,
  143
HODGES RECOVERY , 9
HODGSON, John, 65
  Nicholas, 46
  Robert, 166
HOGANS, William,
  186
HOLDEN, John, 183
HOLDER, John, 172
HOLEADGER, Jno.,
  163
HOLEAGER, John, 18
  Phillip, 42,
  63, 65
HOLEMAN, Abraham,
  116
  Edward, 18, 157
HOLLADAY, Francis,
  18
  Henry, 18
HOLLAND, George,
  18, 53
HOLLANDS DELIGHT,
  22
HOLLEADGER,
  Phillip, 63
HOLLEAGER, Phillip,
53, 67
HOLLEGAR, Phillip,
  18
HOL(L)EGER, Philip,
  47, 68
  Phillip, 60
HOLLESIS, Mr., 112
HOLLIDAY, Edward,
  18
HOLLINGSWORTHMORE,
  23
HOLLINSWORTH,
  Charles, 60, 61
  John, 18
  William, 18
HOLLIS, Charles, 18
HOLLMAN, Abraham,
  101
HOLLYDAY, Edward,
  18
  G., 18
HOLLYLAND, 13
HOLMAN, Edward, 156
  Henry, 18
HOLMES, Philip, 181
HOLSE, Abraham, 142
HOLT, 6, 13
  Arthur, 18, 155
HOLTON, Robert,
  105, 114, 127
HOLY LAND, 19, 33,
  56, 80
HOLY LAND, THE, 56
HOLYDAY, Ann, 158
HOLYOAK, Daniel,
  181
HONEST DEALING, 11,
  39, 56, 81
HONEY HILLS, 27
HOOD, Jane, 102
  Joan, 103
  John, 102, 103
  Robert, 103, 123,
  147
HOOPER, Abraham,
  115
  Doctor, 111
  Henry, 18, 178
HOOSIERS ADVENTURE,
  56
HOPE, 10, 12, 18,
  26, 27, 81
HOPE, THE, 56
HOPEFUL UNITY, 16,
38
HOPEFULL, 81
HOPEFULL UNITY, 3
HOPEWELL, 10, 11,
  18, 24, 28, 30,
  39, 81
  Joseph, 55, 56
  Richard, 55, 56
HOPEWELL
  RESURVEYED, 56
HOPEWELL UNITY, 56
HOPEWELLS FARM, 25
HOPKINES, William,
  119
HOPKINGS, Jonathan,
  143
HOPKINS, Benjamin,
  18
  Edward, 155, 184
  Jonathan, 140,
  141
  Joseph, 18, 47,
  56, 180
  Philip, 18
  Phillip, 43, 156
  Sarah, 18
  William, 18, 118,
  119, 179
HOPKINSON,
  Jonathan, 144,
  145
HOPOEWELL, 56
HORNER, James, 101,
  104, 106, 108,
  110, 111
HORNEY, Jeffery, 18
HORNOR, James, 112
HORNY, Thomas, 182
HORWOOD, Robert,
  116
HOSEGOOD, George,
  169
HOSGOOD, George,
  169
HOSIER, Henry, 47,
  143, 144, 146,
  148, 149, 175
  Richard, 153, 156
  Samuel, 98
HOSIERS ADDITION,
  56
HOSIERS FARM, 56,
  81
HOSIERS NEGLECT, 56

INDEX 229

HOSKINS, Stephen, 18
HOSSIER, Henry, 56
HOUADY, William, 169
HOULTON, Robert, 114
HOUSLEYS DISCOVERY, 17
HOUSROFF, John, 181
HOUSTON, William, 190
HOW, Thomas, 169
HOWARD, Ambross, 163
  Benjamin, 18, 153, 186
  Cornelius, 186
  Henry, 135
  James, 76, 185
  Jane, 161
  John, 18, 61, 76, 185, 186
  Joseph, 172, 186
  Linard, 186
  Mathew, 18, 56, 157, 161
  Matthew, 44, 56, 59, 176
  Roger, 50
  Stephen, 186
  Thomas, 126, 186
HOWARD GIFT, 41
HOWARDS ADDITION, 81
HOWARDS ADVENTURE, 18, 56
HOWARDS CHANCE, 9, 25, 56
HOWARDS GIFT, 6, 22, 27, 56, 81
HOWARDS LOT, 18
HOWARDS LOT RESURVEYED, 5
HOWARDS LOTT, 29, 56
HOWARDS LOTT RESURVEYED, 56
HOWARDS POLICY, 18, 56, 81
HOWARDS PURCHASE, 56
HOWELL, 6
  Charles, 64
  John, 18, 56
  Nathaniel, 186
  Thomas, 18, 50, 52, 56, 63
  William, 75, 186
HOWELL RESURVEYED, 41
HOWELLS, 56
HOWELLS ADDITION, 6, 56
HOWELLS ADVENTURE, 6, 21, 26
HOWELLS FARM, 17, 29, 42, 81
HOWELLS OATELAND, 56
HOWELLS OUTLAND, 5, 18, 36
HOWELLS RANGE, 5, 81
HOWELLS RESURVEYED, 56
HOWELS FARM, 17
HOWELS FOLLY, 11
HOWELS OUTLAND, 3
HOWELS RANGE, 5, 14
HOWTEN, Mary, 146
HOZIER, Hannah, 18
  Henry, 18
  Richard, 19
HOZIERS ADDITION, 10
HOZIERS ADVENTURE, 18
HOZIERS FARM, 18
HOZIERS FARM RESURVEYED, 18
HOZIERS NEGLECT, 14
HUBBERD, Humphrey, 138
HUBBERT, Humphrey, 132
HUCHING, Richard, 142
HUCKLEBERRY, 81
HUCKLEBERRY RIDGE, 21, 41, 56, 81
HUD, John, 101, 111
  Robert, 111
HUDD, Joane, 114
HUDDELL, William, 147
HUDDLES NIGHT, 19
HUDDLES RIGHT, 15, 18, 81
HUDLES RIGHT, 13
HUDSON, Elizabeth, 147
  Henery, 133
  Johh, 81
  John, 19, 89, 182
  Philip, 19, 158, 159
  Phillip, 158, 159
  Richard, 144, 146, 147
  Susanna, 160
  Susannah, 160
  William, 163
HUDSON ADVENTURE, 81
HUES, Valentine, 138
HUFE, John, 19
HUFF, John, 19, 42, 43
  Saran, 76, 166
  Thomas, 181
HUFFS ADDITION, 81
HUGHES, John, 172
HULL, Daniel, 19, 96
  David, 19, 56, 179
  Edward, 109, 112, 113, 118, 119, 122, 123, 127, 132, 133, 134, 142, 143, 144, 145
  Elizabeth, 19
  Fardinando, 158, 162
  Ferdinando, 19
  Jos., 161
  Joseph, 19, 56, 157, 179
  Margret, 112, 113, 122
  Nathanell, 123
  Richard, 111
  William, 86, 166, 187
HULLS DESIRE, 56
HULLS PART OF SUFFOLK, 56
HUMBERSON, George, 19

230   INHABITANTS OF KENT COUNTY, MARYLAND, 1637-1787

Jacob, 75, 186
HUMPHREY, Ellis,
  146, 148, 149
Robert, 135
Thomas, 181
HUMPHREYS, Ellis,
  57
Robert, 124, 132,
  133, 134, 135
HUMPHRIES, John,
  174
HUNT, Francis, 102,
  110
John, 66
Morgan, 70, 190,
  191
HUNTER, Charles,
  162, 164
James, 19
John, 19
William, 172, 185
HUNTING FIELD, 36,
  37, 81, 126
HUNTING FIELD AND
  RINGGOLD'S
  CHANCE, 56
HUNTING FIELD
  RESURVEYED, 56
HUNTING FIELDS, 22,
  31, 34
HUNTINGFIELD, 56
HURLEY, Dennis,
  172, 182
Sarah, 19
Timothy, 19
HURLOCK, Jacob, 57
Robert, 19
HURLOCKS CHANCE,
  19, 57
HURLOCKS CHANCE
  RESURVEYED, 57
HURST, William,
  182, 183
HURT, Cornelius, 19
Henry, 19, 81,
  88, 94
James, 73, 76,
  171, 180
John, 19, 57, 74,
  80, 87, 159,
  171, 183, 187,
  189
Jose, 80
Margaret, 69

Martha, 19, 53
Morgan, 19, 57,
  79, 93, 181, 190
HURTLEBERRY TRACT,
  24, 26, 57
HURTS DIRECTION,
  18, 57
HURTS LOT, 11, 19
HURTS LOTT, 57, 81
HUSBAND, Thomas, 57
William, 156
HUSBANDS, Thomas,
  19
HUSBANDS LOTT, 19,
  38, 57, 81
HUSON, Ric:, 115
Richard, 115
HUSSELTON, John,
  172
HUSTABLE, William,
  169
HUTCHENSON, Thomas,
  19
HUTCHESON, Mary, 19
Robert, 159
Vincent, 19
HUTCHESONS
  ADDITION, 17
HUTCHINS, Ellenor,
  132
Richard, 126
HUTCHINSON,
Alexander, 68
James, 19
HUTCHISON, Robert,
  67
Vincent, 57
HUTCHISONS
  ADDITION, 57
HUTSON, John, 43,
  57
Samuel, 181
HUTSONS HILLS, 57
HUXTER, Sabret, 183
HUZBAND, Thomas, 57
HYINSON, Thomas,
  122
HYLAND, John, 171
HYLLING, Nathaniel,
  57
HYLLINGS GROVE, 57
HYNES, Isaac, 185
HYNSON, Andrew, 19,
  161

Benjamin, 81
C. John, 81
Capt., 161
Charles, 19, 45,
  48, 57, 81, 150,
  165, 175, 176,
  178, 181
Francina, 19, 53,
  155
George, 91
James, 19, 77,
  86, 165, 166,
  174, 186, 187
John, 19, 43, 46,
  57, 72, 77, 86,
  148, 150, 151,
  159, 175
John Carvil, 57
John Carvill, 181
Martha, 19, 65
Mary, 83, 90, 98,
  99
Mathias, 19
Nathaniel, 19,
  52, 66, 70, 81,
  98, 99, 150,
  175, 176, 178,
  183
Richard, 72, 77,
  81, 182
Sarah, 20
Thomas, 20, 42,
  48, 57, 61,
  102, 110, 114,
  150, 151, 163,
  166, 175
William, 20, 63,
  172, 176, 183
HYNSONS, James, 89
HYNSONS ADDITION,
  81
HYNSONS ADVENTURE,
  19, 57
HYNSONS CHANCE, 11,
  19, 81
HYNSONS CHANCE
  RESURVEYED, 57
HYNSONS CHOICE, 14,
  57
HYNSONS DESIRE, 19,
  57, 81
HYNSONS DISCOVERY,
  19, 22, 57
HYNSONS DIVISION,

INDEX 231

19, 31, 57, 81
HYNSONS DURLEON, 19

-I-
ILER, Isaac, 103
ILIVE, Is:, 110
Isa., 101
Isack, 109, 110, 112
Isacke, 126
Isake, 106
Izake, 104
ILLCONVENIENT, 14
INCH, John, 20
INCONVENIENCE, 81
INDIAN RANGE, 5, 23, 31, 34, 81
INDIAN RANGE RESURVEYED, 57
INDIAN RANGE, THE, 57
INDIAN SPRING, 57
INGLESBY, Joseph, 136
INGRAM, Elizabeth, 154
  John, 124, 136, 140, 141, 143, 144, 145
  Richard, 169
  Robert, 57
  Thmas, 130
  Thomas, 133, 135, 136, 138, 141
INGRAMS, Elizabeth, 20
INGRAMS LOT, 29
INGRAMS LOTT, 20, 57
INHERITANCE, 81
INTERMIX, 7, 14, 19, 25, 29, 30, 33, 81
INTERMIXT, 57
IRELAND, Joseph, 20, 159, 160, 161, 164, 165
  Thomas, 180
  William, 187
IRONS, Charles, 78, 83, 166, 171, 187, 189
  Simon, 187
ISK, 21

ISKE, 57
ISLAND, 81
ISSELS, Peter, 83
ISTON, Benjamin, 182
IVEY, William, 180
IVINGO, 6, 57, 81

-J-
JACKMAN, William, 148, 149
JACKSON, Abednego, 182
  Abednegoe, 172
  Benjamin, 20, 154
  Jacob, 186
  John, 20, 145, 146
  Martha, 20
  Mary, 74
  Robert, 20
  William, 188
JACOB, Capt., 102
  John, 111
  Thomas, 169
JACOBS, Henry, 20
JAMACO, 8
JAMAICA, 9, 10, 57, 81
JAMES, 28
  Charles, 20, 47, 48, 51, 55, 56, 58
  Edward, 57, 144, 146
  J. Thomas, 80, 81, 86
  Jarvis, 20
  John, 20, 45, 54, 56, 57, 58, 59
  Morgin, 166
  Seney, 20
  Thomas, 148, 184
  William, 84
JAMES ADDITION, 28, 42
JAMES ADVENTURE, 81
JAMES DISCOVEREY, 81
JAMES LOT, 8
JAMES, Negro, 100
JAMES'S ADDITION, 57
JAMES'S ADVENTURE, 57

JAMES'S CHOICE, 57
JAMES'S DISCOVERY, 57
JAMES'S HOPE, 57
JANE BROWN'S PART OF, TRUMPINTON RESURVEYED, 57
JANEFFER, Daniell, 137
JARBO, John, 126
JARMAN, Robert, 20
JARVIS, Edward, 151
  James, 57
  Joseph, 20
  Michael, 169
JEAMES, Owin, 111
JEFFERIES, Jacob, 173
JEFFREY, Richard, 169
JEKYLL, John, 20
  Margaret, 20
JENKENS, John, 127
  Walter, 124
JENKINGS, John, 127
JENKINS, Hannah, 124, 133
  John, 108, 110, 114, 115, 118, 120, 122
  William, 169
JENNINGS, Edmond, 20
  Thomas, 20
JENNYS BEGINNING, 42
JERICHO, 57
JERICO, 16, 82
JERMAN POINT, 57
JERREY, Hugh, 60
JERROM, Sarah, 20
JERROME, 28
JERRUM, Thomas, 20, 79
JERVIS, John, 83
  Mary, 83
JESTER, Jonathan, 73, 187
JOANE, Richard, 144
JOANES, Daved, 141
  David, 137
  Edward, 135, 137, 139, 140, 142, 147, 148

Morgon, 147, 149
Ruth, 139, 147
William, 111,
  137, 145
JOBSON, John, 74,
  84, 186
Jonathan, 187
Michael, 83, 97,
  160, 166, 185
William, 97
JOCE, Margaret, 20
Pasco, 159, 160
Pascoe, 20
Thomas, 20
JOHN, 42
a Dutchman, 104
Edward, 141
James, 39
Sanders, 43
JOHN CARVIL HYNSONS
PART OF HYNSONS
CHANCE, 57
JOHNS, Enoch, 188
Richard, 20
Robert, 169
JOHNS ADDITION, 57,
  82
JOHNS CHANCE, 57
JOHNS CHANCE AND
SALEM
RESURVEYED, 57
JOHNS LOTT, 57
JOHNS NEGLECT, 28,
  57
JOHNS TRIANGLE, 57
JOHNSON, Batrix,
  179
Edward William,
  20, 172
Gabrill, 57
Holeman, 20
Jacob, 139
John, 20, 68,
  157, 160
Josiah, 152, 172,
  177, 192
Mary, 141
Peter, 55, 141,
  142
Petter, 137, 140,
  141
Richard, 20, 53,
  61
Samuel, 20
Susanna, 20
Thomas, 20
William, 20, 106,
  163, 171
JOHNSONS LOT, 9, 14
JOHNSONS LOTT, 57
JOHNSTON, Benjamin,
  185
Edward William,
  185
Jno., 159, 160
Thomas, 20
JOHNSTONE, John,
  159
JOINER, Benjamin,
  183
JOINERS FANCY, 57
JOINGS, 57
JOLLE, John, 169
JOLLY, John, 169
JONES, Anne, 169
Benjamin, 20, 78,
  161, 172, 182
Charles, 172, 186
Darius, 184
David, 20
Edward, 49, 53
George, 173
Griffen, 157
Griffin, 20, 74,
  92
Griffith, 54,
  154, 156, 158,
  186
Henry, 51, 161
Heugh, 131
Jacob, 21, 56,
  57, 158, 159,
  162
James, 81, 185,
  186
Jane, 169
John, 21, 47, 50,
  64, 157, 158,
  159, 160, 169,
  180, 182, 183,
  184, 188
Margarett, 133,
  161
Martha, 76
Mary, 21, 82, 169
Morgan, 51, 65
Morgon, 146
Peter, 21, 57,
  161
Philip, 182
Rice, 21, 150
Richard, 183
Robert, 21, 57
Samuel, 185
Thomas, 21, 45,
  57, 153, 163,
  169, 172, 182,
  186
Will, 101
William, 21, 58,
  66, 72, 102,
  103, 150, 156,
  169, 172, 173,
  187
JONES ADDITION, 21
JONES ADVENTURE,
  21, 31
JONE'S GORE, 57
JONES GORE, 21
JONES INCOGNITO, 57
JONES NEGLECT, 34,
  82
JONE'S VENTURE, 9,
  10
JONES VENTURE, 1,
  34
JONES'S ADDITION,
  57
JONES'S ADVENTURE,
  57
JONES'S NEGLECT, 57
JONES'S PART OF
  BROAD OAK, 57
JONES'S VENTURE, 58
JONNES, Edward,
  123, 124
Elezabeth, 123,
  124
Ruth, 123
JONSON, Alexander,
  123
Peter, 123
Petter, 128, 139
Presillia, 123
JORDAN, John, 21
JOSIAH, Emanuel, 21
JOYANT, John, 185
Stephen, 185
JOYNER, William,
  49, 140, 149
JOYNERS FANCY, 33
JUDD, David, 169

INDEX   233

JUDGKINS, Obadiah, 131
JUNIFER, Daniell, 141
JUREY, Elizabeth, 83, 89
JUSTICE, Peter, 171

-K-
KANNE, Edward, 137
KANSBEARE, Anthony, 169
KATEN, Mary, 21
KATON, William, 21
KEAIN, David, 171
KEAR, Benjamin, 21
  James, 21
KEARE, Thomas, 44
KEARS, Thomas, 21
KEARS ADDITION, 24
KEARTON, John, 90
KEATING, Mary, 159
  William, 159
KEATON, John, 96
  Lambert, 96
  William, 159, 160
KEATTING, William, 166
KEDEDAY, Patrick, 21
KEDGER, Robert, 58
KEDGERSTON, 58
KEELEE, John, 141
KEENE, Mr., 144
KEGGERTON, 36
KELLEY, Alexander, 21, 58
  Andrew, 185
  Benjamin, 154
  James, 154, 186
  Mary, 21
KELLEYS CHOICE, 26
KELLY, Alexander, 58
  Andrew, 86
  Edward, 173
  James, 58, 74, 93, 173, 184
  John, 173
  William, 188
KELLY LANGFORD, 12, 30
KELLY LONGFORD, 58
KELLYS ADDITION,
21, 58
KELLYS CHANCE, 21, 58
KELLYS CHOICE, 23, 58, 82
KELLYS LONGFORD, 10
KEMP, Thomas, 184
KEMPS BEGINNING, 7, 10, 11, 14, 15, 27, 40, 41, 58, 82
KEMPSHEAR, 58
KEMPSTONE, Richard, 141
KENDAL, Robert, 182
  William, 73
KENDALL, William, 21
KENDOLL, James, 180
  William, 180
KENEDY, John, 184
  William, 184
KENNADT, Patrick, 21
KENNARD, Ann, 21, 43, 52
  Daniel, 182
  Dennis, 182
  J., 152
  Jno. Tilden, 152
  John, 21, 58, 74, 76, 90, 152, 153, 156, 163, 182
  John T., 75, 77, 156
  Joseph, 21, 52
  Mary, 43, 52
  Nathan, 76
  Nathaniel, 21, 61, 62, 82, 96, 152, 153, 156, 171, 172
  Owen, 156, 184
  Phil., 154, 160
  Philip, 43, 159, 160, 176
  Phillip, 21, 43, 58, 69
  Richard, 21, 62, 65, 172, 184
  Sarah, 21, 43, 159, 160, 162
  Stephen, 21, 70,
76, 92, 153, 182
  William, 76, 156, 182, 184
KENNARDS DISCOVERY, 21, 58, 82
  alias Chance, 1
KENNARDS DISCOVERY RESURVEYED, 21
KENNARDS FANCY, 21, 58, 82
KENNARDS FARM, 58, 82
KENNARDS POINT, 5, 21, 58, 82
KENNDAY, Edward, 21
  Elizabeth, 21
KENNEDY, Jane, 21
  Patrick, 21
  Roger, 21
KENNY, William, 182
KENSLAUGH,
  Dominick, 21, 70
  John, 22
KENT, Joseph, 107
  Robert, 131, 133, 135, 136, 137, 138, 141, 142
  Thomas, 181
KENT COUNTY, 13, 22
KENT LOT, 12, 82
KENT LOTT, 2, 26, 58
KENT MANNOR, 3
KENT MANOR, 25, 28, 39, 58, 82
KENTON, William, 159
KERR, Andrew, 188
KERRILL, Mary, 169
KERTON, John, 185
  Mary, 161
KEVENTON, 40
KEY, William, 61, 66, 147
KEYBORNS CHOICE, 25
KEYNES, Thomas, 111
KEYS, William, 22
KEYTON, William, 82, 188
KILLEHUNTE,
  Mordecai, 187
KILLENSWORTHMORE, 58
KILLINGSWORTH MORE

ENLARGED, 2
KILLINGSWORTHMORE,
 9, 11, 17, 19,
 26, 27, 28, 34,
 35, 36, 41, 58,
 82
KILLINGSWORTHMORE
 ENLARGED, 13,
 21, 37
KILLINS WORTH MORE,
 58
KILLINSWORTHMORE,
 1, 58
KIMBOLTON, 11, 34,
 39, 58
KINCAID, Peter, 161
KINDAL, William, 96
KINDLE, Stephen,
 172
KINDNESS, 4, 40, 82
KINDNESS, THE, 58
KING, Daniel, 182
 Elias, 46, 63,
 150, 175, 178
 Elioys, 58
 Elizabeth, 22,
 135
 Ellenor, 135, 140
 James, 22, 66
 John, 22
 Joseph, 179
 Mr., 143
 Samuel, 133, 134,
 135, 137, 139,
 140
 Samuell, 135,
 136, 142, 143,
 144, 148
 William, 187
KINGE, Samuell, 139
KINGS PREVENTION,
 26, 33, 36, 58
KINNARD, Ann, 163
 Benjamin, 173
 Mr., 163
 Thomas, 97
 William, 172
KINSEY, Thomas, 22
KINSLAUGH,
 Dominick, 44
 John, 69
KINSON, Stephen, 22
 Thomas, 164, 165
KINVIN WROTH'S LOT,
58
KIRKWOOD, Richard,
 181
KIRTON, William, 98
KITHISON, Benjamin,
 186
KNAP, Robert, 22,
 58, 118
KNAPE, Robert, 125,
 126
KNAPLEY, 22, 58
KNAPLEY GREEN, 23,
 40, 58
KNAPP, Robert, 120,
 121, 122
KNAVE STAND OFF, 1,
 58
KNIGHT, Christ.,
 182
 John, 126
 Peeter, 104
 Richard, 183
 Stephen, 22
KNIGHTON, Isaac,
 169
 Thomas, 136, 137
KNIMPTUM, Thomas,
 172
KNOCK, Benjamin, 22
 Daniel, 172
 Francis, 22, 79,
 88, 185
 Henery, 156
 Henry, 22, 44,
 49, 58, 157, 187
 Jane, 169
 John, 22, 159,
 160
 Nathaniel, 22,
 75, 79, 82, 94,
 165, 166, 171,
 187, 189
 William, 22, 82,
 162, 185, 186,
 190
KNOCK FOLLY, 9
KNOCK HARBOUR, 58
KNOCKS FOLLY, 23,
 58
KNOCKS HARBOUR, 22,
 32
KNOCKS RANGE, 22,
 58, 82
KNOLEMAN, Anthony,
22
 Richard, 22
KNOLMAN, Peter, 169
KNOTS, George, 112
 Jonathan, 158
KNOWLES, Gey, 128
 John, 22, 169
 Ruth, 126
KNOWLMAN, Jane, 22
KNOWLMANS DESIRE,
 17
KNOWLOES, James,
 169
KNOX RANGE, 22

-L-
L---WELL, Edward,
 136
LABOURN, George,
 153
LACY, John, 169
LADAMORE, Mr., 121
LADDS, William,
 144, 145, 146
LADIMOORE, Rogere,
 125
LAMB, Daniel, 92,
 96
 Edward, 22
 Francis, 22, 58,
 172, 186
 George, 22, 78,
 82, 185
 James, 186
 John, 58, 82, 99,
 153, 186
 Joshua, 22, 82
 Pearce, 53, 78,
 90, 183
 Peirce, 22
 Thomas, 74, 80,
 82, 156, 186
LAMBE, Henry, 143
LAMBS MEADOW, 9, 22
LAMBS MEADOW
 RESURVEYED, 58
LAMBS MEADOWS, 22,
 82
LAMBS RANGE, 22, 82
LANCASTER, 22
 John, 22
LANCESTER, George,
 138, 141
LAND, Phillip, 65,

70
LANDERS, William, 169
LANDING, 8
LANDING, THE, 58
LANDOSS, William, 169
LANE, Edward, 169
  Humphrey, 169
  Richard, 172, 180
  Robert, 169
  William, 97
LANG, James, 169
  John, 169
LANGFORD, 9
  John, 58
LANGFORD NECK, 34, 58
LANGFORD NECK RESURVEYED, 9, 15
LANGFORDS NECK, 82
LANGFORDS NECK RESURVEYED, 58
LANHAM, James, 22
LARENHAM, 58
LARKIN, John, 58
  Thomas, 46
LARKINS, Thomas, 22
LARKINS ADDITION, 7, 14, 16, 17, 22, 26, 32, 35, 40, 58
LARKINS ADDITION AND MILLFORK, 33
LARKINS ADDITION TO MILLFORK, 16
LARRANCE, James, 166
  John, 145
LARY, Joseph, 187
LASAELLS, John, 186
LASHBROOK, Abel, 169
LASHINGTON, James, 169
LAST, 1, 82
LAST, THE, 58
LATHAM, Robert, 187
LAUDS MANOR, 82
LAUNDERS, William, 169
LAURENCE, Adam, 172
LAUT, William, 100

INDEX

LAVENHAM, 24
LAWRENCE, James, 183, 187
  John, 133, 135, 137
  Wiliam, 142
  William, 136, 147, 185
LAWSON, Powell, 118
LAYBORNE, John, 95
LAYTON, 25
LAZENBY, William
  John, 173
LEADHORN, James, 169
LEAKE, Edward, 136, 137, 142
  Richard, 54, 55, 60
LEANARD, Joseph, 169
LEANE, Robert, 169
LEATHERBURY,
  Johnathan, 155
  Jonathan, 22, 179
LEE, Arthur, 162, 164, 165
  Hannah, 102
LEEADS, Capt., 129
  William, 128, 130
LEECH, Edward, 22, 178
LEED, William, 114
LEEDES, Will, 101
  William, 106, 107, 113, 114
LEEDS, Wiliam, 109
  William, 105, 107, 113, 118, 127, 175
LEEKE, Edward, 127
LEGG, Grace, 169
  Henry, 169
  William, 169
LELLWOOD, Sarah, 169
LEMON, Francis, 171
  John, 98
LENEGAR, George, 163
LENNAN, Francis, 96, 98
LENNON, Francis, 77, 189

235

LENNOX, Richard, 180
LENOX, Richard, 22
LEO, Valerus, 104, 105, 106, 111
LEONARD, Francis, 187
P., 159
LESLEY, John, 173
LESSENBY, William
  John, 173
LETHERBURY,
  Peregrine, 177, 184
LETTOU, Thomas, 169
LEVEL FIELDS, 58
LEVEL RIDGE, 17, 33
LEVELL, 5, 58
LEVELL RIDGE, 9
LEVES, Thomas, 129
LEVINGHAM, 82
LEVINGTON, 82
LEWELLIN, Andy, 58
LEWIS, Abraham, 22
  Elizabeth, 143
  Evin, 22
  Fanny, 22
  Francis, 22
  John, 135
  Robert, 22
  Thomas, ??, 146, 147
  William, 22
LEYBOURN, George, 22, 154
LIGHT, William, 169
LINCH, Edmond, 159
  Edmund, 74
  Nicholas, 58
LINCHHORN, 82
LINCHS CHANCE, 58
LINCOLN, 8, 40
  John, 156
  Jonathan, 58
LINCOLN INN FIELDS, 41
LINCOLNE, 3, 16, 58
  Jonathan, 22, 58
LINCOLNS INN FIELD, 58
LINCOLNS INN FIELDS, 22
LINEGAR, George, 22
  Jacob, 22

236   INHABITANTS OF KENT COUNTY, MARYLAND, 1637-1787

LINS, Charles, 97
LINSTEAD, Thomas, 134, 136, 137
LINSTED, Thomas, 130
LIPPEN, John, 169
LIPPESLEY, George, 169
LIPPIN, William, 133
LIPPINS, William, 140
LISBEY, James, 22
LISCOMBE, Thomas, 169
LISLE, Rebecca, 22
LITITLEWORTH, 8
LITTLE, Adam, 22
  George, 22, 94, 162, 189
  John, 91, 95, 96
  Mary, 85
  Rebecca, 166
  Rebeckah, 74, 83
  Robert, 23, 94, 172, 186
  Thomas, 165
  William, 83, 85, 166, 186, 190
LITTLE BRITTAIN, 3, 82
LITTLE DRAYTON, 58
LITTLE FORREST, 14, 27, 38, 58
LITTLE GROVE, 2, 3, 7, 21, 22, 23, 24, 28, 31, 39, 58, 83
LITTLE NECK, 58
LITTLES, George, 171
LITTLEWORTH, 8, 58
LIUS, Charles, 97
LIVELY NECK, 20
LLEAGE, Peter, 170
LLOYD, Edward, 23, 118, 119, 121, 130, 153, 177, 178
  James, 23, 77, 177, 184
  Philemon, 137
  Rebecca, 23
  Richard, 23, 76, 80, 154, 156, 174, 176, 177, 179, 190
  Richard B., 75, 77, 93
LOACH, John, 169
LOAN, Richard, 169
LOCKERMAN, John, 23
LOCKETT, Elesabeth, 125
  Elesebeth, 127
  Elisa, 114
LOCUST POINT, 25, 32, 58
LODLINGTON, William, 175
LONDON BRIDGE, 24
LONDON BRIDGE, 2, 7, 10, 12, 14, 25, 83
LONDON BRIDGE RENEWED, 14, 24, 59, 83
LONDON DERRY, 59, 83
LONDONDERRY, 33
LONDONERRY, 21
LONG ACRE, 6, 21, 26, 30, 31, 59, 83
LONG COMPTON, 2, 83
LONG GORE, THE, 59
LONG NEGLECT, 10, 16, 17, 59, 83
LONG SLIPE, 25, 59, 83
LONGCOMPTOR, 59
LONGFORD NECK RESURVEYED, 33
LONGFORDS NECK, 34
LONGTHORNE, John, 115
LORAIN, Thomas, 23
LORD, Thomas, 180
LORDS GIFT, 8, 59, 83
  John, 7
  Williams Lot, 8
LORDS GIFT RESURVEYED, 59
LORDS GRATIOUS GRAND, 11
LORDS GRATIOUS GRANT, 12
LORDS MANOR, 83
LORDSHIPS GRATIOUS GRANT, 11
LORIAN, John, 181
LOTS 5 AND 6 IN CHESTERTOWN, 59
LOTS ADDITION, 84
LOTS IN GEORGETOWN, 59
LOUDWELL, Jane, 169
LOULLIT, James, 23
LOUTILL, James, 159
  Jas., 160
LOVE, Hugh, 103
LOVE AND FRIENDSHIP, 84
LOVEGROVE, James, 180
LOVELL, Robert, 169
LOVELY, Deliverance, 55, 59, 117, 126
  Elizabeth, 117
  Mr., 125
  Mrs., 126
LOVELY NECK, 15, 20, 22, 84
LOVELYS NECK, 20, 59
LOVEMONEY, Simon, 188
LOVERING, Capt., 178
LOVLY, Deliverance, 115, 119, 121
  Dilliverance, 121
  Elizabeth, 121
LOWDER, Ann, 147
  Charles, 23, 147
  Edward, 146, 147
  Richard, 146
LOWE, Henry, 23, 46, 54, 59, 157, 178
  Sussannah, 54
  Sussannah Maria, 46, 59
  Vincent, 146
LOWER, Vincent, 145
LOWER BENNET, 31
LOWER BENNETT, 23, 26
LOWER FORDS, 37
LOWES BENNETT, 46,

59
LOWMAN, John, 180
  Richard, 87, 184
  Samuel, 23
LOWMANS, Richard, 23
LOWMUTH,
  Theophilius, 172
LOYD, Abraham, 43
  Philemon, 71
LOYDD, Edward, 110
LOYDE, Phillamond, 145
  Phillomon, 142
LUCK, 17, 37, 59, 84
LUCYS RECREATION, 25, 59, 84
LUKE, William, 169
LUMBAR, Franchis, 106
  Rebecka, 106
LUMBARD, Francis, 100, 101, 102, 103
  Rebecka, 128
LUMBER, Frances, 103
  Franchis, 111
LUMBURD, Francis, 111
LURAN, Thomas, 154
LUSBY, Draper, 23
  Joseph, 184
LUSSLAKE, John, 169
LUTT, Alse, 114
LUX, Richard, 23
LYNCH, Edmond, 153, 159, 160, 182
  Edmund, 23
  Edward, 156
  James, 184
  John, 23, 172, 174, 180, 182
  Nicholas, 23, 183
  Robert, 23, 51
  Samuel, 188
  Thomas, 23
  William, 153
LYNES, William, 173
LYNN, 21, 59
LYNNS PRIME CHOICE, 24
LYONS, George, 187

LYONS HALL, 11, 15, 59, 84
LYPPINS, Elizabeth, 138
  William, 138, 139

-M-
MACALL, George, 55
MACANY, Isaac, 183
MCCALL, Benjamin, 23
  George, 59
MCCANN, Edward, 23
MCCARTNY, Robert, 129
MCCARTY, Kelly, 181
  Morris, 24
MCCAY, Isaac, 185
MCCAYS PURCHASE, 18, 84
MCCHUSH, Agnes, 169
MCCLACKLAN, James, 23
MCCLAIN, James, 74, 79, 83, 91, 153, 154
MCCLANE, James, 156
  William, 23
MCCLANNAHORN,
  Nathaniel, 23
MCCLEAN, Anna
  Malla, 98
  Hugh, 174
  James, 23, 190
  John, 23
  Margaret, 98
  Mary, 98
  William, 98
MCCLELLAND,
  Nathaniel, 171
MCCLINTOCK, Alex., 23
MCCLURE, James, 87
MCCOMB, Eleazer, 174
MCCOMES, Jacob M., 23
  John, 23
  William, 23
MCCOMES DESIRE, 40
MCCONNAKIN, 84
MCCONNICAN, Daniel, 172
MCCONNOACAN, 5

MCCOPPIN, Thomas, 181
MCCOY, Absalom, 76
  Absolom, 97
  Absolum, 184
MCCOYS PURCHASE, 84
MCCRAKIN, John, 23
MCCUBBIN, Charles, 23
MACCUBBIN,
  Nicholas, 24
MCCUBBIN, Nicholas, 87, 90, 93, 154
MCCUBBINS, Charles, 162, 164
MACCUBINS, Mary, 62
  Nicholas, 62
MCDARMONT, Thomas, 164, 165
MCDARMOTT, Thomas, 165
MCDERMOT, Charles, 98, 164
MCDERMOTT, Daniel, 23
  Sarah, 179
MCDOAL, James, 173
MCDONALD, Jeremiah, 186
MCDONNALD, Sarah, 85
MCDONNOLD, Anguish, 172
MCDOUGALS CHANCE, 25
MCDOUGHAL, John, 163
MCDOWELL, James, 188
  Rebecca, 23
  Samuel, 188
  William, 188
MCDOWGAL, John, 59
MCDOWGALL, John, 23
MCDOWGALLS CHANCE, 23
MCDOWGALS CHANCE, 59
MCDUGALLS CHANCE, 84
MCFALL, Peregrine, 183
MCGOWAN, John, 171
MCGREGORY, John,

238　INHABITANTS OF KENT COUNTY, MARYLAND, 1637-1787

181
MCGUIRE, John, 179
　Patrick, 23
MCHAFFEY, Jere.,
　181
MCHANNY, Dennis,
　161
MACHAR, Thomas, 43
MCHARD, Isaac, 155
　Joseph, 96, 155
　Rosannah, 155
MACHER, Thomas, 48
MCHERD, Joseph, 23
　Samuel, 23
MACHOAKIN, 136
　John, 136
MCHURD, Hugh, 23
MCILVAIN, William,
　23
MACKALL, Susanna,
　193
MACKCONICA, John,
　132
MACKDOWGALLS
　CHANCE, 7
MCKENNY, William,
　23
MACKEY, 4
　Alexander, 24
MCKEY, Elijah, 188
　Jno., 161
MACKEY, John, 24
MCKEY, John, 23
MACKEY, Mary, 24
　William, 24, 59
MACKEYS CHANCE, 59
MACKEYS DESIRE, 11,
　24, 38, 59, 84
MACKEYS PURCHASE,
　11, 18, 37
MCKIM, John, 184
　William, 184
MCKINLEY, Hugh, 96
　Margaret, 96
　Sarah, 76
MCKINLY, Hugh, 184
MCKINNEY, John, 172
MACKLIN, 59
　Robert, 59
MCKNIGHT, George,
　194
　Roger, 194
MACKOAKIN, 59
　John, 59

MCLACHLAN, Henry,
　60
　James, 162, 164,
　165
MCLACKLIN, James,
　23
MCLANE, James, 23
　Neal, 24
MCLEAN, William, 55
MCMANUS, John, 24
MCMULLIN, Andrew,
　186
MCNAMARA, Dennis,
　184
MCNEAL, Bridget, 75
MCNEIL, John M., 24
MACNEMARRA, Thomas,
　53
MACOAKIN, 17, 31,
　35
MACOME, James, 59
MACOMES, James, 24
MACOMES DESIRE, 24,
　59
MACONAKIN, John,
　147
MACONICK, John, 101
MACONIKIN, John,
　128
MCQUEEN, Donald,
　155
MCQUINN, Donald,
　184
MCVENY, Dennis, 24
MADESTARD, Thomas,
　104
MAFFOTT, George, 44
MAGGIES JOYNTURE,
　59
MAGGIES JOYNTURE
　RESURVEYED, 59
MAGGISON, John,
　130, 132, 133,
　137, 138, 139,
　140
MAGGISSON, Abell,
　139
　John, 131
MAGGYS JOINTURE, 25
MAGISON, Abell, 123
　John, 123, 131
MAGISSON, John,
　124, 142
MAGNOR, Edward, 24

　John, 24, 180
MAGRUDERS DELIGHT,
　41
MAHEW, Zacaryah,
　145
MAHON, Thomas, 24
MAIDEN LOT, 5, 14
MAIDEN LOTT, 17, 18
MAIDENS LOT, 19, 38
MAIDENS LOTT, 2,
　22, 26, 31, 59,
　84
MAINE, Abraham, 169
　David, 122
MALLETT, Joseph,
　169
　William, 169
MANCATER,
　Elexander, 126
MANGY PORKY, 7
MANLEY, Peter, 169
MANLOVE, Mary, 24
　Mathews, 24
MANN, G. Vansant,
　24
　George, 190
　Joseph, 24, 99
　William, 172, 188
MANNERING,
　Margreet, 114
MANNING, Mary, 169
MANSELL, Thomas,
　24, 66
MANSFIELD, James,
　181
　Robert, 24, 188
　Samuel, 24, 89,
　158, 159, 160,
　188
　Thomas, 181, 184
　William, 180, 188
MARAH, Timothy, 184
MARBY, Robert, 186
MARCEY, Petter, 157
MARCH, John, 24,
　58, 89, 150,
　153, 162
　Thomas, 126
MARCY, Peter, 24
MARGARETS DELIGHT,
　3, 8, 16, 29,
　38, 40, 84
MARGARETS END, 30,
　33, 40, 84

MARGARETTS DELIGHT, 31, 40, 41
MARGARETTS END, 13, 40, 59
MARIES RAMBLES, 23
MARKET PLACE, 15, 39
MARKET PLACE RESURVEYED, 84
MARKLAND, Ancibel Crampton Blake, 193
  Matthew, 193
MARKS, Nicholas, 169
MARLEY, Robert, 85, 166
MARLIN, William, 156
MARLOW, Benjamin, 163
MARR, William, 48
MARRAH, Morriss, 172
MARRIOTT, Lovering, 153
MARROW BONE, 34, 84
MARROWBONE, 59
MARSH, Margrett, 126
  Mr., 102, 107, 135
  Mrs., 106
  Sarah, 107
  Thomas, 24, 100, 101, 102, 103, 133, 134, 139, 145, 146, 147, 148, 154, 175
MARSH POINT, 84
MARSHALL, Charles, 24
  John, 24
  Thomas, 169
MARSHALLS OUTLETT, 24
MARSHES, 1, 17, 25, 84
MARSHEY POINT, 59
MARSHY HOPE, 59
MARSHY POINT, 84
MARTIN, Andrew, 183
  Barbra, 135
  Elizabeth, 110

Goodie, 109
James, 188
John, 135, 147, 181
Mary, 111
Robert, 101, 103, 106, 107, 109, 110, 112, 113, 116, 121
Thomas, 59
MARTINE, Goodie, 108
  goodman, 108
  Robbine, 108
  Robert, 107, 110, 126
  Robine, 108
MARTINS, 16
MARTINS NEST, 6, 59
MARTYN, William, 169
MARYS PURCHASE, 37
MASEY, Enoch, 171
MASLIN, Britain, 166
  Francis, 98
  James, 24, 84, 165
  Thomas, 24, 48, 74
MASLING, Boutain, 180
  Francis, 180
  Hamon, 180
  James, 180
  Thomas, 180
MASLINS POSSESSION, 84
MAS(S)ON, George, 187
  Hugh, 24, 47
  Joseph, 24
  Mary, 24
  Mathew, 45
  Richard, 148, 150
  Thomas, 144
  William, 91, 180
MASSEY, Abednego, 59, 187
  Ann, 94
  Daniel, 24, 59
  Daniel Toas, 94
  Daniel Toes, 186, 190
  Daniel Tres, 190

Ebenezer, 51, 59, 64, 66, 186
Elijah, 24, 188
Elisha, 188
James, 181
Jane, 161
John, 94, 171
Joseph, 24, 49, 51, 59, 64, 66, 94, 186
Josiah, 94, 96, 185
Katharine, 24
Milcah, 24
Nicholas, 24, 52, 59, 66
Peter, 24, 59, 66, 159, 160
Petter, 157
Rebecca, 94, 96
Samuel, 24, 55, 57
Sarah, 24
Solomon, 162
Stephen, 186
Thomas, 24
William, 24, 59, 163, 169
MASSEYS LOTT, 24, 59
MASSEYS PART OF MERS'S LOCK, 59
MASSEYS VENTURE, 18, 24, 59
MASSEYS VENTURE RESURVEYED, 59
MASSLIN, Thomas, 190
MASSY, Abednego, 166
  Abednego, 92
  Daniel, 163, 164
  Daniel Toas, 86, 99, 172
  Daniel Toes, 166
  Ebenezer, 77, 83, 84, 165
  Elijah, 72, 166
  G. Nathan, 165
  George Nathaniel, 165
  Hannah, 86, 166
  John, 72, 83, 86, 90, 99, 166

INHABITANTS OF KENT COUNTY, MARYLAND, 1637-1787

Joseph, 86, 165
Josiah, 78, 167
Mary, 86
Nicholas, 158, 163
Sarah, 166
Solomon, 163, 164, 165
Stephen, 166
Thomas, 163
William, 163
Zorobable, 164
MASSYS ADVENTURE, 84
MASSYS LOT RESURVEYED, 84
MASTICKE, John, 104
MATCHLER, Daniel, 155
MATHERS, Richard, 169
MATHEWS, Hugh, 25
John, 25
MATHIAS, 10, 32, 84
MATTERS, Richard, 169
MATTHEWS, John, 183
William, 169, 180
MATTHIAS, 59
MATTOCKS, Rice, 121
MATZLER, David, 184
MAULDEN, Francis, 123
MAXFIELD, James, 130
John, 160
MAXWELL,
Allexander, 138, 141
Ann, 25
James, 25
John, 59, 154, 165, 174, 176, 177, 190
Robert, 25, 43, 45, 66, 84, 86, 165, 166, 187, 188, 190, 191
William, 25, 45, 70, 82, 84, 86, 87, 88, 184, 185, 189, 191
MAXWELLS PURCHASE, 59, 84

MAY, Catherine, 169
John, 188
William, 169
MAYFORD, 30
MAYL:, Anto, 139
MAYNARD, Charles, 126
MAYO, Mary, 169
MAYS, William, 169
MEAD, Mother Telah, 169
MEADOW, 8, 28
MEADOWS, 8, 84
MEADOWS, THE, 59, 84
MEAGER, William, 169
MEARS, William, 183
MECANACKEY, John, 117
MECART, Robert, 127
MECARTER, Robert, 117
MECARTNA, Robert, 126
MECAY, Alexander, 63
MECENNY, John, 147
MECHAY, Alexander, 59
MECHAYS PURCHASE, 59
MECONICON, Barbary, 123
John, 123, 124, 131
Mary, 124, 129
MECONNIKIN, John, 114, 118, 122
Mary, 122
MECONNY, Macume, 125, 127
MECONOKIN, John, 51, 53
MEDFORD, Bullman, 25
Bulmer, 53
Buttmer, 162
George, 25, 59, 85, 158, 159, 160, 188
Macall, 151, 153
Marmaduke, 25, 78, 79, 81, 89, 96, 152, 154, 156, 186
McCall, 25, 179, 186
Susanah, 89
Susannah, 78, 80, 84
Thn, 151
Thomas, 25, 76, 80, 81, 85, 153, 157
Unit, 25
Unity, 59
MEDFORDS MISTAKE, 11, 18, 59
MEDFORDS PART OF SUFFOLK, 59
MEEDS, Margaret, 158
MEEK, Walter, 52
MEEKE, Walter, 53
MEEKINS, Frances, 25
MEEKS, Aquila, 93, 183
Aquilla, 73, 79, 80
James, 25
Mary, 78, 156
Robert, 25, 59, 78, 153, 172, 182
St. Leger, 77, 78, 182
William, 172, 182
MEEKS PART OF FORREST OF DEAN RESURVEYED, 59
MEERS INCLOSURE, 14
MEGONIGIL, Morris, 180
MELHUISH, Agnes, 169
MELTON, Abraham, 25
Barbara, 25
Isaac, 25
John, 25
Joseph, 25
Martha, 90
Samuel, 25
MEMENTO MORE, 15
MEMENTO MORI, 34, 59, 84
MERCHANT, George,

INDEX

183
William, 181
MERETON, 36
MERIOTT, Leverings, 59
MERRETT, Lovering, 25
  Lovring, 80
  Sarah, 84
  William, 81, 82, 86, 89
MERRIT, William, 190, 191
MERRITT, Lovering, 60
  Loving, 59
  Lovrin, 180
  Martha, 84, 92
  Mary, 97, 98
  Samuel, 97, 98
  Sarah, 74, 75, 83, 93, 156
  William, 53, 97, 98, 162, 165, 166, 185
MERRITTS ADDITION, 59
MERRITTS DISCOVERY, 60, 84
MERRITTS DISCOVERY RESURVEYED, 60
MERRY, John, 182
MESSETER, Abraham, 148
METCALFE, Rachell, 117
METHAM, John, 100
METZLER, Daniel, 25
MEUSON, William, 169
MICHAY, Robert, 46
MICHELL, W., 130
MICON, William, 169
MIDDLE BRANCH, 3, 10, 27, 35, 60, 84
MIDDLE CHANCE, 9
MIDDLE NECK, 5, 9, 16, 18, 37, 60, 84
MIDDLE NECK, THE, 60
MIDDLE PLANTATION, 13, 19, 33, 84

Thomas, 37
MIDDLE PLANTATION, THE, 60
MIDDLE SPRING, 8, 30, 36, 42, 60, 84, 146
MIDDLEBROOK, Isaac, 186
MIDDLETON, John, 25
  Joseph, 186, 189
  Luke, 179
  Lutener, 25
  Luttner, 156
MIDLETON, Lukener, 49
MIERS, Andrew, 191
  John, 79, 81, 88, 90, 99, 167
  Luke, 25, 60, 73, 83, 84, 100
  Stephen, 60
  William, 83, 171, 189
MIERS CHANCE, 38, 60
MIERS LUCK, 24, 25
MIERS NEGLECT, 84
MIERS RESURVEY, 84
MIFFLIN, Daniel, 25
  Sothey, 25
MIFLIN, Mary, 72, 75
MIKNEY, James, 188
MILBORN, William, 157
MILES, Charles, 60
MILES END, 26, 60
MILESFORD, 60
MILFORD, 4, 84
MILL, 84
  John, 148
MILL FORK, 3, 4, 7, 85
MILL FORKS, 60
MILL HILL, 17, 60
MILL LAND, 85
MILL POINT, 60
MILLBERY, Josh, 25
MILLBORN, John, 25
  Samuel, 25
  William, 157
MILLBURNE, William, 25
MILLER, Arthur, 25,

59, 77, 78, 97, 98, 151, 155, 169
  Charles, 181
  James, 183, 186
  John, 171
  Mi:, 141
  Michael, 25, 42, 43, 44, 45, 49, 50, 51, 60, 61, 71, 85, 142, 143, 145, 148, 150, 151, 175, 183
  Michaell, 64, 142, 143, 144, 145, 147, 148
  Mitchell, 146
  Nathan, 183
  Nathaniel, 26, 60, 85
  Richard, 26, 80, 85, 177, 183, 191
  Samuel, 26, 85, 94, 183
  Thomas, 26, 183
  Walter, 85
MILLERS ADVENTURE, 1
MILLERS CHANCE, 85
MILLERS DELIGHT, 85
MILLERS DELIGHT ENLARGED, 60
MILLERS FANCY, 60
MILLERS PURCHASE, 25, 26, 85
MILLERS PURCHASE RESURVEYED, 60
MILLERS SATISFACTION, 6, 60
MILLFORD, 17, 28, 32, 37, 60, 85
MILLFORK, 12, 24, 25, 32, 36, 39, 40
MILLIGAN, George, 26
MILLON PURCHASE, 8
MILLPOINT, 34
MILLS, 85
MILLS DOWN, 23
MILLWARD, Charles,

26, 82, 85
James, 85
Loverly, 60
MILLWARDS CHOICE,
  26, 60, 85
MILLWOOD, Lowry, 26
MILTON, Abraham,
  58, 180
Richard, 180
Samuel, 66
MILWARD, Charles,
  156, 183
Chs., 154
James, 154
MIRES, John, 185,
  187
Luke, 187
Stephen, 187, 190
William, 187
MIRES RESURVEY, 60
MIRESE, Luke, 60
MISTAKE ALIAS
  PERKINS MISTAKE,
  28, 42
MITCHELL, Edward,
  26, 49, 51, 60,
  63
John, 48, 62,
  144, 179, 187
Richard, 169
William, 65, 70
MITCHELL PARK, 26
MITCHELLS
  ADVENTURE, 26,
  60
MITCHELLS CHANCE,
  6, 35, 39, 40,
  60, 85
MITCHELLS PARK, 35,
  60
MITCHELLS PROPOSAL,
  60
MITCHELLS RANGE, 6
MITCHELLS RUQUE, 60
MITCHELLS VIEW, 60
MITCHELS CHANCE, 7
MITCHELS CHOICE, 5
MITCHELS PARK, 11,
  23
MITCHELS RANGE, 5
MOAD, Mother Telah,
  169
MODE, William, 26
MOFFAT, John, 88

MOFFET, George, 86,
  89
Moses, 94
Richard, 26, 159,
  160
MOFFETS CHANCE, 26
MOFFETT, George,
  26, 52, 73, 75,
  77, 78, 85, 165,
  185
Haley, 185
Jacob, 185
Jesse, 185
Moses, 185
Richard, 85, 165,
  185
Robert, 185
MOFFETTS CHANCE, 85
MOFFETTS LOTT, 26,
  85
MOFFIT, Richard,
  161
MOFFITT, George,
  94, 163, 166
Jesse, 163
Moses, 166
Richard, 166
MOGGYS JOINTURE, 85
MOLL, John, 26,
  148, 150
MOLT, William, 187
MONEY, Robert, 91,
  166, 188
Samuel, 171
William, 180
MONK, Henry, 26
MONRO, Allexander,
  104
MONTEAG,
  Conrelious, 137
MONTROSSE,
  Elizabeth, 139
MOODEY, Robert, 188
MOODY, Robert, 79,
  166
MOOR, Ruloph, 164
William, 158
MOORE, Darcus, 84,
  91
George, 80, 154,
  181, 186
Henry, 26
James, 26, 68,
  93, 154

John, 26, 43, 60,
  72, 75, 93, 94,
  151, 169, 181,
  191
Rebecca, 154
Richard, 142, 148
Ruloph, 165
Simon, 181
Thomas, 144, 148
William, 26, 169
MOORES FISHING
  GROUND, 60
MOORTON, 60
MOR, Richard, 135
MORE, Richard, 138,
  140, 141, 142
MORETON, 4, 7, 14,
  36, 40
MORFETT, George, 60
MORFETTS LOTT, 26,
  60
MORGAN, Barbary,
  115, 123
Charles, 181
Frances, 118
Francis, 106
Henerie, 108
Henery, 103, 104,
  107, 109, 110,
  111
Henry, 26, 57,
  100, 101, 102,
  110, 114, 116,
  117, 118, 119,
  120, 121, 123,
  124, 126, 129,
  175
Jarvis, 57
Job, 169
John, 26, 115,
  117, 121, 124,
  125, 129, 130,
  133, 137, 140
John A., 114
Margret, 115
Margrett, 123
Mary, 124
Mr., 129
William, 26, 130,
  131
MORGANS C. LAND, 85
MORGON, Frances,
  129
Francis, 113

INDEX 243

Henry, 125, 127, 128
John, 125, 128
MORPHEY, George, 60
MORPHEYS CHANCE, 60
MORRIS, Ann, 124
  Ellen, 124
  Jeane, 124
  John, 161
  Joseph, 172
  Mary, 124
  Richard, 124, 184
  Thomas, 169
  William, 169
MORRISON, Hugh, 26
MORRO, John, 169
MORSALL, Thomas, 60
MORSALLS LOT, 60
MORSELL, Thomas, 26, 60
MORSELLS PART OF KILLINGSWORTHMORE, 60
MORTON, 1, 23, 35
  Elizabeth, 136
MORTON RESURVEYED, 14, 60
MOSES, Ruth, 169
MOTHERS CARE, 85
MOTHERS CARE RESURVEYED, 60
MOTHERS GIFT, 3, 15, 60, 85
MOUNT, 25
MOUNT AIREY, 60
MOUNT AIRY, 85
MOUNT HARMAN, 6, 11, 35
MOUNT HARMON, 27, 34, 36, 37, 85
MOUNT HARMON RESURVEYED, 36
MOUNT HERMAN, 10, 26, 27
MOUNT HERMON, 60
MOUNT HOOPE, 37
MOUNT HOPE, 12, 21, 26, 60, 85
MOUNT HOPE RESURVEYED, 60
MOUNT PLEASANT, 8, 9, 10, 60, 85
MOUNTFORD, Thomas, 46

MOUSE, William, 128
MOUSE, 122
MOY, Richard, 144
MUGGERIDGE, Joseph, 169
MULBERRY PLAIN, 19, 60
MULBERRY PLAINS, 5, 11
MULCAHY, Daniel, 172
MULLEN, Patrick, 26
MULLETT, William, 26, 169
MULLICAN, Daniel, 26
MULLINS, Jane, 169
  William, 125
MUMDAY, Thomas, 169
MUNDAY, Thomas, 169
MUNJAR, Richard, 181
  Samuel, 181
MUNTROSE, Janne, 124
MURELL, Ann, 110
  Gregory, 110, 117, 118
MURILL, Ann, 121
  Gregory, 119, 120
MURPHEY, George, 26, 57
  James, 26, 151
  John, 188
  Samuel, 26
MURPHY, Edward, 185
  Mary, 26
MURRAY, Ann, 155
  Catharine, 155
  Elizabeth, 155
  Sarah, 155
  William, 26, 154, 155
MURRELL, Gregory, 125
MUSTIAN, Edmond, 133, 134, 135
  Elizabeth, 135
MY LORDS GIFT, 85
MY LORDS GRACIOUS GRANT, 85
MYARS, John, 26, 81, 166
MYERS, John, 94,

95, 194
  Luke, 61, 165
  Lukeas, 61
MYERS CHANCE, 14, 27
MYERS INCLOSURE, 25, 60
MYERS LOT, 61
MYERS LUCK, 27, 61
MYRES, James, 185

-N-
NAB, Richard, 171
NABB, Elisha, 181
NANCYS CHANCE, 37
NANCYS CHOICE, 12, 61, 85
NANCYS FANCY, 10, 11, 13, 30, 36, 37
NANCYS HOPE, 16, 61
NANCYS HOPE RESURVEYED, 61
NANNYS CHOYCE, 28
NANNYS HOPE, 16
NANSCOYNE, John, 26
NAPLEY GREEN, 85
NASH, Alexander, 42, 123, 124, 133, 134
  Allexander, 137
  Ann, 139
  Elexander, 130
  Fransis, 126
  Richard, 136, 137, 139, 141, 143
  Sarah, 123
NATHANIELS PART OF DANBY RESURVEYED, 61
NEAL, Rubin, 186
NEALE, Edward, 26
  James, 72
  William, 128
NEALL, Edmond, 26
  Edward, 26
NEAVE, Robert, 146
NEAVES, Robert, 65
NECESSITYS HABITATION, 21, 24
NEEDFUL, 11
NEEDFULL, 61

NEEDLES, Edward, 99
NEEFS CHOICE, 85
NEGLECT, 2, 3, 6,
    11, 21, 22, 25,
    26, 28, 36, 37,
    39, 40, 41, 61,
    85
NEGLECT,THE, 61
NEGLIGENCE, 61
NEGRO, William, 100
NEIFE, Robert, 61,
    67, 71
NEIFES CHOICE, 61
NEIFS CHANCE, 39,
    61
NEIFS CHOICE, 2,
    18, 35
NEIGHBOURHOOD, 41,
    61
NEIGHBOURS NEGLECT,
    13, 61
NEIL, Charles, 180
NEIVES, Robert, 65
NEMO, John, 26, 69
NEMOE, John, 160
NEPPS CHOICE, 2
NEUMAN, Willmott,
    169
NEVES CHOICE, 85
NEW ADVENTURE, 86
NEW FORREST, 7, 20,
    61, 86
NEW HARBOUR, 35,
    37, 86
NEW HOLLAND, 27
NEW HUNTING FIELD,
    61
NEW HUNTING FIELDS,
    20
NEW KEY, 13, 16,
    22, 61, 86
NEW M. TAVERN, 86
NEW SCOTLAND, 86
NEW TOWN
    RESURVEYED, 4,
    39, 61
NEW TOWN RESURVYED,
    86
NEW YORK, 13, 18,
    20, 21, 31, 35,
    36, 37, 42, 61,
    86
NEW YORK
    RESURVEYED, 61
NEWBERRY, Thomas,
    169
NEWBOROUGH, 37
NEWCOMB, George,
    87, 91, 185
    John, 97, 98
    Robert, 26, 64
    Thomas, 26, 97,
    98
NEWELL, David, 172,
    185
    John, 186
NEWELS ADVENTURE,
    86
NEWGATE, 36
NEWLAND, Isaac, 188
    John, 171, 188
NEWMAN, Joel, 186
    John, 128
    Joseph, 128
NEWNHAM, Jonathan,
    84
NEWPORT, George,
    169
NEWSOM, Joseph, 171
NEWTON, Jonathan,
    26
    Thomas, 26
NEWTOWN, 61
    Daniel, 169
NEWTOWN RESURVEYED,
    39
NEYSBOROUGH, 61
NICHOLS, James, 26
    Jeremiah, 77, 189
    Jermeiah, 174
NICHOLSON, J., 155
    James, 174
    John, 99, 163,
    173
    Joseph, 26, 45,
    62, 90, 91, 154,
    174, 176, 177,
    190
    William, 26
NICOLS, Jere., 152
    Jeremiah, 180
NIECES CHANCE, 86
NIEFS CHOICE, 22,
    26
NINIVETH, 61
NOALMAN, Anthony,
    26
NOBLE, Elizabeth,
    26
    Mark, 179
NOLAND, Matt, 26
NORBERRY, Thomas,
    169
NORCUTT, 24, 61
    Richard, 27
NORMAN, Elizabeth,
    145
    Henry, 138, 139,
    141
    Peter, 169
    Thomas, 97, 172
NORREST, Robert, 63
NORREST DESIRE, 36
NORRIS, Daniel, 27,
    173
    James, 185
    Richard, 27
    Samuel, 27, 46,
    157, 161, 185
    Sarah, 27
    Thomas, 61, 63,
    141
NORRIS CLAIM, 36
NORRIS FOREST, 86
NORRIS FORREST, 33
NORRIS HIS FORREST,
    61
NORRIS REST, 27, 33
NORRISES FORREST,
    31
NORRIS'S DESIRE,
    18, 40
NORRIS'S DESIRE
    RESURVEYED, 61
NORRIS'S FORREST,
    1, 25
NORTH, William, 145
NORTH ANDOVER, 6,
    12, 61
NORTH EAST
    THICKETT, 61
NORTHCOAT PLAINS,
    24
NORTHERN PART OF
    STRATFORDS
    MANOR, 61
NORTHUMBERLAND, 4
NORTON, Richard, 27
NORWOOD, John, 141
NOVELS ADVENTURE, 1
NOWELL, William,
    27, 61

INDEX 245

NOWELLS ADVENTURE, 27, 61
NOWLAND, Silvester, 27
NUMBERS, John, 183
Joseph, 183
NUSOM, John, 182
NUSUME, John, 27
NUTTWELL, John, 137

-O-
OBRYAN, Laughlin, 27
O'BRYAN, William, 169
O'BRYAND, Timothy, 158
O'BRYANT, Mary Asthr., 161
OFFLEY, John, 184
OGELSBY, Charles, 173
OGILSBY, Charles, 173
OGLE, Samuel, 158
OLD TOWN, 24
OLIVIER, Margaret, 169
OLLIVER, John, 115, 121
OMEALY, Bryan, 44
OMISSION, 19
OMISSION, THE, 61
ONEALL, Hugh, 27
ORCHARD, William, 61
ORCHARDS NECK, 3, 8, 17, 30, 36, 41
OSBORNE, John, 124
Katherin, 124
Kathorine, 133
Rebecka, 123
Thomas, 123, 124, 127, 128, 129, 131, 133, 134, 137, 139, 140
William, 123, 124
OSBOURNE, Thomas, 143
OSBURNE, Thomas, 142
OSMOND, Anne, 169
OSZAKIEWSKI, Robert

Andrew, 168
OUT LETT, 86
OUT RANGE, 5, 20
OUT RANGE, THE, 61
OUTRANGE, 3, 29
OVERSIGHT, 11, 15, 21
Patrick, 21
OVERSIGHT, THE, 61
OVEY, Anthony, 27
OWENS, Richard, 118
OWINES, Mr., 108

-P-
PACA, Aquilla, 27
PACKER, Edward, 61
Walter, 126
PACKERTON, 6, 13, 61, 66, 86
PACOES POOR LOT, 2
PADBURY, Jane, 131
PAGE, Acquilla, 97
Aquila, 166, 185
Aquilla, 82, 93
John, 27, 61, 62, 73, 75, 79, 84, 86, 88, 92, 159, 160, 183, 189, 192
Jonathan, 27
Ralph, 27, 43, 52, 55, 61, 62, 64
PAGE AND MILLER, 89, 92
PAGES DISCOVERY, 61
PAGES FARM, 61
PAGES PURCHASE, 61, 62, 86
PAGES ROAD, 62, 86
PAGGESTY, William, 169
PAINER, Ann, 155
PAINTER, Nicholas, 48, 51, 70
PALMER, Bartley, 185
Benjamin, 27, 43, 44, 62, 75, 77, 86, 161, 166
John, 184, 185
Joseph, 27
Nathaniel, 27
Oliver, 27

Robert, 132, 139, 140, 169
William, 63, 69
PALMERS DESIRE, 27, 62, 86
PALMERS HAZARD, 27, 41, 62, 86
PALPILION, Luis, 114
PAPENFUSE, Edward C., 175
PARISH, John Grey, 180
PARISH OF SHREWSBERRY, 27
PARK, 32
Andrew, 171
PARKER, Derrick William, 166
Henry, 46
Mistris, 123
Peter, 111, 116, 117, 118
Thomas, 144, 146, 147
William, 27, 183, 188
PARKERS REST RESURVEYED, 62
PARKES, Andrew, 187
Robert, 146
PARKINS, Anne, 169
PARKINSON, William, 161
PARKS, John, 27
Patrick, 27, 66
PARK'S REST, 12
PARKS REST, 9
PARL, William, 169
PARONS, John, 64
PARR, John, 27
PARROTT, Abner, 27
PARRY, Mary, 169
PARSONS, Benjamin, 27
John, 27, 45, 48, 62, 63, 70, 185
Joseph, 27, 62, 84, 161, 187
Michael, 188
Nicholas, 179
Rachel, 27
Solomon, 27
PARSONS ADDITION,

11, 62
PARSONS CHANCE, 27
PARSONS MARSH
  ADDITION, 62
PARSONS PART OF
  HOPE RESURVEYED,
  62
PARSONS POINT, 62
PARSONS RECOVERY,
  27, 62
PART OF A LOT IN
  CHESTER TOWN, 62
PART OF DANBY
  RESURVEYED, 62
PART OF HYLENS
  ADVENTURE, 62
PART OF IRVINGS
  RESURVEYED, 62
PART OF LEVEL
  FIELDS, 62
PART OF LOTT 53, 62
PART OF NEW YORK,
  62
PART OF PARTNERSHIP
  RESURVEYED, 62
PART OF THE FORREST
  OF DEAN, 62
  RESURVEYED, 62
PART OF THOMAS'S
  PURCHASE,
  RESURVEYED, 62
PARTNERS ADDITION,
  3, 25, 28, 31,
  40
PARTNERS HELP, 24,
  25
PARTNERSHIP, 2, 3,
  4, 6, 7, 8, 11,
  13, 19, 20, 21,
  24, 27, 29, 31,
  32, 34, 36, 39,
  40, 42, 62, 86
PARTNERSHIP
  ADDITION, 86
PARTNERSHIP POINT,
  6, 17, 22, 31,
  35, 37, 86, 87
PARTNERSHIP POINT
  RESURVEYED, 6,
  29
PARTNERSHIP
  RESURVEYED, 38
PARTNERSHIP, THE,
  62

PARTNERSHIPS POINT,
  62
PARTNERSHIPS POINT
  RESURVEYED, 62
PARTRIDGE, 27
  Love, 169
PASCOE, John, 27,
  62, 169
  Stephen, 27
PASCOE POOR LOTT,
  27
PASCOES POOR LOT,
  37
PASCOES POOR LOTT,
  62
PASCOS POOR LOTT,
  27
PASSINGER,
  Jonathan, 170
PAST HOPE, 136
PASTERNE HOLE, 5
PATTEN, John, 172
PATTIN, William,
  184
PATTON, James, 93
  John, 182
PATTY, Charles, 170
  David, 170
PAUL, William, 173
PAVIN, John, 186
PAVIOR, John, 170
PAYTON, Samuel, 27
PEACH MEADOWS, 23,
  30
PEACOCK, Acquilla,
  95
  George, 93
  John, 27, 164,
  165
  Mary, 95
  Prissilla, 95
  Richard, 27, 68,
  75, 78, 90, 93,
  95, 153, 182,
  185
  Robert, 27, 59,
  74, 76, 90, 95,
  151, 153, 159,
  161
  Sarah, 95
PEARCE, Andrew, 27,
  53, 59, 182
  Ann, 27
  Charles, 180

  Daniel, 27, 157,
  175, 178
  Edward, 182
  George, 28, 162,
  164, 165
  Gideon, 28, 43,
  45, 48, 49, 54,
  59, 62, 65, 67,
  161, 163
  Gidion, 157, 158
  Henry, 98
  Hugh, 173
  James, 28, 62,
  75, 84, 85, 87,
  98, 161, 163,
  164, 165, 174,
  177, 187
  John, 170, 172,
  173, 181
  Mary, 28, 98
  Nathaniel, 43
  Rachell, 28
  Richard, 145, 170
  Sarah, 170
  Thomas, 78, 89,
  170
  William, 3, 28,
  45, 49, 55, 56,
  61, 80, 91, 93,
  153, 156, 158,
  161, 170, 178,
  180, 181, 182
PEARCES ADDITION,
  28
PEARCES ANGLE, 28
PEARCES DESIRE, 62,
  87
PEARCES DESIRE
  RESURVEYED, 24,
  62
PEARCES MEADOW, 62,
  87
PEARCES MEADOWS, 32
PEARCES MILL, 87
PEARCES RAMBLE, 3,
  40, 62, 87
PEARCES RAMBLES, 5,
  24, 26, 28, 30,
  31, 37, 40
PEARCH MEADOW, 39,
  62
PEARCH MEADOWS, 18
PEAREYS MEADOWS, 32
PEARK, Robert, 28

PEARMAN, Jane, 28
PEARSE, Elizabeth, 170
John, 170
William, 170
PECKARD, Nicholas, 103, 111
PEDDAR, Richard, 147
PEDDER, Richard, 148
PEDDLE, James, 170
PEIRCE, George, 170
William, 43, 53
PEIRCIVELL, William, 28
PELL, Mary, 28
William, 28, 85, 88, 166
PENINGTON, Henry, 93
Mr., 129
PENNINGTON, Benedict, 171
Henry, 28, 153, 188
James, 161, 185, 187
John W., 28, 186
John Ward, 74, 83, 166
Joseph, 187
Rachel, 28
Richard, 188
Rosomd, 28
Widdow, 161
William, 94
PENROSE, 35, 62
PENSAX, Marke, 64
Samuel, 67
PENSILVANIA BORDER, 63
PENTRIDGE, 16, 26, 27, 31, 32, 35, 38, 39, 63, 87, 146
PENTROGAY, 63
PERCE, James, 164
PERCH MEADOW, 87
PEREE, William, 63
PEREES ANGLE, 63
PEREGRINE, 36
PERKINS, Daniel, 28, 55, 58, 68, 69, 85, 92, 157, 162
Daniell, 57, 63
Ebenezer, 28, 56, 63, 153
Frederick, 153
G., 28
Isaac, 28, 63, 72, 77, 81, 82, 87, 88, 92, 153, 156, 162, 172, 177, 180, 190, 192
Jacob, 28
John, 173
Joseph, 28
Mary, 93
Samuel, 184
Susanna, 28
Thomas, 28, 54, 63, 151, 153, 159, 160, 165, 179
William, 184
PERKINS ADVENTURE, 28, 63, 87
PERKINS MEADOW, 63
PERKINS MEADOWS, 87
PERKINS MISTAKE, 28, 42, 63, 87
PERKINS POLICY, 87
PERKINS POLLICY, 28, 63
PERKINS POND FIELD NO. 2, 63
PERRY, Daniel, 28
PERY, Ralph, 170
PETERS, Hugh, 170
Richard, 28
PETERS FIELD, 40, 87
PETERS FORREST, 13, 63
PETERS TOWN, 40
PETERSFIELD, 63
PETERSON, Mathias, 136
Matthias, 133
PETHER, Richard, 133, 134, 137, 138, 139, 140, 141, 142
PETT, Thomas, 63, 100, 101, 102, 111
PETTEGREW, William, 171
PETTEN, 20
PETTIT, Barth, 28
PETTS GIFT, 63
PHAROW, Benjamin, 172
PHELP, Cudbeard, 117
Darby, 117
Mary, 117
PHELPE, Cudbeaard, 117
Darby, 115
Edward, 115
PHELPS, Jane, 170
PHILIPS, James, 156
John, 63, 101
Stephen, 187
Thomas, 68
PHILIPS CHOICE, 20, 35, 87
PHILIPS NEGLECT, 4, 18, 63, 87
PHILIPS NEGLECT RESURVEYED, 4
PHILIPSHILL, Charles, 171
PHILLIGEM, Richard, 151
PHILLINGHAM, Richard, 28
PHILLIPPS, Mary, 146
Richard, 146
PHILLIPS, David, 121
Henry, 28, 153
James, 139, 153
John, 28, 53, 127, 172
Lambert, 186
Margaret, 96
Mary, 147
Thomas, 28, 128, 147
PHILLIPS CHANCE, 5
PHILLIPS CHOICE, 19, 28, 32, 63
PHILLIPS NEGLECT, 3, 5, 27, 39
PHILPOT, Robert, 178

248   INHABITANTS OF KENT COUNTY, MARYLAND, 1637-1787

PHILPOTT, Robert, 175
PHLINTHAM, James, 96
PICKARD, Ann, 124
  John, 135
  Nicholas, 106, 121, 135, 142, 143, 175
  Nickholas, 125, 128, 130
  Nickolas, 131, 134
  Nicolas, 109, 116
  Sarah, 135
  William, 115, 135
PICKET, Elizabeth, 105
PICKFORD, Mark, 170
PICMARD, Nicholas, 117
PICURD, Nicholas, 101
PIERCE, William, 51, 63, 66
PIERCES ADDITION, 63
PIG NECK, 19
PIG QUARTER NECK, 63
PIGG NECK, 63
PINAR, Bartus, 28
  Edward, 28
  James, 28, 153
  Matthew, 28
  Thomas, 28, 59, 153
  William, 28
PINE, Francis, 124, 138
PINER, Bartis, 162, 166
  Bartus, 28, 60, 82, 85, 161, 164
  Edward, 159, 160, 161, 162, 164
  Nathaniel, 188
  Sarah, 87, 90, 155
  Thomas, 62, 63, 150, 154
PINERS ADDITION, 28, 63, 87
PINERS GROVE, 28, 63, 87
PINEY GROVE, 31, 40, 63
PINEY NECK, 63
PINEY POINT, 2, 9, 36, 40, 63, 87
PINEY POINT RESURVEYED, 7, 15, 63
PINGSTONE, John, 170
PIPER, J., 152
  James, 155, 184
  Spier, 187
  William, 126, 127
PIRKINS, Thomas, 165
PITT, Christopher, 145
  William, 186
PLAIN DEALING, 24, 29, 31, 39, 63, 87
PLAINE DEALING, 63
PLAINES, THE, 63
PLAINS, 12, 31, 33, 34, 87
PLAINS PARK, 31
PLANES, 87
PLASTOW, Edward, 28
PLATER, George, 28
PLATT, Francis, 170
PLEADE, Mary, 124
  Nicholas, 124
  William, 124
PLEASE, Elizabeth, 170
PLEDGE, William, 132, 140
PLIMPTON, James, 96
PLUMB PARK, 30, 31, 34, 63
POCKARD, William, 170
POIER, Thomas, 106
POINT LOVE, 63
POINTER, Richard, 170
POLLARD, John, 28, 48
  Mary, 28
POLLOWS, John, 28
POMFRETT, Edward, 136, 137
POND SIDE, 14, 63
POND, THE, 63
PONDS, 3, 4, 12
PONDSIDE, 18
PONGSLLY, Alexander, 170
POOL, 29, 38
POOLEY, Mathew, 28
POOR DISCOVERY, 63
POPE, Charles, 28
  Mary, 28
  Matthew, 55, 63
  William, 29, 55, 63, 151
POPES CHANCE, 5, 29, 63
POPES FOREST, 63
POPES FORREST, 7, 12, 19, 32, 35
POPLAR FARM, 3, 6, 9, 12, 14, 31
POPLAR FARME, 17, 63
POPLAR FARMS, 87
POPLAR HILL, 17, 20, 63
POPLAR HILL RESURVEYED, 63, 87
PORTER, Giles, 29
  James, 29, 154, 179
  John, 29, 63
  Joseph, 82
  Richard, 29
  Sarah, 29
  William, 103
PORTER ADDITION, 29
PORTERS ADDITION, 29, 63, 87
PORTERS RESURVEY, 18
POSTERN HOLE, THE, 63
POTTER, Martin, 29, 178
POTTS, William, 29, 150, 178
POVERTY FIELD, 63
POWELL, John, 51
  Nehemiah, 29
  William, 143
POWER, Nichols, 29
PRATT, Philemon, 29

Richard, 187
PRESBURY, 8, 63, 87
  George, 63, 67
PRESBURY DISCOVERY, 87
PRESBURYS DISCOVERY, 63
PRESTON, John, 170
  Richard, 116
PREVENTION, 14, 87
PREVENTION INCONVENIENCY, 40
PREVENTION OF ILLCONVENIENCE, 18
PREVENTION OF INCONVENIENCE, 18, 42, 63
PREVENTION OF INCONVENIENCY, 12
PRICE, Ann, 123
  Benjamin, 188
  Ed, 124
  Edward, 29, 123
  Henry, 180, 181
  James, 29
  John, 29, 63
  Mary, 170
  Moses, 105
  Richard, 29
  Roger, 142, 144
  Thomas, 158, 188
  Will, 101
  William, 29, 104, 106, 107, 108, 109, 112, 117, 118, 119, 123, 124, 128
PRICES LOT, 7
PRICES LOTT, 5, 63, 87
PRICIE, William, 128
PRICKEL PEAR, 26
PRICKLE PEAR, 4, 5, 63
PRICKLE PEARE, 26
PRICKLES PEAR, 8
PRICKLEY PEAR, 15, 38, 87
PRIERS NEGLECT, 5
PRINCE, Caesar, 51

Penellope, 112
PRINCE WILLIAM, 15, 63, 87
PRINCE WILLILAM RESURVEYED, 63
PRINGSTON, John, 170
PRIOR, Thomas, 49
PRIOR NEGLECT, 63
PRITCHET, John, 105
PROBUS, 2, 32, 64, 87
PROBUS RESURVEYED, 64
PROSSER, Henry, 181
  Heugh, 124
PROVIDENCE, 2, 3, 4, 5, 6, 12, 13, 15, 16, 19, 21, 24, 25, 28, 30, 33, 34, 35, 36, 37, 41, 42, 64, 87, 88
PROVIDENCE RESURVEYED, 5, 64
PRYER, Thomas, 162, 166
  William, 166
PRYERS NEGLECT, 6
PRYOR, John, 29
  Phillip, 29
  Thomas, 29, 49, 55
PRYORS NEGLECT, 4, 6, 32, 40, 88
PUDDING DAM, 64
PULLEN, William, 56
PULLENS REFUGE, 5
PULLET, James, 182
PUNNEY, Bartus, 182
  John, 172
  Thomas, 172, 180
PURDEN, Joseph, 171
PURLIN, Edward, 105
PURSE, Bernard, 170
PUSHPIN, Anthony, 186
PUTBERY, Jeane, 124
PYLE, William, 170
PYNE, Francis, 139, 140, 141, 142, 143
PYPER, William, 134

-Q-
QUAIL, Thomas, 99
QUAKER LOT, 11
QUAKERS LOT, 27
QUAKERS LOTT, 64
QUAKES LOTT, 64
QUEEN CARLETON, 9, 12, 14, 16
QUEEN CARLTON, 21, 24, 30, 31
QUEEN CATHERINE, 48
QUEEN CHARLETON, 64
QUEEN CHARLTON, 6, 23, 88
QUEENY, Sutthin, 55
  Suttlan, 45
QUICK, Thomas, 170, 181
QUIGLEY, John, 140
QUILLEN, Wiliam, 185
QUINNEY, John, 29
  Sutton, 29
QUINNY, Sutton, 29

-R-
RABY, John, 110, 114, 117, 118
  Sarah, 127, 128
RACHELLS FARM, 5
RACHELLS FARME, 64
RACHELS FARM, 5, 22, 27, 88
RADCLIFFE CROSS, 64
RADFORD, Anne, 170
  Cornelius, 170
RADWAY, John, 145, 146
RAGAN, James, 172
RAIMON, Michael, 179
RAIN, Ann, 161
RAISIN, George, 64
  John, 64
  Mary, 53, 64
  William, 64, 192
RAISINS DOUBLE PURCHASE, 3, 29, 64
RAISINS LOTT, 64
RAISINS PART OF THE GRANGE, 64
RAISONS PART OF HALES, 64

RALEY, Charles, 94
RALPH, Mary, 29
　Thomas, 83
RALPHS, 64
RAMSEY, William, 184
RAMSSE, William, 127
RANADAM, 29
RANDAL, John, 89, 182
　Pvt., 182
RANDALL, Benjamin, 29, 45
　John, 29
　Robert, 29, 65
　Theophilus, 29, 69, 160, 165
RANDDALL, John, 153
RANDLE, Richard, 170
RANDOLPH, Robert, 95
RANDON, 12
RANGE, THE, 64
RASIN, Abraham, 29, 162, 164
　George, 29, 64, 153, 156
　John, 29, 73
　Joseph, 77, 78, 95, 151, 152, 153, 179, 190
　Joshua, 187
　Mary, 29, 64
　Philip, 153
　Phillip, 29, 45
　Robert, 186
　Sarah, 83
　Thomas, 88, 166, 185
　Warner, 74
　William, 29, 56, 153, 160, 176, 187, 192
RASINS PART OF HALES RESURVEYED, 64
RASINS PURCHASE, 88
RATACLIFFE CROSS, 33
RATCLIFF, 23, 34, 36, 37, 88
RATCLIFF CROSS, 27, 34, 36, 37, 88
RATCLIFFE, 11, 23, 35, 64
RATCLIFFE , 11
RATCLIFFE CROSS, 15, 64
RATCLIFFE'S CROSS, 15
RATLIF, 11
RAWLES, William, 147
RAWLINGS, John, 83
　Selah, 80, 86
RAWLINS, Joseph, 187
　Thomas, 187
RAWLINSON, James, 29
　John, 29
RAWTH, James, 69
RAYMOND, Michael, 29
READ, Francis, 29
　George, 30
　James, 30
　John, 30, 56, 166, 185
　Joseph, 30, 99
　Mathew, 104, 105, 106, 110, 114, 127, 129, 134, 137
　Matshew, 128
　Matthew, 101, 131, 133, 137
　Peregrine, 173
　Thomas, 129, 171
　Tilton, 30
READBOURNE, 64
READE, Ann, 129
　Mathew, 104, 111, 125, 128, 129, 130, 142
　Matthew, 118, 121, 122, 137, 142
　Thomas, 108, 109, 117, 125
READING, 16, 64
　Nathaniel, 151, 159, 160
　William, 30, 64, 179
READINGS ADDITION, 64
READIS, James, 187
REARDEN, 5, 88
REARDEN , 5
REARDIN, Timothy, 30
REARDON, Thomas, 72, 84, 182
REASON, George, 51, 64, 71, 72, 78, 86, 185
　John, 62, 185
　Joseph, 30
　Mary, 30, 51
　Thomas, 30
REASONS PART OF DRAYTON, 64
REBECCAHS DESIRE, 88
REBECCAS DESIRE, 17, 32, 64
RECAUD, L. M., 174
REDDING, John, 30
　Nathaniel, 30, 153
　Richard, 144, 183
　Sarah, 30
　William, 153
REDGRAVE, Abraham, 30, 84, 156, 157, 187
　Ann, 99
　Elizabeth, 53, 78, 99
　Hannah, 30
　Isaac, 30, 73, 99, 182, 185
　James, 185
　John, 30, 48, 55, 64, 69, 161
　Joseph, 30, 78, 159, 160, 163, 165, 166, 187
　Josh., 160
　Polly, 99
　Richard, 188
　Robert, 185
　Sampson, 171, 188
　William, 30, 42, 71, 79, 159, 160, 185, 186
REDGRAVES PART OF CHANCE RESURVEYED, 64

INDEX 251

REDING, Nathanial, 160
Nathaniel, 92, 93
William, 75, 77, 165, 186
REDMONDS SUPPLY, 13, 37
REDMONDS SUPPLY RESURVEYED, 64
REDMONS SUPPLY, 14
REDMORES SUPPLY, 88
REDRIFF, 24, 37
REDRIFFE, 37, 64
REDUE, Isaac, 183
REED, Amos, 94, 185
Araminta, 94
Benjamin, 30, 99
Dean, 184
George, 94, 157, 183
James, 179
John, 30, 99, 182
Joseph, 30, 93, 182
Mathew, 104, 110, 112, 113
Meshach, 99
Peregrine, 94, 173, 188
Phillip, 172
Robert, 155, 184
Samuel, 79, 81, 87, 90, 182
Sarah, 30
Shadrick, 153
Temperance, 93
Tilton, 179
Tom, 109
REEDE, Mathew, 125
REERGARD, 64
REEVES, Enos, 171
REID, Henry, 30
Mathew, 98
Robert, 96
REISEN, Thomas, 30
RELEY, Nicholas, 157
RELIEF, 40, 88
RELIEF, THE, 64
REMAINDER, 6, 8, 19, 25, 88
REMAINDER, THE, 64
REMAINS OF HIS LORDSHIP

GRACIOUS GRANT, THE, 64
RENGATE, 31
RENIPPA WALLS, 40
RENNOULDS, William, 129
RENSLAUGH, Dominick, 45
RENT LOTT, 3
REROGUARD, 8
RESERVE, 3, 7, 8, 30, 33, 64
RESERVE, THE, 64
RESIN, William, 158
RESURVEY, 88
RESURVEY OF ANGELLS REST, 64
RESURVEY OF BROODNOE, 64
RESURVEY OF DRAYTON, 64
RESURVEY OF JERUSALEM, 65
RESURVEY OF MARTHA HYNSONS, PART OF Hinchingham, 65
RESURVEY OF PART OF TILGHMANS FARM AND CHANCE, 65
RESURVEY OF PART OF TRUMPINTON SMITH'S MEADOW, 64
RESURVEY OF TRUMPINTON, 65
RESURVEY OF TRYANGLE, 41
RESURVEY ON PART OF TILGHMANS FARM AND CHANCE, 36
RESURVEY ON TRIANGLE, 36
RESURVEY ON TRYANGLE, 14
RESURVEYED THE CHANCE, 65
REVERSION, 28, 37, 38, 39
REVERSION, THE, 65
REVOIDAN, 5
REWARD, 8, 12, 32, 36, 40
REWARD, THE, 65
REYLE, Benjamin, 166
Nicholas, 166
William, 166
REYLEY, Jacob, 165
James, 172
REYNAR, Ebenezer, 164
REYNEER, Ebenezer, 165
REYNER, Ebenezer, 65, 99, 159, 160, 162, 166, 167
REYNERS ADVENTURE, 65
REYNOLDS, Abraham, 173
James, 173
John, 46, 186
Joseph, 185
Robert, 186
REYNOR, Ebenezer, 88
REYNORS ADVENTURE, 88
RHUE ADAM, 65
RIALY, Charles, 187
RICARD, Benjamin, 30
RICAUD, Benjamin, 51, 59, 64, 150
L. M., 174
Richard, 88, 95
Thomas, 42, 150
RICE, Valentine, 170
RICERDEN, 13
RICH LEVEL, 4, 14, 18, 40, 88
RICH LEVELL, 4, 6, 18, 40
RICH LEVELL, PART OF, 65
RICH MEADOW, 12, 88
RICH MEADOW, THE, 65
RICH MEADOWS, 6
RICH NECK, 65
RICH NECK, THE, 65
RICHARDS, Mary, 124
Samuell, 144
Will, 114, 125
William, 115, 117, 119, 122,

252　INHABITANTS OF KENT COUNTY, MARYLAND, 1637-1787

126, 129, 134, 136
RICHARDS ADVENTURE, 2, 6, 9, 28, 41, 65, 88
RICHARDS PART OF DANBY RESURVEYED, 65
RICHARDSON, Benjamin, 97
Douglas, 30
Jacob, 171
John, 65, 171
Mathew, 89, 163
Matthew, 30, 171
Samuel, 178
Samuel, Capt., 30
Thomas, 30
William, 187
RICHARDSONS SECURITY, 65
RICHARSDS, William, 127
RICHESON, John, 101, 103
RICHFORD, Thomas, 30, 163
RICHUD, Richard, 76, 79, 83, 84, 88
RICKETS, Nathaniel, 45, 88
Philip, 65
RICKETS FARM, 65
RICKETTS, Charlotte, 30
John, 153, 179, 181
John T., 181
Joseph, 30
Nathaniel, 30, 153, 192
Phil., 153
Phillip, 30
RICKETTS FARM, 88
RICKMAN, John, 170
RIDDLE, Andrew, 30
RIDER, Richard, 141
RIDGELEY, 88
RIDGELY, 2, 30
RIDGLEY, 65
Henry, 65, 144
RIDGLY, 8, 28
RIDGWAY, John, 31

RIDIFORD, Thomas, 172
RIDMORE SUPPLY, THE, 65
RIEDDERFORD, James, 181
RIGBY, Charles, 98
James, 110
RILEY, Benjamin, 161, 187
Jacob, 188
John, 159, 160
Jos., 159
Joseph, 159, 160
Nicholas, 65, 99, 161, 163, 188
Richard, 31, 159, 160, 163
William, 182, 188
RILEYS BEGINNING, 20, 31, 65
RILEYS FANCY, 32
RILEYS LAND RESURVEYED, 32
RILEYS RESURVEYED, 88
RINGGOLD, Ann, 78, 87
Anna M., 155
Charles, 31, 65, 150, 151
Christian, 133
Christina, 114
Elias, 31, 52, 56, 180
James, 31, 45, 52, 54, 56, 60, 63, 65, 69, 87, 112, 114, 117, 125, 126, 140, 180
John, 31, 60, 87, 101, 106, 109, 110, 112, 113, 117, 122, 146, 155, 180, 184
Jos., 152
Joseph, 31
Josiah, 155
Josias, 31, 75, 92, 153, 181
Maria Ann, 81
Mary, 31, 87, 93, 155

Mr., 110
Rebeccah, 31
Thomas, 31, 32, 43, 45, 56, 57, 62, 65, 72, 75, 76, 83, 86, 90, 91, 101, 102, 103, 104, 106, 107, 109, 112, 114, 116, 117, 118, 119, 122, 125, 139, 141, 150, 152, 153, 154, 155, 174, 175, 176, 177, 178, 179, 181, 188, 189
William, 31, 59, 73, 81, 91, 150, 151, 153, 154, 155, 174, 176, 177, 183, 188, 189
RINGGOLD FORTUNE, 9
RINGGOLDS CHANCE, 22, 65
RINGGOLDS DISCOVERY, 65
RINGGOLDS FORTUNE, 31, 65, 88
RINGGOLDS LOTT, 9, 31, 88
RINGGOLDS LOTT NO. 55, 65
RINGGOLDS LOTT, SECOND PART OF, 65
RINGGOLDS PART OF POPLAR FARM RESURVEYED, 65
RINGGOLDS PART OF THE ADVENTURE RESURVEYED, 65
RINGGOULD, James, 125, 126, 128, 130
John, 126, 127, 129
Thomas, 56, 125, 126, 128, 130, 133, 135
RINGOLD, James, 63, 144, 145
Rebecca, 63

INDEX

Thomas, 63, 113, 150
William, 151
RINGOULD, Jeames, 143
John, 143
Thomas, 134
RIPPEN, 17, 29
RIPPIN, 88
Henry, 178
RIPPON, 65
Henry, 31
RISBROOKE, Mary, 101
William, 101
RISBY, Elizabeth, 102
William, 102
RISDON, John, 157
ROBAS, James, 31
ROBBINS, George, 148
ROBERTS, Benjamin, 172
Elizabeth, 97
James, 31, 170
John, 182
Robert, 31, 44, 61, 70, 97, 154, 184
Samuel, 184
William, 31, 181
ROBERTSON, William, 182, 184
ROBINETT, Richard, 31
ROBINSON,
Elizabeth, 115
Heneage, 31
Henery, 31
James, 96, 189
Margaret, 31
ROBSON, Charles, 188
ROBY, Charles, 94
ROCH, Henery, 112
ROCHESTER, Francis, 31
Henry, 31
John, 31, 163
ROCK POINT, 65
RODD, Robert, 170
RODGERS, Edward, 144

ROE, Edmond, 147, 148
Edward, 141
ROGER HICKS INTENT, 37, 65
ROGER HIX INTENT, 18
ROGERS, Edward, 31, 106, 107, 117, 118, 143, 148, 151
Elizabeth, 31
Hynson and wife, 31
John, 31, 55, 151, 157, 161, 166, 183
Joseph, 162, 164
Josh., 164
Nathaniel, 183
Ned, 106
William, 83, 85, 165, 170, 174, 187
ROLINSON, John, 185
ROLLINGSON, John, 183
ROLLISON, Charles, 94
James, 191
John, 172
ROLPH, Glanville, 31
John, 31, 84, 172, 180
Thomas, 172
William, 31
RONNETT, Sarah, 170
ROSEMASON, Hans, 134
ROSIER, Henry, 154
ROSIER AND YOUNG, 73
ROSIOR, Parson, 111
Person, 111
ROSS, James, 182
ROSSE, John, 172
ROSSITER, John, 170
ROULINS, John, 187
ROUSBEYS DISCOVERY, 32
ROUSBY,
Christopher, 65
ROUSBY DISCOVERY,

88
ROUSBYS DISCOVERY, 26
ROUSBYS RECOVERY, 6, 65
ROWELL, William, 184
ROWLISON, James, 75
ROYDEN, William, 138
ROZIER, Henry, 31
RUABON, 2, 29
RUARDON, 7, 35
RUDDLE, Andrew, 31
RUDREN, 5
RUE ADAM, 29, 89
RUERDEN, 5, 19
RUERDON, 35, 65
RULE ADAM, 89
RUMFORD, 26, 27, 34, 41, 65, 89
RUMFORD RESURVEYED, 89
RUMNEY, Joseph, 182
RUNNELS, John, 166
RUSELL, John, 102
RUSEMORE, 65
RUSH, Thomas, 31
RUSH MORE, 13
RUSHMORE, 15, 18, 19, 65
RUSSEL, William, 155
RUSSELL, Capt., 109, 114
Francis, 137
James, 188
John, 61, 101, 103, 104, 106, 107, 109, 110, 114, 118, 119, 122, 175, 183
Mr., 112
William, 184
RUTH, Thomas, 55
RUTTER, Amy, 170
Francis, 76, 87, 185
Philop, 170
RYE, John, 148
RYE:, John, 140
RYLEY, 89
Benjamin, 89
Cornelius, 75

John, 31
Mary, 31
Nicholas, 31
Richard, 32, 65
Sarah, 32
RYLEYS BEGINNING,
    31, 65, 89
RYLEYS FANCY, 65
RYLEYS LAND, 34
RYLEYS LAND
    RESURVEYED, 5,
    30, 65
RYLEYS LANDS
    RESURVEYED, 31
RYLEYS RESURVEYED,
    89
RYLYS BEGINNING, 32
RYNER, Ebenezer, 93

-S-
SACLE, Mary, 132
SADLER, Joseph, 32
SADLERS LOTT, 14,
    31, 65
ST. ALBANS
    ADDITION, 89
ST. ANDREWS CROSS,
    16, 17, 18, 28,
    89
SAINT ANDREWS
    CROSSE, 66
SAINT ANTONI, 3
SAINT ANTONIA, 3
ST. CLAIR, Mary, 94
ST. CLEAR, William,
    66, 165
ST. CLEARS
    DISCOVERY, 66
ST. CLEARS
    RESURVEY, 66
ST. CLEARS VENTURE,
    66
ST. EPHRAIM, 89
ST. JOHNS FIELDS,
    89
ST. MARGARETS, 17
SAINT MARGARETTS, 3
SAINT MARTINE, 66
ST. MARTINS, 1, 8,
    12, 89
ST. MARTINS
    ADDITION, 89
SAINT MARY'S, 66
ST. MARYS, 12

SAINT PATRICKS
    GARDEN, 66
SAINT PAULS, 66
ST. TANTANS, 89
SAINT TANTONS, 66
ST. TANTONS, 41
SAINT TAUNTONS, 66
SALISBURY, 13
    William, 32, 52,
    163
SALKELD, 19, 66
SALLVATORY, 66
SALLY'S CHANCE, 2
SALSBURY, Isabella,
    96
    James, 96, 99
    William, 161
SALTER, Jane, 106,
    107
    Janne, 128
    John, 32, 43, 44,
    45, 52, 56, 57,
    62, 70, 103,
    104, 106, 107,
    108, 109, 110,
    111, 113, 114,
    116, 118, 120,
    121, 125, 127,
    128, 175
    Maria, 115
    Marie, 115
SALTERS LAND
    RESURVEYED, 66
SALTERS LOAD, 66,
    89
SALTERS LOAD
    RESURVEYED, 6
SAMFIELD MOORE, 4
SAMPSON, Ambrose,
    170
    William, 32
SAMPSONS ADDITION,
    19, 32
SAMPSONS EDITION,
    32
SANDERS, Abraham,
    188
    George, 32, 94,
    156, 166, 187
    John, 57
    Thomas, 32, 166,
    188
    William, 32
SANDERS ADDITION,
    32
SANDFORD, 66
SANDY HILL, 89
SANDY PLANTATION,
    19, 39
SANER, Thomas, 170
SAP, Shadrick, 173
SAPPINGTON,
    Hartley, 172,
    188
    James, 166, 188
    Thomas, 32, 171
SARAHS LOT, 14, 37
SARAHS LOTT, 14,
    66, 89
SAUGHIER, George,
    66
SAUL, Sarah, 170
SAUNDERS, Abraham,
    83
    Hannah, 90
    James, 172, 182
    Martha, 85
    Robert, 56
    Thomas, 85, 88,
    163
    William, 66, 163
SAUNDERS ADDITION,
    66
SAUNTER, Hannah, 99
    Negro, 99
SAVAGE, 32
SAVIDGE, William,
    144
SAVORIES FARM, 89
SAVORY, William,
    32, 66
SAVORYS FARM, 6,
    31, 66
SAYER, Andrew, 170
    Peter, 130, 143
SCAGGS, Richard,
    32, 166, 185
    William, 32
SCAGS, Richard, 74,
    77, 86
SCALE, Kathorine,
    131, 133
    Mary, 139
    Peter, 131, 133,
    139
SCALES, Peter, 132
SCANDLAN, Ann, 98
    James, 98

INDEX 255

SCANDLEN, Edward, 77
SCANLAN, Ann, 98
  Catharine, 98
SCANTLAN, Edward, 94
SCARBOROUGH, Joseph, 170
SCHAGS, Elizabeth, 158
SCHARF, J. Thomas, 174
SCHAW, John, 162, 164
SCHAWHAN, Darby, 162
SCHEE, Hermanus, 32, 64
SCIDMORE, 89
SCINCOCK, Mary, 60
SCIPWITH, Samuel, 125
  Samuell, 125
SCONE, George, 172
  James, 183
SCOONE, Charles, 172
SCOT, Edward, 150
SCOTLAND, 29
SCOTS FOLLY, 35
  William, 35
SCOTT, Absolom, 173
  Andrew, 183
  Ann, 32
  Charles, 32, 172
  Col., 32
  David, 32, 163
  Edward, 32, 43, 66, 150, 175, 178
  Francis, 32
  George, 32
  John, 32, 43, 46, 87, 91, 96, 152, 154, 155, 159, 162, 174, 177, 181, 190, 191
  Lambert, 188
  Mary, 32, 129
  Nathaniel, 32
  Timothy, 83
  Walter, 32
  William, 150, 178
SCOTTS CHANCE, 32

SCOTTS FANCY, 16
SCOTTS FOLLY, 19, 20, 22, 27, 32, 66, 89
SCOTTS LOT, 26
SCOTTS LOTT, 19, 32, 66, 89
SCOW, Joseph, 180
SCRAP, 8, 66, 89
SCUDDAMORE, 66
SEALY, Robert, 170
  Thomas, 32
SEAMANS, Henry, 32
  Jeremiah, 32
  Lambert, 74
  Sarah, 32
  Solomon, 32
  William, 32
SEAMANS FOLLY, 32, 89
SEARELL, Daniel, 170
SEARES, Janne, 129
SEARS, John, 192
SEAVER, Thomas, 170
SEAWALL ALIAS
  ULRICK, 8
SEAWARD, Thomas, 66
SEAWARDS HOPE, 66
SEAWELL, 66, 89
SECOND ADDITION, 25, 66
SECOND CHANCE, 66
SEDGEWICK, James, 48
SELBEY, Thomas, 32
SELBY, 66
SELVESTER, John, 126
SEMANS, Asher, 97
  David, 94
  Gilbert, 73, 89
  Lambert, 73
  Mary, 97
  Richard, 73, 94
  Sarah, 73, 97
  Solomon, 73, 87, 97
  William, 73
SEMBRECK, Frances, 131
SENBY, William, 181
SEPSEN, John, 101
SERELL, Daniel, 172

SEVELL, Daniel, 172
SEVERNTON, 89
SEVIER, Elizabeth, 170
SEWALL, 69
SEWALL ALIAS
  ULRICK, 7, 13, 21
SEWALLS MANOR, 11, 35
SEWARDS HOPE, 15, 24, 89
SEWEL, 89
SEWELL, 10
  Frances, 131
  John, 32, 66
  Mary, 32
  Richard, 32, 43, 157, 158, 185
  Thomas, 32, 161, 171, 185
SEWELL ALIAS
  ULRICK, 9, 10, 12, 17, 24, 39
SEWELLS CHANCE, 89
SEWELLS MANNOR, 13
SEWELLS MANOR, 13
SEWISTERN, 13
SEWSTERN, 66
SEWSTERNE, 13
SHAD HOLE, 82
SHADFORD MANNOR, 14, 24
SHADS HOLD, 30
SHADS HOLE, 3, 4, 8, 33, 89
SHADSHOLD, 33, 66
SHADSHOLE, 8, 19
SHAFFER, Jacob, 184
SHAHAWN, Daniel, 97
  Diana, 88
  John, 82, 89
  Thomas, 74, 81
SHAKES, George, 182
SHAMBROOKE,
  Frances, 132
SHANHANE, James, 33
SHARPLESS, Robert, 173
SHART, Robert, 103
SHAUGHEN, Dennis, 160
SHAVES, John, 181
SHAW, John, 66, 148

Matthew, 52
Nathan, 183
William, 72, 180, 182
SHAWAH, Darby, 165
SHAWAN, John, 153
SHAWE, Matthew, 33
SHAWHAN, Darby, 164
SHAWHAWN, John, 33
Miles Mason, 33
SHAWHORN, Daniel, 187
Isaac, 185
Joseph, 49
Thomas, 185
SHAWN, Darby, 33
SHAWS CHANCE, 28, 66
SHEARES, Ann, 115
William, 144
SHEARING, John, 138
SHEARS, Janne, 124
William, 144
SHEERS, William, 145
SHEHAN, Thomas, 33, 57
SHEHAWN, Daniel, 33, 97
John, 33
SHEIGHANE, Darby, 50
SHEMBROOKE, Frances, 139
SHEPPARD, James, 173
SHERIN, 28
SHERRARD, Francis, 185
SHEURTY, Hanna, 142
Hannah, 142
SHIELD, William, 180
SHIELD, THE, 66
SHIELDS, 7, 40
John, 33
William, 87
SHIP-POYNT, 138
SHIRKEY, Patrick, 161
SHOOBROOK, Thomas, 33
SHORT, Mary, 115
Robert, 103, 104, 111
Tabitha, 110, 111
Tabytha, 116
SHREWSBURY PARISH VESTRY, 33
SHURMUR, Benjamin, 67
SHUTE, Henry, 170
SIBERY, Johnathan, 137
SIGLYE, William, 33
SILBREY, Jonathana, 134
SILL, Benjamin, 187
Joseph, 183
Robert, 33
SILLIMI, 66
SILLIVIN, John, 172
SILVESTER, John, 117, 121, 125
SIMCOCK, William, 33, 51
SIMCOCKS, William, 151, 161
SIMMES PRIME CHOICE, 66
SIMMINS PARK, 25
SIMMOND, Dr., 66
SIMMONDS, John, 72, 180
Noble, 183
Richard, 150
Sarah, 86
SIMMONS, Archibald, 186
Henry, 66
Lambert, 186
Richard, 33
William, 68, 186
SIMMONS FOLLY, 66
SIMMONS PRIME CHOICE, 20
SIMMONSON, 66
SIMMS FARM, 27, 66
SIMMS PRIME CHOICE, 39
SIMONDS, Lawrence, 146
Seath, 146
SIMONS, David, 188
Larrence, 145
Lawrence, 145
Richard, 188
Thomas, 112
SIMPSON, James, 184
Thomas, 33
SIMPSONS ADDITION, 35, 36, 89
SIMPSONS ADVENTURE, 32, 34
SIMS, Alexander, 56, 66
Edward, 156
SIMS FARM, 25, 89
SIMS FARME, 66
SIMS PRIME CHOICE, 28, 66
SIMSON, William, 66
SINGLETON, Jacob, 148
SINNETT, Samuel, 172, 181, 190
SKAGGS, John, 186
SKEGGS, Richard, 157
SKERVIN, Francis, 180
SKIDDIMORE, Edward, 156
SKIDMORE, 4, 19, 23, 31, 33, 35, 38
Edward, 66, 135, 146, 147
Joseph, 33
Jucley, 33
SKIDMORE AND BLUNTWELL, 17
SKINNER, Andrew, 33, 51, 66, 68, 70
Anthony, 170
Thomas, 33
William, 33
SKINNERS MARSH, 25, 33, 42, 66, 89
SKINNERS NECK, 89
SKIPWITH, George, 135
SKIPWORTH, George, 135
SKIRTON, George, 156
SKIRVEN, George, 49
Percy G., 171
Sarah, 33
SKIRVENS NEGLECT, 66

SKIRVIN, George, 33
  William, 184
SKIRVINS, 39
SKIWINS, 39
SLADES CHANCE, 2,
  40
SLATER, Richard,
  101
SLAUGHTER, John,
  148
SLAYDE CHANCE, 66
SLEE, Thomas, 170
SLIP, 66
SLIPE, 27, 28, 34,
  66, 89
SLIPE ALONG SIDE OF
  MASSEYS VENTURE,
  66
SLIPPER, Thomas, 33
SLOSS, Samuel, 33,
  162, 164, 165
SLUBEY, William,
  155
SLUBY, Mr., 189
  William, 177
SLY, John, 170
SMALL, Robert, 115
SMALLEY, 34, 89
SMALLY, 15, 26, 34,
  66
SMETHERS, 89
  William, 157
SMITH, Anne, 170
  Charles, 33, 163
  Daniel, 174
  Edward, 180
  George, 33, 83,
    150, 184, 185
  Isaac, 172
  James, 33, 54,
    67, 68, 88, 93,
    99, 150, 152,
    153, 176, 180,
    181, 184, 185,
    186, 188
  Jenkins, 148
  Joan, 144
  John, 33, 67, 73,
    93, 101, 105,
    107, 108, 111,
    117, 121, 122,
    125, 127, 128,
    129, 142, 156,
    159, 160, 161,
    163, 164, 170,
    172, 181, 184,
    185, 186, 188
  John Worldly, 33
  Jokhn, 112
  Jonathan, 33,
    159, 160
  Joseph, 33
  Joyce, 33
  Lambert, 86, 185,
    187
  Margret, 122
  Mary, 95
  Matthew, 33, 95,
    185
  Matthias, 132,
    141
  Nicholas, 33, 67,
    159, 161, 162,
    163, 165, 173,
    176, 185
  Oliver, 83, 88,
    91, 92, 160,
    161, 164
  Renatus, 42
  Richard, 33, 52,
    113, 178, 184
  Richard G., 67
  Robert, 48, 51,
    61, 64
  Rosamond, 33
  Samuel, 33, 76,
    80
  Simon, 184
  Stephen, 184
  Sutton, 184
  Thomas, 33, 43,
    62, 65, 67, 72,
    95, 99, 150,
    153, 155, 175,
    176, 183, 188
  Walter, 101, 114
  William, 34, 49,
    68, 75, 83, 92,
    95, 143, 144,
    145, 147, 150,
    156, 158, 159,
    160, 162, 166,
    172, 180, 183,
    185, 187
  Zephania, 102
SMITH DESART, 15
SMITHERS, John, 34,
  58
  William, 34, 56,
    67
SMITHERS PLAINS,
  41, 67
SMITH'S BAY, 25
SMITHS BAY, 23, 67
SMITHS CHANCE, 25,
  33, 34, 67
SMITHS DESART, 34,
  67
SMITHS MEADOW, 39
SMITHS MEADOWS, 5,
  33, 34, 67
SMITHS MEADOWS
  RESURVEYED, 67
SMITHS PARK, 19,
  67, 89
SMITHS PARKE, 67
SMITHS PART OF
  WORTHS FOLLY, 67
SMITHS PLAINS, 67
SMITHS POINT, 33,
  67, 89
SMITH'S RANGE, 12
SMITHS RANGE, 5
SMITHS VENTURE, 33,
  67
SMITHS VENTURE AND
  ADDITION
  RESURVEYED, 67
SMITHSBY, 129
SMOTHERS, 89
SMOTHERS PLAINS, 89
SMYTH, Hynson, 88,
  184
  James, 89
  John, 101
  Mathew, 161
  Matthew, 172
  Nicholas, 161
  Richard, 180
  Simon, 191
  Thomas, 67, 75,
    79, 80, 81, 82,
    84, 90, 92, 95,
    96, 150, 154,
    155, 171, 172,
    174, 177, 178,
    189, 191
  William, 34, 51,
    62, 154
  Zachariah, 84
SMYTHE, Thomas, 176
SMYTHERS, Mary, 161

William, 163
SMYTHES DESERT, 90
SMYTHS ADDITION, 90
SMYTHS CHANCE, 90
SMYTHS MEADOWS, 90
SMYTHS PARK, 67
SMYTHS PART OF
  STANDAWAY, 67
SMYTHS VENTURE, 90
SMYTHSTON, 67
SNAVELYS LOTT, 19
SNOCKES, Thomas,
  113
SNOOKES, Thomas,
  117, 127
SNOW, Prince, 34
  Silas, 190
  Thomas, 125, 128,
  141
SNOW HILL, 17, 67
SOLBEY, 34
SOLE, 8, 21, 42, 90
SOLE, THE, 67
SOLWAY, William,
  180
SOMERHAYS, John,
  170
SOMERS, John, 170
SOULE, THE, 67
SOUTH, Thomas, 69,
  101, 104, 107,
  109, 110, 112,
  114, 116, 120,
  143
SOUTHERAN, Mary,
  136
SOUTHERN, Thomas,
  131, 134
SOUTHERNE, Mary,
  133
  Valentine, 131
SOUTHREN, Mary, 123
  Valentine, 123
SOUTHWARD, 67
SOWLY, Robert, 170
SPALDEN, 34, 67
  Andrew, 67
SPALDING, 3
  Andrew, 34
SPARKE, John, 170
SPARKES, Edward,
  67, 117
SPARKES POINT, 67
SPARLES, Mary, 170

SPAULDING, 90
SPEAR, David, 166
SPEARE, Robert, 34
SPEARMAN, Abraham,
  161
  Abram, 34
  Ann, 34
  Charity, 34
  Francis, 34, 156
  John, 34, 165,
  186
  Philip, 34
  William, 34, 86,
  164, 166
SPEER, James, 99,
  186
SPEERMAN, Francis,
  50
SPEERS, Robert, 34
SPENCER, Augusteen,
  172
  Capt., 163, 178
  Daniel, 182
  Eliza, 34
  Elizabeth, 59
  Hannah, 98, 99
  Henry, 34, 161
  Hugh, 182
  Isaac, 34, 73,
  76, 78, 83, 84,
  85, 89, 92, 97,
  98, 99, 164,
  165, 174, 185,
  189
  Jane, 145
  Jarvice, 157
  Jarvies, 157
  Jarvis, 34, 50,
  59, 66, 157,
  158, 162
  Jervis, 61
  John, 34, 59, 67,
  158, 161, 170
  Jonathan, 182
  Martha, 170
  Pere., 182
  Richard, 34, 75,
  76, 87, 182
  Sarah, 170
  Thomas, 34, 57,
  59, 178, 179
  Walter, 145
SPENCERS PART OF
  FRIENDSHIP, 67

SPENDLOVE, Jacob,
  163
SPERMAN, John, 165
SPETTIGUE,
  Burchett, 170
SPICIE GROVE, 67
SPINCKE, Thomas,
  141
SPORTMANS HALL, 67
SPRATT, Sarah, 170
SPRING GARDEN, 13,
  15, 16, 17, 23,
  24, 25, 27, 29,
  32, 33, 67, 90
  George, 22
SPRING HILL, 19, 67
SPROT, William, 171
SPRUSEBANKS,
  Francis, 72
SPRY, Francis, 85,
  185
  Oliver, 126
SPRYE, Oliver, 102,
  108, 129
SPUR, David, 85
SPURDANCE, John,
  125
SQUARE, 40
SQUIBB, John, 110
STACKNEY, 8
STADFORD MANNOR, 30
STADTS HOLD, 67
STAFFORD, Richard,
  43
STAGGALL, Moses,
  136
STAGGOLL, Thomas,
  143
STAGOLL, Moses, 148
  Mosses, 137
  Moyses, 143
  Thomas, 143
STAGWELL, Moyses,
  128
  Thomas, 127, 129,
  175
  William, 126
STAIRES, Bennett,
  145, 146
STALKER, Martha, 34
  Thomas, 34
STANAWAY, 10, 17,
  19, 31, 33, 67,
  90

STAND OFF, 7, 27, 67
STANDAWAY, 6, 11, 23, 36, 67, 90
STANDFORD, 16, 22, 90
STANDLEY, William, 67
STANDLEYS HOPE, 24, 29, 67
STANDOFF, 27, 90
STANFORD, 14, 90
STANHAM, 25
STANLEY, Ebenezer, 186
  Isaac, 85, 186
  John, 85, 186
  Richard, 85
  William, 136
STANLEYS HOPE, 29, 30, 38, 90
STANLY, An:, 113
  Isaac, 166
  John, 163
STANLYS HOPE, 2, 24
STANNAWAY, 1, 11, 13, 28
STANSBURY, William, 170
STANTON, Mary, 34
STAPLE, James, 185
STAPLE WARREN, 90
STAPLEFORD, Thomas, 180
STAPLES, Henry, 44, 58, 67
STAPLES CHOICE, 17, 41, 67
STAPLES WARREN, 3, 28, 31, 67
STARKEY, John, 173
STATES, James, 185
STAVELY, Eliza, 34
  James, 34, 67, 68, 73, 79, 90, 157
  John, 34, 67, 94, 166
  Joseph, 71, 82, 91, 185
  William, 94, 95
STAVELYS LOT, 17, 34
STAVELYS LOTT, 67, 90
STAVELYS LOTT RESURVEYED, 67
STAVELYS PART OF BROAD OAK, 67
STAVELYS PART OF SUFFOLK, 67
STAVLY, Jno., 100
STEAD, James, 34
STEDHED, Mary, 129
STEDMAN, John, 143
STEEL, James, 78, 188
STEIN, James, 182
STENT, Thomas, 107
STEPHEN HEATH MANNOR, 67
STEPHEN HEATH MANOR, 26, 27, 32
STEPHEN HEATHS MANOR, 13, 16
STEPHENS, John, 133
  Thomas, 170
  William, 34, 170
STEPHENS INHERITANCE, 67
STEPHENSON, John, 171
STEPNEY, 1, 3, 4, 7, 9, 13, 14, 17, 20, 22, 23, 25, 28, 29, 33, 38, 40, 67, 90
STEPNEY FIELDS, 1, 67, 90
STEPNEY HEATH MANOR, 31, 90
STEPNEY POINT LOTT, 30
STERLING, James, 34, 46
STEUARD, Ann, 123
  Charles, 123, 131, 137
STEVENS, Alice, 142, 143
  Griffen, 140
  John, 34, 130, 134, 139, 162
  Richard, 143
  Thomas, 188
  William, 34, 183
STEVENSON, 34, 90
  John, 34, 55, 140
  Symond, 148
  William, 34, 177
STEVENTON, 67, 68
  William, 68
STEWARD, Charles, 106, 107, 109, 114, 127, 131, 134, 147
STEWARDS HOPE, 3
STEWART, Alexander, 187
  Asa, 185
  Edward, 172, 183, 188
  John, 81, 180, 185
  Major, 180
  William, 166, 185
STILDS, Nathauniall, 122
STILE, Natthaniell, 145
STILES, Nathaniel, 34, 50
  Nathaniell, 68
STILES ADDITION, 34, 68, 90
STILES ADDITION CORRECTED, 15, 68
STILL, George, 34, 64
STINCHCOMB, Nathaniell, 137
STINCHCOMBE, Nathaniel, 133
STINSON, John, 183
STINTON ERICKSON, 68
STIVENS, William, 183
STOCKTON, 33
STOCTON, 68
STOILL, Ann, 121
  John, 121
STOKE, 33
STOKER, Ephraim, 182
STONE, Gov., 102
  Richard, 68
  Thomas, 170
  William, 101
  Wm., 193

STONE TOWER, 24
STONETON, 7, 29, 30, 68, 90
STONETOWN, 30
STONEY HILL, 90
STONEY HILLS, 27, 68
STONNAWAY, 68
STONY HILLS, 27
STOOP, Phil, 35
STOOPE, Henry, 117, 118, 130
STOOPLEY GIBSON, 68
STOOPS, Benjamin, 171
　Benjamin Townsend, 35
　David, 95, 185
　Ephraim, 94, 95
　Henry, 68
　John, 35, 160, 171
　Nicholas, 185
　William, 35, 79, 159, 160, 163
STOPE, Elesabeth, 126
STOPPE, Henry, 121
STOUPE, Henery, 113
STOURTON, George, 156
STOWELL, John, 125, 128
STOYLES, Nathaniel, 129
STRADFORD MANNOR, 14
STRADFORD MANOR, 25, 90
STRADFORD MANOR RESURVEYED, 68
STRAFFORD MANNOR, 25, 31
STRAFFORD MANOR, 3, 14, 33
STRAFFORD RESURVEYED, 14
STRAGHON, Jas., 159
STRAHAN, James, 35
　John, 183
STRATFORD MANNOR, 12, 14, 25, 68
STRATFORD MANOR, 36, 37, 90

STRATTON, George, 35
STRAUGHAN, James, 160
STREATOR, Edward, 130
　Elezabeth, 130
STREET, Edith, 170
　Jacob, 35
　Lady, 170
　Robert, 35
STREETT, Robert, 158
STRICKLANDS REST, 17
STRINGFELLOW, Elisha, 35, 178
STRONG, Benjamin, 72
　George, 60
　James, 186
　Leonard, 103
　Micajah, 35
　Thomas, 35
　William, 75, 180
STRONGE, Leo:, 126
STROUD, Abraham, 68
STROUDS WHITE STABLE, 68
STUARD, Charles, 116, 119, 122, 124, 125, 140
　Eadey, 124
　John, 121, 122
　Tabytha, 124, 125
STUART, Alexander, 78
　Charles, 106
STURGES, John, 181
　William, 190
STURGIS, Jno., 152
　John, 155, 189
STURTS LOTT, 41
STYLES, Nathaniel, 71
SUBBARDS, 30
SUBBURBS, 30
SUBURBS, 29, 30, 90
SUBURNS, 90
SUDLER, Emory, 82, 88, 153, 154, 155, 174, 176, 177
　Thomas, 180

SUDLERS LOTT, 90
SUDWARD, James, 67
SUFFOLK, 1, 2, 5, 13, 15, 17, 19, 25, 26, 34, 35, 37, 68, 91
SUFFOLK RESURVEYED, 15
SULLAVANT, Patrick, 148
SULLIVAN, James, 185
　John, 181, 183, 186
　Mary, 170
SULLIVANE, Dennis, 35
SUMMERS, John, 144
　Robert, 35, 75, 183
SUMNERS, Sarah, 170
SURPLUS, 39
SURPRISE, 68
SURVEYORS LIGHT, 68
SUSQUEHANNAH, 68
SUTHERIN, Dorethy, 123
　Mary, 123, 124
　Valentine, 124, 139
　Vallentine, 140
　Vallentyne, 123
SUTHERNE, Thomas, 125, 135
SUTTEN, Burgin, 157
SUTTON, 33, 68
　Benjamin, 35
　Caesar, 140, 142
　Edward, 188
　John, 35, 44, 72, 91, 110, 180
　Joseph, 35
　Richard, 35
　Samuel, 35
SUTTON UNDERHILL, 19, 68
SWAIN, John, 50
SWAMP, 17
SWAMP RESURVEYED, 7, 17, 68
SWAMP, THE, 68
SWAMPS RESURVEYED, 91
SWAN ISLAND, 13, 68

SWANEY, James, 75
SWANSON, Swan, 104
SWEATMAN, Edward,
    44, 47
SWEATMANS ADDITION,
    41
SWEATMANS INSULA,
    13, 41
SWEATNAM, Edward,
    68
SWEATNAMS ADDITION,
    68, 91
SWEET HALL NECK, 68
SWEET HARBOUR, 18,
    68
SWEETHALL, 28
SWEETHALL NECK, 39
SWEETMAN, Edward,
    55, 68
SWEETMANS INSULA,
    68
SWEETMANS
    PENINSULA, 91
SWENHAM, 30
SWERSTUN, 6
SWETTNAM, Edward,
    147
SWIFT, John, 35,
    80, 184
    Samuel, 35
SWINEY, James, 35
SYBREY, Johnathan,
    138
SYMOND, Alexander,
    170
SYMONDS, William,
    164
SYMONDS ADDITION,
    20
SYMONS FARM, 27
SYMPSON, Mary, 158
    William, 35, 68
SYMPSONS ADDITION,
    68
SYMPSONS ADVENTURE,
    68
SYMS'S PRIME
    CHOICE, 7

-T-
TAILER, Henry, 117,
    119, 120, 122
    Sarah, 120
TAIMBIN, Edward,
    170
TALBOTT, Henry, 179
TALLENT, Robert,
    141
TALLEY FANCY, 15
TAMBIN, Edward, 170
TAMFIELD, 33
TANFIELD MOORE, 91
TARANT, Edward,
    105, 106
    Elizabeth, 106
    Rebecka, 106
TARENT, Edward, 106
TARKINTON, John,
    145, 147
TARR KILL, THE, 68
TARRANT, Edd, 115
    Edward, 107
TARRENT, Edward,
    107
TARRINGTON, James,
    79, 84
    Thomas, 35
TASKER, Benjamin,
    35
TASSELL, John, 131,
    133, 138, 140,
    143
TATOM, John, 186
TATUM, John, 35, 68
TATUMS MEADOW, 25,
    68
TATUMS MOUNT, 35,
    68, 91
TAUTON, Phillip,
    170
TAYLER, Sarah, 127,
    128, 130
    Sarye, 130
    Will, 125
TAYLOR, Abraham,
    89, 183, 188
    Andrew, 149
    Henry, 101
    Hyth., 184
    James, 185
    John, 35, 74, 83,
    151, 182, 186
    Marlow, 171
    Michaell, 148
    Philip, 77, 184
    Phillip, 35
    Rebecca, 35
    Robert, 183
    Samuel, 183
    Thomas, 35, 101,
    137, 138, 141,
    170, 187
    William, 35, 165,
    170, 173, 183,
    187
TEAGE, Peter, 170
TEAGUE, Peter, 170
TEBBALS AND CASTLE
    CAREY, 40
TEBBATS, 13
TELIOR, Henerie,
    106
    Henery, 104
TEMBRULL, William,
    35
TEMPLE, John, 118
TEMPLE PATRICK, 68
TENANT, James, 187
TENNANT, James, 35
    John, 35, 51, 178
    Mary, 133
    Moses, 35
    William, 183
TERRY, Ann, 35
    Benjamin, 35, 91,
    153, 156, 166
    Hugh, 35
    John, 35, 68
    Jonathan, 91
    William, 35
TERRYS PART OF
    SUFFOLK, 68
TERSON, Andrew, 68
TERSONS ADDITION,
    68
TERSONS NECK, 68
TERSONS NEGLECT, 16
TEYLER, Henery, 110
THACKISTON, Mary,
    35
THACKSTONE, Thomas,
    35
THARP, John, 184
THE NEW INVENTION,
    126
THECHILEY, Thomas,
    132
THEXSTON, Thomas,
    144, 146
THOMAS, Ann, 35
    Beal, 173
    Ebenezer, 35

262 INHABITANTS OF KENT COUNTY, MARYLAND, 1637-1787

Elizabeth, 170
Francis, 35
George, 173
Henry, 35, 68, 72, 173
J. Exel, 72
James, 35, 68
James Earle, 181
Joanna, 36
John, 36, 170, 173, 187
Margaret, 36
Martha, 115
Mary, 36, 147
Michael, 172
Mr., 108
Philip, 143
Richard, 175, 184
Samuel, 36, 68, 86, 90, 150, 178, 180
Starling, 173
Sterling, 184
Thomas, 36, 181
William, 36, 43, 58, 60, 64, 65, 68, 71, 82
THOMAS HYNSONS LAND RESURVEYED, 19
THOMAS PURCHASE, 26, 35, 42, 91
THOMAS'S ADDITION, 68
THOMAS'S FOLLY, 68
THOMAS'S LANDING, 35, 68
THOMAS'S PURCHASE, 13, 32, 68
THOMAS'S SLIPE, 68
THOMPSON,
  Augustine, 36
  Barnett, 187
  Dowdall, 36
  Eliza, 36
  Elizabeth, 92
  James, 141, 182
  Mary, 36
  Richard, 175
  Samuel, 36, 70, 159, 165
THOMSON, James, 129
THORN, William, 170
THORNE, Richard, 170
William, 170
THORNTON, 3, 13, 18, 20, 29, 68, 91
  John, 36
  Mary, 69
  Richard, 48
  Thomas, 36, 184
  William, 157, 161
THORNTON ADDITION, 29
THORNTONS ADDITION, 20, 68
THORP, Alice, 36
  John, 36
THORTON, 14
THOURSON,
  Allexander, 131
  Andrew, 132
THRAP, James, 182
THREE FRIENDS, 2, 5, 14, 26, 38, 68, 91
THRIFT, John, 36, 158, 159, 160
  Mary Anne, 36
  Pere., 185
  William
    Peregrine, 171
THROP, Alice, 36
  John, 36
THRUSH, Clem:, 115
THURSTON, Thomas, 134, 135
THURSTONE, Thomas, 62
TIBBALDS, 27, 91
TIBBALLS, 16, 28, 68
TIBBET, James, 68
  Richard, 68
TIBBETS ADVENTURE, 31
TIBBETS VENTURE, 37, 68
TIBBETT, James, 36
  Samuel, 36
TIBBETTS VENTURE, 36
TIBBIT, Grace, 36
TIBBITS VENTURE, 36
TIDMASH, William, 36
TILDEN, Capt., 191
Charles, 36, 46, 79, 80, 87, 91, 93, 97, 147, 150, 153, 156, 182, 184
Elizabeth, 36
J., 62
John, 36, 43, 44, 46, 69, 151, 159, 160, 162, 176, 178
Mar., 152
Marmaduke, 36, 79, 94, 95, 150, 151, 152, 153, 154, 156, 176, 177, 182, 190, 191
Rebeckah, 158
Sarah, 153
William B., 72, 74
William Blay, 36, 165
TILDEN AND RAISIN, 36
TILDENS AND BROWNS PART OF BLAYS RANGE AND BLAYS, 68
TILDENS FARM, 91
TILDENS FORREST, 69
TILDENS MEADOWS, 69
TILDENS PART OF BLAYS PARK RESURVEYED, 69
TILDLENS MEADOWS, 36
TILEY, Hannah, 170
TILGHMAN, 36
  Edward, 36, 53, 74, 85
  James, 36, 65, 155
  Mary, 69
  Philemon, 184
  Richard, 36, 69, 133, 141, 144, 145
TILGHMAN AND FOXLEYS GROVE, 69
TILGHMANS & FOXLEYS GROVE, 7, 13

INDEX 263

TILGHMANS AND
  FOXLEYS GROVE,
  33, 39, 40, 41,
  91
TILGHMANS CHOICE,
  3, 28, 31, 69,
  91
TILGHMANS FARM, 1,
  27, 28, 31, 36,
  38, 91
TILGHMANS FARM AND
  CHANCE, 25
TILGHMANS FOLLY, 11
TILGHMANS GROVE, 31
TILLAR, Edward, 159
  George, 94, 160
  James, 94
  Josias, 94
  Samuel, 94
TILLARD, Edward,
  37, 159
  Forgitt, 37
  Frogget, 183
  Froggett, 73
  Froggitt, 172
  Frogitt, 69
  George, 37
  John, 37
TILLARDS ADDITION,
  37, 69
TILLER, Edward, 108
  George, 46, 85,
  88, 185
  John, 98, 182
  Jonas, 185
  Samuel, 98
TILLMAN, Richard,
  141, 142
TILLOTSON, William,
  171
TILLTON, Humphrey,
  57, 156
TILTON, Humphrey,
  37
TIMBER LEVELL, 13,
  69, 91
TIMBIN, Edward, 170
TIMBRELL, William,
  37
TIMELY DISCOVERY,
  31
TIMELY DISCOVERY,
  THE, 69
TIMMS, John, 182

TIPPETS ADVENTURE,
  91
TIPPETT, James, 37
  Martha, 170
  Samuel, 37
  Thomas, 170
TISHE, Samuel, 182
TITTLE, John, 95,
  184
  Lazarius, 184
TO KEEP BLACKISTON
  HONEST, 69
TOALSON, Andrew,
  179
TOAS, Daniel, 37,
  62
  John, 37
TOBBINS LOTT, 37,
  69
TOBENS FOLLY, 13
TOBENS LOTT, 13
TOBIN, Richard, 37,
  161
TOBINS, 91
TOBINS FOLLY, 69,
  91
TOBINS LOT, 91
TOLCHESTER, 10, 13,
  15, 16, 17, 19,
  22, 23, 27, 28,
  29, 31, 33, 34,
  35, 36, 38, 39,
  41, 49, 69, 75,
  91
TOLCHESTER , 10
TOLCHESTER AND
  TOMB, 22, 42
TOLESON, Andrew,
  159, 160
  Nathaniel, 84,
  166
TOLL CHESTER, 91
TOLLEY, Thomas, 48
TOLLEY AND HODGES,
  48
TOLLSON, William,
  69
TOLSON, Andrew, 37
  George, 172
  Nathaniel, 84
TOMB, 16
TOMBE, 69
TOMBS, Charles, 179
TOMSON, Elizabeth,

  170
TONEY, Isaac, 187
TOOLE, Christopher,
  170
TOULSON, Andrew,
  154, 160
  Ann, 158
  Nathaniel, 185
  William, 51, 67,
  69
TOURSON, Alexander,
  134
  Allexander, 128
  Sarah, 126, 127
TOVEY, Samuel, 37,
  64, 69, 150, 175
TOVEYS LOT, 37
TOVEYS LOTT, 69, 91
TOVY, Samuell, 145,
  147, 148
TOWCESTER, 69
TOWER HILL, 69, 91
TOWERSON,
  Alexander, 147
  Allexander, 139
  Sarah, 137
TOWLSON, William,
  137
TOWN HILL, 21, 22
TOWN RELICT, 1, 7
TOWN RELIEF, 7, 13,
  23, 29, 32, 42,
  91
TOWN SIDE, 10
TOWN SIDE REBUILT,
  69
TOWNE RELIEF, THE,
  69
TOWNSEND, Mary, 170
TOWNSIDE, 69
TOWRSON,
  Allexander, 137
  Allexsander, 120,
  122
  Sara, 142
TRANGE, 32
TRAVELLERS
  REFRESHMENT,
  THE, 69
TRAVELORS
  REFRESHMENT, 10
TREANY, Mary, 170
TREISE, John, 170
TRENCHARDS

MEMORIAL, 91
TRENCHER, Aaron,
  180
TREVASCUS, Arthur,
  170
TREVASEUS, Arthur,
  170
TREVSTUS, Arthur,
  170
TREW, John, 61,
  131, 132
  Thomas, 182, 183
  William, 64, 132,
  180, 181
TREWS, William, 147
TRIANGLE, 10, 12,
  69, 91
TRIANGLE
  RESURVEYED, 92
TRIANGLE
  RESURVEYED, THE,
  69
TROIFE, John, 170
TROTH, Henry, 180
TROTTLE, Robert,
  170
TRUE, John, 37, 43,
  89, 90, 137,
  138, 139, 140
  William, 37, 79,
  88, 138
TRUE GIFT, 26
TRUELOCK, Henry,
  69, 72, 79, 85,
  92, 153, 156,
  173, 190
  Joseph, 69
  William, 62
TRUELOCKS
  ADVENTURE, 69,
  92
TRUELOCKS RIGHT OF
  HALES
  RESURVEYED, 69
TRULOCK, Henry, 37,
  158, 179
  Jacob, 179, 183
  Joseph, 37, 179
  William, 37
TRULOCKS RIGHT, 37
TRUMAN, Thomas, 134
TRUMPINGTON, 5, 33,
  39, 69, 92
TRUSTY, Richard,
  186
TRYANGLE, 7, 10,
  21, 36, 41, 69
TRYANGLE, THE, 69
TUCK, James, 170
TUCKER, George, 182
  John, 37, 48
  Peter, 170
TUCKOR, Richard,
  170
TUCKWELL, John, 179
TULLEY, David, 172
TULLEY FANCY, 15
TULLEYS FANCY, 15
TULLY, John, 69
TULLYS CHOICE, 27
TULLYS FANCY, 4,
  15, 18, 25, 32,
  40, 69, 92
TUMBLES, Michael,
  37
TUMEES, Ann, 145
TUMES, Ann, 149
TURBOTT, William,
  37
TURBUTT, William,
  178
TUREY, Lewis, 187
TURNER, Araminta,
  98
  Daniel, 96, 172,
  183
  Ebenezer, 186
  Jane, 37
  John, 37, 78,
  183, 185
  Jonathan, 37, 69,
  93, 153, 156,
  159, 160
  Joseph, 86, 98,
  186
  Martha, 98
  William, 85, 100,
  166, 185, 186
TURNERS PART OF
  SUFFOLK, 69
TURNEY, Richard, 47
TURNY, Richard, 118
TUSH, John, 170
TWEEG, John, 64
TWIGG, John, 37
  Mary, 37
TWILLYS FANCY, 36
TYLER, Edward, 188
  James, 170
  Robert, 117, 118
TYLOR, Francis, 170
-U-
ULRICK, 7, 8, 9,
  10, 12, 13, 17,
  21, 24, 39
UNDERHILL, 19
  John, 68
  Mich., 184
  Richard, 37
  Robert, 170
UNDERSTONE, George,
  37
UNICE, John, 37
UNICK, Thomas, 37
UNITT, Richard, 37
UNITY, 14, 15, 28
UNITY, THE, 69
UPPER BLOUNT POINT,
  69
UPPER PART OF
  DARNALLS FARM,
  (THE), 69
URIE, Thomas, 37,
  75, 76
USHER, George, 37,
  69
  James, 37
  John, 37
  Thomas, 37, 61,
  69
USHERS LOTT, 37, 69
USHERS PART OF
  KILLINSWORTHMORE
  , 69
USILTON, Robert,
  186
USLINGTON, James,
  185
USSELTON, Francis,
  186
  William, 186
USTLETON, John, 183
UTIE, Nathanell,
  110
  Nathaniel, 50, 69
UTIESLEY
  KILLINSWORTHMORE
  , 69
UTRICK ALIAS
  SEWALL, 69
UTY, Nathanniall,
  116

INDEX 265

Nathanuniall, 122
-V-
VALLEY, 92
VAN DYKE, Thomas,
  152, 156
VANBEBBER, Adam, 37
VANDEKE, Thomas, 37
VANDYCKE, Thomas,
  189
VANDYKE, Thomas,
  72, 76, 80
VANHECK, John, 54
VANSANT, Albertus,
  37
  Benjamin, 37, 171
  Christopher, 162,
    171, 187
  Cornelius, 37,
    70, 72, 75, 78
  Ephraim, 37, 78,
    166
  Garradus, 83
  Garrett, 171, 187
  George, 37, 83,
    89, 161, 171,
    185, 187
  Jacob, 83, 166,
    187
  James, 78, 188
  John, 38, 57, 60,
    69, 171, 188
  Joshua, 38, 49,
    51, 57, 69, 70,
    75, 78, 161, 172
  Lambert, 185
  Mary, 38
  Nicholas, 38
  Rosata, 38
  William, 188
VANSANTS BING, 69
VANSANTS FERRY, 69
VANSANTS LANDING,
  38, 69
VANSANTS PART OF
  ENDEAVOUR AND
  CHESTER GROVE,
  69
  RESURVEY, 69
VANSANTS PART OF
  FORK RESURVEYED,
  70
VANSANTS RING, 69
VANSTONE, Jonas,
  170
VANSWARINGEN, Mr.,
  144
VARINE, Jane, 158
VAUGHAN, Capt.,
  105, 109
  Charles, 105
  Mary, 133
  Robert, 62, 65,
    100, 101, 102,
    106, 107, 110,
    111, 112, 113,
    114, 116, 119,
    120, 122, 125,
    126, 127, 128,
    129, 130, 131,
    132, 133, 175,
    178
  William, 145
VAUGHANA, Robert,
  108
VAUGHN, Robert, 58
VEAVIN, 92
VEAZEY, Edward, 171
VENISON, 28
VERIAN, 13
VERINA, 21, 27, 40,
  41, 70, 92
VERINE, 19
VERINNIA, 92
VESTRY OF CHESTER
  PARISH, 38
VESTRY OF
  SHREWSBURY
  PARISH, 38
VESTRY OF ST.
  PAUL'S PARISH,
  38
VIAL, Judeth, 130
VIANA, 92
VIANEM, 70
VIANNA, 70
VIAVAN, 31
VIAVEN, 3, 31, 70
VIAVEN RESURVEYED,
  32, 70
VICARIGE, John, 134
VICARIS, John, 124,
  131, 132, 133,
  134, 135, 138,
  139
  Mary, 124, 133,
    137, 138
VICARY, Hugh, 170
VICKERICE, John,
  131
VICKERS, Abner, 183
  James, 184
  Joseph, 183
  William, 96, 155,
    184
VIENNA, 7, 12, 22,
  24, 33, 34, 41,
  42
VINCENT, Henry, 109
  Richard, 170
VISITORS OF KENT
  COUNTY FREE
  SCHOOL, 38
VIVIAN, William,
  170
VOORHEES, John, 83,
  165, 192
VORHEES, John, 174
VUETT, Richard, 156
-W-
W. CLIFT, 92
WADDY, Thomas, 53
WADE, John, 46
  Zachary, 45, 100,
    101
WADELOE, Nicholas,
  118
WADES, 38
WADILA, Nicholas,
  118
WADING PLACE
  NECK,THE, 70
WADING PLACE, THE,
  70
WAITING PLACE NECK,
  70
WALDEN, Edward, 38
WALDROND, Grace,
  170
WALKER, Daniel, 127
  Nicholas, 38
  William, 38
WALL, Hugh, 170
  Renippa, 38
WALLACE, Francis,
  66, 72, 86
  Hannah, 38, 43
  Henry, 70, 82,
    88, 93
  Hugh, 38, 158
  John, 70, 81, 84,

86, 91, 92, 93,
  153, 188
John and Co., 38
Ruth, 38
Samuel, 38, 67,
  76, 86
Samuell, 44, 49,
  62, 64
WALLACE CHANCE, 92
WALLACES FANCY, 38,
  70
WALLACES MEADOW, 70
WALLER, George, 181
WALLICE, Hannah, 38
John, 38
William, 38
WALLIS, Francis,
  188
Henry, 95, 188
Hugh, 159, 160,
  176, 188
John, 165, 188
Samuel, 62, 95,
  155, 156, 157,
  161, 175, 176,
  181, 188
William, 184
WALLMUTT, John, 170
WALLNUTT NECK, 70
WALLS, John, 38,
  172, 187
Renippa, 38
Samuel, 162, 164,
  165
William, 38, 159,
  160, 172, 187
WALLTERS,
  Alexander, 124
Ellin, 124
Margret, 124
WALLTON, John, 136,
  138
WALNUT NECK, 19, 92
WALNUT NECK
  RESURVEYED, 70
WALROND, Grace, 170
WALTER, Owen, 145
Patrick, 70
WALTERS, Alexander,
  140
Allexander, 140
Richard, 170
Walter, 38
WALTERS LOTT, 70

WALTHAM, Edward, 38
John, 38
William, 38
WALTON, John, 138
WARD, Anna, 170
Anne, 170
Elisabeth, 114
Elizabeth, 115
Job, 170
John, 38
Matthew, 49, 60,
  70, 150
Mr., 102, 109
Mrs., 114
Ralph, 124
Samuel, 135
Thomas, 38, 70,
  101, 102, 104,
  105, 109, 111,
  114, 116, 117
William, 186
WARD OAK, 11, 70,
  92
WARD OAK
  RESURVEYED, 70
WARDE, Matthew, 145
Thomas, 110
WARDENS LOTT, 14
WARDNER, George,
  56, 70
WARDNERS ADVENTURE,
  70
WARDS HOPE, 28, 42,
  70
WARDS OAK, 36
WARE, James, 74,
  183
John, 38, 154
WARNER, Elizabeth,
  52
George, 38, 52,
  70
Hannah, 82, 89,
  93
Joseph, 38
Mary, 70
Phil., 165
Philip, 154
Samuel, 179
WARNERS, 92
WARNERS ADDITION,
  2, 18, 19, 21,
  22, 26, 37, 38,
  70, 92

WARNERS ADVENTURE,
  2, 11, 18, 21,
  22, 30, 34, 37,
  38, 92
WARNERS ADVISER, 26
WARNERS LEVEL, 30,
  35, 38
WARNERS LEVEL
  RESURVEYED, 70
WARNERS LEVELL, 28
WARNERS LEVELS, 92
WARNERS MARSH, 3,
  11, 29, 70
WARNERS PART OF
  DRAYTON
  RESURVEYED, 70
WARRELL, William,
  190
WARREN, Robert, 170
Thomas, 145, 146,
  148, 149
WARUM, Valentine,
  180
WATERMAN, Nicholas,
  38
WATERS, Alexander,
  51, 63, 71, 133
Francis, 138
James, 186
WATERS LOTT, 70
WATKINS, Esau, 38
John, 38, 154,
  184
WATSON, James, 150
John, 38, 52,
  159, 183
Peter, 188
William, 182
WATTS, Charles, 87,
  188
George, 38, 76,
  182
John, 38
William, 154
WATTSON, James, 38
John, 39, 163,
  178
Thomas, 129
WAXFORD, 11, 21,
  22, 70, 92
WEATHERED, John,
  153
WEATHERELL, George,
  39

INDEX

Samuel, 39
WEATHERHEAD,
  Isabella, 179
  William, 179
WEATHERLEYS, 19
WEAVER, Celia, 96
  Isaac, 187
  John, 85, 185
  Thomas, 96, 181
WEBB, Amerial, 39
  Benjamin, 188
  Edmund, 128
  Edward, 70
  Giles, 115
  James, 39
  John, 39, 85, 86,
    163, 166, 186
  Richard, 170
  Robert, 39, 61,
    70, 187
  Thomas, 170
  Timothy, 170
WEBBER, Humphrey,
  170
WEBBS CHANCE, 70
WEBLEY, 35, 70
WEBSTER, John, 141,
  142, 143
WEDG, John, 127
WEDGE, John, 60,
  70, 147
WEDGES DISCOVERY,
  8, 9, 19
WEDGES RECOVERY, 5,
  26, 92
WEDGES RECOVERY
  RESURVEYED, 70
WEDGES RESURVEY, 70
WEEB, Edmund, 128
WEEBE, Edmt., 101
WEECKES, Joseph,
  103, 104
  Mr., 114
WEECKS, Samuel, 70
WEECKS MARSH, 70
WEEKES, Joseph,
  125, 127, 137
  Mr., 129
WEEKS, John, 64
  Joseph, 62
  Mary, 165
  Robert, 191
  Walter, 100
WEELLS, Tobye, 129

WEEST, Henry, 101
  Thomas, 101, 102
WEHILL DOWN, 70
WEICKES, Joseph,
  106, 107, 109
WEICKS, Capt., 106
  Joseph, 144
WEIKES, Joseph, 105
  Mr., 105
WEITHRED, John, 165
  William, 165
WELCH, James, 39,
  70, 95
  Mary, 78
WELCHES PURCHASE,
  70
WELCOCKS, Philip,
  170
WELL, William, 110
WELL MEANING, 27,
  32, 70
WELLDIN, David, 187
WELLES, James, 170
WELLS, David, 186
  Hugh, 170
  John, 39, 67,
    144, 145, 147,
    148, 150, 175,
    178
  Joseph, 170
  Mary, 170
  Richard, 39, 51
  Ruth, 39
  Tobias, 115, 120,
    122, 123, 126,
    130, 136, 142,
    144, 148
  Toby, 61, 124,
    126, 131, 132,
    133
  Tobyas, 136, 137,
    138, 139, 140,
    142, 143, 145
  Tobye, 126, 128
WELSH, James, 70
  Lawrence, 165
  Lewis, 39
WELSHS PART OF
  AGREEMENT
  RESURVEYED, 70
WENDALS CHANCE, 40
WEST, John, 51
  Peter, 48
  Richard, 39

WESTLAKE, Joseph,
  170
WESTLEY, John, 116
WETHERALLS HOPE, 22
WETHERED, Isabella,
  162
  John, 39, 77, 85,
    94, 97, 163,
    165, 181
  Mary, 95
  Richard, 39, 94,
    97, 162
  William, 94, 163,
    165
WETHERELL, 70
  Thomas, 70, 101,
    113, 117
WETHERELLS HOPE, 39
WETHERHEAD, John,
  186
  Samuel, 39
  William, 39
WETHERILL, 70
  Samuel, 70
  Thomas, 114, 120
WETHERLY, Thomas,
  106
WETHERS, Sammuell,
  127
WETHERSPONE, David,
  39
  Thomas, 39
WEXFORD, 11
WEYHILL DOWN, 70
WEYMOUTH, 35, 70
  Thomas, 70
WHALAND, Edward,
  182
  John, 39, 182
  Owen, 39, 172,
    184
  Thomas, 182, 184
WHALEY, 92
  Ann, 39
  Daniel, 70
  David, 39
  Owen, 39
WHALEYS ADVENTURE,
  24, 39, 70
WHALON, Thomas, 80
WHARTON, Henery,
  112
  Joseph, 136
  Robert, 182

Thomas, 182
WHATLY, William, 132
WHEALER, Charles, 181
WHEATFIELD, 92
WHEATHERED, Richard, 73
WHEATHERSPOON, Thomas, 83
WHEELER, James, 170
Mr., 144
Samuel, 96, 175
William, 170
WHEELRIGHT SWAMP, 92
WHEELWRIGHT SWAMP, 21, 22
WHEELWRIGHTS SWAMP, 70
WHELER, Mary, 96
Samuel, 96
Thomas, 96
WHETFIELD, 92
WHETHERILS HOPE, 9
WHETSTON, Steven, 145
WHETTSTON, Steven, 145
Stevens, 147
WHETTSTONE, Stephen, 39
WHICHCOAT, Ann Maria, 87
WHICHCOTE, Peregrine, 98
Rebecca, 98
WHIT, John, 129
WHITCHCOAT, Paul, 39
WHITE, Eli, 188
Elizabeth, 125
Henry, 170
John, 80, 93, 120, 125, 127, 144, 147, 187, 188
Martha, 39
Richard, 39, 68
Robert, 39
WHITE CLIFT, 92
WHITE MARSH, 2, 9, 92
WHITE MARSH, THE, 70
WHITEFIELD, 1, 10, 16
WHITEHEAD, George, 43
George and Co., 39
WHITEHOUSE, Samuel, 173, 182
WHITEMAN, Conrod, 172
WHITEMARSH, 28
WHITFIELD, 1, 5, 20, 33, 34, 36, 37, 40, 70
WHITTEN, Richard, 131
WHITTFIELD, 9, 16, 29, 36, 41
WHITTINGTON, 12, 70
Abraham, 99, 187
I., 39
James, 39, 99
John, 39, 81, 99, 175, 187
WICKE, Joseph, 109
WICKERS, Joseph, 183
WICKES, Ann, 92
Benjamin, 74
Capt., 110
Joseph, 45, 60, 75, 76, 77, 89, 101, 102, 106, 109, 110, 113, 114, 116, 119, 121, 132, 142, 143, 144, 153, 175, 182
Lambert, 39
Mary, 81, 92, 154
Mr., 113
Samuel, 151, 154, 182
Simon, 72, 73, 84, 87, 92, 152, 154, 155, 182, 190
William, 119
WICKES LAND, 92
WICKLIFF, 15, 39, 70
WICKLIFFE, 8, 15, 39, 92
Market Place, 8
WICKS, Benjamin, 39
John, 147
Joseph, 39, 70, 138, 145, 146, 147, 148, 149, 191
Lambert, 39
Mrs., 115
Samuel, 39
Simon, 62, 191
William, 98
WICKS PART OF BUCKINGHAM RESURVEYED, 70
WIDDOWS REST, THE, 70
WIDGIN, Edward, 39
WIDOWS CHANCE, 19, 31, 41, 70
WIDOWS REST, 2, 31, 34
WILDE, Abraham, 148
WILES, John, 180
WILKENS, Thomas, 49
WILKERSON, Mary, 170
Richard, 170
WILKESON, William, 111
WILKINS, Ann, 96
Bartus, 49, 88, 89, 96
John, 39
Mary, 39, 95, 134
Philis, 170
Samuel, 95, 98, 170
Thomas, 39, 43, 48, 64, 66, 75, 96, 98, 151, 152, 153
WILKINSON, Joseph, 99, 187
Richard, 40
WILLAN, Richard, 126
WILLIAH, John, 70
WILLIAM, Lewis, 115
WILLIAM AND MARY, 92
WILLIAM AND MARYS ADVENTURE, 42, 70, 92

WILLIAM THOMAS'S
  PART OF
  TILGHMANS FARM,
  71
WILLIAMES, Henry,
  124
WILLIAMS, Abraham,
  40
  Charles, 40
  Christopher, 40,
    66, 185
  Dorethy, 124
  Dorothy, 133
  Edward, 127, 164
  Eli, 188
  Henry, 173
  Hopkins, 40
  Hopton, 40
  Isaac, 44
  Jane, 170
  John, 40, 71, 75,
    76, 78, 80, 150,
    153, 156, 164,
    166, 170, 172,
    183, 188, 190
  Joseph, 73, 87,
    90, 95, 185
  Lewis, 40
  Mary, 40
  Morgan, 105, 114,
    124, 129, 131,
    132, 133, 134,
    136, 142
  Morgane, 125
  Morgon, 113, 125,
    127, 145
  Sarah, 114, 124
  Thomas, 40, 66,
    126, 127, 147,
    148, 158, 161,
    162, 170
  William, 117,
    118, 119, 187
WILLIAMS ADDITION,
  70
WILLIAMS ADVENTURE,
  4, 31
WILLIAMS FANCY, 40,
  71
WILLIAMS LOT, 8
WILLIAMS LOTT, 71,
  92
WILLIAMS LOTT
  RESURVEYD, 71

WILLIAMS VENTURE,
  12, 17, 21, 71,
  92
WILLIAMSON, 92
  Alexander, 40, 43,
    44, 150, 176
  Capt., 191
  Eliza, 82, 90
  Elizabeth, 155
  George, 40, 188
  James, 40, 85,
    87, 155, 157,
    171, 172, 183,
    190
  John, 40, 75, 85,
    94, 154, 158,
    188
  Richard, 170
  Sarah, 40
WILLIAMSTON, 71
WILLIS, Cornelius,
  100
  James, 170
  Joel, 72, 184,
    191
  John, 49, 183
  Joshua, 100, 182
  Martha, 100
  Richard, 40, 98,
    153, 184
  Ruben, 100
WILLKINSON,
  Christopher, 40
WILLMER, James, 188
  Lambert, 157, 158
  Rebecca, 150
  Simon, 150
  Symon, 47, 58, 66
WILLMERS FARME, 71
WILLMORE, Simon, 71
WILLMORES ARCADIA,
  71
WILLSON, George,
  40, 157, 176
  Isaac, 40
  James, 40, 156,
    157, 188
  John, 40, 74, 85,
    88, 156, 157
  Mary, 40
  Peter, 40
  Richard, 40
  Robert, 138
  Sarah, 40

WILMER, B., 152,
  156
  Blackiston, 155,
    184
  Charles, 40
  Edward Price,
    161, 165
  James, 181
  James J., 166
  John, 166, 171,
    189, 190
  John Lambert,
    177, 188
  Lambert, 40, 65,
    71, 157, 158,
    176
  Mary Ann, 40
  Rose, 66
  Simon, 40, 44,
    46, 49, 55, 56,
    71, 150, 152,
    154, 156, 159,
    163, 164, 175,
    176, 179
  William, 41, 66,
    71, 166, 184
WILMERS ADDITION,
  9, 71
WILMERS ADVENTURE,
  71
WILMERS ARCADIA, 10
WILMERS CHANCE, 40,
  71
WILMERS FARM, 41
WILMERS GIFT, 25,
  31, 71
WILMERS GROVE, 41,
  71
WILMERS GROVE
  ADDITION, 71
WILMORE, Darcus, 41
  John, 73, 74, 75,
    77, 80, 82, 85,
    88, 90
  Lambert, 89
  Mary, 41
  Rosanna, 89
  Simon, 90, 91
  William, 41, 84,
    88, 89, 92
WILMORE FARM, 92
WILMORE GROVE, 92
WILMORES FARM, 41
WILSHARE, William,

270 INHABITANTS OF KENT COUNTY, MARYLAND, 1637-1787

41
WILSON, Frances,
 87, 92
George, 41, 44,
 71, 73, 75, 84,
 92, 161, 163,
 166, 180, 187
Hiram, 188
Isaac, 161
James, 41, 92,
 102, 156, 171,
 172, 173, 181,
 182, 187
John, 41, 59, 63,
 72, 73, 79, 87,
 88, 92, 156,
 165, 166, 171,
 187, 188
Joseph, 94
Mary, 41
Richard, 159,
 160, 163, 180
Samuel, 188
Sarah, 41
William, 72, 74,
 91, 166, 171,
 173, 182, 187,
 191
WILSONS NEGLECT,
 40, 71, 92
WILTSHIRE, Eliz, 41
 William, 172
WINCESTER, John,
 102
WINCHESTER, 71
 Edward, 115
 Elizabeth, 133
 Goodie, 106
 Isaac, 132, 136,
  137, 140, 141,
  142
 Issack, 145
 John, 71, 100,
  101, 103, 105,
  106, 111, 113,
  118, 120, 121,
  124, 125, 127,
  128, 130, 133,
  134, 137, 138,
  139, 140, 141,
  142, 143
 Margarett, 128
 Margret, 120
 Mr., 148

WINCKLES, Edward,
 140
WIND MILL HILL, 71
WINDALE, 40
WINDALL, 41
 Edward, 162
 Thomas, 66, 71
WINDALLS CHANCE, 71
WINDMILL HILL, 39
WINFIELD, 10
WINN, Penelope, 41
WINTERS, Elisha,
 182, 189
WINTERS FIELD, 8
WINTONS ADDITION,
 71
WIONDALL, Thomas,
 156
WISE, James, 172
 William, 187
WITHERELL, Thomas,
 106, 107, 108
WITHERIDGE, Jane,
 170
WITHERS, Samuel,
 41, 52, 71, 110
WITHERSPOON, David,
 71
WMITH, Thomas, 95
WOBBLER, Thomas,
 170
WODDALL, Thomas,
 153
WOLF HEAD, 27
WOLF HOOK, 93
WOLF TRAP BRIDGE,
 THE, 71
WOLFE HEAD, 71
WOLFS HUCK, 3, 38
WOLFS HUKE, THE, 71
WOMSLEY, Thomas,
 170
WONSLEY, Thomas,
 170
WOOD, Abraham, 179
 John, 170
 Robert, 41
 Thomas, 173
WOODAL, James, 183
 Thomas, 181
WOODALL, Edward,
 185
 James, 41, 78,
  185

 John, 41, 78, 92,
  159, 160, 172,
  185
 Thomas, 41, 78,
  91, 156, 185
 William, 41, 71,
  78, 89, 92, 185
WOODALLS HAZARD, 71
WOODARD, Thomas,
 181
WOODLAND, Abraham,
 41, 79, 80, 86,
 87, 163, 166,
 187
 Abrm., 161
 Christian, 41
 James, 41, 71,
  84, 166, 171,
  187, 191
 John, 87, 166,
  167, 188
 Jonathan, 41
 Katharine, 41
 Wiliam, 61
 William, 41, 48,
  68, 71, 157,
  158, 159, 160,
  163, 164
WOODLAND NECK, 19,
 29, 71, 93
WOODLAND NECK, THE,
 71
WOODLANDS
 DISCOVERY, 71
WOODLANDS FOLLY,
 41, 71, 93
WOODLANDS GIFT, 41
WOODLANDS HAZARD,
 41
WOODLANDS
 INTENTION, 23,
 39, 71
WOODLANDS
 INTENTIONS, 23
WOODLANDS RISQUE,
 71
WOODSON, Richard,
 41
WOODYARD THICKET,
 THE, 71
WOOLACUTT, John,
 170
WOOLASTON, William,
 184

INDEX

WOOLCHURCH, Henry, 49, 56
WOOLCOTT, John, 132, 135
WOOLMAN, Alice, 129
WOOLMUTT, John, 170
WOOLSY, Mary, 170
WOOMS, John, 170
WOOTEN, Michael, 170
WOOTON, Michael, 170
WORKEMAN, Anthony, 144
WORRAL, Joseph, 41
WORRALL, Mary, 41
  William, 154
WORREL, Simon, 41
WORRELL, Benjamin, 73, 94
  Edward, 41, 88, 150, 151, 155, 172, 174
  S. or G., 154
  Simon, 152, 154, 155, 181
  William, 41, 92, 150, 156, 181
WORREN, Thomas, 147
WORSLEY, George, 150
WORTH, James, 78, 92
  John, 71
  Jonathan, 89, 189, 190, 191
  William, 188
WORTHS FOLLY, 11, 22, 30, 33, 38, 71, 93
WORTON MANNOR, 25, 71, 93
WORTON MANOR, 23, 71
WORTON MEADOW, 1
WRIGHT, Archibald, 187
  Arthur, 71, 136, 137, 140, 141, 142, 143, 144, 146, 147, 148, 175
  Catharin, 142
  Edward, 155, 167, 171, 192
  Gideon, 53
  James, 41
  John, 41, 44, 68, 130, 131, 132, 133, 134, 136, 137, 139, 140, 141, 142, 143, 144, 145, 146, 159, 166, 184, 187
  Joseph, 41
  Katherin, 141
  Margaret, 83
  Mrs., 144
  Nathaniel, 41, 159
  Robert, 177
  Samuel Turbutt, 171
  Solomon, 41, 50, 53, 154, 175
  Thomas, 41
  Turbutt, 79, 80, 177
  William, 41, 92
WRIGHTS CHANCE, 41
WRIGHTS FORTUNE, 71
WRIGHTS NECK, 9
WRIGHTS REST, 5, 9
WRITB, Arthur, 125
WRITES REST, 93
WRITSON, John, 95, 98
WRITTE, Arthur, 127
WROTH, Benjamin, 181
  Hensin, 79, 80, 89, 90, 91, 92
  Ishmael, 173
  J., 152
  James, 42, 92, 151, 156, 182
  John, 42, 153
  Jonathan, 89
  Kelvin, 42
  Kinvan, 153
  Kinvin, 58, 79, 89, 90, 91, 92, 156, 181, 182
  William, 188
WYATT, Henry, 188
  James, 42, 71
  Jane, 42
  John, 42, 63, 178
  Samuel, 188
  Thomas, 42, 57, 161
  William, 188
WYATTS ADDITION, 28, 42, 71
WYATTS CHANCE, 28, 42, 93
WYDALL, John, 42
WYDDALL, John, 48
WYE, Rebecca, 161
WYE HILL DOWN, 15
WYE HILL DOWNS, 93
WYFALL, 71
WYLMER, Symon, 63
WYOTT, James, 71
  Nicholas, 143
WYOTTS CHANCE, 71
WYTHELL, Thomas, 168

-Y-

YAPP, 24, 25, 71, 93
  William, 71
YARDSLEY, James, 97
  William, 155, 184
YATE, George, 136, 137, 138
YATES, Donaldson, 189
YEAMANS, William, 140
YEARLEY, John, 87, 183
YEARLY, John, 81
  William, 42, 62, 70, 71
YEARLYS BEGINNING, 71
YEATES, Donaldson, 93, 160, 174, 177, 184, 190
  William, 184
YEATES AND GRINDAGE, 93
YEATES PURCHASE, 93
YOARKLEY, John, 179
YORK, 28
  William, 170
YOUNG, David, 42
  John, 42, 75, 182
  Joseph, 42, 170

Mary, 42
Robert, 171
Thomas, 42
William, 42
YOUNGER, Frogget,
 172
 Humphrey, 42, 67
 James, 42
 John, 42
 Joseph, 90
 -Z-
ZELEFRO, John, 186
ZELEFROTH, John,
 188
ZELEFROW, John, 188
ZELEPHROW, John,
 73, 83
ZELLEFROE, Joseph,
 164, 165
ZELOFROW, John, 94

Other books by the author:

A Closer Look at St. John's Parish Registers [Baltimore County, Maryland], 1701-1801
A Collection of Maryland Church Records
A Guide to Genealogical Research in Maryland: 5th Edition, Revised and Enlarged
Abstracts of the Ledgers and Accounts of the Bush Store and Rock Run Store, 1759-1771
Abstracts of the Orphans Court Proceedings of Harford County, 1778-1800
Abstracts of Wills, Harford County, Maryland, 1800-1805
Baltimore City [Maryland] Deaths and Burials, 1834-1840
Baltimore County, Maryland, Overseers of Roads, 1693-1793
Bastardy Cases in Baltimore County, Maryland, 1673-1783
Bastardy Cases in Harford County, Maryland, 1774-1844
Bible and Family Records of Harford County, Maryland Families: Volume V
Children of Harford County: Indentures and Guardianships, 1801-1830
Colonial Delaware Soldiers and Sailors, 1638-1776
Colonial Families of the Eastern Shore of Maryland
Volumes 5, 6, 7, 8, 9, 11, 12, 13, 14, and 16
Colonial Maryland Soldiers and Sailors, 1634-1734
Dr. John Archer's First Medical Ledger, 1767-1769, Annotated Abstracts
Early Anglican Records of Cecil County
Early Harford Countians, Individuals Living in Harford County, Maryland in Its Formative Years
Volume 1: A to K, Volume 2: L to Z, and Volume 3: Supplement
Harford County Taxpayers in 1870, 1872 and 1883
Harford County, Maryland Divorce Cases, 1827-1912: An Annotated Index
Heirs and Legatees of Harford County, Maryland, 1774-1802
Heirs and Legatees of Harford County, Maryland, 1802-1846
Inhabitants of Baltimore County, Maryland, 1763-1774
Inhabitants of Cecil County, Maryland, 1649-1774
Inhabitants of Harford County, Maryland, 1791-1800
Inhabitants of Kent County, Maryland, 1637-1787
Joseph A. Pennington & Co., Havre De Grace, Maryland Funeral Home Records:
Volume II, 1877-1882, 1893-1900
Maryland Bible Records, Volume 1: Baltimore and Harford Counties
Maryland Bible Records, Volume 2: Baltimore and Harford Counties
Maryland Bible Records, Volume 3: Carroll County
Maryland Bible Records, Volume 4: Eastern Shore
Maryland Deponents, 1634-1799
Maryland Deponents: Volume 3, 1634-1776
Maryland Public Service Records, 1775-1783: A Compendium of Men and Women of
Maryland Who Rendered Aid in Support of the American Cause against
Great Britain during the Revolutionary War
Marylanders to Carolina: Migration of Marylanders to
North Carolina and South Carolina prior to 1800

Marylanders to Kentucky, 1775-1825
Methodist Records of Baltimore City, Maryland: Volume 1, 1799-1829
Methodist Records of Baltimore City, Maryland: Volume 2, 1830-1839
*Methodist Records of Baltimore City, Maryland: Volume 3, 1840-1850
(East City Station)*
More Maryland Deponents, 1716-1799
*More Marylanders to Carolina: Migration of Marylanders to
North Carolina and South Carolina prior to 1800*
More Marylanders to Kentucky, 1778-1828
Outpensioners of Harford County, Maryland, 1856-1896
Presbyterian Records of Baltimore City, Maryland, 1765-1840
Quaker Records of Baltimore and Harford Counties, Maryland, 1801-1825
Quaker Records of Northern Maryland, 1716-1800
Quaker Records of Southern Maryland, 1658-1800
Revolutionary Patriots of Anne Arundel County, Maryland
Revolutionary Patriots of Baltimore Town and Baltimore County, 1775-1783
Revolutionary Patriots of Calvert and St. Mary's Counties, Maryland, 1775-1783
Revolutionary Patriots of Caroline County, Maryland, 1775-1783
Revolutionary Patriots of Cecil County, Maryland
Revolutionary Patriots of Charles County, Maryland, 1775-1783
Revolutionary Patriots of Delaware, 1775-1783
Revolutionary Patriots of Dorchester County, Maryland, 1775-1783
Revolutionary Patriots of Frederick County, Maryland, 1775-1783
Revolutionary Patriots of Harford County, Maryland, 1775-1783
Revolutionary Patriots of Kent and Queen Anne's Counties
Revolutionary Patriots of Lancaster County, Pennsylvania
Revolutionary Patriots of Maryland, 1775-1783: A Supplement
Revolutionary Patriots of Maryland, 1775-1783: Second Supplement
Revolutionary Patriots of Montgomery County, Maryland, 1776-1783
Revolutionary Patriots of Prince George's County, Maryland, 1775-1783
Revolutionary Patriots of Talbot County, Maryland, 1775-1783
Revolutionary Patriots of Worcester and Somerset Counties, Maryland, 1775-1783
Revolutionary Patriots of Washington County, Maryland, 1776-1783
*St. George's (Old Spesutia) Parish, Harford County, Maryland:
Church and Cemetery Records, 1820-1920*
St. John's and St. George's Parish Registers, 1696-1851
Survey Field Book of David and William Clark in Harford County, Maryland, 1770-1812
The Crenshaws of Kentucky, 1800-1995
The Delaware Militia in the War of 1812
*Union Chapel United Methodist Church Cemetery Tombstone Inscriptions,
Wilna, Harford County, Maryland*

www.ingramcontent.com/pod-product-compliance
Lightning Source LLC
Chambersburg PA
CBHW050132170426
43197CB00011B/1807